MACROECONOMICS

SECOND EDITION

ROBERT J. BARRO
UNIVERSITY OF ROCHESTER

JOHN WILEY & SONS
NEW YORK CHICHESTER BRISBANE TORONTO SINGAPORE

To Elisabeth—

It's economics, but it really is interesting.

Copyright © 1984, 1987 by John Wiley & Sons, Inc.

All rights reserved. Published simultaneously in Canada.

Reproduction or translation of any part of
this work beyond that permitted by Sections
107 and 108 of the 1976 United States Copyright
Act without the permission of the copyright
owner is unlawful. Requests for permission
or further information should be addressed to
the Permissions Department, John Wiley & Sons.

Library of Congress Cataloging-in-Publication Data:

Barro, Robert J.
  Macroeconomics.

  Includes indexes.
  Bibliography: P. 571
  1. Macroeconomics. I. Title.

HB172.5.B36   1987   339   86-24667
ISBN 0-471-85125-6

Printed in the United States of America

10 9 8 7 6 5 4 3 2

PREFACE

Macroeconomics is in a state of flux. The Keynesian model, which was almost universally accepted as the basic paradigm until the late 1960s, has become increasingly less popular. This loss in popularity reflects embarrassments over past economic events—especially the failure of the model to deal satisfactorily with inflation and supply shocks. It also reflects the theoretical and empirical progress of an alternative "market-clearing approach," which is more closely related to the microeconomics that economists use successfully to study the behavior of individual households and businesses. Although some important problems remain, this approach provides a much more satisfactory macroeconomics than the one we had before. By more satisfactory, I mean that the approach avoids internal inconsistencies and also provides a better understanding of the real world.

Although the Keynesian model has been subject to increasing skepticism by economists, it has nevertheless continued to reign supreme in most textbooks. As a result, it has continued to organize the way the subject has been taught to the majority of students. Many textbooks present aspects of market-clearing models, but these models have not been taken seriously when it comes to studying real-world events or policy proposals. This gap between textbook material and the knowledge gained in the last 20 years motivated me to write the first edition of this book.

Here, I present the market-clearing approach as a general method for analyzing real-world macroeconomic problems. The stress on this approach means that the book is not a "balanced" treatment of alternative macroeconomic models. There is no book—and probably could be none of substance—that is balanced in this respect. Although I deal in a serious manner with the Keynesian model, and show carefully how it relates to the market-clearing approach, I do not use the Keynesian framework for most of the analyses of economic events or policies. In any case, whatever one's ultimate judgment about the value of the Keynesian model, there is a very good reason not to start the study of macroeconomics with it. The Keynesian theory is an advanced topic that involves specific assumptions about the ways that private markets malfunction. The nature of these malfunctions and the special features of the Keynesian model cannot be fully understood and appreciated until the market-clearing analysis has been worked out.

I have been very encouraged by the market's reception of the first edition. This favorable reception shows up directly in the large and growing usage of the book in undergraduate courses at many colleges. But the book has also received a lot of attention in the national press. Positive reviews appeared in *Newsweek, Fortune, The Wall Street Journal, Newsday, The Boston Globe, The Washington Times, The Rochester Democrat and Chronicle,* and *The Financial Times.* Reviews of textbooks in the media are rare, and these were a pleasant surprise to me (and my publisher).

I think that the favorable reception reflects the widespread eagerness for a macroeconomic framework that outperforms the Keynesian model. For although the Keynesian model can be appealing as a teaching device, it tends to leave students with a poor understanding of how the economy works and how governmental policies can make things better or worse. In addition, I sense that, after some initial skepticism, many instructors have become convinced that the more satisfactory market-clearing approach really is accessible to undergraduates.

The second edition maintains the theme of the first, but makes a number of improvements. Perhaps the most important is the expanded treatment of employment and unemployment. The book now discusses the market-clearing approach to the labor market in Chapter 6, and develops the distinction between firms and households at that point. Then Chapter 10 contains a much improved analysis of unemployment.

Another major revision concerns the material on "rational-expectations macroeconomics," which now appears in Chapter 17. The exposition has been improved substantially, without any loss of substance. The discussion of the Keynesian model in Chapter 18 has been enlarged to include a more satisfactory analysis of investment, as well as fuller expositions of the IS/LM model and the contracting approach to macroeconomics.

Another change is the shortening of the material on microeconomic foundations, which resulted in the combination of the old Chapters 3 and 4 into the new Chapter 3. Similarly, the two chapters on investment were condensed to form the new Chapter 9.

As with the first edition, I discuss the material in as simple a fashion as I have found possible, so that the book will be usable for undergraduate courses in intermediate macroeconomics. Three years of experience have demonstrated that the book works well for these courses. However, the feedback from users has helped me to simplify the exposition in many places. Therefore, I am confident that students will find the second edition even more accessible than the first.

In writing this book I have benefited from an unusual amount of excellent advice, as well as encouragement to carry out the project. Since regular revision is a part of textbook writing, I would appreciate further suggestions from readers. I am particularly grateful to Mark Rush, who provided valuable and detailed comments on several versions of both editions. Chitra Ramaswami, who is responsible for many of the end-of-chapter problems and the glossary, has also been a great help. Jennifer Barro was an excellent assistant in the construction of the index, and Jason Barro showed remarkable skill in the preparation of the bibliography.

I thank for their helpful comments my colleagues and reviewers, including David Aschauer, Alan Auerbach, James Barth, Marianne Baxter, Gary Becker, Steve Bronars, A. Edward Day, Dave Denslow, William Dougan, Steve Easton, Jonathan Eaton, Sebastian Edwards, Stan Engerman, Gene Fama, Lauren Feinstone, Mark Fisher, Jacob Frenkel, Peter Garber, Ron Gilbert, Jeremy Greenwood, Gene Grossman, Herschel Grossman, Sanford Grossman, John Haltiwanger, Gary Hansen, Alan Hess, Greg Huffman, Bo Ickes, Bob King, Roger Kormendi, John Laitner, George Lamson, Stephen LeRoy, Michael Lovell, Bob Lucas, Randall Mariger, Sule Ozler, John Pettengill, Tim Roth, Chaipat Sahasakul, Michael Salemi, Dave Saurman, Jeremy Siegel, Dave Spencer, Dennis Starleaf, J. Kirker Stephens, Alan Stockman, Marc Vellrath, Henry Wan, Jr., Raburn Williams, Michael Wiseman, and Geoffrey Wood.

I am also grateful to Neil Howe and Les Lenkowsky, who argued early on that this book was a good idea. Terry Fisher has continued to perform as an understanding and efficient secretary. I express my appreciation to Rich Esposito, who had a great career as an editor. (Despite the disincentives from the new tax law, he has now become a full-time real estate tycoon.) He in turn would like to thank Alan Stockman and Bob Lucas for first bringing us together. Finally, thanks go to my wife Judy, who exhibited even more patience and encouragement than before. She proofread the final manuscript and cheerfully offers $1 for each report of a (previously unnoticed) typo.

Robert J. Barro

CONTENTS

CHAPTER 1
THE APPROACH TO MACROECONOMICS

In macroeconomics we study the overall or aggregate performance of an economy. For example, we consider the total output of goods and services as measured by the **gross national product (GNP).** Similarly, we look at the aggregates of employment and unemployment, and at the breakdown of GNP into consumer expenditures, investment (which are purchases of new capital goods), government purchases of goods and services, and net exports.

The above terms refer to the quantities of goods or work effort. We shall also be interested in the prices that relate to these quantities. For example, we consider the dollar prices of the goods and services that the economy produces. When we look at the price of the typical or average item, we refer to the **general price level.** But we are also interested in the **wage rate,** which is the price of labor services, **the interest rate,** which determines the cost of borrowing and the return to lending, and the **exchange rate** between the currencies of different countries.

We shall want to know first how the private economy determines the various quantities and prices that we just mentioned. In addition, we want to know how government policies affect these variables. Specifically, we shall consider monetary policy, which involves the determination of the quantity of money and the design of monetary institutions, and fiscal policy, which pertains to the government's expenditures, taxes, and budget deficits.

The performance of the overall economy is a substantial concern for everyone. This performance influences our job prospects, our incomes, and the prices that we face. Thus, it is important for us—and even more important for our government policymakers—to undersand how the macroeconomy works. Unfortunately, as is obvious from reading the newspapers, the theory of macroeconomics is not a settled scientific field. In fact, there is much controversy among economists about what is a useful basic approach as well as about the detailed analysis of particular economic events and policy proposals. However, there has been a great deal of progress in recent years in designing a more satisfactory macroeconomic theory. The main objective of this book is to convey that progress to students in an accessible form.

The Behavior of Output, Unemployment, and the Price Level in the United States

To get an overview of the subject matter, let's look at the historical record on some of the major macroeconomic variables for the United States. Figure 1.1 shows the total output of goods and services in the United States from 1872 to 1985. (The starting date is determined by the available data.) The measure of aggregate output is the gross national product, expressed in terms of values for a base year, which happens to be 1972. This measure, which we discuss in a later section on national-income accounting, is called **real GNP.**[1]

Two features of the graph of real GNP stand out. First, there is the general upward trend, which reflects the long-term growth or economic development of the U.S. economy. In particular, the average growth rate of real GNP from 1872 to 1985 was 3.2% per year. Thus, over 113 years, the total output increased 35-fold. If we divide through by population to determine real per capita GNP, then we find that the average growth rate was 1.7% per year—the 3.2% average growth rate of real GNP less the 1.5% average growth rate of population. Hence, over 113 years, output per person increased by a factor of 7.

The second striking feature of Figure 1.1 is the recurring ups and downs in real GNP over periods of roughly 1 to 5 years. These movements are called aggregate business fluctuations or the business cycle.[2] We can see these movements in Figure 1.1 and also in Figure 1.2, which shows the growth rate of real GNP for each year. When real GNP falls toward a low point or trough, the economy is in a **recession** or an economic contraction. Conversely, when real GNP expands toward a high point or peak, the economy is in a **boom** or an economic expansion.

Figures 1.1 and 1.2 show the major U.S. recessions since 1872. Note especially the **Great Depression** of 1930–33, where output fell 30% below the peak value reached in 1929. The other major economic contractions before World War II occurred in 1893–94, 1907–08, 1914, 1920–21, and 1937–38. For the post-World War II period, the most significant recessions were those for 1958, 1974–75, and the most recent one, 1980–82.

On the up side, note first the high rates of growth in output during World Wars I and II and the Korean War. Other periods of economic boom—in the

---

[1]The figure uses a proportionate (or logarithmic) scale on the vertical axis. Hence, each unit on the axis corresponds to an equal percentage change in real GNP.

[2]The term *business cycle* is somewhat misleading since it suggests a more regular pattern of ups and down in economic activity than actually appears in the data. But the term is too entrenched in economics literature to avoid entirely.

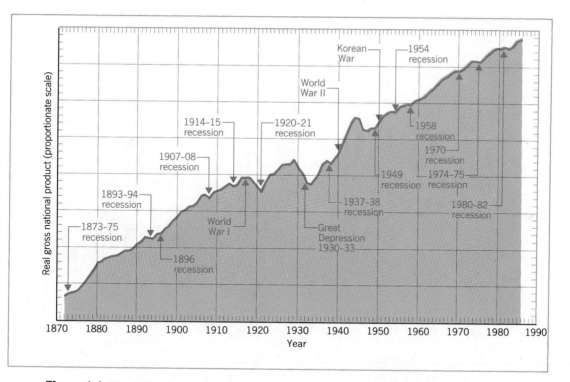

Figure 1.1 **The Behavior of Output in the United States, 1872–1985**
Sources for Figures 1.1–1.5:
For real GNP—Recent values are from the U.S. Commerce Department, *U.S. Survey of Current Business*. Figures back to 1918 are from the U.S. Commerce Department, *National Income and Product Accounts of the U.S., 1929–76*. For 1872–1917, the values are from Christina Romer, "The Prewar Business Cycle Reconsidered: New Estimates of Gross National Product, 1872–1918," Princeton University, May 1985, Table 1.

For the GNP deflator—Sources as above since 1918. For 1909–17, figures are from the U.S. Commerce Department, *National Income and Product Accounts of the U.S., 1929–76*. For 1889–1908, the numbers are based on John Kendrick, *Productivity Trends in the United States*, Princeton University Press, Princeton, N.J., 1961, Tables A-1 and A-III. For 1869–88, the data are unpublished estimates of Robert Gallman.

For the unemployment rate—The figures are the number unemployed divided by the total labor force, which includes military personnel. Data since 1930 are from *Economic Report of the President*, 1985, Table B-29; 1983, Table B-29; 1970, Table C-22. The data from 1933–43 are adjusted to classify federal emergency workers as employed, as discussed in Michael Darby, "Three-and-a-Half Million U.S. Employees Have been Mislaid: Or, an Explanation of Unemployment, 1934–1941," *Journal of Political Economy*, February 1976. Values for 1890–1929 are based on Christina Romer, "Spurious Volatility in Historical Unemployment Data," *Journal of Political Economy*, February 1986, Table 9.

Figure 1.2 Growth Rates of Output in the United States, 1873–1985

sense of unusually high growth rates of real GNP—were 1982–85, 1975–79, 1961–73 (except for the brief recession in 1970), the recovery from the Great Depression from 1933–40 (aside from the recession of 1937–38), much of the 1920s, the period from 1896 to 1906, and the years from 1875 to 1880.

Figure 1.3, which reports the unemployment rate for each year, gives us another way to look at recessions and booms. The unemployment rate is the fraction of the total labor force that has no job. (We discuss the precise meaning of this variable in Chapter 10.) Over the period from 1890 to 1985, for which data are available, the median unemployment rate was 5.3%. (The mean was 6.4%.) But during recessions the unemployment rate rises above the median. The extreme is the Great Depression, where unemployment reached 22% of the labor force in 1932. But also noteworthy are the average rates of 18% for 1931–35, 12% for 1938–39, 11% for 1894–98, 9% for 1982–83 and 1921, and 8% for 1975–76.

Figures 1.1–1.3 show the turbulence of the economy during the two world wars and the 1930s. But suppose that we abstract from these episodes and compare the post-World War II performance with that from before World War I. Then the major message from the data is the similarity between the post-World War II and pre-World War I experiences. For example, the average growth rate of real GNP was 3.4% per year from 1947 to 1985 and 3.6% from 1872 to 1914. The median unemployment rate was 5.3% for 1947–85 and 5.2%

Figure 1.3 The United States Unemployment Rate, 1890–1985

for 1890–1914 (the means were 5.4% and 6.4%, respectively). Further, the extent of fluctuations—in terms of the severity of recessions and booms—was only slightly greater in the earlier period than in the later one.[3] Therefore, although the economy has changed greatly over a century—including a much larger role for government, a diminished share of agriculture in the GNP, and dramatic alterations in the monetary system—the data suggest no major change in the intensity of business fluctuations.[4]

---

[3]For a detailed comparison of real GNP over the different periods, see Christina Romer, *The Prewar Business Cycle Reconsidered: New Estimates of Gross National Product, 1872–1918*, Princeton University, May 1985. On the unemployment rate, see Christina Romer, "Spurious Volatility in Historical Unemployment Data," *Journal of Political Economy*, February 1986.

[4]Until recently economists believed that the post-World War II period exhibited milder business fluctuations than the pre-World War I period. (For example, Chapter 1 of the first edition of this book accepted this viewpoint.) However, this comparison depended on using data for the earlier period that were constructed differently from those for the later period. Christina Romer's research (see footnote 3 above) demonstrated that these data problems were crucial. She constructed estimates since the late 19th century on a consistent basis for real GNP, the unemployment rate, and industrial production. Her measures show little change in the volatility of these variables from before World War I to after World War II. Note that we use her estimates in the construction of Figures 1.1–1.3.

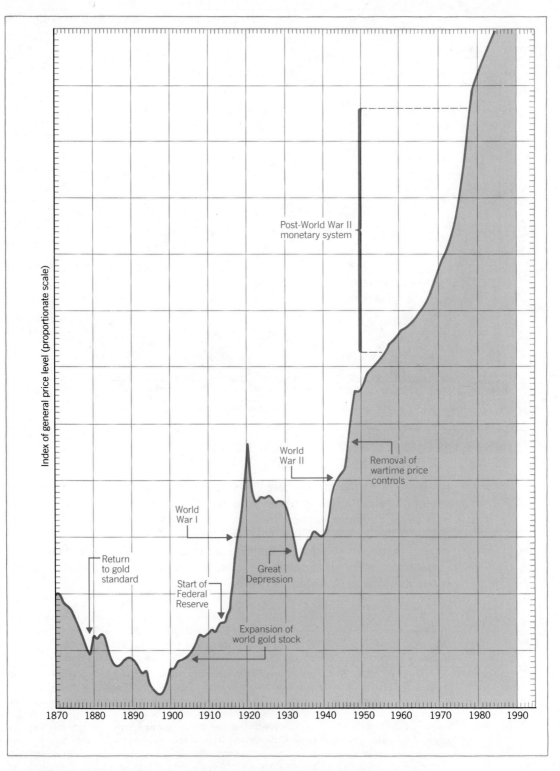

Figure 1.4 The Price Level in the United States, 1870–1985

Overall, when looking at Figures 1.1–1.3, we should recall the two main features that we would like to use economic analysis to understand. One is the long-term growth and the other is the short-term pattern of business fluctuations. As we develop our macroeconomic model in subsequent chapters, we shall frequently compare the theoretical propositions about these phenomena with the patterns that appear in the real-world data.

Figure 1.4 shows an index of the general level of prices in the United States from 1870 to 1985. (We discuss the details of the particular measure—the deflator for the gross national product—toward the end of this chapter.) One striking observation is the persistent rise in prices since World War II, as contrasted with the movements up and down from before the war. In fact, there are long periods in the earlier history—1870–92 and 1920–33—during which prices fell persistently.

Figure 1.5 looks at the year-to-year growth rate of the general price level—that is, the **inflation rate.** As already suggested, we find that almost all of the inflation rates since World War II were positive, as contrasted with a mixture of positive and negative values from earlier periods. Note also that the inflation rate fell sharply from a peak of nearly 10% in 1980–81 to values below 5% for 1982–85.

In subsequent chapters we relate the behavior of the general price level to monetary developments, especially to changes in the quantity of money. It turns out that this analysis interacts with the nature of monetary institutions, such as whether the United States was on the **gold standard** (as it was from 1879 until World War I and, to some extent, from World War I until 1933). Also important is the nature of the banking system, which has become much less vulnerable to financial crises since the 1930s. In any event, when we discuss the general price level and inflation, we shall keep in mind the behavior that shows up in Figures 1.4 and 1.5.

The Approach to Macroeconomics

This section describes the basic theoretical approach that we shall use to design a useful macroeconomic model. In setting up this model, we spend a good deal of time on economic theory. In this context we worry about whether the theory seems sensible, whether it is internally consistent, and so on. But we should always remember that the main test of the model will be its ability to explain the behavior of macroeconomic variables in the real world. Therefore, especially after the basic theoretical framework is complete, we devote considerable space to comparisons of the theory with the real world—that is, with empirical evidence.

Microeconomic Foundations of Macroeconomics

We begin by developing the basic price theory—or **microeconomic foundations**—which underlies the macroeconomic analysis of the aggregate variables

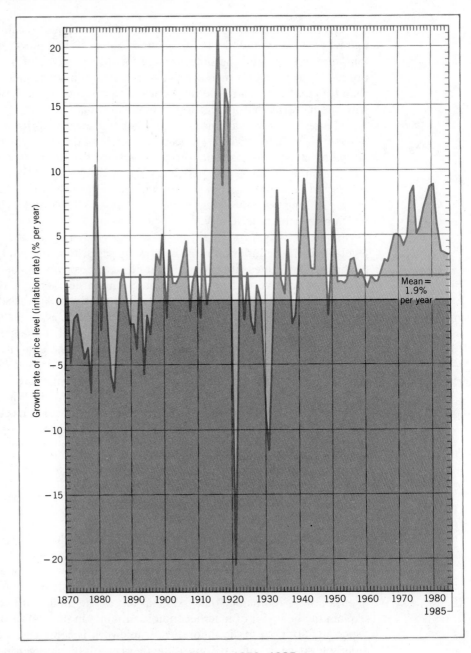

Figure 1.5 Inflation Rates in the United States, 1870–1985

in an economy. Much of this microeconomics will be familiar to students from previous courses in economics. In that sense, the macroeconomic approach in this book is a continuation of the economic reasoning that was used before to explain the behavior of individual households and businesses. Here, we apply this same economic science to understand the workings of the overall economy—that is, to study such things as real GNP, employment and unemployment, the general price level and inflation, the wage rate, the interest rate, the exchange rate, and so on. Unfortunately, many basic courses in economics do not follow this general approach when dealing with macroeconomics. In fact, students could easily reach the conclusion that macroeconomics and microeconomics were two entirely distinct fields. A central theme of this book is that a more satisfactory macroeconomics emerges when it is linked to the underlying microeconomics. By more satisfactory, we mean first that the macroeconomic theory avoids internal inconsistencies, and second, that we obtain a better understanding of the real world.

In Chapter 2 we examine the choice problems of an isolated individual, Robinson Crusoe. Naturally, we assume that Crusoe's choices are guided by enlightened self-interest—that is, we exploit the central economic postulate of optimizing behavior. In the initial framework, the only choice problem concerns the level of work effort, which then determines the quantities of production and consumption. But by studying Crusoe's behavior, we can understand the trade-off between leisure and consumption that also applies in complicated market economies. Also, by looking at an isolated individual, we bring out the role of a resource or **budget constraint** in its simplest form. Here, when goods cannot be stored over time, Crusoe's budget constraint dictates that his consumption equals his production. As we shall see, extensions of this simple constraint are central to correct macroeconomic analyses in economies that include many consumers and producers, as well as a government.

We can use the model of Robinson Crusoe to predict his responses to changes in production opportunities—for example, to harvest failures or to discoveries of new goods or methods of production. Many of these results carry over to the predictions for aggregate output and employment in more realistic settings. In particular, when we consider the economy's responses to changes in production opportunities—such as the recent oil crises—we usually get the right answer by thinking of the parallel situation for Robinson Crusoe.

Chapter 3 develops the microeconomic foundations that we need to go from an analysis of Robinson Crusoe to a study of many persons who interact in various marketplaces. Once again we exploit the postulate of optimizing behavior, subject to budget constraints, to assess the responses of individuals to different circumstances.

To simplify matters, we start with only two markets. On the first market, people buy and sell goods in exchange for money. The dollar cost on this market is the theoretical counterpart of the general price level. On the other market, people can borrow and lend. This credit or loan market establishes an interest rate, which borrowers must pay to lenders.

The introduction of the goods market allows people to specialize in their production activities, which adds to the economy's productivity. (Robinson Crusoe did not have this option.) The existence of the credit market means that a person's expenditure during any period can diverge from his or her income during that period. Thus, unlike Robinson Crusoe, a person with a given income has choices about consuming now versus later. Similarly, people can choose between working now versus later. We discuss these choices by considering people's incentives to save—that is, to accumulate assets that pay interest income. Here, we stress the idea that a higher interest rate motivates people to save more, which means that they consume less today and plan to consume more later on. Similarly, we show that various forces can induce people to rearrange their work and production from one period to another.

Later on (in Chapter 6), we introduce a labor market on which labor services are bought and sold at an established wage rate. But to simplify the basic model, we do not include this market at the outset. Rather, we pretend that people work only on their own production processes—that is, each person owns his or her own business and is the only employee. For many purposes—such as studying the main determinants of aggregate output and work effort, the general price level, and the interest rate—we find that this simplification is satisfactory. But to explore some other topics—such as the behavior of unemployment and the determination of wage rates—we have to deal explicitly with the labor market.

Throughout our analysis, we stress the role of budget constraints. Namely, over one or many periods, there must be a balance between each person's sources of funds and his or her uses of these funds. Although these budget conditions may seem tedious at times, it is important to keep these matters straight. In fact, many serious errors in macroeconomic reasoning occur when economic theorists forget to impose the appropriate budget constraints in their models. We shall see that these conditions are especially important in evaluating temporary versus permanent changes in income, in studying the effects of interest rates on lenders and borrowers, and in evaluating the effects of people's money holdings. Also, when we introduce government policies in later chapters, we find it crucial to impose the government's budget constraint. Many errors in analyses of the government's expenditures and deficits result from a failure to impose this budget constraint.

In Chapter 4 we complete our discussion of microfoundations by exploring people's incentives to hold non-interest-bearing paper money, rather than financial assets that bear interest. We assume that the **demand for money** arises out of the process of carrying out transactions, which use money as a **medium of exchange.** In particular, since people use money when they buy or sell goods or financial assets, it would require a great deal of planning and effort for someone to hold little or no cash. We then discuss how the quantity of money demanded depends on the price level, the interest rate, the level of income, and other variables.

Market-Clearing Conditions

We note in Chapter 5 that certain conditions must hold when we add up the actions of all individuals. For example, the total of goods sold by suppliers must equal the total bought by demanders. Similarly, the total amount loaned out by people on the credit market must equal the total borrowed by others. We refer to conditions such as these as **aggregate-consistency conditions.** These conditions tell us something about how aggregate quantities must behave in order for the analysis to be internally consistent. Any reasonable macromodel must satisfy these conditions.

One way to ensure that the aggregate-consistency conditions hold is to assume that the various markets—say, for goods and credit—always clear. Clearing means here that the price level and the interest rate adjust simultaneously so that the aggregate demand for goods equals the aggregate supply, and the aggregate of desired lending equals the aggregate of desired borrowing. We use this **market-clearing approach** for satisfying the aggregate-consistency conditions in the basic model.

The idea that markets clear is closely related to the notion that private markets function efficiently. Specifically, with cleared markets, it is impossible to improve on any outcomes by matching potential borrowers and lenders or by bringing together potential buyers and sellers of goods. Cleared markets already accomplish all of these mutually advantageous trades. We can see that market clearing is reminiscent of the optimizing behavior of individuals, which we exploited when working out the microfoundations of the model. On the one hand, people determine their individual choices of work, consumption, and so on, to make themselves as well off as possible. On the other hand, market clearing means that the people who participate in and organize markets—and are guided by the pursuit of their own interests—do not waste resources, and thereby end up achieving efficient outcomes. Thus, market clearing is the natural macrocomplement to the microfoundations that underlie the model.

It is possible to satisfy the aggregate-consistency conditions without imposing market clearing in the sense described above. One important idea is that imperfect information makes it impossible to make the best decisions about production and work at all times. Later on, we explore some macroeconomic models that incorporate incomplete information (particularly in Chapter 17). But it is best to explore the workings of the economy under full information before going on to this advanced topic. Thus, we do not introduce incomplete information into the model at the outset.

Another alternative to market clearing is the **Keynesian model.** This model assumes that some prices (usually of labor services or commodities) are sticky and that some rationing of quantities bought or sold comes into play. It turns out that outcomes are generally inefficient in the Keynesian model. Notably, some mutually advantageous trades do not take place. As a reflection of this "market failure," there tends to be chronic unemployment and underproduction. These conclusions from the Keynesian model have led many economists to advocate "corrective" policy actions by the government.

The Keynesian model depends crucially on the assumption that prices are sticky. Thus, not surprisingly, the rationale for price stickiness has been a subject of substantial debate, which is still unresolved. In any event, just as in the case of models with incomplete information, the Keynesian theory is an advanced topic that cannot be appreciated without first working through the logic of a market-clearing model. Thus, we take up the Keynesian model (in Chapter 18) after the market-clearing analysis is completed.

To summarize, the basic model relies on two key elements for making predictions about the behavior of quantities and prices in the real world. First, we use the microfoundations of the model, which stem from the optimizing behavior of individuals subject to budget constraints. Second, we exploit the notion of market clearing. As mentioned, this idea reflects the smooth operation of markets—that is, the efficient matching of potential buyers and sellers of goods, credit, labor services, and so on.

Using the Market-Clearing Model

In Chapter 5 we construct the central theoretical apparatus that we use throughout the remainder of the book. After this point, the discussion amounts to extensions of the basic model in order to apply the reasoning to various topics in macroeconomics. Thus, our list of applications eventually includes supply shocks, business fluctuations, long-term economic growth, the role of government purchases and public services, monetary and fiscal policies, financial intermediation, incomplete information, the Keynesian model, and aspects of the international economy.

We first use the model in Chapter 5 to study various disturbances that affect opportunities for production. Specifically, we assess the effects of supply shocks on output, employment, the price level, and the interest rate.

In Chapter 6 we bring in a labor market, and allow for business firms as distinct economic units. With this extension of the model, we show how the clearing of the labor market determines the wage rate and the quantity of employment. However, for most purposes, the extended model yields results that coincide with those in Chapter 5. Therefore, for most of the subsequent analysis, we return to the setting that neglects the labor market and considers only one type of economic unit. We can think of this unit as a combination of a household and a firm. That is, we merge into this unit the consumption and working activities of households with the production and hiring activities of businesses. The main reason we proceed this way is that it greatly simplifies the analysis without leading us into any mistakes.

In Chapters 7 and 8 we introduce the possibility of chronic rises in the general price level—that is, inflation. We look at inflation as primarily a monetary phenomenon. One of the major themes is that inflation and monetary growth can be largely independent of the variations in output and employment, which are examples of "real" variables. The interaction of monetary phenomena with output, employment, and other real variables is a major issue in macroeconomics, but one that is not fully resolved. In this book we deal first with simple models where the interaction between monetary forces and the real variables is unimportant. Then we extend the analysis to bring in more interesting possibilities for this interaction (in Chapters 15–18).

In Chapters 9–11 we apply the theory to aspects of business fluctuations and economic growth. First, we allow for investment, which is the accumulation of capital goods. By looking at actual recessions in the United States, we find that aggregate business fluctuations involve mainly variations in investment, rather than consumption. Then we show how the theory is consistent with this important empirical observation. To demonstrate this consistency, we rely on two aspects of the microfoundations of the model. First, we utilize the forms of households' budget constraints, and second, we consider the incentives that people have to shift their investment and consumption from one period to another.

In Chapter 10 we expand the model to allow for unemployment. We view unemployment as arising from the problem of matching workers to jobs. Specifically, we relate the average level and dynamics of unemployment to the rates at which people find and lose jobs. Then we show how various economic forces influence the rates of job finding and job separation. In particular, we show why unemployment rises during a recession.

In Chapter 11 we study how investment shows up over the longer term as an increase in the stock of capital and thereby in economic growth. By allowing also for growth in population and for improvements in technology, we can apply the theory to a country's long-term economic development. Accordingly, we are able to use the model to study the behavior of the major macroeconomic variables in the United States over the past century. In addition, we apply the theory to a comparison of the growth experiences of a number of industrialized countries since World War II.

Chapters 12–14 bring in government expenditures, taxes, and public debt, which allow us to consider fiscal policies. First, we introduce government purchases of goods and services, which we assume are used to provide public services to consumers and producers. Then we consider how people react to income taxes and to transfer programs, such as social security. Finally, by introducing the public debt, we can evaluate the economic consequences of the government's financing its spending by deficits rather than taxes.

To assess changes in government activity, we again rely on the microfoundations of the model. First, we analyze individuals' incentives to react to taxes, to the provisions of various transfer programs, and to the services that they get "free of charge" from the government. Second, we use the budget constraints that face households and the government. It is these constraints that tell us the main difference between temporary and permanent changes in government expenditures—results that we illustrate by considering the behavior of the economy during wartime. In addition, the careful analysis of budget constraints gives us a perspective on government deficits that differs substantially from the popular view. Namely, in many circumstances, there is little economic difference between taxes and deficits.

Chapters 15–18 deal with interactions between monetary forces and real economic activity. In Chapter 15 we introduce financial intermediaries, which allows us to study the creation of deposits and the lending operations of banks and other institutions. We stress here the role of intermediaries in promoting economic efficiency. Thus, a contraction in the amount of financial intermediation—such as that during the Great Depression and in other periods of financial crisis—tends to reduce the levels of production and employment. In addition, there are important effects of changes in financial intermediation on the general price level.

Chapter 16 explores the main pieces of empirical evidence that concern the interaction between monetary variables and the real economy. Our theory can explain much of the evidence, but not all of it. Specifically, using the model that we have developed up to this point, we cannot rationalize significant effects of purely monetary shocks on real economic activity, which seem to apply at least since World War II.

In Chapter 17 we extend the market-clearing model to account for the observed economic effects of monetary disturbances. The new feature is that individuals have incomplete information about prices in various markets and about the overall monetary picture. However, when people do not observe something directly—such as the general price level—they are still motivated to form their expectations rationally. Because of this feature, the approach is often called "rational-expectations macroeconomics." The important idea is that people use their available information to forecast unobserved variables as well as possible. In this setting we find that monetary disturbances can affect real economic activity more or less as appears in the U.S. data on business fluctuations. However, some empirical puzzles remain.

The theory in Chapter 17 has some intriguing implications for monetary policy. Namely, there are effects on real variables only from the erratic part of this policy, and the effects tend to be adverse. Thus, the main message is that monetary policy should be predictable, rather than erratic.

In Chapter 18 we develop the model of business fluctuations that was stimulated by the research during the 1930s of the British economist, John Maynard Keynes. This theory departs from our previous analysis by assuming that some prices do not adjust instantaneously to clear all markets. That is, the prices of goods or wages of labor are assumed to be sticky, rather than perfectly flexible. We begin with a simple version of the Keynesian model, which brings out the idea that shocks to the economy can have multiplicative effects on output. Then we work out a popular extended version of this theory, which is called the **IS/LM model.**

A basic conclusion from the Keynesian model is that recessions can result from decreases in the aggregate demand for goods, which might result from monetary contractions. Also, there is more scope for active monetary and fiscal policies in this model than there was in our market-clearing framework.

For many years, the Keynesian model was the most popular tool of macroeconomic analysis. However, the popularity of this model has diminished since the late 1960s, especially at the frontiers of macroeconomic research. There are two main reasons for this decreased popularity. First, the Keynesian model did not deal very well with inflation or supply shocks, both of which have been important since the late 1960s. Second, economists have not found satisfactory ways to provide the Keynesian macromodel with internally consistent microfoundations. In any event, there is another good reason to postpone our consideration of the Keynesian model until late in the book. Namely, the model cannot really be fully understood—and the distinctive features of it cannot be appreciated—until the market-clearing analysis has been worked out. Thus, whatever one's ultimate judgment about the value of the Keynesian model, it is a great mistake to begin a study of macroeconomics with this model.

Finally, Chapter 19 extends the theory from the economy of one country to that of many countries, which interact on international markets. In many respects there is a parallel between a single country in the world economy and an individual in the economy of one country. Thus, we can readily apply our prior analysis to study such things as international lending and borrowing, changes in the prices of commodities such as oil, and the behavior of a country's **balance of international payments.** Then we carry out some new analysis to consider the determination of exchange rates among different currencies, as well as the interplay among price levels and interest rates across countries.

A Note on Mathematics and Economic Reasoning

This book does not use any advanced mathematics. Rather it relies on graphical methods and occasional algebraic derivations. Although calculus would speed up the presentation in some places, this higher mathematics turns out to be unnecessary for the main economic arguments. Therefore, students should not find the book difficult on technical grounds.

What will be demanding from time to time is the economic reasoning. But it is this aspect of economics that really is the most difficult, as well as the most rewarding. Unfortunately, not all of this difficulty can be avoided if we wish to understand the economic events that take place in the real world. The feature that should help students to master the material is the use of a single, consistent model, which is then successively refined and applied to a variety of macroeconomic problems. Anyone who invests enough effort to understand the basic model will eventually see the simplicity of the approach, as well as the applicability to a wide variety of real-world issues.

Elements of National-Income Accounting

Up to this point, we have used terms such as *gross national product* (*GNP*), *consumer expenditure, investment*, the *general price level*, and so on without defining them precisely. Now, by looking at the **national-income accounts,** we develop the meanings of these terms. There are many difficult issues that arise in the construction of these accounts. Here, we consider only the basic concepts, which will be adequate for our subsequent analysis.

Nominal and Real GNP

We begin with the GNP. Nominal GNP measures the dollar value of all the goods and services that an economy produces during a specified time period. For example, in 1985 the nominal GNP in the United States was $3989 billion. During the first quarter of 1986, the nominal GNP was $4117 billion when expressed at an annual rate—that is, 1986's GNP would equal this amount if the dollar value of production throughout the year remained at the same rate as that for the first 3 months.

Let's examine the definition of nominal GNP one step at a time. The word *nominal* means that the GNP is measured in units of dollars—or, more generally, in units of some currency, such as pounds, marks, yen, and so on.

Next, for most goods and services—such as pencils, automobiles, haircuts, and so on—the dollar value is the price for which these items sell in the marketplace. However, governmental services, which include national defense, the justice system, and police services, are not exchanged in markets. These items are included in nominal GNP at their dollar cost of production.

It is important to understand that the GNP includes only the goods and services that an economy produces during a given time period. In other words, current GNP measures only current production. For example, the construction and sale of a new house counts in GNP, but the sale of a second-hand house (which was produced earlier) does not count.

If we are interested in measures of production, then the nominal GNP can be misleading. That is because this measure depends on the overall level of prices, as well as on the physical amounts of output. The top part of Table 1.1 illustrates this problem. Think about a simple economy that produces only butter and golf balls. We show the hypothetical quantities and prices of these goods for 1986 in the first columns of the table. Notice that the nominal GNP for 1986 is $500. The columns labeled 1987A and 1987B show two possibilities for prices and outputs in 1987. In both cases nominal GNP rises by 10% to $550. However, in case A the production of both goods has declined, while in case B the production of both has increased. Thus, identical figures on nominal GNP can conceal very different underlying movements in production.

We construct a measure of real GNP to solve the problem of changing price levels. Real GNP uses prices from only 1 year, which is called the base year. For example, if the base year is 1980, then we refer to real GNP as "GNP in 1980 dollars" or as "GNP in constant dollars," since we use a set of constant (1980) prices. Similarly, we refer to nominal GNP as "GNP in current dollars," since it uses the prices of the current period.

We compute real GNP by multiplying the current quantity of output of each good by the price of that good in the base year. Then we sum up over

Table 1.1 **The Calculation of Nominal and Real GNP**

	1986			1987A			1987B		
	P_{1986}	Q_{1986}	Market Value at 1986 Prices	P_{1987A}	Q_{1987A}	Market Value at 1987A Prices	P_{1987B}	Q_{1987B}	Market Value at 1987B Prices
Butter	$2.00/lb	50 lb	$100	$2.30/lb	44 lb	$101.20	$1.80/lb	70 lb	$126
Golf balls	$1.00/ball	400 balls	$400	$1.20/ball	374 balls	$448.80	$0.80/ball	530 balls	$424
Nominal GNP			$500			$550.00			$550
	P_{1986}	Q_{1986}	Market Value at 1986 Prices	P_{1986}	Q_{1987A}	Market Value at 1986 Prices	P_{1986}	Q_{1987B}	Market Value at 1986 Prices
Butter	$2.00/lb	50 lb	$100	$2.00/lb	44 lb	$ 88	$2.00/lb	70 lb	$140
Golf balls	$1.00/ball	400 balls	$400	$1.00/ball	374 balls	$374	$1.00/ball	530 balls	$530
Real GNP (1986 base)			$500			$462			$670

all these multiples to get the economy's aggregate real GNP. Because the prices used in this calculation do not vary from year to year, we end up with a reasonable measure for the changes over time in the overall level of production.

The bottom portion of Table 1.1 illustrates this calculation, using 1986 as the base year. Consider the values of real GNP for the cases labeled 1987A and 1987B. These values differ substantially, even though the values of nominal GNP are the same. In the 1987A example, real GNP falls below the 1986 level by 7.6%. This figure is a weighted average of the fall in butter production by 12% and that in golf ball production by 6.5%. Thus, real GNP gives a more accurate picture of the change in output than does the 10% increase in nominal GNP. Similarly, for the 1987B case, real GNP rises by 34% (which is a remarkable achievement for 1 year!). This figure is a weighted average of the rise in butter production by 40% and that in golf ball production by 32%.

Notice that the proportional change in real GNP gives us a weighted average of the proportional changes in production for the various goods, which are butter and golf balls in the example. Generally, there would be many ways to define the weights in this calculation. It turns out that the standard method for computing real GNP—which we employed in Table 1.1—uses as weights the shares of each good (butter or golf balls) in GNP for the base year. That is, as seems reasonable, we give more weight to the goods that account for a larger share of the economy's output (in the base year). But as we move away from the base year, these shares can change significantly. For that reason, the

U.S. Commerce Department changes the designation of the base year from time to time. (For example, in 1986 they shifted from 1972 to 1982.)

Although it reveals a lot about the economy's overall performance, the real GNP is not a perfect measure of welfare. Some of the problems with using real GNP as a measure of well-being are the following:

- Aggregate GNP does not consider changes in the distribution of income across households.
- The calculated GNP excludes a variety of nonmarket goods. These include legal and illegal transactions in the "underground economy," as well as the services that people perform in their homes. For example, if someone mows his or her own lawn, then GNP does not increase—but if the person hires someone to mow the lawn (and the transaction is reported to the government), then GNP increases.
- The GNP assigns no value to leisure time.

Despite these shortcomings, we typically learn a great deal about an economy—both in terms of short-run fluctuations and in the context of long-term development—by studying the changes in aggregate real GNP.

The Gross National Product—Expenditure, Production, and Income

We can think about GNP in three different ways. First, we can consider the expenditures on goods and services by different groups—households, businesses, all levels of government, and foreigners. Second, we can measure the production of goods by various industries—agriculture, manufacturing, wholesale and retail trade, and so on. Finally, we can calculate the incomes earned in the production of goods—compensation of employees, rental income, corporate profits, etc. The important point is that all three approaches will end up with the same total for GNP. To see this, we take up each approach in turn, beginning with a breakdown by type of expenditure.

Measuring GNP by Expenditures

The national accounts divide GNP into four parts, depending upon who or what buys the goods or services. The four sectors are households, businesses, all levels of government, and foreigners. Table 1.2 shows the details of this breakdown for 1985. The first column lists values in current dollars, while the second refers to real dollars—that is, values for the base year, 1982.

The purchases of goods and services by households for their own use is called **personal consumption expenditure.** This spending accounts for the bulk of GNP—for example, for $2313 billion out of a total $3570 billion or 65% of real GNP in 1985 (see Table 1.2).

The national accounts distinguish between purchases of consumer goods

Table 1.2 **Expenditure Components of the Gross National Product for 1985**

Category of Expenditures	Billions of Dollars	Billions of 1982 Dollars
Gross national product	3988	3570
Personal consumption expenditure	2582	2313
Durable goods	362	345
Nondurable goods	912	847
Services	1309	1121
Gross private domestic investment	669	649
Fixed investment	662	643
Nonresidential	476	472
Residential	186	171
Change in business inventories	8	6
Government purchases of goods and services	815	716
Federal	355	323
State and local	460	394
Net exports of goods and services	−78	−108
Exports	370	360
Imports	448	468

Source: *U.S. Survey of Current Business*, March 1986, Tables 1.1, 1.2.

that will be used fairly quickly, such as toothpaste and various services, and those that will last for a substantial time, such as automobiles and appliances. The first group is called **consumer nondurables and services,** while the second is called **consumer durables.** The important point is that consumer durables yield a flow of services in future periods, as well as currently. Table 1.2 shows the division of consumer expenditures among durable goods, nondurable goods, and services.

The second major category of GNP is **gross private domestic investment,** which is the purchase of goods and services by businesses. The "fixed" part of these investments comprises firms' purchases of new capital goods, such as factories and machines. Note that business's capital goods are durables, which enhance production opportunities over many years. Thus, investment goods are similar to the consumer durables that we mentioned before. In fact, in the national accounts, an individual's purchase of a new home—which might be considered the ultimate consumer durable—is counted as part of fixed business investment, rather than as personal consumer expenditure. For many purposes, we might add the other purchases of consumer durables to the national accounts' measure of gross investment to get a broader concept of investment.

Total investment is the sum of fixed investment and the net change in business's inventories of goods. In 1985 this total investment was 18% of real GNP, or 28% if we include the purchases of consumer durables (see Table 1.2).

The third component of GNP is **government purchases of goods and services.** This category combines governmental consumption expenditures with public investment. However, it is possible to get a rough breakdown into the two components. There are two points about the government sector that sometimes cause confusion. First, it includes all levels of government, whether federal, state, or local. Second, it includes purchases of goods and services, but excludes the government's **transfer payments.** (Examples of transfer payments are social security benefits and welfare payments.) The idea is that transfers do not represent payments to individuals in exchange for currently produced goods or services. Hence, they should not appear in GNP. In 1985 government purchases of goods and services accounted for 18% of real GNP (see Table 1.2).

Finally, some of the goods and services produced in an economy are exported to foreign users. **Exports** must be added to domestic purchases to compute the economy's total production (GNP). But in addition to buying goods and services that are produced domestically, foreigners also produce goods and services that are imported into the domestic country. **Imports** must be subtracted from domestic purchases to calculate GNP. So the foreign component appears in GNP as **net exports**—that is, the spending by foreigners on domestic production (exports) less the domestic spending on foreign production (imports). Notice that net exports may be either positive or negative. In 1985 this component was negative, and equal to -3% of real GNP. (Real exports were 10% of real GNP while real imports were 13%.)

Economists often omit net exports when they construct a macroeconomic model for a single economy. Then the model applies to a **closed economy,** rather than an **open economy,** which includes the foreign sector. The rationale for assuming a closed economy is first, to simplify the theory, and second, at least for the United States, that exports and imports are small relative to GNP. We follow this tradition until Chapter 19, where we consider the role of foreign trade. When we omit the foreign sector, we get the familiar division of GNP into three parts, namely

GNP = consumer expenditure + gross investment + government purchases

One common error about national accounting arises because the spending on new physical capital is called "investment." This terminology differs from the concept of investment in ordinary conversation, which refers to the allocation of saving among different financial assets, such as stocks, bonds, savings accounts, and so on. When we speak of a firm's investment, we mean the purchase of physical goods, such as a factory. Do not be confused by these two different meanings of investment.

Another point about investment concerns **depreciation.** During any period, some of the existing stock of capital tends to wear out or depreciate. Thus, a part of gross investment merely replaces the old capital that has depreciated. If we subtract depreciation from gross investment, then the remainder—called **net investment**—equals the net change in the stock of capital goods. We shall discuss the difference between gross and net investment in Chapter 9. For now, we note that the sum of consumption expenditures, *net* investment, government purchases of goods and services, and net exports is called **net national product (NNP).** The difference between GNP and NNP reflects the difference between gross and net investment, which is the amount of depreciation. Hence, we have the condition

$$NNP = GNP - depreciation$$

Measuring GNP by Production

Instead of breaking down GNP into the sectors that do the spending, we can look at a breakdown by the sectors that do the producing (and selling). Table 1.3 shows such a breakdown for 1984. In terms of shares of real GNP, the breakdown was 22% in manufacturing, 17% in wholesale and retail trade, 15% in finance, insurance and real estate, 15% in services, 11% in production by government and government enterprises, 9% in transportation and public utilities, 4% in construction, 4% in mining, and 2% in agriculture.

In many cases a firm produces **intermediate goods,** which another business uses as an input. In order not to double count intermediate goods in GNP, we give each unit credit only for its **value added** to production. The value added by a firm is the difference between its revenues and the cost of goods that it buys from other firms. An example of an intermediate good is flour that a baker uses to make bread. The baker's value added is the market value of the bread less the value of the flour used up to produce the bread. The amounts shown in Table 1.3 are the value added to production by each industry.

Table 1.3 Production Components of the Gross National Product for 1984

Category of Production	Billions of Dollars	Billions of 1982 Dollars
Gross national product	3775	3492
Domestic industries (gross domestic product)	3727	3448
Agriculture	95	85
Mining	121	133
Construction	168	157
Manufacturing	780	761
Transportation and public utilities	345	313
Wholesale and retail trade	620	585
Finance, insurance, real estate	580	513
Services	576	510
Government	443	391
Rest of the world	48	44

Source: U.S. Survey of Current Business, March 1986, Table 6.1.

The last figure shown in Table 1.3 refers to the rest of the world. This amount is the value added to production by the U.S. labor and capital that is used in other countries, net of the contribution of foreign labor and capital to domestic production. (The figure is also called the "net factor income from abroad.") If we deduct this item from GNP, then what remains is the production by domestic industries. This total is called **gross domestic product,** or **GDP.**

Income

The third way to look at GNP is in terms of the income earned in this production. This income is called **national income.** To make clear the relation between production and income, let's think of a simple economy that has one firm producing bread as the only final product, and another firm producing flour as the only intermediate good. Suppose that the miller uses only labor to produce flour, while the baker uses labor and flour to produce bread. Sample income statements for these firms appear in Table 1.4. In this table the only sources of income are labor income and profits. We see also that total (nominal) GNP, which is the market value of the bread, is $600. This amount also equals the total revenue of the baker. The income statement shows that this revenue divides up into $350 for the cost of flour, $200 for payments to labor (or, from the workers' standpoint, $200 of labor income), and $50 of profits. For the miller, the revenue of $350 goes for $250 of labor costs (or labor income) and $100 of profits. Thus, national income equals the total labor income of $450 plus total profits of $150, which equals the $600 of GNP.

Table 1.5 shows the breakdown of national income in the United States for 1985. 74% of the total is compensation of employees, 8% is income of proprietors (owners of farms and small businesses), less than 1% is personal rental income (net of estimated depreciation on rental property), 9% is corporate profits, and 9% is net interest income.

Two complications disturb the equality between GNP and national income in the real world. First, suppose that the baker uses some capital goods in the production process. Then, as the capital wears out, the baker subtracts depreciation charges from profits. Hence, the total income for labor and profit

Table 1.4 Data for Calculation of Gross National Product and National Income

Baker			Miller		
Revenue	Costs and Profits		Revenue	Costs and Profits	
Total revenue from sale of bread	$600	Labor $200 Flour $350 Profit $ 50	Total revenue from sale of flour	$350	Labor $250 Profit $100

Table 1.5 Breakdown of National Income in 1985

Category of Income	Billions of Dollars
National income	3213
Compensation of employees	2372
Proprietors' income	242
Rental income of persons	14
Corporate profits	297
Net interest	287

Source: U.S. Survey of Current Business, March 1986, Table 1.14.

equals the baker's total revenue, which equals GNP, less the depreciation charges. That is, national income equals GNP less depreciation, which is NNP.

A second adjustment arises because of sales and excise taxes, which are called indirect taxes. These levies create a gap between the market price of a good—which includes the tax—and the revenue received by the producer. (The gap shows up as revenue for the government.) In our example from Table 1.4, if there had been a 5% sales tax on bread, then the consumer would have paid $630 for the bread, while the baker's total revenue would have remained at $600. As a result, national income would still be $600, while GNP would be $630. Generally, we find that national income equals GNP less depreciation and less these indirect taxes. Table 1.6 demonstrates this calculation using U.S. data for 1985.

Recall that the definition of national income includes only the amounts earned in the production of output. Often economists also calculate the amount of income that people actually receive, which is called **personal income.** This concept differs from national income for several reasons. First, only a portion of firms' profits are paid out as dividends to individuals. Second, we subtract from national income the contributions paid for social insurance, since people do not receive these amounts directly as income. Next there are a series of adjustments to ensure that the amount of interest income in personal income corresponds to the amount that individuals receive. Finally, we add various transfer payments, which are not included in national income, to calculate personal income. All of these adjustments are detailed in Table 1.6.

We can also determine the amount of income that people have left after paying personal taxes, which is called **disposable personal income.** Table 1.6 shows the calculation of disposable personal income from personal income.

Prices

One objective of macroeconomic theory is to explain the general level of prices and the changes in the price level over time. To use our theory, we need an empirical measure (or measures) of the general price level. Our analysis of

Table 1.6 **Data for Calculation of Net National Product, National Income, Personal Income, and Disposable Personal Income in 1985 (Billions of Dollars)**

Gross national product (GNP)	3988
less	
Depreciation	438
equals	
Net national product (NNP)	3550
less	
Indirect business taxes and nontax liability	319
equals	
National income	3213
less	
Corporate profits	297
Contributions for social insurance	355
plus	
Government transfer payments	465
Net adjustment for interest income	169
Personal dividend income	79
Business transfer payments	19
equals	
Personal income	3294
less	
Personal tax and nontax payments	493
equals	
Disposable personal income	2801

Source: U.S. Survey of Current Business, U.S. Department of Commerce, March 1986, Tables 1.9 and 2.1.

real and nominal GNP provides one such measure. The **implicit GNP price deflator** can be calculated as

$$\text{Implicit GNP price deflator} = \left[\frac{\text{nominal GNP}}{\text{real GNP}} \right] \times 100$$

It is conventional to multiply by 100 to obtain an index number that takes on the value 100 for the base year (for which nominal GNP equals real GNP).

For a concrete example, consider again the data from Table 1.1. For the 1987A case, we find that the GNP deflator is (nominal GNP/real GNP) × 100 = (550/462) × 100 = 119. In other words, the price of the "average item" increased by 19% from 1986 to 1987. This number is a weighted average of the percentage increase in the price of butter, which is 15%, and that of golf balls, which is 20%. It turns out that the weights used to compute the average percentage change are the shares of the two goods in the real GNP for 1987. Thus, by using the GNP deflator to measure the general level of prices, we give more weight to the items that are currently more important in the economy's market basket of produced goods.[5]

The formula for the implicit price deflator can be rearranged to see why we call it a price deflator. The rearranged equation is

$$\text{Real GNP} = \left[\frac{\text{nominal GNP}}{\text{implicit GNP price deflator}}\right] \times 100$$

Thus, we effectively divide or deflate the nominal GNP by the price deflator to compute the real GNP.

This implicit GNP price deflator is called "implicit" because it is not directly or explicitly calculated. Real GNP and nominal GNP are computed directly and the GNP deflator is calculated by dividing the two as we have done. There are also explicit indices of the general price level. Two important examples are the **consumer price index (CPI),** and the **producer price index (PPI),** which is also called a wholesale price index. These are explicit indices since they are calculated directly.

The CPI is based on a fixed market basket of consumer goods. Every few years the government takes a statistical survey to compile the base-year prices and expenditures on about 400 goods that are consumed by typical individuals. The expenditure shares serve as fixed weights until the next survey is taken. In order to calculate the CPI we first compute the ratio of the current market price of each good to its base-year price. Then we sum up over the ratios, weighting each by the share of the good in base-year expenditures. Typically, we also multiply the result by 100, so that the CPI for the base year is 100.

The PPI is computed in a similar manner. This index measures prices at an early stage of production, so the "basket" in the PPI consists of about 2800 items sold at wholesale. These goods are primarily raw materials and semifinished goods.[6]

We shall use primarily the implicit GNP price deflator, which appears in Figure 1.4, as our empirical measure of the general level of prices. There are several reasons for this choice. First, the PPI is too narrow a concept to reflect the general level of prices. Second, the GNP deflator reflects the importance of the various items in current market baskets of produced goods, whereas the CPI refers to base-year market baskets, which can become less relevant over time. Third, the GNP deflator contains only the prices of goods that are produced domestically, whereas the CPI includes prices of imported goods. Our attempt to understand the domestic forces that contribute to changes in the domestic price level can be confused if we use the CPI. Finally, until

---

[5]The GNP deflator, which weights by the importance of goods in current market baskets, is an example of a Paasche index of prices. For a discussion, see Edwin Mansfield, *Microeconomics*, 5th ed., Norton, New York, 1985, pp. 105ff.

[6]The CPI and PPI, which weight by the importance of goods in the base year, are examples of Laspeyres indices of prices. See Mansfield, op. cit., for a discussion.

recently, the treatment of housing costs in the CPI was inappropriate. In particular, the index was unduly responsive to changes in mortgage interest rates.

Important Terms and Concepts

gross national product (GNP)
general price level
wage rate
interest rate
exchange rate
real GNP
recession
boom
Great Depression
gold standard
inflation rate
microeconomic foundations
budget constraint
demand for money
medium of exchange
aggregate-consistency conditions
market-clearing approach
Keynesian model
IS/LM curve
balance of international payments
national-income accounts
personal consumption expenditure
consumer nondurables and services

consumer durables
gross investment
government purchases of goods and services
transfer payments
exports
imports
net exports
closed economy
open economy
depreciation
net investment
net national product (NNP)
intermediate goods
value added
gross domestic product (GDP)
national income
personal income
disposable personal income
implicit GNP price deflator
consumer price index (CPI)
producer price index (PPI)

PART I

MICROECONOMIC FOUNDATIONS AND THE BASIC MARKET-CLEARING MODEL

CHAPTER 2

Work Effort, Production, and Consumption— The Economics of Robinson Crusoe

In this chapter we develop parts of the basic theoretical structural or microeconomic foundations that we use throughout this book. First, we describe a simple production function, which relates the quantity of output to the amount of work effort. We focus on the productivity of labor—that is, on how much extra output people generate by working more. Then we discuss people's preferences for consumption and leisure. Basically, people increase their work effort and accept less leisure only if they receive a sufficient addition to consumption.

In any economic analysis, the interaction of opportunities for production with people's preferences determines the choices of work effort, production, and consumption. To bring out this basic interaction clearly, we begin with the simplest possible framework—namely, an economy of isolated households, each of which resembles Robinson Crusoe. Within this setting we can readily analyze the responses to changed opportunities in terms of **wealth effects** and **substitution effects.** It turns out that the primitive environment of Robinson Crusoe contains the essence of choice problems that arise in complicated market economies. Therefore, the principal findings from this chapter remain valid when we extend the analysis in later chapters to settings that look more like modern industrialized economies.

Production Technology

The basic theoretical model contains one type of economic unit, which we can think of as a combination of a household and a firm. Thus, this single unit combines the consuming and working activities of households with the production and hiring activities of businesses. For most purposes, this abstraction will be satisfactory because some households ultimately own the private businesses. Further, by merging the functions of households and businesses, we achieve some major simplifications of the analysis. From now on we refer to this composite unit as simply a household.

— Each household uses its labor effort as an input to production. Note that, to simplify matters, we do not yet consider stocks of capital as inputs to the production process. In this chapter we concentrate on the economic incentives that make people work more or less in order to produce and consume more or fewer goods.

Formally, the quantity of a household's commodity output per period, denoted by y, is a function of the quantity of labor input n. We write this relation as

$$y_t = f(n_t) \tag{2.1}$$

where f is the household's production function, which specifies the relation between the amount of work and the quantity of goods produced. The subscript t, which indicates the time period, is omitted when no ambiguity results.

Since our abstract model includes a single physical type of commodity, there are no problems in measuring each household's output. The real world counterpart of this output, when added up over all producers, is the gross national product (GNP). Many practical problems arise in using price indices to add up goods that are physically different. Also, the standard concept of GNP is limited to the flows of commodities that go through the organized market sector.[1] From an economic standpoint, several adjustments are in order. First, we would add the real value of the services that people produce at home, such as preparation of meals and housecleaning. Second, we might include the products from various "black markets"—including victimless crimes like prostitution and gambling, and activities such as baby-sitting and home repair work—which the official statistics exclude. Third, we might subtract from output any additions to air and water pollution, and the like. Although attempts have been made to expand the definition of GNP along these lines, there are some severe problems of concept and measurement. In any case, these difficulties do not arise in our simplified theoretical framework.

— We assume also in the basic model that people cannot store commodities from one period to the next, and thus, we neglect inventories of goods. We can think of the commodities in our model as perishable consumer goods. Examples include personal services, restaurant meals, and so on.

Work is productive in the sense that more work effort, n, means more output, y. The extra output produced by one more unit of work is called the

---

[1] One significant exception concerns owner-occupied housing. The U.S. Department of Commerce estimates the flow of rentals that could have been obtained if these houses had been offered on rental markets. The national accounts treat this *rental equivalent* as an imputed flow of output, which appears as a component of the economy's GNP.

[handwritten margin notes:]
1st add real value of services people produce at home
2nd include products from various black mkts
3rd Subtract from output any additions to air and water pollution

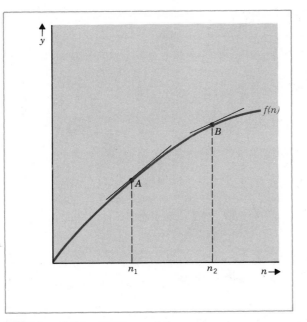

Output is zero when labor effort is nil.

Figure 2.1 Graph of Production Function
The curve shows the level of output as a function of the quantity of labor input. At point A, the slope of the tangent straight line equals the marginal product of labor when $n = n_1$. Similarly, for point B where $n = n_2$.

marginal (physical) product of labor, henceforth designated **MPL.** However, we assume **diminishing marginal productivity,** which means that each successive unit of work effort generates progressively smaller, but still positive, responses of output.

Figure 2.1, which is the graphical representation of equation (2.1), shows the relation of output to the quantity of labor input. Note that the curve goes through the origin, which means that output is zero when labor effort is nil. The positive slope of the curve (that is, of a straight line that is tangent to the curve) at any point indicates the relation between increments of output and increments in labor input, which is the marginal product of labor. For example, at the employment level n_1, the MPL equals the slope of the straight line that is tangent to the production function at point A.

The shape of the production function in Figure 2.1 implies that the slope becomes less steep as work effort increases. This property reflects the assumption of diminishing marginal productivity of labor. For example, at the employment level n_2, which exceeds n_1, the slope of the tangent straight line at point B is smaller than at point A.

Figure 2.2 clarifies the nature of diminishing marginal productivity. If we work 1 hour per day, so that $n = 1$ in the figure, then we produce the quantity Δy^1. (The symbol Δ is the Greek capital letter delta. The symbol denotes the

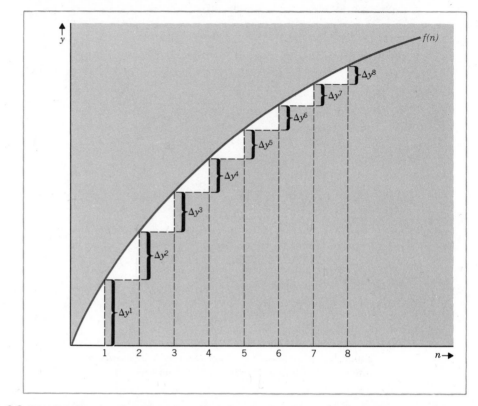

Figure 2.2 Graph of Production Function, Showing the Declining Marginal Product of Labor
The curve has the property, $\Delta y^1 > \Delta y^2 > \Delta y^3 > \ldots > \Delta y^8$. That is, the marginal product of labor declines as work effort increases.

increment in some quantity—in this case, the increment in output.) So in the interval up to 1 hour of work, the amount Δy^1 is a reasonable approximation to the marginal product of labor.

Now, if we work another hour, so that $n = 2$, then we produce the additional amount, Δy^2. Therefore, Δy^2 approximates the marginal product in the interval between 1 and 2 hours of work per day. Notice that the shape of the production function implies $\Delta y^1 > \Delta y^2$. Therefore, Figure 2.2 shows geometrically that the marginal product of labor declines as the amount of work effort rises. This property holds as work increases from 2 to 3 hours, from 3 to 4 hours, and so on. In Figure 2.2 the successive additions to output satisfy the property, $\Delta y^1 > \Delta y^2 > \Delta y^3 \ldots > \Delta y^8$.

The full relation of the marginal product of labor to the amount of work appears in Figure 2.3. Note that the marginal product declines steadily as work effort increases.

The curves in Figures 2.1 to 2.3 apply at some initial level of technology, that is, for a given production function $f(n)$. We show this production function again as the solid curve in Figure 2.4. Then the dashed curve in the figure

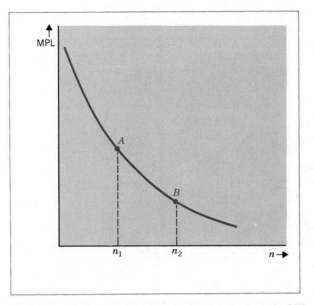

Figure 2.3 Relation of Marginal Product of Labor to Level of Work
Since $n_1 < n_2$, the marginal product of labor at point A exceeds that at point B. That is, the marginal product of labor falls as work effort rises

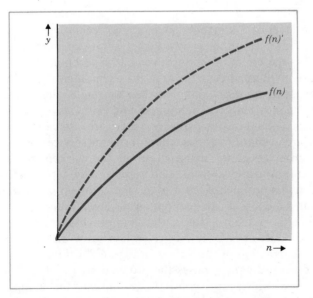

Figure 2.4 Effect of an Improvement in Technology on the Level of Production
The curve labeled $f(n)'$ corresponds to an improved technology, relative to the one labeled $f(n)$. This improvement raises the level of output for a given amount of labor input.

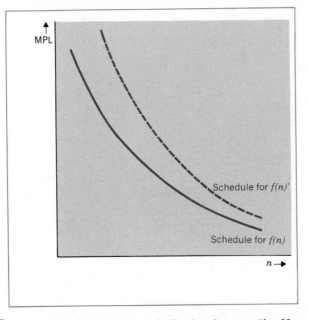

Figure 2.5 Effect of an Improvement in Technology on the Marginal Product of Labor
The dashed curve corresponds to an improved technology, $f(n)'$, relative to the initial one, $f(n)$. The technological advance shifts upward the schedule for the marginal product of labor.

shows the level of output for an improved technology, which we denote by $f(n)'$. The level of output is now higher at any given level of labor input.

What is the effect of an improvement in technology on the MPL? There are two possibilities here. In the first, the technological improvement enhances labor's productivity. For example, when hydraulic mining was applied to gold in the nineteenth century, each miner could process a much larger volume of ore with each hour of work. However, there are also cases where technological advances are primarily a replacement for labor services. For example, the use of robots may reduce the marginal product of workers on assembly lines.

For our purposes, we would like to capture the typical or average response of the marginal product of labor to an improvement in technology. Studies of production functions at an economy-wide level indicate that the first case is typical. That is, in the usual situation an improvement in technology raises the marginal product of labor at any given level of work effort.

The construction of the curves in Figure 2.4 reflects the assumption that the improved technology raises the productivity of labor. Namely, the curve labeled $f(n)'$—which corresponds to the improved technology—is steeper than the initial curve at any level of work effort. Recall that the slopes of the curves measure the marginal product of labor, MPL, at each point. In Figure 2.5 we show explicitly that, for any level of work, the MPL is higher along the new curve than it is along the initial curve. We can say that the technological advance generates an upward shift in the "schedule" for the MPL. By a schedule we mean the functional relation between the MPL and the amount of work, n. This entire relation shifts upward because of the improvement in technology.

Tastes for Consumption and Leisure

Let's pretend now that people have no opportunities to exchange commodities or anything else with other households. That is, consider an environment of Robinson Crusoes where households are isolated from each other. In this case, each household's only option is to consume all the goods that it produces in each period. (Remember, there are no possibilities for storing commodities.) Then in the world of Robinson Crusoe we have

$$c_t = y_t = f(n_t) \tag{2.2}$$

where c_t is the amount of consumption in physical units. The equation says that each household's consumption equals its production, which depends on its quantity of work effort.

Consumption in each period is a source of happiness or **utility** for households. (Henceforth, we use the economist's standard jargon, *utility*.) Equation (2.2) implies that people can consume more only if they raise their production. Further, for a given technology, the quantity of goods produced, y_t, depends on the level of work effort n_t. So the amount of work in each period is the key decision that households make in this model.

In the real world, households have a lot of flexibility in their choices of work effort. For example, someone might work 4 hours per day or 8 hours. A person can pick a job that requires lots of hard work or one that does not. Someone might work for only part of the year, as is often the case for construction workers and professional sports figures. From the perspective of a family, there is a decision on how many members participate in the labor force. For example, there has been a strong increase over the last 40 years in the number of families with two full-time workers. One evidence of this trend is the growing rate of participation of women in the civilian labor force. This participation rate grew from 28% in 1940 to 54% in 1985 (while that for males declined from 84 to 76%).[2] In a longer time perspective, the amount of time spent at work depends also on the typical length of retirement and on the number of years that people spend in school.

We capture this real-world flexibility on work effort in the model by allowing people freely to choose their hours of work in each period. Thus, we

---

[2]These figures refer to persons aged 16 years or more (14 years or more for 1940) who are neither full-time students nor members of the military. See *Economic Report of the President,* 1985, Table B-34, and U.S. Bureau of Labor Statistics, *Employment and Earnings,* January 1986, Table 2.

neglect any constraints that, for example, permit people to work on some jobs for 8 hours per day or 4 hours, but not $7\frac{1}{2}$ or 2. This abstraction will be satisfactory when we think about the overall behavior of work effort for a large number of households. In this context the constraints tend to average out.

Households have a fixed amount of time in each period, which they can divide between work and leisure. By the term *leisure*, we mean to capture the full array of activities—other than work to produce goods—on which people spend their time. We assume that leisure time is intrinsically more enjoyable than time at work. In other words, leisure is a source of utility for households.

Suppose that we can define a function to measure the amount of utility that derives each period from consumption and leisure. The form of this **utility function** is

$$u_t = u(c_t, n_t) \tag{2.3}$$
$$(+)(-)$$

where u_t is the amount of utility (in units of happiness, which are sometimes called *utils*) that someone obtains for period t. We assume that the form of the utility function, u, is the same for all periods. The positive sign under the quantity of consumption, c_t, indicates that utility rises with consumption. The negative sign under work effort, n_t, signifies the negative effect on utility of more work (that is, of less leisure).

We simplify matters by assuming a type of independence for utility at different dates. Specifically, the way in which people get utility, u_t, from consumption and leisure at date t does not depend on their consumption and work during other periods. So, if someone works a lot this period, we ignore the possibility of fatigue for the next period. Similarly, if someone consumes a lot this period, we assume that the memory of this consumption binge does not make consumption any less enjoyable next period.

In the present setting, a household's decisions for any period have nothing to do with choices made at other points in time. This result follows because goods are not storable and because the utility generated at one date does not depend on choices made for other dates. Therefore, we can focus on the selections of work effort and consumption for a single period. For convenience, we now drop the time subscripts and refer to period t's consumption and work as c and n, respectively.

We analyze a household's decisions on working and consuming by exploiting the central economic postulate of optimizing behavior. That is, each household opts for the levels of work and consumption that are consistent with the maximization of utility in equation 2.3. Further, we observe that this maximization is subject to the constraint from equation 2.2, which says that each household's consumption in any period equals its production for the same period. We want to use these facts to understand the household's selection of work and consumption.

To make progress in analyzing the household's choices, we must characterize further people's tastes for consumption and leisure. Accordingly, we make some additional assumptions about the form of the utility function, which appears in equation 2.3.

A basic assumption is that the utility gained from an extra unit of leisure, relative to that from an extra unit of consumption, diminishes as the ratio of leisure to consumption rises. In other words, if we have a lot of leisure, but relatively little consumption, then we are more concerned with adding to consumption, rather than leisure. Let's think in terms of how much extra consumption we need to make up for the loss of a unit of leisure time—that is, how much additional consumption we require to make it worthwhile to work an extra hour. If we start with little consumption and a lot of leisure—that is, if we are working only a small amount—then it is important to add to consumption. Therefore, we are willing to work a lot more to get additional consumption. However, if we add more and more to consumption and are already working quite a bit, then leisure becomes more significant. We become less and less willing to work more and give up leisure to obtain extra consumption.

We can summarize this discussion with the curve shown in Figure 2.6. At zero work effort, $n = 0$, the curve specifies a level of consumption, c^0, on the

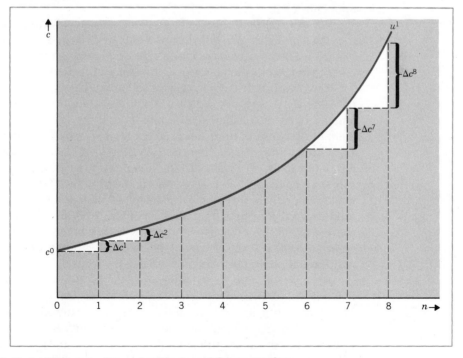

Figure 2.6 An Indifference Curve for Work and Consumption
All points, (n, c), on the curve yield the same level of utility, u^1. Hence, we are indifferent among these pairs of work effort and consumption.

vertical axis. This amount of consumption, together with full-time leisure (that is, $n = 0$), determines some level of utility from equation 2.3. We denote this level of utility by u^1. Then we construct the curve in Figure 2.6 to show all other possible combinations of work and consumption that provide the same level of utility, u^1, as that from the first pair, where $n = 0$ and $c = c^0$.

Suppose now that we work a positive amount, so that leisure becomes less than a full-time activity. For concreteness, assume that we work 1 hour per day, as represented by $n = 1$ in Figure 2.6. By itself, this reduction in leisure lowers utility. But we want to know how much additional consumption is needed to bring us back to the original level of utility. Suppose that we denote by Δc^1 the required amount of extra consumption. Then the new combination of work and consumption, where $n = 1$ and $c = c^0 + \Delta c^1$, yields the same utility as the initial pair, where $n = 0$ and $c = c^0$. Hence, we are indifferent between these two pairs of work and consumption. We show that these two points yield the same level of utility, u^1, by connecting them with the curve shown in Figure 2.6.

If we work another hour—that is, choose $n = 2$—then some additional consumption is again needed to maintain the level of utility. Figure 2.6 assumes that the required extra consumption is the amount Δc^2. Therefore, the position where $n = 2$ and $c = c^0 + \Delta c^1 + \Delta c^2$ again provides the same utility as the initial pair, where $n = 0$ and $c = c^0$.

We can continue this exercise as the amount of work rises. The result is the curve in Figure 2.6, which shows all pairs, (n, c), that yield the same level of utility. Therefore, we are indifferent among these hypothetical pairs of work and consumption. For this reason, the curve is called an **indifference curve.**

The previous discussion tells us something about the shape of an indifference curve. As we work more, each additional unit of work requires a greater amount of extra consumption to maintain utility. Therefore, the size of each addition to consumption, Δc, is larger the higher is the associated number of work hours. In particular, we see that $\Delta c^1 < \Delta c^2 < \ldots < \Delta c^7 < \Delta c^8$ in Figure 2.6. Eventually, if we are talking about working, say, 20 hours per day (or surely 24 hours per day), there will be no amount of extra consumption that makes an extra hour of work worthwhile. These considerations give the indifference curve the shape that it has in Figure 2.6. Specifically, the slope of this curve becomes steeper as we move to higher levels of work effort, n. At a sufficiently high level of work (somewhere less than 24 hours per day), the indifference curve must become essentially vertical.

At any point along the indifference curve, the slope of a tangent straight line tells us the increment in consumption that we require to make up for the loss of a unit of leisure. Each of the additions to consumption, Δc, that appear in Figure 2.6 approximate this slope in the vicinity of the corresponding level of work. For example, the amount Δc^2 is a good measure of the slope when the level of work lies between 1 and 2 hours per day.

The slope of the indifference curve in Figure 2.6 indicates the amount of consumption that we need to make up for the loss of a unit of leisure. Put alternatively, if we receive more than this amount of consumption, then we would be better off. So, for example, when we are already working 7 hours per day, we are willing to work an additional hour if, by doing so, we can raise consumption by at least the amount Δc^8 in Figure 2.6. If it turns out that the extra hour of work enables us to expand consumption by an amount greater than Δc^8, then economic reasoning predicts that we work that extra hour. This viewpoint allows us to determine the number of hours that people actually work.

All points on the curve in Figure 2.6 yield the same level of utility u^1. But suppose that we look along the vertical axis and raise the consumption level above c^0; then utility increases. Corresponding to this higher level of utility, say u^2, we can construct another indifference curve. The new curve is similar to the one shown in Figure 2.6, but it lies wholly above this curve. That is, for any level of work, n, the amount of consumption, c, is higher. That is why the new indifference curve corresponds to a higher level of utility. (We can say also that for any level of consumption, c, the amount of work effort, n, is smaller along the new curve.)

Similarly, we could lower the level of consumption below c^0 along the vertical axis. In this case, we can start the construction of an indifference curve for a lower level of utility. As a general matter, we can define a whole "family" or "map" of indifference curves, each of which corresponds to a different level of utility. Figure 2.7 shows five of these curves, labeled by their levels of utility,

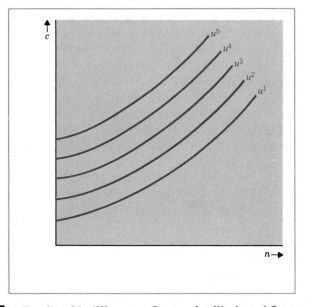

Figure 2.7 **A Family of Indifference Curves for Work and Consumption**
The level of utility rises as we move from the curve labeled u^1 to that labeled u^2, and so on.

where $u^1 < u^2 \ldots < u^5$. Along any curve the level of utility is constant. But as we move vertically from one curve to others—thereby, raising consumption while keeping work fixed—the level of utility increases. So in Figure 2.7, the level of utility rises as we move from the curve labeled u^1 to that labeled u^2, and so on. We have already mentioned the central idea that the household wants to achieve the highest possible level of utility. Therefore, we can also say that the household's objective is to reach the highest possible indifference curve among the family of curves that appears in Figure 2.7.

Deciding How Much to Work

The indifference curves in Figure 2.7 provide information about someone's willingness to give up leisure in exchange for consumption. Now suppose that we begin from a particular combination of work and consumption, (n, c). Then we can consult Figure 2.7 to find the indifference curve to which this point corresponds. The slope of the indifference curve at this point indicates how much extra consumption, Δc, someone insists on to work an additional unit of time.

To determine how much someone actually works, we combine the indifference curves with a description of people's opportunities for raising consumption when work effort rises. In the model these opportunities come from the production function, which we introduced before and graphed in Figure 2.1. The marginal product of labor (MPL) is the amount of extra output generated by an extra unit of work. Further, we know from equation 2.2 that each addition to output corresponds to an equal addition to consumption.

The MPL is the addition to production—and therefore to consumption—that results from an extra unit or work. The slope of the indifference curve is the amount of extra consumption that we need to make up for less leisure time. Therefore, if the MPL exceeds the slope of the indifference curve, then we will be better off if we work more and use the added output to expand consumption. However, as we work more, two things happen. First, the MPL declines (because of diminishing marginal productivity). Second, the slope of the indifference curve, which is the amount of extra consumption that we insist on, tends to rise. Therefore, as we work more and more, we tend to eliminate any initial excess of the MPL over the slope of the indifference curve. When the gap vanishes—that is, when the marginal product equals the slope of the indifference curve—it no longer pays to work more.

The results are in Figure 2.8. There are five indifference curves, just as in Figure 2.7. The figure also shows the household's production function, $y = f(n)$.

Consider the intersection of the production function with indifference curve u^1 at point D. At this position, the slope of the production function—

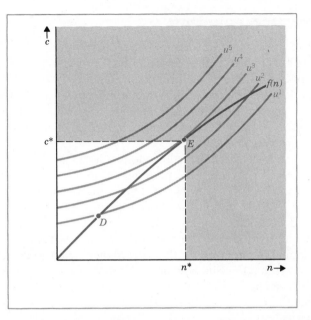

Figure 2.8 **Combining the Indifference Curves with the Production Function**
We move along the production function, $f(n)$, until we reach the highest possible indifference curve. This occurs at point E, where the production function is tangent to indifference curve u^3.

which is the MPL—exceeds the slope of the indifference curve. Therefore, an increase in work expands output—and thereby consumption—by more than enough to maintain the level of utility. Graphically, by raising work and moving along the production function beyond point D, we intersect higher indifference curves. Hence, we raise utility by working more.

Assume that we raise work enough to reach point E in Figure 2.8. Here, we have moved from indifference curve u^1 to indifference curve u^3. But at point E, the slope of the production function has diminished enough to equal the slope of the indifference curve at the same point. We show this graphically by drawing the production function, $f(n)$, as tangent to indifference curve u^3 at point E. Then we designate the associated levels of work and consumption as n^* and c^*. Notice that, at this point, we no longer gain utility by working more. In fact if we move along the production function beyond point E, we intersect lower indifference curves. In other words, the extra output and consumption are now insufficient to make up for the loss of utility from extra work. Therefore, utility declines if we work more than the amount n^*.

To summarize, we choose the combination of work and consumption that maximizes utility. Therefore, we select the pair, (n^*, c^*), at which the production function is tangent to an indifference curve.

Shifts in the Production Function

We want to understand how people alter their work effort and consumption when there are changes in the opportunities for production. Here, we represent these changes by shifts of the production function, $f(n)$. (That is, we have a shift of the entire function, rather than a movement along a single function.) Remember that we are examining the choices of work and consumption for a single period. So think here of changes in the production function that apply for that same period.

There are many examples of economic disturbances that alter production opportunities. For instance, the poor agricultural harvest in the United States for 1973 amounted to a downward shift in the production function—that is, the country had less output for a given input of labor. The oil crises of 1973 to 1974 and 1979 led to increases in the price of oil, which meant that users of energy had to give up more resources to carry out their production. From the standpoint of these users, the disturbance again looks like a downward shift in the production function, $f(n)$. On the other hand, discoveries of new technology—such as practical uses of electricity, nuclear energy, computer chips, and fiber optics—amount to upward shifts of the production function.

In analyzing the reaction of households to economic changes, we shall find it useful to place the responses into two categories:

• wealth effects
• substitution effects

For example, we will be able to decompose any kind of shift to the production function into wealth and substitution effects. Briefly, a **wealth effect** (which economists also call an **income effect**) concerns the overall scale of opportunities. If a change allows us to obtain more of the things that provide utility, then our wealth increases. Note that we define wealth here in terms of the utility that we can attain. On the other hand, a **substitution effect** refers to the relative ease or cost with which we can obtain the different items that give us utility. For example, in the case we have been discussing, we might have a change in the possibilities for transforming more work (and, hence, less leisure) into more consumption. More generally, we could have a change in the relative costs of obtaining any two goods, such as bread and television sets.

We shall use the concepts of wealth and substitution effects extensively throughout this book. Here, we start with the details of wealth effects for the model that we have been analyzing. Throughout this discussion we assume that people have a given pattern of tastes for consumption and leisure. Specifically, people's indifference curves, which appear in Figures 2.7 and 2.8, do not move around when the production function shifts.

Wealth Effects

As a general definition some change raises our wealth if it enables us to reach a higher level of utility. On the other hand, wealth declines if the change forces us to a lower level of utility.[3] Unfortunately, this definition may be difficult to apply in some circumstances. We want to use the notions of wealth and substitution effects to assist in analyses of various economic changes, such as a harvest failure. In some cases, we do not know at the start whether a particular change will end up raising or lowering our utility. So if we have to solve the whole problem to determine what happens to wealth, then there may not be much point in using the concept.

We can usually test for the sign of the change in wealth by the following method. Start with a household's initial choices of work and consumption at the position, (n^*, c^*), in Figure 2.8. Then see how the economic change alters opportunities in the vicinity of this initial point.[4] For example, we may find that the initial quantity of work effort, n^*, now allows us to consume at a higher level than before. Then wealth surely increases (because we shall be able to attain a higher level of utility). On the other hand, we may find that the initial level of work effort, n^*, now allows only a smaller quantity of consumption than before. In this case wealth probably declines.

Let's be more concrete about this method for the case of a shift to the production function. An increase in wealth arises if we can produce and consume more goods for the same amount of work effort. In the simplest case of a pure wealth effect, there is a parallel upward shift of the production function, at least in the vicinity of the initial level of work, n^*. A parallel upward shift means more output for a given amount of input, but no change in the slope of the production function at each level of work. That is, the marginal product of labor does not change if we maintain the level of work. We show this case in Figure 2.9. Here, the initial production function is $f(n)$, while the new one is $f(n)'$. Note that the new production function parallels the old one.

Recall that our previous cases of shifts to the production function—as shown in Figures 2.4 and 2.5—involve changes in the slope of the function. For example, a 10% rise in output at all levels of work means that the marginal product of labor is higher by 10% at each level of work. For the moment we neglect this type of change in the schedule for labor's marginal product, because it brings in substitution effects. The parallel shift shown in Figure 2.9 is easier because it involves only a wealth effect.

How do people respond to an increase in wealth? We can find the answer

---

[3]This viewpoint comes from John Hicks, as developed in his classic book, *Value and Capital*, 2nd ed., Oxford University Press, Oxford, 1946, Chapter 2.

[4]This general approach derives from the work of the Russian economist, Eugen Slutsky. For a discussion (in the context of markets for goods), see Heinz Kohler, *Intermediate Microeconomics*, Scott, Foresman, Glenview, Il., 1982, p. 82.

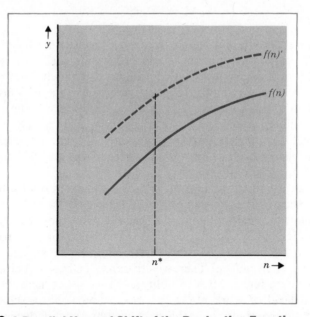

Figure 2.9 **A Parallel Upward Shift of the Production Function**
The new production function, $f(n)'$, lies everywhere above the old one, $f(n)$. With this
type of parallel shift, the two functions have the same slope at any given level of work
effort.

by combining the change to the production function from Figure 2.9 with the
indifference curves in Figure 2.8. The results are in Figure 2.10. For clarity,
we reproduce in this diagram only two indifference curves. Initially, the production function is tangent to an indifference curve at the point, (n^*, c^*).
Then, as mentioned before, the upward shift of the production function enables
us to reach a higher indifference curve. The new production function, $f(n)'$,
is tangent to a higher indifference curve at the point, $[(n^*)', (c^*)']$. The figure
indicates that consumption increases—$(c^*)' > c^*$—while work effort decreases—$(n^*)' < n^*$. In other words, we respond to the increase in wealth by
raising the quantities of both things that provide utility—here, consumption
and leisure. We say that consumption and leisure are **superior goods** because
the quantities of both rise in response to an increase in wealth. (Sometimes
economists use the term, **normal goods,** rather than superior goods.) Alternatively, we can say that the wealth effect is positive for consumption and
negative for work.

Generally, when there are many types of goods, we cannot be sure that
the wealth effect is positive for all of them. Some goods may be **"inferior,"**
which means that people desire less of them when wealth rises. (Often, economists pick on potatoes and margarine as candidates.) But when thinking of
only two broad categories of things that provide utility—namely, consumption
and leisure—we can be pretty sure that both goods are superior. That is, some

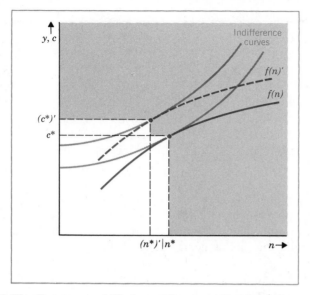

Figure 2.10 **The Response of Work and Consumption to an Increase in Wealth**
The parallel upward shift of the production function motivates us to consume more
and work less. ~~This has a L.R. negative influence of econ. development~~

reasonable assumptions about the nature of preferences guarantee this result.
Hence, from now on, we assume that consumption and leisure are superior
goods.

It is not surprising that the wealth effect on consumption is positive. Casual
observation across families or countries immediately supports this proposition.
Similarly, we can look over time for the United States as the economy has
developed. It is no surprise that consumption per person has grown along with
the rise in output per capita.

The negative effect of wealth on work effort is somewhat harder to verify.
But it does show up in the long-run negative influence of economic development on average hours of work. In the United States the average hours
worked per week for workers in manufacturing declined from 55 to 60 in 1890
to about 50 in 1914, 44 in 1929, and 40 in 1985.[5] Similarly, in the United
Kingdom the average weekly hours of male manual workers fell from 60 in
1850 to 55 in 1890, 54 in 1910, 48 in 1938, and 47 in 1965.[6]

---

[5]The data are from U.S. Department of Commerce, *Historical Statistics of the U.S., Colonial
Times to 1970,* pp. 168, 169; and *Economic Report of the President, 1986,* Table B-41. For a full
analysis, we should also consider changes in labor-force participation. See problem 2.10 below.

[6]The earlier data are rough averages from M. A. Bienefeld, *Working Hours in British Industry,*
Weidenfeld and Nicolson, London, 1972, Chapters 4 and 5. Figures since 1938 are from B. R.
Mitchell and H.G. Jones, *Second Abstract of British Historical Statistics,* Cambridge University
Press, Cambridge, 1971, p. 148.

If we look across countries at a point in time, we get some further indication of a negative wealth effect on work effort. For example, over the period from 1953 to 1960, the mean over 10 industrialized countries for the average weekly hours in manufacturing was 43.9. (The 10 are the United States, Canada, Switzerland, Sweden, New Zealand, the United Kingdom, Norway, France, West Germany, and the Netherlands.) But the mean over 10 less-developed countries was 47.4. (These 10 are Yugoslavia, Colombia, the Philippines, El Salvador, Ecuador, Guatemala, Peru, Taiwan, Egypt, and Ceylon.)[7]

On the other hand, the negative effect of economic development on average hours of work seems to weaken at high levels of development. In the United States the long-term downward trend in average hours worked per week in manufacturing apparently ended around World War II—the figure of 40.4 average hours per week for 1947 is nearly equal to that of 40.5 for 1985.[8] Similarly, for male manual workers in the United Kingdom, the value of 47.0 average hours for 1965 is nearly equal to that of 47.6 for 1946 and 47.7 for 1938.

We have to go further with our economic analysis to explain these observations for the recent period. As mentioned before, we want to bring in substitution effects as influences on the choices of work and consumption.

Substitution Effects for Work versus Consumption

We started with the case of a pure wealth effect where the production function shifted upward in a parallel manner, as shown in Figure 2.9. This change in technology allows people to produce more goods for a given amount of work. However, there is no change in the schedule for the marginal product of labor, MPL. This last condition is unrealistic, since technological advances tend to raise the MPL at each level of work.

Suppose that we want to understand the effects on households' choices from the type of upward shift to the production function that appears in Figure 2.11. (Once we understand this case, we can apply our methods to any kind of shift in the production function.) The new function, $f(n)'$, is proportionately higher than the initial one, $f(n)$, at each level of work. Therefore, the slope of the new curve exceeds that of the initial one at each level of work. For example, when work effort is the amount n^*, the slope of the new function

---

[7]The data are in Gordon Winston, "An International Comparison of Income and Hours of Work," *Review of Economics and Statistics*, February 1966, Table 1. His study deals also with cross-country differences in labor-force participation.

[8]However, the available statistics refer to hours paid by employers. The actual decline in hours worked may be greater than the data indicate because of the increasing importance of vacations and sick days. Also, more of a decline shows up when we look at the total private, nonagricultural economy. Here, average hours fell from 40.3 in 1947 to 35.1 in 1985. But these data partly reflect the changing composition of the labor force, especially toward more female workers.

additional output

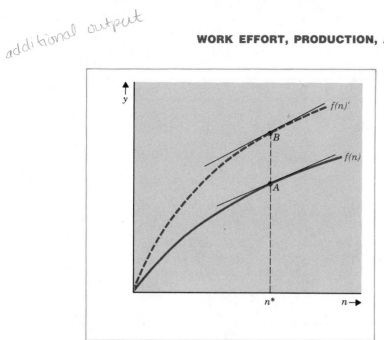

no Δ in output
more work
more consumption

Figure 2.11 A Proportional Upward Shift of the Production Function
The new production function, $f(n)'$, is higher and more steeply sloped than the old one, $f(n)$, at each level of work.

at point B exceeds that of the old one at point A. This increase in the slope of the production function means that the change is not a pure wealth effect. The change in slope brings in a substitution effect, which we now have to consider.

The proportional shift in Figure 2.11 combines the parallel shift in Figure 2.9 with a counterclockwise twist of the new function, $f(n)'$. Recall that we already understand the pure wealth effects from the parallel shift; therefore, we need only to study the consequences of a counterclockwise twist of the production function to assess the type of proportional shift that appears in Figure 2.11. Therefore, we now isolate this twist in Figure 2.12. Because the twist occurs at the employment level n^*, there is no change in output at this point. However, the new production function, $f(n)'$, is more steeply sloped than the old one, $f(n)$, at each level of work. For example, at the work level n^*, the dashed line labeled *new slope* in Figure 2.12 is steeper than the one labeled *old slope*. Hence, the twist raises the marginal product of labor at any level of work.

Figure 2.13 shows the response to a twist of the production function. The initial function, $f(n)$, is tangent to an indifference curve at the point, (n^*, c^*). Since the new function, $f(n)'$, passes through this point, it would still be possible to work the amount n^* and consume the amount c^*. Initially, we were happy to stay at this point because the MPL equaled the slope of the indifference curve, but the MPL is now higher. Therefore, more work now generates enough additional output (and consumption) to raise utility. That is, a

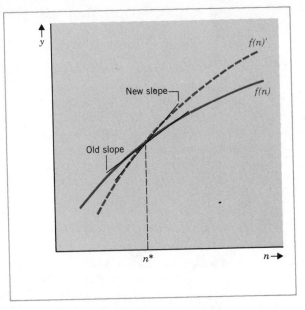

Figure 2.12 A Twist of the Production Function
At n^* the level of output is the same for the two production functions. However, the new function, $f(n)'$, is more steeply sloped than the old one, $f(n)$, at any level of work.

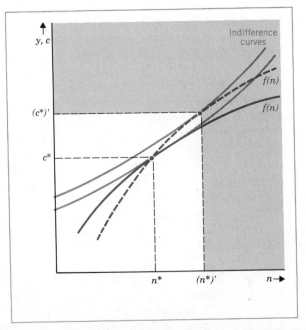

Figure 2.13 Response of Work and Consumption to a Substitution Effect
The schedule for the marginal product of labor shifts upward when we move from the old production function, $f(n)$, to the new one, $f(n)'$. The response is an increase in work—from n^* to $(n^*)'$—and a rise in consumption—from c^* to $(c^*)'$.

move along the new production function, $f(n)'$, in Figure 2.13, reaches higher indifference curves. Eventually, we get to one that is tangent to the new production function at the point, $[(n^*)', (c^*)']$. Then, any more work would lower utility.

We have shown that a rise in the schedule for the marginal product of labor induces more work, $(n^*)' > n^*$, and more consumption, $(c^*)' > c^*$. Recall that we always have the opportunity to work one more unit of time and use the additional MPL units of output to raise consumption. In terms of the two things that provide utility—leisure and consumption—we have the option to give up 1 unit of leisure in exchange for MPL extra units of consumption. When the schedule for labor's marginal product shifts upward, this deal becomes more favorable. We can now get more consumption, MPL, when we give up a unit of leisure. Or, to put this another way, consumption has become less costly relative to leisure. A rational person who wants to maximize utility finds it desirable to substitute toward the things that have become less costly. In our example, this substitution effect motivates more consumption and less leisure (which means more work).[9]

Combining the Wealth and Substitution Effects

We can now work out the full effects from a proportional upward shift of the production function, which appears in Figure 2.11. As mentioned before, this change amounts to a parallel upward shift of the production function, combined with a counterclockwise twist. That is, we have an increase in wealth, as well as a substitution effect from the rise in the schedule for the marginal product of labor.

Figure 2.14 shows the effects on the household's choices. Notice that consumption increases, $c^{*\prime} > c^*$. However, the effect on work effort is ambiguous. Let's consider the nature of this ambiguity. The positive wealth effects lead to more consumption and more leisure, which means *less* work. However, the substitution effect from the higher schedule for the MPL implies more consumption and less leisure, which means *more* work. Note that the wealth and substitution effects reinforce themselves with respect to consumption, but oppose each other with respect to work and leisure. The proportional shift of the production function leads to less work and more leisure only if the wealth

---

[9]Figure 2.13 shows that the household reaches a higher indifference curve. Therefore, the disturbance involves an increase in wealth as well as a substitution effect. However, it turns out that the wealth effect is relatively unimportant, which means that the example provides a close approximation to a pure substitution effect. To isolate the substitution effect exactly, we would have to include a small, parallel downward shift of the production function along with the twist shown in Figure 2.13. If this small shift were the right size, the household would remain on the initial indifference curve. But this minor modification would still leave people with higher levels of work effort and consumption. Thus, the elimination of the small wealth effect would not change any qualitative results.

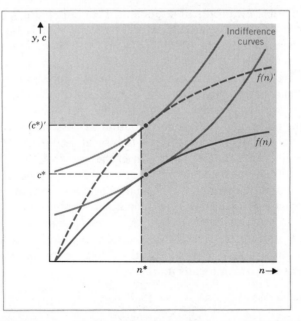

Figure 2.14 Response of Work and Consumption to Combined Wealth and Substitution Effects
When the production function shifts upward proportionately, there is an increase in consumption, but an ambiguous change in work effort.

effect dominates the substitution effect. We cannot say in general which force will be more important.

Let's use the perspective of wealth and substitution effects to reconsider the facts on work hours that we looked at before. Recall that over the last 40 years or so, there has been no strong trend in average hours worked per week in industry for the United States and the United Kingdom. However, there was a major decline in average hours worked at earlier stages of economic development.

Suppose that we think of economic development in the United States and the United Kingdom as represented by a series of proportional upward shifts to production functions. Figure 2.15 picks out three stages of economic development. These are a low level where the production function (for the typical producer) is $f(n)^I$, a middle level at $f(n)^{II}$, and a high level at $f(n)^{III}$. We can think of the first curve as applying to the United States before World War I, of the second curve as applying at the end of World War II, and of the third as applying in 1987.

Let's consider the patterns for households' tastes that would be consistent with the data on average work hours. Consider first an economy at a low level of development—that is, a situation where the production function allows the typical person to reach only a low indifference curve. In this circumstance

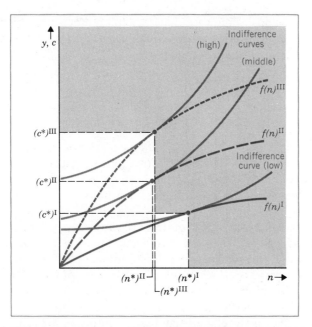

Figure 2.15 Effect of Long-Term Economic Development on Average Work Hours
The figure shows three levels of the production function as the economy develops from
$f(n)^{\text{I}}$ to $f(n)^{\text{II}}$ to $f(n)^{\text{III}}$. The indifference curves in the corresponding regions are labeled
as "low," "middle," and "high." Notice that work effort falls at early stages of economic
development, but changes little at more advanced stages.

people are likely to be willing to work long hours to maintain their consumption
levels, even if their marginal products are low and although they are already
working a lot. Diagrammatically, the indifference curve marked *low* in Figure
2.15 is extremely flat up to a high level of work effort. The flat slope means
that people are willing to work a lot to gain a small amount of extra consumption. Notice that the first production function is tangent to the low indifference curve at the point, $[(n^*)^{\text{I}},\ (c^*)^{\text{I}}]$. Here, people work many hours,
but produce and consume relatively little because of the low level of the
production function.

When production opportunities improve to the second level, $f(n)^{\text{II}}$, the
production function is tangent to the indifference curve labeled *middle* at the
point, $[(n^*),^{\text{II}}\ (c^*)^{\text{II}}]$, in Figure 2.15. The figure shows this middle indifference
curve with a slope that is generally higher and more steeply rising than that
for the low indifference curve. This shape means that extra leisure has become
more important relative to additional consumption. For this reason a reduction
in hours worked, $(n^*)^{\text{II}} < (n^*)^{\text{I}}$, accompanies the rise in consumption, $(c^*)^{\text{II}}$
$> (c^*)^{\text{I}}$. In this range of economic development, the negative wealth effect on
work effort dominates the substitution effect.

Finally, the move from the second production function, $f(n)^{\text{II}}$, to the third,

$f(n)^{\text{III}}$, corresponds to the case that we explored before in Figure 2.14. Here, the wealth and substitution effects roughly cancel to yield little change in work hours. But consumption again increases, $(c^*)^{\text{III}} > (c^*)^{\text{II}}$.

Summary

In this chapter, households are isolated from each other, and therefore behave like Robinson Crusoes. There are no markets on which people can trade, and each household uses its own labor to produce goods via a production function. Since we treat goods as nonstorable, each household consumes what it produces.

We can express people's preferences in terms of their utility for consumption and leisure. Then we can translate these preferences into indifference curves for work and consumption. Basically, people are willing to work more only if they receive a sufficient addition to their consumption.

The combination of households' preferences with their opportunities for production determines the choices of work, production, and consumption. For convenience we analyze these choices in terms of wealth and substitution effects. An improvement in the production function increases wealth, which motivates less work and more consumption. That is, the wealth effect is positive for consumption and leisure. The only substitution effect in the model involves the productivity of labor. If the schedule for labor's marginal product shifts upward, then households can obtain more consumption for an extra hour of work. Since consumption becomes cheaper relative to leisure, households work more to raise their consumption. In other words, they substitute away from leisure and toward consumption.

Toward the end, we use the apparatus to analyze the long-term behavior of work hours. Initially, as an economy develops, the increase in wealth motivates people to consume more, and to work fewer hours per week. As the economy develops further, the substitution effect from labor's higher productivity tends roughly to offset the wealth effect. Hence, there is little change in work hours, but consumption continues to rise.

Important Terms and Concepts

production function	utility
wealth effect	utility function
substitution effect	indifference curve
marginal product of labor (MPL)	superior goods (or normal goods)
diminishing marginal productivity	inferior goods

QUESTIONS AND PROBLEMS

Mainly for Review

2.1 What is a production function? How does it represent a trade-off that the individual *has* to make between work (and consumption) and leisure?

2.2 Distinguish between total product and marginal product. What are the implications for total product if marginal product is (*a*) positive and increasing, (*b*) positive and diminishing, and (*c*) negative?

2.3 What is a utility function? Show how to represent different levels of utility by a family of indifference curves. Can these curves shift in the way that the production function can?

2.4 Show how the slope of each indifference curve indicates the trade-off that the individual is willing to make between work (and consumption) and leisure. Explain why it may not be equal to the trade-off represented by the slope of the production function.

2.5 Suppose that to remain at the same level of utility an individual would have to receive one additional unit of consumption as compensation for one less unit of leisure. Would it be utility-maximizing for the individual to work more if at that point the additional output obtained is more than one? If it is less than one? Restate your answer using the concepts of indifference curves and the production function.

2.6 Suppose there is an improvement in the production function, which is accompanied by an increase in the marginal product of labor. Will the individual work more to obtain more output; or work less, obtain the same or a greater amount of output, and enjoy more leisure than before? Explain your answer in terms of wealth and substitution effects. How does your answer change if either consumption or leisure is an inferior good?

Problems for Discussion

2.7 Properties of a Specific Production Function

Suppose that the production function has the form,

$$y = A \cdot \sqrt{n} + B$$

where y is output, n is labor input, A is a positive constant, and B is another constant, which may be positive, negative, or zero.

a. Graph the level of output, y, versus the quantity of labor input, n.

b. Is the marginal product of labor positive? Is it diminishing in n?

c. Describe the wealth and substitution effects from an increase in the coefficient, A.

d. Describe the wealth and substitution effects from an increase in the coefficient, B.

2.8 Effects of Shifts in the Production Function on the Choice of Work Effort

Assume again that the production function is $y = A \cdot \sqrt{n} + B$. What are the effects on a household's work effort, n, output, y, and consumption, c, from

a. an increase in the coefficient A?

b. an increase in the coefficient B?

2.9 Temporary Versus Permanent Changes in the Production Function

Suppose that the production function shifts upward. Assume, as in Figure 2.9, that the shift is parallel, so that no change occurs in the schedule for labor's marginal product. Recall that we showed in Figure 2.10 that people respond by raising consumption and reducing work.

The improvement in the production function could be permanent—as in the case of a discovery of some new technology—or it might be temporary—as in the case of good weather for this period. What difference does it make for our results whether the change is permanent or temporary? That is, do we predict different responses of consumption and work effort in the two cases?

2.10 Changes in Labor-Force Participation

In the text we mentioned some variations over time in average hours worked per week. But we also see important changes in aggregate work effort that reflect shifts in labor-force participation. For example, people may alter their time spent at school or in retirement. Also, especially for married women in recent years, people may choose to work in the market, rather than at home. Overall, we can assess the changes in labor-force participation from the following table, which shows the ratio of the total labor force (including the military) to the adult population aged less than 65.[10]

Total Labor Force ÷ Population Aged 16–64 (%)	
1980	76
1960	69
1940	64
1920	63
1900	63

Notice that labor-force participation rose sharply during the post-World War II period. Further, most of this change reflected the increased activity of women, especially married women, in the market sector.

What does our analysis of wealth and substitution effects say about this

---

[10]The data are from the U.S. Department of Commerce, *Historical Statistics of the U.S. Colonial Times to 1970*, pp. 10 and 128, and *Economic Report of the President, 1983*, pp. 195 and 196.

behavior of labor-force participation? (Think here of effects on a family, which includes more than one potential worker.) Can we reconcile the rising rate of labor-force participation with the tendency of average hours worked per worker to stay constant or fall slowly? (*Note:* This question does not have a clear-cut answer!)

(2.11) Productivity

A popular measure of productivity is the ratio of output (say, real GNP) to employment (say, worker hours). In the graph of the production function below, this concept of productivity at the employment level n^I is given by the ratio, y^I/n^I. Productivity at this point equals the slope of the dashed line that is drawn from the origin to intersect the production function at the employment level n^I.

a. For the production function that is shown below and for any employment level n, show graphically that productivity, y/n, always exceeds the marginal product of labor, MPL.

b. Consider a technological change that shifts the production function upward proportionately at all levels of n (as shown in Figure 2.11). What happens to the choices of work effort, n, and output, y? What happens to productivity, y/n? (Empirically, long-run economic development is associated with a sustained rise in output per worker hour.)

c. Assume now that the form of the production function does not change. But suppose that people shift their tastes and become more willing to work. That is, at the initial levels of work and consumption, each person requires a smaller addition in consumption to give up a unit of leisure. What happens here to the choices of work effort, n, and output, y? What happens to productivity, y/n?

work effort same
output ↑
productivity ↑

CHAPTER 3

THE BEHAVIOR OF HOUSEHOLDS WITH MARKETS FOR COMMODITIES AND CREDIT

In the previous chapter, households were Robinson Crusoe-like producers and consumers. Hence, there were no possibilities for trade between one household and another. Now we introduce two types of opportunities for exchange. First, there is a commodity market where people can sell their outputs and buy those of others. On this market, the price level is the amount of money that exchanges for a unit of commodities. One important aspect of this market is that it allows people to specialize in their type of production. This specialization is a major element in efficient economic organization.

Second, there is a credit market on which people can borrow and lend. Here, the interest rate determines the cost of borrowing and the return to lending. By using the credit market, individuals can smooth out consumption even if their incomes vary from period to period. The effect of the interest rate on the time pattern of consumption and work is one of the key relations that we study in this chapter.

The Commodity Market

In the real world people consume very little of most of the goods that they help to produce in the marketplace. For example, an auto worker's contribution to the output of cars is much greater than that worker's expenditure on cars. Typically, people work on one or a few products and receive income from the sale of these products or from the sale of their labor services, which help to create the products. Then they use this income to purchase a wide range of consumer goods. As Adam Smith observed, people tend to specialize with respect to occupations and production activities. This specialization aids efficiency—in fact, the national output would be many times smaller if everyone participated in the production of all goods. In this case, people would learn each job badly and would spend most of their time shifting from task to task.

In the theoretical model we want to capture the feature that individuals consume little of what they produce. To keep things workable it is convenient to go to the extreme and assume that producers sell their entire output on a market where people buy and sell commodities. Then sellers use their proceeds to buy other goods for consumption purposes.

Our model would become unmanageable if we tried to keep track of the physical differences among many kinds of goods. Therefore, we continue to pretend that there is a single physical type of good, which households produce via one type of production process. Hence, as before, the production function is

$$y_t = f(n_t) \tag{3.1}$$

Money

Consider the sales and purchases of goods on the commodity market. We assume that it is inconvenient to trade one type of good directly for another. As economists have noted for hundreds of years, this form of **barter** exchange would require us to find someone who wants exactly the goods that we have and has exactly the goods that we want. Therefore, we assume that society has settled on a **medium of exchange,** called money. People sell their outputs for money and use money to buy other goods for consumption purposes. The use of money facilitates the exchange of one good for another.

The money in our model is analogous to a paper **currency** that is issued by a government. At the present time, almost all governments issue this type of currency. (Two exceptions are Panama and Liberia, which use U.S. currency. Some others that lack their own paper money are Andorra, Greenland, Guadalupe, and Liechtenstein.)

Money is denominated in an arbitrary unit, such as a "dollar." We shall often refer to dollar amounts as **nominal** magnitudes. One important feature of money is that it maintains its value in dollar terms if someone holds it. That is, unlike some assets that we introduce later, money does not bear interest.[1]

As mentioned, money takes a paper form in the model, with no backing

---

[1]Historically, it is rare for currency to pay interest. Some early forms of U.S. Treasury notes, such as those issued from 1812–15, paid interest and also had some limited use as media of exchange. However, because no denomination below $100 was issued, these notes were used mostly as bank reserves. For a discussion, see Richard Timberlake, *The Origins of Central Banking in the United States*, Harvard University Press, Cambridge, Mass. 1978, pp. 13–17.

by gold or other commodities. The monetary roles of gold and silver were important historically, but are much less significant under present-day arrangements.

Let's denote the dollar quantity of money that someone holds during period t by m_t. Then the change in someone's cash position for period t is the difference between today's money, m_t, and the amount held over from the previous period, m_{t-1}. If people add to their cash position, so that $m_t - m_{t-1} > 0$, then they are positive savers in money during period t. But, if $m_t - m_{t-1} < 0$, then they dissave in money during period t.

The aggregate quantity of money equals the sum of the holdings by all individuals. Here, we adopt the general convention of using a capital letter to denote an aggregate quantity. Therefore, M_t is the total of money held by all households during period t. For now, we assume that the aggregate quantity of money does not change over time. Therefore, $M_t - M_{t-1} = 0$ holds for all periods. This condition means that the total over households of saving in monetary form will be zero at all times.

The Price Level

We mentioned that goods sell for money on the commodity market. How much money do people get for each unit of goods sold? Since goods are physically the same, we expect that all can be sold for the same number of dollars. The number of dollars that people receive for each unit of goods sold is the dollar *price* of the good. We denote the price by P and measure it in units of dollars per good. Often, we refer to P as the general price level.

From the standpoint of a seller of commodities, the price P is the number of dollars obtained for each unit of goods sold. From the viewpoint of a buyer of commodities, the price is the number of dollars paid per unit of goods. Since P dollars buy 1 unit of goods, we see that \$1 buys $1/P$ units of goods. Therefore, the expression, $1/P$, is the value of \$1 in units of the commodities that it buys. Similarly, if we have \$$m$, rather than \$1, then we can exchange this money for $(m) \times 1/P$ units of commodities. Whereas the quantity m defines the value of money in terms of dollars, the quantity m/P measures the value of this money in terms of the quantity of commodities that it buys. Expressions like m/P, which are in commodity units, are often described as being in **real terms.** By contrast, a quantity like m is in dollar or nominal terms.

Because there is only one physical good in the model, there is only one dollar price for commodities at any point in time. But in the real world there are lots of commodities, each of which has a different price. Economists measure the general level of prices at each date by averaging over all of the individual prices for that date. Then they use this average to form a **price index,** which indicates how the average price has changed since some base year. For example, the consumer price index (CPI) in the United States stood at 322 in 1985, relative to 100 for the base year 1967. Thus, the dollar price of the typical item more than tripled from 1967 to 1985.

Many problems arise in calculating price indices. By an average price we seek to measure the dollar cost of a typical market basket of goods. So, we have to know what weights to assign to each good in constructing this market basket. To have a good price index, we also have to allow these weights to change over time. As an additional problem, we have to decide how to compare goods from one year with those from another. But in what sense is a car or a computer from 1987 the same as one from 1967? Although these issues are important and interesting, we shall not spend time on them in this book. That is because we can satisfactorily avoid these hard problems for many interesting macroeconomic questions.

One important thing to keep in mind is the distinction between the general price level and the **relative prices** of different goods. In the model we shall talk about the price level, which corresponds in the real world to a general index of prices. By a relative price we mean the dollar cost of one good expressed as a ratio to the dollar cost of another good. So we can say that the price of oil rose in 1973 relative to the price of hamburger or relative to the general level of prices. With only one physical good in the model, we cannot talk about changes in relative prices. But occasionally, we shall stretch our imaginations by referring to real-world examples where relative prices do change.

In the present chapter, we assume that people perceive the price level to be constant over time. However, we drop this unrealistic assumption in Chapter 7, which begins the study of inflation. In any case, we assume throughout the analysis that each household views itself as sufficiently small that it can buy or sell any amount of goods in the commodity market without influencing the established price. Economists call this **perfect competition.**

The Credit Market

In the Robinson Crusoe model of Chapter 2, people had no way to shift resources over time. For example, individuals could not borrow from others and repay these loans later. Also people were unable to store goods from one period to the next.

For now, we retain the assumption that goods cannot be stored over time. However, we introduce possibilities for borrowing and lending on a credit market. This market will enable individuals to shift resources from one period to another. For example, borrowing now and repaying later allows people to consume now rather than later. On the other hand, lending now and collecting later permits people to consume later instead of now.

Lenders receive a piece of paper that indicates the terms of the contract.

Table 3.1 Breakdown of Debt for Private, Domestic, Nonfinancial Borrowers in the United States at the End of 1984

Borrowing Sector	Amount of Debt ($ Billion)	% of Total	Type of Debt	Amount of Debt ($ Billion)	% of Total
Households	2134	51	Residential mortgages	1508	36
Corporate business	1307	31	Consumer credit	594	14
Noncorporate,			Corporate bonds	453	11
nonfarm business	563	13½	Commercial mortgages	403	9
Farms	186	4½	Farm mortgages	111	3
			Bank loans (other than those included above)	580	14
			Other	541	13
Total	4190	100		4190	100

Source: Board of Governors of the Federal Reserve System, flow-of-funds accounts.

In our model we call this piece of paper a **bond.** The holder of a bond has a claim to the amount owed by the borrower. The borrower is the issuer of the bond.

Recall that we are dealing with households that proxy for the array of firms and households in the real world. Therefore, the bonds in our model might correspond to securities issued by corporations, business loans made by banks, residential mortgages, or various personal loans.

As a general background for our theoretical concept of loans, we can refer to Table 3.1. This table gives a breakdown for 1984 of the outstanding debt of private domestic, nonfinancial borrowers. Hence, the table excludes the obligations of governments, foreigners, and financial institutions, such as banks and insurance companies. From the standpoint of the identity of the borrower, the total debt breaks down into 51% for households,[2] 31% for corporations, and 18% for noncorporate businesses including farms. Expressed in terms of the type of debt, there is 36% in mortgages, 14% in consumer credit (which includes installment loans on automobiles and other purchases, personal loans, and charge accounts), 11% in corporate bonds, 12% in commercial and farm mortgages, 14% in bank loans (aside from those included in other categories), and 13% in other forms.

In the theoretical model, business loans become more interesting in later chapters when we introduce possiblities for financing investments. At present,

[2]Since the households own the various corporations and noncorporate businesses, they ultimately also owe these other components of the debt.

we can think of bonds as consumer loans that people arrange on a credit market. Households use this market to achieve a desired pattern of consumption over time. For example, an individual can borrow or lend to smooth consumption, even if income varies from period to period.

Bonds in our model come in units of dollars. When we buy 1 unit of bonds with $1 of money, we lend $1 on the credit market. On the other hand, if we issue 1 unit of bonds in exchange for $1 of money, then we borrow $1.

For convenience, assume that all bonds have a maturity of one period. Then each dollar unit of these bonds commits the borrower to pay the lender the **principal**, $1, plus interest, R, in the next period. The variable R is the **interest rate**—that is, the ratio of the interest payments, R, to the amount borrowed, which is $1. For the buyer of a bond, the interest rate is the return per period to lending, while for the issuer of the bond, the interest rate is the cost per period of borrowing.

We assume that the credit market treats all bonds alike, regardless of the issuer. That is, to keep things manageable, we do not differentiate among persons with respect to their credit-worthiness, the type of collateral that they put up for a loan, and so on. Accordingly, the interest rate, R, must be the same for all bonds. Further, any household is small enough to be able to buy or sell any amount of bonds without affecting the interest rate. Again, this is an assumption of perfect competition. Later on, we can modify this framework to bring in various real-world complications, such as limitations on individuals' access to borrowing. Also, we can readily consider loans with different payment streams, such as mortgages or securities with long maturities.

Suppose that we look at the borrowing or lending status of various households at any point in time. Some people have a history of borrowing on the credit market—for example, students who are financing their college education may have taken out a large amount of loans. Similarly, individuals who have recently purchased homes or automobiles are likely to have incurred substantial debts. On the other side of the credit market, there are people who have positive holdings of bonds. For example, those who are nearing retirement or have already retired are likely to have accumulated financial assets. Also persons who are near their peak earning years—such as business executives, middle-aged college professors, and unionized workers with seniority—are likely to have amassed substantial assets.

Let b_t represent the number of bonds in dollar units that a household holds during period t. Recall that the amount of bonds may be either positive or negative for an individual household. Notice, however, that for any dollar borrowed by one person, there must be a corresponding dollar lent by someone else. Hence, the total of positive bond holdings for lenders must exactly match the aggregate of negative bond holdings for borrowers. In our model we allow only one type of economic unit, namely households, to borrow and lend. In particular, we do not yet deal with governments, foreigners, financial institutions, or corporations as participants in the credit market. (We shall see later that the essential ideas do not change when we make these additions.) There-fore, in our model the total of bonds held by all households must always be zero.

Recall that a capital letter designates the aggregate value of a variable. Accordingly, B_t represents the total of bond holdings of all households during period t. We have just shown that $B_t = 0$ holds at all points in time in our model.

As noted before, b_{t-1} is the dollar amount of bonds that someone holds during period $t - 1$. In period t these bonds pay the interest, Rb_{t-1}, and principal, b_{t-1}. Thus, the receipts from bonds are positive for lenders—for whom b_{t-1} is positive—and negative for borrowers. Recall that the aggregate stock of bonds for period $t - 1$, B_{t-1}, is zero. Therefore, the aggregates of interest and principal payments for period t must also be zero. The total of interest receipts always balances the total of interest expenses.

We measure **saving** in the form of bonds as the net change in someone's asset position, $b_t - b_{t-1}$. This saving is positive for some persons and negative for others. However, when we sum up across households, we know that $B_t = B_{t-1} = 0$. Therefore, the aggregate of saving in bonds, $B_t - B_{t-1}$, must also be zero in each period. In the aggregate the additions to loans balance the additions to debts.

In our model an individual's total of financial assets equals the sum of money and bonds, $m_t + b_t$. Recall that money holdings are nonnegative for all persons—that is, $m_t \geq 0$. (Only the government can issue money!) How-ever, bond holdings can be either positive or negative. In the aggregate, since $B_t = 0$, the stock of financial assets in our model equals the total money stock, M_t.

The change in an individual's financial assets, $(m_t + b_t) - (m_{t-1} + b_{t-1})$, determines that individual's total saving for period t. When summing up across all households, we know that $M_t - M_{t-1} = 0$ (because the total stock of money is constant), and $B_t - B_{t-1} = 0$. Therefore, the aggregate of total saving is zero at all points in time in the present model. (When we introduce investment in Chapter 9, this result will change.)

Budget Constraints

Budget Constraints for One Period

Each household receives income from sales of output, y_t, to the commodity market. As before, the quantity of output depends on the amount of labor input, n_t, through the production function, $y_t = f(n_t)$. Since the price of goods is P, the dollar income from selling output is Py_t. Recall that interest income from the bond market, Rb_{t-1}, is positive for lenders and negative for borrowers. Also, remember that people receive no interest income from their holdings of money.

Each household purchases the quantity of consumable goods, c_t, from the commodity market. Since the price of goods is P, the amount of consumption expenditure in dollars is Pc_t.

If someone's total income exceeds his or her consumption expenditures, then he or she is a positive saver and experiences an increase over time in the dollar value of total financial assets, money plus bonds. Similarly, households whose total income is below their consumption expenditures are dissavers.

For a given total of financial assets, a household can use the credit market to exchange money for bonds, or vice versa, and thereby achieve the desired composition of assets between bonds and money. Recall that the amount held as bonds, b_t, determines the interest income (positive or negative) for period $t + 1$. The motivation for holding money—which does not bear interest—concerns money's convenience in carrying out exchanges. However, for expositional purposes, we shall not deal explicitly with the demand for money until Chapter 4. So, for now, we just assume that people hold part of their assets as money.

We can express the equality between a household's total sources and uses of funds in the form of a budget constraint. The condition for period t is

$$Py_t + b_{t-1}(1 + R) + m_{t-1} = Pc_t + b_t + m_t \qquad (3.2)$$

The left side of equation 3.2 contains sources of funds, which include income from the commodity market, Py_t, the principal received on last period's bonds, b_{t-1}, the interest receipts from these bonds, Rb_{t-1}, and the stock of money held over from the previous period, m_{t-1}. The right side of the equation comprises uses of funds, which are consumption expenditures, Pc_t, holdings of bonds, b_t, and holdings of money, m_t. Since we treat the price level and interest rate as constants, these variables appear without time subscripts in the equation.

If we rearrange equation 3.2, then we obtain an expression for a household's nominal saving, which equals the change over time in the dollar value of financial assets.

$$\text{Nominal saving} = (b_t + m_t) - (b_{t-1} + m_{t-1}) = Py_t + Rb_{t-1} - Pc_t \qquad (3.3)$$

Notice that nominal saving equals the income from the commodity market plus interest receipts less consumption expenditures. One thing to stress is the connection between consumption and saving. If we spend more on consumption, Pc_t, then saving falls one-to-one. Correspondingly, we carry over less assets, $b_t + m_t$, to the future.

Households can leave saving intact while making simultaneous changes in income and consumption. For example, suppose that we work more in period t and raise income, Py_t, by \$1000. Then, if we also raise consumption spending, Pc_t, by \$1000, savings does not change. Therefore, the budget constraint allows people to work more and raise consumption during any period, without altering the amounts of assets that they carry over to the following period. This choice beween consumption and leisure in a single period was the only one available to Robinson Crusoe in the model from Chapter 2. The expanded model retains this option but introduces new possibilities that exploit the credit market. Specifically, individuals can vary current saving, which is the difference between income and expenditure. Thereby, people alter the amount of assets that they carry over to the future.

Recall that equation 3.3 specifies the saving for one household. As mentioned before, the total of this saving across households is zero in our model. When we add up the right side of equation 3.3 over all households, we find that aggregate income equals aggregate spending, $PY_t = PC_t$. (Note that the aggregate stock of bonds, B_{t-1}, is zero.) For Robinson Crusoe, the equality between production and consumption holds individually at every point in time. Now, because of the credit market, some people can consume more than their income (dissave), while others consume less (save). But it is still true for the economy as a whole that total output cannot depart from total consumption. Consumption is the only use for commodities in the present model.

Budget Constraints for Two Periods

The previous discussion brought out the effects of current consumption and work on the assets that someone carried over to the future. We can clarify this process by studying a household's choices over more than one period. We can go a long way by considering just two periods.

The budget constraint from equation 3.2 holds for any period. For example, for period 1, the condition is

$$Py_1 + b_0(1+R) + m_0 = Pc_1 + b_1 + m_1 \qquad (3.4)$$

Now we shall find it convenient to assume that each household's cash holdings are constant over time—that is, $m_1 = m_0$. Anyone who maintains a constant quantity of money carries out any saving or dissaving in the form of bonds. By making this assumption, we avoid a clutter of minor terms in the household's budget constraint over more than one period. But we shall return later (in Chapter 4) to reconsider the case where someone's holdings of money change over time.

Using the condition, $m_1 = m_0$, the budget constraint from equation 3.4 simplifies to

$$Py_1 + b_0(1+R) = Pc_1 + b_1 \qquad (3.5)$$

There is a similar one-period budget constraint for period 2,

$$Py_2 + b_1(1+R) = Pc_2 + b_2 \qquad (3.6)$$

Note that the two budget constraints are not independent. In particular, b_1 is a use of funds in the budget constraint for period 1, but a source of funds in the constraint for period 2. Thus, b_1 (which is the amount of interest-bearing assets carried over from period 1 to period 2) provides the link between the two periods.

We can combine the two one-period budget constraints into a single two-period budget constraint. First, solve equation 3.6 for b_1 to get

$$b_1 = \frac{Pc_2}{(1+R)} + \frac{b_2}{(1+R)} - \frac{Py_2}{(1+R)} \qquad (3.7)$$

Next, substitute the right-hand side of equation 3.7 for b_1 in equation 3.5 and collect terms into sources and uses of funds to get

Sources of funds   Uses of funds

$$Py_1 + \frac{Py_2}{(1+R)} + b_0(1+R) = Pc_1 + \frac{Pc_2}{(1+R)} + \frac{b_2}{(1+R)} \qquad (3.8)$$

The left side of equation 3.8 contains the income from the commodity market for periods one and two, Py_1 and Py_2, and the initial stock of bonds, b_0. On the right side are terms that involve consumption expenditures over the two periods, Pc_1 and Pc_2, and the stock of bonds held at the end of the second period, b_2. Recall that we already substituted out for the interim bond stock, b_1, which does not appear in equation 3.8.

Observe the manner in which the incomes, Py_1 and Py_2, appear in equation 3.8. We divide next period's amount, Py_2, by the term, $(1+R)$, before adding it to this period's, Py_1. It is important to understand why incomes from the two periods, Py_1 and Py_2, are not just added together in the household's two-period budget constraint. Similarly, on the right side of equation 3.8, we divide next period's expenditure, Pc_2, by the term, $(1+R)$, before adding it to this period's, Pc_1. Again, we want to understand why we combine expenditures from different dates in this manner.

Present Values

If the interest rate is positive—that is, $R > 0$—then a given dollar amount of today's bonds translates into a larger number of dollars next period. Accordingly, individuals who can buy or sell bonds on the economy-wide credit market (that is, people who can lend or borrow) regard a dollar's worth of income or expenses differently depending on when it arises. Specifically, a dollar received or spent earlier is equivalent to more than one dollar later. Or, viewed in reverse, dollars received or spent in the future must be discounted to express them in terms that are comparable to dollars in the present.

Suppose, for example, that $R = 10\%$ per year. Assume that we have $100 of income today, but plan to spend these funds in the future. Then we can buy $100 of bonds now and have $110 available next year. Hence, $100 today is worth just as much as $110 next year. Equivalently, we discount the $110 by asking how much income would we need today to generate $110 next year.

We find the answer by solving the equation,

$$\text{(Income needed today)} \times (1 + 10\%) = \$110$$

The required amount of current income is $\$110/(1.1) = \$100$.

More generally, if we substitute any value of the interest rate, R, for 10%, then we divide the income for next period, Py_2, by the term, $(1+R)$, to find the equivalent amount for this period. The result, $Py_2/(1+R)$, is the **present value** of the future income. Economists also call the term, $(1+R)$, the **discount factor.** When we discount by this factor—that is, when we divide by the term, $1+R$—we determine the present value of next period's income.

Equation 3.8 shows that we express the second period's income as a present value, $Py_2/(1+R)$, before combining it with the first period's income, Py_1. Thus, the sum, $Py_1 + Py_2/(1+R)$, is the total present value of income from the commodity market over periods 1 and 2.

So far, the discussion refers to present values of incomes. But the same reasoning applies to expenditures. Equation 3.8 shows that we express next period's expenditure as the present value, $Pc_2/(1+R)$, before adding it to this period's spending, Pc_1. Hence, the sum, $Pc_1 + Pc_2/(1+R)$, is the total present value of consumption expenditures over periods 1 and 2.

The Household's Budget Line

We now begin our analysis of how individuals choose their levels of consumption and work over two periods. In doing so, we assume that people face a given price level, P, and interest rate, R. In particular, an individual can save either a positive or negative amount in each period. However, remember that saving must add to zero in each period when we sum up across all of the households. Later (in Chapter 5), we shall see how to ensure that aggregate saving is always zero. But for the moment, we ignore this aggregate condition and consider only the behavior of individuals.

The two-period budget constraint in equation 3.8 brings out the choices that a credit market allows to a household. The interesting new element is the choice between consuming now or later—that is, Pc_1 versus Pc_2—and earning income (by working) now or later—that is, Py_1 versus Py_2. Assume, for example, that we raise today's spending, Pc_1, by $1000, and thereby cut today's saving by $1000. This change reduces assets at the end of the first period, b_1, by $1000 (see equation 3.5). For the second period, we lose $1000 in receipts of principal from bonds and $100 in receipts of interest (assuming that $R = 10\%$). Since we have $1100 less during the second period, we can decrease next period's spending, Pc_2, by this amount to keep the final asset position, b_2, intact. Therefore, the increase in today's spending by $1000 balances against a decrease in next period's spending by $1100.

Put alternatively, to offset the increase by $1000 in period 1's spending, we must lower the present value of period 2's spending, $Pc_2/(1+R)$, by $1000.

But, with an interest rate of 10%, this requires a decrease in next period's spending by $1100. Generally, the required decrease in spending for the next period, Pc_2, equals the increase in this period's spending, Pc_1, multiplied by the discount factor, $(1+R)$.

Let's focus now on the choices of consumption over two periods, c_1 and c_2. For this purpose, it is convenient to divide through equation 3.8 by the price level P. Then, if we rearrange terms to place those involving consumption on the left side, we get

$$c_1 + \frac{c_2}{(1+R)} = y_1 + \frac{y_2}{(1+R)} + b_0(1+R)/P - \frac{b_2}{P(1+R)} \qquad (3.9)$$

Each term in equation 3.9 appears in units of commodities, rather than as dollar values. For example, y_1 is period 1's real income from the commodity market, in the sense of indicating the number of commodity units that we can buy during period 1 with the dollar income of Py_1. Similarly, y_2 is the real income for period 2. Also, the quantities, c_1 and c_2, are the real expenditures for consumption during periods 1 and 2.

The dollar amount of the initial principal and interest receipts from bonds is $b_0(1+R)$. When we divide this amount by the price level, P, in equation 3.9, we determine the real value of these principal and interest payments. Similarly, we divide the dollar value of the final stock of bonds, b_2, by the price level in equation 3.9. (Notice that the division by the discount factor, $(1+R)$, converts this amount into a present value. We discount b_2 by $1+R$ because b_2 is the amount of bonds in the *second* period. $b_0(1+R)$ is not discounted because it measures funds available during the *first* period.)

Suppose that we fix the total of the items on the right side of equation 3.9 at some amount, which we can call x. So we can think of fixing the starting real value of bonds, $b_0(1+R)/P$, the real present value of bonds carried over to period 3, $b_2/P(1+R)$, and the total present value of real income from the commodity market, $y_1 + y_2/(1+R)$. Then we can rewrite equation 3.9 as

$$c_1 + \frac{c_2}{(1+R)} = x \qquad (3.10)$$

where $x = b_0(1+R)/P - b_2/P(1+R) + y_1 + y_2/(1+R)$. Equation 3.10 makes clear that for a given quantity x, we can change today's consumption, c_1, if we make the appropriate adjustment in next period's consumption, c_2.

The straight line in Figure 3.1 shows the possibilities. Notice that if we consume nothing in the second period, so that $c_2 = 0$ (which would probably cause us to starve and therefore be undesirable), then equation 3.10 says that today's consumption, c_1, equals x. Hence, the line in the figure intersects the horizontal axis at this point. Alternatively, if we consume nothing today, so that $c_1 = 0$, then the real present value of next period's consumption, $c_2/(1+R)$, equals x. In this case, next period's consumption is given by

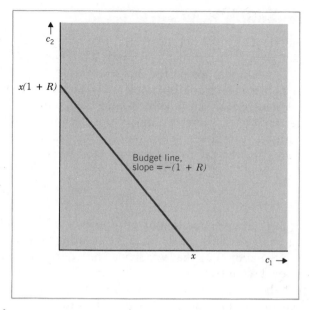

Figure 3.1

The budget line with slope $-(1+R)$ shows the attainable combinations of consumption levels, c_1 and c_2. Along this line, the total real present value of expenditures over the two periods equals the fixed amount, x.

$c_2 = x \cdot (1+R)$. Therefore, the line in the figure intersects the vertical axis at this point.

The straight line in Figure 3.1 connects the value x on the horizontal axis to the value $x(1+R)$ on the vertical. This **budget line** shows all the combinations of consumptions, c_1 and c_2, that satisfy the household's budget condition from equation 3.10. The important point is that the budget line shows the attainable pairs of consumption, c_1 and c_2, for a given value of x—that is, for a given real present value of spending over the two periods.

The budget line in Figure 3.1 has the slope of $-(1+R)$. (The magnitude of the slope is the ratio of the vertical intercept, $x[1+R]$, to the horizontal, x.) Along this line, a decrease by 1 unit in today's real spending, c_1, is matched by an increase of $(1+R)$ units in next period's real spending, c_2. To put it another way, the interest rate R is the premium that we get in future consumption by saving today, rather than consuming.

So far, our analysis describes a household's opportunities for consuming in one period versus another. But we have not yet studied people's preferences for consumption at different dates. When we combine the opportunities with the preferences, we shall determine the actual choices of consumption over time. Thus, we now turn our attention to these preferences.

Preferences for Consuming Now versus Later

We mentioned in Chapter 2 that people receive utility from consumption and leisure in each period. In particular, a family's utility for period 1 is given by $u_1 = u(c_1, n_1)$, while that for period 2 is $u_2 = u(c_2, n_2)$. But how do people weigh the units of utility or utils obtained today, u_1, versus those received next period, u_2? Usually, economists assume that people prefer to get their utils earlier rather than later. Here, we model this preference by discounting the units of future utility in a simple manner. Specifically, we assume that each household cares about total utility, U, over the two periods, as measured by

$$U = u(c_1, n_1) + \frac{1}{(1+\rho)} u(c_2, n_2) \qquad (3.11)$$

Note that at this stage, we do not look beyond period 2. Implicitly, we assume for now that people's choices from date 3 onward are givens.

Notice in equation 3.11 that we divide the utility received during period 2 by a type of discount factor, $(1+\rho)$, where the parameter ρ is a positive constant (ρ is the Greek letter *rho*). In effect, we calculate the present value of utility, but we use the number ρ, rather than the market interest rate, R, to calculate the present value. We shall call the number ρ the **rate of time preference.** The higher the rate of time preference, the greater is the discount applied to future utility. Put another way, for each unit of utility that we give up today, we need $(1+\rho)$ extra units next period to maintain total utility, U. So a higher value of ρ signifies a greater preference for current utils relative to future ones. We assume here that all households have the same rate of time preference, ρ.

Suppose for the moment that we have already decided on our levels of work effort, n_1 and n_2. To keep things simple, assume for now that we work the same amount in each period, so that $n_1 = n_2$. Then we want to model our attitude toward different combinations of consumption for the two periods, c_1 and c_2. In the language of Chapter 2, we want to draw indifference curves for consumption now versus consumption next period. These curves will reveal the different combinations of consumptions, c_1 and c_2, that yield the same level of total utility, U, as defined in equation 3.11.

Figure 3.2 shows an indifference curve for consumption today versus consumption next period. Here the level of total utility is the amount U^1. For very high levels of today's consumption, relative to next period's—for example, at point A in the figure—we are much more interested in adding to next period's consumption rather than this period's. Hence, a small increase in c_2 makes up for the loss of a unit of c_1. Thus, in the figure the curve has a relatively flat slope at point A. Similarly, the indifference curve has a steep slope when today's consumption, c_1, is relatively low, as at point B in the figure. Here, we need a large addition to next period's consumption, c_2, to make up for the loss of a unit of this period's consumption, c_1.

The slope of the indifference curve at any point reveals the amount of

Figure 3.2 **An Indifference Curve for Consumption Now versus Consumption Next Period**
We are equally happy with any combination of consumptions, c_1 and c_2, that lie along the curve. Today's consumption is high relative to next period's at point A, and low relative to next period's at point B. Hence, the curve is steeper at point B than at point A.

next period's consumption that we need to make up for the loss of a unit of current consumption. Generally, this slope depends on two factors. First, as shown in Figure 3.2, the slope steepens as current consumption, c_1, falls relative to future consumption, c_2. Second, the slope depends on the rate of time preference, ρ, which appears in expression 3.11. For any given combination of consumptions, c_1 and c_2, a rise in ρ means that we value future consumption less relative to current consumption. So, for given c_1 and c_2, an increase in ρ raises the number of units of future consumption that we need to make up for the loss of a unit of current consumption. Hence, the indifference curve shown in Figure 3.2 becomes steeper throughout if ρ rises.

As in Chapter 2, we can define a family of indifference curves, each one applying to a different level of utility. Figure 3.3 shows three of these curves, labeled by their levels of total utility, where $U^1 < U^2 < U^3$.

Choosing Consumption over Two Periods

The budget line in Figure 3.1 describes how people can use the credit market to shift between consumption now and consumption next period. The family of indifference curves shown in Figure 3.3 describes people's willingness to exchange consumption now for consumption next period. Therefore, if we

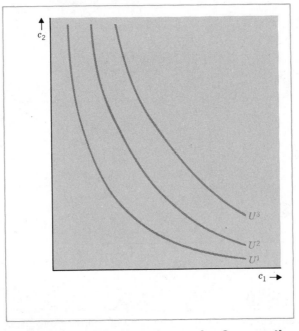

Figure 3.3 **A Family of Indifference Curves for Consumption Now versus Consumption Next Period**
Along each curve the level of utility is constant. Utility increases as we move from the curve labeled U^1 to that labeled U^2, and so on.

combine the market opportunities from Figure 3.1 with the indifference map from Figure 3.3, we can determine the choices of consumption over the two periods.[3]

Figure 3.4 combines the budget line from Figure 3.1 with the indifference curves shown in Figure 3.3. Note that we move along the budget line until we reach the highest possible indifference curve. This occurs at the point of tangency, shown in the figure, where the slope of the budget line equals the slope of an indifference curve. We label the corresponding levels of consumption for the two periods as c_1^* and c_2^*.

Recall that the slope of an indifference curve measures the bonus in next period's consumption that we need to compensate for giving up a unit of this period's consumption. On the other hand, the slope of the budget line is $-(1+R)$, which tells us the premium, R, that we get if we save more. Therefore, at the point of tangency shown in Figure 3.4 the premium from saving more just balances the willingness to defer consumption. For this reason, any

---

[3]This method comes from Irving Fisher, *The Theory of Interest*, Macmillian, New York, 1930, especially Chapter 10. (Interestingly, Fisher—who did his main work at Yale University— is one of the few macroeconomists who is popular today at both Yale and Chicago.)

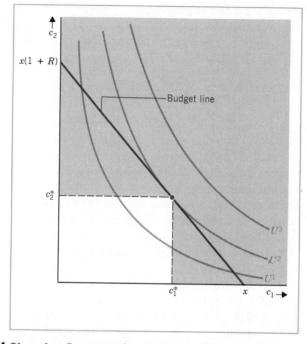

Figure 3.4 Choosing Consumption Today and Next Period
The choice of consumption levels, c_1^* and c_2^*, occurs where the budget line is tangent to an indifference curve.

choice along the budget line other than the point (c_1^*, c_2^*) leads to lower utility. This result is clear geometrically from Figure 3.4.

To sum up, we combined people's opportunities (the budget line) with their preferences (the indifference curves) to determine the choices of consumption over two periods. At the same time, we determined how much people save today. We can use this analysis to see how the time pattern of consumption and saving changes when there are shifts in the interest rate or other variables. The effects of changes in the interest rate turn out to be especially important for our subsequent macroeconomic analysis.

Wealth and Substitution Effects

As in Chapter 2, we can use the notions of wealth and substitution effects to analyze people's choices. In the present setting wealth effects relate to the quantity previously denoted as x, which is the total present value of real consumption expenditures for periods 1 and 2. The important substitution variable for consuming now versus later, or for how much to save, turns out to be the interest rate, R.

Wealth Effects on Consumption

Before, we found that parallel shifts of the production function implied pure wealth effects. Here, these wealth effects show up as shifts in the total real present value of expenditures, x, which is given by

$$x = c_1 + \frac{c_2}{(1+R)} = y_1 + \frac{y_2}{(1+R)} + b_0(1+R)/P - \frac{b_2}{P(1+R)} \quad (3.12)$$

Also, recall that the amounts of real income from the commodity market come from the production function as $y_1 = f(n_1)$ and $y_2 = f(n_2)$.

Assume that the production function shifts upward for periods 1 and 2. Think of parallel shifts that do not change the schedule for labor's marginal product. Assuming for the moment that we do not change the levels of work, n_1 and n_2, there are increases in the amounts of real income, y_1 and y_2. Now suppose that we hold constant the initial and final stocks of bonds, b_0 and b_2. In particular, by holding fixed b_2 we do not change the provision of assets for the future. Then the increases in y_1 and y_2 raise the total real present value of spending, x, from equation 3.12. Now we have to decide how to allocate this increase in total spending between c_1 and c_2.

Figure 3.5 shows that the increase in the total real present value of spending generates a parallel outward shift of the budget line. (The slope stays the same because the interest rate does not change.) The new budget line allows us to

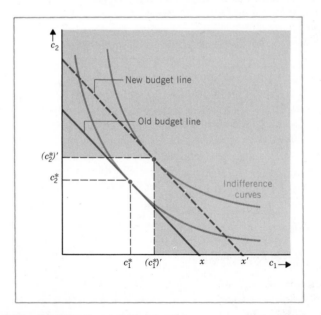

Figure 3.5 Wealth Effects on Consumption
The total real present value of consumption expenditures for periods 1 and 2 rises from x to x'. Consumption increases from c_1^* to $(c_1^*)'$ in period 1, and from c_2^* to $(c_2^*)'$, in period 2.

reach a higher indifference curve than before. Note especially that the new point of tangency between the budget line and an indifference curve occurs at higher levels of consumption for each period. Hence, the wealth effect is positive for c_1 and c_2—or equivalently, c_1 and c_2 are both superior goods.

The Interest Rate and Intertemporal Substitution

If the interest rate is R, then each household faces the budget line that we label as "old" in Figure 3.6. Given the total real present value of spending for periods 1 and 2, which equals x, the household selects the consumption pair, (c_1^*, c_2^*).

If the interest rate rises to R', then the new budget line is steeper than the old one. However, there are many places that we could draw this new line in Figure 3.6. For present purposes, we want to draw the new line so as to isolate the substitution effect from a higher interest rate. Suppose that we tried

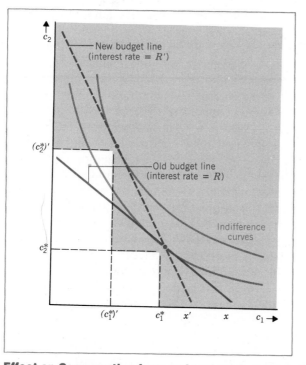

Figure 3.6 Effect on Consumption from an Increase in the Interest Rate

When the interest rate is R on the old budget line, the household chooses the consumption pair, (c_1^*, c_2^*). But if the interest rate rises to R' on the new budget line, the household opts for the pair, $[(c_1^*)', (c_2^*)']$. Notice that the increase in the interest rate motivates people to choose a higher ratio of consumption next period to consumption this period.

holding fixed the overall real present value of spending, x. Then the new budget line would start from the value x on the horizontal axis, but otherwise lie everywhere to the right of the old budget line. But then the new budget line would allow us to consume the same amount today, c_1^*, and more next period. Hence, as in our previous example, there would be an increase in wealth. Accordingly, this sort of shift would not give us a pure substitution effect.

We can approximate a pure substitution effect by rotating the budget line around the point where we initially chose the levels of consumption. Therefore, as shown in Figure 3.6, the new budget line intersects the old one at the point, (c_1^*, c_2^*). Then we can still buy this initial pair of consumptions if we wish. But we cannot increase either quantity unless we give up some of the other. (Notice that this construction implies a decrease in the total real present value of spending—that is, $x' < x$ on the horizontal axis.)

Although the new budget line passes through the point (c_1^*, c_2^*) in Figure 3.6, the line is not tangent to an indifference curve at this point. Rather, the new budget line is steeper than the indifference curve, which means that the premium to saving more, R', exceeds the amount needed to motivate more saving. It follows that each household would raise saving—that is, c_1 falls and c_2 rises. The new choices, labeled $[(c_1^*)', (c_2^*)']$ in Figure 3.6, are where the new budget line is tangent to an indifference curve.[4] The important point is that the increase in the interest rate motivates people to raise future consumption, c_2, relative to current consumption, c_1. Equivalently, the rise in the interest rate induces people to save a larger fraction of current income.

Let's look at the results from another perspective. Recall that the total real present value of spending over periods 1 and 2 is $c_1 + c_2/(1+R)$. Note again that we divide the next period's consumption, c_2, by the discount factor, $(1+R)$, before adding it to current consumption, c_1. Therefore, a rise in the interest rate effectively lowers the cost of next period's consumption relative to that of current consumption. Specifically, we can obtain more units of consumption next period for each unit of current consumption than we forego. It is this change in relative costs that motivates us to substitute future goods, c_2, for the relatively more expensive current ones, c_1. Economists often refer to this mechanism as an **intertemporal-substitution effect.** Namely, the rise in the interest rate induces us to postpone spending from the present to the future. Equivalently, the higher interest rate makes it worthwhile for us to save more of our current income in order to consume more goods later.

---

[4]Note that we reach a higher indifference curve. Hence, wealth increases, even though we rotated the budget line through the point where we initially chose consumption, (c_1^*, c_2^*). But it turns out that this wealth effect becomes negligible, relative to the substitution effect, when we look at smaller and smaller changes in the interest rate. So, at least when we consider small changes, we can neglect the wealth effect as a satisfactory approximation.

Choosing Work Effort at Different Dates

In Chapter 2 we studied the choice of work and consumption for a single period. There we stressed substitution effects from changes in the schedule for labor's marginal product. Also, we explored wealth effects from shifts in the position of the production function.

In the present chapter we examined an individual's choices of consumption over time. But so far we have held fixed the behavior of work effort. However, if we combine the previous analysis of work and consumption with the present analysis of consumption over time, then we shall also understand how people choose work effort over time.

Wealth Effects on Work Effort

We can write the household's budget constraint over two periods as

$$f(n_1) + \frac{f(n_2)}{(1+R)} + \frac{b_0(1+R)}{P} = c_1 + \frac{c_2}{(1+R)} + \frac{b_2}{P(1+R)} \qquad (3.13)$$

Note the substitutions, $y_1 = f(n_1)$ and $y_2 = f(n_2)$, in the expression for the real sources of funds on the left side.

Suppose that the production function shifts up in a parallel fashion for periods 1 and 2. Then, if we hold fixed the amounts of work, n_1 and n_2, we increase the real sources of funds on the left side of equation 3.13. As we saw before, people respond by raising c_1 and c_2.

Recall from Chapter 2 that people also react to more wealth by taking more leisure. Hence, the levels of work, n_1 and n_2, tend to decline, rather than stay fixed.

Often, macroeconomists stress the positive wealth effect on consumption, but neglect the effect on leisure. However, the evidence on hours of work, which we reviewed in Chapter 2, indicates that this effect on leisure is important. For example, at early stages of economic development, the wealth effect is strong enough that average hours worked tend to diminish as an economy develops.

The Interest Rate and Choices of Work Effort

Figure 3.6 shows that an increase in the interest rate motivates us to reduce current consumption, c_1, and raise next period's consumption, c_2. Equivalently, by reducing c_1, we save more in period 1. So far, we held fixed the amounts of work, n_1 and n_2. Let's see now whether this is correct.

Notice from the right side of equation 3.13 that an increase in the interest rate, R, makes next period's consumption, c_2, cheaper relative to this period's, c_1. That is why we substitute toward c_2 and away from c_1 when the interest rate rises. But the same argument holds for leisure in the two periods. If we take leisure in period 2, then we discount the loss in output, $f(n_2)$, by the factor, $(1+R)$. Therefore, when the interest rate rises, the leisure from period 2 becomes cheaper relative to that in period 1. That is, the future output that we lose by working less in period 2 has a smaller present value than before. The conclusion is that an increase in the interest rate motivates us to substitute toward next period's leisure and away from this period's. Or, equivalently, we raise this period's work, n_1, relative to next period's, n_2. Note also that the increase in n_1 reinforces the decrease in c_1 in the sense of raising current saving.

Overall, an increase in the interest rate has two types of intertemporal-substitution effects. First, we reduce today's consumption, c_1, relative to next period's, c_2. Second, we raise today's work, n_1, relative to next period's, n_2. Both effects—the reduction in current spending and the increase in current income—show up as an increase in current saving. Thus, both responses reflect the positive response of an individual's desired saving to the return from saving, which is the interest rate. Typically, macroeconomists stress the effect on saving that results from intertemporal substitution of consumption, but neglect the effect from changes in work effort. However, there is some evidence for the United States that intertemporal substitution of work effort is also significant.[5]

Budget Constraints over Many Periods

Thus far, we have examined the behavior of households over two periods. But to carry out this analysis, we had to hold fixed the amount of bonds that someone carries over to later periods. In fact, this amount is not a given, since it depends on people's plans for consuming and earning income later on. Now, we make this connection explicit by dealing with households' plans over many periods.

Budget Constraints for Three Periods

To proceed, we have to examine people's behavior for more than two periods. We start by extending a household's budget constraint from two periods to three. Then we can readily expand to any number of periods.

Start with the two-period budget constraint from equation 3.8:

$$Py_1 + \frac{Py_2}{(1+R)} + b_0(1+R) = Pc_1 + \frac{Pc_2}{(1+R)} + \frac{b_2}{(1+R)}$$

The final stock of bonds from the second period, b_2, determines the initial stock for period 3. Specifically, for period 3 the budget constraint is

$$Py_3 + b_2(1+R) = Pc_3 + b_3 \tag{3.14}$$

(Note that we still assume constancy of money balances, so that $m_2 = m_3$.)

---

[5]See Thomas MaCurdy, "An Empirical Model of Labor Supply in a Life-Cycle Setting," *Journal of Political Economy*, December 1981.

We can solve out for the stock of bonds, b_2, from equation 3.14 and substitute the result into the two-period budget constraint. Then we find that the three-period budget constraint is

$$Py_1 + \frac{Py_2}{(1+R)} + \frac{Py_3}{(1+R)^2} + b_0(1+R)$$

$$= Pc_1 + \frac{Pc_2}{(1+R)} + \frac{Pc_3}{(1+R)^2} + \frac{b_3}{(1+R)^2} \quad (3.15)$$

There are two main differences between the three-period budget constraint from equation 3.15 and the two-period constraint from equation 3.8. First, the right side of the three-period constraint involves the amount of bonds, b_3, held at the end of the third period, rather than the second. Second, the three-period constraint shows how to include the incomes and expenses from period 3. Notice that we divide these amounts, Py_3 and Pc_3, by the factor, $(1+R)^2$, before adding them to the present values of incomes and expenses, respectively, for the first two periods. In other words, we calculate the present values of income and expenditure for period 3 by dividing by the factor $(1+R)^2$. This factor represents the accumulation of interest income or expense from period 1 to period 3—that is, over two periods.

Budget Constraints for Any Number of Periods

By now we see how to construct a budget constraint for any number of periods. For example, the budget constraint for n periods is

$$Py_1 + \frac{Py_2}{(1+R)} + \frac{Py_3}{(1+R)^2} + \cdots + \frac{Py_n}{(1+R)^{n-1}} + b_0(1+R)$$
$$= Pc_1 + \frac{Pc_2}{(1+R)} + \frac{Pc_3}{(1+R)^2} + \cdots + \frac{Pc_n}{(1+R)^{n-1}} + \frac{b_n}{(1+R)^{n-1}} \quad (3.16)$$

(We again assume constancy of money balances, so that $m_0 = m_1 = m_2 = \cdots = m_n$.) Note that our previous examples of budget constraints are special cases of equation 3.16. For $n = 2$ we get the two-period budget constraint in equation 3.8, while for $n = 3$ we get the three-period constraint in equation 3.15.

Notice two things about the budget constraint for n periods in equation 3.16. First, the right side involves the stock of bonds, b_n, held at the end of period n. Second, we calculate the present value of income or expense for any period t by dividing by the factor $(1+R)^{t-1}$. This factor represents the accumulation of interest between period 1 and period t—that is, over $(t - 1)$ periods.

The Household's Planning Horizon

Suppose that someone is choosing today's consumption and work effort, c_1 and n_1. Typically, people make these choices in the context of a long-term plan that considers future levels of consumption and income. In particular, these future values relate to the current choices through the n-period budget constraint in equation 3.16. Here, we can refer to the number, n, as someone's **planning horizon.**

How long a horizon should someone consider in making current decisions? Because we are dealing with people who have access to a credit market, a long planning horizon generally applies. That is, by borrowing or lending people effectively use future income to finance current spending, or current income to pay for future spending. When expressed as a present value, prospective incomes and expenses from the distant future are just as pertinent for current decisions as are today's incomes and expenses.

Economists often assume that the planning horizon is long, but finite. For example, in a class of theories called **life-cycle models,**[6] the horizon, n, represents an individual's expected remaining lifetime. If people do not care about things that occur after their death, then they have no reason to carry assets beyond period n. Therefore, they set to zero the final asset stock, b_n, which appears on the right side of the budget constraint in equation 3.16. (We also have to rule out the possibility of dying in debt, which would correspond to $b_n < 0$.)

Usually, researchers who use life-cycle models assume that the working span, which is the interval where $n_t > 0$, is shorter than the length of life. In this case, people have retirement periods during which consumption must be financed either from savings accumulated during working years or from transfer payments. These transfers could come from the government (**social security**) or from one's children.

It is reasonably straightforward to define the anticipated lifetime—and thereby a finite planning horizon—for an isolated individual who has no concern for descendants. However, the appropriate horizon is not obvious for a family in which the parents care about their children. (The children may also care about their parents!) In this context, the applicable horizon extends beyond someone's expected lifetime, and people would give some weight to the expected future incomes and expenses of their children. Further, since children care about the welfare of their children—should they have any—and so on for each subsequent generation, there is no clear point at which to terminate the planning period. Of course, this argument does not imply that anticipated incomes and expenses for the distant future count as much as those for a few years off. But by using present values, we already place a large—and perhaps sufficient—discount on incomes and expenses from the distant future.

Instead of imposing a finite horizon, we can allow the household's plan to extend into the indefinite future. That is, we can treat the length of the

---

[6]See Franco Modigliani and Richard Brumberg, "Utility Analysis and the Consumption Function: An Interpretation of Cross-Section Data," in K. Kurihara (Ed.), *Post-Keynesian Economics*, Rutgers University Press, New Brunswick, N.J., 1954; and Albert Ando and Franco Modigliani, "The 'Life Cycle' Hypothesis of Saving: Aggregate Implications and Tests," *American Economic Review*, March 1963.

planning interval, n, as though it were infinite. There are two good reasons for proceeding in this way:

- First, if we think of the typical person as part of a family that has concerns about the members of future generations—such as children, grandchildren, etc.—into the indefinite future, then this setup is the correct one. In particular, it would be inappropriate to identify the horizon with the typical person's expected lifetime.
- Second, although it is not obvious at this point, an infinite horizon is the easiest thing to work with.

Budget Constraints for an Infinite Horizon

When the planning horizon is infinite, the budget constraint includes the present values of incomes and expenses for the indefinite future. Then, using equation 3.16, we have

$$Py_1 + \frac{Py_2}{(1+R)} + \frac{Py_3}{(1+R)^2} + \cdots + b_0(1+R)$$
$$= Pc_1 + \frac{Pc_2}{(1+R)} + \frac{Pc_3}{(1+R)^2} + \cdots \quad (3.17)$$

We no longer terminate the sums for incomes and expenses at some finite date, n, as we did in equation 3.16. Notice also that the final stock of bonds, b_n, does not appear in the budget constraint. In effect, there is no "final" period to consider here.

For most purposes, we prefer to deal with the budget constraint when expressed in real terms. If we divide through equation 3.17 by the price level, P, we get

$$y_1 + \frac{y_2}{(1+R)} + \frac{y_3}{(1+R)^2} + \cdots \frac{b_0(1+R)}{P}$$
$$= c_1 + \frac{c_2}{(1+R)} + \frac{c_3}{(1+R)^2} + \cdots \quad (3.18)$$

Equation 3.18 says that the present value of real income from sales to the commodity market over an infinite horizon, plus the real value of the receipts from the initial stock of bonds, equals the present value of real consumption expenditure over an infinite horizon. We shall use this form of the budget constraint when studying the households' choices over many periods.

Preferences Over an Infinite Horizon

Here, we extend our earlier ideas about time preference from two periods to an infinite horizon. We assume now that each household cares about total utility, U, as defined by the sum,

$$U = u(c_1, n_1) + \frac{u(c_2, n_2)}{(1+\rho)} + \frac{u(c_3, n_3)}{(1+\rho)^2} + \cdots \quad (3.19)$$

Again, the expression looks like a present value, but with the rate of time preference, ρ, replacing the interest rate.

The use of an infinite horizon gives us an interesting way to interpret the rate of time preference. This rate may not be positive just because an individual prefers to get his or her utils earlier rather than later. Rather, particularly for the distant future, we can think of people as preferring their own utils to those of their children, grandchildren, and so on. Therefore, they discount the utils of these later generations. In other words, people care about their descendants, but not quite as much as they do about themselves.

Choices over Many Periods

Before, we discussed the choices of consumption over two periods, c_1 and c_2. Now we consider the entire path of consumption, $c_1, c_2, c_3, \ldots$. Let's start by holding fixed the path of work. In particular, suppose that work is the same in each period, $n_1 = n_2 = n_3 = \ldots$.

In some of our previous discussion, we thought about a given total present value of real spending over two periods, $x = c_1 + c_2/(1+R)$. Here, we proceed analogously by looking at the total present value of real spending over an infinite horizon. That is, we consider the expression,

$$x = c_1 + \frac{c_2}{(1+R)} + \frac{c_3}{(1+R)^2} + \cdots \tag{3.20}$$

Notice from equation 3.18 that the quantity x equals the total real present value of income from the commodity market plus the real value of the receipts from the initial stock of bonds.

The Interest Rate and Intertemporal Substitution

Given the total present value of real spending over an infinite horizon, we can still substitute between c_1 and c_2. For each unit of c_1 that we forego, we can obtain $(1+R)$ additional units of c_2. But there is nothing special about periods 1 and 2. We can substitute in a similar manner between c_2 and c_3, c_3 and c_4, and so on. In general, if we give up 1 unit of c_t, then the credit market allows us to raise c_{t+1} by $(1+R)$ units.

Consider an increase in the interest rate, R. As before, we want to abstract from wealth effects to isolate the substitution effect from this change. Then in the two-period case we know that an increase in R motivates people to reduce c_1 relative to c_2. That is because the higher interest rate makes today's consumption more expensive relative to the next period's. But the same reasoning applies to any pair of consumptions, c_t and c_{t+1}. An increase in R lowers c_t relative to c_{t+1}. In other words, since c_{t+1}/c_t rises, the higher interest rate motivates people to plan for a more steeply rising time path of consumption.

We show these results in Figure 3.7. We assume that the initial plan, shown by the solid line, dictates constant levels of consumption, $c_1 = c_2 = c_3 = \ldots$.

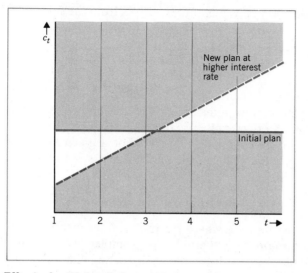

Figure 3.7 Effect of a Higher Interest Rate on the Path of Consumption
An increase in the interest rate motivates people to defer consumption. Therefore, the new path is more steeply sloped than the old one.

Then an increase in R causes the time path of consumption to tilt upward, as shown by the dotted line in the figure. In comparison with the initial plan, the new one involves a higher ratio, c_{t+1}/c_t, at any date.

Observe from Figure 3.7 that the quantity consumed falls during the early periods and rises during the later ones. (Recall that, with no change in wealth, the amounts consumed cannot all increase or decrease.) Further, the decrease in consumption is greater for the current period, c_1, while the increase in consumption becomes larger the further out we look. In general, the inter-temporal-substitution effect from a higher interest rate motivates us to shift consumption away from the near term and toward the future.

When we allow for variable work effort we find that changes in the interest rate also have intertemporal-substitution effects on work and leisure. The generalization from the two-period model is that an increase in R motivates people to take less leisure now and more leisure later. Correspondingly, current work, n_1, rises relative to that in the future.

Finally, note that the decrease in c_1 and increase in n_1 both imply an increase in current saving. Thus, as in the two-period case, a higher interest rate motivates people to save more.

Wealth Effects

As before, wealth effects involve changes in the total present value of real spending, x. Recall from the household's budget constraint (equation 3.18) that this total equals the present value of real income from the commodity market plus the real value of the receipts from the initial stock of bonds, that is,

$$x = y_1 + \frac{y_2}{(1+R)} + \cdots + \frac{b_0(1+R)}{P} \qquad (3.21)$$

Remember that the aggregate value of the initial stock of bonds, B_0, is zero. Therefore, if we think about the typical or average household, for whom $b_0 = 0$, wealth effects will arise only from changes in the present value of real income from the commodity market. For a given amount of work effort in each period, these changes must involve shifts in the production function.

Permanent Shifts of the Production Function

Consider first the case where the production function, $f(n_t)$, shifts upward in a parallel fashion for all periods. As examples, we can think of discoveries of new technology or natural resources—that is, changes that create permanent improvements in productive capacity. If we hold constant each period's amount of work, n_t, then we raise each period's level of output, y_t. Hence, the total real present value of spending, x, increases in equation 3.21.

As a generalization of the results for two periods, we find that the increase in the present value of real spending, x, leads to increases in consumption, c_t, for each period. Consumption in any period is a superior good, which means that the wealth effect is positive.

Similarly, when we allow work effort to vary, we find that more wealth leads to more leisure in each period. Therefore, an increase in wealth implies less work effort, n_t, at each date.

increase in consumption

The Propensity to Consume

Suppose, as an example, that real income, y_t, ends up rising by 1 unit in each period. (The change in y_t is the upward shift in the production function, $f(n_t)$, net of the downward effect on income from the reduction in work effort, n_t.) Then, as one possibility, a person can also raise consumption, c_t, by 1 unit in each period. This response satisfies the budget constraint, which is again

$$y_1 + \frac{y_2}{(1+R)} + \cdots + \frac{b_0(1+R)}{P} = c_1 + \frac{c_2}{(1+R)} + \cdots$$

If someone does respond in this way, then we say that his or her **marginal propensity to consume** is one—that is, current consumption, c_1, rises by the same amount as current real income, y_1. Since consumption and income change by equal amounts, there is no change in saving—in other words, the **marginal propensity to save** is zero.

If someone increases current consumption, c_1, by less than 1 unit, then the current marginal propensity to consume is less than one and the current marginal propensity to save is positive. However, people must use this extra saving to expand some future level of consumption. Then there must be at least one period later on during which consumption, c_t, rises by even more than one unit.

Suppose that we planned initially for a constant time path of consumption, as in the solid line shown in Figure 3.7. Then the increase in period t's consumption, c_t, by more than 1 unit means that this consumption increases relative to today's, c_1. That is, consumption shifts away from the present and toward the future. Now we know that this type of shift is appropriate if the interest rate increases. But since the interest rate does not change here, we would want to maintain the relative amounts of consumption at different dates. For the case at hand, this happens only if we increase consumption in every period by 1 unit. Hence, if the improvement in the production function is permanent, then the marginal propensity to consume is one. Correspondingly, the marginal propensity to save is zero.[7]

Permanent Income

Our findings correspond to Milton Friedman's concept of **permanent income**.[8] The general idea is that people care about a long-term average of income. Specifically, permanent income is the hypothetical, constant flow of income that has the same present value as someone's actual sources of funds. But recall from equation 3.21 that the present value of the sources of funds equals the present value of consumption expenditures, x. Therefore, the present value of permanent income equals the present value of consumption expenditures. For the case where consumption is constant, it follows that permanent income equals consumption. In other words, we can think of permanent income as the amount of constant consumption that a person can sustain forever.

More formally, we define permanent income, $\bar{y}$, by the condition

$$x = \bar{y} + \frac{\bar{y}}{(1+R)} + \frac{\bar{y}}{(1+R)^2} + \cdots$$

$$= \bar{y}\left[1 + \frac{1}{(1+R)} + \frac{1}{(1+R)^2} + \cdots\right] = \frac{\bar{y}(1+R)}{R}$$

---

[7] We have to modify the conclusions somewhat if the initial path of consumption is either rising or falling over time. Then proportionately equal changes in consumption for each period no longer imply that each quantity of consumption rises by precisely 1 unit. Typically, we can still say as an approximation that the marginal propensity to save will be small if the improvement in the production function is permanent. However, the true propensity may be either slightly positive or slightly negative. Correspondingly, the marginal propensity to consume will now be either slightly below or slightly above one.

[8] He developed the idea in his book, *A Theory of the Consumption Function*, Princeton University Press, Princeton, New Jersey, 1957, especially Chapters 2 and 3.

We get the last term on the right from the formula for a geometric progression, which we describe in the box below. Solving out for $\bar{y}$ and substituting for the variable x from equation 3.21 leads to

$$\bar{y} = x \cdot \frac{R}{(1+R)} = \left[\frac{R}{(1+R)}\right] \cdot \left[y_1 + \frac{y_2}{(1+R)} + \cdots\right] + \frac{Rb_0}{P} \quad (3.22)$$

Geometric Progression

Consider the geometric progression, $1 + z + z^2 + \cdots$. If $-1 < z < 1$, this sum equals $1/(1 - z)$. We can verify this answer by multiplying the expression, $(1 + z + z^2 + \cdots)$, by the term, $(1 - z)$. Then we get $1 - z + z - z^2 + z^2 - \cdots = 1$. (If the magnitude of z is one or greater, then the sum is unbounded.) In the present case, $z = 1/(1+R)$, which is between 0 and 1. Therefore, $1 + 1/(1+R) + 1/(1+R)^2 + \cdots = 1/[1 - 1/(1+R)] = (1 + R)/R$.

The term on the extreme right of equation 3.22 is the real income received as interest on the initial stock of bonds, b_0. We can think of the other term on the right side in a parallel fashion. Suppose that we take the entire present value of real income from the commodity market, $y_1 + y_2/(1+R) + \cdots$, and use it to buy bonds today. Then the first term on the right side of equation 3.22 is the real income that we would receive each period as interest on these bonds. (We divide by the discount factor, $(1+R)$, because the interest income does not start until the second period.) Therefore, permanent income is the real interest receipts from this hypothetical stock of bonds plus that on the initial stock, b_0.

For someone who consumes the same amount in each period, the level of consumption equals the level of permanent income, $\bar{y}$. Hence, for this person, the marginal propensity to consume out of permanent income equals one.

Recall that in our previous example the level of real income from the commodity market increased by 1 unit in every period. But then permanent income also increases by 1 unit. (We can verify this result from equation 3.22.) Since permanent income rises by 1 unit, we conclude that—at least for someone whose consumption is the same in each period—consumption increases by 1 unit. So, the concept of permanent income gives us the same answer that we found earlier.

Temporary Shifts of the Production Function

In this section we contrast the results for permanent changes in the production function with those for temporary changes. Suppose now that the parallel upward shift to the production function lasts only for the current period. So instead of discoveries of new technologies or resources, we can think of the effects of weather, temporary changes in the supply of raw materials, strikes, and so on.

If work efforts do not change, then the increase in real income occurs only in the current period. Typically, people would want to spread this extra income over consumption in all periods. But to raise future consumption, people now have to raise current saving. Hence, current consumption, c_1, rises by much less than the increase in current real income, y_1. In other words, for the case of a temporary improvement in the production function, the marginal propensity to consume is small. Consequently, the marginal propensity to save is positive and nearly equal to one.

In terms of permanent income, we see from equation 3.22 that the change would be the fraction, $R/(1+R)$, of the change in y_1. For example, if $R = 10\%$ per year, then an increase in this year's real income by 1 unit means that permanent income rises by only 0.09 units. Hence, we predict that the marginal propensity to consume is only about 0.09, while the marginal propensity to save is about 0.91.

Since the temporary improvement of the production function implies an increase in wealth, we predict that leisure would rise in each period. In particular, current work effort n_1 would decline. However, as with consumption, this response is much weaker than that in the case of a permanent improvement of the production function.

Empirical Evidence on the Permanent Income Hypothesis

There have been many attempts to test the permanent income hypothesis. Overall, the results of empirical tests indicate strongly that the marginal propensity to consume out of permanent income is much greater than that out of temporary income. However, the marginal propensity to consume out to temporary income seems to be somewhat higher than the theory would suggest.

Some of the clearest evidence comes from special circumstances where there are windfalls of income, which people surely regard as temporary. One example is the receipt by Israeli citizens of lump-sum, non-recurring restitution payments from Germany in 1957–58. The payments were large, with an average value that roughly equaled the average family income for a year. For this case, the data indicate that the typical family's consumption expenditure during the year of the windfall rose by no more than 20% of the amount received.[9] Further, the measure of consumer

---

[9]The results are in Mordechai Kreinin, "Windfall Income and Consumption—Additional Evidence," *American Economic Review*, June 1961; and Michael Landsberger, "Restitution Receipts, Household Savings and Consumption Behavior in Israel," Research Department, Bank of Israel, 1970.

spending includes purchases of consumer durables. Since these goods last for many years, we should view these purchases as partly saving, rather than consumption. Therefore, the marginal propensity to consume out of the windfall would actually be substantially less than 20%.

Another example is the 1950 payment to U.S. World War II veterans of an unanticipated, one-time life insurance dividend of about $175. At the time, this amount represented about 4% of the average family's annual income. In this case, the statistical estimates indicate that consumption rose by 30 to 40% of the windfall.[10] But since the data again include purchases of consumer durables, the true marginal propensity to consume would be substantially lower than these values.

More generally, statistical studies of consumer spending over time indicate that the marginal propensity to consume out of permanent income is large and not much different from one. By contrast, the marginal propensity to consume out of temporary income is only about 20 to 30%.[11] Although this response to temporary changes is somewhat greater than that predicted by the permanent-income theory, the important point for our theoretical analysis is that the response of consumer spending to permanent changes in income is much greater than that to temporary changes.

Wealth Effects from Changes in the Interest Rate

This far, we have looked only at intertemporal-substitution effects from changes in the interest rate. Now let's see whether a change in the interest rate leads to a wealth effect.

We can test for the effect on wealth by using the budget constraint, which is again

$$y_1 + \frac{y_2}{(1+R)} + \cdots \frac{b_0(1+R)}{P} = c_1 + \frac{c_2}{(1+R)} + \cdots$$

Abstract from the term that involves the initial stock of bonds, $b_0(1+R)/P$. Remember that this term will, in any case, equal zero when we sum up over all households.

Suppose that we hypothetically hold fixed the paths of real incomes, y_1, $y_2, \ldots$, and expenditures, $c_1, c_2, \ldots$ Then consider the separate effects of

[10]See Roger C. Bird and Ronald G. Bodkin, "The National Service Life Insurance Dividend of 1950 and Consumption: A further Test of the 'Strict' Permanent Income Hypothesis," *Journal of Political Economy*, October 1965.

[11]Two of the more important studies (which are demanding in terms of knowledge of econometrics) are Marjorie Flavin, "The Adjustment of Consumption to Changing Expectations about Future Income," *Journal of Political Economy*, October 1981; and Robert Hall and Frederic Mishkin, "The Sensitivity of Consumption to Transitory Income: Estimates from Panel Data on Households," *Econometrica*, March 1982.

an increase in the interest rate on the left and right sides of the budget constraint. The rise in the interest rate reduces the present values of real income, $y_1 + y_2/(1+R) + \cdots$, and of real spending, $c_1 + c_2/(1+R) \ldots$. But the important question is which sum falls by the greater amount. If the present value of real spending falls by more, then the given path of real income would be sufficient to continue purchasing these goods and still have something left over. Then we could increase consumption for some periods without *necessarily* decreasing it for others.[12] Hence, wealth increases. However, the opposite conclusion obtains if the present value of real spending falls by less than that of real income.

The budget constraint indicates that the terms that decline most with the rise in the interest rate are those that are most distant into the future. That is, the discount factor for period t is $1/(1+R)^{t-1}$, which is more sensitive to changes in R the higher the value of t. Therefore, when the interest rate rises, the present value of real spending declines by more than that of real income if the path of spending is more heavily concentrated in the future than is the path of income. For the case where the initial bonds, b_0, equal zero, this property applies for someone who has positive saving in most of the earlier years and negative saving in most of the later years. In other words, people who plan usually to be lenders experience an increase in wealth when the interest rate rises. Conversely, those who plan usually to be borrowers have a decline in wealth.

Although either situation may hold for an individual, neither case can apply for the average person. Since the aggregate stock of bonds is always zero in our model, we know that the average household is neither typically a lender nor typically a borrower. Therefore, in the aggregate, the wealth effect from a change in the interest rate is nil.[13] So for the purposes of aggregate analysis, we shall find it satisfactory to neglect wealth effects from changes in the interest rate. This result is important. It says that for aggregate purposes we should focus on the intertemporal-substitution effects from changes in the interest rate.

Shifts in the Schedule for Labor's Marginal Product

Consider now a rise in the schedule for labor's marginal product, which usually accompanies an improvement in the production function. As we know, a higher schedule for labor's marginal product motivates people to work more. If the change is the same for each period, then work and hence output rise by roughly

---

[12]The change in the interest rate has intertemporal-substitution effects, which may motivate us to decrease consumption at some dates. But for assessing the wealth effect, the important point is the capacity to raise consumption for some periods without necessarily lowering it for others. This perspective makes it clear that overall utility—and hence, wealth—must increase.

[13]For further discussion of this result, see Martin J. Bailey, *National Income and the Price Level*, 2nd ed., McGraw-Hill, New York, 1971, pp. 106–108.

equal amounts in each period. It follows that permanent income, and therefore each period's consumption, increase by the same amount as output. In other words, saving does not change.

A permanent improvement in labor's productivity, as above, means that consumption becomes cheaper relative to leisure at each date. Therefore, people work and consume more in every period. However, there are no changes in the relative costs of consumption or leisure for different periods. So the responses in work and consumption are the same in each period, and there are no effects on saving.

We should be careful to distinguish the substitution between consumption and leisure from the intertemporal-substitution effect. The intertemporal effect involves the cost of taking consumption or leisure in one period rather than another. For example, an increase in the interest rate motivates people to reduce today's consumption and leisure relative to those later on. In contrast, the schedule for labor's marginal product determines the relative cost of consumption and leisure at a point in time. Therefore, a shift in this schedule induces changes in the relative amounts of consumption and leisure. But, if the change in labor's productivity is permanent, there are no intertemporal-substitution effects.

The results are different if the change in productivity is temporary. As an example, think of a gold rush or other temporary profit opportunity, which makes the reward for today's effort unusually high. We can represent this case by shifting the schedule for labor's marginal product only for the current period. Then the new element is that today's leisure becomes more expensive relative to future leisure or consumption. Therefore, people have an incentive to expand work today in order to increase consumption and leisure later on. Thus, a temporary improvement of productivity stimulates saving. That is, today's output rises by more than today's consumption.

Note especially that the temporary boost to productivity raises the cost of leisure today relative to leisure later. This change looks like the intertemporal-substitution effect on work effort that arises from an increase in the interest rate. Thus, we can look at a temporary improvement in productivity as the combination of two positive substitution effects on current work. First, there is the rise in the cost of leisure relative to consumption, which arises also when the improvement is permanent. Then second, there is the intertemporal-substitution effect, which works like an increase in the interest rate. It is this last element that stimulates saving.

Summary

We introduced a commodity market on which people buy and sell goods at the price, P. The existence of this market allows producers to specialize, which aids efficiency.

We also introduced a credit market on which people borrow and lend at the interest rate R. By using this market, individuals can choose a time pattern for consumption that differs from that for income.

We began with a budget constraint over two periods, but then extended the analysis to any number of periods. For most purposes we can think of the behavior of households over an infinite horizon. We motivated the infinite planning period by thinking about a family in which parents care about their children, who care about their children, and so on.

An increase in the interest rate motivates people to shift away from consumption over the near term and toward that in the future. The opposite responses apply to work effort. These intertemporal-substitution effects mean that a higher interest rate raises an individual's current saving.

Improvements in the production function have wealth effects that are positive on consumption and negative on work for each period. If the shift is permanent, then permanent income increases by as much as current income. Hence, the marginal propensity to consume out of current income is near one and the marginal propensity to save is near zero. But if the shift is temporary, then permanent income changes little. Therefore, the marginal propensity to consume is small and the marginal propensity to save is almost one. Finally, we showed that a change in the interest rate has no aggregate wealth effect.

A permanent upward shift in the schedule for labor's marginal product raises work and consumption in each period, but does not affect saving. However, a temporary upward shift in the schedule raises current output by more than current consumption, and thereby raises saving.

Important Terms and Concepts

barter

medium of exchange

nominal terms

currency

general price level

interest rate

principal of bond

budget constraint

saving

present value

real terms

price index

deflator for GNP

CPI

perfect competition

bond

discount factor

budget line

rate of time preference

intertemporal-substitution effect

planning horizon

life-cycle model

social security

infinite horizon

marginal propensity to consume

marginal propensity to save

permanent income

QUESTIONS AND PROBLEMS

Mainly for Review

3.1 Why would individuals be interested only in the real value of consumption expenditures, income, and assets such as money and bonds? Would a fall in the dollar amount of consumption spending leave the individual worse off when it is accompanied by an equi-proportionate fall in the price level?

3.2 Distinguish clearly between an individual's initial asset position and the change in that position. Which is affected by current consumption and saving decisions? Is an individual who is undertaking negative saving necessarily a borrower in the sense of having a negative position in bonds?

3.3 Derive the two-period budget constraint, and draw a graph of it. Why are there no terms involving money holdings on the side of sources of funds?

3.4 Show how taking a present value involves giving different weights to dollar values in different periods. Why is income in the present more "valuable" than income in the future? Why is consumption in the future "cheaper" than consumption in the present?

3.5 Review the factors that determine an individual's choice of consumption over two periods, c_1 and c_2, and show this choice graphically. Why is the individual best off where the budget line is tangent to an indifference curve?

3.6 What factors determine whether the marginal propensity to consume is less than one or equal to one? Can the marginal propensity to consume be greater than one?

3.7 Review the effects of the following changes on current consumption and work, distinguishing clearly between wealth effects and substitution effects.
  a. A permanent parallel shift of the production function.
  b. A change in the interest rate.
  c. A temporary change in the marginal product of labor.

Problems for Discussion

3.8 Discount Bonds
The one-period bonds in our model pay a single interest payment or "coupon" of $\$R$ and a principal of $\$1$. Alternatively, we could consider a one-period discount bond like a U.S. treasury bill. This type of asset has no coupons, but pays a principal of $\$1$ (or, more realistically, $\$10,000$) next period. Let P^B be the dollar price for each unit of discount bonds, where each unit is a claim to $\$1$ next period.
  a. Is P^B greater or less than $\$1$?
  b. What is the one-period rate of interest that we get from holding discount bonds?

c. How does the price, P^B, relate to this one-period rate of interest?

d. Suppose that, instead of coming due next period, the discount bond comes due (matures) two periods from now. What is the interest rate *per period* that we get from holding this bond? How do the results generalize if the bond matures n periods from now?

3.9 Financial Intermediaries

Consider a financial intermediary, such as a bank or savings and loan association, that enters the credit market. This intermediary borrows from some people and lends the proceeds to others. (The loan to a bank from its customers often takes the form of a "deposit.")

a. How does the existence of intermediaries affect our result that the aggregate amount of loans is zero?

b. What interest rate would the intermediary charge to its borrowers and pay to its lenders? Why must there be some spread between these two rates?

c. Can you give some reasons to explain why intermediaries might be useful?

3.10 Permanent Income With No Receipts From the Commodity Market

Suppose that our initial bond holdings are $b_0 = \$1000$. All commodity market receipts, Py_t, are zero. The interest rate is $R = 10\%$ per year and the price level is constant over time.

a. What is the level of permanent income? If consumption is constant, what is the amount of saving each year? What is the level of permanent income when we calculate it during period 2?

b. Suppose now that $c_1 = 0$. What is permanent income when we calculate it during the second period? Explain this result.

3.11 Wealth Effects

Consider the household's budget constraint in real terms over an infinite horizon, $y_1 + y_2/(1+R) + \cdots + b_0(1+R)/P = c_1 + c_2/(1+R) + \cdots$. Using this condition, evaluate the wealth effect of the following:

a. An increase in the price level, P, for a household that has a positive value of initial bonds, b_0. (The result has implications for the effects of unexpected price changes on the wealth of nominal creditors and nominal debtors.)

b. An increase in the interest rate, R, for a household that has $b_0 = 0$ and $c_t = y_t$ in each period.

c. An increase in the interest rate, R, for a household that has $b_0 = 0$, $c_t > y_t$ for $t \geq T$, and $c_t < y_t$ for $t < T$, where T is some date in the future.

3.12 Short-Term and Long-Term Interest Rates

Assume that \$1 worth of one-period bonds issued at the end of period 0 pays out $\$1(1+R_1)$ during period 1—that is, the principal of \$1 plus the interest payment of $\$R_1$. Assume that \$1 worth of one-period bonds issued at the end of period 1 will pay out $\$(1+R_2)$ during period 2. Suppose that people also market a two-period bond at the end of period 0. \$1 worth of this asset pays out $\$(1 + 2R)$ during period 2. Lenders from date 0 to date 2 have the option of holding a two-period bond or a succession of one-period bonds. Borrowers have a similar choice between negotiating a two-period loan or two successive one-period loans.

a. What must be the relation of R to R_1 and R_2? Explain the answer from the standpoint of borrowers and lenders.

b. If $R_2 > R_1$, what is the relation between R (the current "long-term" interest rate) and R_1 (the current short rate)? (The answer is an important result about the "term structure of interest rates.")

c. In March 1980 the yield on Aaa-rated (premium grade, long-term) corporate bonds was 13% per year, while that on three-month maturity prime commercial paper (short-term notes issued by large corporations) was 17% per year. What does this relation suggest for March 1980 about the financial markets' prediction of subsequent yields on commercial paper? (You can consult the *Federal Reserve Bulletin* to see what actually happened.)

3.13 The Household's Budget Constraint with a Finite Horizon

Consider the household's budget constraint for n periods from equation 3.16,

$$Py_1 + \frac{Py_2}{(1+R)} + \cdots + \frac{Py_n}{(1+R)^{n-1}} + b_0(1+R)$$

$$= Pc_1 + \frac{Pc_2}{(1+R)} + \cdots + \frac{Pc_n}{(1+R)^{n-1}} + \frac{b_n}{(1+R)^{n-1}}$$

Assume that $y_t = 0$ for $t > T_1$, and $c_t = 0$ for $t > T_2$. Here, T_2 might represent the expected lifetime and T_1 the anticipated working span for an individual.

a. Assume that we use the planning horizon, $n = T_2$. Why might we want to do this? What value would we select for b_n? What does the n-period budget constraint look like in this case?

b. Discuss the pattern of saving, $b_t - b_{t-1}$, for the "retirement period," where $T_1 < t \leq T_2$. What can be said about saving for the "typical" working year where $0 < t \leq T_1$? (This result concerns the "life-cycle" motivation for household saving.)

c. Suppose that the government forces people to retire earlier than they would otherwise choose. How would this action affect the choices of work effort, consumption, and desired saving for people who are still working, but anticipating an earlier retirement?

d. Given that individuals care about their children (and parents), what difficulties arise in specifying a value for the finite planning horizon, $n = T_2$?

CHAPTER 4
THE DEMAND FOR MONEY

Our model includes two forms of financial assets, money and bonds. But so far, we have not analyzed how much money people hold or how these holdings change over time. Thus, we carried out the analysis in the previous chapter under the assumption that each household maintained a constant stock of money. Whenever people changed their saving they altered their holdings of bonds, but not their holdings of money.

Now we provide the remaining building block in the model by explaining people's willingness to place part of their assets into money; that is, we explain the demand for money. Later on, we shall see that this demand is a crucial determinant of the price level.

The Nature of a Monetary Economy

As mentioned before, we assume that money is the sole medium of exchange in the economy. Trades occur between money and commodities and between money and bonds, but not directly between bonds and commodities or between the commodities that different households produce. The direct exchange of goods for goods, which is called barter, is inefficient for many types of transactions.[1] Barter requires a **double coincidence of wants,** which is a situation where one person has the goods that someone else desires and vice versa. A general means of payments, such as money, avoids this problem. Buyers use money to purchase goods or bonds. Sellers receive money in exchange for goods or bonds. In this environment people accept money because they can use it later to buy something else. As long as people hold money they know

---

[1]The classic discussion of the difficulties with barter exchange is W. Stanley Jevons, *Money and the Mechanism of Exchange,* Appleton, New York, 1896, Chapters 1–3. An interesting model of the evolution of specialized media of exchange appears in Robert Jones, "The Origin and Development of Media of Exchange," *Journal of Political Economy,* August 1976.

that they can buy goods or bonds. The problem of double coincidence of wants does not arise.

Historically, commodities such as gold and silver served as money. These precious metals possess attractive physical characteristics, which classical economists enumerated as portability, indestructibility, homogeneity, divisibility, and cognizability.[2] But when paper money—such as U.S. dollar bills—replaces commodity money, these physical characteristics no longer enter into the analysis. In our model we think of money as these paper notes, rather than gold, silver, or other commodities.

We assume that the interest-bearing bonds in the model are not money— that is, these paper claims do not function as media of exchange. There are several reasons for this. First, the government may impose legal restrictions that prevent private parties, such as General Motors, from issuing small-size, interest-bearing notes that could serve conveniently as hand-to-hand currency. Further, the government may enact statutes that reinforce the use of its money. As an example, there is the proclamation that the U.S. dollar is "**legal tender** for all debts public and private."[3] Also, U.S. courts are more willing to enforce contracts that are denominated in U.S. dollars, rather than in some other unit. Second, there are costs of establishing one's money as reliable and convenient. These include the prevention of counterfeiting, the replacement of worn-out notes, the willingness to convert notes into different denominations and possibly into other assets, and so on. These costs suggest that money would tend to bear interest at a rate lower than bonds. In fact, because of the inconvenience of paying interest on hand-to-hand currency, the interest rate on currency is typically zero.

Table 4.1 allows us to relate our abstract concept of money to a conventional measure of the money stock for the present-day United States. Our theoretical construct corresponds closely to currency held outside of commercial banks. For 1985 the average amount of this currency was $165 billion, which amounted to 4.1% of the nominal gross national product (GNP). That is, people held a little more than 2 weeks' worth of the GNP as currency in 1985.

The term *money* typically refers to a monetary aggregate that is broader than currency. The standard definition, called *M*1, attempts to classify as money the assets that serve regularly as media of exchange. Specifically, this concept includes the checkable deposits that people hold at banks and some other financial institutions. The average amount of these checkable deposits in 1985 was $423 billion, or 10.6% of annual GNP. Therefore, *M*1—the sum of currency and checkable deposits (plus about $6 billion in travelers' checks)—

---

[2]See Jevons, op. cit., Chapter 5 and—for an earlier discussion—John Law, *Money and Trade Considered* (1705), Augustus Kelley, New York, 1966, Chapter 1.

[3]Notice that this provision does not determine the price at which currency exchanges for goods. If the price level were infinite, what would the legal-tender property mean?

Table 4.1 The Money Stock in 1985

	United States		United Kingdom	
	Components of the Money Stock ($ billion)	Ratio to Annual GNP (%)	Components of the Money Stock (£ billion)	Ratio to Annual GNP (%)
Currency	165	4.1	12.5	3.6
Checkable Deposits	423	10.6	45.3	13.0
$M1$ Definition of Money Stock	594	14.9	57.8	16.6

Note: The U.S. data are averages of monthly figures from the *Federal Reserve Bulletin*. For 1985, $M1$ includes about $6 billion in travelers' checks (of non-bank issuers). The U.K. data are averages of monthly values from the Bank of England's *Quarterly Bulletin*. In the United Kingdom checkable deposits are called "sight deposits."

equaled $594 billion in 1985, or 14.9% of GNP. Put alternatively, $M1$ amounted to about 8 weeks' worth of the GNP in 1985.

Table 4.1 also shows comparable data for 1985 on money in the United Kingdom. Notice that the ratio of currency to annual GNP (3.6%) is somewhat lower than that in the United States, while the ratio of checkable deposits to annual GNP (13.0%) is higher.

As mentioned, we can readily identify the money in our theoretical model with currency, but our concept does not correspond precisely to a broader monetary aggregate, such as $M1$. When we expand the theoretical framework to incorporate financial institutions, such as banks (in Chapter 15), we can deal with checkable deposits. For now, however, we should think of money as being currency. We also assume that the government has a monopoly in the issue of money, and that the interest rate on money is zero.

Given that people use money to transact, how much money should they hold? Suppose that everyone synchronized each sale of goods or bonds with an equal-size purchase of some other good or bond. Then, although people used money for all exchanges, they would end up holding virtually zero cash. But to hold this low average money balance each person would have to spend a lot of effort on financial planning. They would have to synchronize the timing of sales and purchases, and they would have to carry out a large number of transactions. Typically, it is more convenient to allow receipts to accumulate for awhile as cash before spending these funds or converting them into bonds. As Milton Friedman put it, money serves as a *temporary abode of purchasing power*. As a general statement, people can reduce their average holdings of cash only by incurring more costs. These costs are often called **transaction costs,** which refer to the expenses of carrying out trades, as well as the costs of making financial decisions.

Given the total of financial assets, a lower average cash balance means a higher average stock of bonds. Hence, by economizing on money, people earn more interest (or pay less interest if they are borrowing). The demand for money reflects this trade-off between transaction costs and interest earnings. In the next section we illustrate this trade-off in a simple model of cash management.

A Model of Optimal Cash Management

Consider a retired person, who is living off previously accumulated assets. This person keeps financial assets primarily in bonds, but holds some cash to facilitate purchases of consumer goods. For simplicity, assume that consumption expenditure is constant at the amount Pc dollars per year. (We still pretend that the price level, P, does not change over time.) The retiree makes occasional withdrawals of funds from the stock of interest-bearing assets. Suppose that these withdrawals occur at the interval ϕ (ϕ is the Greek letter *phi*). For example, if an exchange occurs every month, then $\phi = \frac{1}{12}$ of a year. Equivalently, the frequency of exchange is 12 per year. Note that this frequency is the reciprocal of the period between withdrawals, $1/\phi$.

Each exchange of interest-bearing assets for cash involves a transaction cost. There may be explicit brokerage changes, but, more likely, the main expense is the time and trouble for carrying out the transfer. If people spend more time transacting, they have less time remaining for work or leisure. Suppose that each exchange costs $\$\gamma$, where γ is the Greek letter *gamma*. (This cost includes the dollar value that people attach to the time needed for the exchange.) We assume a lump-sum transaction cost, which means that the charge is independent of the number of dollars withdrawn. If the retiree transacts at the frequency $1/\phi$ per year, then the total of transaction costs per year is the dollar amount $\gamma \cdot (1/\phi)$. Dividing by the price level, P, we find that the real transaction cost per year is

$$\text{real transaction cost} = \left(\frac{\gamma}{P}\right) \cdot \left(\frac{1}{\phi}\right) \tag{4.1}$$

The term, γ/P, is the real cost per transaction.

When the retiree makes a withdrawal, he or she obtains the amount of cash needed to meet expenses until the next withdrawal. In the present case, the money must cover the expenditures over an interval of length ϕ. Since the person spends at the rate $\$Pc$ per year, the amount needed is $Pc \cdot \phi$. The retiree spends these funds gradually to buy goods, running out of money when the time ϕ has elapsed. At that point, he or she replenishes cash by making the next withdrawal from the stock of interest-bearing assets.

We show the time pattern of money holdings in Figure 4.1. Notice that a withdrawal of $\$Pc \cdot \phi$ occurs at date 0. The retiree spends gradually out of cash at the rate $\$Pc$ per year, which just exhausts the stock of money at time ϕ. Therefore, between dates 0 and ϕ, the level of money is shown by the downward-sloping line in the figure. At date ϕ there is another withdrawal of size $\$Pc \cdot \phi$. Hence, cash jumps upward—along the dashed line in the

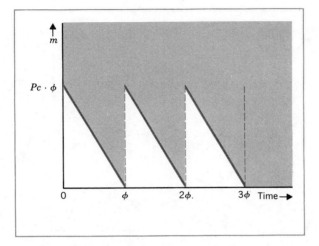

Figure 4.1 The Time Pattern of Money Holdings
Money holdings reach a peak, $Pc \cdot \phi$, just after each withdrawal. Then money declines gradually, reaching zero when it is time to make the next withdrawal. Notice that the withdrawals occur at the interval ϕ.

figure—to the level $Pc \cdot \phi$. Then cash declines steadily again until the time for a new withdrawal at 2ϕ. This sawtooth pattern for cash holdings keeps repeating with the peaks spaced at interval ϕ.

Given the form of cash management from Figure 4.1, the average cash balance is half the vertical distance to the peak, which is

$$\overline{m} = \frac{1}{2} Pc \cdot \phi \qquad (4.2)$$

where $\overline{m}$ denotes the average holding of cash. If we divide by the price level, P, we can express the average holdings of cash in real terms as

$$\frac{\overline{m}}{P} = \frac{1}{2} c\phi \qquad (4.3)$$

Suppose that the retiree has already determined the amount of his or her total financial assets for each period. Then an increase in the average money balance must imply a reduction in the average holdings of bonds, and hence a decline in interest income. If the interest rate is R, then the dollar magnitude of interest earnings foregone per year is the quantity $R \cdot \overline{m} = R \cdot (\frac{1}{2}) Pc\phi$. If all financial assets had been held as bonds, then the interest income would have increased by this amount. As usual, we can divide through by the price level to express this dollar magnitude in real terms. Therefore, the real amount of interest income foregone per year is given by

$$\text{interest foregone in real terms} = R \cdot \frac{M}{P} = R \cdot \frac{1}{2} c\phi \qquad (4.4)$$

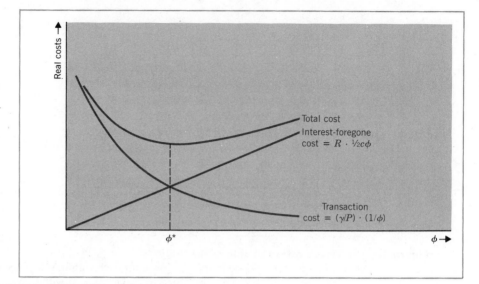

Figure 4.2 The Costs of Cash Management
The interest foregone by holding money, $R \cdot \frac{1}{2}c\phi$, increases with the period between withdrawals, ϕ. Transaction costs, $(\gamma/P) \cdot (1/\phi)$, decline as the period rises. Note that total costs reach a minimum at the point ϕ^*.

There are two types of costs in our cash-management problem.[4] First we can think of the interest foregone in real terms, $R \cdot \frac{1}{2}c\phi$, as a cost of holding money. We graph this cost versus the transaction interval, ϕ, in Figure 4.2. Note that this cost is a straight line from the origin with slope equal to $R \cdot \frac{1}{2}c$. Second, there is the real transaction cost, which is given in equation 4.1 as $(\gamma/P) \cdot (1/\phi)$. This cost appears as the rectangular hyperbola in Figure 4.2. Transaction costs approach zero as the interval between transactions tends toward infinity, and approach infinity as the interval tends toward zero.

We show also the total of interest and transaction costs in Figure 4.2. This curve is U-shaped. Costs decline initially as the transaction interval rises above zero, because transaction costs decline by more than interest costs increase.

---

[4]The model is an example of the "inventory approach" to money demand, which was pioneered by William Baumol, "The Transactions Demand for Cash: An Inventory Approach," *Quarterly Journal of Economics,* November 1952; and James Tobin, "The Interest-Elasticity of Transactions Demand for Cash," *Review of Economics and Statistics,* August 1956. (The approach is often called the "Baumol-Tobin" model.) The two costs for holding money are analogous to those that arise when a firm holds an inventory of its product. The interest-foregone cost for money parallels the costs of foregone interest, storage, and depreciation, which apply to inventories of goods. The transaction cost for financial exchanges corresponds to the costs of restocking— that is, the transaction cost for ordering, shipping, and processing new goods from a supplier. More complicated models of inventories—whether of goods or money—stress the uncertainties in receipts and expenditures.

Eventually, we find that transaction costs do not fall as fast as interest costs rise. Therefore, total costs start to increase with increases in the interval, ϕ. There is some amount of time between trips, denoted by ϕ^* in the figure, which minimizes total costs.[5] Hence, a rational person chooses the interval ϕ^*.[6]

For later purposes, the important point is that the choice of transaction interval, ϕ, determines the average holding of real cash from equation 4.3 as the amount, $\overline{m}/P = (\frac{1}{2}) c\phi$. Therefore, a person's choice of transaction interval translates into that person's choice of an average real money balance. Our main concern now is how various changes in the economy affect the transaction interval and thereby a person's average real money holding.

There are three variables that determine the transaction interval, ϕ^*, in the model. These are the interest rate, R, the real flow of expenditures, c, and the real cost per transaction, γ/P. We can use graphical methods to study the effects of changes in any of these variables.

We consider in Figure 4.3 an increase in the interest rate from R to R'. This change steepens the slope of the line that describes interest-foregone costs. In calculating total costs we find that the interest component has become more important relative to the transaction-cost component. Hence, we reach sooner the position where increasing interest costs dominate over falling transaction costs. It follows that the minimum of total costs occurs at a shorter interval between withdrawals—that is, $(\phi^*)' < \phi^*$ in the figure.

We can interpret the result as follows. An increase in the interest rate makes it more important to economize on cash in order to avoid large amounts of foregone interest income. In our simple model, people can reduce average holdings of money only by transacting more frequently—that is, by shortening the period between financial exchanges, ϕ. Although this process entails a higher transaction cost, people are motivated by the rise in the interest rate to incur these costs. Hence, the rise in the interest rate, R, leads to a decline in the interval between transactions.

Recall from equation 4.3 that the average real money balance equals $\frac{1}{2}$ $c\phi$. Since the increase in the interest rate lowers the period, ϕ, it follows that average real money holdings decline. In other words, a higher cost of holding money—that is, a rise in the interest rate—reduces the real demand for money. We shall use this important result many times in our subsequent analysis.

We can use a similiar method to assess changes in the real flow of spending, c. A rise in the spending flow shifts the interest-foregone cost exactly as shown

---

[5] The answer can also be found using calculus. We want the value of ϕ that minimizes total costs, $R \cdot \frac{1}{2} c\phi + (\gamma/P) \cdot (1/\phi)$. The result from calculus is $\phi^* = \sqrt{2(\gamma/P)/Rc}$. Since $\overline{m}/P = \frac{1}{2}$ $c\phi$, the solution for ϕ^* implies $\overline{m}/P = \sqrt{c(\gamma/P)/2R}$. The last result is sometimes called the "square-root formula" because it relates $\overline{m}/P$ positively to $\sqrt{c}$.

[6] In our example, the period ϕ^* turns out to equalize the two components of the total costs. That is, in Figure 4.2, the interest-foregone line intersects the curve for transaction costs at the point ϕ^*. This property depends on the details of our example—it does not hold more generally.

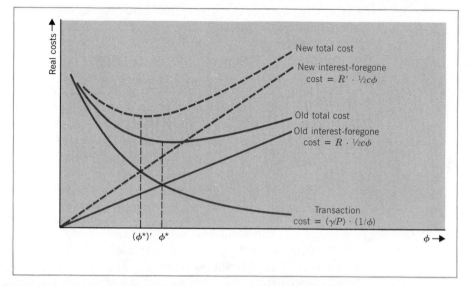

Figure 4.3 **Effect on the Transaction Interval of an Increase in the Interest Rate**
An increase in the interest rate from R to R' steepens the line that describes interest-foregone costs. Therefore, people respond by lowering the period between withdrawals from ϕ^* to $(\phi^*)'$.

in Figure 4.3. Hence, someone with a greater annual flow of real expenditure chooses a shorter interval between withdrawals, ϕ. This result obtains because an increase in the real volume of spending, c, makes the interest-foregone cost more important relative to the transaction cost. Households with more real spending—typically, households with higher income—find it worthwhile to devote more effort to financial planning in order to economize on their cash.

Average real cash balances equal the quantity, $\frac{1}{2}c\phi$. For a given choice of transaction interval, ϕ, a rise in real spending, c, increases average real cash balances proportionately. But we have just shown that the period, ϕ, declines as the volume of spending increases. This response means that a rise in real spending leads to a less-than-proportionate increase in the average holding of real cash.[7] Sometimes, people refer to this result as **"economies of scale"** in cash holding. This property means that households with a larger scale of spending hold less cash when expressed as a ratio to their expenditures.

Finally, we can consider an increase in the real cost of transacting, γ/P. We can show graphically that this change leads to a lengthening of the period between exchanges, ϕ. People transact less frequently when the cost of each

---

[7]We can show that the decline in the transaction interval, ϕ, is by a smaller proportion than the increase in real spending, c. Therefore, the average real cash balance does rise on net. See footnote 5 above.

exchange rises. Because the period, ϕ, lengthens, we know also that average real money balances, $\frac{1}{2} c\phi$, increase.

Properties of the Demand for Money

The results tell us the effects on average real money balances from changes in the interest rate, R, the real volume of spending, c, and the real cost of transacting, γ/P. We can summarize these findings in the form of a function, ℓ, for average real money demanded,

$$\overline{m}/P = \ell(R, c, \quad \gamma/P) \tag{4.5}$$
$$(-)(+)(+)$$

Again the signs indicate the effect of each independent variable on the dependent variable, $\overline{m}/P$.

To find the average money balance in nominal terms, we can multiply through equation 4.5 by the price level. Then we get

$$\overline{m} = P \cdot \ell(R, c, \quad \gamma/P) \tag{4.6}$$
$$(-)(+)(+)$$

Consider what happens if we double the price level, P, but hold fixed R, c, and γ/P. (Note that nominal spending, Pc, and the dollar cost of transacting, γ, both double along with the doubling of the general price level.) These changes leave unaltered the curves in Figure 4.2, which describe the real cost of transacting and the real value of interest income foregone. Therefore, people do not change their choice of transaction interval, ϕ. It follows that average *real* balances, $\overline{m}/P = \frac{1}{2} c\phi$, do not change in equation 4.5. But average *nominal* balances, $\overline{m} = \frac{1}{2} Pc \cdot \phi$, double along with the doubling of the price level, as shown in equation 4.6.

The Aggregate Demand for Money

For an individual in our model, the level of real cash follows a sawtooth pattern and varies between zero and the amount, $c \cdot \phi$. Equation 4.5 determines the average level of real cash, $\overline{m}/P = \frac{1}{2} c \cdot \phi$. Suppose that we sum up over many households, each of which has the same average real balance. Then, unless the timing of transactions is synchronized across households, this aggregation smooths out the sawtooth pattern. In particular, aggregate real cash balances at any date look like an individual's average amount, $\overline{m}/P$, multiplied by the number of people.

We can write out a function, L, for aggregate real money demanded as

$$M/P = L(R, C, \quad \gamma/P) \tag{4.7}$$
$$(-)(+)(+)$$

The function L looks like the individual's function ℓ in equation 4.5, but magnified to incorporate the adding up across many people. Similarly, the aggregate version of equation 4.6 for nominal money demand is

$$M = P \cdot L(R, \ C, \ \gamma/P) \qquad\qquad (4.8)$$

$$(-)(+)(+)$$

Generalizations of the Simple Model

Although we can complicate the theory of money demand in many ways, the properties that we derived from the simple model still tend to hold. That is because the simple model captures the basic trade-off that determines the demand for money. Namely, if people put more effort into transacting and financial planning, then they can lower their average holding of cash. A lower cash balance means, in turn, a greater amount of interest earnings. Someone engages in various aspects of cash management up to the point where the gain in interest income just compensates for the added transaction costs. Consequently, an increase in the interest rate motivates people to incur more costs in order to economize on cash. Similarly, an increase in the volume of expenditures raises the benefits from financial planning. Therefore, although a higher level of spending means more money held, we predict that money balances rise less than proportionately with the scale of spending. Finally, the theory relates the demand for money in real terms to a set of real variables, which include the real flow of spending, the real costs of transacting and financial planning, and the interest rate. A change in the general price level— with all the real variables held fixed—does not change the demand for money in real terms. Therefore, the nominal demand for money rises by the same proportion as the price level if all real variables do not change.

In our simple model, the real transaction costs incurred per year, $(\gamma/P) \cdot (1/\phi)$, pertain to transfers from interest-bearing assets to money. More generally, transaction costs apply also to other forms of exchanges, such as the costs of buying commodities with money and the costs of making wage payments to workers.[8] We would want also to bring in the costs of financial

---

[8]Irving Fisher, in *The Purchasing Power of Money* (1922), Augustus Kelley, New York, 1971, pp. 83–85, stressed the effect of the payment period for wages on workers' demand for money. The effects of this period are analogous to those we discussed for the case of the period between withdrawals from a financial asset. In particular, a shorter period reduces the average holding of real balances. This effect is important during extreme inflations—for example, during the German hyperinflation after World War I. In such situations the cost of holding money becomes very high. Therefore, people incur more transaction costs—such as the costs of making more frequent wage payments—to reduce their average holdings of real cash. For 1923, the final year of the German hyperinflation, an observer reported, "it became the custom to make an advance of wages on Tuesday, the balance being paid on Friday. Later, some firms used to pay wages three times a

planning and decision making. Typically, people who do more calculating manage to maintain a smaller average cash balance and thereby achieve a greater amount of interest earnings. But this broader view of transaction costs does not alter our main conclusions with respect to the form of the functions for aggregate money demand in equations 4.7 and 4.8.

The costs of transacting change when there are technological innovations in the financial sector. For example, the use of computers by financial institutions makes it easier to shift between money and alternative assets. These improvements tend to lower the demand for money. Similarly, the development of convenient checkable deposits in the late nineteenth and early twentieth centuries in the United States had a negative effect on the demand for currency (and a positive effect on the holdings of demand deposits). The possibilities for economizing on cash holdings are influenced also by the use of credit. It may be easier to synchronize receipts and payments—thereby resulting in a lower average money balance—when we buy with credit rather than cash. In any case, credit favors the use of checks, rather than currency.

A broader model would bring in uncertainties associated with the timing and size of receipts and expenditures. An increase in these uncertainties tends to raise the average holding of money, since people hold cash partly because of the possibility that a desirable purchase opportunity will materialize or because of the chance that an income receipt will be late. But the introduction of uncertainty does not eliminate the types of influences on aggregate money demand that we summarized in equations 4.7 and 4.8, and which we shall use later on.

The Velocity of Money

Economists often think of the relation between the average amount of money that someone holds, $\overline{m}$, and the amount of transactions carried out by that money. In our simple model, the dollar volume of transactions equals the amount of consumption expenditure, Pc. The ratio of transactions to the average money balance, $Pc/\overline{m}$, is called the **velocity of money.** The velocity is the number of times per unit of time, such as a year, that the typical piece of money turns over.

In our model, a person's average real balance is given from equation 4.3 by $\overline{m}/P. = \frac{1}{2} c\phi$. Therefore, velocity is $c/[\overline{m}/P] = 2 \cdot (1/\phi)$. Notice that the velocity of money depends directly on the frequency of exchange, $1/\phi$, between alternative financial assets and cash. One variable that has an important effect

---

week or even daily" (Costantino Bresciani-Turroni, *The Economics of Inflation* (1931), Allen & Unwin, London, 1937, p. 303). Similarly, during the Austrian hyperinflation after World War I, "the salaries of the state officials, which used to be issued at the end of the month, were paid to them during 1922 in installments three times per month" (J. van Walre de Bordes, *The Austrian Crown*, King, London, 1927, p. 163).

on velocity is the interest rate, R. An increase in the interest rate motivates a higher frequency of financial exchanges, $1/\phi$, and therefore a higher velocity.

The Velocity of Money in the United States

Figure 4.4 shows the velocity of money in the United States from 1890 to 1985. (The data are plotted at 5-year intervals.) Velocity is defined here as the ratio of aggregate personal consumption expenditures for the year, PC, to the annual average of the money stock.[9] For the upper curve in the figure we define money as the public's holding of currency. However, it is more common to use the broader monetary aggregate, $M1$, which includes checkable deposits. Since these checkable deposits are an alternative to currency as a medium of exchange, we can readily apply our theory of the demand for money to the broader concept, $M1$. The lower curve in the figure uses the $M1$ definition of money.

One thing to notice from Figure 4.4 is the upward movement in velocity since the end of World War II. This pattern appears whether we define money as currency or as $M1$. Two main factors account for this behavior. First, interest rates have risen substantially since 1945. For example, the interest rate paid on 3-month maturity U.S. treasury bills rose from 0.4% in 1945 to 2.9% in 1960, 6.5% in 1970, and a peak of 14.0% in 1981, but then declined to 7.5% in 1985. The overall rise in interest rates motivated a reduction in real cash balances, relative to the volume of real spending, which meant an increase in velocity. Second, there have been technological advances in financial management, which enabled people to economize more easily on their cash.[10] In our simple model, these developments appear as reductions in the real cost of financial exchanges, γ/P. Such changes induce people to switch from money to alternative financial assets, which again implies a higher velocity of money.

The velocity of currency rose also over most of the period from 1890 to 1930. Changes in interest rates were not a major element here. However, checkable deposits became a convenient alternative to currency over this pe-

---

[9]More often, economists use gross national product (GNP), rather than consumer spending, to measure aggregate velocity. However, the pattern of results is similar if we use GNP. Although GNP is broader than consumer spending, it still covers only the final goods that an economy produces. Total transactions include intermediate exchanges, such as sales from suppliers to producers, from wholesalers to retailers, and so on. These trades are netted out in GNP. Also, a large and rapidly increasing volume of monetary exchange involves financial trades—such as purchases or sales of stocks and bonds. We do not have data on the total volume of transactions. However, we do know the quantity of expenditures that are made via checks, which are called debits to demand deposits. For 1985, these debits totaled $110 trillion, which was 31 times the GNP of $4.0 trillion! The ratio of debits to GNP has increased dramatically in recent years—it was about 16 in 1975, 11 in 1970, 8 in 1965, and between 5 and 7 from 1945 to 1960. The main reason for this change was the explosion of various types of financial transactions. (The data on debits are in issues of the *Federal Reserve Bulletin*.)

[10]Some of these advances—particularly the ready availability of money-market funds—were triggered by the rise in interest rates. Therefore, the second factor for explaining the rise in velocity is partly related to the first one.

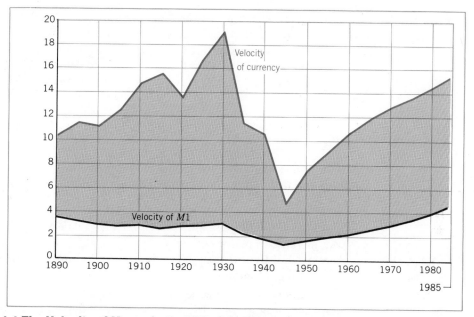

Figure 4.4 The Velocity of Money in the United States, 1890–1985

The upper curve is the ratio of consumption expenditure for the year to the annual average of currency held by the public. The lower curve uses $M1$, rather than currency. (Prior to 1915, the numbers are based on the broader monetary aggregate, $M2$, which includes all deposits at commercial banks.) *Sources:* the data on currency and $M1$ are from Milton Friedman and Anna Schwartz, *Monetary Statistics of the United States,* Columbia University Press, New York, 1970, Table 2; and Board of Governors of the Federal Reserve System, *Banking and Monetary Statistics* 1941–1970, *Annual Statistical Digest* 1970–1979, and the *Federal Reserve Bulletin,* various issues.

riod. It is interesting that the peak of currency velocity around 1930 actually exceeded that for 1985. Although there has been much talk recently about the economy's learning to dispense with currency, we see that there was actually less currency outstanding relative to the volume of consumer spending in 1930 than in 1985.

The broader monetary aggregate, $M1$, includes checkable deposits, which became increasingly popular from 1890 to 1930. Therefore, the velocity of $M1$ behaved very differently from that of currency during this period. In fact, there was a small decline in the velocity of $M1$ from 1890 to 1930.

Major declines in the velocity of currency occurred during World Wars I and II. The demand for currency rises during wartime because there are more transactions with strangers, reduced desires to leave records of transactions from checking accounts (because of rationing, higher income taxes, and other legal restrictions on private activities), and increased demand for currency by foreigners.[11] There was also a sharp decrease in the velocity of currency during

---

[11]For a discussion of these matters, see Phillip Cagan, "The Demand for Currency Relative to the Total Money Supply," *Journal of Political Economy,*. August 1958.

the Great Depression. In this case, the major financial collapse lessened the attractiveness of alternatives to currency, including demand deposits. Therefore, the velocity of currency fell dramatically from 1930 to 1935.

The influences of the Great Depression and World War II led also to declines in the velocity of $M1$. However, there was no noticeable effect during World War I.

Empirical Evidence on the Demand for Money

Our simple model provides a number of conclusions about the factors that influence the demand for money. We can summarize the main results as follows:

- An increase in the interest rate, R, reduces the real demand for money.
- An increase in real spending, C, say by 10%, raises the real demand for money, but by less than 10%—that is, there are economies of scale in the holding of money.
- An increase in the price level, P, say again by 10%, raises the nominal demand for money by 10%—hence, the real demand for money does not change.
- An increase in real transaction costs, γ/P, raises the real demand for money.

We want to know how these propositions accord with the facts. Over the past 25 years, there have been many statistical studies of the demand for money, so that a good deal of empirical evidence is available.[12]

The negative effect of interest rates on the demand for money is confirmed by investigators whether they measure money by $M1$ or currency. For example, Steve Goldfeld[13] used a variety of specifications for the United States from 1952 to 1973. He found that a 10% increase in interest rates (for example, a rise from 10 to 11%) on time deposits and on commercial paper reduced the real demand for $M1$ in the long run by about 3%. The reduction in $M1$ reflected roughly the same proportionate declines in currency and in checkable deposits.[14]

---

[12]For surveys of the evidence see David Laidler, *The Demand for Money: Theories and Evidence,* 3rd ed., Harper & Row, New York, 1985, Chapter IV, and John P. Judd and John L. Scadding, "The Search for a Stable Money Demand Function," *Journal of Economic Literature,* September 1982.

[13]Steven M. Goldfeld, "The Case of the Missing Money," *Brookings Papers on Economic Activity,* 1976:3, and "The Demand for Money Revisited," *Brookings Papers on Economic Activity,* 1973:3.

[14]For the effects on currency, see Jack Ochs and Mark Rush, "The Persistence of Interest Rate Effects on the Demand for Currency," *Journal of Money, Credit and Banking,* November 1983.

There is strong evidence for a positive effect of real spending on the real demand for money, and weaker evidence of economies of scale in this relation. For example, Goldfeld found that an increase by 10% in real GNP led in the long run to an increase by 6 to 7% in the real demand for $M1$. (A somewhat larger response of $M1$ shows up if we consider a 10% increase in real consumer expenditure, rather than real GNP.) The appearance of economies of scale—that is, a less than 10% response of real $M1$—turns out to reflect the behavior of checkable deposits. An increase by 10% in real GNP implies a long-run expansion of real currency by roughly 10%, but a rise in real checkable deposits by only about 6%.

Our model claims that an increase in the price level raises the nominal demand for money by the same proportion. This proposition receives strong empirical support. For example, Goldfeld found that an increase of the price level by 10% led to a 10% increase in the nominal demand for $M1$.

Finally, our theory predicts that a decrease in transaction costs lowers the demand for money. This effect has been important since the early 1970s because a variety of financial innovations have made it easier for people to hold less currency and checkable deposits. The innovations include automatic-teller machines, the spread of credit cards, and various accounts that allow inexpensive computerized transfers between checkable and noncheckable deposits.

Most economists, when trying to estimate the demand for money, ignored these financial innovations. Until about the mid 1970s, the estimated equations seemed to work well in that their predictions about the demand for money were fairly accurate. However, most of the developments that substantially reduced transaction costs have occurred only since the mid 1970s, which is also when the estimates that ignored these innovations started to fail. In particular, the actual amount of money that people held was substantially less than the amount predicted by earlier estimates. (This has sometimes been referred to as "missing money.")

Michael Dotsey[15] found that the volume of electronic funds transfers was a good proxy for the state of financial innovation. Thereby he showed that recent financial innovations had a strong downward effect on holdings of checkable deposits.[16] Further, by including his measure of financial innovation, he derived a money-demand equation that looked stable before and after the early 1970s. His fitted equation showed effects from interest rates and real spending that were similar to those, such as Goldfeld's, that included data only up to the early 1970s.

---

[15]"The Use of Electronic Funds Transfers to Capture the Effect of Cash Management Practices on the Demand for Demand Deposits," *Journal of Finance*, December 1985.

[16]Differences in financial sophistication are also important when considering the demand for money across countries. For some empirical estimates over the long term see Michael Bordo and Lars Jonung, "The Long-Run Behavior of the Income Velocity of Money in Five Advanced Countries, 1870–1975: An Institutional Approach," *Economic Inquiry*, January 1981.

Money and Households' Budget Constraints

We want now to incorporate the discussion of money demand into our treatment of households' budget constraints. Recall the form of the budget condition for period t,

$$Py_t + (1 + R)b_{t-1} + m_{t-1} = Pc_t + b_t + m_t \qquad (4.9)$$

Before, we simplified the analysis by pretending that each household's cash balance was constant over time—that is, $m_t = m_{t-1}$. Then the cash-balance terms on each side of equation 4.9 canceled. Therefore, terms involving money did not appear in the derivation of the budget constraint over an infinite horizon. Now, we want to reconsider this analysis when households can alter their holdings of cash.

In our model of the demand for money, the cash position moves up and down during a period in accordance with the sawtooth pattern shown in Figure 4.1. But for the purpose of constructing a budget constraint over an infinite horizon, it is satisfactory to neglect these ups and downs of money within a period. Hence we now pretend that a household's money holding is constant during a period, although it can change from one period to the next.

As before, we can use the one-period budget constraint from equation 4.9 to derive a budget condition that applies for any number of periods. When we consider an infinite horizon and express things in real terms, the results are

$$y_1 + \frac{y_2}{(1 + R)} + \cdots + \frac{b_0(1 + R)}{P} + \frac{m_0}{P}$$

$$= c_1 + \frac{c_2}{(1 + R)} + \cdots + \frac{R(m_1/P)}{(1 + R)} + \frac{R(m_2/P)}{(1 + R)^2} + \cdots \qquad (4.10)$$

Consider the role of the monetary terms in equation 4.10. First, the sources of funds on the left side include the initial real balance, m_0/P. People can use their initial cash to pay for goods, just as they can use their initial bonds, $b_0(1 + R)/P$. Second, the uses of funds on the right side include a series of terms that reflect the interest foregone by holding money rather than bonds. The first term is $R(m_1/P)/(1 + R)$. The household could have held the real quantity of assets, m_1/P, as bonds rather than money during period 1. Then the real interest income during period 2 would have increased by the amount, $R(m_1/P)$. The term, $R(m_1/P)/(1 + R)$, is the real present value of this foregone interest. Similarly, the expression, $R(m_2/P)/(1 + R)^2$, is the real present value of the interest foregone during period 3. Overall, the series of monetary terms on the right side of equation 4.10 equals the real present value of interest foregone by holding money.

Let's think about the effect of the monetary terms on the sources of funds, which appear on the left side of equation 4.10, net of that on the uses of funds, which appear on the right side. This net effect equals the difference between the initial real balance and the present-value sum of interest foregone. That is, the net effect is

$$\frac{m_0}{P} - \left[\frac{R}{(1 + R)}\right]\left[\frac{m_1}{P} + \frac{m_2}{P(1 + R)} + \frac{m_3}{P(1 + R)^2} + \cdots\right] \quad (4.11)$$

Recall that all of the terms within the brackets relate to planned holdings of real balances, m_1/P, m_2/P, . . . To understand the nature of expression 4.11, suppose that these planned real balances were all the same—that is, $m_1/P = m_2/P = \ldots$. Then we can evaluate the sum within the brackets in expression 4.11 as

$$\left(\frac{m_1}{P}\right)\left[1 + \frac{1}{(1 + R)} + \frac{1}{(1 + R)^2} + \cdots\right] = \left(\frac{m_1}{P}\right)\left[\frac{(1 + R)}{R}\right]^{17}$$

Substituting back into expression 4.11, we find that the net monetary term is $m_0/P - .m_1/P$. The net of sources and uses of funds depends on the difference between the initial real balance, m_0/P, and the real balance that someone plans to hold in future periods, m_1/P. To get this answer, we assumed that all future real balances equaled the amount, m_1/P. But more generally, some average of planned future holdings would appear, rather than just the next period's, m_1/P.

We see now what happens when we include the monetary terms in the household's budget constraint, as we do in equation 4.10. The sources of funds on the left side rise relative to the uses of funds on the right side only if the initial real cash balance, m_0/P, exceeds the amount that someone plans to hold on average in the future. For someone who plans to maintain a constant real balance over time, the net effect is nil.

The Real-Balance Effect

Let's calculate the wealth effect from a change in the price level, P. Look at the household's budget condition in real terms from equation 4.10. Suppose that we hold fixed the levels of output, y_1, y_2, . . . , and consumption, c_1, c_2, ... Also, hold constant the interest rate, R, the planned levels of real balances, m_1/P, m_2/P, . . . , and the initial *nominal* money holding, m_0. Finally, let's look at the average person, for whom the initial bonds, b_0, equal zero.

Consider the effects on the left and right sides of equation 4.10 from a decline in the price level. Given our assumptions, nothing changes on the right side, which measures the uses of funds in real terms. The only effect on the left side (since $b_0 = 0$) is an increase in the real value of the initial money

---

[17]We again use the condition for a geometric sum, $1 + z + z^2 + \cdots = 1/(1 - z)$ if $-1 < z < 1$. In our case, $z = 1/(1 + R)$.

balance, m_0/P. Thus, wealth increases[18] because people can use these higher initial real balances either to raise some levels of consumption or to lower some levels of work effort. The increase in wealth from a decline in the price level is called the **real-balance effect**.[19] As with other wealth effects, we predict that this one leads to increased consumption and reduced work effort at all dates.

The real-balance effect operates only when there is a change in initial real cash, m_0/P, relative to the average of planned holdings, m_1/P, m_2/P . . . . In most of our subsequent analyses, we shall look at situations where the aggregates of actual and planned real balances move by equal amounts. Then, as mentioned before, there are equal changes to the left and right sides of the aggregate form of the budget constraint in equation 4.10. In these cases, the change in real balances will not involve wealth effects on the aggregates of consumption and work effort.[20]

Wealth Effects from Transaction Costs

In our simple model of the demand for money, we considered transaction costs and interest-foregone costs. The interest foregone from holding money appears on the right side of the budget constraint in equation 4.10. However, we have not yet incorporated any transaction costs.

Recall from our simple model that each household picks a frequency of transacting, $1/\phi$. Suppose that the chosen frequency during period t is $(1/\phi_t)$. Then, if the real cost of each transaction is (γ/P), the total of transaction costs incurred for period t is $(\gamma/P)(1/\phi_t)$. In terms of the household's budget constraint, these transaction costs are just like the real expenditure on consumption, c_t. (At least this is true if the transaction costs represent payments for financial services, which people buy from the producers of these services.) Therefore, we should augment the right side of equation 4.10 to include the

---

[18]We can modify these results to accommodate a nonzero value for the initial level of bonds, b_0. Lenders, for whom $b_0 > 0$, benefit from a decline in the price level. Borrowers lose out by a corresponding amount. In the aggregate, since $B_0 = 0$, the only effect comes from the change in real money balances, M_0/P.

[19]The effect has been stressed by many economists. See, for example, Gottfried Haberler, *Prosperity and Depression,* 2nd ed., League of Nations, Geneva, 1939, Chapters 8 and 11; A. C. Pigou, "Economic Progress in a Stable Environment," *Economica,* August 1947; Don Patinkin, "Price Flexibility and Full Employment," *American Economic Review,* September 1948; and Robert Mundell, "Money, Debt and the Rate of Interest," in *Monetary Theory,* Goodyear, Pacific Palisades, Calif., 1971.

[20]For related discussions of real-balance effects, see G. C. Archibald and Richard Lipsey, "Monetary and Value Theory: A Critique of Lange and Patinkin," *Review of Economic Studies,* October 1958; and E. J. Mishan, "A Fallacy in the Interpretation of the Cash Balance Effect," *Econometrica,* May 1958.

present value of real transaction costs. Assuming that the real cost per transaction, γ/P, is constant over time, this present value equals

$$\frac{\gamma}{P}\left[\frac{1}{\phi_1} + \frac{1}{\phi_2\,(1 + R)} + \cdots\right]$$

Other things equal, an increase in the present value of real transaction costs reduces wealth. However, most economists believe that in normal times these costs are small relative to a household's total present value of real expenditure, which appears in equation 4.10. Therefore, it is customary to neglect changes in transaction costs when analyzing the determination of work effort, consumption, and saving. For most purposes, we shall follow this practice.

Summary

In this chapter, we explained why people hold part of their financial assets as money, rather than interest-bearing bonds. The explanation involves, first, the role of money (but not bonds) as a medium of exchange, and, second, the extra transaction costs that arise when people economize more on their holdings of cash. We showed that the average amount of real money held involves a trade-off between transaction costs and interest-income foregone. A higher interest rate motivates people to incur more transaction costs in order to achieve a lower average real cash balance.

Our theoretical model has the following major implications for the aggregate demand for money:

- An increase in the interest rate reduces the real demand for money.
- An increase in the volume of real spending raises the real demand for money, but by a smaller proportion.
- An increase in the price level raises the nominal demand for money by the same proportion.
- An increase in real transaction costs raises the real demand for money.

The empirical evidence generally supports these propositions.

We incorporated the holdings of money into households' budget constraints over an infinite horizon. If the average of planned future holdings of real cash equals the initial holding, then there is no impact on the net of sources and uses of funds. Therefore, in these cases, we do not have to worry about wealth effects from real cash balances on the aggregates of consumer demand and work effort. On the other hand, an increase in the present value of real transaction costs reduces wealth. But in most instances, we assume that this wealth effect is small enough to neglect.

Important Terms and Concepts

double coincidence of wants

legal tender

transaction costs

M1

economies of scale in the demand for money

velocity of money

real-balance effect

QUESTIONS AND PROBLEMS

Due 9/27

Mainly for Review

4.1 What are the costs of transacting between money and financial assets? (You may want to make a list and include such items as the cost of a trip to the bank and the time spent waiting in line.) How would the development of electronic teller services affect this cost?

4.2 Suppose that an individual's consumption expenditure is $6000 per year and that it is financed by monthly withdrawals of money from a savings account.

  a. Depict on a graph the pattern of the person's money holdings over a period of 1 year. What is the average money balance?

  b. Graph the pattern of money holdings when withdrawals of money are made only once in 2 months. Show that the average money balance is higher.

4.3 Refer to question 4.2. If consumption expenditure rises to $9000 per year and withdrawals continue to be made monthly, what is the average money holding? Is it optimal for the frequency of withdrawals to remain the same when consumption increases? Explain.

4.4 What is the definition of the aggregate velocity of money? Use the concept of velocity to explain how a given aggregate quantity of money balances can be used to pay for a relatively large volume of consumption expenditure over a year.

4.5 Consider the following changes and state whether their effect on the real demand for money is an increase, a decrease, or uncertain.

  a. A decrease in the interest rate.

  b. An increase in real transaction costs.

  c. An increase in real consumption.

  d. An increase in the price level.

4.6 Consider again the changes listed in question 4.5, and describe their effect on velocity.

Problems for Discussion

4.7 **Transaction Costs and Households' Budget Constraints**

Assume that the real cost of transacting between bonds and money, γ/P, rises.

a. How does this change show up in households' budget constraints? What is the effect on wealth?

b. We neglected transaction costs when considering households' choices of work effort, consumption, and saving. Suppose now that we bring in the wealth effect from part a. What then is the effect of an increase in the real cost of transacting, γ/P, on households' work effort, consumption, and saving?

c. Have we left out a new substitution effect in part b? Think about the choice between consumption and leisure. Consumption involves market exchange, which requires us to use money. But we can "buy" leisure without using money! So what substitution effect arises for consumption versus leisure when the real cost of transacting, γ/P, rises? How does this affect the answer to part b?

4.8 **Further Aspects of Transaction Costs**

In problem 4.7 we considered the effects of transaction costs on households' budget constraints. These costs might show up as purchases of financial services—for example, as brokerage fees or service charges by banks. Alternatively, transaction costs might just represent the time that it takes to go to the bank or to make a decision.

a. How do these two different views of transaction costs affect the way that the costs appear in households' budget constraints?

b. Do these differences affect our other answers to problem 4.7?

c. How should we think about the production of financial services? That is, how can we incorporate this "good" into the model?

4.9 **Effects of the Payment Interval on the Demand for Money**

Think of a worker with an annual income of $12,000. Suppose that he or she receives wage payments once per month. Consumption spending is constant at $12,000 per year. Assume that the worker holds no bonds—that is, he or she holds all financial assets in the form of cash.

a. What is the worker's average cash balance?

b. What would the average cash balance be if the worker were paid twice per month, instead of once per month?

c. What is the general relation between the average money balance and the interval between wage payments?

4.10 **Effects of Shopping Trips on the Demand for Money**

Assume again the conditions of problem 4.9 with workers paid once per month. But instead of carrying out consumption expenditures in a uniform flow, the worker now makes periodic shopping trips. At each trip he or she buys enough goods (for example, groceries) to last until the next trip.

a. If the worker shops 4 times each month, what is the average cash balance? Why is the answer different from that in part a of problem 4.9?

b. What happens if he or she shops only twice each month?

c. What is the general effect on the average cash balance of the interval between shopping trips? Compare the answer with that for part c of problem 4.9.

d. Suppose that the cost of making shopping trips rises—for example, because of an increase in the relative price of gasoline. How would this affect the frequency of shopping trips? What does this tell us about the effect of an increase in the cost of making shopping trips on the average real holding of money? How does this result compare with the effect of financial transaction costs, γ/P, which we explored in the text?

4.11 Expenditures and the Demand for Money

a. Consider an increase in the aggregate of real spending, C. What is the effect on the aggregate demand for real cash balances, M/P? Notice that aggregate real spending can rise for two reasons. First, there could be an increase in everyone's real spending with no change in the number of people. Second, there could be an increase in the number of people with no change in each person's level of real spending. How does the response of aggregate real cash, M/P, depend on which case applies?

b. What should happen to the velocity of money as an economy develops? (Take a look at Figure 4.4 to see the history of velocity in the United States.) In answering, be sure to specify what happens to the interest rate, R, and the real cost of transacting between money and interest-bearing assets, γ/P.

4.12 The Denominations of Currency (optional)

Consider how people divide their holdings of currency between large bills (say, of $100 and over) versus small ones. How would the fraction of the value of currency that someone holds as large bills change with.

a. an increase in the price level?

b. an increase in a person's real income?

c. an increase in the interest rate?

d. a greater incentive to avoid records of payments (for example, to evade taxes or to engage in criminal transactions)?

Given the results above, the facts for the United States are not so easy to explain. The fraction of currency held as large bills (denominations of $100 and over) stayed nearly constant—between 20 and 22%—from 1944 to 1970. Then the fraction rose steadily to about 44% in June 1984. What do you think explains these numbers?

CHAPTER 5

THE BASIC MARKET-CLEARING MODEL

Aggregate-Consistency Conditions and the Clearing of Markets

In Chapter 2, we discussed households' choices of work efforts, which determined their production of commodities. In the Robinson Crusoe environment with no possibilities for storing goods, production was equal to consumption for each household. In Chapter 3 we allowed people to buy and sell goods at the price P, and to borrow and lend at the interest rate R. With these market opportunities, a household could save or dissave, so that consumption and production need not be equal in every period. The accumulation of saving over time determined a household's stock of financial assets, which could be held as money or bonds. Finally, by studying the demand for money in Chapter 4, we saw how people divided their assets between money and bonds.

During our discussion of a market economy in Chapter 3, we mentioned three conditions that must hold when we sum up over all households. First, because each dollar lent by someone on the credit market corresponds to a dollar borrowed by someone else, the aggregate stock of bonds, B_t, equals zero in every period. Second, since the stock of money does not change over time, the total that people hold in each period, M_t, equals the given quantity, M_0. Finally, since consumption is the only use for output in the model, total production, Y_t, equals total consumption, C_t. We shall refer to the three conditions just mentioned as aggregate-consistency conditions.

How do we know that the totals of individuals' choices satisfy the three aggregate-consistency conditions? For example, on the credit market, each person thinks that he or she can borrow or lend any amount at the going interest rate R. For a particular interest rate, there is no reason to think that the total of desired holding of bonds, B_t, would be zero. But then we have an inconsistency, because the total that people want to borrow does not equal the total that others want to lend. One way or another the credit market has to operate to balance the overall amounts of borrowing and lending.

Similarly, with respect to money, each person believes that he or she can

[handwritten margin notes: "aggregate stocks of bonds, B_t equals zero in every period." / "$Y_t = C_t$" / "→total people hold in each period" / "$M_t = M_0$"]

117

hold the quantity demanded. Yet somehow the total of these demands must equal the given aggregate quantity of money. Finally, on the commodity market, individuals think that they can sell or *supply* a desired quantity of goods, and also buy or *demand* a desired quantity. Once again, we need something to guarantee that the total of commodities supplied equals the total demanded.

The classical solution is that the interest rate, R, and the price of commodities, P, adjust to ensure the following:

- The total of desired holdings of bonds is zero.
- The total of money demanded equals the aggregate quantity of money.
- The total of commodities supplied equals the total demanded.

This viewpoint is called the market-clearing approach. In this approach the various prices, which are R and P in our model, adjust so that each market clears. By clearing we mean that the quantity supplied of each good—bonds, money or commodities—equals the quantity demanded. When this condition holds simultaneously for every good, we say that **general market clearing** obtains.

Note that when all markets clear, no one is unable to buy or sell commodities at the going price, or unable to extend or receive credit at the going interest rate. When markets clear, everyone can buy and sell as much as they want of each good at the market-clearing prices.

Recall that each household regards the interest rate, R, and the price level, P, as givens. However, the aggregates of households' choices determine R and P to satisfy the market-clearing conditions. Hence, R and P cannot be independent of the aggregate of people's choices about bonds, money, and commodities. But any individual's transactions are assumed to be a small fraction of the totals on any market. Therefore, as a good approximation, each person can disregard the effects of his or her behavior on the market-clearing values of R and P. So we can continue to use the analyses of individual choices that we worked out in Chapters 3 and 4.

As mentioned before, we need to ensure that the three aggregate-consistency conditions hold. But why do we use the postulate of market clearing to ensure these conditions? It turns out that this postulate amounts to assuming that *private markets function to allocate resources efficiently*. When the markets clear, it would be impossible to improve on any outcomes by matching potential borrowers and lenders or by bringing together potential buyers and sellers of commodities. Cleared markets already accomplish all of these *mutually advantageous trades*. Thus, the assumption that markets clear is tied closely to the view that the individuals who participate in and organize markets—and who are guided by the pursuit of their own interests—end up generating efficient outcomes.

We could use some other concept, instead of market clearing, to ensure that the aggregate-consistency conditions hold. One alternative is the Keynesian model, where some markets do not clear in the sense of our concept of cleared markets. Rather, some prices are sticky and some rationing of quantities comes into play. For example, people may be unable to sell all of the goods or labor services that they desire at the going price. We explore this viewpoint in detail in Chapter 18. But the subtleties of Keynesian arguments cannot be appreciated without first understanding the workings of a market-clearing model. Therefore, it is best to begin by studying a framework where markets clear.

People often use the term, *equilibrium,* to signify market clearing. But because the concept of an equilibrium has been used in so many different ways in the economics literature, its meaning has become unclear. For example, some people think of the Keynesian model as a *disequilibrium* framework, while others view it as a different concept of equilibrium. We shall avoid the terms equilibrium and disequilibrium in our discussion. But let's emphasize two basic ideas that are central to our thinking about markets. First, we have some aggregate-consistency conditions, which must be satisfied by any reasonable model. Second, we assume in most of the analysis that the interest rate, price level, and so on, adjust to clear markets. That is how we satisfy the aggregate-consistency conditions in the market-clearing model. We shall see later how the Keynesian model modifies the second idea, but not the first one.

Walras' Law of Markets

Consider again an individual who faces a given price level, P, and interest rate, R. Let's label as y_1^s the quantity of goods that the individual decides to produce and *supply* to the commodity market during period 1. By the amount supplied, we mean the quantity that someone offers to sell at a particular price. Similarly, let c_1^d represent the quantity of goods that an individual offers to buy—or *demands*—from the commodity market. Finally, let b_1^d and m_1^d denote the person's planned stocks of financial assets for period 1—that is, b_1^d is the demand for bonds and m_1^d is the demand for money.

Suppose that a household carries over from period 0 the stocks of financial assets, b_0 and m_0. Then the household's budget constraint in real terms for period 1 is

$$y_1^s + \frac{b_0(1+R)}{P} + \frac{m_0}{P} = c_1^d + \frac{b_1^d}{P} + \frac{m_1^d}{P} \tag{5.1}$$

If we sum up equation 5.1 over all households, then we get the aggregate form of the budget constraint for period 1,

$$Y_1^s + \frac{B_0(1+R)}{P} + \frac{M_0}{P} = C_1^d + \frac{B_1^d}{P} + \frac{M_1^d}{P} \tag{5.2}$$

During period zero, we must have that every dollar lent corresponds to a dollar borrowed, so that $B_0 = 0$. Using this condition, we can simplify equation 5.2 to

$$Y_1^s + \frac{M_0}{P} = C_1^d + \frac{B_1^d}{P} + \frac{M_1^d}{P} \tag{5.3}$$

Let's use equation 5.3 to see how the market-clearing model deals with the three aggregate-consistency conditions, which we mentioned before. For period 1, these conditions are

- $B_1^d = 0$—any dollar that someone wants to lend corresponds to a dollar that someone else wants to borrow,
- $M_1^d = M_0$—people willingly hold the outstanding stock of money, M_0, and
- $Y_1^s = C_1^d$—the total supply of commodities equals the total demand for commodities.

But look at equation 5.3. Suppose that the first two aggregate-consistency conditions hold—that is, $B_1^d = 0$ and $M_1^d = M_0$. Then equation 5.3 guarantees that the third condition, $Y_1^s = C_1^d$, holds also. In fact, if any two of the three conditions hold, then the third one must hold. Thus, we have to worry about satisfying only two of the three conditions for aggregate consistency. The third one follows automatically from the aggregate form of households' budget constraints in equation 5.3. This result is called **Walras' Law of Markets,** in honor of the nineteenth-century French economist, Leon Walras, who pioneered the study of models under conditions of general market clearing. (Economists refer to his analysis as *general equilibrium theory*.)

We shall obtain the same results regardless of which pair of aggregate-consistency conditions that we examine. Usually, macroeconomists look at the condition for clearing the commodity market, $Y_1^s = C_1^d$, and at the one for money to be willingly held, $M_1^d = M_0$. We shall find it convenient to follow this practice in our analysis. However, remember that the results would not change if we substituted for one of these conditions the condition that the credit market clear, $B_1^d = 0$.

Clearing the Commodity Market

We want to ensure that the aggregate quantity of commodities supplied, Y_1^s, equals the aggregate quantity demanded, C_1^d. We refer here to quantities for the current period, which is period 1. But it is convenient now to drop the time subscripts.

Our previous analysis pinpoints several variables that influence the aggregate supply and demand for commodities. These include the following:

- The interest rate, R—a higher rate implies intertemporal-substitution effects, which reduce current demand, C^d, and raise current supply, Y^s (by raising current work).
- Wealth effects from changes in the position of the production function—an increase in wealth raises demand, C^d, but lowers work effort. This decline in work offsets the direct effect from an improvement in the production function on the supply of goods, Y^s.

• Substitution effects from changes in the schedule for the marginal product of labor—an upward shift leads to an increase in supply Y^s (because people work more), and an increase in demand, C^d.

We can write out the condition for clearing the commodity market during the current period as *agg*.

$$Y^s(R, \ldots) = C^d(R, \ldots) \qquad (5.4)$$
$$(+) \qquad\qquad (-)$$

The function Y^s refers to the aggregate supply of commodities, while the function C^d refers to the aggregate demand. We indicate explicitly only the effects of the interest rate in these functions. The omitted variables in the functions, denoted by . . . , include the wealth and substitution effects that arise from changes in the production function.

Equation 5.4 deals with the summation over a large number of households. We would like to use this analysis even when households are not identical— for example, when they differ by productivity, age, tastes, initial assets, and so on. In some cases, the aggregation over different types of people will not cause major problems. For example, a change in the interest rate implies the same type of intertemporal-substitution effect for everyone. Similarly, we can handle shifts in the characteristics of the production functions when these shifts are similar for all producers. However, some changes benefit some people and harm others. For instance, we discussed before how movements in the price level or the interest rate have positive or negative effects on wealth, depending on someone's status in the credit market. Thus, these types of changes shift the distribution of resources across households, without changing the aggregate value of these resources. Economists call these kinds of changes **distributional effects.** Typically, we have no presumption about how distributional effects influence the aggregates of commodities supplied or demanded. So, as is customary in macroeconomics, we assume (hope) that we can neglect distributional effects for the purpose of aggregate analysis.

Let's be clear about some variables that do not influence aggregate supply and demand in equation 5.4. We discussed in Chapter 4 how the monetary terms enter into households' budget constraints. Specifically, these terms exert no wealth effects on the aggregates of consumption and work effort when the initial real balances, M_0/P, equal the quantity that people plan to hold in all future periods. Because this condition holds in our model (when all markets clear), we do not incorporate real-balance terms into the functions in equation 5.4.

Δ in price level have no effect on aggregate real value of these bonds

The aggregate quantity of bonds, B_0, is zero. Therefore, changes in the price level, P, have no effect on the aggregate real value of these bonds. Hence, on this count, there is no aggregate wealth effect from changes in P. Remember that we also have no effects from the monetary terms. Therefore, P does not appear at all in the condition for clearing the commodity market, equation 5.4.

no aggregate wealth effect from Δ's in P

$r\uparrow \Rightarrow C^d\downarrow$
$\quad\quad\quad Y^s\uparrow$

P'

S

P

$P\downarrow$

D

Y^s, Y^d

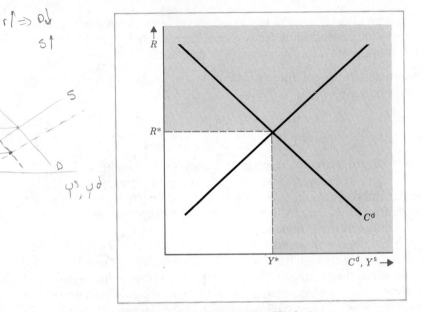

Figure 5.1 Clearing of the Commodity Market
Clearing of the commodity market, $C^d = Y^s$, occurs at the interest rate, R^*. At this point the level of aggregate output is $Y^* = C^*$.

We discussed some types of transaction costs in Chapter 4. Generally, there are wealth and substitution effects associated with these transaction costs. But as mentioned in Chapter 4, we assume that these effects are small enough to neglect for most purposes. Hence, these effects are also absent from equation 5.4.

Δin R has no aggregate wealth effect

Finally, we demonstrated in Chapter 3 that a change in the interest rate, R, has no aggregate wealth effect. (A rise in R is good for people who are usually lenders, but correspondingly bad for those who are usually borrowers.) Therefore, the effects of R on aggregate supply and demand, which appear in equation 5.4, refer only to intertemporal-substitution effects. For this reason, we know that a rise in R lowers current consumer demand, C^d, and raises current commodity supply, Y^s.

Because the interest rate has important influences on commodities supplied and demanded, we shall find it convenient to depict equation 5.4 graphically with R on the vertical axis. In Figure 5.1 we show that the interest rate has a positive effect on aggregate supply, Y^s, and a negative effect on aggregate demand, C^d. When R changes, the responses of supply and demand show up as movements along the curves in the figure. (We show the curves as straight lines only for convenience.)

The positions of the supply and demand curves in Figure 5.1 depend on the omitted elements, denoted by . . . , in equation 5.4. When any of these elements change, the effects on commodity supply and demand show up as shifts of the curves in the figure. Then for given values of these elements, we can read off from the figure the value of the interest rate, R^*, which corresponds to clearing of the commodity market, $Y^s = C^d$. Generally, we use an asterisk to signal that the value of a variable, such as $R = R^*$, derives from a market-clearing condition. Notice from the figure that the market-clearing level of output is the quantity, $Y^* = C^*$.

Remember that each household's quantity of output, y, depends on the level of work, n, through the production function, $y = f(n)$. Here we assume that we can use an aggregate form of this relation

$$Y = F(N) \tag{5.5}$$

The aggregate production function connects the aggregate amount of work, N, to the aggregate quantity of output, Y. Once we know the market-clearing level of output Y^* from Figure 5.1, we can use equation 5.5 to compute the corresponding level of aggregate work effort, N^*.

The market-clearing diagram in Figure 5.1 is the central graphical tool for our subsequent study of macroeconomic disturbances. Even when we complicate the model, we shall be able to use a version of this diagram to derive the main results. Therefore, let's stress the basic ideas behind this diagram. First, a higher interest rate stimulates the desire to produce and sell goods today, but deters the desire to buy goods. Second, we determine the market-clearing values of the interest rate and the quantity of output by equating aggregate supply to aggregate demand.

The Quantity of Money Equals the Quantity Demanded

The second aggregate-consistency condition requires the stock of money, M_0, to equal the aggregate quantity demanded during period 1, M_1^d. For convenience, we again drop the time subscripts.

In Chapter 4 we derived a function for the aggregate demand for money. When expressed in real terms—that is, as M^d/P—this demand depends negatively on the interest rate, R, and positively on the real amount of spending, C. We also discussed some effects of the real transaction cost, γ/P, although we hold this element fixed for most of our analysis. Therefore, we can write the condition for money to be willingly held as

$$M = P \cdot L(R, \quad Y, \ldots)$$
$$(-) \, (+) \tag{5.6}$$

Note that the function, L, on the right side of equation 5.6 describes the demand for money in real terms, M^d/P. Therefore, $P \cdot L(R, Y, \ldots)$ is the nominal demand for money, M^d. For convenience, we replace aggregate real expenditure, C, in the money-demand function by aggregate output, Y. (When the commodity market clears, real expenditure, C, equals real output, Y.) The omitted terms, denoted by . . . , include any effects on real money demanded

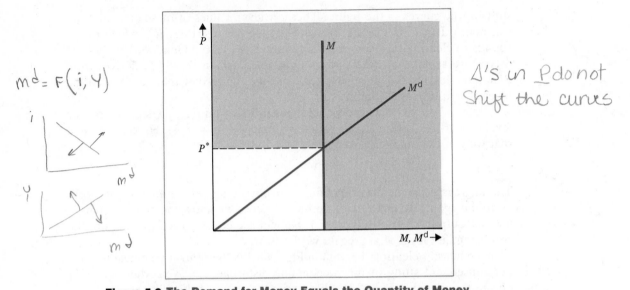

Handwritten notes (left margin):

$m^d = F(i, Y)$

Handwritten notes (right):

Δ's in P do not shift the curves

Figure 5.2 The Demand for Money Equals the Quantity of Money
The nominal demand for money is $M^d = P \cdot L(R, Y, \ldots)$. For given values of Y and R, this demand is a straight line starting from the origin. The nominal quantity of money is the constant M. The amount of money demanded equals the quantity of money when the price level is the value P^*.

other than the interest rate and the level of output. For example, the level of real transaction costs, γ/P, enters here.

Figure 5.2 shows graphically the equality between the quantity of money and the quantity demanded. We shall find it convenient to put the price level, P, on the vertical axis. Then the quantity of money is the constant, M, which appears as a vertical line in the figure. The nominal demand for money is $M^d = P \cdot L(R, Y, \ldots)$. For given values of R and Y, this demand is directly proportional to P. Hence, we show it in the figure as a positively sloped straight line, starting from the origin. Notice that the quantity of money equals the quantity demanded when the price level is the value P^*.

General Market Clearing

We want to determine the values of the interest rate, R^*, and the price level, P^*, that are consistent with the two aggregate-consistency conditions:

- the commodity market clears, as in Figure 5.1, and
- the quantity of money equals the quantity demanded, as in Figure 5.2.

Remember that these two conditions ensure that the credit market clears—that is, $B^d = 0$. We know that from Walras' Law of Markets. So we can refer to R^* and P^* as the general-market-clearing values of the interest rate and the price level.

We can readily see the basic workings of the model. To start with, the market-clearing diagram from Figure 5.1 determines the interest rate, R^*. Then we know also the levels of aggregate output and consumption, $Y^* = C^*$. Hence, we can substitute the values for R^* and Y^* into the money-demand function on the right side of equation 5.6. Then, for a given quantity of money, M, Figure 5.2 determines the general-market-clearing value of the price level, P^*.

The procedure for solving the model is this simple because the price level does not appear in equation 5.4, which is the condition for clearing the commodity market. Or, to put things another way, changes in P do not shift the curves in Figure 5.1. For this reason, we do not have to know the general-market-clearing value of the price level, P^*, when we determine the interest rate, R^*. Rather, we can just look at Figure 5.1 to determine R^*. Then, conditional on this result, we can use equation 5.6 and Figure 5.2 to solve out for P^*. But the best way to clarify the workings of the model is to work through some examples, which are of substantial interest for their own sake.

Supply Shocks

Economists use the term, **supply shock,** to refer to sudden changes in the conditions of production. Adverse effects include harvest failures, strikes, natural disasters, epidemics, and political disruptions. However, the most important recent examples of supply shocks were the oil crises of 1973–74 and 1979–81. In fact, most economists became interested in supply shocks only after these dramatic changes in the market for oil. We examine the empirical significance of oil shocks in Chapter 10.

For some reason, the term "supply shock" always refers to a negative effect on the supply of goods. But there can also be positive developments, such as technical innovations, bountiful harvests, or a run of good luck in labor relations. Our analysis can be applied either to favorable or unfavorable changes in productive conditions. However, as in some previous discussion, we shall find it important to distinguish temporary changes from permanent changes.

A Temporary Shift of the Production Function

Let's start with a temporary change to the production function—specifically, let's consider a shift that lasts only for the current period. As examples, we can think of bad weather that limits the production of coffee in Brazil, or a coal strike that lowers production in Britain.

Consider first a purely parallel downward shift of the production function, as shown in Figure 5.3. This case is the simplest example of a supply shock, because it does not alter the schedule for the marginal product of labor. Hence,

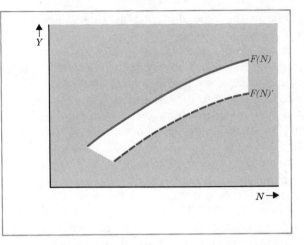

Figure 5.3 A Parallel Downward Shift of the Production Function
We examine here a parallel downward shift of the production function from $F(N)$ to $F(N)'$.

there are no substitution effects from changes in the relative costs of consumption and leisure.

Effects on the Interest Rate and Output

One effect of the supply shock is that output decreases for a given level of work effort. On this count, the supply of goods, Y^s, falls.

Second, the disturbance reduces wealth. However, because the change is short-lived, the wealth effects will be small. So we predict a small negative response of aggregate consumer demand, C^d, and a small positive response of aggregate work effort. The increase in work implies a rise in goods supplied, Y^s. But, since the wealth effect is weak, this increase offsets only a small part of the initial cutback in supply. Thus, there is a net decrease in aggregate supply, Y^s, which exceeds the small decline in aggregate demand, C^d.

We show the changes to the commodity market in Figure 5.4. Before the shift, the market cleared at the interest rate R^*. Then the disturbance causes the aggregate supply curve to shift leftward from the one labeled Y^s to that labeled $(Y^s)'$. Also, the aggregate demand curve shifts leftward from the one marked C^d to that marked $(C^d)'$. As discussed before, the shift of the supply curve is larger than that of the demand curve. Hence, there is **excess demand** for commodities—$(C^d)' > (Y^s)'$— at the initial interest rate R^*. (In the opposite situation there would be **excess supply** of commodities.)

The excess of goods demanded over those supplied means that—at the going interest rate—everybody would like to reduce their saving or borrow more. That is because the worsening of the production function is temporary. As we know from before, individuals desire to take out most of their tem-

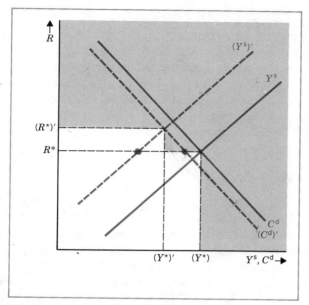

Figure 5.4 Effect of a Supply Shock on the Commodity Market
The temporary worsening of the production function lowers aggregate supply by more than demand. Therefore, clearing of the commodity market requires the interest rate to rise.

porarily depressed income in the form of less current saving or more current borrowing. People plan to repay their debts or build up their assets later when income is higher. But we know also that everybody cannot actually reduce their saving or increase borrowing because aggregate saving must end up being zero. So the interest rate has to adjust to make the aggregate of people's desired saving conform to the economy's possibilities—namely, zero total saving. To put this point another way, the interest rate must change to clear the commodity market.

We see from the diagram in Figure 5.4 that the new interest rate, $(R^*)'$, exceeds the initial one, R^*. This rise in the interest rate eliminates people's desires to carry out negative aggregate saving. Equivalently, we see that the increase in the interest rate lowers the quantity of goods demanded along the curve $(C^d)'$ and raises the quantity supplied along the curve $(Y^s)'$. Note that at the new interest rate, $(R^*)'$, the commodity market again clears—that is, $(Y^s)' = (C^d)'$.

The new level of output, $(Y^*)'$, can be read off the intersection of the new supply and demand curves in Figure 5.4. Notice that the disturbance— the temporary worsening of the production function—leads to a fall in output. From the perspective of commodity demand, $(C^d)'$, it is clear that output must be lower. First, there is the decrease in wealth, which shifts the demand curve leftward. Then second, there is the increase in the interest rate, which reduces the quantity demanded along the new curve, $(C^d)'$. So aggregate demand—and hence output, which equals the quantity demanded—must decline overall.

From the standpoint of commodity supply, $(Y^s)'$, there is the initial leftward shift of the curve. Then the rise in the interest rate raises the amount supplied along the curve $(Y^s)'$. However, this increase in quantity supplied can only partially offset the initial decrease. This result follows since supply and demand are again equal at the new interest rate, $(R^*)'$, and we have just shown that demand is lower.

Effects on Work Effort

The forces that operate on work effort are closely related to those that affect consumer demand. First, the decline in wealth leads to more work and less leisure. Second, the rise in the interest rate reinforces these effects on current work and leisure. So aggregate work effort rises, while aggregate leisure falls. This result makes sense because the disturbance does not change the terms on which people can transform leisure into consumption—that is, the schedule for labor's marginal product does not shift. If the quantities of consumption and leisure change, we would expect them to change in the same direction. In the present example, the aggregates of consumption and leisure both decrease.

Overall, the supply shock leads to less output and consumption, but to more work. Recall from the analysis in Chapter 2 that we reached similar conclusions when we confronted Robinson Crusoe with a downward shift of the production function. We might have expected some differences because people can use the credit market to borrow and lend in the present model, whereas Robinson Crusoe could not borrow and lend. But the interest rate adjusts in the market economy to ensure that the aggregate of desired saving is zero. Therefore, the typical person ends up saving zero, just like Robinson Crusoe. For this reason, we end up with similar predictions about the effects of a worsening of the production function on work effort, production, and consumption.

Effects on the Price Level

To determine the price level, we use the condition that all cash be willingly held. Recall that this condition is

$$M = P \cdot L(R, \ Y, \ldots)$$
$$(-) \, (+)$$

We know that the disturbance lowers aggregate output and raises the interest rate. Both of these changes reduce the real demand for money, which appears on the right side of the equation. Therefore, Figure 5.5 shows that the demand for money shifts leftward from the line labeled M^d to that labeled $(M^d)'$. Notice that the price level rises from the initial value P^* to the higher value $(P^*)'$.

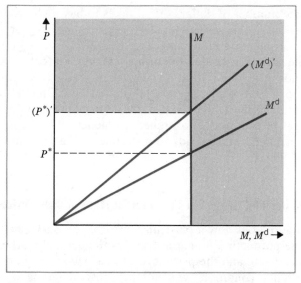

Figure 5.5 Effect of a Supply Shock on the Price Level
The increase in the interest rate and the fall in output imply a leftward shift to money demand. The price level rises from P^* to $(P^*)'$ to restore equality between the amount of money demanded and the fixed quantity of money, M.

This change is necessary to restore equality between the amount of money demanded and the fixed quantity of money, M.

We can use this analysis to understand the effects on the general price level in the United States from the oil crises of the 1970s. Sharp increases in the price of oil, relative to that of other goods, occurred in 1973–74 and 1979–81. For two reasons, this disturbance resembles an adverse shock to production functions. First, oil is an important input to production. Therefore, a cutback in the supply of oil—as reflected in an increase in its relative price—tends to deter the production of other goods. Second, because the United States imports a lot of oil, an increase in oil's relative price means that the United States pays out more of its income to foreigners per unit of oil purchased. Therefore, for a given amount of work effort and production, the United States ends up with less income to spend on consumption.

Overall, the oil crises created adverse shifts of the type shown in Figure 5.4. (At least, these changes apply if people perceived the increase in oil's relative price to be temporary.) Then we find again that output falls, the interest rate rises, and the real demand for money declines. Hence, for a given quantity of money, the general price level increases. By similar reasoning, we find that the reductions in the relative price of oil in 1983–84 helped to hold down the overall level of prices in the United States.

We should not conclude that an increase in the relative price of any commodity leads to a rise in the general price level. By the general price level, we mean the number of dollars that it takes to buy a typical market basket of goods. Obviously, this general level of prices can move up or down while some relative prices increase and some decrease.

As an example, consider a poor harvest of grain that affects foreign countries, but not the United States. The price of grain rises, relative to the price of other goods. But as a large exporter of grain, the United States gains. From the standpoint of the United States, the disturbance amounts to a temporary upward shift of the production function. Hence, there is an increase in real money demanded, which leads to a decline in the general level of prices in the United States.

The Dynamics of Changes in the Interest Rate and the Price Level

We have figured out how a particular disturbance, such as a temporary worsening of the production function, changes the general-market-clearing values of the interest rate and the price level. In particular, we know that the aggregate-consistency conditions will not be satisfied unless we get to the new position of general market clearing. But we have not really explained how R and P move from one position of market clearing to another.

We mentioned before that a temporary worsening of the production function makes everyone want to save less at the initial interest rate. Consequently, there are less offers to lend funds than there are offers to borrow. Therefore, we anticipate that the interest rate on loans will be bid up. This observation is consistent with the increase in the market-clearing value of the interest rate.

We noted also that the disturbance creates excess demand for commodities. Hence, we can think of suppliers as raising the price, P, at which they are willing to sell. This response accords with the increase in the market-clearing value of the price level.

The above sketch suggests that some plausible stories about market pressures would lead the economy toward the new position of general market clearing. In fact, researchers have constructed some elaborate models of these dynamics. But it remains true that economists do not understand these processes very well. For one thing, we have trouble explaining how people behave along the way while the aggregate-consistency conditions do not hold.[1] But if we look only at positions where these conditions hold, then we limit our attention to situations of general market clearing.

In the subsequent analysis we focus on the characteristics of market-clear-

---

[1]Walras thought of an auctioneer who adjusted various prices along the lines of our dynamic sketch. But no trades were concluded until a position of general market clearing was achieved. With this view we do not have to worry much about how people behave in situations where the markets do not clear. Of course, the device of an auctioneer who adjusts prices should not be taken literally for most markets. Rather, the idea is that buyers and sellers will manage quickly to establish prices that accord with the aggregate-consistency conditions—that is, which clear markets.

ing positions. Along the way, we sometimes provide dynamic stories to motivate the changes in the price level and the interest rate. But these stories should be treated with caution, since they do not correspond to fully worked-out models. Our main propositions about the real world come from seeing how particular disturbances influence the conditions for general market clearing. Often, this method provides answers that accord well with real-world observations. So from an empirical standpoint, the lack of a formal dynamic theory of price changes may not be that much of a shortcoming.

Summarizing the Results

Let's review our findings for a temporary worsening of the production function. We found that this disturbance leads to cutbacks in output and consumption, but to a rise in work effort. The interest rate and the price level both rise.

Consider why the interest rate rises. Because everyone regards the fall in output as temporary, they would like to borrow funds to maintain their levels of consumption. Since not everyone can borrow at once, the interest rate increases to restore the balance between desired borrowing and lending. Anyone who lends funds in this depressed situation receives a premium in terms of a high rate of interest.

Consider why the price level rises. The decline in current consumption and output, combined with the rise in the interest rate, reduce the demand for money. Therefore, the price level must rise for the amount of money demanded to equal the fixed quantity of money, M.

Including a Shift to the Schedule for the Marginal Product of Labor

We have just studied an example where the production function shifted downward in a parallel fashion. But we are usually interested in situations where the cutback in the production function involves also a worsening in the schedule for labor's marginal product. For example, there may be a proportional downward shift of the production function, as shown in Figure 5.6. Here, the marginal product of labor falls at any given level of work effort. But we assume again that the change to the production function applies only for the current period—that is, people still perceive the disturbance to be temporary.

We again have the effects on the commodity market that appear in Figure 5.4. However, we have to add some new effects, which concern the decrease in labor's marginal product. Because of this lower productivity, people want to work less now in order to shift from consumption to leisure. Also, because the worsening in production opportunities is temporary, people want to shift toward current leisure and away from future leisure and consumption. That

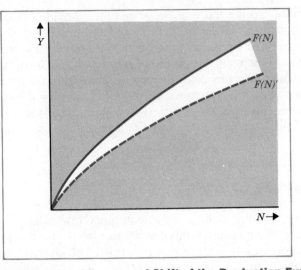

Figure 5.6 A Proportional Downward Shift of the Production Function
We examine here a proportional downward shift of the production function from $F(N)$ to $F(N)'$.

is, an intertemporal-substitution effect applies. Overall, there is a strong incentive to cut current work, N, and a weaker incentive to reduce current demand for goods, C^d. Note that the decrease in current work means a cutback of current goods supplied, Y^s.

To incorporate the new effects, we have to make modifications to Figure 5.4. First, we add a large leftward shift to the supply curve, $(Y^s)'$. Second, we add a small leftward shift to the demand curve, $(C^d)'$. Notice that these changes do not alter the general configuration of the curves shown in Figure 5.4. Hence, we still conclude that output and consumption decrease, while the interest rate rises. But because of the fall in the schedule for labor's marginal product, these effects are all larger than before.

The only qualitative difference in the results concerns the behavior of work effort. We found before that work effort increased. Recall that this response reflected the decrease in wealth and the increase in the interest rate. But now people want to work less because of the fall in the marginal product of labor (MPL). Overall, it is now uncertain whether work effort rises or falls on net.

Think of this last result again in terms of a harvest failure. People want to work a lot today because output is low (the wealth effect) and because the interest rate is high (an intertemporal-substitution effect). But if the harvest failure makes additional labor today relatively unproductive, then people prefer to take leisure instead of work. Overall, it is unclear whether the net of these forces leads people to work more or less.

When we look at the condition that money be willingly held, equation 5.6

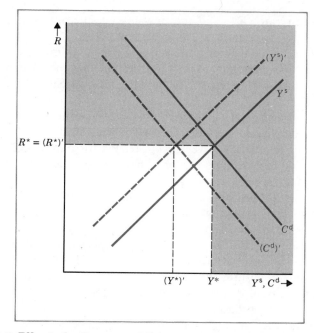

Figure 5.7 Effect of a Permanent Downward Shift of the Production Function on the Commodity Market

The permanent worsening of the production function reduces aggregate supply and demand by comparable amounts. Therefore, the interest rate does not change.

and Figure 5.5, we again find that the disturbance raises the price level. However, because output and the interest rate move by more than before, we also conclude that the increase in the price level is greater than previously.

A Permanent Shift of the Production Function

Let's return to the case of a parallel downward shift of the production function, where labor's marginal product does not change. But suppose now that this change is permanent, rather than lasting just for one period.

The difference from the previous case concerns the size of the wealth effects. Now, there is a strong negative effect on consumer demand. Also, there is a strong positive effect on work effort, so that the supply of goods falls by less than before. Recall that the permanent income hypothesis implies that a permanent shift in the production function has little effect on desired saving. In particular, people do not want to borrow more today, because future income will be just as low as current income. It follows, for a given interest rate, that the decreases in commodities supplied and demanded would be roughly equal. We use the market-clearing diagram in Figure 5.7 to illustrate this case. Notice that the leftward shifts to the supply and demand curves are the same. Therefore, commodity supply still equals commodity demand at the initial interest rate, R^*, and the new market-clearing interest rate, $(R^*)'$, equals R^*.

We again have declines in output and consumption. Note that, since the interest rate does not change, the reduction in consumer demand now reflects only the decrease in wealth. Similarly, the fall in wealth implies an increase in work effort.

Since output declines and the interest rate does not change, we know that real money demanded declines. Therefore, we can still use Figure 5.5 to see that the price level rises. Overall, the results for output and the price level resemble those that we found before when the change in the production function was temporary.

The major difference in results is the rise in the interest rate when the worsening of the production function is temporary, but no change when the worsening is permanent. The interest rate is a signal that tells people the cost of using resources now rather than later. Specifically, a high interest rate attaches a high cost to current consumption and leisure, relative to future consumption and leisure. When the production function worsens temporarily, there is a scarcity of goods today relative to the future. Thus, a high interest rate makes sense because it makes people take today's relative scarcity into account when they decide how much to consume and work. On the other hand, a permanent worsening of the production function means that fewer goods are available at all times. In particular, there is no change in today's position relative to tomorrow's. The interest rate does not change because there is no change in the cost of using resources today rather than tomorrow.

The results tell us something important about movements in interest rates. Mostly, we expect interest rates to change when there are economic disturbances that alter present conditions relative to prospective ones. Harvest failures, natural disasters, and major strikes fall into this category. As we stress in a later chapter, war may be empirically the most important example of a disturbance that has a temporary effect on the overall economy. On the other hand, for disturbances that have permanent effects, we do not predict large changes in interest rates. (*Warning*: The analysis has so far left out the important influence of inflation on interest rates. We cover this topic in Chapters 7 and 8.)

As before, we can modify the analysis to include a downward shift to the schedule for the marginal product of labor. Then we find that this extension does not change most of the results. We still predict that a permanent worsening of the production function has no effect on the interest rate. However, as in the analysis of a temporary shift, we now find that the response of work effort is ambiguous. That is because the reduction in wealth motivates more work, while the fall in labor's marginal product motivates less work. Recall that we discussed the essence of this case in Chapter 2, where we considered the influence of economic development on hours worked. (However, that analysis dealt with upward shifts to the production function, rather than downward shifts.) Economic development leads to less hours worked over time if the wealth effect dominates over the substitution effect from higher productivity.

Changes in the Stock of Money

In our previous examples, we deduced the change in the price level by examining the condition that money be willingly held. We found that changes in output and the interest rate altered the demand for real cash balances. Then the price level changed to equate the nominal quantity of money demanded to the given nominal quantity of money. Essentially, we have dealt with changes in the demand for money, while holding fixed the aggregate supply of nominal money, M.

Many economists have argued that changes in the quantity of money, M, are empirically the major source of variations in the price level. To study this linkage, we have to allow for changes in the stock of money. Therefore, we now construct a simple device that enables us to study these changes.

Think of a case where the initial stock of money, M_0, and all subsequent stocks M_t for $t > 0$, rise by the same amount. In this case there is a once-and-for-all increase in the quantity of money, which might arise by the government printing up the extra money and giving it to people. In Chapters 7 and 15 we shall examine further how new money gets into the economy. For now, we assume that the government will never repeat this odd business of printing money and giving it away. So nobody expects to receive any more cash later on.

The condition for clearing the commodity market, $Y^s(R, \ldots) = C^d(R, \ldots)$, does not involve the level of the money stock, M. Therefore, we know right away that the change in the number of dollars bills outstanding does not change the market-clearing value of the interest rate, R^*. Further, there are no effects on the levels of output and consumption, $Y^* = C^*$.

Consider again the condition that the money stock be willingly held,

$$M = P \cdot L(R, \; Y, \ldots)$$
$$(-)\,(+)$$

Since the interest rate and the level of aggregate output do not change, there is no change in the real demand for money, $L(R, Y, \ldots)$, which appears on the right side of the equation. Therefore, the line labeled M^d in Figure 5.8 does not shift. However, the figure shows that the nominal quantity of money increases from M to M'. It follows that the price level rises from P^* to $(P^*)'$. For the change in the nominal amount of money demanded, M^d, to equal the change in the quantity of money, this increase in the price level must be in the same proportion as the change in the money stock. In other words, the real quantity of money, M/P, does not change. This result makes sense since the real amount of money demanded, $L(R, Y, \ldots)$, is the same.

As before, we can outline a dynamic story that makes plausible the increase in the price level. At the initial level of prices, people have more money than they wish to hold; so everyone tries to spend their excess cash, partly on goods and leisure and partly on bonds. The positive effect on goods and leisure is the real-balance effect. Remember that this effect operates when—as in the present case—people have more cash than they plan to hold in the future.

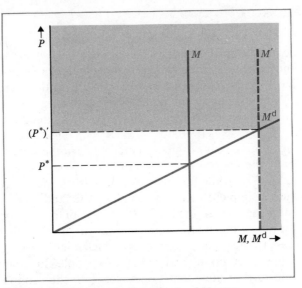

Figure 5.8 Effect of a Change in the Stock of Money
The quantity of money rises from M to M'. For this money to be willingly held, the price level rises from P^* to $(P^*)'$.

Since the real-balance effect raises the aggregate demand for goods above the supply, there is upward pressure on the price level.[2] Further, this increase in prices continues until the outstanding amount of money is willingly held. At this point, people no longer have excess cash that they wish to spend and there is no further pressure for the price level to rise.

The Neutrality of Money

Our results exhibit an important property that is called the **neutrality of money.** Once-and-for-all changes in the aggregate quantity of money affect nominal variables, but leave real variables unchanged. For example, if we double the money stock, then we double the price level, P, the nominal value of production and consumption, $PY = PC$, and so on. But we leave unchanged the real variables, such as output and consumption, $Y = C$, real cash balances, M/P, and the quantity of work, N. Also we do not affect the interest rate, R. Note that the interest rate is a real variable, which signals the cost of buying consumption or leisure today, rather than tomorrow. In later chapters, we explore further aspects of monetary neutrality.

---

[2] We noted that people attempt to spend some of their excess cash on bonds. This increase in the demand for bonds tends to drive down the interest rate. A lower interest rate leads, in turn, to excess demand for commodities. Therefore, this channel reinforces the pressure toward higher prices. Note, however, that there is no net change in the interest rate at the new position of general market clearing.

The Quantity Theory of Money and Monetarism

The **quantity theory of money** refers to a body of thinking about the relation between money and prices. This viewpoint goes back hundreds of years, with some of the most interesting statements coming from David Hume, Henry Thornton, and Irving Fisher.[3] There are two common elements in these analyses. First, changes in the quantity of money have a positive effect on the general price level. Second, as an empirical matter, movements in the money stock account for the major longer-run movements in the price level.

Some writers refined the quantity theory to apply to changes in the stock of money relative to changes in the quantity of goods on which people could spend their money. The last element corresponds in our model to the total output of goods, Y. But output is only one variable that affects the demand for real cash balances. So, to go further, some quantity theorists stress that the price level increases when the quantity of money rises in relation to the real balances that people want to hold. Empirically then, most movements in prices would reflect movements in money if the variations in the nominal quantity of money were much greater than the fluctuations in the demand for real cash balances.[4]

Sometimes economists identify the quantity theory of money with the statement that monetary changes are neutral. Then we have our previous proposition that shifts in the stock of money have proportional effects on the price level, but no effects on real variables. Many quantity theorists regard this hypothesis as accurate in the long run, but not for short-run fluctuations in money. In particular, the quantity theory allows for the possibility that fluctuations in money have temporary effects on real economic activity. So far, our model does not admit these short-run effects of money. But we reexamine this possibility in later chapters.

More recently, economists have used the term **monetarism,** to describe a school of thought that is similar to modern versions of the quantity theory of money. As with most terms that are popular in the newspapers, this one has been used in contradictory ways. But it is clear that monetarists regard the quantity of money as the major determinant of the price level, especially over the long run. Thus, monetarists stress control of the money supply as the central requirement for price stability. Also, monetarism allows for important short-term effects of monetary fluctuations on real economic activity. But monetarists typically regard these effects as unpredictable—therefore, they

---

[3]David Hume, "Of Money" (1752), in Eugene Rotwein, ed., *David Hume—Writings on Economics*, University of Wisconsin Press, Madison, 1970; Henry Thornton, *An Enquiry into the Nature and Effects of the Paper Credit of Great Britain* (1802), Augustus Kelley, Fairfield, N. J., 1978; and Irving Fisher, *The Purchasing Power of Money*, 2nd ed. (1922), Augustus Kelley, New York, 1963, Chapters 2 and 8.

[4]Milton Friedman stresses the stability of the demand for money as the hallmark of a modern quantity theorist. See his "The Quantity of Money—A Restatement," in M. Friedman, ed., *Studies in the Quantity Theory of Money*, University of Chicago Press, Chicago, 1956, p. 16.

argue that stable money is also the best policy for avoiding erratic movements of the real variables.[5]

Changes in the Demand for Money

As mentioned, we can determine the price level by looking at the condition that money be willingly held

$$M = P \cdot L(R, \ Y, \ . \ . \ .)$$
$$(-) \ (+)$$

We have just studied changes in the money stock. Shifts in money change the price level in the same direction. Earlier, we examined disturbances to the production function, which ended up changing output, Y, or the interest rate, R. With the money stock held constant, these changes affect the price level by shifting the real demand for money. Notice that the price level moves in the direction opposite to changes in the real demand for money.

An economy may experience changes in the demand for money that do not reflect movements in output or the interest rate. For example, in our model of the demand for money from Chapter 4, there may be changes in the cost of transacting between interest-bearing assets and money. These costs have declined significantly in recent years with the development of money-market funds, automated bank tellers, and other financial innovations. We predict that these types of changes reduce the demand for real cash balances.

To represent this type of change, suppose that the real demand function for money, $L(R, Y, \ . \ . \ .)$, shifts leftward, as shown in Figure 5.9. The result is that the price level must rise for the nominal amount of money demanded to remain equal to the given nominal quantity, M. Hence, we predict that the financial innovations of recent years—which reduced the demand for real cash balances—raise the price level for a given behavior of the nominal stock of money. Notice also that these innovations lead to a lower level of real balances, M/P.

In our model the change in the real demand for money—and the resulting change in real balances—do not influence the condition for clearing the commodity market, $Y^s(R, \ . \ . \ .) = C^d(R, \ . \ . \ .)$. Therefore, there are no changes in the market-clearing values of output or the interest rate. This conclusion depends on our earlier approximation, which neglected the role of transaction costs in households' decisions for work effort, consumption, and saving. In

---

[5]The term, monetarism, apparently originates from Karl Brunner, "The Role of Money and Monetary Policy," Federal Reserve Bank of St. Louis, *Review*, July 1968. Brunner (p. 9) stresses three major features of the monetarist position: "First, monetary impulses are a major factor accounting for variations in output, employment and prices. Second, movements in the money stock are the most reliable measure of the thrust of monetary impulses. Third, the behavior of the monetary authorities dominates movements in the money stock over business cycles."

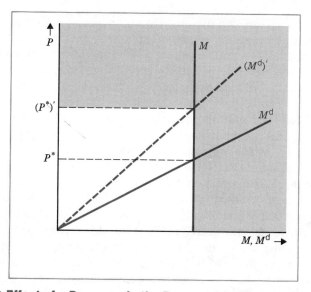

Figure 5.9 Effect of a Decrease in the Demand for Money on the Price Level
The demand for money shifts leftward from M^d to $(M^d)'$. The price level rises from P^* to $(P^*)'$ to restore equality between the amount of money demanded and the fixed quantity of money, M.

particular, we neglected the wealth effects from changes in transaction costs. More generally, if we took account of the resources that people use up in transacting, then financial innovations could affect real variables like output and the interest rate.[6] However, we continue to assume that these effects are small enough to neglect for present purposes.

Summary

Any macroeconomic model must satisfy some conditions for aggregate consistency. In our context these are first, any dollar that someone lends corresponds to a dollar that someone else borrows; second, people hold the outstanding stock of money; and third, total output equals total consumption. We use the idea of market clearing to satisfy these conditions. Specifically, we require that first, the aggregate demand for bonds is zero; second, that the amount of money demanded equals the quantity outstanding; and third, the supply of commodities equals the demand. Because of the budget constraints of households, these three conditions are not independent. In particular, Wal-

---

[6]The change in the nominal stock of money, M, is different. In this case, people end up holding the same real balances, M/P, and incurring the same real flow of transaction costs. Hence, the change in the money stock is neutral even if we take account of the resources used up in transacting.

ras' law says that we can use any two of the three conditions. We focus on the condition for clearing the commodity market—that the supply of commodities equals the demand—and on the condition that the stock of money be willingly held.

We constructed a market-clearing diagram to show how the condition for clearing the commodity market determines the interest rate and the level of output. Then the condition that money be willingly held determines the price level for a given nominal quantity of money. We use this apparatus to analyze supply shocks, which we represent as shifts to the production function. For example, a temporary adverse shock lowers output and raises the interest rate and price level. The effect on work is ambiguous. When the unfavorable shift to the production function is permanent, rather than temporary, the main difference is that the interest rate does not increase. That is because a higher interest rate signals the scarcity of goods today relative to later. When things get permanently worse, there is no reason for the interest rate to change.

Shifts in the nominal quantity of money are neutral in our model. Specifically, the price level changes in the same proportion as money, but no real variables change. Finally, if we neglect transaction costs, then shifts to the demand for money do not influence any real variables, except for the quantity of real cash balances. But the price level falls when the real demand for money increases.

Important Terms and Concepts

general market clearing	excess supply
Walras' Law of Markets	neutrality of money
distributional effects	quantity theory of money
supply shock	monetarism
excess demand	

QUESTIONS AND PROBLEMS

Mainly for Review

5.1 How are transactions in different markets, such as consumption and borrowing, linked in individual budget constraints? How does Walras' law show that this linkage carries over to the markets as a whole?

5.2 How does a change in (*a*) the interest rate, (*b*) wealth, and (*c*) the production function affect the aggregate demand and supply of commodities? Describe the effects graphically, making sure to distinguish between *shifts in* and *movements along* the demand and supply curves.

5.3 Why is a change in the price level not effective in reducing excess demand or supply in the commodity market? Explain how a change in the price level can ensure that the outstanding quantity of money is held willingly.

5.4 Consider a parallel upward shift of the production function, which raises the aggregate supply of commodities. Use a graph to convince yourself that
  a. If consumption demand shifts by an equivalent amount, the interest rate does not change.
  b. If consumption demand shifts by a smaller amount, the interest rate declines.

5.5 Describe your results in question 5.4 in terms of the marginal propensity to consume. Which of the two possibilities is likely to hold when the shift in the production function is temporary?

5.6 What is meant by the neutrality of money? Explain its implications for the popular notion that an increase in the quantity of money will reduce the interest rate.

5.7 Consider a decline in the transaction cost of converting financial assets into money. Describe its effect on (a) the price level, (b) the real quantity of money, and (c) velocity. Do these effects contradict the neutrality of monetary changes?

Problems for Discussion

5.8 Walras' Law of Markets
  a. Show how to derive Walras' Law of Markets (equation 5.3) by using the household's budget constraints.
  b. We seem to have three independent conditions for aggregate consistency: zero aggregate demand for bonds, $B_1^d = 0$; the money stock is willingly held, $M_0 = M_1^d$; and equality between commodities supplied and demanded, $Y_1^s = C_1^d$. Walras' law says that only two of these conditions are independent. Explain this result.
  c. How do the number of independent conditions for aggregate consistency compare with the number of market prices that we have to determine in the model? By the term, *market prices,* we mean to include both the price level, P, and the interest rate, R. That is, the interest rate is the price of credit.
  d. Write out Walras' law in the form of a sum of aggregate excess demands, $C^d - Y^s$, $M_1^d/P - M_0/P$, and B_1^d/P. What does the law say in this form?

5.9 Aggregate-Consistency Conditions for Robinson Crusoe
  We discussed several conditions for aggregate consistency in this chapter. These conditions arise because we have many individuals who come together to trade at marketplaces for commodities and credit. We did not have these markets in Chapter 2, where we discussed the behavior of an isolated individual, such as Robinson Crusoe.
  How would you think about aggregate-consistency conditions for Robinson Crusoe? What parallels and differences are there with the conditions that arise in the present chapter?

5.10 Effects of a Change in Population

Assume a one-time decrease in population, possibly caused by an onset of plague or a sudden out-migration. The people who left are the same as those who remain in terms of productivity and tastes. The aggregate quantity of money does not change.

What happens to the values of aggregate output, Y, work effort, N, the interest rate, R, and the price level, P?

5.11 Effects of a Change in the Willingness to Work

Suppose (in a magical, unexplained fashion) that all households change their preferences to favor consumption over leisure. That is, people raise their willingness to work. Assume that no change occurs in preferences for expenditures now versus later, so that aggregate desired saving does not change at the initial interest rate.

What happens to the values of aggregate output, Y, work effort, N, the interest rate, R, and the price level, P?

Can you think of some real-world events that might raise everybody's willingness to work?

Note: We will be in trouble if we permit unrestricted fluctuations in preferences. A basic strength of the economic approach—and the basis for forming hypotheses that we can conceivably reject from observed data—is the assumption of stable tastes. Then we can analyze changes to production possibilities and other disturbances in terms of wealth and substitution effects, as we did in the text. In this manner, we end up with predictable influences on observable variables, such as output and the price level. But if tastes are unstable, then we can reconcile any observed behavior by assuming the appropriate shift in unobservable preferences. This capacity for explaining all data means that the model has no predictive value. Also, unaccountable shifts in preferences are more plausible for an individual than for the aggregate of households. Usually, there is no good reason for everyone to become more eager to work precisely at the same time.

5.12 Effects of a Shift in the Rate of Time Preference

Suppose that all households increase their preference for current expenditures over future expenditures. In terms of the language that we used in Chapter 3, there is an increase in the rate of time preference, ρ.

What happens to the values of aggregate output, Y, work effort, N, the interest rate, R, and the price level, P?

(The note attached to problem 5.11 applies also to the change in tastes that we assumed in this problem.)

5.13 Temporary Changes in the Price Level

Consider again the analysis of a temporary worsening of the production function (Figures 5.4 and 5.5). We showed that the price level rises from its initial value, P^*, to a higher value, $(P^*)'$. But since the disturbance is temporary, we expect the price level to return in later periods to the initial value, P^*. At least, this should happen if nothing else changes, including the quantity of money.

So far, the analysis assumes that people expect the price level to remain constant over time. But we just showed that the current price level is above its expected future values when there is a temporary worsening of the production function. Think about how to modify the analysis to take account of expected future changes in the price level. (Do not spend too much time on this problem, since we shall study this topic in detail in Chapters 7 and 8.)

5.14 Consumption, Saving, and the Interest Rate (optional)

According to the theory, an increase in the interest rate motivates people to reduce current consumption, relative to current income. Correspondingly, people increase current saving. Yet although a temporary downward shift of the production function leads to an increase in the interest rate, it does not lead to any change in the ratio of aggregate consumption to aggregate income (which equals one in this model). Also, there is no change in aggregate saving, which equals zero.

a. Explain these results.

b. Researchers often attempt to estimate the effects of a change in the interest rate on an individual's choices of consumption and saving. Many studies look at the relation between the interest rate and either the ratio of aggregate consumption to aggregate income or the amount of aggregate saving. What does the theory predict for this relation? Why does it not reveal the effect of a change in the interest rate on an individual's desire to consume and save?

c. The theory says that an increase in the interest rate motivates people to raise next period's consumption, c_2, relative to this period's, c_1. Suppose that we look at the relation of the interest rate, R_1, to the ratio of aggregate consumptions, C_2/C_1. Does this relation reveal something about the behavior of individuals?

d. Suppose that we want to use aggregate data to figure out the effects of the interest rate on an individual's choices of consumption and saving. What do the answers to this question suggest that we should look at?

5.15 The Dynamics of Changes in the Price Level

In the text, we examined a case where the real demand for money declined. Then the price level increased, but the interest rate did not change.

a. Outline a dynamic story that describes the pressures for the price level to rise.

b. Does the interest rate stay fixed or move around while the price level adjusts in part a?

c. Can you tell a story where the price level jumps immediately to its new market-clearing position, rather than adjusting gradually in accordance with the sketch in part a?

5.16 A Currency Reform

Suppose that the government replaces the existing monetary unit with a new one. For example, the United States might shift from the old dollar to the Reagan dollar, which equals 10 old dollars. People can exchange their old currency for the new one at a ratio of 10 to 1. Also, any contracts that were written in terms of old dollars are converted at the ratio of 10 to 1 into Reagan dollars.

a. What happens to the price level and the interest rate?

b. What happens to the quantities of output, consumption, and work effort?

c. Do the results exhibit the neutrality of money?

5.17 Temporary versus Permanent Changes of the Production Function (optional) Consider the parallel downward shift of the production function in Figure 5.3. This type of change does not affect the schedule for labor's marginal product. Suppose first that this change is permanent.

a. We dealt with this type of disturbance for an isolated individual, Robinson Crusoe, in Chapter 2. We found that Crusoe reduced output and consumption, but raised work effort. How do these results compare with those we obtained in the present chapter, which includes markets for commodities and credit? Think of the typical or representative household: Does that household's responses of output, consumption, and work effort differ from those of Robinson Crusoe?

b. Suppose now that the change to the production function is temporary. Compare again Robinson Crusoe's responses of output, consumption, and work effort with those of the typical household in the model from the present chapter.

c. For Robinson Crusoe, how do the responses of output, consumption, and work effort depend on whether the improvement to the production function is temporary or permanent? (Problem 2.9 in Chapter 2 deals with this matter.)

d. Put together the results from parts a, b, and c. They tell us how to compare temporary and permanent changes in the production function for the model in the present chapter, which includes markets for commodities and credit. How do the responses of output, consumption, and work effort for the typical household depend on whether the change in the production function is permanent or temporary?

CHAPTER 6

THE LABOR MARKET

To simplify matters, we pretended that households used only their own labor to produce goods. Now we make things more realistic by introducing a market where people exchange labor services. We can think of the people who buy labor services as firms or employers. Those who sell services are the employees in the economy.

We shall think of the labor market as a place where people supply and demand labor services. Then the clearing of this market—along with those for commodities and credit—determines the aggregates of work and output. One objective of the present chapter is to see how the presence of the labor market and the existence of firms changes the way that work and output are determined. For most macroeconomic questions, it turns out that the answer is not much. The simplified setting in which people work only on their own production processes is satisfactory for most purposes. However, the extensions in this chapter do allow us to explore the determination of wage rates and the manner in which a labor market promotes economic efficiency. Also, the extended framework will be essential later on when we study unemployment (in Chapter 10).

Setup of the Labor Market

Suppose for simplicity that everyone's labor services are physically the same. But instead of working on one's own production process, people now sell all of their labor services on the labor market. This market establishes a single wage rate, which we denote by w and measure in units of dollars per person-hour. (For convenience, we omit subscripts here.) By the wage rate we mean that buyers of labor services pay w dollars for each hour that someone works for them. Correspondingly, sellers of labor services receive w dollars for each hour of work. As in our treatment of the commodity market, we assume that individual buyers and sellers regard the wage rate, w, as a given.

Denote by n^s the number of person-hours of labor services that a household supplies to the labor market during a period. Correspondingly, this household receives the dollar quantity, $w \cdot n^s$, of labor income.

Suppose that some of the households—who are inclined to be entrepreneurs—set themselves up as **firms.** These firms hire other people as workers. Let n^d denote the number of person-hours of labor services that a firm demands from the labor market. Correspondingly, the firm pays the dollar amount, $w \cdot n^d$, as wage payments to its workers.

Each firm uses its input of labor services, n^d, to produce commodities. The quantity produced and supplied to the commodity market is

$$y^s = f(n^d) \tag{6.1}$$

where f is again the production function. Since the goods sell at the price P, the firm's gross revenue from sales is $P \cdot y^s$. The firms's **profit** is gross revenue less wage payments—that is,

$$\text{profit} = P \cdot y^s - w \cdot n^d = P \cdot f(n^d) - w \cdot n^d \tag{6.2}$$

The profit from this business goes to the household or households that own the firm. Therefore, a household's total income now includes its share of profits from firms, as well as wage income, $w \cdot n^s$, plus interest income.

The Demand for Labor

Think about a household that owns all or part of a firm. The household's utility depends on its paths of consumption, c^d, and work, n^s. Hence, the demand for labor, n^d, matters to the household only through its effect on the firm's profit, which appears in equation 6.2. If the firm acts to benefit its owners—which we assume—then it sets its demand for labor, n^d, to maximize profit in each period.

An increase in labor input, n^d, has two effects on profit. First, an extra hour of work means that output, $f(n^d)$, increases by the marginal product of labor, MPL. Hence, gross sales revenue rises by the dollar amount, $P \cdot$ MPL. Second, the wage bill increases by the dollar wage rate, w. Therefore, profit rises if the value of labor's marginal product, $P \cdot$ MPL, exceeds w. To maximize profit a firm expands employment, n^d, up to the point where the value of the marginal product just equals the wage rate—that is, where $P \cdot \text{MPL} = w$. (Recall that as work increases, the marginal product of labor declines.) If we divide through by the price level, the condition that each firm satisfies in every period is

$$\text{MPL} = \frac{w}{P} \tag{6.3}$$

Notice that the right side of equation 6.3 is the **real wage rate**, w/P. This variable is the quantity of commodities that someone can buy with the dollar amount, w. Equation 6.3 says that a producer chooses the quantity of labor input, n^d, so that the marginal product, MPL, equals the real wage rate. At that point, the last unit of labor contributes just enough to output, MPL, so

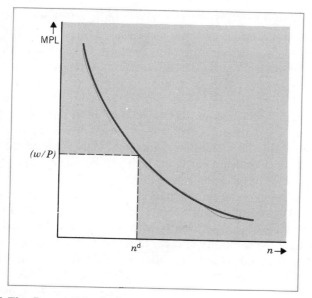

Figure 6.1 The Demand for Labor

Labor's marginal product, MPL, declines as the quantity of labor increases. Producers set the demand for labor, n^d, at the point where the marginal product equals the real wage rate, w/P.

as to cover the extra cost of this labor in units of commodities, which is the real wage rate.

We illustrate the results in Figure 6.1. The curve shows the negative effect of more labor input on the marginal product, MPL. Notice that firms set their demand for labor, n^d, at the point where the marginal product equals the real wage rate, w/P.

At a point in time each person receives the same real wage rate since we assume that all labor services are identical. Hence, labor's marginal product ends up being the same on all production processes. This result holds even if there are differences across firms in production functions or across households in the willingness to work. It is efficient to equalize these marginal products. Otherwise, the economy's total output could rise, without changing total work effort, by shifting workers from one production process to another. In particular, this increase in output would result if a worker moved from an activity where his or her marginal product was low to one where it was high. But it is only the existence of the labor market that ensures the equality in marginal products. In our earlier model, where people worked only on their own production processes, we might end up with large differences in marginal products. Since one person could not work on another's production activity, there was no mechanism to equalize the marginal products.

For example, think of two isolated regions, A and B. The technology in A is primitive, so that workers end up with the low marginal product and real wage rate, $MPL^A = (w/P)^A$. Region B is more advanced and ends up with a higher marginal product and real wage rate, $MPL^B = (w/P)^B$. Now suppose that an economy-wide labor market develops, which means that people from region A can work in region B and vice versa. As we set things up, the workers from the low-wage region A would migrate to region B. Then, by working with the better technology, these workers can produce more goods without working any harder. In fact, the movement of workers out of A and into B continues until the marginal products and real wage rates are equalized in the two regions. This happens partly through a higher marginal product in A (where work declines) and partly through a lower marginal product in B (where work increases). But for our purposes, the important point is that the opening up of the economy-wide labor market allows for an expansion of aggregate output without requiring an increase in total work effort. In that sense the economy operates more efficiently when the labor market exists.

As with the commodity and credit markets, we find that the existence of the labor market aids economic efficiency. Specifically, this market exhausts all the potential gains from movements of workers from one place to another. Because everyone's marginal product and real wage rate end up being the same, there are no gains of this type that remain unexploited.

Properties of the Demand for Labor

We can use Figure 6.1 to see how various changes affect the demand for labor. It follows at once that a decrease in the real wage rate, w/P, means a higher quantity of labor demanded. That is, when the real cost of hiring workers decreases, firms expand employment until labor's marginal product falls by as much as the decrease in w/P.

Second, an upward shift in the schedule for labor's marginal product—that is, an upward shift of the curve in Figure 6.1—leads to a greater quantity of labor demanded for any given real wage rate. Specifically, employment expands until the marginal product again equals w/P.

We can summarize the results by writing down a function for the aggregate demand for labor. This function takes the form

$$N^d = N^d \left(\underset{(-)}{\frac{w}{P}}, \dots \right) \tag{6.4}$$

where the expression . . . again refers to characteristics of the production function.

Recall that each firm's choice of labor input determines its supply of goods through the production function, $y^s = f(n^d)$. Since labor demanded decreases with the real wage rate, we can write the function for the aggregate supply of goods as

$$Y^s = Y^s \left(\underset{(-)}{\frac{w}{P}}, \dots \right) \tag{6.5}$$

Labor Supply and Consumption Demand

The introduction of the labor market does not greatly alter the analysis of work effort and consumption demand. The main modification concerns the household's choice between consumption and leisure at a point in time. In our previous model the schedule for labor's marginal product, MPL, tells people the terms on which they can substitute consumption for leisure. When someone works an extra hour on his or her own production process, he or she can use the additional output (of MPL units) to raise consumption. Now people sell their labor services at the real wage rate, w/P, rather than working on their own production. So the real wage rate tells people the terms on which they can substitute consumption for leisure. If someone works an extra hour, then he or she can use the additional w/P units of real income to expand consumption.

For an individual, the real wage rate appears where previously the schedule for labor's marginal product appeared. Specifically, an increase in the real wage rate motivates people to increase labor supply and consumption demand. But recall that the choice of labor demand by firms guarantees that the real wage rate equals the economy-wide marginal product of labor. Therefore, the effects from the real wage amount, ultimately, to corresponding effects from the schedule for labor's marginal product. The only difference is that the real wage rate and the marginal product of labor must be the same for everyone. In our earlier analysis these marginal products could be unequal, unless all people and production functions happened to be identical.

As before, wealth effects can arise from shifts in production functions. These effects show up first on firms' profits. But it is important to remember that the profits go to the households that own the firms. Therefore, the shifts in production functions ultimately have wealth effects on households, as in our earlier model that ignored firms.

One new consideration is the wealth effect from a change in the real wage rate, given the position of the production function. An increase in w/P benefits the households who sell labor services. But this benefit is matched by an extra cost for the firms, who buy labor services. Since the firms are owned by households, the overall wealth effect on households from a change in w/P is nil. (There would be distributional effects if households differ by their relative amounts of wage and profit income. But we follow our usual practice of neglecting distributional effects on the aggregates of labor supply and consumption demand.)

The interest rate, R, has the same intertemporal-substitution effects as before. An increase in R motivates households to save more by reducing current consumption demand and raising current labor supply. An additional intertemporal-substitution effect arises if people anticipate variations over time in the real wage rate. Suppose, for example, that workers regard the current real wage rate as high relative to future values. Then they increase current labor supply and plan to reduce labor supply in the future. Before, we found similar effects if people anticipated changes in the schedule for labor's marginal product.

We can summarize the results in this section by writing down functions for the aggregates of labor supply and consumption demand. These take the forms

$$N^s = N^s \left(\underset{(+)}{\frac{w}{P}}, \underset{(+)}{R}, \ldots \right) \tag{6.6}$$

and

$$C^d = C^d \left(\underset{(+)}{\frac{w}{P}}, \underset{(-)}{R}, \ldots \right) \tag{6.7}$$

The omitted terms, denoted by . . . , include characteristics of the production function, as well as any elements that generate departures of expected future real wage rates from the current value.

Clearing of the Labor Market

The labor market clears when the aggregate supply of labor, N^s, equals the aggregate demand, N^d. Therefore, using equations 6.4 and 6.6, the condition for clearing the labor market is

$$N^d \left(\underset{(-)}{\frac{w}{P}}, \ldots \right) = N^s \left(\underset{(+)}{\frac{w}{P}}, \underset{(+)}{R}, \ldots \right) \tag{6.8}$$

Recall that the terms denoted by . . . include characteristics of the production function.

As before, there are also conditions for clearing the commodity market and for ensuring that all money is willingly held. These conditions must hold along with equation 6.8 to ensure the clearing of all markets. When we take these conditions together we shall be able to determine the nominal wage rate, w, as well as the interest rate, R, and the price level, P. In other words, we add one new market-clearing condition, equation 6.8, and thereby determine one more "price"—namely, the price of labor services, w. For now, we focus on the new condition for clearing the labor market.

Figure 6.2 shows the clearing of the labor market. For convenience, we place the real wage rate, w/P, on the vertical axis, while we put labor demand and supply on the horizontal. Notice that the quantity of labor demanded by firms rises as w/P falls, assuming a given form for the production function. For the case of households' labor supply, we hold fixed the interest rate, R, and the forms of production functions. (We assume also that prospective values of real wage rates equal the current value.) Then an increase in w/P means a larger quantity of labor supplied.

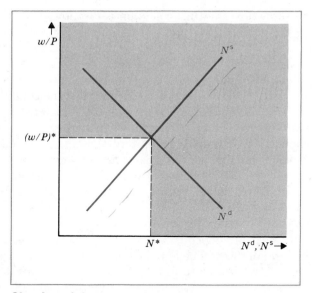

Figure 6.2 Clearing of the Labor Market
For a given value of the interest rate, R, and for a given form of the production function, the labor market clears when the real wage rate is $(w/P)^*$ and the quantity of work is N^*.

Notice from Figure 6.2 that the aggregates of labor demand and supply are equal when the real wage rate is $(w/P)^*$ and the level of work is N^*. We can think of this overall level of work effort as corresponding to aggregate **employment.**[1] Figure 6.2 allows us to relate the market-clearing values of the real wage rate and employment to variables that shift either the labor-demand curve or the labor-supply curve. These variables include the interest rate, R, the forms of production functions, and prospective changes in the real wage rate. For example, an increase in the interest rate shifts the labor-supply curve rightward in Figure 6.2. Hence, employment, N^*, rises, while the real wage rate, $(w/P)^*$, declines.

Clearing of the Commodity Market

Using equations 6.5 and 6.7, we can write the condition for clearing the commodity market as

$$C^d\left(\frac{w}{P}, R, \ldots\right) = Y^s\left(\frac{w}{P}, \ldots\right)$$
$$(+)(-) \qquad\qquad (-)$$

(6.9)

---

[1] Usually economists measure employment by the number of people working in the market, without taking account of hours on the job. Total hours worked by all persons would be a better counterpart of N.

We want to show now that this condition is essentially the same as the one for clearing the commodity market in Chapter 5. That is, we want to demonstrate that the introduction of the labor market and firms leaves intact our previous analysis of the commodity market.

We proceed by using our analysis of the labor market to substitute out for the real wage rate, w/P, in equation 6.9. Recall that the condition for clearing the labor market in equation 6.8 (and Figure 6.2) determines w/P. We can use this condition to see how w/P changes when there are shifts in labor demand or labor supply. For example, an upward shift in the schedule for labor's marginal product shifts the labor-demand curve rightward in Figure 6.2. Consequently, w/P increases. As another example, a rise in the interest rate, R, shifts the labor-supply curve rightward in Figure 6.2. Hence, w/P falls in this case.

By using the condition for clearing the labor market, we can figure out how the real wage rate depends on the various factors—such as the interest rate and the form of the production function—that affect labor supply or labor demand. Then if we use these results to substitute out for w/P in equation 6.9, we get the simplified condition for clearing the commodity market.

$$C^d(R, \ldots) = Y^s(R, \ldots) \qquad (6.10)$$
$$(-) \qquad\quad (+)$$

As usual, the expression . . . includes characteristics of the production function. Note that w/P does not appear in equation 6.10 because we have replaced it by the various elements—including R and the form of the production function—that determine the real wage rate. In particular, since Y^s depends on w/P in equation 6.9, and since w/P depends on R, Y^s depends indirectly on R. Therefore, when we solve out for w/P, Y^s depends directly on R in equation 6.10.

Let's examine in detail how the interest rate enters into the condition for clearing the commodity market in equation 6.10. Recall that an increase in R shifts the labor-supply curve rightward in Figure 6.2, which leads to a decline in w/P. This decline in w/P leads, as shown in equation 6.9, to an expansion of goods supply, Y^s. Therefore, the positive effect of R on Y^s in equation 6.10 picks up this channel of effects.

On the demand side, the change in the interest rate has two effects. First, from equation 6.9, an increase in R lowers consumer demand, C^d, for a given value of w/P. Second, because an increase in R leads to a lower value of w/P, there is a further decline in consumer demand. Therefore, the negative effect of R on C^d in equation 6.10 picks up both channels of effect.

We can proceed in a similar way to analyze changes in other variables, including the form of the production function. Equation 6.10 combines the direct effects of these changes with those that arise from movements in the real wage rate.

The important point is that equation 6.10 looks just like the condition for clearing the commodity market that we used in Chapter 5. The only difference

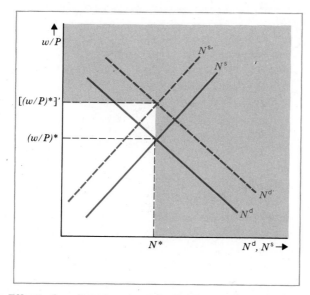

Figure 6.3 **Effect of an Improvement in the Production Function on the Labor Market**
The permanent upward shift of the production function raises the demand for labor,
but lowers the supply. Therefore, the real wage rate increases, but the change in work
is uncertain.

is that the labor market ensures that everybody's marginal product of labor,
which equals the real wage rate, is the same. (Recall that we assume that
everyone's labor services are physically identical.[2]) Since the condition for
clearing the commodity market looks as it did before, we can still use our
previous analysis to determine the interest rate and the quantities of output
and work effort for each period. To see how this works, let's reconsider the
example of a shift in the production function.

An Improvement in the Production Function

Assume a permanent proportional upward shift of the production function.
This change means that the level of aggregate output and the marginal product
of labor increase for any given amount of aggregate work effort.

Figure 6.3 shows the effects on the labor market. Since the disturbance
raises wealth, the supply of labor declines for a given value of w/P. (Recall
that we hold constant the interest rate, R, when drawing the labor supply
curve.) Because of the upward shift to the schedule for labor's marginal prod-

---

[2]We could expand our analysis to deal with different levels of skills and different characteristics
of jobs. Then we would find that real wage rates are higher first, for people who are more
productive, and second, on jobs that are less pleasant. But these considerations would not change
the major macroeconomic results.

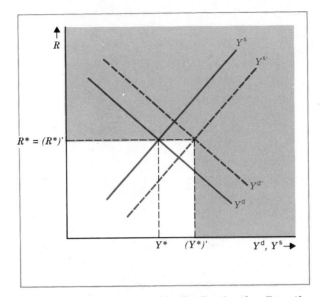

Figure 6.4 **Effect of an Improvement in the Production Function on the Commodity Market**
The permanent upward shift of the production function raises the demand and supply
of commodities by roughly equal amounts. Hence, output increases, but the interest
rate does not change.

uct, the demand for labor rises for a given value of w/P. Hence, Figure 6.3
shows that the real wage rate increases, but the change in the quantity of work
in uncertain. As in some previous cases, the wealth effect suggests less work,
but the improvement in productivity suggests more work.

Figure 6.4 shows the effect on the commodity market. We use the market-
clearing condition from equation 6.10, which takes account of the determination of the real wage rate from the labor market. Notice first the rightward
shift in consumer demand. This shift reflects partly the wealth effect from the
improvement in the production function and partly the substitution effect
(toward consumption and away from leisure) from the rise in the real wage
rate.

The supply of goods rises with the improvement in the production function,
but falls because of the increase in the real wage rate. However, recall that
the shift in the production function and the resulting change in w/P are permanent in this example. Therefore, the aggregate of desired saving would
change little, if at all, at the initial interest rate. This means that goods supply,
Y^s, shifts rightward on net by roughly the same amount as C^d. We conclude
from Figure 6.4 that output increases, but the interest rate does not change.[3]

[3]Since the interest rate does not change, we do not have to modify the analysis of the labor
market in Figure 6.3. Recall that this diagram applies for a given value of R.

An important observation is that the basic results coincide with those that we reached earlier, when people worked only on their own production processes. A permanent improvement in production opportunities raises aggregate output, but has an ambiguous effect on work effort. Further, because the shift in the production function is permanent, there is no change in the interest rate.

The introduction of the labor market does deliver an important result about the behavior of the real wage rate. Suppose that economic development involves a series of permanent improvements to the production function of the sort that we considered in Figures 6.3 and 6.4. Then the analysis shows that economic development leads to continuing increases in the real wage rate. This proposition accords with data for a large number of countries. For example, in the United States, the average hourly real wage rate rose at an average rate of 1.1% per year from 1948 to 1985.[4]

Nominal Wage Rates

To determine nominal wage rates and other nominal variables, we again consider the condition for money to be willingly held. This condition looks as in Chapter 5,

$$M = P \cdot L(\underset{(-)}{R}, \underset{(+)}{Y}, \ldots) \tag{6.11}$$

The aggregate real demand for money, $L(\cdot)$, now includes money held by firms as well as households. However, the form of this function would not differ greatly from that in our earlier analysis. In particular, the amount of real money demanded still falls with an increase in the interest rate, R, and rises with an increase in real transactions as measured by real output, Y.

The full market-clearing model now consists of equation 6.11 plus the conditions derived earlier for clearing the labor and commodity markets.

$$N^d\left(\underset{(-)}{\frac{w}{P}}, \ldots\right) = N^s\left(\underset{(+)}{\frac{w}{P}}, \underset{(+)}{R}, \ldots\right) \tag{6.12}$$

and

$$C^d\left(\underset{(+)}{\frac{w}{P}}, \underset{(-)}{R}, \ldots\right) = Y^s\left(\underset{(-)}{\frac{w}{P}}, \ldots\right) \tag{6.13}$$

---

[4]The wage rate refers to average hourly earnings (adjusted for overtime and interindustry shifts) in the total private nonagricultural economy. The real wage rate is the ratio of the nominal wage to the GNP deflator. For the data, see *Economic Report of the President*, 1986, Tables B-41 and B-3.

We have already seen that equations 6.12 and 6.13 determine the real wage rate, w/P, the interest rate, R, and the levels of output, Y, and employment, N.

We showed in Chapter 5 that an increase in the quantity of money, M, was neutral. Namely, the price level, P, rose in the same proportion, but all real variables were unchanged. These real variables included output, Y, work effort, N, the interest rate, R, and real cash balances, M/P. This property of monetary neutrality still holds in the model that includes a labor market. However, we have to add the real wage rate, w/P, to the list of real variables that do not change. Then we have to include the nominal wage rate, w, along with the nominal variables that rise in the same proportion as the quantity of money.

To verify these results, remember that equations 6.12 and 6.13 determine R and Y. These variables then determine the real demand for money, $L(\cdot)$. Given this real demand, equation (6.11) implies that an increase in M raises P in the same proportion. Thereby real cash balances, M/P, do not change when there is a once-and-for-all shift in the nominal quantity of money.

Recall that equations (6.12) and (6.13) determine w/P and N. In fact, the real wage rate equals the marginal product of labor at this value of N. We can find the nominal wage rate, w, by multiplying the real wage rate, w/P, by the price level, P, which we have also determined. Notice that an increase in M raises P in the same proportion but does not change w/P. Therefore, an increase in M must raise the nominal wage rate w (as well as P) in the same proportion.

The Labor Market in the Macroeconomic Model

Let's consider how the introduction of the labor market and firms affects our analysis. We have shown that these new features do not change the way that shifts to the production function affect the interest rate and the aggregate quantities of output and work effort. We also found that the extensions did not change the interaction between money and prices. In other words, our earlier simplification—which neglected the labor market and the existence of firms—allows us to get reasonable answers to many important questions. Therefore, for most of our subsequent analysis, we find it satisfactory to return to the simpler framework, which does not deal explicitly with the labor market or firms. The main place where we reintroduce firms and the labor market is in Chapter 10, where we study unemployment.

Summary

We introduced a labor market in which firms demand labor and households supply labor at a going wage rate. This market clears when the aggregate demand for labor equals the aggregate supply. One important aspect of a cleared labor market is that it equates each worker's marginal product to the real wage rate. Thereby, this market exhausts all the gains in output that can result by shifting workers from one production activity to another.

The requirements for general market clearing are that the labor market clear along with the markets for commodities and credit. In comparison with our previous analysis, we have added one new condition—that the labor market clear—and one new "price," which is the wage rate for labor services.

The conditions for determining the aggregate quantities of output and work, as well as the interest rate and the price level, turn out to be similar to those from before. Therefore, for many purposes, we can carry out the analysis by pretending, as before, that households work only on their own production processes. However, we have to consider firms and a labor market later on when we study unemployment. In addition, the inclusion of the labor market enables us to determine the wage rate. The theory predicts that the real wage rate will increase as an economy develops, which accords with empirical evidence.

Important Terms and Concepts

real wage rate	profit
firm	employment

QUESTIONS AND PROBLEMS

Mainly for Review

6.1 How does an increase in the real wage rate affect the demand for labor? Where does the assumption of diminishing marginal productivity of labor come in?

6.2 Consider two individuals, A and B; they have the same production function, but A has a greater willingness to work. If each individual is isolated on an island, who will work more? Who will have the higher marginal product? Show how total output can increase, with no increase in total labor, by exchanging labor services for goods between the two islands—that is, by opening up a labor market.

6.3 Suppose that the interest rate increases. How does this change affect the supply of labor and hence the real wage rate?

6.4 Explain why economic development tends to raise the real wage rate. causes ↑Y

6.5 Suppose that the quantity of money, M, increases.

   a. The increase in the nominal wage rate suggests that workers would be better off. Why is this not so?

b. The increase in the price level suggests that workers would be worse off. Is this correct?

Problems for Discussion

6.6 The Labor Market and Efficiency

In the text we considered two isolated regions, A and B. The technology in A was inferior to that in B. Therefore, we found that the opening up of an economy-wide labor market led to higher aggregate output without requiring an increase in aggregate work effort. In this sense the new market improved the economy's efficiency.

a. Does the result mean that everyone is better off? In answering, consider the position of workers and firms (and the owners of firms) in both regions.

b. Does your answer suggest that some groups might oppose moves to free up markets, even when there would be gains in the aggregate? Can you think of any real-world examples of this behavior?

6.7 Walras' Law

a. When we introduce the labor market what new aggregate-consistency condition arises?

b. Use the aggregate form of households' budget constraints to derive Walras' Law of Markets. How does the Law differ from that in Chapter 5?

6.8 Wealth Effects from Changes in the Real Wage Rate

Suppose that the real wage rate, w/P, increases.

a. Why are there offsetting effects on wealth? What would you predict for the wealth effect on aggregate consumption demand and labor supply?

b. Suppose that most suppliers of labor own relatively little of the ownership rights in firms. Then what would you predict for the wealth effect on aggregate labor supply?

6.9 Temporary Shifts of the Production Function

Consider a temporary, parallel downward shift of the production function.

a. What are the effects on the interest rate, the real wage rate, and the quantities of output and employment?

b. Do the results differ from those in Chapter 5, where people worked only on their own production processes?

c. How do the answers change if the shift of the production function is proportional, rather than parallel?

6.10 Short-Run Movements of the Real Wage Rate (optional)

Consider again a temporary, parallel downward shift of the production function.

a. Using the results from problem 6.9, what is the pattern of association between changes in the real wage rate and changes in the quantities of employment and output?

b. Assume, more realistically, that the schedule for labor's marginal product shifts downward. In particular, assume that this shift is large enough so that work effort declines. In this case what is the pattern of association between changes in the real wage rate and changes in the quantities of employment and output?

c. Suppose that business fluctuations result from temporary shifts of the production function. Then what do you predict for the "cyclical" behavior of real wage rates? That is, do they move together with or inversely to output and employment? (There is much empirical debate about the cyclical behavior of real wage rates. However, most researchers find a weak "procyclical" pattern, which means that real wage rates tend to be high when output and employment are high.)

6.11 The Short-Run Behavior of Productivity (optional)

Suppose that we use the popular definition of labor productivity as the ratio of output to employment, Y/N.

a. How does this measure of productivity relate to the marginal product of labor?

b. Assume, as in problem 6.10, that business fluctuations result from shifts of the production function. Then how would productivity behave? In particular, is productivity high or low when output is high?

PART II
INFLATION

Thus far, we have simplified the analysis by holding fixed the general price level. Although this assumption was convenient, it conflicts dramatically with real-world experience, especially in recent years. These days, prices tend to rise over time—that is, there tends to be inflation. Therefore, it is important to modify the model to allow for the effects of changing price levels.

Chapter 7 begins by noting the empirical association between inflation and monetary growth. Then we discuss the important distinctions between expected and unexpected inflation, and between nominal and real interest rates.

Chapter 8 incorporates the new tools into the market-clearing model. With these extensions we can study the effects of monetary growth on inflation, interest rates, and other variables. One important finding is that fluctuations in monetary growth can be the principal source of variations in inflation. Nevertheless, these movements in monetary growth and inflation may have little to do with the behavior of real variables. That is, money can still be approximately neutral in the model.

CHAPTER 7

INFLATION AND INTEREST RATES

In this chapter we begin the study of **inflation**. By inflation, we mean a continuing upward movement in the general price level. The theoretical analysis suggests some possible sources of inflation. To sort out the possibilities we shall find it convenient to think about the condition that all money be willingly held

$$M = P \cdot L(R, Y, \ldots) \qquad (7.1)$$
$$(-)(+)$$

One way for the price level to increase is through a downward movement in the real demand for money. For example, there can be a permanent downward shift in the production function, which lowers aggregate output, Y. But notice that a single disturbance of this type creates a single increase in the price level, rather than a continuing series of increases in prices. To generate inflation along this line, we would need a succession of downward shifts to the production function. There is no doubt that adverse shocks to the production function—such as oil crises, harvest failures, and strikes—can influence the general level of prices over short periods. But there is no evidence that these forces can account for inflation in the sense of persistent rises in prices. In fact, the typical pattern in most countries is one of growing output. Since this growth raises the real demand for money, we predict that prices would fall over time if the nominal stock of money, M, did not change.

There can also be reductions in the real demand for money that reflect increasing financial sophistication. For example, in recent years many countries have developed financial instruments and procedures that make it easier for people to economize on cash. In the United States in the post-World War II period, this factor has led to a downward trend in the real demand for money. However, this element can account only for a small amount of inflation—something like 1 to 2% per year is a reasonable estimate. Therefore, we cannot use this idea to explain the persistently high rates of inflation that have occurred since the late 1960s.

The remaining suggestion from the previous analysis is a link between inflation and increases in the quantity of paper money, M. At an empirical level it is clear first, that the quantity of money often grows at a high rate over long periods of time, and second, that **rates of monetary growth** differ substantially across countries and over time for a single country. Therefore, monetary growth is a good candidate as a source of inflation.

Cross-Country Data on Inflation and Monetary Growth

To assess the role of money as a determinant of inflation, let's examine some data. Table 7.1 shows the experiences of 83 countries during the post-World War II period. The table reports the average growth rates of an index of consumer prices and of money, which we define as hand-to-hand currency. (The results are similar if we use the broader monetary aggregate, $M1$, which includes checkable deposits. However, because of differences in the nature of financial institutions, the meaning of $M1$ varies more across countries than does that of currency.) The table arranges the countries in descending order with respect to their average rates of inflation. Note the following:

- The average growth rates of prices and money are positive for all countries since World War II.
- The average growth rates are typically high. For example, the median inflation rate for the 83 countries is 7.1% per year, with 19 of them exceeding 10%. For the average growth rate of currency, the median is 11.6% per year, with 53 of the countries above 10%.
- There is a broad cross-sectional range for the average growth rates of prices and money. The average inflation rates vary from 81% for Argentina, 72% for Chile, and 43% for Uruguay, to about 3% for Switzerland and West Germany. The rate for the United States is 4.3%. Notice that the growth rates of currency have a comparable range, varying from 79% for Argentina, 77% for Chile, and 43% for Uruguay, to about 5% for Belgium, Switzerland, and the United States.
- The average growth rate of currency exceeds that of prices in almost all cases. That is, growing real cash balances is typical in the post-World War II period. The median growth rate of real currency across the countries is 3.6% per year.
- Most significantly, there is a strong positive association across countries between the average rates of price change and the average rates of monetary growth.

Figure 7.1 brings out the nature of the association between inflation and monetary growth. The graph shows the positive correlation between inflation and the growth rate of currency. Further, each increase by 1 percentage point per year in the rate of monetary growth is associated with an increase by

Table 7.1 Annual Growth Rates of Prices, Money, and Output for 83 Countries in the Post-World War II Period (Arranged by Decreasing Order of the Inflation Rate)

Country	ΔP	ΔM	$\Delta M - \Delta P$	ΔY	Time Span
Argentina	80.6	79.3	−1.3	1.2	1969–1983
Chile	71.7	77.3	5.6	1.3	1970–1982
Uruguay	42.6	42.7	0.1	2.3	1960–1980
Brazil	37.9	38.6	0.7	6.6	1963–1983
Zaire	28.2	26.8	−1.4	2.5	1963–1982
Bolivia	25.0	29.6	4.6	3.1	1950–1982
Israel	23.5	23.2	−0.3	7.3	1950–1983
Peru	20.8	24.0	3.2	4.2	1960–1982
Ghana	18.4	15.7	−2.7	2.1	1950–1983
Iceland	18.3	18.0	−2.3	4.3[a]	1950–1983
Turkey	16.0	19.9	3.9	4.9[a]	1953–1982
Yugoslavia	15.8	21.1	5.3	5.6	1960–1982
Korea (S.)	14.8	24.2	9.4	7.2	1953–1983
Colombia	13.0	17.8	4.8	4.7	1950–1983
Sierra Leone	12.1	13.6	1.5	3.8	1963–1983
Mexico	11.9	16.5	4.6	5.9	1950–1983
Paraguay	10.9	15.2	4.3	5.3	1952–1982
Somalia	10.9	15.5	4.6	—	1960–1982
Jamaica	10.1	13.9	3.8	1.9	1960–1982
Spain	9.6	12.8	3.2	4.6	1954–1983
Mauritius	9.3	11.9	2.6	3.6[b]	1963–1981
Portugal	9.1	11.0	1.9	5.1	1953–1982
Madagascar	8.8	9.5	0.7	1.1	1964–1983
Central African Republic	8.4	13.8	5.4	—	1963–1983
Saudi Arabia	8.2	21.4	13.2	7.9	1968–1983
Gabon	8.1	11.9	3.8	8.8[b]	1962–1982
Greece	8.1	15.4	7.3	5.3	1953–1982
Nigeria	8.0	14.1	6.1	4.0	1955–1982
Trinidad and Tobago	8.0	14.0	6.0	3.9	1960–1983
Niger	7.9	11.5	3.6	—	1960–1983
Senegal	7.8	14.1	6.3	2.1	1967–1981
Ivory Coast	7.8	12.2	4.4	5.4[b]	1962–1983
Cameroon	7.7	12.1	4.4	14.4[b]	1963–1983
Ireland	7.7	8.2	0.5	3.4	1950–1983
Nepal	7.6	13.4	5.8	2.4	1964–1983
Iran	7.6	20.3	12.7	5.6	1959–1981
Italy	7.4	10.7	3.3	4.4	1950–1983
Ecuador	7.4	12.5	5.1	5.6	1951–1983
Togo	7.3	14.9	7.6	3.3[b]	1963–1983
New Zealand	7.2	5.8	−1.4	3.1	1954–1982
Guyana	7.2	10.6	3.4	1.8	1960–1982
India	7.1	9.5	2.4	3.5	1960–1982
Pakistan	7.0	9.8	2.8	4.2	1955–1983
Finland	7.0	8.8	1.8	4.3	1950–1983
Sudan	6.9	9.7	2.8	3.5[b]	1951–1979

Country	ΔP	ΔM	$\Delta M - \Delta P$	ΔY	Time Span
Gambia	6.9	11.3	4.4	5.1[b]	1964–1982
Congo	6.8	11.5	4.7	—	1960–1983
United Kingdom	6.7	6.7	0.0	2.3	1951–1983
France	6.6	7.5	0.9	4.3	1950–1983
Philippines	6.6	10.2	3.6	5.5	1950–1983
Denmark	6.4	6.7	0.3	3.2	1950–1983
Australia	6.3	8.0	1.7	3.9	1950–1983
Costa Rica	6.3	12.2	5.9	5.7	1960–1980
Norway	6.1	6.8	0.7	4.1	1950–1983
Sweden	6.1	7.5	1.4	3.0	1950–1983
South Africa	6.1	9.0	2.9	4.1	1950–1983
Egypt	6.0	12.7	6.7	4.9	1955–1983
Upper Volta	5.9	11.1	5.2	4.0[b]	1962–1983
Syria	5.9	14.5	8.6	6.1	1957–1982
Chad	5.8	7.2	1.4	—	1960–1977
Japan	5.5	11.8	6.3	7.3[a]	1953–1983
Libya	5.4	25.0	19.6	14.2[b]	1964–1979
Morocco	5.4	11.3	5.9	3.7	1958–1983
Thailand	5.3	8.7	3.4	6.5	1955–1983
Haiti	5.2	8.1	2.9	2.1	1953–1983
Tunisia	5.0	11.6	6.6	6.5	1960–1983
Austria	4.9	7.9	3.0	4.1	1950–1983
Netherlands	4.8	6.6	1.8	4.0	1950–1983
Sri Lanka	4.8	9.4	4.6	4.6	1950–1983
Iraq	4.7	14.1	9.7	6.6	1965–1975
Belgium	4.7	4.6	−0.1	3.4	1955–1983
Canada	4.7	7.1	2.4	4.2	1950–1983
El Salvador	4.7	7.2	2.5	3.3	1951–1982
Cyprus	4.4	10.5	6.1	4.2	1958–1983
Dominican Republic	4.3	9.1	4.8	5.4	1950–1982
United States	4.3	5.3	1.0	3.2	1950–1983
Malta	4.3	11.1	6.8	6.7	1960–1983
Honduras	4.3	8.6	4.3	3.8	1950–1982
Singapore	4.2	11.9	7.7	8.7	1963–1983
Venezuela	4.1	8.7	4.6	5.2	1950–1982
Guatemala	3.7	7.3	3.6	4.5[a]	1950–1982
West Germany	3.4	7.0	3.6	4.3	1953–1983
Switzerland	3.3	5.0	1.7	3.1	1950–1983

Note: All growth rates are annual averages for the sample periods shown in the right column. ΔP is the growth rate of consumer prices. ΔM is the growth rate of the stock of currency. ΔY is the growth rate of real gross domestic product. All data are from issues of *International Financial Statistics*.

[a]Real gross national product was used instead of real gross domestic product.

[b]Data on real domestic product were unavailable for these countries. ΔY was calculated by subtracting the average growth rate of consumer prices, ΔP, from the average growth rate of nominal gross domestic product.

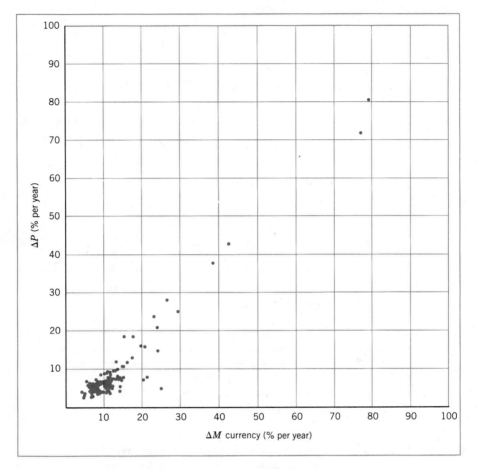

Graph of the Inflation Rate versus the Growth Rate of Currency for 83 Countries
We show here the positive relation between inflation and the growth rate of currency.

roughly 1 percentage point per year in the rate of inflation. However, the relation is closer for the more extreme cases than for the moderate ones. For example, the association is less dramatic if we look only at countries where the average rate of monetary growth is between 5 and 15% per year.

If the growth rate of money exceeds the growth rate of prices, then real cash balances, M/P, increase over time. Since money is willingly held at each date, the growth rate of real balances must equal the growth rate of real money demanded. Recall that our previous analysis of the demand for money suggests several factors that could lead to increases over time in the quantity of real money demanded. The most important is the growth rate of output. Table 7.1 shows the average growth rate of output for 78 countries (those for which data are available), while Figure 7.2 graphs these growth rates along with the

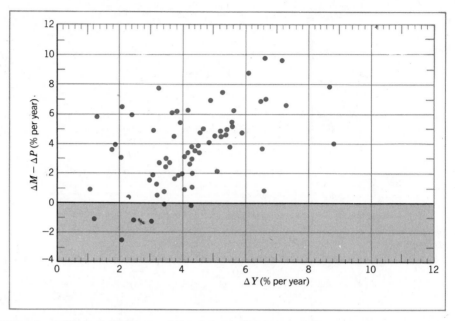

Figure 7.2 Graph of the Growth Rate of Real Cash Balances versus the Growth Rate of Output for 74 Countries
We show here the positive relation between the growth rate of real currency and the growth rate of output. To provide a clearer picture, we omit four outlying countries: Zaire, Nigeria, Saudi Arabia, and Libya. The inclusion of these countries would not change the basic relationship.

average growth rate of real cash balances. Notice the positive association between the growth rate of output and the growth rate of real balances. Also, observe from the table that the median growth rate of output, which is 4.2% per year, accords with the median growth rate of real cash balances, which is 3.6% per year. These findings imply that a country with a higher growth rate of output tends to have a lower rate of inflation for a given rate of monetary growth. Therefore, differences in the growth rates of output explain some of the imperfect association between monetary growth and inflation, which shows up in Figure 7.1.

Another variable that influences the demand for money is the interest rate, R, which determines the cost of holding money. Other things equal, we predict that the average growth rate of real cash balances will be lower for countries in which the interest rate has increased, and vice versa. Notice that the change in the interest rate matters here, rather than the average level of the interest rate. Although researchers have verified this proposition for industrialized countries, we cannot demonstrate it for the substantial number of countries that lack organized securities markets on which interest rates are quoted. However, we shall see in this and the next chapter that interest rates and inflation rates are closely related. In particular, increases in the rate of inflation also mean greater costs of holding money—that is, a higher rate of inflation means that money depreciates in real terms at a faster rate. It follows that an increase in the rate of inflation tends to reduce the real demand for money. Therefore, we predict that the average growth rate of real cash balances will be lower for countries in which the inflation rate has increased. (Notice again that what matters here is the change in the inflation rate, rather than the average level of the rate.) As examples, the sharp rises in inflation rates explain the negative growth rates of real cash balances that show up in Table 7.1 for Argentina, Zaire, and Israel.

Overall, the cross-country data suggest a significant, positive association between monetary growth and inflation. Furthermore, this relation is closer than it first appears if we consider additional variables, such as the growth rate of output and changes in interest rates and inflation rates, which affect the real demand for money.

U.S. Time Series Data on Inflation and Monetary Growth

Table 7.2 reports data for the United States on average rates of inflation and monetary growth over 20-year periods from 1860 to 1980. Over the entire 120-year span, the average inflation rate was 2.1% per year, while the average

Table 7.2 U.S. Time Series Data on Inflation and Monetary Growth: Averages for 20-Year Periods (All Figures are Average Growth Rates in % per Year)

	ΔP	ΔM (Currency)	$\Delta M - \Delta P$	ΔY
1860–1880	1.1	3.4	2.3	4.3
1880–1900	−0.6	3.2	3.8	3.0
1900–1920	4.6	6.5	1.9	2.8
1920–1940	−1.6	2.4	4.0	2.4
1940–1960	4.3	6.8	2.5	3.8
1960–1980	2.1	6.9	2.1	3.5
1860–1980	2.1	4.9	2.8	3.3

Note: All growth rates are annual averages for the period shown in the first column. ΔP is the growth rate of the deflator for the gross national product. ΔM is the growth rate of currency. ΔY is the growth rate of real gross national product. All data before 1890 are rough estimates.

Sources: For the price level and real GNP, see Figures 1.1 and 1.4 of Chapter 1. For money, see Milton Friedman and Anna Schwartz, *Monetary Statistics of the United States,* Columbia University Press, New York, 1970, Tables 1 and 13, and *Federal Reserve Bulletin,* various issues.

growth rate of currency was 4.8% per year. Correspondingly, the average growth rate of real cash balances was 2.7% per year. Notice that this figure accords with the average growth rate of output, which was 3.3% per year. (Again, the results are similar if we look at the broader monetary aggregate, $M1$, rather than currency.)

Although the time series data for the United States do not provide the range of experience that appears in the cross-country sample, there are substantial differences in the various 20-year periods. For example, the average inflation rate was negative over two intervals: -1.6% for 1920–40 (which includes the Great Depression) and -0.6% for 1880–1900. But the rate exceeded 4% in three of the cases: 4.8% for 1960–80, 4.6% for 1900–20, and 4.3% for 1940–60. Note that the world wars strongly influence the observations for the last two subperiods. For currency, the range of growth rates was from 2.4% for 1920–40 to 6.9% for 1960–80.

There is a positive, though imperfect, association between monetary growth and inflation over the different 20-year periods. As in our previous analysis, we can explain some of the divergences between monetary growth and inflation by considering variables that alter the demand for money. These include the growth rate of output, changes in interest rates, and the development of financial institutions.

Inflation as a Monetary Phenomenon

Casual observation of two types of data—across countries and over time for the United States—suggests that we should consider seriously Milton Friedman's famous statement, "Inflation is always and everywhere a monetary phenomenon."[1] However, we should remember some important points. First, the analysis will not rule our effects of real disturbances, such as supply shocks, on the price level. But we expect that these effects will be more important for isolated episodes of price changes than for chronic inflation. Second, we should view the expression, *monetary phenomenon,* as incorporating variables that influence the real demand for money, as well as the nominal supply of money. Third, we would eventually like to know why monetary growth behaves differently in different countries and at different times. This question would require us to explore a number of new subjects, including governmental incentives to print more or less money. We sidestep the theory of money supply in this and the next chapter. Here, we look at the consequences for inflation and other variables of a given—unexplained—time path of money. This type of analysis is crucial for an understanding of inflation, although it does not constitute a full study of the topic.

---

[1]Milton Friedman, "Inflation: Causes and Consequences," in *Dollars and Deficits*, Prentice-Hall, Englewood Cliffs, New Jersey, 1968, p. 29.

Actual and Expected Inflation

Here we begin the process of incorporating inflation into the theoretical model. The inflation rate between periods t and $t + 1$ is

$$\pi_t = \left(\frac{P_{t+1} - P_t}{P_t}\right) \tag{7.2}$$

where π is the Greek letter *pi*. Notice that the inflation rate equals the rate of change of the price level between periods t and $t + 1$. By rearranging equation 7.2, we can solve out for the next period's price level as

$$P_{t+1} = (1 + \pi_t)P_t \tag{7.3}$$

Hence, prices rise over one period by the factor, $1 + \pi_t$. Although we focus on rising prices—that is, positive rates of inflation—we can also consider declining prices. These cases are called **deflations.**

In making various decisions, such as the choice between consuming now or later, people want to know how prices will change over time. Therefore, people form forecasts or **expectations of inflation.** We use the symbol π_t^e to denote an expectation for the inflation rate, π_t. Usually, we think of someone as forming this expectation during period t. Since people already know the current price level, P_t, the expectation of inflation, π_t^e, corresponds to a forecast of the next period's price level, P_{t+1}.

In general, forecasts of inflation are imperfect. That is, the actual rate of inflation is typically higher or lower than the representative person's expectation. Hence, the forecast error—or **unexpected inflation**—is usually nonzero. However, people have incentives to form their expectations *rationally*—making efficient use of the available information on past inflation and other variables— to avoid systematic mistakes. Therefore, we should not find that unexpected inflation is either typically positive or typically negative. Further, there ought not to be a systematic pattern of errors over time. For example, if unexpected inflation is positive this period, then it may be either positive or negative in the next period.

Real and Nominal Interest Rates

As before, let R_t be the interest rate on bonds. Then if a person buys $1 worth of bonds during period t, he or she gets $(1 + R_t)$ as receipts of principal plus interest during period $t + 1$. This means that the dollar value of assets held as bonds rises over one period by the factor $(1 + R_t)$. Accordingly, we can think of the rate R_t as the dollar or **nominal interest rate.**

What happens over time to the real value of assets that people hold as bonds? If the price level is constant, as in previous chapters, then the real value of these assets also grows at the rate R_t. Thus, in a world of constant prices, the nominal interest rate, R_t, is also the **real interest rate,** which determines the growth over time in the real value of assets.

But what happens if the inflation rate is positive? Then goods next period cost more than those this period. If the inflation rate is π_t, then equation 7.3 says that the price level rises over one period by the factor, $(1+\pi_t)$. Hence, if the dollar value of assets rises over one period by the factor, $(1+R_t)$, then the real value rises by the proportion, $(1+R_t)/(1+\pi_t)$. Here, we consider that the dollars available next period—which grow by the factor, $(1+R_t)$—face a price level that is higher by the factor, $(1+\pi_t)$.

If people hold assets in the form of bonds, then the real value of these assets rises over one period by the factor, $(1+R_t)/(1+\pi_t)$. Let's define the real interest rate, r_t, to be the rate at which assets held as bonds grow in real terms. Then the real interest rate satisfies the condition

$$(1+r_t) = \left(\frac{1+R_t}{1+\pi_t}\right) \tag{7.4}$$

The important point is that the real interest rate, rather than the nominal rate, tells people the amount of extra consumption that they can get in period $t + 1$ if they forego a unit of consumption in period t. For example, if someone lowers c_t by one unit, then he or she saves P_t extra dollars (in the form of bonds), and thereby has an additional $P_t(1+R_t)$ dollars to spend in period $t + 1$. This amount buys $P_t(1+R_t)/P_{t+1}$ units of additional consumption in period $t + 1$. Finally, this term equals $(1+R_t)/(1+\pi_t)$, which equals $1+r_t$ from equation 7.4.

These results mean that, in deciding how much to consume (or work) in one period versus another—that is, in deciding how much to save—people will look at the real interest rate, rather than the nominal rate. For this reason we want to explore further the meaning and measurement of the real interest rate.

We can obtain a more useful expression for the real interest rate, r_t, if we manipulate equation 7.4. Multiply through on both sides by the term, $(1+\pi_t)$, and then simplify the result to get the condition

$$r_t + \pi_t + r_t\pi_t = R_t \tag{7.5}$$

Recall that we measure each variable—R_t, π_t, and r_t—as a growth rate per "period." For example, suppose that a period is a month. Then think of nominal interest rates and inflation rates that are no larger than, say, 10 to 20% per year. In this case, the various rates per month—R_t, π_t and r_t—will be no greater than 1 to 2%. It follows that the interaction term, $r_t\pi_t$, will be very small in equation 7.5. In particular, it will be smaller than the amount, $0.02 \cdot 0.02 = 0.0004$. Therefore, we can neglect this term and satisfactorily approximate the real interest rate as

$$r_t \approx R_t - \pi_t \qquad (7.6)$$

where the symbol, $\approx$, means approximately equal to.[2]

Recall that the nominal interest rate, R_t, tells people how the dollar value of assets held as bonds grows over time. By contrast, the real interest rate, r_t, determines how fast these assets grow in real terms. Equation 7.6 says that the real interest rate, r_t, equals the nominal rate, R_t, less the rate of inflation, π_t. Thus, the real rate is lower than the nominal rate if the inflation rate is positive. Further, the real rate is positive only if the nominal rate exceeds the inflation rate. Otherwise—that is, when the nominal rate is less than the inflation rate—the real interest rate is negative. In this case the rise in dollar value at the rate R_t does not cover the rise in prices at the rate π_t.

Actual and Expected Real Interest Rates

Usually, we think of situations where people observe the nominal interest rate on bonds, R_t. Then, to calculate the **expected real interest rate** between periods t and $t + 1$, people have to subtract from the nominal interest rate their expectation of inflation, π_t^e. The expected real interest rate, which we denote by r_t^e, is

$$r_t^e \approx R_t - \pi_t^e \qquad (7.7)$$

Recall that the actual inflation rate, π_t, can be above or below its expectation, π_t^e. If inflation turns out to be surprisingly high—that is, $\pi_t > \pi_t^e$—we find that the real interest rate r_t is less than its expectation, r_t^e. In other words if we combine equations 7.6 and 7.7, then the unexpected part of the real interest rate, $r_t - r_t^e$, is

$$r_t - r_t^e \approx -(\pi_t - \pi_t^e) \qquad (7.8)$$

Errors in forecasts of inflation, $\pi_t - \pi_t^e$, generate errors of the opposite sign in forecasts of the real interest rate.

It is possible to have different institutional arrangements where borrowers and lenders specify in advance the real interest rate, r_t, rather than the nominal rate, R_t. In this case the nominal payments for principal and interest adjust to compensate for inflation. These adjustments would ensure that the actual real interest rate equaled the prespecified value. Therefore, people would

---

[2]The approximation becomes better the shorter the length of the period. In fact, the length of the period plays no economic role in the model. Rather, we carry out the analysis in terms of periods—which economists call "discrete time"—solely for covenience. Therefore, we can reasonably assume that a period is extremely brief. Then equation 7.6 is a very accurate approximation.

know the real interest rate in advance, but would be uncertain about the nominal interest rate.

The financial arrangements where people contract in advance for real interest rates are called **indexation** or **inflation correction.** These systems tend to exist in countries, such as Brazil and Israel, in which extreme inflation is chronic. Recently, the British government issued a long-term indexed bond of this type, which we discuss below. But the U.S. government has thus far resisted suggestions to issue this kind of security. Economists do not know why private parties and governments typically prefer to borrow and lend at prespecified nominal interest rates, rather than real rates.[3]

Nominal and Real Interest Rates in the Post-World War II United States

Table 7.3 shows the relation between nominal and real interest rates for the United States over the post-World War II period. The nominal rate, R_t, is the average for each year on 3-month maturity treasury bills (short-term U.S. government securities). The inflation rate for each year, π_t, is the rate of change of the general price level, as measured by the consumer price index (CPI). The real interest rate for each year comes from the formula, $r_t = R_t - \pi_t$.

The actual rate of inflation, π_t, may diverge substantially from the rate that people expected, π_t^e. In that case the real interest rate, r_t, differs from the expected rate, r_t^e. Since the expected real interest rate will be important for our subsequent analysis, we should make some effort to measure expected inflation.

Measures of Expected Inflation

Economists have employed at least three methods to measure expectations of a variable like inflation or the real interest rate.

- First, ask a sample of people about their beliefs.
- Second, use the hypothesis of **rational expectations,** which says that peo-

[3]There have been some suggestions: (1) People use and hold money—an asset that is denominated in nominal units—which makes it desirable to borrow and lend in the same units. (2) The government enforces contracts in nominal units more diligently than contracts in other units. (3) The tax treatment of indexed bonds is unclear. And (4) it is hard to agree on a price index to use in making inflation corrections. In his article, "The Ban on Indexed Bonds, 1933–77," *American Economic Review,* December 1980, Huston McCulloch came up with another reason; namely U.S. courts were unwilling to enforce indexing provisions on bonds after 1933. In that year Congress resolved not to honor the "gold clauses" that appeared in some previously issued bonds. These clauses—which were a form of indexing—committed borrowers to repay in a stated amount of gold, rather than U.S. dollars. When the Congress voided these gold clauses, the courts interpreted the restriction as applying to all types of indexed bonds. However, Congress rescinded this resolution in 1977, so the ban on indexed bonds no longer applies.

Table 7.3 Inflation Rates, Nominal Interest Rates, and Real Interest Rates for Recent U.S. Experience (% per year)

Year	R_t	π_t	r_t	π_t^e	r_t^e
1948	1.0	0.8	0.2	1.2	−0.2
9	1.1	−3.0	4.1	−4.0	5.1
1950	1.2	8.2	−7.0	−0.2	1.4
1	1.6	4.1	−2.5	3.1	−1.5
2	1.8	0.2	1.6	1.1	0.7
3	1.9	0.7	1.2	−0.6	2.5
4	1.0	−1.2	2.2	−0.9	1.9
1955	1.8	0.0	1.8	0.3	1.5
6	2.7	3.3	−0.6	0.5	2.2
7	3.3	3.4	−0.1	1.3	2.0
8	1.8	1.3	0.5	0.1	1.7
9	3.4	1.1	2.3	0.6	2.8
1960	2.9	1.6	1.3	0.7	2.2
1	2.4	0.7	1.7	0.6	1.8
2	2.8	1.4	1.4	1.0	1.8
3	3.2	1.5	1.7	1.0	2.2
4	3.6	1.0	2.6	1.0	2.6
1965	4.0	2.0	2.0	1.1	2.9
6	4.9	3.0	1.9	1.7	3.2
7	4.3	3.5	0.8	2.1	2.2
8	5.3	4.0	1.3	2.8	2.5
9	6.7	5.3	1.4	2.9	3.8
1970	6.5	4.4	2.1	3.6	2.9
1	4.4	3.3	1.1	3.8	0.6
2	4.1	3.6	0.5	3.3	0.8
3	7.0	9.5	−2.5	3.6	3.4
4	7.9	11.2	−3.3	6.2	2.7
1975	5.8	6.5	−0.7	6.7	−0.9
6	5.0	5.2	−0.2	5.6	−0.6
7	5.3	6.0	−0.7	5.6	−0.3
8	7.2	8.2	−1.0	6.2	1.0
9	10.1	11.3	−1.2	7.6	2.5
1980	11.4	10.3	1.1	10.4	1.0
1.	14.0	7.7	6.3	9.7	4.3
2	10.7	4.1	6.6	6.1	4.6
3	8.6	4.0	4.6	4.5	4.1
4	9.6	3.1	6.5	5.3	4.3
1985	7.5	3.3	4.2	4.0	3.5

Note: The inflation rate, π_t, refers to the change in the CPI from January of each year to January of the next year. We use the figures that exclude the shelter component to avoid some problems of measuring mortgage interest costs. The nominal interest rate, R_t, is the average annual rate on secondary markets for U.S. treasury bills with three-month maturity. The real interest rate, r_t, equals $R_t - \pi_t$. The data on prices are from *U.S. Survey of Current Business* and the U.S. Labor Department. Data on interest rates are from issues of the *Federal Reserve Bulletin* and U.S. Board of Governors of the Federal Reserve System, *Banking and Monetary Statistics, 1941–1970*. The variable π_t^e, from the Livingston survey, comes from the Federal Reserve Bank of Philadelphia. We use an average for each year of the 6-month forecasts (from December of the previous year and June of the current year).

ple's beliefs correspond to optimal predictions, given the available information. Then use statistical techniques to figure out these optimal predictions.

• Third, use market data, such as interest rates or prices of financial contracts, to infer what people believe.

The main shortcoming of the first approach is that the sample may not be representative of the whole economy. Also, economists have a better theory of how people take actions than of how they answer questions on surveys. Unlike in a market where the participants back up their statements with money, it is less clear what it means when someone just expresses opinions about inflation or other variables.

The second approach, based on rational expectations, has produced some successes and some difficulties.[4] One problem arises in figuring out what information people have when they form expectations. Another concerns the choice among statistical models. In any event, the results about expected inflation from some of these studies do not differ in many respects from the survey findings that we consider below.

The third approach, which relies on market data, has had limited success thus far for measuring expected inflation.[5] The main problem has been lack of applicable data, but this situation may be changing. An exciting recent source of data is the futures contract based on the CPI that is traded on the Coffee, Sugar & Cocoa Exchange. Traders in this market essentially bet on the value of the CPI in future periods. Then these traders win or lose money depending on the value that the CPI actually takes later on. By looking at the current bets (in the *Wall Street Journal*) we can infer traders' expectations of future changes in the price level. For example, in February 1986, people anticipated an inflation rate of 4.5% for the remainder of 1986, but expected much higher rates later on. Expected inflation was 7.3% for 1987 and 8.1% for 1988. However, by June 1986, the expected inflation rates had fallen to 4.4% for 1987 and 6.6% for 1988. If these data become available for a long period (that is, if there is enough trading volume for the exchange to make a profit), then economists will make great use of them. We also consider later on the recent data on British indexed bonds, which are available for a somewhat longer period and are also useful for measuring expected inflation.

---

[4]For uses of this approach to measure expected inflation, see, for example, Robert Barro, "U.S. Deficits since World War I," *Scandinavian Journal of Economics,* 1986, Table 4; and James Hamilton, "Uncovering Financial Market Expectations of Inflation," *Journal of Political Economy,* December 1985.

[5]Eugene Fama, in his article, "Short-Term Interest Rates as Predictors of Inflation," *American Economic Review,* June 1975, suggested that nominal interest rates were good measures of expected inflation. But his estimated relationships broke down after the early 1970s. For some discussion of this topic see Charles Nelson and G. William Schwert, "Short-Term Interest Rates as Predictors of Inflation: On Testing the Hypothesis That the Real Rate of Interest is Constant," *American Economic Review,* June 1977.

Let's return now to the first approach, which uses survey data to measure expected inflation. Joseph Livingston, a Philadelphia journalist, began in 1946 to survey about 50 economists (fewer in the early years of the sample) for their forecasts of the CPI 6 to 12 months in the future. The variable denoted π_t^e in Table 7.3 is the average of the two 6-month-ahead forecasts for each year, when expressed as the implied prediction for the annual rate of inflation.[6] The last column in Table 7.3 shows the corresponding value of the expected real interest rate, $r_t^e = R_t - \pi_t^e$.

Interest Rates and Expected Inflation in the Post-World War II Period

One thing to notice from Table 7.3 is that the nominal interest rate rose dramatically in the post-World War II period. This rate increased from 1% per year in 1948 to about 3% in the early 1960s, 5–6% in the late 1960s, 10% in 1979, and 14% in 1981, but then fell to 7% in 1985. Note that the increase was not steady—for example, the interest rate declined from 3.3% in 1957 to 1.8% in 1958, from 6.5% in 1970 to 4.1% in 1972, from 7.9% in 1974 to 5.0% in 1976, and from 14.0% in 1981 to 7.5% in 1985. Further, despite the appearance of a generally upward drift in interest rates, it would not have been easy to forecast this "trend." In any event someone who foresaw this pattern could have made a fortune by speculating on bond prices.

Figure 7.3 plots the data from Table 7.3 on the nominal interest rate, R_t, the expected inflation rate, π_t^e, and the expected real interest rate, r_t^e. A striking feature of this graph is the tendency for the nominal interest rate and the expected inflation rate to move together. Especially from the early 1950s until 1980, expected inflation increased roughly in parallel with the nominal interest rate. The same is true for actual inflation, although it showed more fluctuation from year to year. In our subsequent analysis (in Chapter 8) we shall want to understand why nominal interest rates and inflation rates tend to move together on roughly a one-to-one basis.

The behavior of expected real interest rates differs markedly from that of nominal rates. Since expected inflation and nominal interest rates moved together nearly one-for-one, there was no regular pattern for expected real interest rates, r_t^e, at least through 1980. For example, for 1948–64 the average value of r_t^e was 1.8%, while that for 1965–80 was 1.7%.

For 1981–85 the average value of r_t^e was 4.2%—or 2.4 percentage points above that for 1948–80. From Table 7.3 we see that the sharp decline in expected inflation from 10.4% in 1980 to 4.0% in 1985 was not matched by a comparable decline in nominal interest rates (which fell from 11.4 to 7.5%). We should retain an historical perspective by noting that the expected real interest rates for 1981–85 would not stand out relative to those before World War II (as we shall see in Chapter 11). But there is no question that the real

---

[6]For a discussion of the Livingston Survey, see John A. Carlson, "A Study of Price Forecasts," *Annals of Economic and Social Measurement,* Winter 1977.

Figure 7.3 **Behavior of the Inflation Rate, Nominal Interest Rate, and Real Interest Rate in the United States**

The expected inflation rate and the nominal interest rate rose over the post-World War II period. Expected real interest rates increased after 1980.

rates after 1980 were well above the average of the previous 30 years. We shall try to understand this phenomenon as we carry out our analysis in this book, but a full explanation turns out to be unavailable.

Another thing to note from Table 7.3 is that deviations of actual from expected inflation, $\pi_t - \pi_t^e$, explain some of the behavior of actual real interest rates, r_t. Remember that, for a given value of r_t^e, the inflation surprise, $\pi_t - \pi_t^e$, reduces r_t one-to-one.

As an example, surprise inflation—where $\pi_t > \pi_t^e$—accounts for some of the smallest real interest rates. In 1950, the inflation rate of 8.2%—as compared to the expected rate of −0.2%—was a surprise associated with the start of the Korean War. Therefore, the real interest rate of −7.0% was well below the anticipated rate (1.4%). Similarly, for 1973 to 1974, the inflation rates of 9.5 and 11.2%—as compared to expectations of 3.6 and 6.2%—were surprises related to the first oil crisis. Thus, the real interest rates, −2.5% and −3.3%, were again well below expectations.

In a longer run context, the average of the Livingston survey's measure of expected inflation from 1948 to 1980 was 2.4%, as compared to an average for actual inflation of 3.7%. Correspondingly, the average expected real interest rate, r_t^e, of 1.8% was well above the average of the actual rate, r_t, of 0.5%. In other words, the persisting tendency—through 1980—to underpredict inflation is a partial explanation for why r_t averaged only slightly above zero.[7]

Finally, to use inflation surprises to explain high real interest rates, we have to search for unexpectedly low inflation. Mainly we find this pattern in the period 1981–85. The actual inflation rates for 1981, 1982, and 1984 were each about 2 percentage points below the expected rates. For this reason, the average of r_t for 1981–85 was 5.6%, as compared to 4.2% for r_t^e. In other words, unexpectedly low inflation accounts for 1.4 percentage points of the high average for r_t in 1981–85.

Indexed Bonds in the United Kingdom

We mentioned before that indexed bonds adjust their nominal payments to provide a known real interest rate. Therefore we do not have to measure expected inflation to compute expected real interest rates (which equal the actual rates in this case). Although indexed bonds do not exist currently in the United States,[8] it is worthwhile to study the British experience.

The British government began in March 1981 to issue marketable bonds ("gilts") that linked the nominal interest payments and principal to a broad index of retail prices.[9] Table 7.4 shows how real interest rates on British indexed bonds have behaved since April 1981. The rates rose from 2.4% in 1981 to 3.4% in 1984. For 1982–84 the average value of 3.0% compares with an average of 4.3% for expected real interest rates, r_t^e, in the United States (see Table 7.3).

---

[7]Conceivably the chronic tendency to underpredict inflation means that the respondents to the Livingston survey were irrational. But this assessment depends heavily on hindsight. In fact, as we mentioned in Chapter 1 and showed in Table 7.2, the high average inflation of the post-World War II period was a dramatic departure from the U.S. history during peacetime. Statistical models that forecast a lot better than the Livingston survey might not have been used by people who had access only to historical data. For some discussion of the rationality of the Livingston survey, see Carlson, op. cit; and John Caskey, "Modeling the Formation of Price Expectations: a Bayesian Approach," *American Economic Review,* September 1985.

[8]The famous economist, Irving Fisher, had his company, Cardex Rand, issue an indexed bond in the 1920s. But it was not very popular. Recently, the First City National Bank of Houston has offered (to pension funds) certificates of deposits with a maturity of up to 30 years, for which the real interest rate is fixed at about 4%. It will be interesting to see whether these instruments are popular.

[9]Because the index linking involves a lag of 8 months, the real yield varies somewhat with actual inflation. But, as a first approximation, we can treat the real interest rate as known in advance.

**Table 7.4 Real Interest Rates on Indexed Bonds
in the United Kingdom**

Period	Real Interest Rate[a] (%)
April to December 1981	2.4
1982	2.8
1983	2.9
1984	3.4

[a]The rate applies to bonds with roughly a 25-year maturity. From April 1981 to March 1982, the values are estimated from the yield on bonds due in 1996.
Source: Buckmaster and Moore, *Index-Linked Gilt Book*, May 1985.

Since there are participants in the financial markets who can move readily between U.K. indexed bonds and U.S. nominal bonds, we would anticipate that the expected real interest rates on these assets would be similar. Otherwise, some people would switch to the bond that promised the higher real yield. This process of switching would continue until the prices of the bonds adjusted to equalize the expected real interest rates.[10] In any event, the data shown in Table 7.4 give us another measure of expected real interest rates after 1980.

Interest Rates on Money

We have discussed the nominal and real interest rates on bonds. But the same analysis applies to money, once we specify that the nominal interest rate on money is zero, rather than R_t. Recall that the real interest rate on any asset equals the nominal rate less the rate of inflation, π_t. Therefore, for bonds, the real rate is $r_t = R_t - \pi_t$. Similarly, for money, the real interest rate is $-\pi_t$. Positive inflation means that the purchasing power of money erodes over time.

---

[10]There are some elements that would allow the real interest rate on the British government's indexed bonds to differ from the expected real interest rate on U.S. government bonds. First, the returns on U.S. bonds are more risky because of the uncertainty of inflation. Second, the British bonds have a more favorable tax treatment because only the earnings corresponding to the real interest rate are taxable. Third, the British bonds are tied to an index of British prices, which may behave differently from U.S. prices. Finally, the debt studied in Table 7.4 has a maturity of 25 years, whereas the U.S. treasury bills in Table 7.3 have a maturity of 3 months.

As with bonds, we can distinguish the expected real interest rate on money from the actual rate. The expected real interest rate on money is just the negative of the expected inflation rate, $-\pi_t^e$. Given the persistent increase in U.S. inflation rates over the post-World War II period, as shown in Table 7.3, it follows that the expected real interest rate on money is much lower than it used to be.

Remember that the money in our model is like currency, which pays a zero nominal interest rate. Recently, most forms of checkable deposits have started to pay interest. For these types of "moneys," we would calculate the real interest rate just as we do for bonds. That is, the real rate on these deposits equals the nominal interest rate less the rate of inflation.

Summary

We began by examining data on monetary growth and inflation across countries and over time for the United States. These data suggest that variations in monetary growth account for a good deal of the variations in inflation rates.

The real interest rate on bonds, r_t, equals the nominal rate, R_t, less the inflation rate, π_t. If a bond specifies the nominal interest rate in advance, then the expected real interest rate, r_t^e, depends inversely on the expected inflation rate, π_t^e. We examined the United States data since World War II on treasury bills and on the Livingston survey of inflationary expectations. We found that nominal interest rates and the expected rate of inflation have risen dramatically and by roughly equal amounts. For 1948–80 expected real interest rates averaged just below 2%, but have increased to over 4% for 1981–85. The real interest rates on British indexed bonds averaged a little over 3% for 1981–84.

Important Terms and Concepts

inflation	real interest rate
rate of monetary growth	expected real interest rate
deflation	indexation
expectation of inflation	inflation correction
unexpected inflation	rational expectations
nominal interest rate	

QUESTIONS AND PROBLEMS

Mainly for Review

7.1 Monetarists hold that changes in the price level are primarily the results of changes in the quantity of money. Can this conclusion be based solely on theoretical reasoning? Explain.

7.2 Define the real interest rate. Why does it differ from the nominal interest rate in the presence of inflation?

7.3 Why does the actual real interest rate generally differ from the expected rate? How does this relation depend on whether bonds prescribe the nominal interest rate or the real interest rate?

7.4 Consider the Livingston survey of inflationary expectations. What are the pluses and minuses of using this type of information to measure expected rates of inflation?

Problems for Discussion

7.5 Monetary Growth and Inflation

Suppose that the money-demand function takes the form

$$(M/P)^d = L(Y, R, \ldots) = Y \cdot H(R)$$
$$(+)(-)$$

where H is some function. This form says that an increase in real output by, say, 10% raises the real demand for money by 10%.

a. Is it possible that this form of the demand for money accords with our theory of money demand from Chapter 4?

b. Consider the relation across countries between the average growth rates of money and prices. If the functional form shown above for money demand applies, then how does the average growth rate of real output affect the relation between the growth rates of money and prices?

c. What is the relation between the average growth rates of money and prices for a country where the nominal interest rate, R, has increased?

d. If the expected real interest rate is constant, what is the relation between the average growth rates of money and prices for a country where the expected inflation rate, π^e, has increased? How does this result apply to countries for which we do not observe the nominal interest rate, R, on an organized credit market?

7.6 Prepayments of Mortgages and Callability of Bonds

Mortgages typically allow the borrower to make early payments of principal, which are called *prepayments*. Sometimes the mortgage contract specifies a penalty for prepayments, while sometimes there is no penalty. In recent years many state governments have prohibited prepayment penalties on mortgages.

(However, there are generally some fees for negotiating a new mortgage.) Similarly most long-term bonds—although not those of the U.S. government— allow the issuer to prepay the principal after a prescribed date and with a specified penalty. When the bond issuer exercises this option to prepay, he or she is said to "call" the bond. Bonds that allow this option are said to be *callable* or to have a *call provision.*

   a. When would a borrower want to prepay (or call) his or her mortgage or bond? Would we see more prepayments when nominal interest rates had unexpectedly increased or decreased?

   b. From the late 1970s until 1982 banks and savings and loans were especially eager for their customers to prepay their mortgages. Why was this the case?

   c. Suppose that there is an increase in the year-to-year fluctuations of nominal interest rates, as is true since the early 1970s. From the standpoint of a borrower, how does this change affect the value of having a prepayment option—that is, callability—in his or her mortgage or bond?

7.7 Rational Expectations and Measures of Expected Inflation

How would the hypothesis of rational expectations help us to measure inflationary expectations? What seem to be the pluses and minuses of this approach?

7.8 Indexed Bonds

Consider a bond that costs $1000. Suppose that the bond pays a year later the principal of $1000 plus interest of $100.

   a. What is the nominal interest rate on the bond? What are the actual and expected real interest rates? Why is the nominal rate known, but the real rate uncertain?

   Suppose that someone issues an indexed bond, which adjusts the payments to compensate for inflation. For example, assume that the total amount paid a year later is the quantity $\$1100 \cdot (1+\pi)$, where π is the inflation rate over the year.

   b. What is the real interest rate on the indexed bond? Are the real and nominal interest rates both uncertain in some cases?

7.9 The Term Structure of Real Interest Rates

In February 1985 the real interest rates on British indexed bonds with a 5-year maturity were about $4\frac{1}{2}\%$, whereas those with a 20-year maturity were about $3\frac{1}{2}\%$.

   a. What does this pattern suggest for people's expectations of future real interest rates—for example, on bonds with a 5-year maturity when issued in 1990?

   b. For the United States we would like to know whether the high real interest rates for 1981–85 represent a temporary or a permanent change. How do the British data bear on this question?

CHAPTER 8

MONEY, INFLATION, AND INTEREST RATES IN THE MARKET-CLEARING MODEL

In this chapter, we use the market-clearing model to determine inflation and interest rates. For the main analysis we return to the setting from Chapter 5 that does not deal explicitly with a labor market or firms. As we saw in Chapter 6, this simplification will be satisfactory for most purposes. Our basic approach will be to specify a given time path of the money stock, M_t. Then we figure out what time path of the price level, P_t—hence, of the inflation rate, π_t—and of the nominal and real interest rates, R_t and r_t, satisfy the conditions for general market clearing.

Here, we focus on the consequences of different rates of anticipated inflation and monetary growth. Even when the inflation rate, π_t, varies over time, we assume that people forecast these changes accurately. Put another way, people have **perfect foresight** about future price levels, so that there is always equality between the actual and expected inflation rates, $\pi_t = \pi_t^e$. Accordingly, if people know the nominal interest rate, R_t, then there is also equality between actual and expected real interest rates, $r_t = r_t^e$.

On the one hand, the analysis is limited since it does not address unanticipated inflation and monetary growth. (Later on, we shall explore these matters.) But it is useful to study anticipated inflation as a separate topic. In particular, the changes in anticipated inflation explain the principal longer term movements in U.S. nominal interest rates since World War II.

Incorporation of Inflation and Monetary Growth into the Model

We want to incorporate into the model the various new elements that we introduced in Chapter 7. These include inflation and the distinction between real and nominal interest rates. Also, to analyze the link between monetary growth and inflation, we have to extend the model to allow for changes in the stock of money.

For simplicity, we begin with situations where the nominal interest rate, R, and the inflation rate, π, are constant over time. Therefore, the real interest rate, $r = R - \pi$, is also constant. Since we assumed equality between actual and expected inflation, $\pi = \pi^e$, there is also equality between actual and expected real interest rates, $r = r^e$.

Monetary Growth and Transfer Payments

We choose the simplest possible way to introduce monetary growth into the model. Namely, we assume that new money shows up as transfers from the government to households. Later on, when we study more realistic ways by which money enters the economy, we shall see that this simple device captures the essence of monetary changes. In particular, the main results still hold for other methods of introducing new money into the economy.

Let's denote by v_t the dollar amount of transfer that a household receives during period t. Note that this amount need not be the same for everyone. The government finances the total of transfers, V_t, by printing and distributing new money. Therefore, the change in the aggregate quantity of money, $M_t - M_{t-1}$, equals the aggregate amount of transfers

$$V_t = M_t - M_{t-1} \tag{8.1}$$

Equation 8.1 is a simple version of a **governmental budget constraint.** The left side is total government expenditures, all of which take the form of transfers, V_t, at this point. The right side lists government revenues. At present, this revenue derives solely from the printing of new paper money in the amount, $M_t - M_{t-1}$.

We can think of transfer payments as arising via a "helicopter drop" of cash.[1] Thus, our public officials effectively stuff a helicopter full of paper currency and fly around dropping money randomly over the countryside. The transfer payments occur when people pick up the money. Despite the unrealistic flavor of this story, the only important aspect of it is that each person's transfer is independent of his or her level of income, previous amount of money holdings, and so on. (Let's ignore any dependence on the effort that people exert in searching the countryside for currency.) Economists refer to these kinds of transfers as **lump sum,** by which we mean that the amount someone receives is independent of his or her level of work effort, holdings of money, or other choices. Since the transfers are lump-sum, an individual understands

---

[1] I think that the original source of this popular story is Milton Friedman, "The Optimum Quantity of Money," in his *The Optimum Quantity of Money and Other Essays*, Chicago, Aldine, 1969, pp. 4–5.

that changes in his or her holdings of money, m_t and m_{t-1}, have no impact on the size of his or her transfer, v_t.[2]

We have to modify households' budget constraints to include the transfer payments. Now, each household's budget constraint for period t is, when expressed in nominal terms

$$P_t y_t + b_{t-1}(1+R) + m_{t-1} + v_t = P_t c_t + b_t + m_t \qquad (8.2)$$

As before, the sources of funds on the left side include the dollar receipts from the commodity market, $P_t y_t$, plus the values of the bonds and money that were held last period, $b_{t-1}(1+R) + m_{t-1}$. The new element is the dollar amount of transfer, v_t, which is an additional source of funds for a household. The right side of equation (8.2) contains the same uses of funds as before. These are the nominal purchases of commodities, $P_t c_t$, plus this period's holdings of bonds and money, $b_t + m_t$. Notice that we date the price level, P_t, since it will no longer be constant over time. However, since we assume that the nominal interest rate, R, is constant, we do not have to date it.

Inflation and Saving

The national accounts define a household's saving, as we did before, to equal the change in nominal assets, which in the model consist of money and bonds. Using this definition and rearranging the budget constraint from equation 8.2 we get

Nominal saving (national accounts' version)
$$= (b_t + m_t) - (b_{t-1} + m_{t-1}) = P_t y_t + Rb_{t-1} + v_t - P_t c_t \qquad (8.3)$$

The expression on the right side differs from that in earlier chapters only by the inclusion of the transfers, v_t, and by the dating of the price level, P_t.

National income accounting—and standard accounting practices for businesses or governments—do not deal correctly with changing price levels when they measure saving as in equation 8.3. A meaningful concept of someone's dollar saving would—when divided by the price level, P_t—equal the change in the real purchasing power of that person's assets. The standard definition does this when the price level is constant, but does not when the price level changes.

Consider an alternative approach, where we start by defining a household's **real saving** to be the change in the real value of assets—that is

$$\text{real saving} = \frac{(b_t + m_t)}{P_t} - \frac{(b_{t-1} + m_{t-1})}{P_{t-1}}$$

---

[2]The discussion assumes positive transfers, although we could deal with negative ones. Negative transfers are taxes, which can also be lump-sum—that is, independent of individuals' levels of income, amount of money holdings, and so on. While we view transfers as financed by a helicopter drop of cash, we can view taxes as collected by a giant vacuum cleaner.

Now we want to use a version of the budget constraint where everything appears in real terms. So if we divide through equation 8.2 by the price level, P_t, we get the condition in real terms

$$y_t + \frac{b_{t-1}(1+R)}{P_t} + \frac{m_{t-1}}{P_t} + \frac{v_t}{P_t} = c_t + \frac{b_t}{P_t} + \frac{m_t}{P_t} \qquad (8.4)$$

If we rearrange terms, we determine the real value of assets held for period t

$$\frac{(b_t + m_t)}{P_t} = y_t + \frac{b_{t-1}(1+R)}{P_t} + \frac{m_{t-1}}{P_t} + \frac{v_t}{P_t} - c_t$$

To calculate real saving we have to subtract from both sides of the equation the initial real assets, $(b_{t-1} + m_{t-1})/P_{t-1}$. Then we get

$$\frac{(b_t + m_t)}{P_t} - \frac{(b_{t-1} + m_{t-1})}{P_{t-1}}$$
$$= y_t + \frac{b_{t-1}(1+R)}{P_t} + \frac{m_{t-1}}{P_t} + \frac{v_t}{P_t} - c_t - \frac{(b_{t-1} + m_{t-1})}{P_{t-1}}$$

Finally, we can combine terms on the right side, taking account of the relation, $P_t = (1+\pi)P_{t-1}$. When we carry out the algebra, we end up with the following expression for real saving

$$\text{real saving} = \frac{(b_t + m_t)}{P_t} - \frac{(b_{t-1} + m_{t-1})}{P_{t-1}}$$
$$= y_t + (R - \pi)\left(\frac{b_{t-1}}{P_t}\right) - \pi\left(\frac{m_{t-1}}{P_t}\right) + \frac{v_t}{P_t} - c_t \qquad (8.5)$$

The important property of the formula for real saving in equation 8.5 is the way that it calculates returns on assets. For bonds, we use the real interest rate, $r = R - \pi$. For money, we use the real interest rate on money, which is $-\pi$. Real saving still equals real income less real expenditures, c_t. But real income must be defined carefully. It equals the real receipts from the commodity market, y_t, plus the real value of transfers, v_t/P_t, plus the real returns on assets, which are $(R - \pi)(b_{t-1}/P_t)$ for bonds and $-\pi(m_{t-1}/P_t)$ for money.

Once we know a person's real saving from equation 8.5 we can calculate the dollar value of this saving from multiplication by the price level, P_t. Then we have

$$\text{nominal saving} = P_t y_t + (R - \pi)b_{t-1} - \pi m_{t-1} + v_t - P_t c_t \qquad (8.6)$$

Compare this result with the standard definition of nominal saving in equation 8.3. The differences involve the measures of returns on assets. Specifically, the standard definition uses nominal interest rates, which are R for bonds and zero for money. But our concept of saving uses real interest rates, which are $(R - \pi)$ for bonds and $-\pi$ for money.

Inflation and the Definition of Saving: Some Examples

Consider some examples to clarify the results about saving. Suppose that in each period someone's receipts from the commodity market plus transfers, $P_t y_t + v_t$, just cover consumption expenditure, $P_t c_t$. Assume that the person starts with $1000 in bonds—that is, $b_0 = \$1000$. For simplicity, suppose that he or she holds no money. Then assume that the nominal interest rate, R, and the inflation rate, π, are both 10% per year. Hence, the initial nominal interest income, Rb_0, is $100.

The standard definition, equation 8.3, calculates nominal saving for the first period as $100. This saving shows up as an increase in the dollar value of bonds to $b_1 = \$1100$. Hence, the dollar value of bond holdings goes up by 10% from period zero. But the price level also rises by 10%. So the $1100 of bonds in period 1 buys no more than does the $1000 in period 0. Apparently, the person does a lot of "saving," but has added nothing to the purchasing power of his or her assets.

We get a more reasonable answer by using the definition of saving from equation 8.6. Since the real interest rate, $R - \pi$, is zero we find that this version of nominal saving is zero. (Note that real saving, as calculated from equation 8.5, is also zero.) This answer tells us, correctly, that the purchasing power of assets does not change over time.

Suppose now that we change the example by having all assets—initially $1000—held each period as money, rather than bonds. Then the nominal interest income is zero in each period. Given the other conditions that we assumed before, the standard definition of saving from equation 8.3 says that saving is zero. Correspondingly, the person's nominal assets—all held as money—remain at $1000 over time. But with 10% inflation, these dollars buy progressively less goods. According to the standard definition, the person does zero saving—yet, the real value of his or her assets deteriorates over time.

Again, we get a more reasonable answer from the definition of saving in equation 8.6. Here, we apply the real interest rate, $-\pi = -10\%$, to the holdings of money. The effective interest earnings on money are initially $-\$100$, because $1000 of money loses $100 of real value over a year. Thus, nominal saving for the first period is $-\$100$, rather than zero.

So far, the examples have assumed that the holdings of bonds were nonnegative. But the adjustments for inflation reverse if a person is a debtor. For example, suppose that someone takes out a mortgage on a house for $100,000 at an interest rate, R, of 15%. Then he or she makes annual interest payments of $15,000. (Assume that the mortgage has a long maturity, in which case there is very little repayment of nominal principal.) But the true interest costs are much less than $15,000 per year. If the inflation rate is 10%, then the real value of the outstanding principal on the loan declines by 10% in each year. Hence, the true annual interest costs are $15,000 in explicit payments less $10,000 for the decline in the real value of debt, for a net amount of $5,000.

Aggregate Real Saving

We define an individual's real saving to be the change in his or her holdings of real bonds and money. When we sum up over all households, we find that aggregate real saving equals the change in the aggregate real stock of bonds, $B_t/P_t - B_{t-1}/P_{t-1}$, plus the change in the aggregate real stock of money, $M_t/P_t - M_{t-1}/P_{t-1}$. Since the total stock of bonds, B_t, still equals zero in each period, it follows that the aggregate of real saving equals the change in the aggregate of real cash balances. So if total real money balances change over time, then the aggregate of real saving is now nonzero.

Budget Constraints over an Infinite Horizon

We have to make some adjustments to incorporate inflation into households' budget constraints over an infinite horizon. For the moment, let's put aside the various monetary terms, which include the initial stock of real cash balances, the transfers received from the government, and the interest foregone by holding money. Then, when written in terms of nominal present values, the budget constraint over an infinite horizon looks basically like it did before. Since we assume that the nominal interest rate R is constant, the condition is

$$
P_1 y_1 + \frac{P_2 y_2}{(1+R)} + \frac{P_3 y_3}{(1+R)^2} + \cdots + b_0(1+R)
$$

$$
= P_1 c_1 + \frac{P_2 c_2}{(1+R)} + \frac{P_3 c_3}{(1+R)^2} + \cdots \quad (8.7)
$$

The only new element in equation 8.7 is the dating of the price level.

Recall that we assume a constant rate of inflation, π. Therefore the price levels for any two adjacent periods satisfy the condition, $P_t = (1+\pi)P_{t-1}$. We can use this condition repeatedly to express each future level of prices in terms of the current price, P_1, and the constant inflation rate π. Then we get the sequence

$$
P_2 = (1+\pi)P_1,
$$

$$
P_3 = (1+\pi)^2 P_1,
$$

.

.

.

If we substitute these results into the budget constraint from equation 8.7, we get the revised condition

$$P_1\left[y_1 + y_2 \cdot \frac{(1+\pi)}{(1+R)} + y_3 \cdot \frac{(1+\pi)^2}{(1+R)^2} + \cdots\right] + b_0(1+R)$$

$$= P_1\left[c_1 + c_2 \cdot \frac{(1+\pi)}{(1+R)} + c_3 \cdot \frac{(1+\pi)^2}{(1+R)^2} + \cdots\right] \quad (8.8)$$

Notice that the next period's real income and spending, y_2 and c_2, enter multiplicatively with the factor, $(1+\pi)/(1+R)$. But recall from Chapter 7 that the relation between real and nominal interest rates is $(1+r) = (1+R)/(1+\pi)$. Therefore, the term in equation 8.8, $(1+\pi)/(1+R)$, is equal to $1/(1+r)$. Hence, to express the next period's real income and spending, y_2 and c_2, as present values we divide by the discount factor, $(1+r)$. But this makes sense since the real interest rate tells people how they can exchange goods of one period for those of another. In particular, it is the real interest rate, rather than the nominal rate, that matters here.

The same idea applies for any future period. For example, the real income and spending for period 3, y_3 and c_3, enter into equation 8.8 as a multiple of the factor, $(1+\pi)^2/(1+R)^2$, which equals $1/(1+r)^2$. If we make all these substitutions into equation 8.8—and also divide through by the current price level, P_1—we end up with a simplified form of the budget constraint

$$y_1 + \frac{y_2}{(1+r)} + \frac{y_3}{(1+r)^2} + \cdots + \frac{b_0(1+R)}{P_1}$$

$$= c_1 + \frac{c_2}{(1+r)} + \frac{c_3}{(1+r)^2} + \cdots \quad (8.9)$$

(The nominal interest rate appears in the term, $b_0(1+R)$, because this term is the nominal value of the bonds carried over to period 1.)

Equation 8.9 is the budget constraint in real terms over an infinite horizon. The new element is that the real interest rate, r, appears, instead of the nominal rate, R, in the various discount factors.

Finally, let's recall our assumption that the real interest rate, $r = R - \pi$, is known. Given this condition, there is no distinction between the expected real interest rate and the actual rate. More realistically, when people express prospective real incomes and expenses as present values they must use anticipated real interest rates, rather than the actual values. Therefore, we can think of the real interest rate, r, that appears in equation 8.9 as an expected rate, $r^e = R - \pi^e$.

Intertemporal-Substitution Effects

We discussed before how the interest rate has intertemporal-substitution effects on people's choices of consumption, work, and saving. These effects involve the relative costs of taking consumption or leisure at one date rather than another. In making these comparisons an individual wants to know, for example, how much extra consumption he or she can get next period by reducing consumption this period. But as we worked out before, an individual can save and thus transform each unit of consumption foregone this period into $(1+r)$ units of added consumption for the next period. An increase in the real interest rate, r, motivates people to reduce current consumption and leisure in order to raise future consumption and leisure. In other words, a higher r motivates people to save more today. The important point is that the real interest rate matters here, rather than the nominal rate. Thus, our previous discussions of intertemporal-substitution effects remain valid, as long as we replace the nominal interest rate by the real rate.

Finally, remember again that we treat the real interest rate, r, as a known quantity. More generally, the expected real interest rate, $r^e = R - \pi^e$, is what matters for intertemporal-substitution effects. No one shifts their planned time paths of consumption and leisure, and hence their saving, unless they anticipate that the real interest rate will be either higher or lower. For example, if surprisingly low inflation makes the real interest rate unexpectedly high, then we do not predict a major intertemporal-substitution effect. After all, people could not have expected this unexpectedly low inflation when they decided on their current levels of consumption, work, and saving. For intertemporal-substitution effects to arise, there must be changes in the expected real interest rate, $r^e = R - \pi^e$. That is, there must be changes in the nominal interest rate, R, relative to the expected rate of inflation, π^e.

Money and Households' Budget Constraints

Now we can incorporate the various monetary terms into households' budget constraints. Recall that these terms involve initial real cash balances, transfers from the government, and interest foregone on future holdings of money. Before, we considered these terms when the price level was constant and transfers were zero. We found that the monetary terms had no effect in the aggregate on the real present value of households' sources of funds net of the uses of these funds. Hence, wealth effects on the aggregates of consumption and leisure arose only if we brought in the present value of real transaction costs. But we assumed that these costs were small enough to neglect for most purposes.

The previous results still hold in our extended framework. Specifically, variations in prices and in the quantity of paper money—which show up as transfer payments—cannot, by themselves, create or destroy wealth in the aggregate. As before, wealth effects on the aggregates of consumption and leisure emerge only when we bring in changes in the present value of real transaction costs. In the appendix to this chapter we go through a fair amount of algebra to prove these results. However, it is possible to skip this material without losing any continuity.

Interest Rates and the Demand for Money

Recall that the demand for money involves a trade-off between transaction costs and interest foregone. Further, the interest foregone depends on the differential between the interest rate on bonds and that on money. For example, if we think of nominal interest rates, then we care about the rate on bonds, R, less that on money, which is zero. The differential between the nominal interest rates is the amount R, just as in our previous analysis.

We can also make the calculation in terms of real interest rates. Then we take the real interest rate on bonds, r, less that on money, which is $-\pi$. So, the differential is again the amount, $R = r + \pi$.

Since the interest-income foregone still depends on the rate, R, we conclude that the demand-for-money function looks the same as before. Namely, the aggregate real demand again takes the form

$$\left(\frac{M_t}{P_t}\right)^d = L(Y_t, R, \ldots)$$
$$(+) \;(-) \tag{8.10}$$

Notice an important point. It is the (expected) real interest rate, r, that exerts intertemporal-substitution effects on consumption and work. But it is the nominal interest rate, R, that influences the real demand for money.

Market-Clearing Conditions

We know from Chapter 5 how to write down the conditions for general market clearing in the model that excludes the labor market. First, the aggregate supply of goods for period t, Y_t^s, equals the demand, C_t^d. Here we write this condition as

$$\underset{\text{supply of goods}}{Y^s(r_t, \ldots)} = \underset{\text{demand}}{C^d(r_t, \ldots)} \quad \underset{\substack{\text{Intertemporal} \\ \text{Substitution effect}}}{}$$
$$(+)_r \qquad\qquad (-)_r \tag{8.11}$$

Equation 8.11 shows the intertemporal-substitution effects from the real interest rate, r_t. As usual, this effect is positive on the supply of goods for period t, and negative on the demand.

The omitted terms, denoted by . . . in equation 8.11, include various properties of the production function. For example, shifts in this function can exert wealth and substitution effects. However, we know that no wealth effects on the aggregate of consumption and leisure arise from the combination of three monetary terms—initial real cash balances, the present value of real transfers, and the present value of interest foregone on future money. Therefore, we do not have to consider these terms in the condition for clearing the commodity market. On the other hand, transaction costs generally have some influence on commodities supplied and demanded. As before, we neglect these effects as an approximation.

Second, we have the condition that all money be willingly held. We can write this condition for period t as

$$M_t = P_t \cdot L(Y_t, R_t, \ldots)$$
$$(+)(-) \qquad (8.12)$$

On the left, we have the actual quantity of money. On the right, we have the nominal demand for money, which depends positively on the price level, P_t, and aggregate output, Y_t, and negatively on the nominal interest rate, R_t. Any other factors that influence money demand, such as the degree of financial sophistication, are denoted by the expression . . . in equation 8.12. Here, we assume that these factors do not change over time.

The Superneutrality of Money

Before we explore the details of the link between monetary behavior and inflation, we can already see an important property from the condition for clearing the commodity market. Consider the underlying real factors in the model, which include such things as the forms of production functions, population, and the preferences of households. These elements enter into the demand and supply of commodities through the omitted terms, which we denote by . . . in equation 8.11. For given values of these elements, equation 8.11 determines the real interest rate, r_t, and the level of aggregate output, $Y_t = C_t$, at each date. Further, if the underlying real elements do not change over time, then the market-clearing values of the real interest rate and output are constants.

The important point is that we determine the real interest rate and output independently of the path of money. Although changes in money will end up affecting the paths of the price level and the nominal interest rate, they will not affect at least some of the real variables in the model. If all real variables were invariant with the behavior of money, we would say that money was **superneutral.** Note that this term suggests an extension of another concept, the neutrality of money, which we discussed before. Neutrality of money means that once-and-for-all changes in the quantity of money affect nominal variables, but not real variables. Superneutrality extends this idea from one-time changes in the stock of money to arbitrary variations in the entire path of money.

We know from before that money is neutral in our model. One thing we want to study in this chapter is whether money is superneutral. To the extent that money is not superneutral, we shall find some effects of money and inflation on real variables.

Monetary Growth, Inflation, and the Nominal Interest Rate

We want now to examine the details of the linkages among monetary growth, inflation, and the nominal interest rate. We carry out this analysis for given values of the real interest rate, r, and output, Y. By holding these variables fixed, we are making two types of assumptions. First, we use the property that anticipated variations in money and prices do not affect the real interest rate and output. Second, we assume that no other shifts occur over time to the functions for aggregate commodity demand or supply. Generally, these types of changes would lead to movements in the real interest rate and output.

More specifically, the analysis neglects any systematic growth of output. Recall from Chapter 7 that countries with higher average growth rates of output tend to have less inflation for a given average growth rate of money. Although it is not hard to incorporate this feature into the analysis, we assume that output is constant to bring out the major points in the easiest possible way.

We can illustrate the main results by assuming a constant rate of monetary growth. In this case we have

$$M_t = (1+\mu)M_{t-1} \qquad \mu = \text{monetary growth rate} \qquad (8.13)$$

where μ (the Greek letter *mu*) is the monetary growth rate. We assume that equation 8.13 governs the behavior of money at least from the current date, which we label as $t = 1$, and out into the indefinite future.

We want to calculate the price level at each date, given that money grows at a constant rate. Generally, the model determines the time path of prices from the market-clearing conditions that we mentioned before. But we already determined the real interest rate and output to equate aggregate commodity supply and demand in equation 8.11. Further, if the supply and demand functions do not shift over time, then the real interest rate, r, and output, Y, are constants. Given these results, the price level, P_t, must satisfy the condition that money be willingly held. Writing this condition in real terms, we have

$$\frac{M_t}{P_t} = L(Y,\ R_t,\ \ldots)$$
$$(+)\ (-) \qquad\qquad\qquad (8.14)$$

In Chapter 5 we found that once-and-for-all increases in the quantity of money raised the price level in the same proportion. Therefore, it is reasonable to consider the possibility that the price level, P_t, grows at the same rate as the money stock, M_t. In this case the inflation rate, π, is constant and equal to the rate of monetary growth, μ. So let's make this guess and see whether it accords with the condition from equation 8.14 that all money be willingly held.

If money and prices grow at the same rate, the ratio of these two, which is the level of real cash balances, M_t/P_t, does not change over time. Therefore, the amount of real cash, which appears on the left side of equation 8.14, is constant.

Recall that the nominal interest rate, R_t, equals the quantity, $r_t + \pi_t$. But we already know that the real interest rate is constant. Therefore, if the inflation rate is constant, then the nominal interest rate is also constant. Finally, this result means that the real demand for money, $L(\cdot)$, which appears on the right side of equation 8.14, is constant. (Remember that output, Y, does not change over time.)

Since actual and desired real cash balances are constant, we have only to be sure that the two constants are the same. But this condition holds if we determine the current price level, P_1, to equate the amount of real cash balances, M_1/P_1, to the real quantity demanded, $L(\cdot)$. Then, since actual and desired real cash do not vary over time, we can be sure that all money will be willingly held at each date. That is, equation 8.14 holds in every period.

We have now verified that our guess—where prices grow at the same rate as money—satisfies the conditions for general market clearing. Therefore, this path of prices is the one that our model says will prevail. To summarize, the results are as follows:

- Prices grow at the same rate as the money stock—that is, $\pi = \mu$.
- Aggregate real money balances, M_t/P_t, are constant.
- The nominal interest rate, R, is constant and equal to the quantity, $r + \pi$.
- The aggregate demand for real balances, $L(Y, R, \ldots)$, is constant.
- The current price level, P_1, equates the quantity of real cash balances, M_1/P_1, to the real amount demanded, $L(Y, R)$.

Notice that the results imply that the growth rate of money, μ, shows up one-for-one in the inflation rate, π, and in the nominal interest rate, $R = r + \pi$. But recall that a higher nominal interest rate means a lower level of real money demanded. Therefore, a higher growth rate of money corresponds to a lower level of aggregate real cash balances, M_t/P_t.

A Shift in the Monetary Growth Rate

We can better understand the results about inflation and the nominal interest rate by studying a change in the monetary growth rate. Suppose that the money stock has been growing for a long time at the constant rate, μ. Further, everyone expects this behavior to persist indefinitely. Hence, the inflation rate is the constant, $\pi = \mu$, and the nominal interest rate is given by

$$R = r + \pi = r + \mu$$

We show this initial situation on the left side of Figure 8.1.

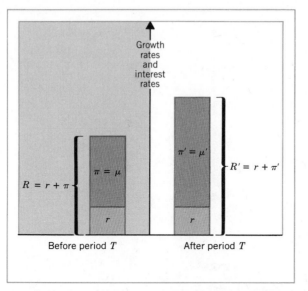

Figure 8.1 Growth Rates of Money and Prices and Levels of Interest Rates: Effects of an Increase in the Monetary Growth Rate

Before period T, the growth rate of money is μ. Hence, the left side of the figure shows that the inflation rate is $\pi = \mu$, and the nominal interest rate is $R = r + \pi = r + \mu$. After period T, the growth rate of money is the higher value μ'. Consequently, the new inflation rate is $\pi' = \mu'$, and the new nominal interest rate is $R' = r + \pi' = r + \mu'$.

Consider how the quantity of money, M_t, behaves over time. We have the sequence

$$M_1 = (1+\mu)M_0$$
$$M_2 = (1+\mu)M_1 = (1+\mu)^2 M_0$$

.

.

.

Therefore, for any period t, the quantity of money is given by

$$M_t = (1+\mu)^t M_0 \tag{8.15}$$

We shall find it convenient to graph the quantity of money, M_t, on a proportionate scale. On this type of scale (which is also called a logarithmic scale), each unit on the vertical axis corresponds to an equal proportional change in a variable—say, a 1% change in the stock of money. Since money grows at the constant proportionate rate μ, the graph of money versus time is a straight line on a proportionate scale. Further, the slope of the line equals

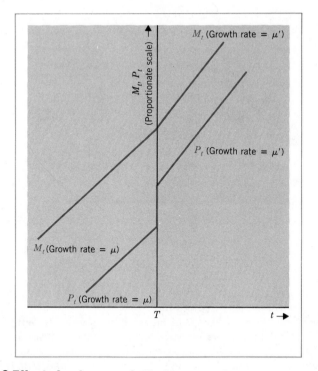

Figure 8.2 **Effect of an Increase in the Monetary Growth Rate on the Path of the Price Level**
We show the behavior of money and prices before and after an increase in the monetary growth rate at date T. Notice that a jump in the price level occurs at date T.

the growth rate, μ. Accordingly, on the left side of Figure 8.2, we graph the quantity of money, M_t, as a straight line with slope μ.[3]

We found before that the price level grows also at the constant rate, $\pi = \mu$—that is,

$$P_t = (1+\pi)^t P_0 = (1+\mu)^t P_0 \qquad (8.16)$$

Therefore, the graph of the price level, P_t, on the left side of Figure 8.2 is a straight line with slope μ. Note that this line parallels the one for the stock of money, M_t.

Assume now that the growth rate of money rises from μ to μ' at some date T. Here, we think of this change as a surprise—that is, before date T no one anticipated the acceleration of money. But once it happens, we assume that everyone expects that the new monetary growth rate, μ', will persist indefinitely. Hence, we study here the consequences of a once-and-for-all increase in the rate of monetary expansion.

---

[3]We ignore the discrete length of periods in this graph. In effect, we treat this length as being extremely brief.

After the change in the monetary growth rate, the economy is in the same type of situation as before. The only difference is that the growth rate of money is μ', rather than μ. Therefore, we show on the right side of Figure 8.1 that the new inflation rate is $\pi' = \mu'$. Also, we know that the change in monetary behavior does not affect the real interest rate, which remains at the value r. Therefore, the new nominal interest rate is $R' = r + \pi' = r + \mu'$. In other words, the inflation rate and the nominal interest rate each rise by as much as the increase in the monetary growth rate.

We show the levels of money and prices after date T (on a proportionate scale) on the right side of Figure 8.2. Because the growth rate of money rises after date T, the line for the money stock, M_t, has the slope, μ', which exceeds the original slope. Note, however, that there is no immediate jump in the stock of money at date T—money just starts to grow faster at this point.

Since prices grow at the rate $\pi' = \mu'$ after date T, we again show the line for the price level, P_t, as parallel to that for the money stock. But notice an important complication in the graph of P_t in Figure 8.2. Namely, we show a jump in P_t at date T. Let's see why this jump occurs.

The acceleration of money at date T raises the nominal interest rate from the value, $R = r + \mu$, to the higher value, $R' = r + \mu'$. But recall that an increase in the nominal interest rate reduces the real demand for money. Hence, the existing amount of cash will be willingly held at date T only if the actual real cash balances, M_T/P_T, fall by as much as the real demand. But there is no sudden change in the nominal quantity of money at date T—only an increase in the rate of growth. Therefore, real balances can fall to equal the smaller amount demanded only if there is an upward jump in the price level at date T.

We can also say something about the size of the jump in the price level at date T. The proportionate rise in the price level equals the proportionate fall in real cash balances, which equals the proportionate decline in the real demand for money. Further, the magnitude of the decline in money demand depends on two things: first, the change in the nominal interest rate, which is $\mu' - \mu$, and second, the sensitivity of real money demanded to changes in the nominal interest rate. Therefore, the jump in the price level is greater the larger is the acceleration of money, $\mu' - \mu$, and the greater is the sensitivity of money demand to changes in the nominal interest rate.

The Increase in the Nominal Interest Rate

Let's think about why the acceleration of money at date T leads to a rise in the nominal interest rate. At date T, people learn that the government will, henceforth, pursue a more expansionary monetary policy. They know also that this policy means a rate of inflation, $\pi' = \mu'$, which exceeds the initial rate, $\pi = \mu$. Consider what the higher expected rate of inflation does at date T in the credit market. Borrowers now regard the old nominal interest rate, R, as a better deal. That is because the real interest rate that they must pay has fallen from the value, $R - \mu$, to the lower value, $R - \mu'$. Hence, if the nominal interest rate did not change, borrowers would raise their demand for loans. On the other side, lenders see that their real rate of return has deteriorated. Therefore, if the nominal interest rate did not change, lenders would decrease their supply of loans. Overall, we can reattain balance between the demand and supply for loans—that is, clear the credit market—only if the nominal interest rate rises.

The new nominal interest rate, R', exceeds the old one, R, by the amount of the increase in the inflation rate, $\mu' - \mu$. Lenders view this rise in the nominal rate as just sufficient to compensate them for the loss of purchasing power over time because of the higher inflation rate. Similarly, borrowers are willing to pay the higher nominal interest rate because they expect to repay their loans with more heavily deflated dollars. In other words, the increase in the nominal interest rate incorporates fully the change in expected inflation. Thereby, the acceleration of money and prices does not change the real interest rate, r.

The Jump in the Price Level

Let's examine now why the price level jumps upward at date T. The sudden prospect of higher inflation and the consequent rise in the nominal interest rate lead to a fall in the real demand for money at date T. Therefore, if the price level did not adjust, people's actual real cash balances, M_T/P_T, would exceed their desired amount. Consequently, everyone would attempt to spend this excess cash by buying either goods or bonds. (The impact on the demand for goods is the real-balance effect.) The rise in the demand for goods puts upward pressure on the price level. In fact, the economy returns to a position of general market clearing only when the price level rises enough to equate actual and desired real cash. This condition is the one that we used to determine the size of the jump in the price level in Figure 8.2.

Wage Rates

If we added a labor market to the model, we would find again that the real wage rate, w/P, and the quantity of employment, N, were independent of money. Therefore, the path of nominal wage rates must parallel the path of prices, which appears in Figure 8.2. This means that nominal wages grow at rate μ up to date T, and at the higher rate μ' after date T. Further, we must have an upward jump in the nominal wage rate at date T.

Summarizing the Results for an Acceleration of Money

Let's summarize the results for a once-and-for-all increase in the growth rate of money. (A decrease in the growth rate of money just reverses the signs of all effects.)

- There are no changes in the real interest rate, the real wage rate, or the levels of output and employment.
- The inflation rate and the nominal interest rate (and the growth rate of nominal wages) rise by as much as the increase in the growth rate of money.
- The real demand for money and the actual quantity of real cash balances decrease.
- The price level jumps upward to equate actual real cash balances to the smaller quantity demanded.

Let's use these results to see whether money is superneutral—that is, whether the path of money matters for real variables. Recall that the path of money does not affect the real interest rate, the real wage rate, and the quantities of output and employment. However, because the acceleration of money raises the inflation rate, it also raises the nominal interest rate, and thereby lowers the amount of real money demanded. The resulting fall in real cash balances is one real effect of the change in monetary behavior. Therefore, money is not quite superneutral in the model.

Underlying the decline in real money demanded is an increase in the transaction costs that people incur in order to economize on cash. These costs absorb resources—therefore, the increase in these costs is an adverse real effect from the increase in monetary growth. Further, we neglected any effects of transaction costs on households' choices of work effort, consumption, and saving. If we took account of these effects, then we would find that an acceleration of money might influence the real interest rate, the real wage rate, and the quantities of output and employment. The independence of these real variables from the path of money is only an approximation, which is satisfactory when transaction costs are small.

Finally, we should stress that the present analysis assumes perfect foresight about future price levels (except for the jump in prices that accompanies the surprise acceleration of money at date T). Hence (except at date T), there is equality between actual and expected inflation, and thereby between actual and expected real interest rates. But we already saw in Chapter 7 that unexpected inflation has important effects on realized real interest rates. If inflation and hence future real interest rates are uncertain, there are a variety of real effects that would arise (some of which we shall explore in Chapter 18). At this point we have considered only the effects from anticipated variations in money and prices.

The Dynamics of Inflation

Consider again the case where monetary growth rises at date T from the initial value, μ, to the higher value, μ'. Let's think further about the transition from the initial rate of inflation, $\pi = \mu$, to the subsequent rate, $\pi' = \mu'$. Because the nominal interest rate increases, the level of real cash balances decreases. Hence, for real cash to fall, there must be a transition period during which prices rise by proportionately more than money. So far our analysis says that this transition occurs in an instant at date T via an upward jump in the price level. But in the real world there are a number of considerations that stretch out the transition over several periods. Here, we introduce some of these features to study some aspects of the dynamics of inflation.

Anticipated Changes in Monetary Growth

Our analysis can deal with situations where the growth rate of money either rises or falls. But so far, we have looked only at cases where the change in actual monetary growth coincides with the change in perceptions about future monetary growth. That is, two things happen at date T in the previous examples. First, money accelerates or decelerates permanently. Second, people first learn at date T that this acceleration or deceleration will occur.

Sometimes, people receive information in advance that allows them to forecast increases or decreases in the rate of monetary growth. For example, if the end of a war is imminent, then people would project a likely decline in the growth rate of money. Alternatively, during an extreme inflation, there may be promises of a change to a stable monetary regime. For instance, toward the end of the post-World War I **hyperinflation** in Germany, people apparently anticipated that a **monetary reform** was coming.[4] It is also possible that political events—such as the outcomes of elections—signal that the government plans to shift to a more or less expansionary monetary policy. For example, William Jennings Bryan campaigned for president in the 1890s on a program of easy money (free coinage of silver). His defeat probably lowered expectations of future monetary growth and inflation—presumably, these expectations would have increased if he had been elected. Similarly, it may be that the election of Ronald Reagan, rather than Jimmy Carter, in 1980 lowered expectations of future monetary growth and inflation.

If people forecast an acceleration or deceleration of money, then the path of inflation differs from those already discussed. To avoid a good deal of complicated details, we just sketch the types of effects that can arise.

Suppose, as an example, that people learn currently that an acceleration of money is coming at the future date T. Then they know also that inflation rates and nominal interest rates will be higher in the future. But because the cost of holding money rises from date T onward, people tend to reduce their demand for money even before date T. Otherwise, they will get caught holding money at date T when the big increase in prices occurs. Thus, the expectation

---

[4]Robert Flood and Peter Garber quantify these expectations of impending monetary reform in their paper, "An Economic Theory of Monetary Reform," *Journal of Political Economy*, February 1980. See also Laura Lahaye, "Inflation and Currency Reform," *Journal of Political Economy*, June 1985.

of future inflation has a negative effect on people's willingness to hold cash today. Then the reduction in today's demand for money means that today's price level must rise. In other words, even though the acceleration of money has not yet occurred, the expectation of the future monetary acceleration shows up today as a higher rate of inflation. Finally, since this higher rate of inflation becomes anticipated, the nominal interest rate also rises before the acceleration of money.

The precise path of inflation depends on when people learn about the acceleration of money. But, as mentioned, one general point is that changes in expectations about future money can generate variations in inflation and the nominal interest rate that precede the changes in monetary growth. Thus, although the analysis stresses monetary factors as the source of inflation, we find that significant divergences can arise in the short run between the growth rates of money and prices. Also, these divergences are likely to be important in an environment—such as those present today in the industrialized countries—where a volatile monetary policy induces frequent revisions in people's forecasts of monetary behavior. Such an environment would also be marked by volatility in inflation rates and nominal interest rates.

Gradual Adjustment of the Demand for Money

Let's return to the case where people first learn at date T that money will be growing at a higher rate. Recall that the size of the jump in the price level at date T depends on the extent of the fall in real money demanded. But suppose that people reduce their demand for money only gradually when the nominal interest rates increases. Then we may find only a small jump—or no jump at all—in the price level at date T. Instead, the extra upward kick to the price level shows up only gradually as people reduce their real demand for money. (Given the value of the real wage rate, the path of the nominal wage rate would parallel this path for the price level.)

Recall that a person's real demand for money reflects some underlying decisions about the frequency of transactions, financial planning, and so on. If the nominal interest rate rises, it is reasonable that people would take some time to modify these aspects of their behavior.[5] Hence, in the aggregate, the real demand for money would decline gradually in response to an increase in the nominal interest rate.

Slow adjustment in the demand for money effectively spreads out the jump in the price level over a transition interval. Now, when money accelerates at time T, the inflation rate reacts something like the solid line shown in Figure 8.3. Here, the inflation rate, π_t, exceeds the new growth rate of money, μ',

[5]Gradual adjustment to changed circumstances could also apply to households' decisions about work effort and consumption. We focus on slow adjustment of the demand for money for two reasons: first, there is empirical evidence that this lag in adjustment is significant, and second, the existence of this lag has a qualitative effect on the behavior of the price level.

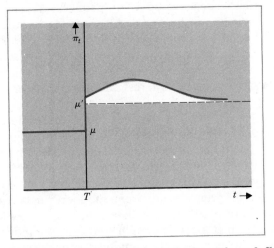

Figure 8.3 **The Effect of Higher Monetary Growth on Inflation, Including Gradual Adjustment of the Demand for Money**
The growth rate of money rises from μ to μ' at date T. The solid line shows that the inflation rate, μ_t, stays above μ' for awhile, but eventually approaches μ'.

over an extended interval.[6] Throughout this period, real cash balances fall gradually as the real demand for money declines. Eventually, the inflation rate approaches its new long-term value, μ'. Then the level of real cash again remains constant, but at a lower level than initially.

Let's stress a basic feature of these results. Although jumps in the price level need not occur, the acceleration of money must involve a transition during which prices rise by proportionately more than money. This conclusion follows inevitably from the eventual decline in real cash balances.

We can also turn the results around to deal with the case where money decelerates. Then, although a downward jump in the price level need not occur, we find that the transition must involve a period where prices grow by proportionately less than money. This result holds because the lower nominal interest rate raises the real demand for money.

As an example, consider a contractionary monetary policy where the government reduces monetary growth permanently from 10% per year to 5%. Presumably, the objective of this policy is to reduce inflation. Our analysis implies that there is a transition period during which the inflation rate is even less than 5% per year. In fact, there may be a deflation—that is, falling prices—for awhile. Thus, when contemplating a monetary policy to end inflation, we have to think about the potential for very low or negative rates of inflation as a temporary side effect.

---

[6]The figure shows that the inflation rate rises for awhile after date T, and later falls toward the value μ'. The details of this path depend on the precise specification of gradual adjustment in the demand for money.

Money and Prices During the German Hyperinflation

We can assess some of the theoretical results by examining the data on the post-World War I German hyperinflation. Here, we have something close to a laboratory experiment for studying the consequences of high and variable rates of monetary growth and inflation.[7] Over the period from 1921 to 1923, the rates of inflation ranged from near zero to over 500% per month! Further, the available data suggest that relatively small changes occurred in aggregate real variables, such as total output and employment. (However, the unanticipated part of inflation did cause major redistributions of income, especially in favor of people who began with large nominal debts.) Here, we use the data to focus on the interaction between monetary growth and inflation.

When inflation rates are volatile, it is impossible to predict accurately the real interest rate on loans that prescribe nominal interest rates. Therefore, this type of lending tends to disappear during hyperinflations, such as the one in Germany. Also, unlike Israel, Brazil, and some other high-inflation countries at the present day, Germany in the 1920s had no organized credit market in terms of indexed loans. (However, there was an active stock market and much dealing in assets that were denominated in foreign currencies.) So in terms of analyzing the demand for money during the German hyperinflation, we have no useful measures of the nominal interest rate. In this environment the best indicator of the cost of holding money comes directly from the expected rate of inflation, π^e. This rate tells people how much they lose by holding cash, rather than consuming or holding a durable good that maintains its value in real terms.

Table 8.1 summarizes the behavior of the monetary growth rate, μ, the inflation rate, π, and real cash balances, M/P, in Germany from 1920 until 1925. In most cases the table indicates the average growth rates of money and prices over 6-month intervals. Then the level of real money balances pertains to the ends of each of these intervals.

At the beginning of 1920 the growth rates of money and prices were already at the very high rate of about 6% per month. (Typically, when talking about hyperinflations, people measure these rates per month, rather than per year!) Then there was a deceleration of money to an average rate of less than 1% per month for the first half of 1921. Notice that, as our theory predicts, the growth rate of prices, π, fell by more

---

[7]Not surprisingly, the topic has fascinated many economists. Two of the more important studies are Costantino Bresciani-Turroni, *The Economics of Inflation*, Allen & Unwin, London, 1937; and Phillip Cagan, "The Monetary Dynamics of Hyperinflation," in M. Friedman, ed., *Studies in the Quantity Theory of Money*, University of Chicago Press, Chicago, 1956.

Table 8.1 Monetary Growth, Inflation, and Real Cash Balances during the German Hyperinflation

Period	μ (% per month)	π (% per month)	M/P (end-of-period) (1913 = 1.0)
2/20– 6/20	5.7	6.0	1.01
6/20–12/20	3.0	1.1	1.13
12/20– 6/21	0.8	0.1	1.18
6/21–12/21	5.5	8.4	0.99
12/21– 6/22	6.5	12.8	0.68
6/22–12/22	29.4	46.7	0.24
12/22– 6/23	40.0	40.0	0.24
6/23–10/23	233	286	0.03
Reform Period			
12/23– 6/24	5.9	−0.6	0.44
6/24–12/24	5.3	1.4	0.56
12/24– 6/25	2.0	1.6	0.57
6/25–12/25	1.2	0.4	0.60

Note: M is an estimate of the total circulation of currency. Until late 1923 the figures refer to total legal tender, most of which consists of notes issued by the Reichsbank. Later, the data include issues of the Rentenbank, private bank notes, and various "emergency moneys." However, especially in late 1923, many unofficial emergency currencies, as well as circulating foreign currencies, are not counted. We standardize the numbers so that the quantity outstanding in 1913 is 1.0. P is an index of the cost of living, based on 1913 = 1.0.

than the growth rate of money, μ, when money decelerated. Correspondingly, real cash balances increased by about 20% from early 1920 to early 1921. (The level of real cash in early 1920 was roughly equal to that from before the war in 1913.)

In 1922 money accelerated dramatically to an average growth rate of nearly 30% per month toward the end of the year. Note that during this period the growth rate of prices, π, exceeded that of money, μ. Hence, by late 1922 real cash balances fell to about one-fourth of the level prevailing in early 1920.

During the first half of 1923 there was some letup in the acceleration of money. Here money and prices grew together at the extraordinary average rate of 40% per month. Correspondingly, although the rate of inflation was enormous, the level of real cash remained fairly stable. But late in 1923 the hyperinflation built to its climax with rates of monetary expansion of 300 to 600% per month for October–November. Again, the acceleration of money led to rates of inflation that exceeded the growth rates of money. Therefore, real cash balances reached their low point in October 1923 at about 3% of the level for early 1920. So, if we neglect variations in aggregate real income from 1920 to 1923—which is satisfactory as a first-order approximation—then the reduction in real cash implies a rise in velocity by over 30-fold. In other words, if in 1920 people held the typical piece of currency for 2 weeks before spending it, then in October 1923 they held it for about half a day.

A major monetary reform occurred in Germany during November 1923. This reform included the introduction of a new type of currency, a promise not to print new money beyond a specified limit to finance government expenditures or for other purposes, some changes in government spending and taxes, and a commitment to back the new currency by gold.[8] In any event, there was a sharp curtailment in monetary growth and inflation after December 1923. For example, during 1924 monetary growth averaged 5–6% per month. But because of the deceleration of money after November 1923, the average inflation rate was even less—below 1% per month for 1924. Most dramatically, the quantity of real cash balances rose from 3% of the early-1920 level in October 1923 to 56% of that level by December 1924. (Much of the increase in real cash arose as an infusion of new types of currency during the reform months of November to December 1923.)

Finally, in 1925 the growth rate of money fell to 1–2% per month, while the inflation rate remained at roughly 1% per month. Correspondingly, there was a slow rise in real cash, which reached 60% of the early-1920 level by late 1925. Interestingly, although the inflation rate remained low for the remainder of the 1920s, the level of real cash did not reattain the early-1920 level. Perhaps this discrepancy reflects a long-lasting negative influence of the hyperinflation on people's willingness to hold money.

Some Real Effects of Anticipated Inflation

Real Cash Balances and Transaction Costs

In our discussion of superneutrality we mentioned that some real variables, such as aggregate output, were at least approximately independent of anticipated variations in money. But recall that we have not considered real effects from the unpredictability of inflation. During the German hyperinflation, these effects included massive redistribution of wealth and the disappearance of most

---

[8]For a discussion of the reform, see Costantino Bresciani-Turroni, op. cit., Chapter IX, and Peter Garber, "Transition from Inflation to Price Stability," *Carnegie-Rochester Conference Series on Public Policy*, Spring 1982.

organized loan markets. Also, there are some indications that the process of dealing with the severe inflation in late 1923 had adverse effects on aggregate output. But in any case, one clear real effect from inflation is the reduction of real cash balances. During the German hyperinflation this response was dramatic, with aggregate real cash falling to about 3% of its initial level.

Corresponding to the increase in expected inflation and the reduction in real cash, people expend more resources on transaction costs. Although we regard these costs as small in normal times, we cannot neglect them during extreme circumstances, such as the German hyperinflation. For example, people spent a significant portion of their time on the process of receiving wage and other payments once or twice per day and in searching rapidly to find outlets for their cash. Given these magnitudes, we would also predict that extreme inflation would have significant effects on aggregate output.

The Revenue from Money Creation

A different real effect from inflation concerns the **government's revenue from printing money.** In our theory the government uses this income solely to finance transfers. But more generally, governments use the printing press to pay for a variety of expenditures.

Recall that the real amount of revenue for period t is the quantity, $(M_t - M_{t-1})/P_t$. Using the condition, $M_t = (1 + \mu)M_{t-1}$, we can rewrite this expression as

$$\text{real revenue from printing money} = \frac{(M_t - M_{t-1})}{P_t} = \mu \cdot \frac{M_{t-1}}{P_t} \quad (8.17)$$

Economists often refer to the government's revenue from money creation as the **inflation tax.** A higher value of μ implies a higher value of the inflation rate, π, which implies a higher value for the nominal interest rate, $R = r + \pi$. Therefore, a higher growth rate of money generates a higher rate of tax on the holding of cash—people must forego interest at a higher rate in order to hold money. (We can also say that the higher value of π means that the real value of money declines at a faster rate.)

Note from equation 8.17 that the real revenue from money creation is the product of the growth rate of money, μ, and a term that approximates the level of aggregate real money held, M_{t-1}/P_t. Recall that an increase in μ leads to a reduction in real cash balances. Hence, if μ rises by, say, 10%, then real revenue increases only if the magnitude of the proportionate decline in real cash is by less than 10%. Empirically, this condition holds except for the most extreme cases. For example, during the German hyperinflation, the condition was apparently not violated until the growth rate of money approached 100% per month between July and August 1923. Until then, the government successfully extracted more real income by printing money at higher rates.

In normal times for most countries, the government obtains only a small portion of its revenue from printing money. For example, in recent years the Federal Reserve obtained about $10 to 15 billion from this source. These amounts correspond to between 1 and 3% of total U.S. government revenues, and to less than 1% of the GNP.[9] More broadly, for 14 industrialized countries over the period 1960–78, the revenue from money creation averaged about 1% of the GNP.[10]

In a few high-inflation countries, the revenue from money creation is far more important. As an extreme example, for Argentina over 1960–75, money creation accounted for nearly half of government revenues and for about 6% of the GNP. Some other countries where the revenue from printing money is important include Chile (5% of the GNP over 1960–77), Libya (3% of the GNP over 1960–77), and Brazil (3% of the GNP over 1960–78).[11]

During the German hyperinflation and in some other hyperinflations (such as Austria, Hungary, Poland, and Russia after World War I), money creation became the primary source of government revenue. Eventually, the amounts obtained approached 10 to 15% of the GNP, which appears to be about the maximum obtainable from printing money.[12] Also, there was a close month-to-month connection in Germany between the volume of real government spending and the growth rate of the money supply. That is, the variations in monetary growth—and hence, inflation—were driven in this case by shifts in real government spending.[13] Interestingly, much of the government spending over this period went to reparations payments associated with World War I. Therefore, the reduction in these payments after November 1923 was probably a major factor in the success of the German monetary reform.

Summary

We introduced monetary growth into the model by allowing for governmental transfer payments. By considering the government's budget constraint, we found that the aggregate of these transfers equals the change in the stock of

---

[9]See Robert Barro, "Measuring the Fed's Revenue from Money Creation," *Economics Letters*, 1982, Tables 2 and 3.

[10]See Stanley Fischer, "Seigniorage and the Case for a National Money," *Journal of Political Economy*, April 1982, Table A2.

[11]These figures are from Stanley Fischer, op. cit.

[12]These results come from Robert Barro, "Inflationary Finance and the Welfare Cost of Inflation," *Journal of Political Economy*, September/October 1972.

[13]For a detailed analysis of this process, see Zvi Hercowitz, "Money and the Dispersion of Relative Prices," *Journal of Political Economy*, April 1981.

money. Then we modified the concept of saving and the formulation of house-holds' budget constraints to include inflation. The main result is that saving and budget constraints involve the real interest rate, rather than the nominal rate. Similarly, the intertemporal-substitution effects on consumption and lei-sure depend on the real interest rate. When there is uncertainty about inflation, it is the expected real interest rate that matters for intertemporal-substitution effects.

We discussed how the various monetary terms—initial real cash, the pres-ent value of real transfers, and the interest foregone on future money—enter into households' budget constraints. Unless we bring in transaction costs, we find that there are no wealth effects from these terms on the aggregates of consumption and leisure.

The nominal interest rate, R, still determines the cost of holding money rather than bonds. Therefore, although the real interest rate matters for choices of consumption and work, it is the nominal rate that appears in the demand-for-money function.

We used the market-clearing model to analyze the interactions among monetary growth, inflation, and nominal and real interest rates. An important result is that the real interest rate, the real wage rate, and the aggregates of output and employment are invariant with anticipated variations in the quantity of money. However, money is not superneutral in the model. (By superneutral, we mean that variations in the path of money have no real effects.) The behavior of money influences the level of real cash balances, the nominal interest rate, and the volume of transaction costs. Further, the invariance of the real interest rate and aggregate output holds only as an approximation.

An increase in the growth rate of money shows up in the long run as parallel increases in the inflation rate, the nominal interest rate, and the growth rate of nominal wages. However, because the higher nominal interest rate reduces the real demand for money, there must be a transition interval during which the rate of inflation exceeds the growth rate of money. In a simple case the transition occurs in an instant via an upward jump in the price level. But if we bring in some realistic extensions of the model—such as foreknowledge of the acceleration of money and gradual adjustment of money demand—then we find a richer dynamics of prices during the transition. Here, the inflation rate exceeds the growth rate of money for awhile.

Similar results obtain for a decrease in the growth rate of money. Then the process of reducing inflation involves a transition period with unusually low rates of inflation, which may even be negative.

We illustrated some of the results by observing the dynamics of monetary growth and inflation during the post-World War I German hyperinflation. The data show that higher rates of monetary growth led to lower levels of real cash balances, while reductions in monetary growth had the opposite effect. We also discussed the effects of inflation on transaction costs and on the real revenue that the government obtains from printing money.

Appendix
The Wealth Effects from the Monetary Terms

Consider the right side of equation 8.9, which shows the real present value of a household's uses of funds over an infinite horizon. If we neglect transaction costs, we have to add the real present value of interest foregone from holding money. Thus, the new terms are

$$R \cdot \frac{m_1}{P_2(1+r)} + R \cdot \frac{m_2}{P_3(1+r)^2} + \cdots \tag{8.18}$$

where . . . represents similar terms involving m_3, m_4, and so on. To understand this series of terms, let's consider the first one. The term, Rm_1, is the dollar interest earnings that someone forgoes during period 2 because he or she holds the quantity of money, m_1, rather than bonds during period 1. Since the foregone interest income applies to period 2, we divide by period 2's price level, P_2, to convert to real terms. Then we divide by the discount factor, $(1+r)$, to express the result as a present value. Notice that the subsequent terms in expression 8.18 are similar, except for the discount factor. For example, for the second term, the discount factor is $(1+r)^2$.

For subsequent purposes, it is convenient to modify expression 8.18. Note that the first part of the expression involves the term, $P_2(1+r)$. But the price level for period 2, P_2, equals the quantity, $(1+\pi)P_1$, where π is the constant rate of inflation. Therefore we have

$$P_2(1+r) = P_1(1+\pi)(1+r) = P_1(1+R)$$

If we make this type of substitution for the price level in each term of expression 8.18, we obtain the simplified formula

$$\frac{R}{(1+R)} \cdot \left[\frac{m_1}{P_1} + \frac{(m_2/P_2)}{(1+r)} + \cdots \right] \tag{8.19}$$

Now consider the left side of equation 8.9, which shows the real present value of a household's sources of funds. To these terms we have to add the real value of the initial cash balances plus the present value of real transfers received from the government. Thus, the additional terms are

$$\frac{m_0}{P_1} + \left(\frac{v_1}{P_1} \right) + \frac{(v_2/P_2)}{(1+r)} + \frac{(v_3/P_3)}{(1+r)^2} + \cdots \tag{8.20}$$

We can sum up across households in expression 8.20 to determine the aggregate real present value of the new sources of funds. Then we get the expression

$$\frac{M_0}{P_1} + \left(\frac{V_1}{P_1} \right) + \frac{(V_2/P_2)}{(1+r)} + \frac{(V_3/P_3)}{(1+r)^2} + \cdots$$

But recall from the government's budget constraint that the aggregate transfer for each period, V_t, equals the change in the stock of money, $M_t - M_{t-1}$. If we make this substitution above, we obtain the revised form,

$$\left(\frac{M_0}{P_1}\right) + \left\{\frac{(M_1 - M_0)}{P_1} + \frac{(M_2 - M_1)}{[P_2(1+r)]} + \frac{(M_3 - M_2)}{[P_3(1+r)^2]} + \cdots\right\}$$

Observe that the first term, M_0/P_1, cancels with one of the terms inside the brackets. Hence we can rewrite the expression as

$$\left(\frac{M_1}{P_1}\right) - \frac{M_1}{[P_2(1+r)]} + \frac{M_2}{[P_2(1+r)]} - \frac{M_2}{[P_3(1+r)^2]}$$
$$+ \text{ terms that involve } M_3, M_4, \ldots$$

Recall that we can make the substitution

$$P_2(1+r) = P_1(1+\pi)(1+r) = P_1(1+R)$$

Therefore, we can combine the terms that involve M_1 in the above expression to get

$$\left(\frac{M_1}{P_1}\right)\left[1 - \frac{1}{(1+R)}\right] = \left(\frac{M_1}{P_1}\right) \cdot \frac{R}{(1+R)}$$

Similarly, the terms that involve M_2 simplify to

$$\left(\frac{M_2}{P_2}\right) \cdot \frac{[R/(1+R)]}{(1+r)}$$

If we put this all together, then the expression for the aggregate real present value of the new sources of funds becomes

$$\left[\frac{R}{(1+R)}\right]\left[\frac{M_1}{P_1} + \frac{(M_2/P_2)}{(1+r)} + \text{ similar terms that involve } M_3, M_4, \ldots\right]$$
$$(8.21)$$

But look at expression 8.19, which shows the real present value of a household's new uses of funds. The aggregate of these new uses coincides with the aggregate of the new sources, which appears in expression 8.21. Hence, as we wanted to show, the monetary terms have no impact in the aggregate on the sources net of the uses. Accordingly, we do not have to consider wealth effects on the aggregates of consumption and leisure from the combination of first, real cash balances; second, the present value of real transfers; and third, the interest foregone from future holdings of money.

Finally, let's stress again that aggregate wealth effects do arise when we consider the present value of real transaction costs. But as before, we assume as an approximation that we can neglect these effects.

Important Terms and Concepts

governmental budget constraint

lump-sum transfer

real saving

nominal saving

perfect foresight

superneutrality of money

hyperinflation

monetary reform

government's revenue from printing money

inflation tax

Mainly for Review

8.1 Consider an individual who lives for two periods, earns a nominal income of $1000 in each period, and has zero initial and terminal assets. The nominal interest rate, R, on dollar loans is 15%, and the expected rate of inflation, π^e, between the two periods is 10%. Assume that the price level in the first period is 1.

25%

a. What is the real value of period 1 income? $r = \pi^e + R$

b. What is the maximum amount of dollars that could be borrowed in period 1? Find the real value of this amount, and add it to the real value of period 1 income to see the maximum amount of (real) consumption possible in period 1.

c. What is the price level in period 2? What is the real value of period 2 income?

d. What is the maximum amount of dollars that can be obtained in period 2 by saving in period 1? Find the real value (in period 2) of this amount and add it to the real value of period 2 income to see the maximum amount of (real) consumption possible in period 2.

e. As in question 3.3 of Chapter 3, plot a graph showing the consumption possibilities in the two periods.

f. What is the slope of the budget line that you drew in part e? Show that it is equal to $-(1+R)/(1+\pi^e)$.

8.2 Based on your answer to question 8.1, explain why $(1+R)/(1+\pi^e)$, rather than one plus the nominal interest rate, is the correct measure of the trade-off between real consumption in the two periods. In what situation would it be appropriate to use the nominal interest rate? *current $ prices*

8.3 Distinguish bweeen the measures of nominal saving given in equations 8.3 and 8.6. Explain why, when inflation is positive, the first measure is an overestimate of saving for a net lender (an individual for whom $b_{t-1} > 0$). Can we make a similar comparison for a net debtor (an individual for whom $b_{t-1} < 0$)?

8.4 Suppose that the commodity market clears at a real interest rate of 4%.
   a. If the inflation rate is zero, what is the nominal interest rate? If the inflation rate is 10%, what is the nominal interest rate?
   b. If the nominal interest rate did not go up by the same amount as the inflation rate, what would happen to the commodity market—that is, would there be excess supply or excess demand?

8.5 Which of the following statements is correct?
   a. A constant rate of increase in the price level will lead to a continuous rise in the nominal interest rate.
   b. A continuous increase in the inflation rate will lead to a continuous rise in the nominal interest rate.

8.6 What would be the effect on the nominal interest rate of each of the following events?
   a. The announcement of a one-time increase in the money stock.
   b. The announcement of a planned increase in the rate of monetary growth.
   Why does the price level jump in both instances? Does the velocity of money increase in both cases?

8.7 Critically review the following statement: "The quantity theory of money predicts that the rate of inflation must equal the rate of monetary growth. In fact, the two are not equal; therefore the theory is wrong." How do factors such as an anticipated increase in inflation or gradual adjustment in the demand for money alter the prediction? What about factors considered in Chapter 7, such as growth in output?

8.8 Can the government always increase its revenue by raising the rate of monetary growth? How does the answer depend on the response of money demanded to the nominal interest rate?

Problems for Discussion

8.9 Inflation and the Demand for Money
   Suppose that households hold stocks of goods—for example, groceries—as well as money and bonds. Assume that these goods depreciate in a physical sense at the rate δ per year (δ is the Greek letter *delta*).
   a. What is the "nominal interest rate" on holdings of these goods? Does this interest rate affect the demands for stocks of goods and money?
   b. Assume that the nominal interest rate on bonds, R, does not change, but the expected inflation rate, π^e, rises. What happens to the demand for money?
   Note: This problem shows that the demand for money can involve substitution between money and goods, as well as between money and bonds. Therefore, the demand for money may change with a shift in the expected inflation rate, even if the nominal interest rate on bonds does not change.

8.10 Wealth and Substitution Effects from Inflation (optional)
   Suppose that the expected inflation rate, π^e, and the nominal interest rate, R,

each increase by 1 percentage point. Thus, the expected real interest rate on bonds does not change.

a. What happens to the real demand for money?

b. Underlying this demand for money, what happens to the real amount of transaction costs that people incur?

Assume now that we do not neglect the role of transaction costs in households' budget constraints.

c. What is the effect of higher inflation on people's wealth? Therefore, how do consumption and leisure respond?

d. Does higher expected inflation also exert substitution effects on consumption and leisure? (Note that, unlike consumption, leisure does not require people to use money.) Therefore, what is the overall effect of higher expected inflation on consumption and leisure?

8.11 The Superneutrality of Money

a. What is the meaning of the term, *superneutrality of money?*

b. Is money superneutral in our model? In particular, if the behavior of money changes, then which real variables change and which do not change? Explain the factors that underlie these results.

PART III

BUSINESS FLUCTUATIONS AND ECONOMIC GROWTH

This part of the book applies the model to the important problems of business fluctuations and economic growth. We start in Chapter 9 by incorporating investment, which plays a key role in the short-term fluctuations of an economy. We then consider the extent to which the model can explain some observed features of business cycles.

At this stage our model does not include the government's spending, taxes, and debt (which we take up in Chapters 12–14). Also, we do not allow any role for monetary disturbances as sources of changes in real economic activity (which we consider in Chapters 15–18). Thus, business fluctuations can arise in the model only because of supply shocks (that is, shifts in the production function) and perhaps from changes in preferences. Models that rely on these kinds of disturbances to explain economic fluctuations are called "real theories of business cycles." (Economists who use these models should perhaps be called "realists," as opposed to monetarists.) Such theories are receiving a lot of attention recently from researchers.[1] Later we shall build on the form of the analysis that we carry out here to understand business fluctuations that originate either from movements in the government's spending, taxes, and debt or from monetary changes.

---

[1]The term, "real business cycles," originates from John Long and Charles Plosser, "Real Business Cycles," *Journal of Political Economy*, February 1983. For a general discussion and an extension to include monetary disturbances, see Robert King and Charles Plosser, "Money, Credit and Prices in a Real Business Cycle," *American Economic Review*, June 1984.

In Chapter 10 we show that fluctuations in economic activity involve variations in unemployment. As a related matter we discuss the average or "natural" rate of unemployment, and show why it will be positive.

Finally, in Chapter 11, we take up the longer-term aspect of investment—namely, its manifestation over time as the accumulation of productive capital. This accumulation plays a central role in the process of long-term economic growth.

CHAPTER 9
INVESTMENT

Thus far we have simplified matters by pretending that labor services were the only variable input to the production process. Now we want to be more realistic by including capital services as well. We shall think primarily of **physical capital,** such as machines and buildings used by producers. In the national accounts this category is called **producer's durable equipment and structures.** But we can broaden this concept of capital to include the goods held as **inventories** by businesses. We might also add consumer durables, such as homes (called residential structures in the national accounts), automobiles, and appliances. In fact, we could usefully go further to include **human capital,** which measures the effects of education and training on the skills of workers. But while the main analysis applies also to human capital, we shall confine most of our thinking here to physical capital.

The Capital Stock in the United States

Let's start with an overview of the U.S. capital stock. Figure 9.1 shows how a standard concept of physical capital evolved from 1926 until 1985. This concept, called **private fixed capital,** includes producers' durable equipment and structures, plus residential structures.[2] It turns out that the residential component accounts for about half the total throughout the period, 1926–85. Note that this definition of capital excludes business inventories (which are

---

[2]The data are from John Musgrave, "Fixed Capital Stock in the United States: Revised Estimates," *U.S. Survey of Current Business,* February 1981, and "Fixed Reproducible Tangible Wealth in the United States," *U.S. Survey of Current Business,* August 1984. The figure for the end of 1984 is estimated by using the value of net fixed investment for 1984 (from *U.S. Survey of Current Business,* March 1986, Tables 1.2 and 1.10).

Figure 9.1 The Stock of Private Fixed Capital in the United States
The figure shows the quantity of capital on a proportionate scale. The data run from the start of 1926 until the start of 1985.

not part of "fixed" capital), as well as consumer durables other than homes. Also, the measure ignores any capital that is owned by governments. The data are in real terms—that is, they express the quantity of capital in terms of dollar values for the base year, 1972. In addition the numbers are net of depreciation, which we shall discuss later.

Notice that the quantity of capital grew throughout the post-World War II period. In particular, from 1946 to 1985, the average growth rate was 3.7% per year. However, the capital stock behaved very differently before 1946. After growing for most of the 1920s (only partially shown in the figure), the stock declined during the depressed years of the 1930s. Then, after some growth for 1940–41, the stock declined again during World War II.

Capital in the Production Function

Here, we begin to incorporate capital into the theoretical model. To keep things manageable, we pretend that there is a single type of capital, which we can measure in physical units—for example, as a number of standard-type machines. Denote by k_{t-1} the quantity of capital that a producer has at the end of period $t-1$. Because it takes time to make new capital operational, we assume that the stock from period $t-1$ is available for use in production during period t. In other words, it takes one period for newly acquired capital to become on line.

The production function is now

$$y_t = f(k_{t-1}, n_t) \qquad (9.1)$$
$$(+)\,(+)$$

where the variable, k_{t-1}, is capital input and the variable, n_t, is labor input. In the real world there are variations in the **utilization rate** of capital. For example, a factory, which is a type of capital, may operate for one shift per day or two. But we neglect these possibilities for the production function shown in equation 9.1. Here, we can think of the quantity of capital, k_{t-1}, as always operating for one standard-length shift per day.

The plus signs under the two inputs in equation 9.1 signify that each is productive at the margin. That is, an increase in either input, with the other held fixed, leads to more output. Remember that the marginal product of labor for period t, MPL_t, is the effect on output, y_t, from an extra unit of work, n_t. Note that we hold fixed the quantity of capital, k_{t-1}, when we measure the marginal product of labor. Hence, this marginal product indicates the response of output when labor increases by 1 unit, while capital does not change.

We define the **marginal product of capital** in a similar manner. This marginal product, MPK_{t-1}, is the response of output, y_t, when capital, k_{t-1}, increases by 1 unit, while the amount of work, n_t, does not change. Notice that the dating on this marginal product shows that it relates to the quantity of capital, k_{t-1}, from the end of period $t-1$. However, because of the lag in making new capital operational, this marginal product refers to the effect on output for period t.

We discussed before the diminishing marginal productivity of labor. Specifically, labor's marginal product, MPL_t, falls as the amount of work increases, at least if the quantity of capital does not change. Now we make a parallel assumption about the marginal product of capital. This marginal product, MPK_{t-1}, declines as the quantity of capital, k_{t-1}, increases, at least if the amount of labor does not change.

Figure 9.2 shows how output responds as a producer uses more capital. Here, we hold fixed the quantity of labor. Notice that the curve goes through the origin, which means that a producer gets no output if the capital stock is zero. The slope of the curve is the marginal product of capital, MPK_{t-1}. Note

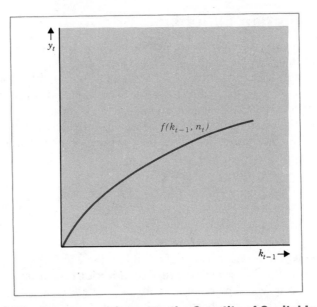

Figure 9.2 The Response of Output to the Quantity of Capital Input
The graph shows the effect on output, y_t, of a change in capital input, k_{t-1}. Here, the quantity of labor, n_t, does not change.

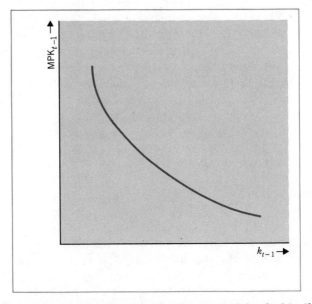

Figure 9.3 The Relation of the Marginal Product of Capital to the Quantity of Capital
The graph shows that the marginal product of capital, MPK_{t-1}, declines as the amount of capital, k_{t-1}, increases.

that the slope is positive throughout, but declines as the amount of capital increases. To stress this relationship, we show it explicitly in Figure 9.3. Here, the marginal product, MPK_{t-1}, declines as the quantity of capital, k_{t-1}, rises. (Recall that the curve assumes a fixed amount of labor, n_t.)

Investment Goods and Consumer Goods

We define investment to be the purchase of capital goods—for example, machines or buildings—from the commodity market. With firms in the model, we would think of most investment as being carried out by firms. But, as before, we find it simpler to neglect firms. Then we think of households in their role of producers as carrying out investment.

Generally, capital goods differ physically from consumer goods. But to keep things simple, we assume that there is only one physical good that people produce and exchange on the commodity market. One person buys this good for consumption purposes, while another buys it to accumulate more capital— that is, for investment purposes.

The analysis does not actually require consumer goods and capital goods to be physically the same. Instead, we are assuming something about the way people can shift from producing consumables to producing capital goods. For example, suppose that someone can use a combination of the productive inputs to make either X_1 units of consumables or X_2 units of capital. The ratio, X_2/X_1, indicates the terms on which the producer can substitute output of capital goods for output of consumables. Then our basic assumption is that the ratio, X_2/X_1, is constant. The terms on which production of capital goods can be substituted for production of consumables do not depend on either the producer's or the economy's level of production for the two types of goods. Also, we do not allow for any time to elapse while people shift from one type of production to another.[3]

If the substitution ratio for producers, X_2/X_1, is constant, then we may as well pick physical units for consumer goods and capital so that this ratio equals one. That is, we can measure things so that people can shift from producing one unit of consumer goods into producing one unit of capital goods and vice versa. But then this setup amounts to the one that we described before, in which the two types of goods were physically identical. So from now on, we pretend that these two goods are physically the same.

---

[3]Our setup is called a *one-sector production technology*. This specification, which appears in most macroanalyses, has only one process that allows people to use inputs to produce goods. Some economists use a *two-sector production model*. Then there is one process for producing consumer goods and another for capital goods. (However, there is still only one physical type of capital and only one physical type of consumable.) For an example of a model with a two-sector production technology, see Duncan Foley and Miguel Sidrauski, *Monetary and Fiscal Policy in a Growing Economy,* Macmillan, New York, 1971, especially Chapter 2.

As before, producers sell all of their output, y_t, on the commodity market at the price, P_t. People buy these goods either for consumption, c_t, or investment, which we denote by i_t. Therefore, a household's total demand for goods, y_t^d, equals the sum of consumption demand, c_t^d, and investment demand, i_t^d. (We can add these two magnitudes since they are measured in the same physical unit.) Because all goods sell at the same price, suppliers do not care whether their goods are labeled as consumer goods or investment goods. Therefore, we shall focus on a producer's total supply of goods, y_t^s.

Depreciation

Capital goods do not last forever, but rather tend to depreciate—or wear out—over time. We model this process in a simple form, where the amount of depreciation during period t is a constant fraction of the stock of capital carried over from period $t-1$. In other words, if d_t denotes the amount of depreciation in units of commodities, then

$$d_t = \delta k_{t-1} \qquad (9.2)$$

where δ (the Greek letter *delta*) is the constant rate of depreciation per period. For example, the depreciation rate δ might be 10% per year. Here we can think of the quantity of capital goods, d_t, as effectively disappearing or "evaporating" during period t.

We still assume that the capital held over from period $t-1$, k_{t-1}, is the pertinent input for production during period t. Then, to calculate the stock that is available for the next period's production, we have to add investment, i_t, and subtract depreciation, d_t. Therefore, the capital stock at the end of period t and available for production in period $t+1$ is

$$k_t = k_{t-1} + i_t - \delta k_{t-1} \qquad (9.3)$$

Recall that a producer purchases the quantity of investment goods, i_t, during period t. But the change in the capital stock, $k_t - k_{t-1}$, equals these purchases less the depreciation of existing stocks, δk_{t-1}. Hence, there are two concepts of investment, as follows:

- Gross investment is the quantity of capital goods purchased, i_t.
- Net investment is the change in the capital stock, $k_t - k_{t-1}$, which equals gross investment, i_t, less the amount of depreciation, δk_{t-1}.

Correspondingly, there are also two concepts of output:

- Gross product is the total amount produced, y_t.
- Net product equals gross product less depreciation, $y_t - \delta k_{t-1}$. That is, net product is the quantity of goods that someone produces net of the amount needed to replace the capital goods that wear out during the period.

Gross Investment, Depreciation, and Net Investment in the United States

Figure 9.4 shows the behavior of aggregate real gross investment, I_t, depreciation, D_t, and net investment, $I_t - D_t$, in the United States from 1929 to 1985. The numbers refer to private fixed domestic investment, which includes purchases of business plant and equipment, plus residential construction. Thus, the concept of investment corresponds to the measure of the capital stock that we looked at before in Figure 9.1. In Figure 9.4 we express the amounts of

Figure 9.4 **The Ratios of Investment and Depreciation to the Capital Stock**
The graph shows the ratios to the capital stock, K_{t-1}, of gross investment, I_t, depreciation, D_t, and net investment, $I_t - D_t$. The data on investment and depreciation run from 1929 until 1985.

investment as ratios to the stock of capital from the end of the previous year, K_{t-1}.

The numbers for depreciation are rough estimates that assume specified service lives for different types of capital. Therefore, the ratio of measured depreciation to the capital stock changes only when there are shifts in the average service life of the existing capital. The ratio of measured depreciation to the capital stock is relatively stable, ranging between 4.9 and 7.2% from 1929 to 1985. However, because of a recent shift away from investment in plant and toward investment in shorter-lived equipment, the ratio rose from 5.8% in 1967 to 7.2% in 1985.

By contrast, the ratio of net investment to the capital stock is volatile. From 1946 to 1985, the mean of this ratio was 3.8%. But the numbers ranged from 1.8% in 1982 to 5.8% in 1948. In fact, low numbers for this ratio identify years of recession—that is, times where output has been growing at a relatively low rate, which is sometimes negative. The list of the lowest ratios for net investment to the capital stock—1.8% for 1982, 2.1% for 1975, 2.4% for 1983, 2.6% for 1976, 2.8% for 1981, 2.8% for 1980, and 2.8% for 1958—picks out the main recessions of the post-World War II period. Conversely, the ratio tends to be high in years of economic boom, where total output grows rapidly.

We see a stronger version of the same pattern before World War II. Notice that net investment was negative during the years of the Great Depression, 1931–33. In fact, net investment did not become positive again until 1937. Then the recession of 1938 generated another year of negative net investment. Note also that net investment was negative during World War II. However, we shall postpone our consideration of this behavior until we study government expenditures in Chapter 12.

Another thing to note from Figure 9.4 is that the fluctuations in the ratio for gross investment parallel those in the ratio for net investment. This property holds because the ratio for depreciation (as measured) is relatively stable.

Figure 9.5 shows the ratios of gross investment, depreciation, and net investment to real gross national product (GNP). Again, the movements in the investment ratios indicate the recessions. Because investment fluctuates by proportionately more than total output, we find that investment's share of output declines during a recession. For example, from 1946 to 1985, the mean of the ratio of net investment to GNP was 5.6%. But the lowest values of this ratio—again the years of major recession—were 2.9% for 1982, 3.3% for 1975, 3.7% for 1983, 4.0% for 1976, 4.2% for 1981, 4.3% for 1980, and 4.3% for 1958. Conversely, the ratio of net investment to GNP tends to be high in years where total output grows rapidly.

Real GNP and its Components during Recessions

In this section we explore the behavior of real GNP, and especially of its investment component, during economic downturns in the United States. If we examined times of economic upturn, then we would reach similar conclu-

Figure 9.5 The Ratios of Investment and Depreciation to GNP
The graphs show the ratios to real GNP of gross investment, I_t, depreciation, D_t, and net investment, $I_t - D_t$. The data run from 1929 until 1985.

sions, except that all signs would be reversed. (Perhaps the tendency to focus on recessions rather than booms reflects the sour disposition of economists.)

Table 9.1 shows how real GNP behaved during recent recessions in the United States. Consider, for example, the recession of 1957–58. Real GNP for 1958 was $680.9 billion. Using real GNP for 1956 as a benchmark, we can calculate the real GNP that would have resulted in 1958 if output had grown at the annual rate of 3.0% (the average rate for 1929–85). This value, labeled Y^0 in the table, is $713.1 billion. Hence, the gap between this value and actual real GNP is $32.2 billion, which constitutes a shortfall in output of 4.5%. Overall, this concept of a shortfall in output gives us a reasonable estimate for the magnitude of a recession. However, the precise numbers are sensitive to the choices for benchmark years and for the trend growth rate of output.

Table 9.1 shows the results of this calculation for the seven U.S. recessions since World War II and for the Great Depression of 1929–33. Notice that

Table 9.1 Consumption and Investment during Recessions

Final Year of Recession Benchmark Year for Comparison	1933 1929	1949 1948	1954 1953	1958 1956	1961 1959	1970 1969	1975 1973	1982 1979	Mean for 7 Post-War Recessions
Shortfall of Real GNP (billions of 1972 dollars)	133.9	12.5	26.6	32.2	9.7	35.1	100.3	138.7	—
Shortfall as % of Trend Real GNP	37.6	2.5	4.1	4.5	1.3	3.1	7.5	8.6	4.5
% of shortfall in real GNP accounted for by:									
Personal consumption									
Expenditures	54	19	17	39	64	16	36	37	33
Durables	10	−16	3	20	46	16	16	15	14
Nondurables and services	44	34	14	19	19	−1	20	22	19
Gross fixed investment	33	73	4	42	64	30	51	33	42
Nonresidential	24	53	10	31	8	19	27	14	23
Residential	9	21	−6	10	56	11	24	19	19
Change in business inventories	8	81	11	25	45	22	25	13	32
Other[a]	5	−73	68	−6	−73	32	−12	17	−7
Total investment[b]	51	138	18	87	155	68	92	61	88

[a]Government purchases and exports less imports.

[b]Purchases of consumer durables plus gross fixed investment plus change in business inventories.

Note: The method for calculating the shortfall in each component is discussed in the text.

Source: Economic Report of the President, 1985, Table B-2.

the sharpest post-war contractions were the ones for 1982[4] and 1975, where the shortfalls in output were by 8.6 and 7.5%, respectively. On average for the seven cases, the shortfall in real GNP was by 4.5%. By contrast, for 1933, the estimated shortfall was a remarkable 38%.

We use the same method in Table 9.1 to compute the shortfalls in the main components of real GNP.[5] For the seven post-war recessions we find that the mean shares for the shortfall in real GNP were 33% in personal consumption expenditures, 42% in gross fixed investment, 32% in changes in business inventories, and −7% in other categories (government purchases and

---

[4]There is some controversy as to whether to treat 1980 and 1982 as the final years of two distinct recessions, or to consider 1980–82 as one prolonged contraction. (The "official" verdict on such matters is decided at a festive dinner hosted by the National Bureau of Economic Research.) Since the intervening recovery in late 1980 and early 1981 was so brief, we treat 1980–82 as a single recession.

[5]Except for the category labeled *other,* the calculated shortfall in any component is the difference of a trend value from the actual. The trend value assumes 3% annual growth from the benchmark year. For the category labeled other, the estimated shortfall is the total shortfall in GNP less the sum of the components calculated separately.

exports less imports).[6] To put the results another way, although the mean ratio of consumption expenditures to GNP over the post-war period was 62%, the fluctuations in these expenditures accounted on average for only 33% of the fall in output during recessions. The reason is that consumption fluctuates proportionately much less than total output, which in turn fluctuates much less than gross (or net) investment.

By using personal consumption expenditures, we substantially overstate the fluctuations in consumption. This category includes purchases of consumer durables (except for residences), such as automobiles and home appliances. These goods last for many years and are used to provide flows of services, such as transportation, food preparation, house cleaning, and so on. We should view these durables as forms of capital goods that happen to be owned and used in the real world by households, rather than businesses. Hence, we should treat purchases of consumer durables as a form of gross investment.

The last line of Table 9.1 adds together all the investment components—gross fixed investment, changes in business inventories, and purchases of consumer durables. Notice that this total accounts on average for 88% of the shortfall in real GNP during recessions. By contrast, although the mean ratio of consumer expenditures on nondurables and services to GNP was 54%, this component accounts on average for only 19% of the shortfall in output. To put this result another way, the shortfall in the consumption of nondurables and services during recessions turns out to average only 1.7% of the trend value of this component. The main point is that consumption is remarkably stable. As a first approximation, explaining recessions amounts to explaining the sharp contractions in the investment components.

Finally, notice the figures for the Great Depression of 1929–33. In this case the consumption of nondurables and services accounted for 44% of the shortfall in real GNP, while the total of the investment components accounted for 51%. Thus, the cutback in consumption was relatively more important during the Depression than it has been for the milder contractions since World War II.

Overall, there are several features of the data that we would like our theory to explain. In particular, we want to know why

- Investment is far more volatile than consumption.
- The ratio of investment to GNP or the stock of capital is low during recessions and high in booms.
- Consumption expenditures—especially on nondurables and services—decline little in proportional terms during mild recessions, but fall significantly during a severe contraction.

---

[6]For the 1954 and 1970 recessions, the large contribution from the other category reflects the sharp cutbacks in military spending after the Korean and Vietnam Wars, respectively. For the 1949 and 1961 recessions, there were substantial increases in government purchases. Therefore, the other category shows large negative contributions to the shortfall of real GNP.

Characteristics of Existing Capital

Let's return now to the theoretical analysis. Remember that producers can call their output either consumables or capital. But once a purchaser has put capital into place—for example, as a factory—it would be unrealistic to assume that these goods can be reclassified as consumables and then eaten up. Hence, we assume that the initial labeling choice as consumables or capital is irreversible. In other words, producers cannot consume their capital at a later date. However, they can allow capital to depreciate and not replace it.

A second issue concerns the possibilities for moving capital goods from one production activity to another. Here, we simplify the analysis by assuming that these movements are possible at negligible cost. This mobility of capital ensures that producers place all existing stocks in their most favorable use. Otherwise, someone could do better by shifting capital to another location. Recall also that we treat all units of capital as physically identical. Therefore, each unit must end up with the same physical marginal product.

Sometimes, we shall find it convenient to think of a resale market for used capital. Then, if a piece of capital has a low marginal product for one person, he or she will find it advantageous to sell the capital to someone else. But since old and new capital are identical, the price of a unit of capital during period t on the resale market must equal that for new units, which is P_t. Given this result, we can think of old capital goods as being sold along with new ones on the commodity market. Hence, we do not have to worry about a separate market for resales.

Investment Demand

Consider a producer's incentive to invest during period t. Recall that the stock of capital that will be available for production next period is the quantity

$$k_t = k_{t-1} + i_t - \delta k_{t-1}$$

At date t, the previous stock, k_{t-1}, and the amount of depreciation, δk_{t-1}, are givens. Therefore, an increase by 1 unit in gross investment, i_t, means an increase by 1 unit in net investment, $i_t - \delta k_{t-1}$, and also an increase by 1 unit in the stock of capital, k_t. Hence, each producer decides how much to invest during period t by weighing the cost of this investment against the return from having more capital, k_t.

To raise investment by 1 unit, a producer must purchase an additional unit of goods from the commodity market at the price, P_t. Hence, P_t is the dollar cost of an extra unit of investment.

There are two components of the return to investment. First, an additional unit of investment raises capital, k_t, by 1 unit. If we hold fixed the quantity of work for the next period, n_{t+1}, then next period's output, y_{t+1}, rises by the marginal product of capital, MPK_t. Since producers sell this output at the price, P_{t+1}, the additional dollar sales revenue is the amount, $P_{t+1} \cdot \text{MPK}_t$.

Remember that the fraction, δ, of each unit of capital disappears after one period because of depreciation. But the remaining fraction, $1 - δ$, is still around. We can simplify the analysis, without harming anything, by pretending that producers sell their old capital on the commodity market at date $t+1$. (If they like, they can "buy back" this capital during period $t+1$ to use for production at date $t+2$. But that decision is separate from the choice of investment at date t, which we are now considering.) Since goods sell at price P_{t+1} during period $t+1$, the dollar revenue from the sale of used capital is the amount, $(1 - δ)P_{t+1}$. Hence, this term is the second part of the return to investment.

Overall, an additional unit of investment costs P_t during period t and yields the amount, $P_{t+1}(\text{MPK}_t + 1 - δ)$ in period $t+1$. Therefore the dollar return on the investment is the difference, $P_{t+1}(\text{MPK}_t + 1 - δ) - P_t$. If we divide by the number of dollars invested, P_t, we determine the nominal rate of return to investment, which is

$$\frac{P_{t+1}(\text{MPK}_t + 1 - δ) - P_t}{P_t} = (1 + π_t)(\text{MPK}_t + 1 - δ) - 1$$

Here, we use the condition, $P_{t+1} = (1 + π_t)P_t$, where $π_t$ is the inflation rate for period t.

The nominal rate of return from investment looks good or bad depending on its relation to other available returns. Specifically, people can earn the nominal interest rate, R_t, on bonds. Also, they would pay this rate if they decide to borrow funds to finance investment. If the nominal rate of return from investment exceeds the nominal interest rate, R_t, producers would like to raise investment—that is, buy more capital goods. But as the capital stock rises, diminishing marginal productivity implies that capital's marginal product, MPK_t, falls. Eventually, this decline in the marginal product reduces the nominal rate of return to investment enough to equal the nominal interest rate, R_t. Then producers have no further incentive to expand investment.

Algebraically, investors act to satisfy the condition

$$(1+π_t)(\text{MPK}_t + 1 - δ) - 1 = R_t$$

where the left side is the nominal rate of return from investment. However, recall that the real rate of return on bonds, r_t, satisfies the relation, $(1+r_t) = (1+R_t)/(1+π_t)$. Using this condition, we can simplify the above result to the form

$$\text{MPK}_t - δ = r_t \tag{9.4}$$

Equation 9.4 is the basic condition for determining investment demand.

The left side of equation 9.4 is the real rate of return from an additional unit of investment. In the absence of depreciation—that is, $δ = 0$—this rate of return would be the marginal product of capital, MPK_t. But, when there is depreciation, we lose δ units of goods per year for each unit of investment. Therefore, we have to subtract the rate of depreciation, δ, from the marginal product, MPK_t, to calculate the net **real rate of return from investment.**

Equation 9.4 says that investors act to equate the real rate of return from investment to the real rate of return on bonds, r_t. Any difference between these two rates makes it profitable to select either a higher or lower amount of investment. Therefore, the amount of investment that people choose generates a marginal product, MPK_t, that equates the two real rates of return.

We show the results graphically in Figure 9.6. As the quantity of capital k_t rises, the marginal product MPK_t declines, as shown in the upper curve in the figure. The real rate of return from an extra unit of investment is the amount, $MPK_t - \delta$, which we show on the lower curve in the figure. A producer chooses the quantity of capital, denoted by $\hat{k}_t$, where the real rate of return from investment, $MPK_t - \delta$, equals the real interest rate, r_t.

Given the schedule for capital's marginal product, the **desired stock of capital**, $\hat{k}_t$, depends on the real interest rate, r_t, and the depreciation rate, δ. Hence, we can write the desired stock of capital as the function

$$\hat{k}_t = \hat{k}_t(r_t, \ \delta, \ \ldots) \qquad (9.5)$$
$$(-)(-)$$

The expression . . . represents the characteristics of the production function that affect the schedule for capital's marginal product. Note that an increase in r_t or δ means that the marginal product of capital, MPK_t, must be higher in equation 9.4. Therefore, for a given schedule of capital's marginal product (Figure 9.6), the desired stock of capital declines. To put it another way, we can think of capital and bonds as alternative assets that someone can hold.

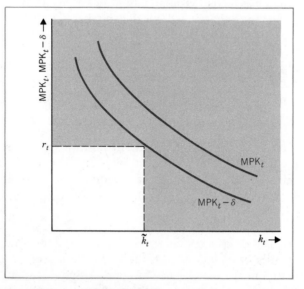

Figure 9.6 The Choice of Capital Stock
Producers aim for the quantity of capital, $\hat{k}_t$, where the real rate of return from investment, $MPK_t - \delta$, equals the real interest rate on bonds, r_t.

Accordingly, an increase in the real interest rate on bonds makes it less attractive for investors to accumulate capital, rather than holding bonds.

For given values of the real interest rate and the rate of depreciation, an upward shift in the schedule for capital's marginal product raises the desired stock of capital. We can show this result graphically by shifting the two curves upward in Figure 9.6.

Once we know the desired stock of capital, $\hat{k}_t$, we know also the choice of gross investment, i_t. Specifically, to attain the stock $\hat{k}_t$, a producer demands for investment purposes the quantity of goods i_t^d, where

$$i_t^d = \hat{k}_t - (1 - \delta)k_{t-1}$$

Notice that, for given values of the starting capital stock, k_{t-1}, and depreciation, δk_{t-1}, gross **investment demand** varies one-to-one with changes in the desired stock of capital $\hat{k}_t$.

Using equation 9.5, we can write out a function for gross investment demand as

$$i_t^d = \hat{k}(r_t, \ \delta, \ldots) - (1 - \delta)k_{t-1} = i^d(r_t, \ \delta, k_{t-1}, \ldots) \qquad (9.6)$$
$$(-)(-) \qquad\qquad\qquad\qquad (-)(?)(-)$$

The implied amount of net investment demand is

$$i_t^d - \delta k_{t-1} = \hat{k}(r_t, \ \delta, \ldots) - k_{t-1} \qquad (9.7)$$
$$(-)(-)$$

Properties of Investment Demand

Here, we summarize the main implications of the analysis for investment demand.

- A reduction in the real interest rate, r_t, raises the desired stock of capital, $\hat{k}_t$. Therefore, given the initial stock k_{t-1}, investment demand rises.

- Given the real interest rate, an upward shift in the schedule for capital's marginal product, MPK$_t$, raises the desired stock of capital, $\hat{k}_t$. Hence, given the initial stock of capital, k_{t-1}, investment demand increases.

- Other things equal, investment demand declines if the previous stock of capital, k_{t-1}, rises. By "other things equal," we mean to include the various elements that determine the desired stock of capital, $\hat{k}_t$. Recall that net investment demand equals the quantity, $\hat{k}_t - k_{t-1}$. Therefore, this demand falls with a rise in the initial stock, k_{t-1}. Gross investment demand equals the quantity, $\hat{k}_t - (1-\delta)k_{t-1}$. As long as the depreciation rate, δ, is less than 100%, a rise in the initial stock, k_{t-1}, means less gross investment demand, i_t^d.

- An increase in the rate of depreciation, δ, lowers the desired stock of capital, $\hat{k}_t$. Therefore, net investment demand, $\hat{k}_t - k_{t-1}$, declines. However, recall again that gross investment demand equals the quantity, $\hat{k}_t - (1-\delta)k_{t-1}$. Because the desired capital stock declines, while depreciation rises, the overall effect on gross investment demand is ambiguous.

- Gross investment demand is positive as long as the desired stock, $\hat{k}_t$, exceeds the fraction, $1-\delta$, of the initial stock, k_{t-1}. Negative gross investment means that someone's sales of old capital goods exceeds his or her purchases of new ones.

We assumed before that capital goods cannot be converted back into consumables. Therefore, one person's negative gross investment (sales of capital goods) must correspond to someone else's positive gross investment. Hence, when we aggregate over all producers, we cannot have negative gross investment, I_t. To put this result another way, the aggregate stock of capital, K_t, cannot fall below the initial stock, K_{t-1}, by more than the amount of depreciation, δK_{t-1}. Correspondingly, aggregate net investment, $K_t - K_{t-1} = I_t - \delta K_{t-1}$, can be negative only up to the magnitude of depreciation, δK_{t-1}.

Recall from Figure 9.4 that the aggregate of private fixed net investment was, in fact, substantially positive for each year since the end of World War II. However, this aggregate was negative during the Great Depression and World War II. Thus, our interpretation is that the aggregate desired stock of capital, $\hat{K}_t$, fell below the initial stock, K_{t-1}, during these years.

Quantitative Effects on Investment Demand

Let's think about the quantitative behavior of net investment demand. Since World War II, aggregate investment has averaged about 4% of the capital stock, K_{t-1}. Consider changes in the real interest rate, r_t, or in the schedule for capital's marginal product, MPK_t. These changes affect the aggregate desired stock of capital, $\hat{K}_t$. Suppose, as an example, that some change occurs that reduces this desired stock by 1%. Then the aggregate of net investment demand—over a period of, say, a year—declines by about 1% of the capital stock. If net investment demand were initially equal to 4% of the capital stock, then this change lowers it to 3% of the stock. Thus, a decline by 1% in the desired stock of capital translates into a fall by roughly 25% in one year's net investment demand. Because one year's net investment is a small fraction—on the average about 4%—of the existing capital stock, small percentage changes in the desired stock generate large percentage changes in net investment demand. Therefore, we should not be surprised by two features of the U.S. data, which appear in Figures 9.4 and 9.5. First, because aggregate net investment demand is volatile, the share of net investment in GNP fluctuates substantially from year to year. Second, the desired stock of capital is sometimes low enough—namely, during the Great Depression and World War II—so that aggregate net investment is negative.

Absence of a Resale Market

In determining the choice of investment, we pretend that producers resell the undepreciated portion of their capital, $(1-\delta)k_{t-1}$, on the commodity market during period t. Then, if they desire, producers can again buy investment goods in period $t+1$, resell them in period $t+2$, and so on. By pretending that people resell their old capital, we can easily calculate the rate of return to investment over one period. But this device is artificial. Typically, a producer keeps a piece of capital for many years. In fact, the sale of used capital goods is unusual for most types of producers' equipment and structures (although it is common for residences and automobiles).

In most cases our analysis of investment goes through even if resales are impossible. In the previous setup, a producer resells the quantity of capital, $(1-\delta)k_{t-1}$, during period t, and then buys back the desired stock, $\hat{k}_t$. The difference between purchases and sales is the quantity, $\hat{k}_t - (1-\delta)k_{t-1}$, which equals gross investment demand, i_t^d.

If we look only at producers who always have positive gross investment demand, then the potential for resale is irrelevant. That is because someone with positive gross investment does not have to resell any capital. The producer just keeps the existing capital, and then buys new goods in the amount, i_t^d. In this case, there are no changes if we eliminate the possibility for resale.[7]

Remember that gross investment demand, i_t^d, equals net investment demand, $\hat{k}_t - k_{t-1}$, plus depreciation, δk_{t-1}. Therefore, for the previous results to hold, we do not need net investment demand to be positive for the typical producer. Rather, we need only to rule out net investment demand being so negative that it outweighs the positive amount of depreciation, δk_{t-1}.

For subsequent purposes, we assume that the previous analysis of investment demand is satisfactory. Recall that this analysis works either if we allow resale of capital or if gross investment demand is always positive for every producer. But, of course, we shall also do okay as an approximation if—as seems plausible—gross investment demand is positive at most times for most producers.

---

[7]For a discussion of this issue and some related topics on investment, see Robert Hall, "Investment, Interest Rates, and the Effects of Stabilization Policies," *Brookings Papers on Economic Activity,* No. 1, 1977, especially pp. 71–74.

Gradual Adjustment of Investment Demand

In our analysis we assume that producers purchase enough goods in a single period—which might be a year—to attain their desired stock of capital. That is, people invest enough to close the gap between the capital carried over from the previous period, $(1-\delta)k_{t-1}$, and the desired stock, $\hat{k}_t$.

We have ignored a variety of costs that arise when producers install new capital goods. For example, to place new plant and equipment into operation, an investor normally goes through a phase of planning and decision making, then a time of building and delivery, and finally an interval where managers and workers familiarize themselves with the new facilities. Producers can speed up parts of this process, but only by incurring extra costs. As examples, quicker decisions mean more mistakes, and faster construction requires larger payments to workers and suppliers.

Because there are costs in adjusting the levels of capital, we predict two types of lags in the investment process. First, a gap between the starting stock of capital, $(1-\delta)k_{t-1}$, and the desired level, $\hat{k}_t$, stimulates higher investment over an extended interval. That is, since it takes time to build and install new plant and equipment, investors stretch out their purchases of new capital goods over an interval of time. Second, the higher capacity for production becomes available only after the investment project is completed. (Note that we capture some of this element by assuming that this period's capital stock affects production for the next period.)

Although adjustment costs for investment are quantitatively important, we continue to ignore these costs to simplify matters.[8] Fortunately, the main features of the results would not change if we brought in these complications. Also, we should note that there are other areas where the analysis omits adjustment costs. For example, we assume that producers can shift without delay from producing consumables to producing capital goods, and vice versa. Also, we assume that the existing capital is highly mobile, which ensures that all units have the same marginal products. Overall, these omissions mean that we should be careful about applying the model in a very short-run context.

---

[8]For discussions of adjustment costs in investment demand, see Robert Eisner and Robert Strotz, "Determinants of Business Investment," in Commission on Money and Credit, *Impacts of Monetary Policy,* Prentice-Hall, Englewood Cliffs, N.J., 1963; and Robert Lucas, "Adjustment Costs and the Theory of Supply," *Journal of Political Economy,* August 1967.

Investment and Households' Budget Constraints

Remember that households, in their role as producers, carry out the investment expenditures in the model. Therefore, these expenditures are another use of households' funds. When we include investment into a household's budget constraint for period t, we get the condition

$$P_t y_t + b_{t-1}(1 + R) + m_{t-1} + v_t = P_t c_t + P_t i_t + b_t + m_t \qquad (9.8)$$

As before, the left side shows the sources of funds, while the right side shows the uses. Note that the new term is the expenditure for investment, $P_t i_t$, on the right side.

Before, we defined real saving as the change in the real value of someone's assets, which could be held as either bonds or money. Aside from these financial assets, people now have another store of value—namely, physical capital goods. Therefore, real saving is now the change in the real value of someone's bonds, money, and capital. Accordingly, we have

$$\text{real saving} = \frac{(b_t + m_t)}{P_t} - \frac{(b_{t-1} + m_{t-1})}{P_{t-1}} + k_t - k_{t-1} \qquad (9.9)$$

Notice that the last term in equation 9.9 is the change in the household's stock of capital—that is, net investment. Hence, net investment is one component of a household's real saving.

As in our previous analysis, we can relate real saving to the flows of income and consumption by using the budget constraint from equation 9.8. Using this equation and the definition of real saving from equation 9.9, we eventually get the result

$$\text{real saving} = y_t - \delta k_{t-1} + (R - \pi)\left(\frac{b_{t-1}}{P_t}\right) - \pi\left(\frac{m_{t-1}}{P_t}\right) + \frac{v_t}{P_t} - c_t \qquad (9.10)$$

We can still interpret real saving as the difference between real income and consumption. But we have to define income carefully. Namely, it equals real *net* product, $y_t - \delta k_{t-1}$, plus the real interest income on bonds, $(R - \pi)(b_{t-1}/P_t)$, and money, $-\pi(m_{t-1}/P_t)$, plus the real value of transfers, v_t/P_t.

Notice that one way for somebody to finance more net investment, $k_t - k_{t-1}$, is to raise his or her real saving. But we see also that people can finance investment by running down the real value of financial assets, bonds and money. For example, people can borrow in order to pay for additional capital goods. Hence, an individual's decision to raise investment does not require a corresponding increase in that person's real saving.

From the standpoint of an individual, there are substantially different forces that influence net investment and real saving. For example, net investment increases with an upward shift in the schedule for capital's marginal product, but falls with a rise in the real interest rate, r_t. On the other hand, desired real saving increases when income is temporarily high or when the real interest rate rises.

If people could not run down financial assets or borrow, then equation 9.9 would say that someone's net investment could be financed only by that person's real saving. Then individuals could exploit productive investment opportunities only if they were willing to abstain from current consumption or leisure. The potential for running down financial assets or borrowing means that people can undertake investments even if they are personally unwilling to save very much. In particular, the opportunities to borrow and lend ensure that all investment projects will be undertaken if the real rate of return to investment is at least as great as the real interest rate, r_t. Hence, the separation of individual decisions to invest from individual decisions to save promotes economic efficiency.[9]

How does aggregate real saving behave? Since the aggregate stock of bonds, B_t, is still zero in each period, we find from equation 9.9 that

$$\text{aggregate real saving} = \frac{M_t}{P_t} - \frac{M_{t-1}}{P_{t-1}} + K_t - K_{t-1} \qquad (9.11)$$

Let's ignore the part of aggregate real saving that consists of changes in aggregate real cash balances. Typically, that part is small relative to aggregate net investment. Then equation 9.11 says that aggregate real saving equals aggregate net investment, $K_t - K_{t-1}$. Recall that individuals can invest by running down bonds or borrowing. But then, others must be expanding their holdings of bonds—that is, lending. So, for society as a whole, the act of greater net investment does require the same addition to aggregate real saving.

Earlier, we did not allow for possibilities of investment. Then, if we neglected changes in aggregate real cash balances, we found that aggregate real saving must be zero. Without investment, there is no way for the whole economy to save—that is, to change its real assets. But when the capital stock can vary, we find that aggregate real saving can be nonzero. In other words, the economy can now adjust aggregate net investment to shift resources from one period to another. These possibilities for shifting resources over time were present before for an individual, who can borrow and lend on the credit market at the given real interest rate, r_t. Hence, the total economy now has opportunities for real saving that resemble those that are available to individuals on the credit market. We shall see that these opportunities have important consequences for the analysis of market-clearing conditions.

Clearing of the Commodity Market

There are still two aggregate-consistency conditions to satisfy—first, that the aggregate demand for commodities equal the supply, and second, that all money be willingly held. The existence of investment has major implications

---

[9]Irving Fisher stresses this feature of a market economy in the *Theory of Interest,* op cit., especially Chapters 7 and 11.

for the first condition, but not the second. So we focus here on the condition for clearing the commodity market.

Clearing of the commodity market requires the aggregate supply of goods to equal the demand—that is

$$Y^s(r_t, \ldots) = C^d(r_t, \ldots) + I^d(r_t, \ldots) \qquad (9.12)$$
$$(+) \qquad\qquad (-) \qquad\qquad (-)$$

The left side of the equation shows the positive intertemporal-substitution effect from the real interest rate, r_t, on the aggregate supply of goods, Y^s_t. As before, this response reflects a positive effect on work effort, N_t. The omitted terms in the function, denoted by . . . , include various characteristics of the production function, as well as the quantity of capital from the previous period, K_{t-1}.

The right side of equation 9.12 contains the two components of aggregate demand, consumption and gross investment. As before, the real interest rate, r_t, has a negative intertemporal-substitution effect on consumer demand, C^d_t.[10] In addition, the real interest rate has a negative effect on gross investment demand, I^d_t. Again, the omitted terms include the characteristics of the production function, as well as the quantity of capital, K_{t-1}, and the depreciation rate, δ.

In Chapter 11, which considers long-term economic growth, it will be important to keep track of how the aggregate capital stock changes over time. Then we have to detail the role of the capital stock, K_{t-1}, in the market-clearing condition from equation 9.12. But for now, we assume a given value of this stock. That is, we carry out a short-run analysis in which changes in the stock of capital are small enough to neglect. It turns out that this setting is adequate to study the main role of investment during business fluctuations.

Figure 9.7 graphs the aggregates of commodities supplied and demanded versus the real interest rate, r_t. Notice that the supply curve, Y^s, slopes upward, while the demand curve, Y^d, slopes downward. Also, the figure breaks down aggregate demand into its two components, which are consumption demand, C^d, and gross investment demand, I^d. Each of these curves slopes downward versus r_t. We discussed before why investment demand would be especially sensitive to variations in the real interest rate. Therefore, the figure shows the I^d curve with more of a negative slope than the C^d curve.

Figure 9.7 shows that the commodity market clears at the real interest

---

[10]We can still neglect any aggregate wealth effect from changes in the real interest rate, r_t. The new element is the wealth that people have in the form of previously accumulated capital, K_{t-1}. But as long as gross investment demand I^d_t is positive, the real value of this capital is fixed. That is, each unit of old capital trades one-for-one with units of goods produced during period t. However, something different happens if the real interest rate rises enough to make gross investment demand negative. If people cannot consume old capital, then aggregate gross investment cannot be negative. Therefore, the overall desire to sell old capital must lead to a fall in the price of old capital relative to that of currently produced goods. In this case an increase in the real interest rate reduces wealth. But note that this case applies only when gross investment is nil.

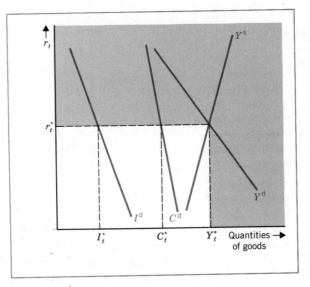

Figure 9.7 Clearing of the Commodity Market
The commodity market clears at the real interest rate, r_t^*. Here, the total output, Y_t^*, breaks down into C_t^* of consumption and I_t^* of gross investment.

rate r_t^*. Correspondingly, we label the level of output as Y_t^*. At this point, the uses of output break down between C_t^* of consumption and I_t^* of gross investment.

Supply Shocks

We want to see how the presence of investment affects our analysis of supply shocks. As before, we distinguish temporary changes from permanent ones.

A Temporary Shift of the Production Function

Consider a temporary downward shift of the production function, such as that caused by a harvest failure. To keep things simple, assume to begin with a parallel downward shift of the production function for period t. Then there are no changes in the schedules for the marginal products of labor, MPL_t, or capital, MPK_{t-1}. Also, we assume that there is no change in the schedule for the prospective marginal product of capital, MPK_t.

The decline in the production function lowers the aggregate supply of goods, Y_t^s, on the left side of equation 9.12. Also, there is a negative effect on wealth, which is small since the disturbance is temporary. Therefore, there is a small decline in consumer demand, C_t^d, and a small increase in work effort,

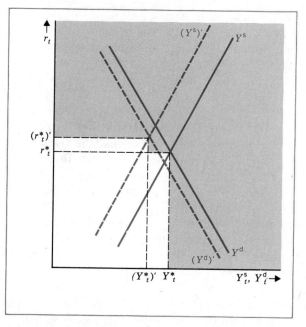

Figure 9.8 **Effects of a Temporary Downward Shift of the Production Function**
There is a leftward shift to aggregate supply, Y^s, which exceeds the leftward shift to
demand, Y^d. Hence, the real interest rate rises, while aggregate output falls.

N_t. Note that this increase in work offsets part of the decline in the supply of
goods. Finally, since the schedule for capital's marginal product, MPK_t, does
not change, there is no shift to gross investment demand, I_t^d.

Figure 9.8 shows the shifts to aggregate supply and demand. There is a
leftward shift in supply and a smaller leftward shift in demand. In the figure
the real interest rate labeled r_t^* is the one that cleared the market in the absence
of the shifts. Therefore, at this real interest rate, there is now an excess of
goods demanded over those supplied—that is, $Y_t^d > Y_t^s$. This excess demand
arises because people react to the temporary shortfall of production by lowering
their desired saving. Thus, we can also say that the disturbance creates an
excess of net investment demand over desired real saving.

As in our previous analysis of this situation, the real interest rate must
rise for the commodity market to clear. Therefore, in Figure 9.8, the new
market-clearing real interest rate, $(r_t^*)'$, exceeds the initial value, r_t^*. We can
think of this increase in the real interest rate as resulting from the excess of
desired borrowing over desired lending.

How does the increase in the real interest rate compare with that in our
earlier analysis, which did not consider investment? In the earlier analysis the
real interest rate had to rise enough to make aggregate desired saving equal

zero.[11] Now, the amount of aggregate real saving equals the quantity of aggregate net investment. Since the rise in the real interest rate reduces investment demand, we do not require as large an increase in the real interest rate as we did before.

Figure 9.8 shows that the new level of output, $(Y_t^*)'$, is below the initial amount, Y_t^*. Further, this drop in output reflects partly a decline in consumption, $(C_t^*)' < C_t^*$, and partly a decline in gross investment, $(I_t^*)' < I_t^*$. (Since depreciation is fixed at the amount, δK_{t-1}, the fall in net investment equals that in gross investment.) Note that the rise in the real interest rate reduces consumption and investment demand. In addition, the decrease in wealth reinforces the decline in consumer demand. Finally, the higher real interest rate and the reduction in wealth imply that the quantity of work effort, $(N_t^*)'$, exceeds the initial amount, N_t^*.

Consider the quantitative responses of consumption and work effort. Because the wealth effect is weak, the changes in consumption and work will be large only if there is a substantial increase in the real interest rate, r_t. However, consider what happens if investment demand is highly responsive to r_t. (We discussed before why this is likely.) Then a small increase in r_t is sufficient to equate desired real saving to net investment demand—that is, to clear the commodity market. In this case, most of the drop in output reflects a decline in investment, and there are only small changes in consumption and work effort.

The important conclusion is that fluctuations in investment partially insulate consumption and work from some types of temporary economic disturbances. Let's explain why this happens. When there is a temporary drop in supply—such as a harvest failure—everybody wants to maintain their levels of consumption and work by saving less or borrowing more at the initial real interest rate. But if there are no possibilities for investment, it is infeasible for everyone to save less or borrow more. In this case the real interest rate rises enough to make the total of desired saving equal zero, which means that people end up making substantial adjustments in their consumption and work. When we introduce investment, it becomes possible for aggregate saving to change. By lowering aggregate net investment, the *economy* does what each individual would like to do at a given real interest rate. In fact, if investment demand is strongly responsive to the real interest rate, as we anticipate, then the bulk of the variation in output shows up as movements in investment. By contrast, consumption and work change relatively little.

Notice that the results imply that investment fluctuates by more than consumption, at least in response to some temporary economic disturbances. In particular, adverse shocks—such as a harvest failure—lead to declines in output and to accompanying decreases in investment as a fraction of GNP. Conversely, favorable shocks lead to higher output and to increases in the

---

[11]By aggregate saving, we refer here to amounts in excess of any changes in aggregate real money balances.

ratio of investment to GNP. Therefore, the theoretical results accord in this respect with the observed behavior of investment during recessions and booms.

The Behavior of Employment

One feature of the results that conflicts with the U.S. data is the behavior of work effort. Recessions are invariably accompanied by declines in employment. But the analysis so far suggests that a temporary adverse shock to the production function leads to a small increase in work.

Work effort rises in our example because we omitted a likely adverse effect on labor's productivity. As mentioned in some earlier cases, a downward shift of the schedule for labor's marginal product, MPL_t, usually accompanies a downward shift of the production function. This change motivates people to reduce work effort, N_t. In fact, because the cutback in productivity is temporary, there is an intertemporal-substitution effect, which reinforces the tendency for work to decline.

The decrease in work effort implies additional leftward shifts to commodity supply and demand of the sort shown in Figure 9.8. Hence, there is a larger decline in output, which reflects the reduction in work effort. Also, there is a larger increase in the real interest rate, which implies a sharper decline in investment. Overall, the main result is the tendency for a reduction in work to accompany the decline in output. We shall reexamine the behavior of employment during recessions in the next chapter, which deals also with unemployment.

A Permanent Shift of the Production Function

Previously, we contrasted permanent shifts of the production function with the type of temporary change that we just examined. Now, consider a permanent downward shift in the presence of investment. But assume again a parallel shift, which leaves unchanged the schedules for the various marginal products. In particular, since there is no change in capital's marginal product, MPK_t, there is again no shift to investment demand, I_t^d.

When the adverse shock is permanent, the wealth effects become important. There is a strong negative effect on consumer demand, C_t^d, and a strong positive effect on work effort, N_t. Recall from our discussion of permanent income that this type of permanent change to the production function exerts little net effect on desired saving. Therefore, in Figure 9.9, we show the leftward shift in demand as equal to that in supply. (This result still obtains if we include a permanent downward shift of the schedule for labor's marginal product, except that the curves shift by greater amounts.)

The main point is that the supply of goods equals the demand at the initial real interest rate, r_t^*. (Equivalently, net investment demand still equals desired real saving.) Since the real interest rate does not change, there is no effect on

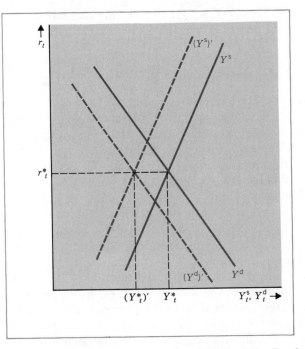

Effects of a Permanent Downward Shift of the Production Function
With a permanent downward shift of the production function, the leftward shifts of
demand and supply are roughly equal. Therefore, output falls, but the real interest
rate does not change.

investment. Hence, in this case, all of the decline in output reflects a fall in
consumption.

    The main new result concerns the role of investment as a buffer for con-
sumption. When there are temporary shocks to the production function, the
sharp fluctuations in investment prevent large changes in consumption. But
movements in investment cannot insulate consumption from permanent changes
in production possibilities. Permanent shifts of the production function, which
have substantial wealth effects, lead to large changes in consumption.

Shifts to the Productivity of Capital
The previous examples dealt with disturbances that left unchanged the schedule
for capital's marginal product, MPK_t. In these cases, there were no shifts to
investment demand. However, shifts in this component of demand can also
be a source of shocks to the economy. In fact, Keynes stressed this element
as a major reason for business fluctuations.[12]

---

[12]John Maynard Keynes, *The General Theory of Employment, Interest and Money*, Harcourt
Brace, New York, 1936, Chapters 11 and 12.

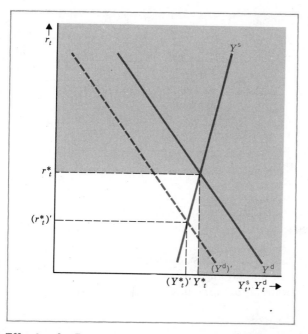

Figure 9.10 Effects of a Decrease in the Marginal Product of Capital
The decrease in the schedule for capital's marginal product reduces investment demand.
Therefore, the real interest rate and the level of output decline.

Consider now a change to the production function that involves a downward shift of the schedule for capital's marginal product, MPK_t. Recall that this marginal product refers to the output for period $t+1$. To keep things simple, assume now that no changes occur to the production function for period t. Also, let's abstract for the moment from any wealth effects (which are likely to be negative here).

Recall that the condition for clearing the commodity market is

$$Y^s(r_t, \ldots) = C^d(r_t, \ldots) + I^d(r_t, \ldots)$$
$$(+) \qquad\qquad (-) \qquad\qquad (-)$$

Given our assumptions, the only initial effect from the disturbance is a decline in gross investment demand, I_t^d, on the right side of the equation. Therefore, Figure 9.10 shows only a leftward shift of the aggregate demand curve, Y^d, which reflects the reduction in investment demand.

We see from the figure that the real interest rate and output decrease. Note that the fall in output reflects the negative effect of the lower real interest rate on work effort. Also, the lower real interest rate means that consumption rises. Therefore, investment falls by more than the decrease in total output.

Let's go back to the temporary supply shock that we considered earlier. Usually, this type of disturbance is accompanied by a worsening of investment opportunities—that is, by a decline in capital's marginal product, MPK_t. So, we should combine the effects from Figure 9.10 with those that we found before in Figure 9.8. When we do this, we reinforce the downward effects on output and investment. However, the downward shift in investment demand tends to lower the real interest rate, which offsets the tendency for consumption to decline. In fact, the overall movement in consumption is now ambiguous.

An important new result concerns the short-run behavior of the real interest rate, r_t. In Figure 9.8 we found that temporary adverse shocks to the production function led to a higher real interest rate. This response reflects everyone's desire to save less in order to maintain their levels of consumption. But an opposing force arises if the shock also lowers the marginal product of capital. Then, as shown in Figure 9.10, the downward shift in investment demand tends to reduce the real interest rate. Thus, the overall effect on the real interest rate is uncertain. The net change depends on whether the decrease in aggregate desired saving is larger or smaller than the fall in net investment demand.

Empirically, real interest rates do not have a clear pattern of association with recessions and booms. Therefore, we should not feel bad that our theory fails to generate an unambiguous prediction for this pattern.

Summary

We began by introducing the stock of capital as an input into the production function. The marginal product of capital is positive, but diminishes as the quantity of capital rises.

Gross investment is the quantity of capital goods that a producer buys from the commodity market. Since we treat capital goods and consumables as physically identical, the total demand for goods is the sum of gross investment demand and consumption demand. The change in a producer's stock of capital—or net investment—equals gross investment less depreciation. In the aggregate, gross investment cannot be negative. However, aggregate investment can be negative—and was in the United States for most of the 1930s and during World War II.

Empirically, investment fluctuates proportionately by much more than total output, which fluctuates by more than consumption. Further, the ratio of investment to either the stock of capital or GNP is low during recessions and high in booms. For seven postwar recessions, the shortfall in total investment—which includes gross fixed investment, changes in business inventories, and purchases of consumer durables—accounted on average for 88% of the shortfall in real GNP. By contrast, consumer expenditures on nondurables and services declined relatively little during these recessions. However, the decline in consumption was relatively more important during the Great Depression.

The real rate of return to investment is the marginal product of capital less the rate of depreciation. Producers determine their desired stocks of capital by equating this rate of return to the real interest rate. It follows that the desired stock of capital rises first, if the real interest falls, or second, if the schedule for capital's marginal product shifts upward, or third, if the depreciation rate declines.

Given their initial stocks, producers invest enough during a period to achieve the desired stock of capital. Therefore, given the initial stock, investment demand rises if the desired stock of capital increases. Also, given the desired stock of capital, a smaller initial stock means a larger investment demand. Finally, we note that small percentage changes in the desired stock of capital translate into large percentages in net investment demand. This property explains why net investment demand is volatile and can sometimes be negative.

We included investment as an item of expenditure in households' budget constraints. Although net investment is one part of an individual's real saving, the existence of the credit market means that an individual's decision to invest does not require that individual to save. However, in the aggregate, real saving equals net investment (plus the change in real cash balances). Therefore, the existence of investment allows the whole economy to change its amount of real saving. This possibility has important implications for the characteristics of short-term business fluctuations.

Aggregate gross investment demand enters as a component of aggregate demand in the condition for clearing the commodity market. Because this component tends to be especially sensitive to variations in the real interest rate, we find that investment absorbs the bulk of short-term fluctuations in output. Specifically, a temporary adverse shock to the production function leads to a major proportionate reduction in investment, but to a relatively small decline in consumption. However, the effect of this supply shock on the real interest rate is uncertain—it depends on whether the decline in desired real saving is larger or smaller than the decrease in net investment demand.

Finally, changes in investment cannot buffer consumption against permanent shifts to the production function. Here, an adverse shock leads to a strong downward response of consumption.

Important Terms and Concepts

physical capital

producers' durable equipment and structures

private fixed capital

inventories

human capital

utilization rate

marginal product of capital (MPK)

real rate of return from investment

desired stock of capital

investment demand

QUESTIONS AND PROBLEMS

Mainly for Review

9.1 What is meant by private domestic fixed investment? Does it include purchases of consumer durables? What about purchases of bonds?

9.2 Distinguish gross investment from net investment. When is net investment negative? Can gross investment be negative if capital goods cannot be resold?

9.3 Suppose producers expect inflation—that is, a higher price level in the next period. Will they want to increase their current purchases of capital goods? What if the nominal interest rate rises to reflect the higher expected inflation?

9.4 Does higher investment require higher saving on the part of an individual household? For the economy as a whole, how do changes in the interest rate ensure that real saving rises to match an increase in investment?

9.5 Show graphically how the division of total output into consumption and investment is achieved through clearing of the commodity market. How does a temporary shift of the production function alter this division? Does your answer depend on the relative sensitivity of consumption demand and investment demand to changes in the interest rate?

9.6 Why does a decline in the productivity of capital reduce the interest rate? Could the interest rate fall so much as to leave the quantity of investment unchanged? Explain.

Problems for Discussion

9.7 The One-Sector Production Function

In our model, output can be labeled as either consumables or capital goods. Economists call this a one-sector production function.

a. Why does the price of a unit of consumables always equal the price of a unit of capital in this model? What would happen if the price of consumables exceeded the price of capital goods, or vice versa?

b. Suppose that everyone wants to undertake negative gross investment—that is, everyone wants to resell old capital on the commodity market. Can the price of capital goods fall below the price of consumables in this case?

c. (optional) Consider a "two-sector model," where different production functions apply to consumables and capital goods. Would the price of a unit of consumables always equal the price of a unit of capital goods in this model?

9.8 Inventory Investment

Businesses hold inventories of goods, partly as finished products and partly as goods-in-process and raw materials. Suppose that we think of inventories as a type of capital, which enters into the production function. Then changes in these stocks represent investment in inventories. (Generally, we assume that the rate of depreciation on inventories is near zero.)

a. How does an increase in the real interest rate affect the quantity of inventories that businesses want to hold? Therefore, what happens to inventory investment?

b. Consider a temporary adverse shock to the production function. What happens to the amount of inventory investment? Therefore, what do we predict for the behavior of inventory investment during recessions?

(Empirically, inventory investment by businesses during the postwar period averaged only 0.7% of GNP. But inventory investment is highly volatile—in fact, during recessions, the change in inventories is often negative. Hence, Table 9.1 indicate that shortfalls in this component accounted, on average over the seven postwar recessions, for 32% of the shortfall in real GNP.)

9.9 The Investment Tax Credit

For most years since 1962 (but not after 1985), some types of investments have qualified for a credit against income taxes. Assume that this governmental program effectively refunds the fraction, a, of investment expenditures. How does the size of the refund percentage, a, influence producers' desired stocks of capital and, hence, their investment demand? (Assume that someone who resells capital has to return the investment credit on the amount sold.)

9.10 Capacity Utilization (optional)

One way for a producer to generate extra output is to use his or her capital more intensively. That is, a producer can run more shifts per day or allow less "down time" for performing maintenance. Assume that more intensive utilization causes capital to depreciate faster.

a. How does a producer determine the best intensity of use for his or her capital?

b. Show that an increase in the real interest rate, r_t, motivates producers to use their capital more intensively. What does this imply for the effect of the real interest rate on the supply of goods, y_t^s?

9.11 The Ownership of Capital (optional)

In our model, the people who use capital also own the capital. Suppose that these people print up certificates, each of which conveys ownership to one unit of capital. Then these certificates can be sold to others (on a "stock market"). But instead of using the capital themselves, the buyers of these certificates may allow other people ("businesses") to use the capital. Then the users pay a fee to holders of certificates. This fee may be either a fixed rental or a share of the profits.

a. Why might it be a good idea to separate the ownership of capital from the use of that capital? (Remember that people can already finance the purchase of capital by borrowing.) Why might it be a bad idea?

b. What determines the nominal and real value of the ownership certificates when each is a claim to 1 unit of capital?

c. In the real world why is the future real value of a certificate subject to great uncertainty? Specifically, why does the value depend on the fortunes of the company that issued it?

9.12 Temporary Shocks to the Production Function and Consumption

Because of the strong response of investment, we found that temporary shocks to the production function had little effect on consumption. Suppose that we look at larger and larger—but still temporary—shocks. How does consumption react as the shocks get bigger? In particular, what happens to the division of the shortfall in output between consumption and investment? How does the answer relate to the Great Depression?

9.13 Investment Opportunities for Robinson Crusoe

In the market economy we found that investment takes the brunt of temporary shocks to the production function. Suppose that we introduce opportunities for investment into the model of Robinson Crusoe, which we constructed in Chapter 2. How would Robinson Crusoe's investment and consumption respond to temporary and permanent shifts to the production function? Are the results basically similar to those for the market economy?

9.14 Saving, Investment, and the Real Interest Rate (optional)

Suppose that shocks to the production function are sometimes favorable and sometimes unfavorable. Also, the shocks are sometimes temporary and sometimes permanent.

a. What pattern of association results between the real interest rate and the aggregate quantities of net investment and real saving?

b. Suppose that we try to deduce the effect of the real interest rate on an individual's desired real saving by examining the relation between the real interest rate and aggregate real saving. What do we find? What is the source of the problem?

c. Suppose that we try to estimate the effect of the real interest rate on investment demand from the relation between the real interest rate and aggregate net investment. What do we find? What is the source of the problem?

d. Suppose that we look at the relation of the real interest rate, r_t, to the ratio of aggregate consumptions, C_{t+1}/C_t. What will this tell us about an individual's saving behavior?

CHAPTER 10
UNEMPLOYMENT

Thus far we have focused on the model's predictions about fluctuations in aggregate output and in the composition of output between investment and consumption. An adverse supply shock can lead to a recession, where output falls and investment declines as a share of output. The model can also explain a decline in aggregate work effort during a recession. In a setting with firms and a separate labor market, as in Chapter 6, the changes in work show up as variations either in employment—that is, the number of persons with jobs— or in the amount of hours worked by those employed.

One thing we have not yet discussed is **unemployment.** Economists define unemployment to be the number of people who are looking for work but have no job. Then the **labor force** is the sum of employment and unemployment. People who neither have a job nor are looking for one are classed as being **outside of the labor force.** Finally, the **unemployment rate** is the ratio of the number unemployed to the labor force.

Whereas unemployment refers to unsuccessful job-seekers, the term **vacancies** describes the number of jobs that firms have been unable to fill. We could define the total of jobs available as the sum of employment and vacancies. Then the vacancy rate would be the ratio of vacancies to the total of jobs available.

In the labor market of Chapter 6, the wage rate adjusted to equate labor supply and demand. Then anyone who sought work at the going wage was able to get a job (and the desired amount of work hours). Similarly, firms managed to hire their desired number of workers (and work hours). Thus, unemployment and vacancies were both zero, and employment equaled the labor force. Although this model of the labor market may account for some of the fluctuations in employment (that is, the labor force), it cannot explain why the quantities of unemployment and vacancies are nonzero. Therefore, the model also cannot tell us why unemployment and vacancies change over time. Given these deficiencies, it is also likely that the model is not yet fully satisfactory for understanding movements in employment and production.

To explain unemployment and vacancies, we have to introduce some type of "friction" into the workings of the labor market. Specifically, we have to explain why people without jobs would take some time to find and accept employment. Similarly, we have to see why businesses with unoccupied positions would take some time to fill them. Thus, the key to unemployment and vacancies is the process of workers searching for jobs and businesses searching for workers.

In our earlier discussion we simplified matters by thinking of all workers as identical. Similarly, by thinking of only one type of production process, we assumed that all jobs were the same. But then the process of search among workers and firms would be trivial. To make the analysis meaningful, we have to allow for differences among workers and jobs. In fact, we can think of the labor market as operating to find good matches between jobs and workers. Because jobs and workers differ, this matching process is difficult and time-consuming. Unemployment and vacancies arise as aspects of this process.

In the next section we develop a simple model of job matching. But let's stress at this point two important objectives of this analysis. First, we want to explain why the levels of unemployment and vacancies are positive. Second, we want to see how these variables change over time, and how they interact with the determination of employment. In particular, we want to understand how unemployment and employment behave during recessions and booms.

A Model of Job Finding

Let's start with a person who has just entered the labor force and is not yet employed. As an example, we can think of a student who has just graduated from school and is seeking his or her first job. Alternatively, we can think of someone who is entering or reentering the labor force after raising a family.

Suppose that this person searches for a position by visiting various firms. Each firm interviews job candidates to assess their likely qualifications for a position. As a result of each inspection, the firm estimates what the value of the candidate's marginal product would be. To keep things simple, we assume that the firm then offers a job with a nominal wage, w, equal to this estimated value of marginal product. (We assume, only for simplicity, that the job entails a standard number of hours worked per week.)

The candidate must decide whether to accept the offer at the wage rate w. In making this decision, he or she takes into account the likely duration of the job, which we treat for now as a given. In particular, because the firm and worker each pay some costs of getting established in a new job, it would usually not pay to take a position for a short period.

The alternative to taking a job is to remain unemployed and continue searching for another one.[1] More search pays off if a subsequent wage offer exceeds the initial one. On the other hand, one cost of turning down an offer is the wage income foregone while not working. However, this income foregone

---

[1]We assume that it does not pay to accept a job and nevertheless keep searching. That is because, first, the costs of getting set up in a job usually make it undesirable to take positions with short expected durations, and second, it may be easier to search while unemployed.

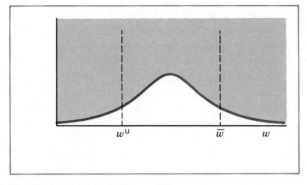

Figure 10.1 **The Distribution of Wage Offers**
The curve shows the chances of receiving wage offers of different sizes. The higher the
curve the more likely that wages of that size will be offered. Note that w^u is the effective
wage while unemployed, and $\overline{w}$ is the reservation wage. Wage offers are accepted if
they are at least as good as $\overline{w}$, and rejected otherwise.

must be measured net of any income that people receive because they are
unemployed. This income includes **unemployment insurance,** which we shall
discuss later, and any value attached to time spent unemployed (and searching
for a job) rather than working.[2]

In evaluating an offer, the first thing to determine is how it compares with
others that might be available. In making this comparison, a job-seeker would
have in mind a distribution of possible wages,[3] given the person's education,
experience, locational preferences, and so on. Figure 10.1 shows a possible
distribution of wage offers. For each value of wages on the horizontal axis,
the height of the curve shows the relative chance or probability of receiving
that wage offer. For the case shown, the offers usually fall in a middle range
of values for w. However, there is a small chance of getting either a very high
wage offer (in the right tail of the distribution) or an offer near zero.

Figure 10.1 shows the value w^u, which is the effective wage received while
unemployed. We know right away that a person would reject any offer that
paid less than w^u. For the case shown in the figure, w^u lies toward the left end
of the distribution of wage offers. This construction implies that most—but
not all—wage offers would exceed w^u. Then a job-seeker's remaining decision
is whether to accept a wage offer w, given that $w > w^u$.

As mentioned before, a person may refuse a wage that exceeds w^u to
preserve the chance of getting a still better offer (see footnote 1). But there

---

[2]Presumably the unemployed have more leisure, even after considering the time required to
search for a job. However, our basic results would not change if people preferred time at work
to time spent unemployed.

[3]We assume for simplicity that the attractiveness of different jobs depends only on the wage
paid. However, we could expand the model to consider an effective wage, which took account
of working conditions, hours, job location, etc.

is a trade-off because the job-seeker then foregoes the income, $w - w^u$, while not working. The balancing of these forces involves what economists call a **reservation wage** (or sometimes an acceptance wage), which we denote by $\bar{w}$. Wage offers below $\bar{w}$ are refused, while those above $\bar{w}$ are accepted. If a person sets a high value of $\bar{w}$, then he or she will probably spend a long time (perhaps forever) unemployed and searching for an acceptable job. On the other hand, a low value of $\bar{w}$ (but still greater than w^u) means that the expected time unemployed will be relatively brief. However, the expected wage on an acceptable job is lower the lower the value of $\bar{w}$.

The optimal value of $\bar{w}$ turns out to depend on the shape of the wage-offer distribution in Figure 10.1, as well as on the value of w^u and the expected duration of jobs.[4] For our purposes we do not have to go through the details of the calculation of the optimal $\bar{w}$. However, we can note some properties that would come out of this calculation.

First, since some wage offers would generally be unacceptable—that is, $w < \bar{w}$ for some offers—it typically takes awhile for a job searcher to find an acceptable job. In the interim the person is "unemployed" (although engaged in job search). Therefore, incomplete information about where to find the best job can explain positive amounts of unemployment.

Second, an increase in the income while unemployed, w^u, motivates job seekers to raise their standards for job acceptance—that is, $\bar{w}$ increases. Given the distribution of wage offers in Figure 10.1, it becomes more likely that $w < \bar{w}$, which means that wage offers are more likely to be rejected. It follows that job searchers tend to take a longer time in finding a job when w^u increases. Hence, for a group of workers, the **job-finding rate** falls, and the expected **duration of unemployment** increases.

Third, suppose that the whole distribution of job offers becomes better. For example, a favorable shock to firms' production functions might mean that marginal products of labor were all 10% higher than before. Then the distribution of wage offers in Figure 10.1 would shift rightward. (The height of the curve at the old wage w is now the height at the wage, $1.1w$.) For a given reservation wage $\bar{w}$, it follows that wage offers are more likely to be in the acceptable range, $w \geq \bar{w}$. Therefore, the job-finding rate rises and the expected duration of unemployment falls.

Generally, a better distribution of wage offers also motivates people to raise their reservation wage $\bar{w}$. However, if the wage while unemployed, w^u, does not change, then the first effect tends to dominate.[5] A shift to a better

---

[4]For a discussion of models of job search that involve an optimal reservation wage, see Belton M. Fleisher and Thomas J. Kniesner, *Labor Economics: Theory, Evidence and Policy*, 3rd ed., Prentice-Hall, Englewood Cliffs, N.J., 1984, pp. 477–507.

[5]If w^u and all wage offers were higher by 10%, then the trade-off between the benefits and costs of accepting a job would not change. Therefore, the job-finding rate and the expected duration of unemployment would also not change. If we instead hold w^u constant—as we did in the text—then the net effect must be equivalent to a fall in w^u. Therefore, the net effect is an increase in the job-finding rate and a decrease in the expected duration of unemployment.

distribution of wage offers—generated, for example, by a favorable shock to productivity—raises the job-finding rate and lowers the expected duration of unemployment.

Search by Firms

Thus far, we have taken an unrealistic view of how firms would contribute to the job-search process. Up to now, firms received job applications, evaluated candidates in terms of likely marginal products, and then expressed wage offers.[6] This process does not allow firms to utilize the information that they have about the characteristics of their jobs, about the traits of workers who are usually productive on these jobs, and about the wages that typically have to be paid for such workers. Firms would communicate this information by advertising job openings that had ranges of requirements for education, experience, and so on, and which also paid a specified range of wages. Such advertisements appropriately screen out most potential applicants, and tend to generate more rapid and better matches of workers to jobs.

Although search by firms is important in a well-functioning labor market, the allowance for this search leaves unaltered our major conclusions. In particular,

- It still takes time for workers to be matched with acceptable jobs, so that the expected durations of unemployment and vacancies are positive.
- An increase in workers' wages while unemployed, w^u, lowers the job-finding rate and raises the anticipated duration of unemployment.
- A favorable shock to productivity raises the job-finding rate and reduces the expected duration of unemployment.

Job Separations

Workers search for jobs that offer high wages, relative to perceived opportunities elsewhere, while employers search for workers with high productivity, given the wages that must be paid. Although workers and firms evaluate their information as well as possible, they often find out later that they made mistakes. For example, an employer may learn that a worker is less productive than anticipated, or a worker may discover that he or she dislikes the job (or his or her boss). When a job match looks significantly poorer later on than it did before, firms are motivated to discharge the worker, or the worker is motivated to quit. In either case there is a job separation, which typically reinstates a vacancy for the firm and unemployment for the worker. The main

---

[6]Since the marginal product of most people on most jobs would be negative (for example, of college professors as the chief executive officer of General Motors), we would have to allow wage offers to be negative. Usually these negative offers would be unacceptable, so we can just as well think of no job being offered in such cases.

point is that a separation restarts the process of job search for firms and workers.

Separations also come about because of changed circumstances, even when firms and workers made accurate initial assessments of each other. For example, an adverse shock to a firm's production function could lower its evaluation of a worker's marginal product, and thereby lead to a discharge (which tends to create unemployment but not a vacancy). If we distinguish the products of firms, then we would get a similar effect from a decline in the relative demand for a firm's product. Also, jobs are sometimes known to be temporary at the outset, as in the case of seasonal workers in agriculture or at sports facilities.

On the other side of the labor market, workers may experience changed circumstances with respect to family, schooling, location, and retirement, as well as alternative job prospects. (Some of these changes would be anticipated, while others would be unanticipated.) Shifts in these factors could induce a worker to quit a job (which may create a vacancy but not unemployment).

For a group of employed workers, we can identify factors that influence the **job-separation rate.** For example, the rate is higher for inexperienced workers who are harder to evaluate initially, or for younger persons who are likely to experience changes in family size or locational preferences. The separation rate would also be higher in industries that are subject to frequent shocks to technology or product demand.

If there were no separations (and no new persons entering the labor force), then the process of job search would tend eventually to eliminate unemployment and vacancies. But the existence of separations means that the finding of new jobs is continually offset by the loss of old ones—that is, by the creation of new unemployment and vacancies. The level and change in unemployment and vacancies involves the interplay between job finding and job separation. We now illustrate this process with a simple example, which focuses on the number of people employed and unemployed.

Job Separations, Job Finding, and the Natural Unemployment Rate

Let N be the number of people employed, and U be the number unemployed. For now, we assume that the labor force, $N + U$, does not change over time. For example, we do not allow for retirements or entry of new persons into the labor force. Because of the reevaluation of jobs and workers, some fraction of those employed experience a job separation in each period. In Figure 10.2 the red box labeled N denotes the number employed, while the white box labeled U shows those unemployed. The arrow from N to U represents the number of job separations. If the labor force is constant, and—also unrealistically—if no job loser finds a new job immediately, then all those who lose jobs move from category N to category U. For the purpose of an example,

Figure 10.2 **Movements between Employment and Unemployment**
In this example, 1% of those employed (N) lose their jobs each period. Simultaneously, 15% of those unemployed (U) find jobs each period. Therefore, the net change in the number unemployed during a period is $15\% \cdot U - 1\% \cdot N$. Also, the change in the number unemployed is the negative of the change in the number employed.

we assume that 1% of those employed lose their jobs each period—that is, the job-separation rate is 1% per period.

As discussed before, the other thing that happens each period is that some fraction of those unemployed find jobs. In Figure 10.2 the arrow pointing from U to N represents the number of unemployed persons who find jobs during a period. Here (in order for the example to generate roughly the right answers later on), we assume that 15% of those unemployed find work each period. In other words, the job-finding rate is 15% per period.

We can work through the process of job separation and job finding to determine the numbers of people employed and unemployed. In Table 10.1 we assume that the labor force is fixed at 100 million people (the actual size of the total labor force in 1985 was 117 million), and the economy starts in period 1 with 90 million employed and 10 million unemployed. Thus, the unemployment rate is initially 10%. Then, of the 90 million workers, 1%— or 0.9 million people—lose their jobs in the first period. Simultaneously, 15% of those unemployed—or 1.5 million people—find jobs. Hence, the net change in employment during period 1 is 0.6 million. Correspondingly, unemployment falls by 0.6 million.

As the number of employed increases and the number of unemployed decreases, the quantity of job separations (1% of those employed) rises, while the quantity of job findings (15% of those unemployed) falls. Therefore, the increase in employment slows down over time. Eventually, the economy approaches levels of employment and unemployment at which the number of job separations and findings are equal. Then, as long as the rates of job separation and job finding do not change, employment and unemployment are constant. In our example the balance between job separations and job findings occurs when employment equals 93.8 million and unemployment equals 6.2 million—that is, when the unemployment rate is 6.2%. Therefore, in this model, we can say that the **natural unemployment rate** is 6.2%. The economy tends toward this rate automatically, given the rates at which people lose and find jobs.

Table 10.1 **The Dynamics of Employment and Unemployment and the Natural Rate of Unemployment**

Period	Number Employed (N)	Number Unemployed (U)	Number Who Lose Jobs	Number Who Find Jobs	Net Change in Employment	Net Change in Unemployment
1	90.0	10.0	0.9	1.5	0.6	−0.6
2	90.6	9.4	0.9	1.4	0.5	−0.5
3	91.1	8.9	0.9	1.3	0.4	−0.4
4	91.5	8.5	0.9	1.3	0.4	−0.4
5	91.9	8.1	0.9	1.2	0.3	−0.3
6	92.2	7.8	0.9	1.2	0.3	−0.3
.	.	.	.	.	.	.
.	.	.	.	.	.	.
.	.	.	.	.	.	.
∞	93.8	6.2	0.9	0.9	0	0

Note: We assume that the economy starts with 90 million people employed (N) and 10 million unemployed (U). Then, from Figure 10.2, 1% of those employed lose their job each period, but 15% of those unemployed find jobs. Therefore, the net change in employment is $15\% \cdot U - 1\% \cdot N$. Also, the change in unemployment is the negative of the change in employment. When the number employed reaches 93.8 million and the number unemployed reaches 6.2 million, the net changes in employment and unemployment are zero. Thus, the natural unemployment rate in this example is 6.2%.

Let's observe some important points about the natural unemployment rate. First, although the unemployment rate eventually stays constant at this value, there is still a substantial amount of *job turnover* going on. Almost a million people lose and find jobs each period in the example when the unemployment rate is 6.2%. In this model—and in the real world—large flows from employment to unemployment and vice versa are a normal part of the operation of the labor market.

Second, the dynamics of employment and unemployment, as well as the value of the natural employment rate, depend on the rates of job separation and job finding. In the example these rates per period were set at 1 and 15%, respectively. More generally, our earlier analysis showed how the rates of job separation and job finding depended on various factors, such as a person's age and experience, the income available while unemployed, and the variability of an industry's supply and demand conditions. To see how these factors influence employment and unemployment, we want to consider alternative values for the rates of job separation and job finding.

Let s be the job-separation rate, and η (the Greek letter *eta*) the job-finding rate. Then the change in the number employed during a period, ΔN, is given by

$$\Delta N = \eta U - sN \qquad (10.1)$$

Note that the first term, ηU, is the number of unemployed who find jobs during a period, while the second term, sN, is the number of employed who lose jobs. Equation 10.1 says that the change in employment equals job findings less job separations.

Equation 10.1 implies that employment increases if job findings, ηU, exceed job separations, sN. In the reverse case employment decreases. To determine the natural levels of employment and unemployment, we set the change in employment, ΔN, to zero in equation 10.1. Then, using the condition that the labor force, $N + U$, is fixed at 100 million, we find that

$$\eta U = sN = s(100 - U)$$

Solving this equation for the number unemployed, U, determines the natural values of unemployment and employment as

$$U = 100 \cdot \frac{s}{(s + \eta)}$$

$$N = 100 \cdot \frac{\eta}{(s + \eta)} \qquad (10.2)$$

Therefore, the natural unemployment rate is

$$u = \frac{U}{100} = \frac{s}{(s + \eta)} \qquad (10.3)$$

Recall that, in our example, $s = 0.01$ per period and $\eta = 0.15$ per period. Thus, $u = 0.01/0.16 = 6.2\%$, as we found before.

Equation 10.3 relates the natural unemployment rate to the rates of job separation, s, and job finding, η.[7] A higher rate of separation, s, raises the natural unemployment rate, while a higher rate of finding, η, lowers it. Thus, when we examine differences in natural unemployment rates—either over groups of people or over time—we should look for differences in the rates of job separation and job finding. People who either lose jobs more frequently or have more trouble in finding jobs will be unemployed a larger fraction of the time.

Movements in and out of the Labor Force

Before applying the theory to data on unemployment rates, we can usefully extend the analysis to include movements in and out of the labor force. Conceptually, we classify people as outside of the labor force if they neither have a market job nor are currently looking for one. (Hence, the category includes

---

[7]For more thorough analyses of this type of model, see Robert Hall, "A Theory of the Natural Unemployment Rate and the Duration of Unemployment," *Journal of Monetary Economics,* April 1979; Chitra Ramaswami, "Equilibrium Unemployment and the Efficient Job-Finding Rate," *Journal of Labor Economics,* April 1983; and Michael Darby, John Haltiwanger, and Mark Plant, "Unemployment Rate Dynamics and Persistent Unemployment under Rational Expectations," *American Economic Review,* September 1985.

full-time students and homemakers, who might reasonably think of themselves as "employed.") In practice, there are sometimes great difficulties in distinguishing those outside the labor force from those unemployed. That is because the distinction comes only from people's answers to a survey question as to whether they are actively "looking for work" during a particular period. To some extent, the number classified as unemployed underestimates the true number because some of those labeled as outside of the labor force would also like market jobs (at some wage rate!). But on the other hand, many of those who are called unemployed are not actually interested in accepting employment on terms that they could reasonably expect to receive.

For our purposes, the important new effects involve movements from inside the labor force to outside and vice versa. There are many good reasons for these movements—for example, when people retire, when they leave or reenter school, when they have changes in marital status or in the number and ages of children, or when the nature of the available jobs changes.

Figure 10.3 shows the possible transitions among the three categories, employment, unemployment, and outside of the labor force. (Notice that the flows labeled 2 and 3 are those that we studied before.) The list of possibilities is as follows:

1. A change in job, without becoming unemployed or leaving the labor force. (This type of shift is especially popular among sports figures and professors of economics—but, more generally, over half of all job changes do not involve any unemployment.[8])
2. A loss of a job with a move to unemployment.
3. The finding of a job from the ranks of the unemployed.
4. A movement from unemployment to outside of the labor force—sometimes described as **discouraged workers.**
5. An entry or reentry to the labor force, but initially unemployed.
6. An entry or reentry to the labor force, with a job obtained at once (as in the case of most graduating majors in business and economics).
7. A loss of a job with a move outside of the labor force (which includes permanent retirements, as well as withdrawals from the labor market to raise a family or return to school).

Notice that total job separations are the sum of flows 1, 2, and 7, while total job findings are the sum of flows 1, 3, and 6. The difference between separations and findings is the change in employment. On the other hand, the change in unemployment is the sum of flows 2 and 5, less the sum of flows 3 and 4. Thus, because of the movements in and out of the labor force, the change in employment no longer coincides with the negative of the change in unemployment.

---

[8]See Kim Clark and Lawrence Summers, "Labor Market Dynamics and Unemployment: a Reconsideration," *Brookings Papers on Economic Activity*, 1:1979, p. 43.

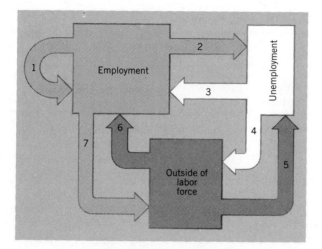

Figure 10.3 The Flows of People among Three Categories: Employment, Unemployment, and Outside of the Labor Force
The diagram shows the possible moves from one category to another.

As before—but with greater complexity—people's tendencies to experience the various transitions shown in Figure 10.3 determine the levels of employment and unemployment over time. It is still true that employment tends to be lower the higher is the rate of job separation. Similarly, employment tends to be higher the greater is the rate of job finding. But the movements in and out of the labor force interact with these tendencies to lose and find jobs. For example, people who move frequently in and out of the labor force build up relatively little work experience. Hence, they tend to be the ones who are terminated first and hired last.

For unemployment the new effects concern the possibilities for moving outside of the labor force. For example, the tendency for the unemployed to cease looking for work (flow 4 in Figure 10.3) reduces the number of persons counted as unemployed. But the tendency for people to shift from employment to outside of the labor force (flow 7) tends to raise unemployment. That is because, first, these people often become unemployed when they reenter the labor force (flow 5), and second, they are more likely to lose a job later on (flows 2 and 7).

The Behavior of U.S. Unemployment Rates by Demographic Groups

Table 10.2 shows unemployment rates for all workers and for various categories of workers by age, sex, and race. The data are averages for 1948–85 and for various subperiods. The average unemployment rate for all civilian workers

Table 10.2 Behavior of U.S. Unemployment Rates

	(% of Civilian Labor Force within Category)					
	All Civilian Workers	Males 20 Years and Older	Females 20 Years and Older	Teenagers (16–19)	White	Black and Other Minorities
1948–54	4.2	3.7	4.2	10.2	3.9	7.0
1955–61	5.3	4.6	5.1	13.2	4.7	10.1
1962–69	4.4	3.2	4.5	14.2	4.0	8.4
1970–77	6.3	4.6	6.1	17.0	5.7	10.9
1978–85	7.6	6.4	6.8	19.1	6.6	14.2
1948–85	5.6	4.5	5.4	14.9	5.0	10.2

Note: The table shows the average unemployment rate over the period indicated for various categories of workers.

Source: Economic Report of the President, 1986, Table B-35.

for 1948–85 was 5.6%. But the average unemployment rates vary substantially by demographic characteristics. For example, among persons 20 years and older, the average rate for females was 5.4%, while that for males was 4.5%. For both sexes, the average unemployment rate declines by age until people reach at least their 50s. But the sharpest distinction applies to teenagers, who had an average unemployment rate of 14.9%, as compared to about 4.7% for those at least 20 years of age. Finally, the average rate for blacks and other minorities of 10.2% was roughly double that for whites, which was 5.0%.

Table 10.2 does not indicate much change over time in the relative unemployment rates for the various demographic groups. For example, the unemployment rate for females over 20 was typically close to the overall rate. That for teenagers averaged 2.7 times the overall rate, with no clear change in this relation over time. Similarly, the rate for blacks was reasonably stable at around 1.8 times the overall rate.

There is some indication from the table that the average rate of unemployment increased by 1–2 percentage points during the 1970s. We discuss this development later on.

Suppose that we think of the variations in average unemployment rates across demographic groups as differences in natural unemployment rates, which derive from differences in the rates of job separation and job finding. To compare the rates of job separation for the various groups, we can look at data on the **duration of jobs.** Basically, people with high rates of job separation end up with short-term jobs, and vice versa. Similarly, to get information about job-finding rates, we consider data on the duration of unemployment.

Those who find jobs quickly end up with brief spells of unemployment, and vice versa.

The Duration of Jobs

The research by Bob Hall[9] on job separations allows us to understand some of the differences in unemployment rates by age, sex, and race. First, most new jobs that people get do not last very long. For example, using data for 1973, Hall estimates that 61% of new jobs last less than one year, while the average duration of a new job is 4 years. But as people get older and try a variety of jobs, most workers eventually find a good job match, which lasts for a long time. In particular (based on data from 1978), by age 50 over 70% of all workers have been on their present job for at least 5 years. Also, by age 40, about 40% of all workers are currently in a very long-term job, which will eventually last at least 20 years. These results mean that job separations (flows 1, 2, and 7 in Figure 10.3) are much more frequent for younger workers, most of whom have not yet found a long-lasting job match. Therefore, this element explains a good deal of the higher unemployment rate for younger persons, especially teenagers.

A lower average duration of jobs can also explain some of the higher average unemployment rate for women than for men. For example, Hall estimates for 1978 that about 50% of women who have jobs will eventually reach a tenure of at least 5 years on their job, while about 15% will reach at least 20 years. But the comparable figures for men are 64% and 37%, respectively. Basically, women move in and out of the labor force (flows 4, 5, 6, and 7 in Figure 10.3) over their lifetime more often than men do.

Contrary to popular belief, Hall's figures suggest that blacks have roughly the same chance as whites to stay on a job for a long time. For example, for 1978, his estimate is that 63% of blacks who have jobs will have an eventual tenure of at least 5 years on their current job, while 26% will reach at least 20 years. The figures for whites—which are 57% and 29%, respectively—are basically similar. However, some other data show that blacks are much more likely than whites to experience a job separation in any given month. In particular, Stephen Marston[10] estimates that this element accounts for about one-third of the higher average unemployment rate for blacks. If we put Marston's observations together with Hall's, the suggestion is that blacks have a strong tendency toward very short-term jobs, although no less of a tendency to achieve jobs with a duration of at least 5 years.

---

[9]"The Importance of Lifetime Jobs in the U.S. Economy," *American Economic Review,* September 1982; and "Employment Fluctuations and Wage Rigidity," *Brookings Papers on Economic Activity,* 1:1980.

[10]Stephen Marston, "Employment Stability and High Unemployment," *Brookings Papers on Economic Activity,* 1:1976, Table 4.

The Duration of Unemployment

The other main element that determines the average unemployment rate is the duration of a typical spell of unemployment. The longer it takes for an unemployed person to find a job or leave the labor force (flows 3 and 4 in Figure 10.3), the greater will be the measured number of unemployed at any point in time.

The research by Clark and Summers (op. cit.) provides some interesting information about the duration of unemployment. One point is that a large fraction of spells end within one month—the percentages were 79% for 1969, 60% for 1974, and 55% for 1975. (Note that 1975 was a year of deep recession, 1974 was an early stage of a recession, and 1969 was a strong boom.) Correspondingly, the average length of a spell is not very long—1.4 months in 1969, 1.9 months in 1974, and 2.2 months in 1975. But Clark and Summers argue that the importance of the long-term unemployed is more significant than these figures suggest. First, in determining the average number of people unemployed at any date, we effectively weight the frequency of each spell by its length. Therefore, although the average length of a spell in 1974 was only 2 months, it also turns out that spells of more than 2 months accounted for 69% of the number employed. Similarly, spells of 6 months or more still accounted for 19% of unemployment in 1974.

Second, roughly half of all spells of unemployment end in withdrawal from the labor force (flow 4 in Figure 10.3), rather than in employment (flow 3 in the figure). Then many of those who leave the labor force soon reappear as job searchers (flow 5 in the figure), which counts as a new spell of unemployment in the data. Clark and Summers argue that these spells of unemployment and the intervening periods outside of the labor force should be counted as long periods of unemployment. But many of these people (as well as some who never leave the labor force) may not be serious job-seekers and should not be counted as unemployed in the first place. This ambiguity points out the fundamental problem of defining and measuring the concept of unemployment. In general, it is easier to define and measure employment than unemployment.

Teenagers tend to find jobs or leave the labor force more quickly than do older persons. For example, for 1974, the average duration of unemployment for teenagers was 1.6 months, as compared with just over 2 months for those over 20. Therefore, the higher unemployment rate for teenagers reflects mostly the short duration of their jobs, rather than a low rate of job finding.

The main difference by sex is the much higher tendency for unemployed females to leave the labor force (flow 4 in Figure 10.3). For example, in 1974, 58% of unemployed females over 20 eventually left the labor force, as contrasted with only 26% of males over 20.

For blacks, particularly those under 25, a greater difficulty in finding jobs accounts for a large part of their higher unemployment rate. For example, Marston (op. cit., Table 4) estimates that this element accounted for two-thirds of the higher average unemployment rate for blacks from 1967 to 1973.

Factors That Influence the
Natural Unemployment Rate

There is a long list of factors—especially government policies—that economists think influence the natural unemployment rate. Here, we consider briefly some of the more important possibilities, which are unemployment insurance, the minimum wage, and labor unions.

Unemployment Insurance

The government's main program of **unemployment insurance** began in 1936. This program provides benefits to eligible persons who have lost their jobs and are currently "looking for work." Hence, those in the category labeled "unemployment" in Figure 10.3 are candidates for these benefits. While the federal government plays some role, the main rules for eligibility and levels of benefits are set by the various state governments. In general, a person's eligibility depends on a long enough work history in a covered job.[11] (In 1984, 92% of all civilian workers were in covered jobs—see *Economic Report of the President,* 1986, Tables B-32 and B-39.) Also, an individual's benefits run out after a period, which typically lasts between 26 and 39 weeks. But in time of recession, such as 1982–83, the federal government typically extends the period of eligibility.

An employed person can compare his or her current wage with the unemployment benefits that he or she could get by not working. The ratio of the potential benefits to the wage is called the **replacement ratio.** For 1978, this ratio averaged about 50% for people who had jobs.[12] Although precise figures are unavailable, there do not seem to have been large changes in this ratio since World War II. For example, a related figure—which is the ratio of the average weekly check from unemployment insurance programs to average weekly earnings for all nonagricultural workers—was 39% in 1947 and 42% in 1984 (*Economic Report of President,* 1986, Tables B-39 and B-42). Over time, the main changes in the unemployment insurance program have been extensions of coverage (especially to small firms and to employees of state and local governments) and increases in the allowable duration of benefits.

Theoretically, the existence of unemployment insurance makes the unemployed who are receiving benefits less eager to accept jobs or leave the labor force (flows 3 and 4 in Figure 10.3). Also, the program makes the

---

[11]In some states people who quit their jobs or are fired for cause are eligible for benefits, while in others they are ineligible. Of course, it is often hard to tell who quits or is fired for cause, and who loses a job for other reasons. For further discussion of this matter and other issues, see Daniel Hamermesh, *Jobless Pay and the Economy,* Johns Hopkins Press, Baltimore, 1977.

[12]See Kim Clark and Lawrence Summers, "Unemployment Insurance and Labor Market Transitions," in Martin N. Baily, ed, *Workers, Jobs and Inflation,* Brookings Institution, Washington, D.C., 1982. Their calculations also consider the taxes that people pay on wages, but not on unemployment benefits.

unemployed persons who will be eligible for benefits more willing to accept job separations (flow 2 in Figure 10.3).[13] In particular, unemployment insurance motivates **temporary layoffs**—that is, short-term job separations during a period of slack production. Overall, a more generous program of unemployment insurance leads to a higher natural rate of unemployment.

Most empirical estimates of the effects of unemployment insurance rely on differences across states in the levels of benefits and in criteria for eligibility. Using these data, some researchers report that the overall program of unemployment insurance in the United States raises the natural unemployment rate by between $\frac{1}{2}$ and 1 percentage point.[14] In a recent study, Gary Solon ("Work Incentive Effects of Taxing Unemployment Benefits," *Econometrica,* March 1985) notes that since 1979 unemployment insurance benefits have been taxable for high-income families. He estimates that the reduction in effective benefits lowered the duration of insured unemployment for high-income persons by about 10%. However, it is hard to translate this figure into an effect on the overall unemployment rate.

Although there is evidence that unemployment insurance raises the unemployment rate, there is no indication that the effect of unemployment insurance has become greater in recent years. Therefore, this program cannot be blamed for the increase in unemployment rates during the 1970s (see Table 10.2).

The Minimum Wage

When considering determinants of the natural unemployment rate, economists often mention the **minimum wage.** Since 1938, the federal government has set minimum wage rates in covered industries. In 1946 this regulation covered about 57% of all nonsupervisory employees. But changes in legislation raised the coverage to roughly 85% in 1975; then some further changes led to a decline in coverage, which reached 78% in 1983 (*Statistical Abstract of the U.S.,* 1985, p. 422, and earlier issues).

Congress has changed the level of the basic hourly minimum wage numerous times, since the initial choice of 25¢ in 1938. For example, the value

---

[13]This tendency diminishes if the worker's employer must pay for the average benefits given to his or her ex-employees through a process called **experience rating.** With experience rating, a business that has a lot of job separations pays a larger amount into the fund that finances the unemployment benefits. Then employers have incentives to hold down their rates of job separation. In the United States there is some experience rating, but it is highly imperfect. For a discussion, see Robert Topel and Finis Welch, "Unemployment Insurance: Survey and Extensions," *Economica,* August 1980.

[14]See Hamermesh, op. cit., p. 52; and Clark and Summers, op. cit., Table 10. Hamermesh focuses on changes in the duration of unemployment. He also distinguishes the effects in a year of high unemployment from those in a year of low unemployment, but the reported differences are small. Clark and Summers' estimates refer to 1978, for which the overall unemployment rate was 5.9%.

was 75¢ in 1950, $1.25 in 1963, $1.60 in 1968, $2.30 in 1977, and $3.35 in 1981. However, no change has occurred since 1981. The ratio of the minimum wage to average hourly nonfarm earnings ranged between 39 and 56% from 1950 to 1985. Although there is no clear trend, the ratio increased each time Congress enacted a new minimum, but then declined gradually as average hourly earnings rose. For example, with no change in the minimum wage, the ratio fell from 46% in 1981 to 39% in 1985.

A higher minimum wage reduces the incentive of employers to hire low-productivity workers in sectors that are covered by the minimum. Empirically, researchers find that a higher minimum wage and greater coverage tend especially to reduce the employment of teenagers. Typical estimates suggest that an increase by 10% in the minimum wage lowers the quantity of teenagers employed by somewhat more than 1%.[15] There is also some indication of a negative effect on the employment of young adults (aged 20–24), but no clear effect on older workers. In fact, since the minimum wage makes the labor of low-productivity workers artificially more expensive, it is likely that businesses would shift to more labor from high-productivity workers. Hence, labor unions tend to favor the minimum wage to protect their high-paid members from the competition of low-productivity, low-wage workers.

The effects of the minimum wage on teenage unemployment rates depend also on the response of labor-force participation. Because a higher minimum wage reduces the chance of finding a job, it turns out also to reduce the number of teenagers who declare themselves as looking for work. This response lessens the tendency for a higher minimum wage to raise the measured unemployed rate of teenagers.

In any event, the behavior of the minimum wage cannot account for the rise in unemployment rates during the 1970s. That is because, first, the minimum wage has not increased relative to average hourly earnings; second, coverage peaked around 1975 and has since declined; and third, the rise in unemployment rates since the early 1970s applies as much to older workers as to teenagers and young adults.

Labor Unions

Sometimes, people argue that labor unions cause unemployment. Mostly, unions can raise real wage rates and hold down the levels of employment in covered industries. Correspondingly, there is a higher supply of labor and lower real wage rates in uncovered sectors. Therefore, unions can create inefficiencies, which include the inappropriate distribution of work and production between covered and uncovered areas. Conceivably, more union power also leads to reductions in aggregate employment and output. But it is less clear

---

[15]For a survey of the evidence, see Charles Brown, Curtis Gilroy, and Andrew Koehn, "The Effect of the Minimum Wage on Employment and Unemployment: A Survey," *Journal of Economic Literature,* June 1982.

Table 10.3 **Behavior of U.S. Employment Ratios**

	Employment Ratio	
	% of Total Population	% of Population Aged 16–64
1948–54	40	64
1955–61	38	65
1962–69	38	65
1970–77	41	66
1978–85	44	69
1948–85	40	66

Note: The table shows the ratio of total employment (including the military) to the total population and to the population aged 16–64.

Source: Economic Report of the President, 1986, Tables B-30, B-31; 1983, Table B-29.

that unions have anything to do with the overall unemployment rate. That is because the adverse effects on total work may correspond mostly to reductions in the labor force.

In any event, we should look for effects of unions by observing the changes in unionization over time. In fact, the fraction of the civilian labor force that is unionized declined from a peak of 27% in the mid 1950s to 21% in 1980 and about 17% in 1984.[16] Therefore, we cannot attribute the increase in unemployment rates since the 1970s to an increase in unionization. (The principal increases in unionization occurred in the first years of the twentieth century, from less than 3 to 6%; in the mid 1930s, from 7 to 15%; and during World War II, from 16 to 26%.)

Changes in Employment Ratios

The increase in unemployment rates for the 1970s contrasts with the behavior of employment when expressed relative to some measure of population. Table 10.3 shows the ratios of total employment (including the military) to total population and to the population aged 16 to 64. The first ratio varied between 38 and 41% until the mid 1970s, but then increased to 46% in 1985. Similarly, the second ratio stayed between 64 and 66% until the mid 1970s, but then rose to 70%. Thus, the high unemployment rates for recent years coexist with peak ratios of employment to population.

The high employment ratios for the recent period reflect mainly the in-

---

[16]*Statistical Abstract of the U.S.,* 1982–83, pp. 408–09. The figure for 1984 is based on data in Larry T. Adams, "Changing Employment Patterns of Organized Workers," *Monthly Labor Review,* February 1985, pp. 25–26.

crease in the labor-force participation of women. Specifically, the fraction of the civilian labor force that is female rose from 28% in 1948 to 38% in 1969 and 44% in 1985. This development means that there are now many more families with more than one income earner. Accordingly, a given overall rate of unemployment does not have as much significance for the typical family's total earnings as it did previously. (The existence of unemployment insurance and other welfare programs also matters here.)

It is possible that the change in labor-force participation has something to do with the increase in the average rates of unemployment for recent years. If someone's spouse is working, then he or she would be less willing to accept work, and more willing to accept a separation from a current job. But, if this effect is important, then we should see an increase in the unemployment rates of married persons relative to those of single people. In fact, this has not happened. Rather, the unemployment rates of married and single people have increased in roughly parallel fashion in recent years.

Employment and Unemployment during Recessions

In Chapter 9 we showed that supply shocks could account for some characteristics of real-world business fluctuations. In particular, adverse shifts of production functions could generate a recession that featured declines in real GNP and in the ratio of investment to GNP. Aggregate work effort might also decline, although this result depended on a balancing of substitution and wealth effects. Now we can use the apparatus from the present chapter to see how supply shocks affect unemployment. We consider the case of a fixed labor force, so that changes in unemployment reflect inverse movements in employment.

Suppose that an adverse shock reduces the marginal product of labor for the typical worker and job. One effect, which we noted earlier, is that the job-finding rate, η, declines. That is because market opportunities—as determined by labor's marginal product—have become poorer relative to the income while unemployed, w^u. For the same reason, existing job matches become less mutually advantageous for firms and workers. Therefore, job separations tend to increase, especially in the form of layoffs or firings by firms. In any event, the job-separation rate, s, tends to rise.

To see the effects on unemployment and employment, let's return to the example where the labor force was fixed at 100 million persons, and where the job-finding rates were initially 15 and 1%, respectively. Table 10.4 assumes that the economy begins in period 1 at the natural unemployment rate, which is 6.2% in this example. Then the adverse shock to production functions—which we think of as initiating a recession—means that the job-separation rate rises from 1% to, say, 1.5%, while, the job-finding rate falls from 15% to, say, 10%.

Table 10.4 **The Dynamics of Employment and Unemployment during a Recession**

Period	Job-Separation Rate (s)	Job-Finding Rate (η)	Number Employed (N)	Number Unemployed (U)	Number Who Lose Jobs	Number Who Find Jobs	Net Change in Employment
1	0.015	0.10	93.8	6.2	1.4	0.6	−0.8
2	0.015	0.10	93.0	7.0	1.4	0.7	−0.7
3	0.015	0.10	92.3	7.7	1.4	0.8	−0.6
4	0.015	0.10	91.7	8.3	1.4	0.8	−0.6
5	0.015	0.10	91.1	8.9	1.4	0.9	−0.5
6	0.01	0.15	90.6	9.4	0.9	1.4	0.5
7	0.01	0.15	91.1	8.9	0.9	1.3	0.4
8	0.01	0.15	91.5	8.5	0.9	1.3	0.4
9	0.01	0.15	91.9	8.1	0.9	1.2	0.3
10	0.01	0.15	92.2	7.8	0.9	1.2	0.3
.	.	.	.	.	.	.	.
.	.	.	.	.	.	.	.
.	.	.	.	.	.	.	.
∞	0.01	0.15	93.8	6.2	0.9	0.9	0

Note: During the recession for periods 1 through 5, the job-separation rate is high—1.5% rather than 1%—and the job-finding rate is low—10% instead of 15%. Consequently, the unemployment rate rises from the natural rate, 6.2%, to 9.4% in period 6. Then, when the job-separation and job-finding rates return to their normal values in period 6, the economy recovers gradually. In particular, the unemployment rate again approaches the natural rate of 6.2%.

Although some people still find jobs, they are outnumbered by those who lose jobs. Hence, Table 10.4 shows that the unemployment rate rises steadily from 6.2% in period 1 to 9.4% in period 6. Correspondingly, the number employed falls from 93.8 million to 90.6 million.

Suppose that the temporary adverse shock to the production function lasts through period 5. Then from period 6 onward the job-separation rate is again 1%, while the job-finding rate is 15%. Now, although some people still lose their jobs, they are outnumbered by those who find jobs. Therefore, the unemployment rate falls gradually toward the natural rate of 6.2%. Correspondingly, employment rises back toward 93.8 million.

We should stress two realistic features of recessions that emerge from this example. First, the buildup of a recession involves a period of gradually rising unemployment and falling employment. Second, even after an economic recovery begins, it takes a substantial period for the unemployment rate to return to its pre-recession level.

In this example, with a fixed labor force, the dynamics of employment is just the reverse of that of unemployment. Further, if we abstract from changes in the stock of capital, the movements in production would parallel those in employment. Although these patterns capture the broad features of business fluctuations, some elements are missing. First, hours worked per worker (and probably the amount of effort expended by each worker) are more flexible than numbers employed. Therefore, hours per worker and the level of production tend to rise or fall before the corresponding changes in employment. Second, since businesses can readily change their utilization of capital, the movements in production again tend to lead the changes in employment. Third, the labor force can vary. However, except for young persons—who tend to drop out of the labor force in bad times—there turns out to be little association of the labor force with the level of real economic activity (see problem 10.7).

Unemployment during Recent U.S. Recessions

Table 10.5 shows the behavior of output, employment, and unemployment during the seven U.S. recessions since World War II. The percentage shortfalls in real GNP are those that we calculated in Chapter 9 (Table 9.1). Now we make similar computations for employment. When using the total number

Table 10.5 The Behavior of Output, Employment, and Unemployment during Recent U.S. Recessions

Year of Recession	1949	1954	1958	1961	1970	1975	1982	Average for 7
Benchmark Year for Comparison	1948	1953	1956	1959	1969	1973	1979	Recessions
% shortfall in real GNP	2.5%	4.1%	4.5%	1.3%	3.1%	7.5%	8.6%	4.5%
No. employed								
N	59.3	63.5	65.7	68.3	81.9	88.0	101.7	
N^0	60.6	65.6	68.6	69.1	82.6	89.9	105.2	
$N^0 - N$	1.3	2.1	2.9	0.8	0.7	1.9	3.5	
% shortfall	2.1%	3.2%	4.2%	1.1%	0.8%	2.1%	3.3%	2.4%
Total hours								
N	2.34	2.48	2.53	2.64	3.04	3.18	3.54	
N^0	2.42	2.59	2.68	2.68	3.11	3.31	3.73	
$N^0 - N$	0.08	0.11	0.15	0.04	0.07	0.13	0.19	
% shortfall	3.3%	4.2%	5.6%	1.5%	2.3%	3.9%	5.1%	3.7%
U	5.8%	5.3%	6.5%	6.5%	4.8%	8.3%	9.5%	
U^0	3.7%	2.8%	4.0%	5.3%	3.4%	4.7%	5.7%	
$U - U^0$	2.1%	2.5%	2.5%	1.2%	1.4%	3.6%	3.8%	2.4%

Note: The shortfall in real GNP comes from Table 9.1. N is total employment (millions) or total weekly hours (billions), and U is the unemployment rate for the total labor force. We calculate the hypothetical levels of employment, N^0, from the benchmark years by the method described in the text. For the unemployment rate, U^0 is the actual value for the base year.

Source of basic data: *Economic Report of the President, 1985.*

employed (including the military), the average shortfall for the seven recessions was by 2.4%.[17] These ranged from less than 1% for 1970 to 4.2% for 1958. Notice that, for each recession, the percentage shortfall in employment was smaller than that in real GNP. As an average for the seven recessions, the percentage shortfall in real GNP (4.5%) exceeded that of employment (2.4%) by about 2 percentage points. Hence, the ratio of real GNP to the number of workers—which is one measure of "productivity"—fell on average by about 2% during these recessions.

From the standpoint of aggregate labor input, a measure of total hours is more pertinent than the number of persons employed. To get the figures for total hours, we multiply the values for numbers employed by an estimate of average weekly hours of persons employed. Since average weekly hours tend to decline during recessions, there are greater percentage shortfalls in total hours[18] than in numbers employed. In fact, for the seven recessions in Table 10.5, the average shortfall of 3.7% for total hours was only a small amount below that of 4.5% for real GNP. Hence, the recessions showed little systematic change in productivity when measured as real GNP per worker-hour. The two cases of substantial decline in this concept of productivity were those for 1975 and 1982.

Finally, Table 10.5 shows the behavior of the unemployment rate during the seven recessions. On average, the unemployment rate increased by 2.4 percentage points. The 1980–82 recession was the worst with an increase by 3.8 percentage points, but 1974–75 was a close second with 3.6 points.

Supply Shocks, Recessions, and Unemployment

Our theory shows how supply shocks could cause recessions, such as those described in Table 10.5. What we would like to know is how much these recessions actually were the result of identifiable supply shocks. Although we cannot give a definite answer to this question, there are some suggestive findings from recent empirical research.

James Hamilton[19] documents the important role of oil shocks. Most economists believe that the dramatic increases in oil prices in 1973–74 and 1979–81 were important factors in the recessions of 1974–75 and 1980–82. Hamilton supports this view, but he also makes the surprising observation that the tendency "for oil price increases to be followed by recessions has in fact characterized every recession in the United States since World War II, with the single exception of the recession of 1960–61" (op. cit., p. 229). For example, the recession of 1957–58 followed the increase in oil prices that stemmed from the Suez crisis, while the downturn of 1954 came after a rise in oil prices

---

[17]We use the trend growth rate of 1.4% per year to calculate the hypothetical level of employment, N^0.

[18]For total hours, we use the trend growth rate of 1.2% per year.

[19]"Oil and the Macroeconomy since World War II," *Journal of Political Economy*, April 1983.

because of the Iranian nationalization of facilities. Overall, Hamilton's statistical results suggest that oil shocks have been important sources of high unemployment and low growth of real GNP. Moreover, the magnitude of the recent shocks—for 1973–74 and 1979–81—can explain why the last two recessions—1974–75 and 1980–82—were the most severe of the post-World War II period. The severity of these recessions explains at least a good part of the higher average unemployment rate since the mid 1970s (see Table 10.2).

Aside from oil, economists have not been successful in pinpointing identifiable shocks as regular elements in U.S. business fluctuations. Of course, it is still possible that an array of disturbances to productive conditions—which macroeconomists cannot identify directly—accounted for the recessions and booms. David Lilien[20] pursued this idea by focusing on the changing composition of U.S. production. Recently this composition has moved away from traditional areas of manufacturing, such as steel and automobiles, and toward high-tech industries and services. (Earlier the dominant movement was from agriculture to manufacturing.) Lilien argues that the process of reallocating labor across sectors means high rates of job separation and therefore high rates of unemployment.[21]

Lilien's empirical results for the post-World War II United States (op. cit., pp. 787–92) show that periods of more rapidly changing industrial composition tend to be times of unusually high unemployment. Thus, the findings suggest that U.S. recessions derive in part from various real shocks—such as technological innovations, changes in foreign competition, or variations in the relative prices of raw materials—that induce shifts in the composition of industry. However, a number of economists have questioned this conclusion. In particular, Prakash Loungani[22] shows that, once we hold fixed the behavior of oil prices, there is no longer much association in the data between changes in the composition of production and the unemployment rate. Thus, at this point, the main evidence on the importance of supply shocks comes from the effects of oil.

Summary

When workers and jobs differ it takes time for people to match up well with jobs. Workers search for positions with high wages (and other desirable characteristics), while businesses search for productive workers. During the process of search, some job-seekers remain unemployed, while some positions remain

---

[20]"Sectoral Shifts and Cyclical Unemployment," *Journal of Political Economy,* August 1982.

[21]Our simple theory, summarized in equation 10.3, says that the natural unemployment rate is $s/(s + \eta)$. Thus, we predict an increase in unemployment if the job-separation rate, s, rises proportionately more than the job-finding rate, η.

[22]"Oil Price Shocks and the Dispersion Hypothesis," *Review of Economics & Statistics,* August 1986. For additional discussion see Katharine Abraham and Larry Katz, "Cyclical Unemployment: Sectoral Shifts or Aggregate Disturbances," *Journal of Political Economy,* June 1986.

vacant. The rate of job finding depends on such things as the income available while unemployed, and the level and shape of the distribution of wage offers.

Because workers or firms make mistakes in their initial assessments, and because circumstances change, existing jobs sometimes end. The job-separation rate depends on workers' characteristics—such as age and experience—and on the variability of an industry's supply and demand conditions.

The dynamics of employment and unemployment depend on the rates of job separation and job finding. If these rates are constant, then the economy tends automatically to a natural rate of unemployment. This natural rate rises with an increase in the job-separation rate, but falls with an increase in the job-finding rate. Also movements in and out of the labor force influence the natural unemployment rate.

We use this framework to analyze differences in average unemployment rates by age, sex, and race. Specifically, we can relate these differences to underlying differences in the duration of jobs and of unemployment. For example, younger workers have much higher job-separation rates and therefore exhibit a higher average unemployment rate.

We found before that supply shocks can generate a recession in the sense that output declines. Now we show that this kind of shock also lowers the job-finding rate and raises the job-separation rate. Thereby unemployment rises and employment falls during a recession. Empirically, the main evidence for these effects from supply shocks concerns changes in oil prices.

On average for the seven postwar recessions in the United States, the increase in the overall unemployment rate was by 2.4 percentage points. Correspondingly, there was a reduction in employment and a proportionately larger reduction in total hours worked. When viewed in conjunction with the shortfall in real GNP, there is some tendency for productivity—that is, output as a ratio to labor input—to fall during recessions. But this tendency is weak if we measure labor input by total hours, rather than by numbers of persons employed.

Important Terms and Concepts

labor force

unemployment

unemployment rate

vacancies

reservation wage

job-separation rate

job-finding rate

natural unemployment rate

outside of the labor force

discouraged workers

duration of jobs

duration of unemployment

unemployment insurance

replacement ratio (for unemployment insurance)

experience rating (for unemployment insurance)

temporary layoffs

minimum wage

Mainly for Review

10.1 What is the definition of the unemployment rate? Since it does not include workers who moved from "unemployment" to "out of the labor force," is it an underestimate of the amount of unemployment in the economy? Can you think of any reason that the unemployment rate overestimates unemployment?

10.2 Suppose that a job-seeker receives a wage offer, w, that exceeds his or her wage while unemployed, w^u. Why might the person reject the offer?

10.3 Once a worker and a firm find a job match, why would they ever choose to end this match? Can you list some elements that influence the rate of job separation?

10.4 What is the natural rate of unemployment? When would unemployment differ from the natural rate? Can the natural rate itself change over time?

Problems for Discussion

10.5 **The Job-Finding Rate**
Discuss the effect on the job-finding rate and the expected duration of unemployment from the following:
a. an increase in unemployment insurance benefits,
b. an increase in the minimum wage,
c. a technological shock that improves the available wage offers.

Consider a group of job seekers whose skills are hard to evaluate. For such people, the distribution of wage offers tends to have a wide dispersion. Would the job-finding rate be high or low for this group?

10.6 **The Job-Separation Rate, the Job-Finding Rate, and the Natural Rate of Unemployment**
Suppose that the labor force has 100 million people, of whom 92 million initially have jobs and 8 million are unemployed. Assume that the job-separation rate is 1% per period and the job-finding rate is 20% per period. Also, suppose that we can neglect movements in and out of the labor force. Trace out the path of employment and unemployment. What is the natural unemployment rate?

10.7 **The Labor Force during Recessions**
The data show little systematic response of the overall civilian labor force to recessions and booms. What response would you predict on theoretical grounds? (*Hint:* Think first about people's incentives to leave the labor force—that is, to stop looking for work—during a recession. But are there also incentives for some people to enter the labor force during bad times?)

On the other hand, the teenage labor force declines during recessions. How can we explain this observation?

10.8 **Women and Teenagers in the Labor Force**
The unemployment rate for women averages about one percentage point higher than that for men (see Table 10.2). Further, the fraction of the civilian labor force that is female rose from 28% in 1948 to 44% in 1985. How would this increased role of women in the labor force affect the overall value of the natural unemployment rate?

For teenagers (aged 16 to 19) the average unemployment rate is about 10 percentage points higher than that for adults. The fraction of the civilian labor force that is teenage rose from about 6.5% in the early 1950s to almost 9.5% in the late 1970s, but then fell to 6.8% in 1985. What do these changes mean for the overall value of the natural unemployment rate?

10.9 **The Minimum Wage Rate**
How does an increase in the minimum wage rate affect the employment of
a. high- and low-productivity workers in covered industries?
b. high- and low-productivity workers in uncovered industries?
What does a higher minimum wage rate mean for the unemployment rate of
a. teenagers?
b. all workers?

10.10 **Okun's Law**
Okun's law (named after the economist, Arthur Okun) states that the ratio of the percentage shortfall in output during a recession to the percentage point increase in the unemployment rate is roughly equal to 3.

Calculate these ratios for the seven post-war recessions covered in Table 10.5. How does Okun's law hold up?

How does Okun's law relate to the behavior of productivity during a recession?

10.11 **Vacancies and Unemployment** (optional)
We considered in the text how an adverse shock to production functions could lead to higher unemployment (as well as lower employment and production).
a. What would this type of disturbance do to the number of job vacancies? Therefore, how would the amount of vacancies relate to the level of real economic activity?
b. Consider a graph of unemployment versus vacancies. (Economists sometimes call such a graph a *Beveridge curve,* after the British economist, William Beveridge.) What would you predict for the slope of this graph?

CHAPTER 11

THE ACCUMULATION OF CAPITAL AND ECONOMIC GROWTH

So far, we have studied investment in a short-run context, where changes in the stock of capital are small enough to neglect. In this context we focused on the role of investment as a component of the aggregate demand for goods. Now we want to allow for the effects of changing capital stocks on productive capacity—that is, on the aggregate supply of goods. Thereby, we bring in one of the central elements that influences a country's economic development over the long term.

Let's be clear about some important elements that we hold constant initially while we study the process of capital accumulation. One of these is population, which is a major determinant of the aggregate labor force. Another is the accumulation of human capital—that is, education and training—which alters the quality of the labor force. But for most purposes, the economic forces that influence the accumulation of human capital are similar to those that affect physical capital. That is, in our theory, we can take a broad view of capital to include education and training along with buildings and machines. (However, although economists have made some estimates, it is difficult to measure human capital empirically.)

Finally, we omit **technological change,** which we might model as shifts in the form of the production function. We can think here of research and experience, which lead over time to better understanding about methods of production and types of goods. For some purposes, we can think of knowledge as another form of capital, which producers can accumulate through expenditures on research and development. But there are some important differences: in particular, it is hard to maintain property rights to knowledge, and an awareness about how to produce things does not tend to diminish as it spreads over more producers or a larger scale of operations.

Effects of the Capital Stock on Production, Work Effort, and Consumption

Until now, we treated the aggregate stock of capital as a constant. But since this stock will change over time, we have to investigate how these changes affect the quantities of goods supplied and demanded. The first thing to consider is how the quantity of capital input interacts with the quantity of labor input.

Interactions between Capital and Labor

How does an increase in capital affect the productivity of labor, and vice versa? We could construct examples where an increase in one input, capital or labor, either raises or lowers the marginal product of the other. But for our purposes, we want to model the typical pattern of interaction between capital and labor. Research on production functions at an economy-wide level indicates that cooperation between the inputs is the usual case. Therefore, we assume in our model that an increase in one factor, capital or labor, raises the marginal product of the other.

Returns to Scale

What happens to output if a producer doubles the quantities of both inputs, capital and labor? Does the producer get twice the output, or more or less than twice the output? If output exactly doubles, then we say that the production function exhibits **constant returns to scale.** Alternatively, there are either **increasing or decreasing returns to scale** as output more or less than doubles, respectively. Of course, there may be increasing returns over some range of operations, constant returns over another range, and decreasing returns over a third range.

Usually, the operation of a business requires some *fixed costs,* such as setting up an assembly line or learning about techniques of production. Since these fixed costs arise only once, there tends to be an interval of increasing returns to scale—in particular, the second unit produced requires fewer inputs than the first. Later on, as the effect of the fixed cost becomes less important and the owner's span of attention and control becomes stretched, there may be a range of decreasing returns.[1] Until they reach this last range, firms in an industry tend to grow larger to exploit the economies of scale. For present purposes, we assume that producing units (still owned by households in our model) are large enough so that diminishing returns apply. That is, in the

---

[1]For discussions of how this and related factors determine the sizes of firms, see Ronald H. Coase, "The Nature of the Firm," *Economica,* November 1937; and Armen A. Alchian and Harold Demsetz, "Production, Information Costs, and Economic Organization," *American Economic Review,* December 1972.

relevant range, a doubling of a producer's capital and labor leads to less than twice as much output.

The Capital Stock and Households' Choices

Remember that a producer's output for period t depends on the previous stock of capital, k_{t-1}, through the production function

$$y_t = f(k_{t-1}, n_t)$$

(Again we neglect firms and think of households as carrying out production.) From the standpoint of a producer during period t, a greater amount of capital, k_{t-1}, looks just like an upward shift in the production function. In particular, given the amount of work effort, n_t, an increase in capital k_{t-1}, means a larger supply of goods, y_t^s.

Other things equal, households are better off at date t if they own a greater amount of capital, k_{t-1}. Of course, to acquire this capital, they had to make investments in the past. These investments had to be financed, possibly by borrowing on the credit market. Thus, in deciding how much to invest, people weighed the benefits from having extra capital against the costs of acquiring it.

From the standpoint of society as a whole, the amounts borrowed and lent cancel. Therefore, the total stock of capital, K_{t-1}, must reflect previous acts of saving—that is, abstinence from either consumption or leisure. However, once period t arrives, these costs associated with acquiring the aggregate stock of capital are bygones. In making decisions, households count the capital as wealth, but make no subtraction in the aggregate for the past hardships that underlie the acquisition of the capital. (An individual subtracts his or her current debts that were incurred to finance investment. But in the aggregate, the stock of debt is zero.) From the perspective of period t, if the capital stock K_{t-1} is higher by 1 unit, then aggregate wealth rises just as it would if people had received 1 unit of goods as a gift from the sky. Therefore, a larger stock of capital, K_{t-1}, means more aggregate consumer demand, C_t^d.

Finally, there are two effects from more capital, K_{t-1}, on aggregate work effort, N_t. First, the wealth effect motivates less work. But second, the increase in capital raises the schedule for labor's marginal product. Since this change raises work effort, the overall response is ambiguous.

Capital in the Market-Clearing Condition

Putting together the results from above, the condition for clearing the commodity market at date t is now

$$Y^s(r_t, K_{t-1}, \ldots) = C^d(r_t, K_{t-1}, \ldots) + I^d(r_t, K_{t-1}, \ldots) \qquad (11.1)$$
$$(+)(+) \qquad\qquad (-)(+) \qquad\qquad (-)(-)$$

Notice the complex role of the capital stock, K_{t-1}, in this equation. First, an increase in this stock raises productive capacity, which underlies the positive effect on goods supplied, Y_t^s. Then, because of the wealth effect, the higher stock of capital raises consumer demand, C_t^d. However, given producers' desired stocks of capital for period t, an increase in the previous stock, K_{t-1}, reduces gross investment demand, I_t^d. Finally, there is also an ambiguous effect of the capital stock on work effort. This effect modifies the overall impact of the capital stock on the supply of goods, Y_t^s, and consumer demand, C_t^d.

The process of capital accumulation works as follows. At date t there is a given stock of capital, K_{t-1}, from the previous period. Then, as in the analysis from the previous chapter, we determine the real interest rate, r_t, and the quantities of output, Y_t, and investment, I_t, from the market-clearing condition in equation 11.1. Thereby, we determine the stock of capital for the next period from the condition

$$K_t = K_{t-1} + I_t - \delta K_{t-1} \qquad (11.2)$$

That is, we add net investment, $I_t - \delta K_{t-1}$, to the previous stock of capital, K_{t-1}, to determine the next period's stock, K_t.

Once we know the capital stock, K_t, we can again use the market-clearing condition to determine the next period's real interest rate, r_{t+1}, and the quantities of output, Y_{t+1}, and investment, I_{t+1}. Thus, we determine a sequence of capital stocks, outputs, and so on. In this way we can use the model to chart out a time path of economic development. (But remember that we do not allow yet for changes in population or technology.)

For subsequent purposes, we shall find it convenient to subtract depreciation, δK_{t-1}, from both sides of equation 11.1. Then the market-clearing condition becomes

$$Y^s(r_t, K_{t-1}, \ldots) - \delta K_{t-1} = C^d(r_t, K_{t-1}, \ldots)$$
$$(+)(+) \qquad\qquad\qquad (-)(+)$$
$$+ I^d(r_t, K_{t-1}, \ldots) - \delta K_{t-1} \quad (11.3)$$
$$(-)(-)$$

Note that the left side is the supply of net product, $Y_t^s - \delta K_{t-1}$, while the right side includes net investment demand, $I_t^d - \delta K_{t-1}$, along with consumption demand, C_t^d.

An Increase in the Capital Stock over One Period

Suppose that at some initial date, $t = 1$, the economy has the aggregate capital stock, K_0. Then, using equation 11.3, the market-clearing condition is

$$Y^s(r_1, K_0, \ldots) - \delta K_0 = C^d(r_1, K_0, \ldots) + I^d(r_1, K_0, \ldots) - \delta K_0$$
$$(+)(+) \qquad\qquad (-)(+) \qquad\qquad (-)(-) \qquad\qquad (11.4)$$

In Figure 11.1 the upward-sloping line shows the supply of net product, $Y_1^s - \delta K_0$, while the downward-sloping line shows the demand, $Y_1^d - \delta K_0$.

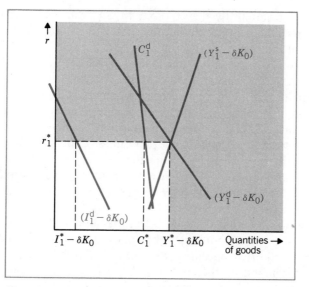

Figure 11.1 Clearing of the Commodity Market
At date 1 the commodity market clears at the real interest rate r_1^*. Net product is $Y_1^* - \delta K_0$, which breaks down into C_1^* of consumption and $I_1^* - \delta K_0$ of net investment.

Hence, the market-clearing real interest rate is the value r_1^*, while the corresponding quantity of net product is the amount, $Y_1^* - \delta K_0$. Note that the figure shows also the two components of demand, which are consumption, C_1^d, and net investment, $I_1^d - \delta K_0$. As before, the figure shows that investment demand is more responsive than consumption demand to variations in the real interest rate. We can use the figure to determine the breakdown of net product into consumption, C_1^*, and net investment, $I_1^* - \delta K_0$.

Assume that aggregate net investment, $I_1^* - \delta K_0$, is positive, as shown in Figure 11.1. Then the next period's stock of capital, K_1, would exceed the initial stock, K_0. Now we have to solve the following problem. How does the increase in the quantity of capital from K_0 to K_1 change the market-clearing condition? In particular, how does the next period's real interest rate, r_2^*, compare with the initial one, r_1^*? Note that in solving this problem we assume that the aggregate capital stock is the only thing that changes between periods 1 and 2.

Using equation 11.3, the market-clearing condition for period 2 is

$$Y^s(r_2, K_1, \ldots) - \delta K_1 = C^d(r_2, K_1, \ldots) + I^d(r_2, K_1, \ldots) - \delta K_1 \quad (11.5)$$
$$(+)(+) \qquad\qquad (-)(+) \qquad\qquad (-)(-)$$

Consider how the increase in capital from K_0 to K_1 changes the various terms. First, for a given amount of work, an increase in capital stock makes the supply of net product, $Y_2^s - \delta K_1$, higher than before. In fact, an extra unit of capital raises this net supply by the amount, $MPK_1 - \delta$, which is the real rate of return to investment. (Recall that investors equate this return to the previous period's real interest rate, r_1^*.)

Next, the increase in capital makes consumer demand, C_2^d, higher than before. To assess the magnitude of this response, we can use the concept of permanent income. If we neglect variations over time in capital's marginal product, then an extra unit of capital provides a constant flow of real income in the amount, $MPK_1 - \delta$. Hence, permanent income increases by this amount. But then if work does not change, consumer demand also rises by approximately the amount, $MPK_1 - \delta$. In other words, the increase in consumption demand roughly equals the increase in the supply of net product. Therefore, the increase in the stock of capital does not lead to a significant change in desired real saving.[2]

So far, we find that the increase in the supply of net product on the left side of equation 11.5 approximately equals the increase in consumer demand on the right side. But the increase in capital from K_0 to K_1 also reduces net investment demand on the right side. Hence, it is uncertain whether the aggregate demand for net product rises or falls. But in any event, we conclude that more capital raises the supply of net product by more than the demand.

The dashed lines in Figure 11.2 show these results for period 2. Note that the rightward shifts to net supply, $Y_2^s - \delta K_1$, and consumer demand, C_2^d, are the same. Net investment demand, $I_2^d - \delta K_1$, shifts leftward. (This demand is zero at the previous real interest rate, r_1^*—if the real interest rate did not change, producers would have no incentive to alter their capital stocks during period 2.) Finally, although the direction of this change is ambiguous, the figure shows a leftward shift in the aggregate demand for net product, $Y_2^d - \delta K_1$.

At the initial real interest rate, r_1^*, the supply of net product during period 2 is greater than the demand—or, equivalently, desired real saving exceeds net investment demand. Therefore, the real interest rate falls to the value, r_2^*. The important point is that an increase in the stock of capital leads to a lower real interest rate.

Now, consider what happens to the various quantities. First, consumption must increase, $C_2^* > C_1^*$. That is because the direct effect from more capital and the decline in the real interest rate combine to raise consumer demand. However, the change in work is ambiguous. Here, the decline in the real interest rate and the wealth effect from more capital motivate less work. But the positive effect of the extra capital on labor's marginal product motivates more work.

Unless work effort falls by a great deal, the increase in capital input means that gross and net product expand. In Figure 11.2 we show that the second period's net product, $Y_2^* - \delta K_1$, exceeds the first, $Y_1^* - \delta K_0$.

---

[2]The change in the amount of work effort is ambiguous. But whatever this change, there will still be little effect on desired real saving.

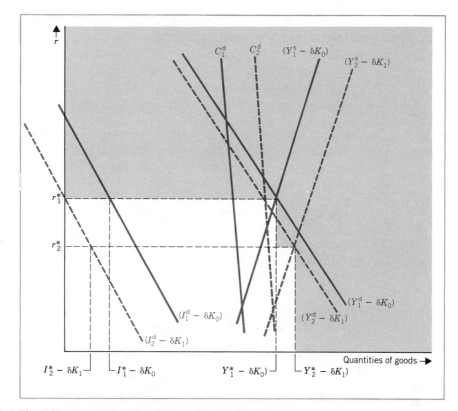

Figure 11.2 The Effects of More Capital on the Commodity Market
We show the effects of an increase in capital from K_0 to K_1. The rightward shifts in the supply of net product and in consumer demand are roughly equal. Therefore, since net investment demand declines, the real interest rate falls from r_1^* to r_2^*. The change in net product (shown as positive) is generally ambiguous.

Figure 11.2 shows graphically that net investment declines—that is, $I_2^* - \delta K_1 < I_1^* - \delta K_0$. We know that this must be the case since otherwise the increase in net product would exceed the rise in consumption. But this outcome is impossible if the rightward shifts to the supply of net product and consumer demand are equal as assumed in the figure. Thus, an increase in the stock of capital leads to less net investment. Moreover, it follows that net investment declines as a ratio to the previous stock of capital—that is, the growth rate of the capital stock falls. Also, there is a reduction in the ratio of net investment to net or gross product.

Finally, since depreciation rises along with the increase in the amount of capital, we cannot say whether gross investment rises or falls. But recall that gross investment equals net investment plus depreciation. Observe that the first part, net investment, declines relative to the previous stock of capital.

Then the second part, depreciation, maintains a constant ratio to this stock. Therefore, gross investment declines overall relative to the previous stock of capital.

Increases in the Capital Stock over Many Periods

As long as net investment is positive, the process described above continues over time. The increase in the capital stock is accompanied by a declining real interest rate, rising consumption, and falling net investment. Also, there are probable increases in net and gross product, but ambiguous changes in work effort.

Recall that the growth rate of capital declines over time. Remember also that the change in the capital stock generates the changes in the other variables. Therefore, the responses of the other quantities—in particular, consumption and total output—tend to become proportionately smaller over time. That is, there are declining growth rates of consumption and of gross and net product.

Let's think about why the real interest rate declines over time. At the start, date 1, the economy has a relatively low capital stock, K_0, and a correspondingly high marginal product of capital, MPK_1. The high real interest rate, r_1^*, signals the cost of using up resources during period 1, rather than later. Specifically, this high cost reflects the favorable investment climate, in the sense of a high level of the investment demand function. Consuming at date 1, rather than later, is justified only if people are willing to forego returns at the rate r_1^*, which equals the real rate of return to investment, $MPK_1 - \delta$.

As the economy matures, the capital stock rises and the marginal product of capital declines. Because of these diminishing opportunities for investment, there is a declining real interest rate, r_t^*, which signals a decreasing return from deferring consumption.

The Steady-State Capital Stock and Real Interest Rate

How long does the process of capital accumulation go on?[3] (Recall again that, so far, we ask this question when population and technology are fixed.) We have already seen that the growth rate of capital tends to fall over time. In fact, this growth rate eventually approaches zero, which means that the capital stock tends to some long-run level. Therefore, net investment eventually becomes zero. Corresponding to the fixed quantity of capital, there are constant levels of output, consumption, gross investment (which equals depreciation here), and work effort. Economists refer to this situation as a **steady state.**

---

[3]The discussion in this section draws on the classic treatment of the dynamics of saving and investment from Frank Ramsey, "A Mathematical Theory of Saving," *Economic Journal*, December 1928.

By a steady state, we mean a position where a set of variables stays constant over time. In our model the growth rates of capital, output, consumption, and work effort are all zero in the steady state. (When we introduce growth of population and technology later on, we shall find that the steady-state growth rates can be positive.)

Now let's examine the real interest rate in the steady state. To carry out this analysis, we have to recall that at any date t, an individual's overall utility is given by

$$U = u(c_t, n_t) + \frac{1}{(1+\rho)} u(c_{t+1}, n_{t+1}) + \cdots$$

where ρ is again the rate of time preference.

In a steady state, people pick the constant values, $c_t = c_{t+1} = \cdots = c$, and $n_t = n_{t+1} = \cdots = n$. Then overall utility is

$$U = u(c, n) + \frac{1}{(1+\rho)} u(c, n) + \cdots$$

But, for this to be the right answer, it must be that a person cannot do better by picking something other than constant values for consumption and work. (Otherwise people could achieve a higher level of overall utility.)

If the steady-state real interest rate is the value r^*, then a person can use the credit market to trade one unit of consumption (or leisure) at date t for $(1+r^*)$ units at date $t+1$. Suppose, for example, that a decrease of c_t by 1 unit would lower period t's utility, $u(c, n)$, by the quantity Δu. Then an increase of the quantity c_{t+1} by $(1+r^*)$ units would raise period $t+1$'s utility by the quantity $(1+r^*)\Delta u$.[4] We multiply this last change by the term, $1/(1+\rho)$, to find the effect on overall utility. Therefore, the full effect on overall utility is given by

$$\Delta u\left[-1 + \frac{1}{(1+\rho)} \cdot (1+r^*)\right]$$

For people to choose constant values of consumption and work, it must be that the term in brackets is zero. This happens when the steady-state real interest rate, r^*, equals the rate of time preference, ρ. Otherwise, people could raise their overall utility by either lowering or raising today's consumption (or leisure) and making the corresponding adjustments to future quantitites.

The conclusion is that, if $r^* = \rho$, people are happy with a constant level of consumption (and work). Further, the level of consumption must equal the level of net product. (Note that net product equals gross product less depreciation, where depreciation equals gross investment in the steady state.) In

---

[4]This calculation works because we start from a position where $c_{t+1} = c_t$ and $n_{t+1} = n_t$. Otherwise, we would have to worry about the relative amounts of consumption and work for the two periods.

other words, real saving is zero in the steady state. This result is consistent with the finding that net investment also equals zero.

Recall that the process of increasing capital stocks involves reductions in the real interest rate, r_t^*. Now we know that the real interest rate eventually approaches the rate of time preference, ρ. Thus, the path of real interest rates looks like the one shown in Figure 11.3. Along the path, where $r_t^* > \rho$, net investment and real saving are positive. But, as the capital stock expands, net investment and real saving decline and the real interest rate approaches the value ρ.

What determines the level of the steady-state capital stock? Recall that, for any period, the real rate of return to investment, $MPK_t - \delta$, equals the real interest rate, r_t^*. Since the steady-state real interest rate equals the rate of time preference, ρ, the condition for the steady state is

$$MPK - \delta = \rho \qquad (11.6)$$

We do not date the marginal product, MPK, since it remains constant in a steady state.

Let's sketch an example to illustrate the nature of the steady-state results. Suppose that at date 1 the economy is in a steady-state position where capital's marginal product, MPK_1, equals the value $\rho + \delta$. Call this steady-state level of capital K_0. Note that during period 1 the real interest rate is the value,

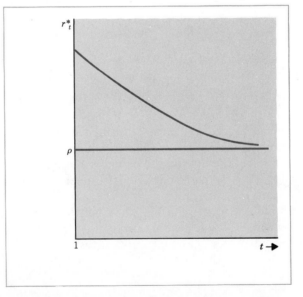

Figure 11.3 The Behavior of the Real Interest Rate over Time
As the capital stock grows over time, the real interest rate declines and approaches the rate of time preference, ρ.

$r_1^* = \text{MPK}_1 - \delta = \rho$. Further, the initial quantitites of net investment and real saving are zero.

Now assume that there is a permanent improvement of the production function during period 2. Hence, producers get more output for given inputs. Also, suppose that there are permanent upward shifts in the schedules for the marginal products of labor and capital. Recall that we carried out a short-run analysis of this type of disturbance in Chapter 9 (although we looked there at a worsening of the production function). Briefly, we get the following effects. Because the change is permanent, there are roughly equal increases in the supply of net product and in consumer demand. That is, desired real saving remains close to zero. However, because of the rise in capital's marginal product, net investment demand becomes positive. Therefore, at the initial real interest rate, $r_1^* = \rho$, there is an excess of commodity demand over supply. Equivalently, net investment demand exceeds desired real saving. Figure 11.4 shows these effects.

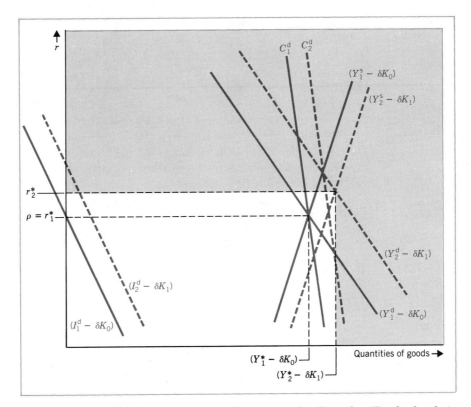

Figure 11.4 Effects of a One-Time Improvement of the Production Function (Beginning from a Steady State)

The permanent improvement of the production function during period 2 causes the demand for goods to exceed the supply at the initial real interest rate, $r_1^* = \rho$. Therefore, the real interest rate increases to r_2^*.

During period 2, the real interest rate, r_2^*, rises above its initial value, $r_1^* = \rho$. Now the economy is in the sort of position where we began our previous analysis of capital accumulation. Net investment is positive and the real interest rate exceeds its steady-state value, ρ. Hence, the stock of capital rises over time, while the real interest rate falls. Eventually, the economy approaches a new steady state, where the stock of capital exceeds the amount, K_0, from the previous steady state. Then the real interest rate returns to the steady-state value, ρ.

To summarize, a permanent improvement in the production function—which includes an upward shift to the schedule for capital's marginal product—raises net investment and the real interest rate in the short run. But in the long run, the economy ends up with more capital—as well as more output and consumption—and no change in the real interest rate.

Changes in Population

A One-Time Increase in Population

Suppose that at date 1 the economy is again in a steady state with the aggregate quantity of capital, K_0. Assume that during period 2 the population increases once and for all by, say, 10%. Let's think of a case where the number of households rises as well by 10%. Then assume that the new households are just like the old ones in terms of average age, tastes, and productivity. Remember that the households are the producing units in the model, so the number of producers also rises by 10%. But the new households might begin life with zero capital. Alternatively, the old households (parents) may provide the new ones (children) with a starting amount of capital. However, the main analysis goes through in either case.

If the aggregate stock of capital does not change, then the typical producer has less capital to work with than before. Therefore, the marginal product of capital exceeds its steady-state value, $\rho + \delta$. In the aggregate, the desired stock of capital increases, which makes aggregate net investment demand positive. There are also increases in the aggregates of work effort, goods supply, and consumer demand. In fact, we can again use Figure 11.4 to show the various responses. In particular, the demand for goods exceeds the supply at the initial real interest rate, r_1^*. Therefore, the real interest rate increases—that is, $r_2^* > r_1^* = \rho$.

The one-time increase in population puts the economy in the familiar position where the real interest rate exceeds its steady-state value, ρ. We can understand this by noting that the rise in population effectively places the typical producer back in an earlier stage of economic development, where he or she has less capital to work with. In this situation the real interest rate exceeds its steady-state value.

Following the increase in the real interest rate for period 2, we can trace out the usual path where the aggregate capital stock increases, while the real interest rate declines toward its steady-state value, ρ. But what can we say about the various quantitites in this new steady state? In particular, do the aggregates of capital, output, consumption, and work all rise by 10%—that is, by the same proportion as population?

The aggregate quantities would all be higher by 10% if production exhibited constant returns to scale. Then a 10% increase in the aggregates of capital and labor would produce 10% more goods. Also, the marginal product of capital would be the same as initially—namely, equal to its steady-state value, $\rho + \delta$.

Since the number of producing units also increases by 10%, why would we expect something other than constant returns? There is some tendency for diminishing returns because there is no change in the aggregate of "land," by which we mean to include various types of natural resoures and physical space. Probably, there is a range of production over which constant returns is a reasonable approximation. That is, returns to scale are nearly constant until the fixed quantity of land becomes a major constraint. Over the range where nearly constant returns applies, we find that an expansion of population by 10% does lead in the long run to nearly 10% increases in the aggregates of capital, output, consumption, and work effort.

Population Growth

We would like now to study continuing growth in population. However, the details of this subject bring in some complications that would take the discussion far afield. So let's just sketch some results, which are only suggestive.

Continue to assume that returns to scale are roughly constant. But assume now that population grows at a steady rate, rather than jumping all at once. For example, growth rates of population between 0 and 2% per year are typical of industrialized countries in the post-World War II period. For the United States, the rate was around 3% per year in the early 19th century, but was only 1.1% between 1960 and 1985.[5]

The growth in population has a continuing upward effect on the aggregates of capital, output, consumption, and work effort. Specifically, the economy no longer approaches a steady state where these aggregates are constant. Instead, we have a situation that economists call **steady-state growth.** Here, the aggregate quantities of capital, output, consumption, and work effort all grow at the same rate as population. Although the levels of these variables change over time, certain ratios are constant in a position of steady-state growth. These include the per capita amounts of capital, output, and con-

---

[5]Immigration accounted for roughly one-third of the growth in population from the mid-nineteenth century until the 1920s. Then immigration was relatively small from the 1930s through the 1960s. But the numbers rose in recent years. In 1983 the reported figures on immigration accounted for 24% of the increase in population. (See *Statistical Abstracts of the U.S.*, 1985, p. 9.) If all illegal immigrants were included, this fraction would be much higher.

sumption. Hence, the per capita growth rates of capital, output, and consumption are all zero in a position of steady-state growth.

Unlike our previous steady states, a position of steady-state growth has positive aggregate net investment and real saving. The net investment provides capital for the new members of society. Thereby, the quantities of capital per person and per worker can remain constant over time. We can think of parents as carrying out the saving in order to provide for their children—in effect, to establish their children in a business (or to provide them with education). Notice that, with a positive growth rate of population, it is not enough for people just to pass on capital to their descendants. There is more than one child per adult on average. Therefore, the typical adult must carry out positive real saving over his or her lifetime.

What is the real interest rate in a position of steady-state growth? Since consumption per person is constant, our previous results suggest that the real interest rate would still equal the rate of time preference, ρ. But remember that the typical parent carries out positive real saving here. The saving goes not to raise consumption per person, but rather to provide for the growing population. For this all to make sense, it must be that parents care about their children. That is, they care to the extent of discounting their children's utility by the rate of time preference, ρ.

Finally, we should mention that the discussion treats the path of population as a given. However, we should also be able to apply economic reasoning to determine population. Some classical economists, such as Malthus, Ricardo, and Marx, regarded this topic as a central element of economic analysis (although their theories did not stand up empirically). Recently, some economists are again using economic analysis to study population growth.[6] Thus far, the empirical results are encouraging, but cannot fully explain the behavior of population growth over time.

Technological Change

Figure 11.4 applies to a permanent improvement of the production function. This type of change leads in the long run to increases in the per capita quantities of capital, output, and consumption. Typically, the process of economic development involves a continuing series of these improvements through a process called technological progress. As in the case of population growth, we shall only sketch some effects from steadily improving technology.

Continuing technological improvements lead to persistent increases in the

---

[6]See, for example, Richard Easterlin, *Population, Labor Force, and Long Swings in Economic Growth*, Columbia University Press, New York, 1968; Gary Becker, "The Demand for Children," in *A Treatise on the Family*, Harvard University Press, Cambridge, Massachusetts, 1981; and Gary Becker and Robert Barro, "A Reformulation of the Economic Theory of Fertility," Rochester Center for Economic Research, Working Paper No. 25, October 1985.

per capita quantities of capital, output, and consumption. In some cases, the economy approaches a position of **steady-state per capita growth,** where the amounts per person of capital, output, and consumption all grow at a constant rate. That is, the economy no longer tends toward per capita growth rates of zero.

What about the real interest rate in a position of steady-state per capita growth? Unlike our previous cases, there is now long-run growth in consumption per person. Therefore, the real interest rate in the steady state must be high enough to motivate people to defer consumption from early dates to later ones. This means that the steady-state real interest rate must exceed the rate of time preference, ρ. (Recall that an interest rate equal to ρ would be just high enough to motivate constant consumption per person.)

Finally, as with population growth, our discussion does not use economic analysis to explain the changes in technology. Ideally, we would like to explain producers' incentives to carry out the research and development that leads to new products and better methods of production. One interesting issue here concerns the property rights that people have in their inventions, production techniques, and so on. We should also consider the eventual limitations on new ideas—that is, the likelihood that technology cannot advance forever. Although there is some promising research in this area, the existing economic theory of technological change is not well developed.

Summarizing Our Conclusions about Economic Development

Before we look at some evidence, let's summarize the main theoretical conclusions about the path of economic development. Suppose first that we abstract from growth in population and technology. Also, assume that the economy begins with a capital stock below its steady-state value. Then we predict positive, but diminishing growth rates of the capital stock, output, and consumption. These growth rates all approach steady-state values of zero. Correspondingly, the real interest rate falls toward its steady-state value, which is the rate of time preference, ρ. We also predict decreases over time in the ratio of net investment to net and gross product, with net investment equaling zero in the steady state. Finally, the levels of capital and the other variables in the steady state depend on the form of the production function and on ρ. (There are also some ambiguous effects that concern the behavior of work effort.)

When we introduce population growth, we find that the economy approaches a position of steady-state growth. Here the per capita growth rates of capital, output, and consumption are all zero. But net investment is positive in this situation. (A higher growth rate of population means a larger ratio of net investment to net and gross product.) Otherwise, the results are similar to those summarized above.

Finally, we can allow for continuing improvements in technology. Then the economy may approach a position of steady-state per capita growth, where the growth rates of capital, output, and consumption per person all equal a positive constant. Now, the steady-state real interest rate exceeds the rate of time preference, ρ. However, suppose that the economy begins with a relatively low capital stock (in relation to the path for steady-state growth). Then we still predict that the various growth rates and the real interest rate will be high initially, but will then decline toward their values under steady-state growth. Also, the ratio of net investment to net and gross product falls over time toward its steady-state value.

Long-Term Evidence for the United States

Let's see how our theory relates to the long-term performance of the U.S. economy. Table 11.1 contains data from the nineteenth and twentieth centuries on the growth rate of real gross national product (GNP), on a measure of the real interest rate, and on the ratios of gross and net investment to real GNP. Here, we examine averages over 20-year periods, excluding the years around the three major wars (1861–66, 1917–19, 1941–46).

To get a long time series, we use the interest rate on prime commercial paper, which covers short-term notes issued by established companies. (U.S. treasury bills were first issued in 1929.) However, we do not know how much the riskiness of commercial paper has changed over time. Recall that during most of the post-World War II period, real interest rates were low—the average for 1947–80 was only 0.6%. However, for 1981–85, the average was much higher—6.4%. Despite these high real interest rates for the last few years, the principal observation from Table 11.1 is the marked decline in real interest rates over the longer term. Specifically, the average value of the real interest rate was 9.1% for 1840–60 and 1867–80, 6.3% for 1880–1900, 3.1% for 1900–16, 4.9% for 1920–40, −0.2% for 1947–60, and 1.2% for 1960–80. In comparison with the numbers from before World War II, the real interest rates for 1981–85 no longer seem dramatic. In any event, the longer term pattern of real interest rates conforms to our theory, which predicts that capital's marginal product and the real interest rate will decline as an economy develops.

The ratios of gross and net fixed private investment to GNP show some decline over the long term. Specifically, the ratio for net investment decreased from 9–10% for 1869–1900 to 6% for 1947–80. Our theory predicts that this decline would accompany the fall in real interest rates.

Table 11.1 shows average growth rates of real GNP, of population, and of real GNP per capita since 1840. (The figures on real GNP for the nineteenth century are rough estimates.) There is a pronounced decline in the growth rate of population—from about 3% per year in the mid-nineteenth century to a little over 1% for 1960–80. There is also some decline in the growth rate of real GNP—from about 5% per year in 1840–60 to 3.5% in 1960–80. But there is no indication of decline since 1880. Finally, there is no clear pattern over

Table 11.1 Growth Rates, Interest Rates, and Investment Ratios for the United States since 1840

	Growth Rates (% per year)			Interest and Inflation Rates[a] (% per year)			Investment Ratios	
	Real GNP	Population	Real GNP per Capita	R	π	$r = R - \pi$	Gross Private Fixed Investment GNP	Net Private Fixed Investment GNP
1840–60	4.9	3.1	1.8	8.6	−0.5	9.1	—	—
1867–80	5.8[b]	2.3[b]	3.5[b]	6.7	−2.4	9.1	0.17[c]	0.09[c]
1880–1900	3.0	2.1	0.9	5.6	−0.7	6.3	0.19[d]	0.10[d]
1900–16	3.3	1.8	1.5	5.5	2.4	3.1	0.17	0.07
1920–40	2.4	1.1	1.3	3.3	−1.6	4.9	0.12	0.01
1947–60	3.5	1.7	1.8	2.3	2.5	−0.2	0.14	0.06
1960–80	3.5	1.2	2.3	5.9	4.7	1.2	0.14	0.06

Notes: The periods exclude the years around three major wars, 1861–66, 1917–19, and 1941–46. For the data on real GNP, see Figure 1.1 of Chapter 1. R is the nominal interest rate on 4 to 6-month prime Commercial Paper. For 1857–89, the variable refers to 60- to 90-day rates, as reported in Frederick R. Macaulay, *The Movements of Interest Rates, Bond Yields and Stock Prices in the United States since 1856*, National Bureau of Economic Research, New York, 1938, Table 10. For 1840–56 the rates are Bigelow's estimates for the "New York and Boston money markets," as reported by Macaulay in Table 25. Interest rates since 1890 are in U.S. Commerce Dept., *Historical Statistics for the U.S., Colonial Times to 1970*, p. 1001. The inflation rate, π, is based on the GNP deflator since 1869. For the data, see Figure 1.4 of Chapter 1. Data on the price level before 1869 refer to the consumer price index, as reported in *Historical Statistics*, p. 211. The investment ratios equal real fixed, private, domestic investment divided by real GNP. Data on investment for 1869–1928 are from John Kendrick, *Productivity Trends in the United States*, Princeton University Press, Princeton, N.J., 1961, Tables A-I and A-III. Data on all variables for recent years are from U.S. Commerce Dept., *The National Income and Product Accounts of the U.S., 1929–76, U.S. Survey of Business*, and the *Federal Reserve Bulletin*.

[a]Dates for the interest rates are 1840–59, 1867–79, 1880–99, 1900–15, 1920–39, 1947–59, and 1960–79. Thereby the periods covered correspond roughly to those for the inflation rate.

[b]1869–80 (data on real GNP for 1867–68 are unavailable).

[c]1869–78.

[d]1879–1900.

time in the growth rates of real GNP per capita. In fact, the value of 2.3% per year for 1960–80 is exceeded only by the value of 3.5% per year for 1869–80.

The strong performance of real GNP per capita during the post-World War II period is a pleasant surprise. In contrast, our theory predicts that a fall in per capita growth rates would accompany the decline in capital's marginal product. We can mention some elements that might account for the facts.

First, there has been no major economic contraction during the post-World War II period. This outcome distinguishes the recent years from two earlier 20-year periods in the table: 1920–40 and 1880–1900.

Second, there has been an unusually large increase in the rate of labor-force participation. The ratio of the total labor force to the population aged 16–64 increased from 66% in 1950 to 68% in 1965 and 76% in 1985. (This ratio varied between 63 and 65% from 1900 to 1940.) The recent change reflects especially the increasing labor-force participation of women, which relates in part to the reduced birth rate.

Finally, it may be that the rate of technological progress was higher than usual during the post-World War II period. We cannot measure the state of technology directly, but there are some interesting proxies to look at. On the one hand, we do not see an unusually large number of patents issued for inventions, when expressed relative to the size of the population. The figures for the post-World War II years were similar to the averages for 1870 to 1940. But total outlays for research and development and for basic research did grow rapidly since World War II. In real terms the average growth rate of these outlays for 1955–84 was 5.0% per year.[7]

If we look ahead, there seems to be limited scope for further increases in the rates of labor-force participation. There is also no reason to anticipate unusually high rates of technological progress. Therefore, even if the economy avoids major economic contractions, we forecast average growth rates of real GNP per capita that are below those experienced for 1960–80.

Nine Industrialized Countries in the Post-World War II Period

Let's try to apply the theory to the experiences of the major industrialized, primarily free-market economies in the post-World War II period. Here, we want to compare the levels of output across different countries at various points in time. To make this comparison we use the results from a research project by Kravis, Heston, and Summers.[8] These researchers measure the price of a market basket of goods in different countries for some benchmark years. Thereby, they can calculate a time series of real gross product for each country, where all magnitudes are expressed in terms of U.S. dollars for the base year, 1975.

We examine the experiences of nine industrialized or semi-industrialized countries, which Kravis *et al.* include in their study.[9] These are the United

---

[7]For the data on patents, see *Historical Statistics of the U.S., Colonial Times to 1970*, pp. 957–58, and *Statistical Abstracts of the U.S.,* 1985, p. 536. Figures for expenditures on research and development are in *Statistical Abstracts of the U.S.,* 1985, p. 574.

[8]Irving Kravis, Alan Heston, and Robert Summers, *World Product and Income, International Comparisons of Real Gross Product,* Johns Hopkins University Press, Baltimore, 1982, Tables 8.3 and 8.4.

[9]They do not include Canada, Sweden, and Switzerland, which we otherwise would have added.

States, Austria, Denmark, France, West Germany, Italy, Japan, Spain, and the United Kingdom.

Suppose that these countries are basically similar in terms of production functions, natural resources, and preferences. But at the starting date, which we take to be 1950, there were major differences across countries in the levels of capital stock per person. (Remember that we take a broad view of capital to include human capital and aspects of technology, as well as machines and buildings.) In fact, a large part of the differences in 1950 stemmed directly from World War II. The losers in that war—Japan, Germany, and Italy—lost a larger fraction of their capital stocks than did the winners and neutrals, of which we consider the United States, the United Kingdom, and Spain. The occupied countries, as represented by Austria, Denmark, and France, are intermediate cases.

The countries that started with more capital per head should have higher initial values for output and consumption per head. But capital's marginal product is greater in the countries with less capital. Hence, these countries would invest a larger fraction of their output and, thereby, experience higher growth rates of capital, output, and consumption. Eventually, we predict that each country would approach the same path of steady-state growth. Therefore, the countries should come together, not only in terms of growth rates and ratios of investment to output, but also in terms of the levels of output and consumption per person. (The last result would not hold exactly if there were long-term differences across countries in natural resources or some other characteristics.)

The results just mentioned can be offset by major shocks, such as war, political upheavals, depressions, or epidemics. In fact, as mentioned before, the effects of wartime account for a significant part of the differences in starting positions among the countries. But, for the countries considered, the post-World War II period was free from major wars, political disturbances, depressions, and so on. Therefore, this period should isolate the effects that we have stressed in this chapter.

Table 11.2 shows for each country the growth rates of real gross product, population, and real gross product per capita, along with the ratios to gross product of gross and net fixed investment.[10] The data refer to averages over three decades—the 1950s, 1960s, and 1970s—as well as to the overall period, which is usually 1950–80. The table also indicates the levels of real gross product per person at four dates: 1950, 1960, 1970, and 1980.

As expected, there was a substantial spread for 1950 in the levels of gross output per person. In terms of 1975 U.S. dollars, the numbers were $4400 for the United States, $2800 for Denmark, $2700 for the United Kingdom, $2300 for France, $2000 for Germany, $1700 for Austria, $1400 for Italy, $1200 for

---

[10]These figures on investment include investment expenditures by governments, except for military purposes.

Table 11.2 The Behavior of Output and Investment in Nine Industrialized Countries

Country/Period		Real GDP per Capita (1000s of 1975 U.S. dollars at start of period)	Growth Rates (% per year)				Investment Ratios	
			Real GDP	Popula-tion	Real GDP per Capita	Period	Gross Fixed Investment/ GDP (period average)	Net Fixed Investment/ GDP (period/ average)
United States	1950–60	4.45	3.2	1.7	1.5	1950–59	0.18	0.07
	1960–70	5.16	3.8	1.3	2.5	1960–69	0.18	0.08
	1970–80	6.64	2.9	1.1	1.8	1970–79	0.17	0.07
	1950–80	7.97 (1980)	3.3	1.4	1.9	1950–79	0.18	0.07
Austria	1950–60	1.73	5.1	0.2	4.9	1950–59	0.21	0.09
	1960–70	2.81	4.5	0.5	4.0	1960–69	0.26	0.14
	1970–80	4.20	3.4	0.2	3.2	1970–79	0.27	0.15
	1950–80	5.78 (1980)	4.3	0.3	4.0	1950–79	0.25	0.13
Denmark	1950–60	2.81	3.3	0.7	2.6	1950–59	0.19	0.13
	1960–70	3.66	4.5	0.7	3.8	1960–69	0.23	0.16
	1970–80	5.36	2.2	0.4	1.8	1970–79	0.24	0.16
	1950–80	6.42 (1980)	3.4	0.6	2.8	1950–79	0.22	0.15
France	1950–60	2.26	4.4	0.9	3.5	1950–59	0.19	0.08
	1960–70	3.21	5.6	1.1	4.5	1960–69	0.22	0.13
	1970–80	5.04	3.4	0.6	2.8	1970–79	0.23	0.14
	1950–80	6.66 (1980)	4.4	0.8	3.6	1950–79	0.21	0.11
Germany (West)	1950–60	1.99	7.5	1.0	6.5	1950–59	0.22	0.14
	1960–70	3.81	4.5	0.9	3.6	1960–69	0.25	0.16
	1970–80	5.46	2.6	0.1	2.5	1970–79	0.23	0.12
	1950–80	6.99 (1980)	5.1	0.9	4.2	1950–79	0.23	0.14
Italy	1950–60	1.37	5.7	0.6	5.1	1950–59	0.20	0.11
	1960–70	2.28	5.3	0.8	4.5	1960–69	0.21	0.13
	1970–80	3.59	2.5	0.6	1.9	1970–79	0.20	0.11
	1950–80	4.35 (1980)	4.6	0.7	3.9	1950–79	0.20	0.12
Japan	1950–60	0.83	8.1	1.2	6.9	1952–59	0.24	0.14
	1960–70	1.65	10.1	0.9	9.2	1960–69	0.32	0.22
	1970–80	4.12	4.7	1.1	3.6	1970–79	0.33	0.20
	1950–80	5.91 (1980)	7.6	1.1	6.5	1952–79	0.30	0.19
Spain	1950–60	1.18	4.9	0.8	4.1	1954–59	0.18	0.08
	1960–70	1.77	7.1	1.1	6.0	1960–69	0.21	0.11
	1970–80	3.24	3.6	1.3	2.3	1970–79	0.22	0.13
	1950–80	4.06 (1980)	5.1	1.0	4.1	1954–79	0.21	0.11
United Kingdom	1950–60	2.74	2.6	0.4	2.2	1950–59	0.15	0.07
	1960–70	3.41	2.8	0.6	2.2	1960–69	0.18	0.10
	1970–80	4.24	2.2	0.1	2.1	1970–79	0.19	0.09
	1950–80	5.24 (1980)	2.5	0.3	2.2	1950–79	0.17	0.08

Notes: GDP is gross domestic product, expressed as U.S. dollars for the base year, 1975. The figures on investment include purchases of capital goods by governments. However, all defense expenditures are excluded. The investment ratios equal nominal investment expenditures divided by nominal GDP.

Sources: The figures on real GDP per capita are from Kravis *et al.*, op. cit., Tables 8-3 and 8-4. Data on population are from the U.N. *Statistical Yearbook*. Figures on nominal investment and GDP are from *OECD, National Accounts of OECD Countries*, V.I., 1981, 1982. For 1950 (and also 1951 for the United Kingdom), the data on investment for Austria, Denmark, France, Germany, Italy, and the United Kingdom are estimated from B. R. Mitchell, *European Historical Statistics*, Macmillan, New York, 1975.

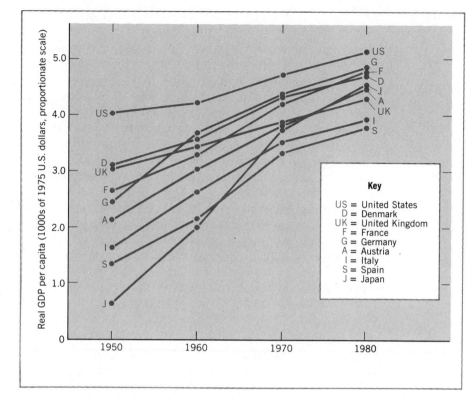

Figure 11.5 Levels of Output per Capita for Nine Industrialized Countries
The figure shows the convergence of output per person across the countries between 1950 and 1980.

Spain, and $800 for Japan. We show these amounts on a proportionate scale on the left part of Figure 11.5.

Consider next the ordering of countries by their average growth rates of output per capita from 1950 to 1980. These numbers were 6.5% per year for Japan, 4.2% for Germany, 4.1% for Spain, 4.0% for Austria, 3.9% for Italy, 3.6% for France, 2.8% for Denmark, 2.2% for the United Kingdom, and 1.9% for the United States. This ranking is nearly the reverse of the first one, which was based on starting levels of output per head. Thus, as predicted, the countries with the lower starting values of output (and capital) per person are the ones that tend to grow faster. Also, the conclusion is similar if we look at growth rates for the levels of output, rather than output per capita.[11]

---

[11]Roger Kormendi and Phillip Meguire ("Macroeconomic Determinants of Growth: Cross-Country Evidence," *Journal of Monetary Economics*, September 1985, p. 147) reach a similar conclusion for a sample of 46 countries in the post-World War II period. They find that countries with a higher initial value of real per capita income tend to have a lower growth rate of real GDP.

Notice that the United States is in last place in terms of the average growth rate of output per capita. (It ranks eighth, ahead of the United Kingdom, if we consider the average growth rate for the level of output.) Although many people criticize this performance, we may not want to take this criticism seriously. First, the theory predicts relatively low growth for the United States because it started with the highest level of output per person. Second, remember that the growth rate of output per capita in the United States since World War II looks good when compared to the historical record. In particular, we commented in the previous section that this growth rate was surprisingly high. Basically, the low ranking for the United States reflects the astonishingly strong performance of the other countries, rather than a low rate of growth in the United States.

The ranking of countries by average growth rates accords reasonably well with a ranking by average ratios of net fixed investment to output. The average values of these ratios for 1950 to 1979 were 0.19 for Japan (for 1952–79), 0.15 for Denmark, 0.14 for Germany, 0.13 for Austria, 0.12 for Italy, 0.11 for Spain (for 1954–79), 0.08 for the United Kingdom, and 0.07 for the United States. In the main, the countries with the higher investment ratios are the ones with first, the lower starting values of output per capita, and second, the higher average growth rates of output per capita.

Figure 11.5 shows how the differences in growth rates led over time to convergences in the levels of output per person. The figures on output per capita for 1980, measured again in 1975 U.S. dollars, were $8000 for the United States, $7000 for Germany, $6700 for France, $6400 for Denmark, $5900 for Japan, $5800 for Austria, $5200 for the United Kingdom, $4400 for Italy, and $4100 for Spain. Thus, for example, output per capita for Japan in 1980 was 74% of the U.S. level, as compared to 19% in 1950. For Germany, the comparison was between 88% of the U.S. level in 1980, versus 45% in 1950. That for Italy was between 55% of the U.S. level in 1980 and 31% in 1950.

Our theory predicts also that growth rates would decline over time for each country, approaching the rates associated with steady-state per capita growth.[12] Figure 11.6 shows the growth rates of output per capita for each country over three decades—the 1950s, 1960s, and 1970s. Similarly, Figure 11.7 shows the growth rates for the levels of output. Overall, there was a tendency for the growth rates to diminish from the 1950s to the 1970s. For example, the simple averages for the growth rates of output per capita over the nine countries were 4.1% in the 1950s, 4.5% in the 1960s, and 2.4% in the 1970s. For the growth rates of levels of output, the corresponding figures were 5.0, 5.4, and 3.1%. Note that the pattern of declining growth rates shows up most clearly for the countries that began with the highest rates of growth,

---

[12]However, these growth rates would not be the same if countries differ by their long-term growth rates of technology or population. As it stands, the theory does not address these questions. With respect to the growth rate of population, the values for the 1970s ranged from 0.1% per year for Germany and the United Kingdom to 1.3% per year for Spain.

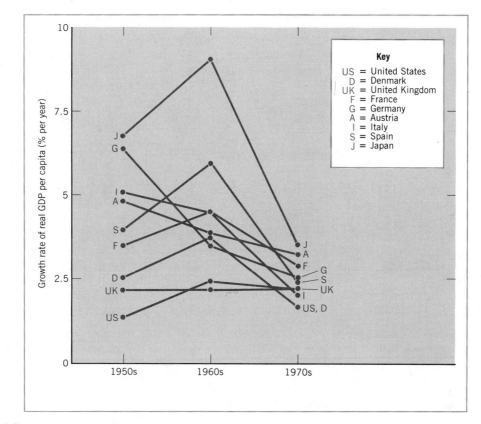

Figure 11.6 **Growth Rates of Output per Capita for Nine Industrialized Countries**
The figure shows the average growth rates of output per capita for the countries during
three decades—the 1950s, 1960s, and 1970s.

which are Japan, Germany, and Italy. In particular, the Japanese growth rate
of output per capita fell from the extraordinary value of 9.2% per year for
the 1960s to 3.6% for the 1970s.

   If we had just extrapolated the Japanese growth rate from the 1950s and
1960s into the 1970s, then we would have predicted that output per person in
Japan in 1980 would have exceeded that in the United States (see Figure 11.5).
Moreover, the gap between Japanese and U.S. output per person would have
widened steadily after 1980. The same type of predictions would have applied
to Germany versus the United States if we had used the German growth rate
of the 1950s to make forecasts. But, because their growth rates have slowed
down, neither Japan nor Germany have yet reached the U.S. level of output
per person. It seems that—at least for the industrialized economies—the theory
that predicts gradual convergence in the levels of output per capita does better
than the mechanical model that just extrapolates the growth rates of various
countries.

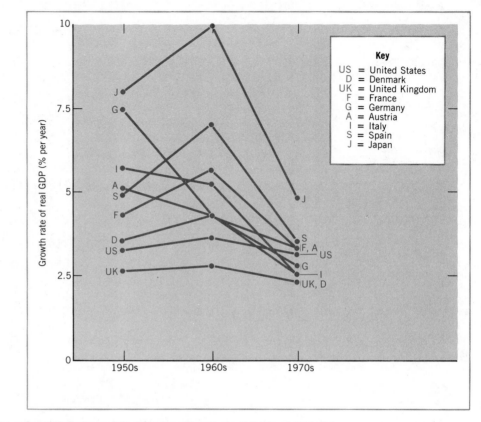

Figure 11.7 Growth Rates of Output for Nine Industrialized Countries
The figure shows the average growth rates of output for the countries during three decades—the 1950s, 1960s, and 1970s.

Contrary to our theory, there was no systematic decline over time in the ratios of net investment to output. The simple averages of these ratios for the nine countries (from Table 11.2) were 10% for the 1950s, 14% for the 1960s, and 13% for the 1970s. Notice that for the 1970s, the ratios were 20% for Japan, 16% for Denmark, 15% for Austria, and 14% for France. These values remained strikingly higher than those for the United States and the United Kingdom, which were 7 and 9%, respectively. Since the growth rates of output across the countries converged substantially, the results on investment ratios are puzzling.

Fumio Hayashi[13] recently carried out a detailed comparison of saving behavior in the United States versus Japan. One of his major observations is

---

[13]See Fumio Hayashi, "Why is Japan's Saving Rate so Apparently High?" presented at the National Bureau of Economic Research Conference on Macroeconomics, Cambridge, Mass., March 1986.

that some serious measurement problems led to a substantial overstatement of the Japanese saving and investment ratios since the early 1970s. The difficulties concern a failure to account for inflation when computing depreciation, and a general tendency to overstate investment in the public sector. For example, for 1979, Hayashi reports the standard figures for the ratio of net national saving to NNP as 8% for the United States and 21% for Japan, which correspond to our figures on net investment ratios in Table 11.2. But, after adjusting the data on depreciation and governmental investment, Hayashi calculates the revised ratios of 9% for the United States and 16% for Japan. Overall, Hayashi's refined calculations show a sharp decline in the Japanese saving ratio since the early 1970s, and a clear convergence toward the U.S. ratio. Thus, at least for the Japanese case, the puzzling behavior of the reported investment ratios seems to be mainly a consequence of bad data.

Looking ahead, a key observation is the relatively small spread for the levels of real output per capita in 1980. Therefore, we predict that the rates of growth for the nine countries in the 1980s will be more similar than they were in the previous three decades. Also, the theory predicts that the ratios of net investment to output (when measured properly) will be closer than they were before.

Summary

This chapter studies the process of capital accumulation over the long term. As the quantity of capital increases, the diminishing marginal product of capital implies that the real interest rate falls. Then we trace out a path of economic development where consumption and output rise, but net investment declines. Work effort may either rise or fall over time. The growth rates of capital, consumption, and output tend to decline, and the economy eventually approaches a steady state in which output and the quantity of capital do not change. In this situation, net investment and real saving are zero, and the real interest rate equals the rate of time preference.

Steadily growing population leads to persistent growth in output and the quantity of capital. Although the economy no longer approaches a position where net investment and real saving are zero, the per capita growth rates of capital, consumption, and output do tend toward zero. If there is continuing technical progress, then these per capita growth rates can be positive in the long run. But if an economy starts with a relatively small amount of capital per person, then economic development still entails decreases over time in the real interest rate, in the growth rates of the capital stock and output, and in the ratio of net investment to output.

For the United States since 1840 we do find a major long-term decline in the real interest rate, and some decrease in the ratio of net fixed investment to GNP. However, while there is some decline over time in the growth rate of output, there is no systematic decline in the growth rate of output per capita.

We also studied the development of nine industrialized countries since 1950. Especially because of World War II, these countries started with major differences in the levels of capital stock and output per person. As the theory predicts, the countries that start with less capital per person experience faster growth rates of output per capita and also invest a larger fraction of their output. Consequently, there is substantial convergence over time in the levels of output per capita among the nine countries. Also, there is a tendency for the growth rates of output to fall over time, at least in the countries that started with the higher rates of growth.

Important Terms and Concepts

constant returns to scale	steady state
increasing or decreasing returns to scale	steady-state growth
technological change	steady-state per capita growth

QUESTIONS AND PROBLEMS

Mainly for Review

11.1 Why does an increase in the capital stock reduce the real interest rate?

11.2 Summarize the effect of a higher capital stock on the quantities of
   a. Consumption
   b. Leisure
   c. Net investment
   Distinguish where necessary between wealth and substitution effects.

11.3 What is the immediate effect of a one-time, permanent improvement in the production function on the real interest rate and net investment? If the rise in the real interest rate were equal to the rise in the marginal product of capital, would net investment rise? Explain why this situation is unlikely to occur.

11.4 What are the long-run effects of the improvement in the production function considered in question 11.3? In particular, why does net investment remain positive in future periods even though there are no more increases in MPK? Why does the economy eventually reach a steady state, where net investment is zero?

11.5 Compare an economy in steady-state growth with one in a steady state. Explain why, in the former, there is positive net investment in every period.

11.6 Should a decline in the investment/GNP ratio be a cause for public concern? Is it inevitably accompanied by lower growth rates of real GNP per capita?

Problems for Discussion

11.7 The Effects of More Capital on the Commodity Market

Figure 11.2 shows the effects of an increase in the capital stock on the commodity market.

a. What determines the direction and magnitude of the shift in the aggregate demand for net product, $Y_2^d - \delta K_1$?

b. Why does the curve for net investment demand, $I_2^d - \delta K_1$, specify zero demand when the real interest rate equals the value r_1^*?

c. Consider the effect of more capital on the quantity of net investment, $I_2^* - \delta K_1$. Why is this effect negative?

11.8 Economic Development and the Real Wage Rate

Suppose that we introduce a separate labor market into the model.

a. Assume that population and technology are fixed, but the economy starts with a capital stock below the steady-state amount. As the economy accumulates capital, what happens to the real wage rate?

b. Suppose that at date 1 the economy is in a steady state. Then there is a once-and-for-all improvement of the production function. Here, the schedules for the marginal products of labor and capital shift upward. (We show this case in Figure 11.4.) What happens to the real wage rate in the short run and the long run?

11.9 Population Growth (optional)

Suppose that technology is fixed, but population grows at the constant rate η (the Greek letter *eta*). Assume that returns to scale in production are nearly constant. How does the value of η affect the following variables *in a position of steady-state growth*:

a. the growth rates of aggregate capital, gross output, consumption, and work effort?

b. the growth rates of capital, gross output, consumption, and work effort per capita?

Assume now that changes in η do not affect the ratio of aggregate capital to either aggregate gross output or aggregate work effort in a position of steady-state growth. Then, how does the value of η affect the following variables under steady-state growth:

c. the ratio of aggregate net investment to the aggregates of capital and gross output?

d. the ratio of aggregate consumption to aggregate gross output? Explain carefully the answers to parts (c) and (d).

11.10 Growth Rates across Countries (optional)

We studied nine industrialized countries in the text. We assumed that these countries were similar in terms of production functions and tastes, but differed by their starting values of capital per head. We assumed also that the primary economic organization in these countries involved free markets. Therefore, we predicted that the countries would all approach the same path of steady-state growth. In particular, countries with lower starting values of output per head would grow more rapidly for awhile.

Would you make the same predictions for all countries, including those that are presently at low levels of economic development? What considerations affect the applicability of the theory to different countries? (No one knows the answer to this!) After you have made your predictions, you can look at data for some cases—for example, for India, Mexico, South Korea, and Brazil. (The data on gross product are in Kravis *et al.* as cited in the text.)

PART IV
GOVERNMENT BEHAVIOR

Up to this point the government does not play much of a role in the model. In fact, all the government does is print money and give away the proceeds as transfer payments. In the real world, governments have important influences on economic activity through their expenditures, taxes, transfer programs, regulations, and debt management. In this part of the book we consider the macroeconomic effects of these governmental activities.

Chapter 12 begins the study by considering government purchases of goods and services and a simple form of tax revenues. With this extension we can analyze how government purchases affect real interest rates, the level of real gross national product, and the split of this product between private and public expenditures. For the United States, short-run changes in government purchases have played a major role during wartime, but otherwise have not been a central element in business fluctuations. However, the longer term increase in the size of government has crowded out private spending.

Chapter 13 introduces income taxes and transfer programs, which affect people's incentives to work, produce, and invest. Here we examine the possibility—stressed by "supply-side economists"—that changes in tax rates have major effects on the level of economic activity.

Chapter 14 discusses the public debt and the related concept of the government's budget deficit. Although these issues have attracted a lot of attention in recent years, our major conclusion is that budget deficits have exerted only minor influences on the U.S. economy.

CHAPTER 12

GOVERNMENT PURCHASES AND PUBLIC SERVICES

In this chapter we introduce government purchases of goods and services and a simple form of tax revenues. But, before considering these extensions to the model, let's get some background by looking at the history of government spending in the United States.

Government Expenditures in the United States

Figures 12.1 and 12.2 show the evolution of government spending in the United States from 1929 to 1985. Excluding the wartime experiences, total dollar government expenditures when expressed as a ratio to nominal GNP rose from 0.10 in 1929 to 0.18 in 1940, 0.21 in 1950, 0.27 in 1960, 0.32 in 1970, 0.33 in 1980, and 0.35 in 1985 (a comparable figure for 1902 is 0.07).

The pattern of steady rise in the relative importance of total government expenditures conceals some different movements in the major underlying components. Figure 12.1 shows how purchases of goods and services have varied over time. Federal purchases rose from 0.01 relative to GNP in 1929 to 0.06 in 1940, but remained at 0.06 in 1950. Following a rise to 0.11 in 1960, the federal purchases' ratio declined to 0.07 in 1979, before rising to 0.09 in 1985. In other words the ratio for 1985 is only 3 percentage points higher than that in 1950 or 1940.

Except during the Great Depression from 1933 to 1940, the dominant component of federal purchases was military spending. This spending was 0.02 relative to GNP in 1940 and 0.09 in 1960, but fell from there to a low point of less than 0.05 in 1979; then this ratio rose to 0.07 for 1985. (As a fraction of total government expenditure, military purchases declined from 33% in 1960 to 19% in 1985.) Notice that Figure 12.1 shows also the peaks in the military

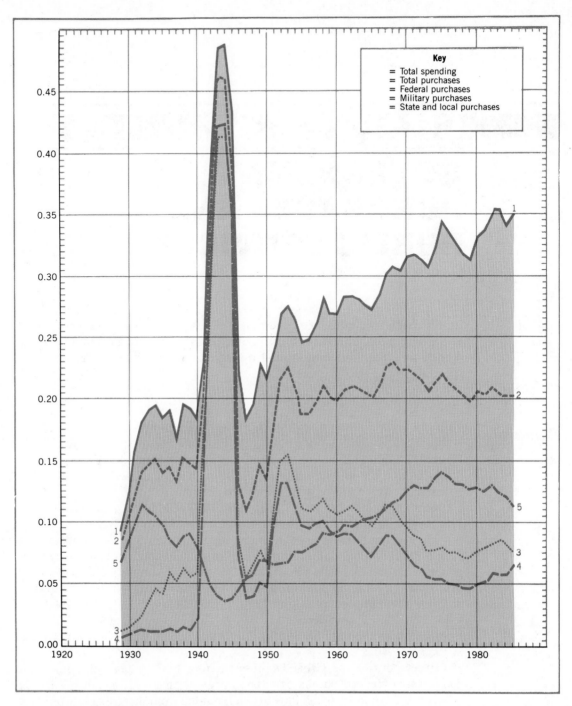

Figure 12.1 **Total Government Spending and Government Purchases, Expressed as Ratios to Nominal GNP**

The data go from 1929 to 1985.

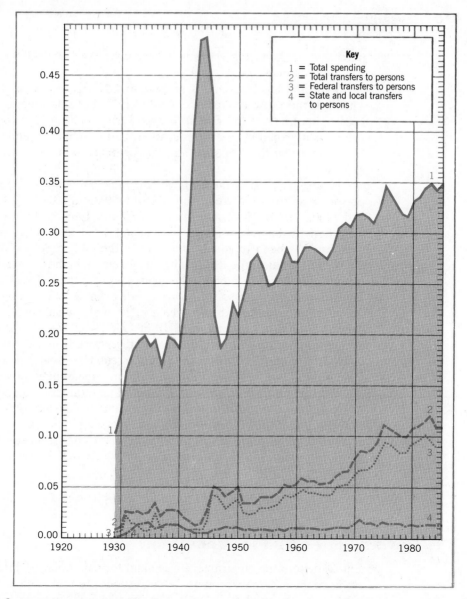

Figure 12.2 Total Government Spending and Transfer Payments, Expressed as Ratios to Nominal GNP
The data go from 1929 to 1985.

purchases' ratio during wartime. These were 0.42 in 1943–44, 0.13 in 1952–53, and 0.09 in 1967–68.

State and local purchases relative to GNP were 0.07 in 1929 and 1950. Then this ratio rose to a peak of 0.14 in 1975, but subsequently fell to 0.12 in 1985. About half of the rise in this ratio from 1950 to 1975 took the form of increases in expenditures for education. (Educational expenditures advanced from about one-third of state and local purchases in the years up to 1950 to 42% in 1975.)

Figure 12.2 shows the behavior of transfers. Total transfer payments to persons rose from 0.01 relative to GNP in 1929 to 0.03 in 1940, 0.05 in 1950 and 1960, 0.08 in 1970, and 0.11 in 1980 and 1985. Note that the state and local part of these transfers (which includes aid to families with dependent children) has been relatively stable since the end of World War II at about 2% of GNP. Hence, the strong upward movement in the transfers' ratio derived from the federal government. The main reason for the increase was the growing benefits paid through social security. For example, the expenditures for old age, survivors, and disability, which is the main social security program, increased from 0.003 relative to GNP in 1950 to 0.047 in 1984. Over the same period, medicare and medicaid expenditures rose from zero to 0.017 relative to GNP. Although there is much recent discussion about social security, there is no indication as yet that the growth of this spending is slowing down.

We can summarize the movements in government expenditures relative to GNP since the 1950s in terms of three major developments: a sharp drop in spending for the military (which was reversed in part after 1979), a roughly compensating increase in social security benefits, and a substantial rise in state and local purchases (a major portion of which was for education) until the mid 1970s.

The Government's Budget Constraint

Let G_t denote the government's demand for commodities during period t. In terms of the national accounts, G_t corresponds to real purchases of goods and services by the total of federal, state, and local governments. Total real government expenditure equals these purchases plus the real value of aggregate transfer payments, V_t/P_t. (We do not yet consider governmental interest payments.)

Thus far, we assumed that the government's only revenue came from printing money. The real value of this revenue is the amount, $(M_t - M_{t-1})/P_t$. Now we assume that the government also levies taxes on households. (Remember that the households are the producers, as well as the consumers, in the model.) Let T_t be the aggregate dollar amount of taxes for period t. Then the real amount of tax revenues is T_t/P_t.

As before, the government's budget constraint equates total real expenditures to total real revenues. Therefore, we have[1]

$$G_t + \frac{V_t}{P_t} = \frac{T_t}{P_t} + \frac{(M_t - M_{t-1})}{P_t} \tag{12.1}$$

Govt. Budget Constraint

Our earlier formulation fits into equation 12.1 if we set real purchases, G_t, and taxes, T_t/P_t, to zero.

Earlier we assumed that transfer payments were lump sum. This means that the amount of an individual's real transfer, v_t/P_t, does not depend on that person's level of income, effort at soliciting transfers, and so on. Now, we assume also that the taxes are lump sum. Hence, an individual's real tax liability, t_t/P_t, is independent of that person's level or type of income, effort at avoiding taxes, and so on.

Of course, in the real world, an elaborate tax law specifies the relation of someone's taxes to their amounts of income, business profits, sales, holdings of property, deductions from taxable income, and so on. Generally, there are lots of things people can do—including hiring accountants, working less, underreporting income, and exploiting tax loopholes—to lower their obligations. These possibilities imply important substitution effects from the tax system on work effort, investment, relative demands for different goods (even including numbers of children!), and so on. In general, people substitute in favor of the activities that lower their taxes.

We shall find it convenient initially to neglect these substitution effects from taxes. That is why we assume **lump-sum taxes,** which do not exert any substitution effects. But we bring in more realistic types of taxes and transfers in the next chapter.

Public Production

The government uses its purchases, G_t, to provide services to households. We assume that the government provides these services free of charge to the users. In most countries public services include national defense, enforcement of laws and private contracts, police and fire protection, elementary education and some parts of higher education, highways, parks, and so on. The range of

---

[1]In the U.S. economy the revenue from printing money accrues directly to the Federal Reserve, which then turns most of its profits over to the U.S. Treasury. However, for historical reasons, the national accounts treat the Fed as though it were a private corporation, rather than a part of the central government. Therefore, the transfer of funds from the Fed to the Treasury appears in the national accounts as a tax on corporate profits! (We can almost feel sorry for the Fed, since its "profits" are taxed at nearly a 100% rate!) This quirk in the national accounts can cause trouble for unwary researchers, since the Fed's payments to the Treasury amounted to 24% of the reported total for federal taxes on corporate profits in 1985 ($16.1 billion out of a total of $67.7 billion).

governmental activities has typically expanded over time, although this range varies significantly from one place to another.

We could model public services as the output from the government's production function. Then the inputs to this function would be the government-owned stock of capital, labor services from public employees, and materials that the government purchases from the private sector. Instead, we simplify matters by neglecting production in the public sector. We do this—as do macromodels generally—by pretending that the government buys only final goods and services on the commodity market. In effect, the government in our model subcontracts all of its production to the private sector. In this setup, public investment, publicly owned capital, and government employment are always zero. Ultimately, the introduction of governmental production would affect the main results only if the public sector's technology or management capability differed from that of the private sector. Otherwise, it will not matter whether the government buys final goods, as we assume, or buys capital and labor to produce things itself.

Before, we assumed that output could be labeled as either consumables or capital goods. Now we introduce a third function for output; namely, the government can purchase goods to provide public services to households. As before, suppliers do not care whether people use the goods for consumption, investment, or to provide public services. The demanders of commodities—which now include the government—determine its use.

Public Services

In our model we consider two types of public services. The first type provides utility directly. As examples we can think of parks, libraries, school lunch programs, subsidized health care and transportation services, and the entertaining parts of the space program. An important feature of these services is that they may substitute closely for private consumer spending. (If the government buys our lunch at school, then we don't buy our own lunch. But we have to be more subtle to find the private substitutes for the space program.)

The second type of service is an input to private production. Examples include the provision and enforcement of laws, aspects of national defense, government sponsored research and development programs, fire and police services, and various regulatory activities. In some cases these services are close substitutes for private inputs of labor and capital. In other cases, such as the provision of a legal system and national defense, the public services are likely to raise the marginal products of private factors.

In many situations a governmental program exhibits features of both types of services that we consider. But the mix varies across the wide range of actual programs. However, in our theory, we proceed as if there were only one type of governmental activity. This activity yields utility directly, and also provides services to producers.

Households' Budget Constraints

Before, we included real transfers, v_t/P_t, as a source of income for a household. Now we also have to subtract real taxes, t_t/P_t, to calculate real income after taxes. For example, the budget constraint in real terms for period t is

$$y_t + \frac{b_{t-1}(1+R)}{P_t} + \frac{m_{t-1}}{P_t} + \frac{(v_t - t_t)}{P_t} = c_t + i_t + \frac{(b_t + m_t)}{P_t} \quad (12.2)$$

As in previous chapters, we can also calculate someone's real saving for period t. The result is now

$$\text{real saving} = y_t - \delta k_{t-1} + (R - \pi)\left(\frac{b_{t-1}}{P_t}\right) - \pi\left(\frac{m_{t-1}}{P_t}\right)$$
$$+ \frac{(v_t - t_t)}{P_t} - c_t \quad (12.3)$$

Before, the household's real income equaled net product, plus the real interest earnings on bonds and money, plus real transfers. Now, we deduct real taxes, t_t/P_t, to compute real income after taxes, which is called disposable real income. Then we subtract real consumption expenditures, c_t, to determine real saving.

Earlier, when we calculated a household's budget constraint over an infinite horizon, we included the present value of real transfers, $v_1/P_1 + (v_2/P_2)/(1+r) + \cdots$. (This expression came up when we added various monetary terms to the budget constraint.) Now, equation 12.2 shows that each period's real transfers net of real taxes, $(v_t - t_t)/P_t$, matters for the household. Therefore, when considering a budget constraint over an infinite horizon, we now have to include the present value of real transfers net of real taxes,

$$\frac{(v_1 - t_1)}{P_1} + \frac{[(v_2 - t_2)/P_2]}{(1+r)} + \cdots$$

Let's consider the aggregate value of this expression. Each term involves the aggregate of real transfers net of real taxes, $(V_t - T_t)/P_t$. But we know from the government's budget constraint in equation 12.1 that this term equals the real revenue from money creation less real government purchases—that is

$$\frac{(V_t - T_t)}{P_t} = \frac{(M_t - M_{t-1})}{P_t} - G_t \quad (12.4)$$

Suppose for the moment that the money stock were constant, so that the condition, $M_t - M_{t-1} = 0$, holds in each period. Then the aggregate real value of transfers net of taxes, $(V_t - T_t)/P_t$, equals the negative of real government purchases, $-G_t$. Therefore, the aggregate of households' budget constraints over an infinite horizon includes the expression

$$\frac{(V_1 - T_1)}{P_1} + \frac{[(V_2 - T_2)/P_2]}{(1+r)} + \cdots = -\left[G_1 + \frac{G_2}{(1+r)} + \cdots\right]$$

Note that the present value of real government purchases tells us the amount to subtract from the aggregate real present value of households' funds. So, on this count, an increase in the present value of real government purchases has a negative effect on households' wealth.

What happens when the money stock varies over time? Then, from equation 12.4, the aggregate real present value of households' funds includes the additional terms

$$\frac{(M_1 - M_0)}{P_1} + \frac{[(M_2 - M_1)/P_2]}{(1+r)} + \cdots$$

But we looked at this expression before (in Chapter 7). We found that it canceled along with two other monetary terms—the aggregate of initial real cash balances less the aggregate real present value of interest foregone on holdings of money. Therefore, the results do not change when we allow for revenue from money creation. Namely, the present value of real government purchases still subtracts from the aggregate of households' available funds.

Let's think about this result. From the aggregate of output in each period, Y_t, the government takes the quantity, G_t. Therefore, the expression, $G_1 + G_2/(1+r) + \cdots$, is the real present value of the goods that the government absorbs. Hence, this expression tells us the real present value of the goods that are not available for the aggregate of households. The important point is that this result does not depend on how much money the government prints in various periods. No matter how much money the government creates, the present value of its purchases measures the resources used by the government, which are therefore unavailable for households.

Permanent Government Purchases

We want to work with a type of average of current and future government purchases, which parallels the concept of permanent income. Specifically, define **permanent government purchases,** $\tilde{G}$, to be the constant flow that has the same present value as the actual path of purchases. In other words,

$$\tilde{G} + \frac{\tilde{G}}{(1+r)} + \cdots = G_1 + \frac{G_2}{(1+r)} + \cdots$$

We know from before that the left side equals $\tilde{G}(1+r)/r$.[2] Therefore, the formula for permanent purchases is

$$\tilde{G} = \frac{r}{(1+r)} \left[G_1 + \frac{G_2}{(1+r)} + \cdots \right] \tag{12.5}$$

A higher value for permanent purchases means a greater present value of government purchases, which means a lower present value of funds available

---

[2]We use the formula for a geometric series, $1 + x + x^2 + \cdots = 1/(1 - x)$ if $0 < x < 1$. In our case $x = 1/(1+r)$.

**Table 12.1 A Time Path for Real
Government Purchases**

Period	G_t
1	100
2	100
3	10
4	10
.	.
.	.
.	.

Note: Real purchases are temporarily high at the value 100 during periods 1 and 2. Then, at date 3, purchases drop to 10, and stay forever at this level. Assuming that the real interest rate, r, is 5%, the present value of purchases is 386.[3] Therefore, permanent purchases are $\tilde{G} = (0.05/1.05) \cdot 386 = 18$.

for households. In fact, if permanent purchases, $\tilde{G}$, rise by 1 unit, then it is just as if the aggregate of households had one less unit of real income available in each period from date 1 onward. On this count, an increase by 1 unit in permanent purchases amounts to a decrease by 1 unit in the aggregate of permanent income.

To illustrate, suppose that the current level of purchases is $G_1 = 100$. But assume that this spending is unusually high because the government is carrying out some foreign military adventure. After period 2, the adventure will end (people think) and purchases will drop forever to 10 units per period. (No more military adventures will ever occur!) We show these numbers for government purchases in Table 12.1. Assume that the real interest rate, r, is 5% per period. Then we can calculate the present value of purchases to be 386. (See the note to Table 12.1.) Using equation 12.5 we find that permanent purchases, $\tilde{G}$, equal 18. Notice that the quantity of purchases during the temporary adventure, $G_1 = G_2 = 100$, is well above the permanent level. Then, after period 2, the quantity of purchases, $G = 10$, falls below the permanent level. But from the standpoint of households' budget constraints, it is just as if the government took away 18 units of goods during each period.

$$[3]\,100 + \frac{100}{1.05} + \frac{10}{(1.05)^2}\left[1 + \frac{1}{(1.05)} + \frac{1}{(1.05)^2} + \cdots\right] = 100 + \frac{100}{1.05} +$$

$$\frac{10}{(1.05)^2}\left[\frac{1}{1 - \dfrac{1}{1.05}}\right] = 100 + 95.2 + 190.5 = 385.7.$$

Effects of Public Services on Private Choices

We want to explore the effects of government purchases on households' choices of consumption, investment, and work effort. For now, we hold fixed the level of permanent purchases, $\bar{G}$. As we shall see, the wealth effects from changes in government purchases involve shifts in permanent purchases. Therefore, with this amount held fixed, we do not get any wealth effects.

Consider an increase in the current level of purchases, G_1. (Notice that, if we hold $\bar{G}$ fixed, then we must reduce some future value(s) of purchases.) The higher current level of purchases means more public services of the two types that we mentioned before.

First, there is a positive effect on utility during the current period. That is because we assume that people like the services that the government provides! Suppose that the public services substitute for some private consumption, but not for leisure.[4] For example, when the government provides free libraries, parks, school lunches, or transportation, then people reduce their private spending in these areas. Let's use the parameter α (the Greek letter *alpha*) to measure the size of this effect. An increase in current purchases, G_1, by 1 unit motivates households to reduce aggregate private consumption demand, C_1^d, by α units. Thus, if public services are a close substitute for private spending, then the parameter α is high.

It is possible for the parameter α to exceed 1. That is, an extra unit of government purchases may substitute for more than 1 unit of aggregate consumer spending. This outcome is possible because people may benefit jointly from some types of government expenditures, such as the Washington Monument. It is this characteristic of joint benefit that economists have in mind when they say that some governmental services are **public goods.** The more the government's services have this characteristic of publicness, the higher the parameter α tends to be.

We assume also that the parameter α declines as the quantity of government purchases rises. That is, as the amount of public services increases, the marginal unit substitutes less closely for private spending. Notice, however, that the value of the parameter α does not necessarily tell us how valuable an extra unit of public services is. People might like these services a lot even if they do not substitute much for private spending—that is, even if α is small.

Some interesting empirical work provides estimates of the parameter α for the U.S. economy in the post-World War II period. The estimates[5] suggest that α is between 0.2 and 0.4. That is, an extra unit of government purchases

---

[4]We follow here the general approach taken in Martin J. Bailey, *National Income and the Price Level,* 2nd ed., McGraw-Hill, New York, 1971, Chapter 9.

[5]See Roger Kormendi, "Government Debt, Government Spending, and Private Sector Behavior," *American Economic Review,* December 1983; and David Aschauer, "Fiscal Policy and Aggregate Demand," *American Economic Review,* March 1985.

substitutes for between 0.2 and 0.4 units of aggregate private consumption. Thus, we are safe in assuming that α is positive but well below unity.

The second type of public service is an input to private production. Let's use the parameter β (the Greek letter *beta*) to measure the marginal product of public services. In other words, if the inputs of labor and capital do not change, then an increase in current purchases, G_1, by 1 unit raises aggregate output, Y_1, by β units. Diminishing marginal productivity suggests that the parameter β would decline as the quantity of government purchases increases. However, for simplicity we treat β as a constant.

Changes in public services may also affect the schedules for the marginal products of labor (MPL) and capital (MPK). In some cases the public services substitute for private inputs. For example, free city police can replace private guards. But more national defense and better enforcement of laws and contracts are likely to raise the marginal products of private factors. So there is no general presumption about the direction of these effects. For want of a better assumption, we neglect any effects on the schedules for the marginal products of labor and capital. In this case current government purchases, G_1, have no direct effect on work effort. Hence, for a given capital stock, an increase by 1 unit in government purchases, G_1, raises the aggregate supply of goods, Y_1^s, by β units.

Recall that net investment demand depends on the schedule for capital's marginal product, on the previous stock of capital, and on the real interest rate. Since we assume that public services do not affect the schedule for capital's marginal product, there is no direct impact of government purchases on investment demand. Any effects that arise must work through changes in the real interest rate.

Clearing of the Commodity Market

Now, we incorporate government purchases into the market-clearing conditions. The main new effects involve the demand and supply of commodities. Therefore, we focus on the condition for clearing the commodity market. The new condition for period 1 is

$$C^d(r_1, \ G_1, \ \ldots) + I^d(r_1, \ \ldots) + G_1 = Y^s(r_1, \ G_1, \ \ldots) \qquad (12.6)$$
$$(-)(-) \qquad\qquad (-) \qquad\qquad\qquad (+)(+)$$

Note that the terms represented by . . . in equation 12.6 include the form of the production function, the initial stock of capital, K_0, and the level of permanent government purchases, $\tilde{G}$.

The aggregate demand for commodities, Y_1^d, consists of consumption demand, C_1^d, gross investment demand, I_1^d, and government purchases, G_1. Hence if consumption and investment demand do not change, aggregate demand increases one-to-one with an increase in government purchases. But an increase by 1 unit in purchases, G_1, reduces aggregate consumer demand, C_1^d, by α units. Since there is no effect on investment demand, we find that an increase by 1 unit in government purchases raises aggregate demand by $(1 - \alpha)$ units. (We assume that $\alpha < 1$ applies.)

Government purchases also influence the supply of commodities. In particular, since public services are productive, an increase in purchases, G_1, by 1 unit raises the supply of goods, Y_1^s, by β units. (*Warning:* Our analysis assumes that taxes are lump sum. When we drop this unrealistic assumption in the next chapter, we introduce some important negative effects from governmental activity on the quantities of goods that people supply and demand.)

Temporary Changes in Government Purchases

Consider a temporary increase in government purchases, where G_1 rises, but permanent purchases, $\tilde{G}$, do not change. Empirically, the most important example of this case is military spending during wars. Permanent purchases typically rise also in this situation, but by less than the increase in current purchases. To simplify matters, we assume here that permanent purchases do not change.

Recall that the government's budget constraint for period 1 is

$$G_1 + \frac{V_1}{P_1} = \frac{T_1}{P_1} + \frac{(M_1 - M_0)}{P_1} \tag{12.7}$$

An increase in purchases, G_1, must involve some combination of an increase in real taxes, T_1/P_1, a decrease in real transfers, V_1/P_1, or an increase in the real revenue from money creation, $(M_1 - M_0)/P_1$. Because we assume lump-sum taxes and transfers, our analysis of the real variables in the commodity market will be the same, regardless of which combination we specify. Therefore, let's think of the extra purchases as financed by more real taxes, T_1/P_1.

We can use the condition for clearing the commodity market, equation 12.6, to find the response to a temporary increase in government purchases. As mentioned before, aggregate demand rises by the fraction $(1 - \alpha)$ of the extra purchases, while aggregate supply rises by the fraction β. Notice that, if $\alpha + \beta < 1$, as we assume below, then the increase in aggregate demand $(1 - \alpha)$ exceeds that in supply (β). This condition turns out to be important for figuring out the effects on the real interest rate.

Consider the inequality, $\alpha + \beta < 1$. This condition says that if government purchases expand by 1 unit, then people get back less than 1 unit in the combined response from the substitution for consumer spending, α, and the increase in private output, β. One easy way to ensure this condition is to assume that public services are useless—that is, the government essentially buys up goods and then throws them into the ocean. In this case we have the condition, $\alpha = \beta = 0$. Although this viewpoint is popular (and appears im-

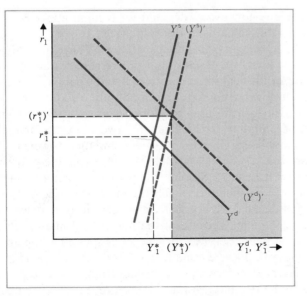

Figure 12.3 Effect on the Commodity Market of a Temporary Rise in Government Purchases
The temporary increase in purchases raises aggregate demand by more than supply. Therefore, the real interest rate and output rise.

plicitly in many macromodels), it may not be the most interesting way to model the functions of government!

More generally, as mentioned before, the two parameters, α and β, tend to decline as the quantity of public services rises. Therefore, our analysis applies in the range where the amount of government purchases is high enough so that the sum, $\alpha + \beta$, is less than one.[6] Notice that, if $\alpha + \beta > 1$, then the typical person would like an increase in public services. That is because the cost—say, 1 unit of goods—is less than what people get back either through services that substitute for consumer spending or through extra production. But the reverse inequality, $\alpha + \beta < 1$, does not necessarily mean that government purchases are too large. Remember that people might like public services a lot even if they substitute little for private spending—that is, even if the parameter α is small.

Figure 12.3 shows the effects on the commodity market when government purchases increase. Without this increase, the market clears at the real interest rate, r_1^*. Then the rise in purchases increases the aggregate quantities of goods demanded and supplied. But notice that the rightward shift of the aggregate demand curve exceeds that of the supply curve. Therefore, at the real interest

---

[6]From an empirical standpoint, we mentioned before that α was estimated to be between 0.2 and 0.4. However, we presently lack estimates of the parameter β.

rate, r_1^*, there is now excess demand for commodities. We conclude that the real interest rate increases to the value $(r_1^*)'$.

Figure 12.3 shows that output increases. There are two elements behind this increase. First, we assume that public services are productive. Second, the increase in the real interest rate motivates people to work more.

Consider now the composition of output. We know that government purchases rise. But private uses of output—for consumption and investment—decline. Consumption demand falls for two reasons. First, there is the substitution of public services for private spending. However, if we are talking about more military spending, then this effect is likely to be weak—that is, the parameter α is small. Second, the higher real interest rate induces people to postpone their expenditures. This second effect accounts also for the drop in investment demand. Notice that the increase in government purchases **crowds out** private spending. Because of the higher real interest rate and the direct substitution of public services for consumer spending, the addition to government purchases induces consumers and investors to spend less.

We suggested before that investment demand is especially sensitive to variations in the real interest rate. Therefore, unless the direct substitution of public services for consumer spending is strong, we predict that the temporary increase in government purchases will mostly crowd out investment (including purchases of consumer durables) rather than consumption.

Since consumption and investment decrease, it follows that total output rises by less than the increase in government purchases. That is, the ratio of the change in output to the change in purchases is positive, but less than one. If the ratio were greater than one, then we would say that a change in government purchases has a multiplicative effect on output. But we do not get this sort of **multiplier** in our model. That is because the economy works to buffer shocks, rather than to magnify them. In particular, the rise in government purchases leads to an increase in work effort, and to decreases in private demands for consumption and investment. Each of these responses serves to alleviate the initial excess demand for goods. (When we study the Keynesian model in Chapter 18 we shall reexamine the potential for a multiplier.)

Let's think about why the temporary increase in government purchases raises the real interest rate. There is a temporarily large governmental demand for goods, which may derive from a war or some other emergency. So, the high real interest rate signals people to work harder, to produce more goods, and to reduce demands for private consumption and investment. In this way the market uses the real interest rate to achieve the appropriate allocations over time for work effort, production, consumption and investment.[7]

Our discussion refers to wars as cases where government purchases are temporarily high. But we have ignored other aspects of major wars that can substantially affect the analysis. For one thing, we neglect any negative effects

---

[7]For some additional discussion, see Robert Hall, "Labor Supply and Aggregate Fluctuations," *Carnegie-Rochester Conference Series on Public Policy,* January 1980.

on productive capacity from military reversals. These resemble adverse supply shocks and would tend to reduce output. Another feature of wartime is the widespread use of rationing to hold down private demands for goods. Others are the military draft, confiscation of property, and appeals to patriotism in order to stimulate work and production. Essentially, direct controls can be a rough substitute for a higher real interest rate as a mechanism for crowding out private spending and for stimulating work and production. These departures from free markets may not affect our general conclusions about the quantities of output, consumption, investment, and employment. But we may not see an increase in the real interest rate during wartime.

Evidence from Wartime Experiences

The Behavior of Output and Other Quantities

We can assess some effects of temporarily high government purchases by looking at the four most recent wars for the United States—World War I, World War II, Korea, and Vietnam. (For these cases we can reasonably neglect any direct effects of combat on productive capacity in the United States.) Table 12.2 describes the behavior of military spending, real gross national product (GNP), and the major components of GNP during these episodes.

The basic method of analysis is similar to one that we used before to examine recessions. For example, we contrast the peak year of the Korean War, 1952, with the benchmark year, 1950. Then we find that real military spending was above its trend value by $56 billion, which was 10% of trend real GNP.[8] On the other hand, real GNP was $33 billion or 6% above its own trend.

Next, we calculate the ratio of excess real GNP and its various components to the excess of real military spending. For GNP the ratio in 1952 was 0.59. Hence—assuming that the boost in military spending was the only major disturbance for the economy—this result supports the theory's predictions. Namely, a temporary increase in government purchases has a positive, but less than one-to-one effect on output.

Since GNP rises by less than the increase in military spending, it follows that the nonmilitary components of GNP must decline overall. The figures shown for 1952 in Table 12.2 indicate that total investment (gross fixed investment, purchases of consumer durables, and changes in business inventories) declined by the fraction, 0.42, of the increase in military spending. In contrast, consumer expenditures for nondurables and services declined by only the fraction, 0.01. Thus, the temporary excess of military purchases crowded out mostly the investment part of private spending. Recall that the theory predicts this outcome since military spending would have little direct substitution for consumer spending.

---

[8]As before, we use a trend growth rate of 3.0% per year for real GNP and its components.

Table 12.2 The Behavior of Output and Its Components during Wartime

Peak Year of War Benchmark Year for Comparison	1918 1916	1944 1947	1952 1950	1968 1965
Excess real military spending (billions of 1972 dollars)	39.7	240.2	56.1	20.0
Excess as % of trend real GNP	18.0	55.9	9.9	2.0
Excess of real GNP (billions of 1972 dollars)	23.2	139.3	32.9	41.3
Excess as % of trend real GNP	10.5	32.4	5.8	4.1
Ratio to excess real military spending for the excess of				
Real GNP	0.58	0.58	0.59	2.06
Real personal consumption expenditures	0.04	−0.10	−0.14	1.22
Durables	—	−0.06	−0.13	0.44
Nondurables and services	—	−0.04	−0.01	0.78
Real gross fixed investment	−0.22	−0.18	−0.17	−0.04
Nonresidential	—	−0.11	−0.02	0.14
Residential	—	−0.07	−0.15	−0.18
Real change in business inventories	−0.09	−0.01	−0.12	−0.20
Other*	−0.15	−0.13	0.02	0.08
Excess of employment (millions)				
Total employment	2.1	8.4	1.5	2.5
Military personnel	2.7	9.9	1.9	0.7
Civilian employment	−0.6	−1.5	−0.4	1.8
Excess of total employment as % of trend value	5.3	14.8	2.4	3.2

*Nonmilitary government purchases and exports less imports.

Note: The method for calculating the excess or shortfall in each component is discussed in the text.

Sources: For World War II, the Korean War, and the Vietnam War, the data are from *Economic Report of the President*, 1983. For 1916 and 1918, the data on real GNP are from the U.S. Department of Commerce, *The National Income & Product Accounts of the U.S., 1929–76*, p. 72. Estimates for the components of real GNP use the data from John W. Kendrick, *Productivity Trends in the U.S.*, Princeton University Press, Princeton, N.J., 1961, Tables A-I and A-IIa. The shares of real GNP shown in each year from Kendrick's data are applied to the Commerce Department's figures on total real GNP to estimate values for military spending, real personal consumption expenditures, real gross fixed investment, and real changes in business inventories.

The final rows of the table show the effects on employment. Notice that total employment (numbers of persons working, including military personnel) in 1952 was above trend by 1.5 million or 2.4% of the trend value. This total divided up between 1.9 million extra military personnel and 0.4 million less civilian workers. (Note that we do not consider here the likely positive effects on hours and effort per worker.)

We apply a similar procedure for World War II. However, since the economy had not yet fully recovered from the Great Depression in 1940, we use 1947 as the benchmark year. Basically, the findings are similar to those from the Korean War, except that the magnitudes are much larger. For example, the excess of real military spending in 1944 was $240 billion, which was 56% of trend real GNP. Then real GNP was $139 billion or 32% above its own trend. Note that the ratio of excess GNP to excess military spending, 0.58, was virtually the same as that for the Korean War.

For World War II, we find that the excess military spending crowded out total investment (gross fixed investment, purchases of consumer durables, and changes in business inventories) by a fraction of 0.25, and consumer purchases of nondurables and services by a fraction of 0.04. Thus, the breakdown was similar to that for the Korean War. Finally, total employment for 1944 exceeded its trend value by 8.4 million or 15%. This total broke down into 9.9 million extra military personnel and 1.5 million less civilian workers.

For World War I, we find that the excess of real GNP above trend in 1918 was again 0.58 times the excess of real military spending. (The closeness of the estimated ratios for 1918, 1944, and 1952 must be a coincidence!) Here, we lack the data to break down consumption into durable and nondurable components. But the total of personal consumption expenditures exceeded its trend by 0.04 times the excess of military spending. In contrast, the shortfall in the sum of gross fixed investment and changes in business inventories was 0.31 times the excess of military spending. Thus, we find again that more government purchases mostly crowds out private investment. (We should be cautious about the detailed results for World War I because the breakdown of GNP into its components is subject to large measurement errors for these years.) Finally, note that total employment in 1918 was above its trend by 2.1 million or 5.3%. In this case there were 2.7 extra military personnel and 0.6 million less civilian workers.

The results for Vietnam differ sharply from those for the other wars. To begin with, using 1965 as the benchmark year, we estimate the excess of real military spending for 1968 as $20 billion, which was only 2% of trend real GNP. Thus, unlike the other cases, it is doubtful that the increase in military spending was the overriding influence on the economy in the middle and late 1960s.

The estimated excess of real GNP for 1968 was $41 billion or 4% of trend real GNP. Thus, the excess real GNP was more than twice as large as the excess real military spending. Correspondingly, we find overall that the non-military components of GNP were above trend in 1968. For example, the ratio to excess military spending was 0.20 for total investment and 0.78 for the consumption of nondurables and services. Hence, the United States really was enjoying "guns and butter" at this time.

The most likely explanation for these results is that the economy was experiencing a boom in the 1960s that had little to do with the Vietnam War. This viewpoint is supported by the high growth rate of output in the period before the main increase in military spending. In particular, from 1961 to 1965, the average annual growth rate for real GNP of 5.1% exceeded that from 1965 to 1968, which was 4.3%.

Suppose now that we focus on the results for the Korean War, World War II, and World War I. Then there is an interesting comparison between the behavior of the economy during wartime booms and during recessions. First, the contrast between wars and recessions concerns the relation between changes in total output and changes in private spending. Total output rises in wars, but falls during recessions. However, private spending declines in both cases. Second, the wartime experiences are similar to recessions in that the major adjustments to private spending occur in the investment components. As with the seven postwar recessions, we find relatively small reductions in consumer purchases of nondurables and services during the Korean War and World War II.

Finally, let's stress the finding that temporarily high government purchases raise total output and employment. But as predicted, the ratio of the excess real GNP to the excess in purchases is less than one.

The Behavior of Real Interest Rates

The theory predicts that temporarily high government purchases, such as in wartime, raise the real interest rate. However, we have to be careful when matching up this prediction with the wartime behavior of interest rates. Recall that our previous theoretical analysis assumes that government purchases are temporarily high only for the current period. But, during wars, military expenditures tend to build up for awhile and then recede at the end of the war. Also, the length of the buildup and the timing of the war's conclusion (or who wins!) are unknown at the outset.

One implication from the theory is that the average real interest rate should be high over the period from the peak of a war until some time after the war finishes. In line with this viewpoint, Table 12.3 reports averages of interest rates over 6-year intervals, beginning with the peak year of each war. Thereby, the figures include beween 1 and 5 years of peacetime after each year. Notice that the table considers the four wars that we just studied, plus the Civil War. In each case we calculate the average for the nominal interest rate on prime commercial paper over 6-year periods. Then we compute real interest rates by subtracting the average rate of change of the GNP deflator. (For the Civil

Table 12.3 Interest Rates During Wartime

Period	π_t	R_t	r_t
1863–68	4.8	7.0	2.2
1918–23	2.7	5.8	3.1
1944–49	6.2	1.0	−5.2
1952–57	2.2	2.6	0.4
1968–73	5.2	6.6	1.4

Note: All values are averages, expressed at annual percentage rates, for the periods indicated. π_t is the inflation rate, based on the consumer price index for the period 1863–68, and on the GNP deflator for the other periods. R_t is the interest rate on 4- to 6-month prime commercial paper, $r_t = R_t - \pi_t$.

Sources: See Table 11.1 of Chapter 11.

War, we lack data on the GNP deflator and therefore use the consumer price index.)

For the Civil War, the average real interest rate over the period 1863–68 was 2.2%. This rate was substantially less than the averages for 1840–60 and 1867–80, which were each 9.1%. For World War I, the average real interest rate over the interval 1918–23 was 3.1%. This value equaled the average for 1900–16, but was below that of 4.9% for 1920–40. Next, for World War II, the average over the period 1944–49 was −5.2%, which was well below the averages of 4.9% for 1920–40 and −0.2% for 1947–60.

For the two most recent wars, Korea and Vietnam, the average real interest rates were 0.4% (for 1952–57) and 1.4% (for 1968–73), respectively. These values do not differ greatly from the average for 1947–80, which was 0.6%.

Overall, the results do not confirm a positive effect of wartime spending on real interest rates. In fact, the real interest rates were, if anything, below average during the wars.

For 1944–49 the substantially negative real interest rates reflect an overstatement of inflation because of the lifting of price controls. (General price controls did not apply to the earlier wars, but were introduced to some extent during the Korean War.) The World War II controls kept the reported price levels below the "true" values especially for 1943–45. Thus inflation was understated for these years. As the controls were gradually eliminated in 1946–48, the reported figures caught up with the true ones and inflation was overstated. My estimate[9] is that, without controls, the inflation rate for 1944–49 would have averaged 1.1% per year, rather than the official value of 6.2%. If the controls merely masked the behavior of the price level, then the lower figure is a reasonable estimate of the true inflation rate. Using this value, the average real interest rate for 1944–49 was −0.1%, rather than −5.2%. Note that the adjusted value of −0.1% is close to the average of real interest rates for 1947–60 (−0.2%).

Even with this adjustment for price controls, we would not conclude that real interest rates were especially high during wars in the United States. A possible explanation is the resort to aspects of a command economy, where governmental decrees on production, work, and expenditures substitute for free markets. Especially during the two world wars, the government exerted direct pressures to work and produce, including the military draft, and also rationed private consumption and investment. With few goods to buy and little option to take leisure, people would hold financial assets even if they paid low real interest rates. In other words, the command economy is in some respects a substitute for free markets with high real interest rates. While this argument may have some validity, it also implies that the data from U.S. wars may not be helpful for testing the theoretical link between temporary government purchases and real interest rates.

---

[9]These estimates, based on the behavior of money and other variables, are discussed in Robert Barro, "Unanticipated Money, Output and the Price Level in the United States," *Journal of Political Economy,* August 1978, p. 572.

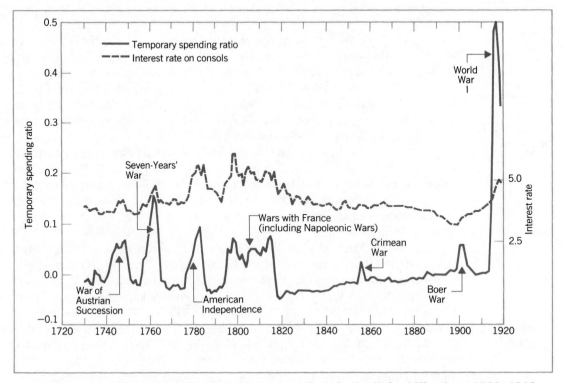

Figure 12.4 **Military Spending and the Interest Rate in the United Kingdom, 1730–1918**

We can get around some of these difficulties by looking at the long-term relation between wartime spending and interest rates in the United Kingdom. From the standpoint of our scientific inquiry, Britain was very cooperative by fighting numerous wars, especially before 1815. Prior to World War I, these wars were not accompanied by the introduction of aspects of a command economy. Thus, unlike the U.S. case, we can be confident of predicting a positive effect of temporary wartime expenditures on real interest rates.[10]

The solid line in Figure 12.4 shows a measure of temporary real military spending expressed as a ratio to trend real GNP.[11] The peaks in this line

---

[10]To use the British data from more than two centuries back, we have to assume that the basic economic forces were the same then as now. However, our approach can be valid even though there have been major changes in technology, the role of government, and so on.

[11]The details of this variable and further results are in Robert Barro, "Government Spending, Interest Rates, Prices and Budget Deficits in the United Kingdom, 1730–1918," Rochester Center for Economic Research, Working Paper No. 1, March 1985. For an earlier discussion of these data, see Dan Benjamin and Levis Kochin, "War, Prices and Interest Rates: Gibson's Paradox Revisited," in Michael D. Bordo and Anna J. Schwartz, eds., *A Retrospective on the Classical Gold Standard, 1821–1931,* University of Chicago Press, Chicago, 1984.

correspond to the seven major wars for the United Kingdom over the period 1730 to 1918. Notice that the high points for temporary spending were 50% of GNP in World War I (1916), 16% in the Seven Years' War (1761), 9% during the War of American Independence (1782), and 7% during the Napoleonic Wars (1814).

The dashed line in the figure is the long-term nominal interest rate.[12] The positive relation of this rate to temporary spending is clear visually and is also confirmed by statistical analysis. Notably, interest rates rose on average by 1.0 percentage points during the seven wars. This change is large relative to the average level of rates, which was 3.5% for 1730 to 1918. Thus, the long-term results for the United Kingdom are more in line with the theory than are those for the United States.[13]

Permanent Changes in Government Purchases

The previous analysis applies to temporary changes in government purchases, such as in wartime. In other cases there are long-lasting shifts in the size of government, with respect to its purchases and public services. For example, the data that we looked at before for the United States show permanent increases in the ratio of total government purchases to GNP during the 1930s and 1950s. But we do not see major changes in this ratio for the 1960s and 1970s.

To study long-run changes in government purchases, we have to allow for a change in permanent purchases, $\tilde{G}$. For convenience, let's now hold fixed the current level of purchases, G_1. (In this case an increase in permanent purchases must reflect a rise in the anticipated values of some future purchases.) Once we work out this case, we can also combine a change in current purchases, G_1, with a change in permanent purchases, $\tilde{G}$.

We found before that an increase by 1 unit in permanent purchases subtracts the equivalent of 1 unit of real income per period from households. However, an increase in permanent purchases also implies an increase in the normal flow of public services. Therefore, in a full sense, an increase by 1 unit in permanent purchases does not subtract the equivalent of 1 unit of real income per period from households. First, if $\tilde{G}$ rises by 1 unit, then in the aggregate households receive α units per period in services that substitute directly for consumer spending. Second, because public services are productive, producers

---

[12]The data are for British consols, which are government bonds that pay a perpetual stream of coupons, but have no maturity date. (The confidence in the durability of the British empire used to be great.)

[13]The results for the United Kingdom refer to nominal interest rates, whereas our theory applies to real interest rates. However, over the period of study, the long-term inflation rate in the United Kingdom was close to zero. For this reason, it is likely that the positive relation beween temporary spending and nominal interest rates also reflects a positive relation with real interest rates.

in the aggregate get β units per period in extra output. On net, an increase by 1 unit in permanent purchases, $\tilde{G}$, subtracts the equivalent of $(1 - \alpha - \beta)$ units of real income per period from households. That is, the aggregate of permanent income effectively declines by $(1 - \alpha - \beta)$ units. Recall that we assume the condition, $\alpha + \beta < 1$, which means that permanent income declines when permanent purchases rise.

Let's think about how people respond to an increase by 1 unit in permanent purchases, $\tilde{G}$. We know that the aggregate of permanent income effectively declines by $(1 - \alpha - \beta)$ units. Suppose for now that work effort, and hence, the supply of goods, Y_1^s, do not change. Then households would reduce aggregate consumption demand, C_1^d, by roughly $(1 - \alpha - \beta)$ units. This follows because the marginal propensity to consume out of permanent income is close to one.

Now, we can incorporate the level of permanent purchases, $\tilde{G}$, into the condition for clearing the commodity market. The expanded condition is

$$C^d(r_1, G_1, \tilde{G}, \ldots) + I^d(r_1, \ldots) + G_1 = Y^s(r_1, G_1, \ldots) \qquad (12.8)$$
$$(-)(-)(-) \qquad\qquad (-) \qquad\qquad\qquad (+)(+)$$

Notice that an increase in permanent purchases, $\tilde{G}$, lowers consumer demand, C_1^d.

To model a permanent increase in government purchases at date 1, we have to allow simultaneously for increases in actual purchases, G_1, and in permanent purchases, $\tilde{G}$. Consider first the effects of this change on consumer demand in equation 12.8. Recall that an increase by 1 unit in actual purchases, G_1, lowers consumer demand, C_1^d, by α units. This reflects the substitution of public services for private spending. Next, an increase by one unit in permanent purchases, $\tilde{G}$, reduces consumer demand by $(1 - \alpha - \beta)$ units. This comes from the fall in permanent income. When we combine the two effects, we find that consumer demand falls by $\alpha + (1 - \alpha - \beta) = 1 - \beta$ units. We summarize these results in the second column of Table 12.4.

Table 12.4 **Effects of Government Purchases on the Excess Demand for Commodities**

(1)	(2)	(3)	(4)	(5)	(6)	(7)
				Impact on		
Increase by 1 Unit in	C_1^d	I_1^d	G_1	Y_1^d	Y_1^s	$Y_1^d - Y_1^s$
G_1	$-\alpha$	0	1	$1 - \alpha$	β	$1 - \alpha - \beta$
$\tilde{G}$	$-(1 - \alpha - \beta)$	0	0	$-(1 - \alpha - \beta)$	0	$-(1 - \alpha - \beta)$
G_1 and $\tilde{G}$	$-(1 - \beta)$	0	1	β	β	0

Note: We show the effects of increases in actual and permanent purchases, G_1 and $\tilde{G}$, on the components of commodity demand—C_1^d, I_1^d, and G_1—and on supply, Y_1^s. The effect on aggregate demand, Y_1^d, is the sum of the effects on the three components of demand. The effect on excess demand, $Y_1^d - Y_1^s$, is the effect on aggregate demand less that on aggregate supply. Notice that a permanent increase in current purchases—where G_1 and $\tilde{G}$ rise together—raises aggregate demand and supply by equal amounts. Hence, excess demand does not change.

Recall that government purchases have no direct impact on investment demand. But government purchases, G_1, enter one-to-one into aggregate demand. Therefore, the net increase in aggregate demand, Y_1^d, is the amount $1 - (1 - \beta) = \beta$. We show this result in column 5 of the table.

Now let's look at aggregate supply in equation 12.8. An increase by one unit in purchases, G_1, raises supply, Y_1^s, by β units, as shown in column 6 of the table. The important finding is that aggregate demand and supply increase by the same amount, β. Therefore, when actual and permanent purchases increase by equal amounts, we end up with no effect on excess demand. The last column of Table 12.4 shows this result.

Figure 12.5 depicts the effects graphically. Notice that the permanent increase in government purchases shifts the demand and supply curves rightward by equal amounts. Therefore, aggregate demand still equals aggregate supply at the initial real interest rate, r_1^*. We conclude that a permanent expansion of government purchases has no effect on the real interest rate.

Figure 12.5 shows that output increases. Since we assumed no change in work effort, this effect depends on the productivity (β) of public services.

Consider next the composition of output. To begin with, government purchases increase. But there are two forces that lower consumer demand. First, public services substitute for private spending, and second, the reduction in permanent income induces people to consume less. However, since the real interest rate does not change there is no effect on investment. Note that this last result differs sharply from that when the change in government purchases

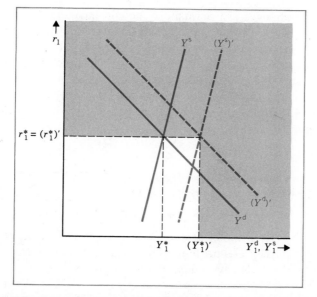

Figure 12.5 Effects on the Commodity Market of a Permanent Rise in Government Purchases
The permanent increase in purchases raises aggregate demand and supply by roughly equal amounts. Therefore, output increases, but the real interest rate does not change.

was temporary. In that case the rise in the real interest rate crowded out both forms of private spending. Now, when the change in purchases is permanent, the extra government purchases crowd out only consumer spending.

Since consumption decreases, while investment does not change, it follows that total output increases by less than the rise in government purchases. That is, the ratio of the change in output to the change in purchases is again positive, but less than one. Thus, we still do not have a multiplier in the model.

Let's think about why the real interest rate increases when the rise in government purchases is temporary, but does not change when the rise in purchases is permanent. A temporary boost in purchases, as in wartime, triggers an incentive to substitute resources intertemporally—in particular, to work and produce more than normal and to consume and invest less than usual during the current period. A higher real interest rate guides people toward these responses. But when the increase in government purchases is permanent, people have fewer resources to spend in every period. While there is an incentive to reduce consumption at all dates, there is no reason to do anything unusual in the current period. Therefore, the real interest rate does not change.

We can readily extend the analysis of permanent changes in government purchases to allow for responses of work effort. Since permanent income declines, we predict that people would take less leisure along with less consumption. The increase in work effort implies a further rightward shift to commodity supply, Y^s, in Figure 12.5.

Since people work more they can reduce consumption by less than before. Therefore, commodity demand, Y^d, also shifts further to the right in Figure 12.5. In fact, this extra shift will be nearly the same as that to supply, Y^s. That is, since the changes are permanent, people have no reason to use the adjustments in work effort to either raise or lower their real saving.

The main point is that, even with the response of work effort, commodity supply and demand are still equal at the initial real interest rate, r_1^*. The new result is that work effort rises, which means that output increases by more than before. (*Warning:* The increase in work effort may not occur if government expenditures are financed by an income tax, rather than a lump-sum tax. We consider more realistic types of taxes in the next chapter.)

Permanent and Temporary Changes in Government Purchases—Statistical Estimates of the Effects on Output

I have carried out a statistical study, which divides the observed values of real government purchases into temporary and permanent parts.[14] When considering the ratio of real government purchases to real GNP in the United States,

---

[14]The results are in Robert Barro, "Output Effects of Government Purchases," *Journal of Political Economy,* December 1981.

it turns out that most of the changes in this ratio are unpredictable. Given the information that people have at any date, it is impossible to forecast the great majority of increases or decreases that occur in this ratio. Therefore, people cannot usually say whether the currently observed ratio of government purchases to GNP is temporarily high or low. As their best guess, people would perceive as permanent most of the observed movements in this ratio. The only systematic exception that I was able to isolate statistically concerns wartime. Not surprisingly, the ratio of defense spending to GNP is unusually high during wars. Therefore, people would anticipate declines in this ratio after each war (they also expect each war to end eventually!).

Figure 12.6 plots from 1930 to 1978 the ratio of real defense purchases to real GNP, which is denoted by G^w/Y. Also plotted are my estimates of the permanent part of this ratio, $(\tilde{G}^w/Y)$, and the temporary part, $G^w/Y - (\tilde{G}^w/Y)$. Notice that the estimates of temporary purchases are positive only during and close to the three wars for the period: from 1940–46 for World War II, 1951–54 for the Korean War, and 1967–69 for the Vietnam War.

There are also some important movements in the permanent part of the ratio for defense purchases. The main ones are the net increase during World War II (from 1940 to 1946), the sharp rise at the end of the Korean War (1952–53), and the decrease from the early 1960s through 1978. (This particular study ends in 1978.)

The ratio of real nondefense government purchases to real GNP, denoted by G^p/Y, appears in Figure 12.7. Here, my statistical analysis did not isolate any temporary variations (except for a temporary reduction during wartime). At any date, the current ratio is also the best forecast for future ratios.

I used statistical techniques to estimate the effects on output from temporary and permanent changes in government purchases. Table 12.5 shows the results over the period 1946–78.[15] In each case there is a range of estimates for the effects of various categories of government purchases on real GNP. But in a statistical sense, we can be reasonably confident that the true effects lie within these intervals.

For defense purchases, the results show a strong positive impact on output. Also, the estimated responses for temporary changes tend to exceed those for permanent changes. Note that the estimates imply that output rises by between 50 and 120% of a temporary increase in defense purchases. These findings are broadly consistent with the less formal results that we observed before during wartime. There we found that the excesses of real GNP—during World Wars I and II and the Korean War—were about 60% of the excesses of real military spending.

Table 12.5 indicates that real GNP rises by between 30 and 70% of a permanent increase in defense purchases. Since the response is again less than

---

[15]Some problems arise in using the data for World War II, although most of the results are similar if the data for 1942–45 are included. The main change is a lower estimate (between 0.5 and 0.8) for the effect of temporary defense purchases on output.

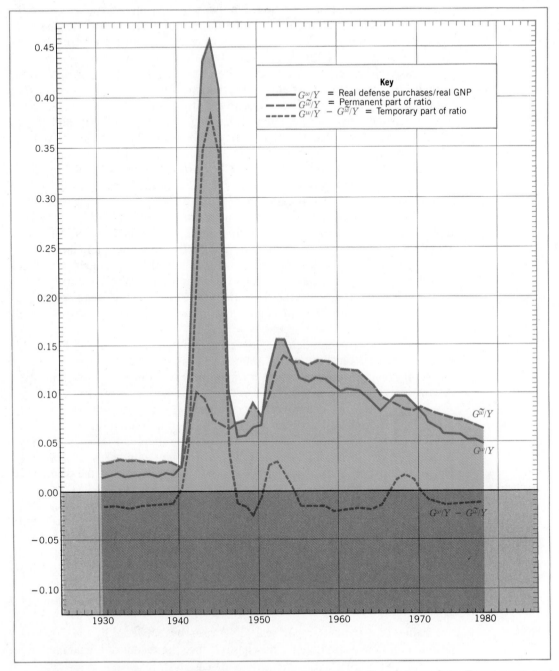

Figure 12.6 The Ratio of Defense Purchases to GNP—A Breakdown into Temporary and Permanent Parts

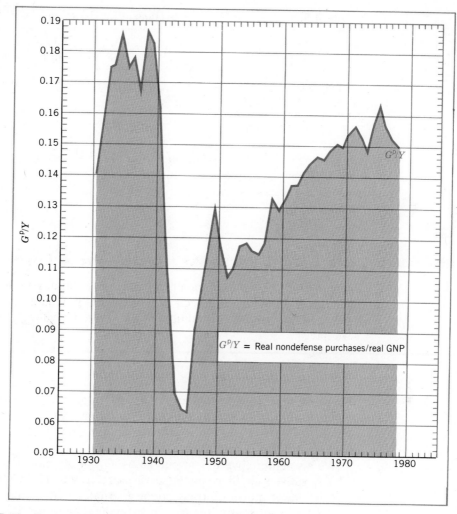

Figure 12.7 The Ratio of Nondefense Purchases to GNP

100%, we find that a permanent rise in purchases must crowd out some private spending.

For nondefense purchases, there were no temporary changes to analyze, and the results apply only to permanent changes. Unfortunately, the estimates are imprecise, covering the range of responses for output from −20 to +130% of the change in purchases. Therefore, while a positive effect is likely, we cannot pinpoint the magnitude.

One final point is that the results suggest little role for government purchases in peacetime business fluctuations. The amount of peacetime variation in purchases, combined with the estimated effects of these purchases on real

Table 12.5 Empirical Estimates of Effects of Government Purchases on Real GNP

Change by 1 Unit in	Estimated Number of Units by which Real GNP Increases
Temporary defense purchases	0.5 to 1.2
Permanent defense purchases	0.3 to 0.7
Permanent nondefense purchases	−0.2 to 1.3

GNP, does not account for much of the observed booms and recessions. In particular, shifts in government purchases have no regular association with the seven U.S. recessions since World War II, which we studied before in Chapters 9 and 10.

Effects of Government Purchases on the Price Level

People often say that government spending is inflationary. So, let's see what the model says about the effects of government purchases on the price level.

We again look at the condition for all cash to be willingly held. For period 1 we have

$$M_1 = P_1 \cdot L(Y_1, R_1, G_1, \ldots) \qquad (12.9)$$
$$(+)(-)(-)$$

where L is again the function for real money demanded. We assume that total output, Y_1, measures real transactions, which have a positive effect on the real demand for money. As before, the nominal interest rate, R_1, has a negative effect on the real demand for money.

We also enter government purchases, G_1, in the money-demand function with a negative sign. Since public services are provided free of charge to users, there are fewer monetary transactions associated with government purchases than with private consumption or investment. Therefore, for a given level of total output, an increase in government purchases, G_1, means less money demanded.

Now, let's explore the consequences for the price level of an increase in government purchases, G_1. If the increase is permanent, there is an increase in output, Y_1, but no change in the real interest rate. Unless the direct negative effect of government purchases on real money demanded is substantial, real money demand would increase. Therefore, if the behavior of the nominal money stock does not change, then we are likely to get a negative effect of government purchases on the price level, P_1.

If the increase in government purchases is temporary, then there is also an increase in the real interest rate, r_1. Hence, for a given expected rate of inflation, π_1^e, the nominal interest rate, R_1, rises. This element lowers the real demand for money, which makes it more likely that the price level would rise.

Overall, for a given behavior of money, there is little basis to predict systematic effects of government purchases on the price level. Moreover, even if there were a positive effect, this channel would not account for chronic rises in prices—that is, for inflation. Rather, each increase in government purchases—relative to the scale of the economy—would generate a one-time rise in the price level. To explain inflation on this basis, we would need continuing expansions in the relative importance of government purchases. Yet, as we saw before, government purchases have not changed much in relation to GNP in the 1960s and 1970s, which are the years when U.S. inflation became significant.

An increase in government purchases may also be inflationary because it stimulates money creation. That is, governments may resort to the inflation tax to finance part of the higher level of purchases. Of course, this argument applies equally well to the government's transfer payments which are another form of government spending. Notice that this mechanism connects a higher level of real spending to a faster growth rate of money and thereby to a higher rate of inflation. Hence, this route does show how higher real government spending can be inflationary.

Empirically, there is not much evidence that changes in government purchases influence the price level, once we hold fixed the behavior of money. But for some countries, there are important linkages between real government spending and the rate of money creation. In other words, when some governments opt to raise real spending, they use the printing press to pay for part of it. For example, as discussed in Chapter 8, the connection between government spending and monetary growth was very close during the German hyperinflation from 1921 to 1923.

For the United States, there is no evidence that long-term changes in government spending as a ratio to GNP have led to higher rates of monetary growth. However, the sharp expansions of spending that occurred during wartime did trigger a lot of money creation. Like most countries, the United States finances part of its wartime spending with the printing press. Hence, this mechanism accounts for some of the inflation that usually accompanies wars.

Summary

We introduced government purchases of goods and services as another use of output. To finance these expenditures and its transfer payments, the government levies lump-sum taxes or prints money. Then the government uses its purchases to provide a flow of public services. An additional unit of these services substitutes for α units of aggregate consumer spending, and also raises production by β units. We assume the condition, $\alpha + \beta < 1$, which means that people get back directly less than the cost of an additional unit of public services.

A temporary increase in government purchases, as in wartime, raises aggregate demand by more than supply. Hence, the real interest rate and output increase. However, the crowding out of investment and consumption means that total output rises by less than the increase in government purchases. That is, there is no multiplier.

Empirically, variations in government purchases play a major role during wartime, but not in peacetime business fluctuations. The U.S. evidence from World Wars I and II and Korea supports the theory's predictions with respect to quantities. In particular, real GNP rises, but by only about 60% of the increase in real military spending. Thus, there is crowding out of private spending, especially investment. However, the real interest rate does not tend to rise during wartime. On the other hand, some long-period evidence for the United Kingdom reveals a positive effect of wartime spending on interest rates.

A permanent increase in government purchases amounts to a reduction in permanent income, which lowers consumer demand and raises work effort. The expansions of aggregate demand and supply turn out to be roughly equal. Therefore, output again increases, but there is no change in the real interest rate. In this case, the crowding out of private spending falls entirely on consumption.

Finally, we examined the connection between government purchases and inflation. For a given behavior of the money stock, the model does not predict any strong linkages. However, more government spending is inflationary if it induces the government to print money at a faster rate.

Important Terms and Concepts

lump-sum taxes

permanent government purchases

public goods

crowding out (from government purchases)

multiplier

QUESTIONS AND PROBLEMS

Mainly for Review

12.1 What are the channels by which government spending affects excess demand in the commodity market? How does it affect utility? Can you think of examples of public services that are not close substitutes for consumption ($\alpha = 0$) but nevertheless provide utility?

12.2 Could government services be a substitute for leisure? If so, what additional channel of effect on the commodity market would you expect?

12.3 Why does the real interest rate rise as a result of a temporary increase in government purchases? Does real saving necessarily decrease?

12.4 Distinguish between (*a*) a rise in permanent government purchases, and (*b*) a permanent rise in government purchases. Which of the two has a wealth effect on consumption? Which has an intertemporal-substitution effect?

12.5 What is crowding out? Does it involve an intertemporal-substitution effect alone? Could there be direct substitution of government purchases for private investment purchases?

Problems for Discussion

12.6 Government Purchases in the National Accounts

The national accounts treat all of government purchases as a part of real GNP. But suppose that these purchases, G_t, are an input to private production—that is, in the aggregate, $Y_t = F(K_{t-1}, N_t, G_t)$. Then public services are an intermediate product—that is, a good that enters as an input into a later stage of production. Hence, we ought not to include these services twice in real GNP—once when the government purchases them, and again when the public services contribute to private production.

  a. Suppose that businesses initially hire private guards. But the government then provides free police protection, which substitutes for the guards. Assume that the private guards and police are equally efficient and receive the same incomes. How does the switch from private to public services affect measured real GNP?

  b. How would you change the treatment of public services in the national accounts? Is your proposal practical?

  (These issues are discussed in Simon Kuznets, "Discussion of the New Department of Commerce Income Series," *Review of Economics and Statistics,* August 1948, pp. 156–57; and Richard Musgrave, *Theory of Public Finance,* McGraw-Hill, New York, 1959, pp. 186–88.)

12.7 Public Ownership of Capital and the National Accounts

When the government produces goods and services, the national accounts measure the contribution to GNP by the government's purchases from the private sector of labor, materials, and new capital goods. But the accounts neglect any contribution to output from the flow of services on government-owned capital. The accounts also do not subtract depreciation of this capital to calculate net product.

  a. What happens to measured GNP if the government gives its capital to a private business and then buys the final goods from that business?

  b. How would you change the treatment of government-owned capital in the national accounts? Is your proposal practical?

12.8 The Role of Public Services

We assume that an additional unit of public services has two direct effects: first, it substitutes for α units of private consumption, and second, it raises production by β units.

a. Consider various categories of government purchases, such as military spending, police, highways, public transit, research and development expenditures, regulatory agencies, etc. How do you think the parameters, α and β, vary across the categories? Are the parameters always positive?

b. Consider a permanent increase in government purchases. How do the sizes of the responses in output and consumption depend on the values of the parameters, α and β? Explain the results.

c. Repeat part b for the case of a temporary increase in government purchases.

12.9 Prospective Changes in Government Purchases

During the current period, date 1, people find out that government purchases will increase permanently in some future period. There is no change in current purchases, or in the paths of the money stock and real transfers.

a. What happens currently to the real interest rate and the quantities of output, consumption, investment, and employment?

b. What happens to the current price level and nominal interest rate?

c. Can you think of some real-world cases where this question applies?

12.10 Effects of Government Purchases on the Real Wage Rate

Suppose that we include a labor market in the model.

a. What is the effect on the real wage rate from a temporary increase in government purchases?

b. What is the effect from a permanent increase in government purchases?

12.11 Government Employment during Wartime (optional)

In the model we assume that the government buys only final product from the commodity market. In particular, the government neither produces goods nor employs people. This assumption is basically satisfactory if the government's production function is similar to that of private producers. But the assumption is troublesome for wartime. For example, suppose that during World War II the government effectively removes 10 million people temporarily from the civilian labor force. But the government takes away no privately owned capital. Then, as before, assume that the government also temporarily raises its purchases of goods by a large amount.

a. Analyze the effects on the real interest rate, and on the quantities of output, investment, and consumption. (How did you count the 10 million conscripts in the measure of output?) What happens to total and private employment?

b. If we include a labor market in the model, what happens to the real wage rate?

12.12 The Price Level during the Korean War

With the start of the Korean War, the price level (GNP deflator) rose at an annual rate of 10% from the second quarter of 1950 to the first quarter of 1951. By contrast, the inflation rate was negative for 1949, 1.4% from the first quarter of 1951 to the first quarter of 1952, and 2.0% from the first quarter of 1952 to the first quarter of 1953.

The table below shows over various periods the inflation rate π_t, the growth rates μ_t of currency and M_1, the growth rate of real government purchases ΔG_t, and the nominal interest rate on 3-month treasury bills, R_t. Using these data, how can we account for the surge in the price level at the start of the Korean War? (This question does not have a definite answer!)

(*Hint:* Price controls were stringent during World War II. People may have expected a return to these controls under the Korean War in 1950.)

		(Figures in % per Year)			
		(M_1)	(Currency)		
Year and Quarter	π_t	μ_t	μ_t	ΔG_t	R_t
1949.1 to 1950.2	−0.3	1.8	−1.6	2.7	1.1
Start of War					
1950.2 to 1951.1	10.0	4.0	−0.5	24.6	1.3
1951.1 to 1952.1	1.4	5.3	4.7	27.9	1.6
1952.1 to 1953.1	2.0	3.2	4.5	9.2	1.8

12.13 The Optimal Level of Public Services (optional)

In our model a permanent increase in government purchases raises output, but lowers consumption and leisure. Recall that we used the condition, $\alpha + \beta < 1$, where α measures the substitution of public services for aggregate consumer spending, and β is the marginal product of public services. We assume also that the parameters, α and β, decline as the quantity of government purchases rises.

Assume first that public services substitute for α units of aggregate consumer spending, but otherwise provide no direct utility. Then

a. What happens to the typical person's utility when the quantity of government purchases rises permanently by 1 unit?

b. If the government wants to maximize the typical person's utility, then where should it set its level of purchases? What condition holds here for the parameters, α and β?

c. Why is it not the right answer in part b to choose the level of government purchases that maximizes aggregate output (as measured by real GNP)?

d. Without working through the details, how does the analysis change if public services provide utility in other ways?

CHAPTER 13

TAXES AND TRANSFERS

Thus far, we have taken an unrealistic view of the way that governments raise tax revenues and make transfer payments. Specifically, we assumed lump-sum taxes and transfers, which means that the amount someone pays or receives has nothing to do with their income or other characteristics. In the real world governments levy a variety of taxes and pay out a lot of transfers, but none of these look like the lump sums in our theory. Generally, a person's taxes and transfers depend on his or her actions. But this dependence motivates changes in behavior. For example, income taxes deter people from working and investing in order to generate income. Similarly, transfers to the unemployed or the poor may motivate people not to work. Overall, the system of taxes and transfers creates a variety of substitution effects on work effort, production, consumption, and investment. In this chapter we extend the theoretical analysis to incorporate some of these effects.

Let's start with an overview of tax collections in the United States. We discuss the different types of levies and indicate how the overall composition has changed over time.

Sources of Government Revenues in the United States

Table 13.1 shows the breakdown of revenues by major types for the federal government since 1929. Individual income taxes (including minor amounts of taxes on estates and gifts) were a reasonably stable share of total federal revenues since World War II. For 1985, this share was 45%. The next component, which is corporate income taxes, declined from about 25% of the total after World War II to only 7% in 1985. Then there are levies for social insurance funds, which increased substantially since World War II. In 1984, 76% of these levies were for social security (including health insurance). The rest were mainly for unemployment insurance and government employees' retirement. Notice that the total of payments into social insurance funds rose from 10% of all federal revenues in 1948 to 39% in 1985. Thus, in 1985, this category was almost as large as the federal income tax on individuals. Another part of federal revenues is excise taxes, customs duties, etc., which fell from about

Table 13.1 The Breakdown of Federal Revenues by Types (Figures Are Percentages of the Total)

	Individual Income Tax, etc.	Corporate Profits Tax	Excise Taxes, Customs Duties, etc.	Social Insurance Levies	Payments from Federal Reserve
1929	33	32	31	3	0
1930	37	24	34	4	0
1	30	21	44	6	0
2	19	19	54	7	0
3	18	17	61	4	0
4	17	18	62	3	0
1935	21	21	55	3	0
6	22	25	45	8	0
7	24	19	34	22	0
8	25	14	34	27	0
9	18	19	35	28	0
1940	16	30	30	23	0
1	13	47	23	16	0
2	21	48	17	14	0
3	42	35	12	11	0
4	43	30	15	12	0
1945	46	24	17	14	0
6	44	22	20	14	0
7	45	25	18	12	0
8	44	27	19	10	0
9	42	24	21	13	1
1950	36	34	18	12	0
1	41	33	15	11	0
2	46	27	15	11	0
3	46	27	16	11	0
4	46	26	15	13	0
1955	43	27	14	12	0
6	45	26	14	14	1
7	46	24	14	15	1
8	47	22	15	16	1
9	44	24	14	17	1
1960	45	21	14	18	1
1	46	21	14	19	1
2	46	20	14	19	1
3	45	21	13	20	1
4	42	21	14	21	1
1965	43	22	13	20	1
6	44	21	11	23	1
7	45	19	11	24	1
8	46	19	10	23	1
9	48	17	10	24	2

Table 13.1 (*Continued*)

	Individual Income Tax, etc.	Corporate Profits Tax	Excise Taxes, Customs Duties, etc.	Social Insurance Levies	Payments from Federal Reserve
1970	48	14	10	26	2
1	45	15	10	27	2
2	48	15	9	28	1
3	44	15	8	31	2
4	46	14	8	31	2
1975	44	13	8	33	2
6	44	15	7	32	2
7	45	15	7	32	2
8	45	15	7	32	2
9	47	13	6	32	2
1980	48	11	8	32	2
1	47	8	10	32	2
2	49	5	8	35	2
3	46	7	8	36	2
4	43	8	8	39	2
1985	45	7	7	39	2

Note: In this table the category, corporate profits taxes, does not include the Federal Reserve's payments to the U.S. Treasury, which are shown separately. These items are combined in the national accounts.

Source: U.S. Department of Commerce, *The National Income and Product Accounts of the U.S., 1929–76,* and *U.S. Survey of Current Business,* various issues.

20% of the total after World War II to 7% in 1985. Finally, the Federal Reserve's payments to the Treasury—which correspond to the government's revenue from printing money—amounted in 1985 to 2% of total federal receipts. These proceeds from money creation were near zero before the mid 1950s.

Before World War II, the excise taxes and customs duties were relatively more important. In fact, these items were the major source of federal revenues before World War I. Individual income taxes began in 1913, except for some levies around the Civil War and in 1895. Corporate taxes started in 1909. Notice also that the levies for social insurance funds were small until the beginning of the unemployment insurance program in 1936 and social security in 1937.

Table 13.2 shows a breakdown for the revenues of state and local governments. Property taxes were traditionally the largest component, but this share fell from about 60% in the early 1930s to less than 40% after World War II, and to 18% in 1985. In the early period the relative decline in property taxes corresponded to the growth in sales taxes. These increased from 6% of state and local revenues in 1929 to 20% in 1941, but maintained a roughly

Table 13.2 **The Breakdown of State and Local Revenues by Types (Figures Are Percentages of the Total)**

	Individual Income Tax, etc.	Corporate Profits Tax	Property Tax	Sales Tax	Social Insurance Levies	Federal Aid	Other
1929	4	2	62	6	2	2	22
1930	4	1	62	7	2	2	22
1	3	1	61	7	2	4	22
2	4	1	62	8	2	2	21
3	2	1	57	9	2	7	22
4	2	1	47	11	2	19	18
1935	3	1	46	13	2	19	16
6	3	2	49	16	2	8	20
7	4	2	47	17	2	8	20
8	4	1	47	17	3	8	20
9	3	2	46	17	3	10	19
1940	3	2	46	18	3	9	19
1	4	3	44	20	3	8	18
2	4	3	43	19	3	8	20
3	4	4	43	18	3	9	19
4	4	4	42	18	3	9	20
1945	5	4	41	20	3	8	19
6	4	4	38	22	5	9	18
7	4	4	36	23	5	11	17
8	4	4	35	23	5	11	18
9	5	3	35	22	5	11	19
1950	4	4	35	23	5	11	18
1	5	4	34	23	6	11	17
2	5	3	34	23	6	10	19
3	5	3	34	23	6	10	19
4	5	3	34	22	7	10	19
1955	5	3	34	22	7	10	19
6	5	3	34	23	7	10	18
7	5	3	34	22	7	11	18
8	5	2	34	24	7	13	15
9	6	3	33	24	7	15	12
1960	6	3	34	24	7	13	13
1	6	2	34	24	7	13	14
2	6	3	33	24	7	14	13
3	6	3	33	24	7	14	13
4	7	3	32	24	7	15	12
1965	7	3	32	24	7	15	12
6	7	3	30	24	7	17	12
7	8	3	30	23	7	17	12
8	8	3	29	23	7	17	13
9	9	3	28	24	7	17	12

Table 13.2 (*Continued*)

	Individual Income Tax, etc.	Corporate Profits Tax	Property Tax	Sales Tax	Social Insurance Levies	Federal Aid	Other
1970	9	3	28	23	7	18	12
1	9	3	27	23	7	19	12
2	11	3	25	22	6	21	12
3	11	3	24	23	7	21	11
4	10	3	24	23	7	21	12
1975	10	3	23	22	7	23	12
6	11	3	22	22	7	23	12
7	11	4	22	21	7	23	12
8	11	4	20	22	8	24	11
9	12	4	19	22	8	23	12
1980	12	3	18	22	8	23	14
1	12	3	18	22	9	21	15
2	12	2	19	22	9	19	17
3	12	3	19	22	8	18	18
4	13	4	19	22	8	17	17
1985	13	3	18	22	8	17	19

Note: Other revenues include hospital and health charges, tuition, fines, motor vehicle licenses, rents and royalties, and some other fees and taxes.

Source: See Table 13.1.

constant share since World War II. More recently, state and local governments have turned to personal income taxes. This category (which includes minor amounts of levies on gifts and estates) constituted 4% of state and local receipts in 1929 and 1948, but then increased to 13% in 1985. The other category of state and local revenues that became more important since World War II is federal grants-in-aid (transfers of funds from the federal government to state and local governments). These climbed from 9% of the total in 1946 to 24% in 1978, but then fell to 17% in 1985. (Federal grants-in-aid are primarily for welfare, medical care, transportation, education, housing, training programs, and general revenue sharing.)

Figure 13.1 indicates the federal share of total government revenues. (Federal grants-in-aid are excluded here from total revenues.) Notice that the federal share was 34% in 1929, then fell to a low point of 19% in 1932, but subsequently rose during the New Deal period to reach 49% by 1940. After a peak of 80% during World War II, the share declined to 62% in the early 1970s. For 1985, the fraction was also 62%.

Figure 13.2 provides one measure of an overall tax rate—the ratio of total government revenues (excluding federal grants-in-aid) to GNP. The ratio rose

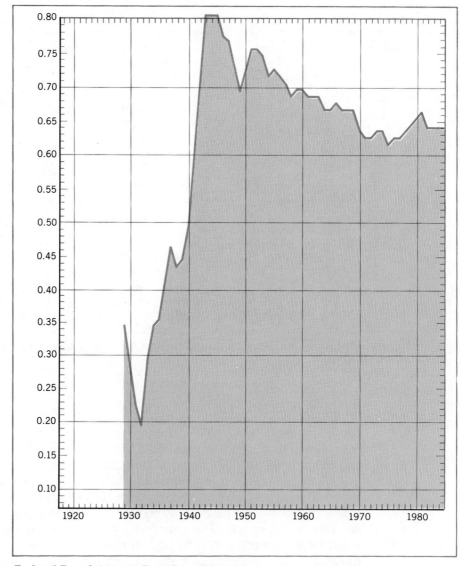

Figure 13.1 Federal Receipts as a Fraction of Total Government Receipts

from 11% in 1929 to 18% in 1940 and 25% in 1945. Then, after a fall to 22% in 1949, the ratio increased slowly to 26% in 1956, 28% in 1960, 31% in 1969, and 32% from 1977 to 1982. Then, with the Reagan tax cuts, the ratio fell (but by only 1 percentage point) to 31% for 1983–84, and then rose back to 32% in 1985. (It is not easy from these figures to detect the Reagan Revolution!)

Figure 13.2 Total Government Receipts as a Ratio to GNP

Types of Taxes

Notice that some taxes fall on income (individual income taxes, corporate profits taxes, and contributions for social security, which are levied on wage earnings), others on expenditures (excise and sales taxes), and some on holdings of property. But one way or another, the amount someone pays depends on his or her economic activity. That is, none of these look like the lump-sum taxes in our theory.

The Federal Individual Income Tax

Let's look at the structure of the federal individual income tax. (In 1985 this category accounted for 44% of federal and 27% of total government receipts.) First, we subtract from someone's reported income the expenses for business purposes, moving, deferred compensation through pension plans, and some other items.[1] That gives us **adjusted gross income.** Then we take out either a standard deduction ($2390 for a single person, $3540 for a married couple in 1985) or the itemized deductions for medical care, interest payments, certain taxes, etc. Then we subtract the value of exemptions, which in 1985 was $1040 per dependent, including oneself. That gives us **taxable income.** Then, aside from any tax credits that apply, the law provides a schedule that relates the amount of tax to taxable income. (Marital status also matters here.) But it is important to note that the tax is not a constant fraction of taxable income— that is, it is not a **flat-rate tax.** Rather, the more income someone receives, the greater is the tax rate on an additional dollar of income. This setup is called a **graduated-rate tax.** (Sometimes, it is called a "progressive tax," which seems to express someone's opinion about its merits. In contrast, a "regressive tax" is one where the rate falls as income rises.)

Figure 13.3 shows the relation of the federal income tax to a family's adjusted gross income. The graph applies in 1985 to a married couple, who have two children and do not itemize deductions. (This assumption is un-realistic at high incomes, where most people do itemize their deductions.) So the graph incorporates a standard deduction of $3540 and an exemption of $4160. The calculations also include the "earned-income credit," which refunds a portion of taxes to families with adjusted gross incomes below $11,000. The maximum credit of $550 applied in 1985 to a family that had only "earned income" (basically labor income) and whose income was between $5000 and $6500. (The total tax due was negative for incomes below $9435.)

For levels of income above $11,000—where the earned-income credit is zero—the tax rises with adjusted gross income at a steadily increasing rate. The slope of the curve in Figure 13.3 indicates the tax rate that attaches to an additional dollar of income. Notice that this slope becomes steeper as income rises above $11,000.

Figure 13.4 shows the tax rates that apply to an additional dollar of income for the various ranges of adjusted gross income. These are called marginal tax rates, because they prescribe the rate of tax on the marginal dollar of income. Notice that the **marginal tax rate** rises from 12% at $11,000 to 14% at $12,070, 16% at $20,710, and so on. Eventually, the rate reaches 49% at an adjusted

---

[1]One of these is the preferential treatment of long-term capital gains. In 1985, when people sold assets that they held for more than 6 months, only 40% of the increase in value was subject to tax.

Figure 13.3 The Tax Schedule from the Federal Individual Income Tax in 1985
The graph shows for 1985 the relation of federal income taxes, net of the earned-income credit, to adjusted gross income for a married couple with two children. We assume that all income is "earned" (at least for levels below $11,000) and that deductions are not itemized.

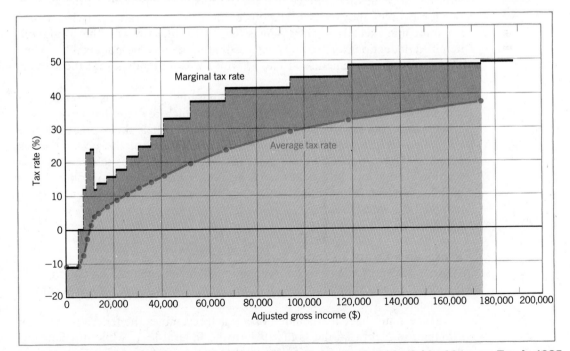

Figure 13.4 Marginal and Average Tax Rates for the Federal Individual Income Tax in 1985
The graph shows for 1985 the relation of marginal and average tax rates to adjusted gross income. We make the same assumptions as in Figure 13.3.

gross income of $118,020, and the maximum of 50% when adjusted gross income hits $173,180. (But recall that we do not allow for itemized deductions, which are almost sure to apply at this level of income.) In years before 1982 the maximum marginal tax rate exceeded 50%.

For incomes below $11,000, we have to consider the earned-income credit, which was introduced in 1975. It is worth looking at some details of this odd feature of the tax law because it helps us to understand better the notion of a marginal tax rate. Until income reaches $5000, the credit rises by 11% of each dollar earned. The effective marginal tax rate is -11%, which means that someone's tax—which happens to be negative here—falls by 11% of each additional dollar of income. Then the credit is constant when income is between $5000 and $6500, so the effective marginal tax rate is zero in this range. Next the credit falls by $12\frac{2}{9}\%$ of each dollar earned above $6500. So, the effective marginal tax rate is $12\frac{2}{9}\%$ until someone's income reaches $7700. Then people start to pay income tax at a marginal rate of 11%, plus they continue to lose the credit at a rate of $12\frac{2}{9}\%$. Hence, the tax system imposes a peculiarly high marginal tax rate of $23\frac{2}{9}\%$ for incomes between $7700 and $9880. At $9880, people start to pay income tax at a marginal rate of 12%—hence, the effective marginal tax rate becomes $24\frac{2}{9}\%$. Then the marginal tax rate falls to 12% at an income of $11,000 when the earned-income credit becomes zero.

Figure 13.4 shows also the **average tax rate,** which is the ratio of taxes to adjusted gross income. Notice that the marginal tax rate is above the average rate for incomes above $5000. Therefore, the average tax rate rises with income when income exceeds $5000. (Why is that?) Recall, however, that we ignore itemized deductions and various devices that make income nontaxable. When we consider these elements, we end up with a weaker tendency for the average tax rate to rise as income increases.

The distinction between average and marginal tax rates is important for our analysis. Average tax rates indicate how much revenue the government collects as a fraction of income—that is, revenue equals the average tax rate multiplied by the amount of income. But the effects of the tax system on people's choices depend on marginal tax rates. These rates tell people what fraction the government takes from an additional dollar of income. So in deciding how much to work, produce, and invest, people take account of these marginal tax rates.

State and Local Income Taxes

Many states and some cities impose individual income taxes. Overall, in 1985, this category accounted for 13% of state and local and 6% of total government revenues.

Some states have a graduated tax, which resembles the federal setup. For example, in Nebraska the tax is 19% of the federal levy, while in California there is a schedule of marginal rates that rise from 0 to 11%. (The highest marginal tax rates seem to be 14% in Minnesota and 18.5% for "unearned" incomes in New York City.) Other states have a flat rate of tax on income, except for a small exemption—for example, the rate is 2.5% in Illinois and 2.35% in Pennsylvania. Finally, there are a few states that have no income tax. For people who are looking for a place to move, these are (in 1985) Alaska, Florida, Nevada, South Dakota, Texas, Washington, and Wyoming. Connecticut, New Hampshire, and Tennessee tax only some forms of property income. (The data in this section are from J. K. Lasser, *Your Income Tax,* Simon & Schuster, New York, 1985, pp. 194–96.)

Social Security Tax

Another important form of tax (which the government amusingly calls a "contribution") is the levy on wage earnings and income from self-employment to finance social security. In 1984 this category accounted for 30% of federal and 18% of total government revenues. At present, almost all workers are covered by social security. The main exceptions are some government employees!

The social security tax is much simpler than the individual income tax. For example, in 1985 covered employees pay 7.05% of earnings up to a ceiling of $39,600. Employers pay an equal amount. Thus, the combined marginal and average tax rates are 14.1% for labor earnings between 0 and $39,600. Then the marginal tax rate falls to zero, so that the average tax rate declines gradually as earnings increase.[2] Overall, except for the ceiling on earnings, the social security tax amounts to a flat-rate levy on labor income. However, the tax rates and ceilings have increased substantially over time—for example, in 1960 the rates were 3% for each employee and employer, with a ceiling of $4800.

Marginal Income Tax Rates

The ratio of goverment receipts to GNP in Figure 13.2 is one measure of an average tax rate. But as mentioned before, we would like to measure marginal tax rates to assess the effect of the tax system on economic activity. Ideally, we would find the marginal tax rate for each family at each point in time. For personal income taxes we would do this by adding the marginal tax rates for each type of tax—the federal and state and local individual income taxes, and

---

[2]In calculating effective marginal tax rates, we should deduct any extra benefits that someone gets *because they pay the tax.* Therefore, some parts of government revenue are not a tax at all—these include charges for school tuition and hospitals, contributions to government employee retirement funds, and some other items. This category accounted for 13% of total government revenues in 1984. For individual income taxes, we treat this extra benefit as nil. That is, even if we like public services, the amounts we get do not depend on the individual taxes that we pay. But for social security, there is some relation of an individual's benefits to that person's lifetime contributions to the program. For an argument that this effect is important for some people, see Roger H. Gordon, "Social Security and Labor Supply Incentives," National Bureau of Economic Research, working paper no. 986, September 1982.

the social security tax. Then we would average these marginal tax rates across families at each date.

Figure 13.5 shows the average marginal tax rate from the federal individual income tax and from the social security tax on employees and employers for 1916–83. These values are averages over families' marginal tax rates, when weighted by the adjusted gross income of each family. Note that the average

Figure 13.5 The Average Marginal Tax Rate from the Federal Individual Income Tax and Social Security

The graph shows the average of marginal tax rates, when weighted by family incomes. The data are from Robert Barro and Chaipat Sahasakul, "Average Marginal Tax Rates from Social Security and the Individual Income Tax," *Journal of Business*, October 1986 marginal tax rates went from 5% in 1920 to 2% in 1930, 6% in 1940, 20% in 1950, 25% in 1960, 27% in 1970, and 36% in 1980. After reaching the all-time peak of 38% in 1981, the average marginal tax rate declined—because of the Reagan tax cuts—to 34% in 1983. As a rough statement, the time pattern of average marginal tax rates in Figure 13.5 parallels that for the ratio of government receipts to GNP in Figure 13.2.

Corporate Profits Taxes

Taxes on corporate profits accounted for 6% of total government revenues in 1985. For large corporations in 1985, the federal marginal tax rate on taxable earnings was 46%. This rate has been close to 50% since World War II, but a complicated "excess profits tax" applied also during the Korean War and World War II. From 1918 to 1938, the tax rates were between 12 and 15%.

The relation of corporate taxes to corporate profits depends also on various tax credits, and on the rules for computing depreciation allowances and for valuing inventories. Figure 13.6 shows how the ratio of corporate taxes (federal plus state and local) to corporate profits changed over time.[3] For 1946–81, this ratio varied between 39 and 59%, with no regular trend. However, the ratio fell to about 30% for 1982–84, and then declined to 23% in 1985. This cut in effective corporate tax rates reflected mainly the more favorable depreciation allowances and some other changes in the 1981 tax law.

Recall that corporate profits taxes have declined sharply as a share of government revenues. These taxes accounted for over 20% of total government receipts in the late 1940s, but only 6% in 1985. There were two main elements behind this change. First—at least until 1982—the ratio of corporate profits taxes to corporate profits did not change greatly since World War II. But other taxes rose substantially relative to income. (Of course, the ratio of corporate profits taxes to corporate profits was already very high—nearly 50%—in the late 1940s.) Second, the ratio of corporate profits to GNP fell significantly in the 1970s. This ratio was about 11% in the late 1940s and was still 10% in 1968. But since then, the ratio fell to 7% in 1985.

We can think of the corporate profits tax as a levy on the capital owned by corporations. But since households ultimately own the corporations, the tax amounts to another levy on individuals' income from capital. In fact, the government taxes the earnings of corporations directly and then taxes them a second time when people receive dividends or capital gains. (Economists call this *double taxation*.) For the purposes of our analysis, we can think of adding the tax on corporate profits to individual income taxes to calculate an overall tax on the income from capital.

---

[3]The figures on corporate profits include adjustments for the valuation of inventories and for the calculation of depreciation.

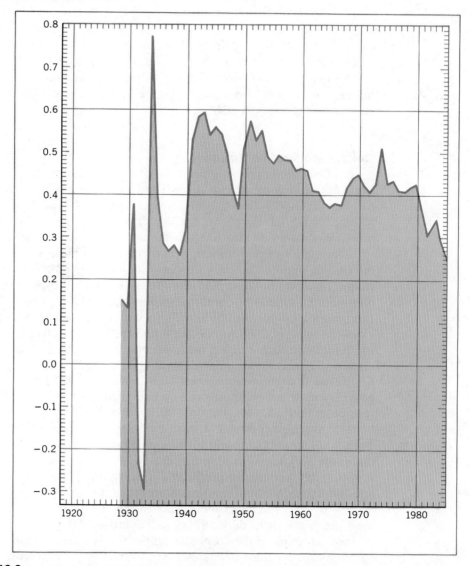

Figure 13.6 Corporate Profits Taxes as a Ratio to Corporate Profits
Corporate profits taxes are amounts paid to federal, state, and local governments. The earnings of the Fed are subtracted from corporate profits, and the Fed's transfers to the Treasury are subtracted from corporate taxes. Data are from *Economic Report of the President,* various issues.

Property Taxes

Property taxes provided 8% of total government revenues in 1985. But the various state and local governments use a bewildering array of procedures to determine the taxes on houses, factories, etc. In a general way we can think of the property tax as another form of tax on capital. Therefore, for most purposes, we can combine this tax with the individual income taxes and the corporate profits tax to find the overall tax on the income from capital.

Sales and Excise Taxes

Finally, we should mention sales and excise taxes, which constituted 13% of total government revenues in 1985. Many states and localities have general sales taxes, but also have special levies on gasoline, alcohol, tobacco, and some other items. The federal government's excise taxes apply to gasoline, alcohol, tobacco, automobiles, tires, and telephone services. As of 1980, the federal government also levies the "windfall-profits tax," which amounts to an excise tax on petroleum products.

The important feature of these taxes is that they apply to types of expenditures, rather than to income or wealth.[4] In the subsequent theoretical analysis, we shall focus on income taxes. Thus, in a broad sense, the analysis encompasses the types of taxes discussed in previous categories. But we should remember that sales and excise taxes operate in a different manner.

An Income Tax in the Theoretical Model

We can evaluate the main effects of taxation by examining a simple form of income tax. Assume that a family's real taxes, t_t/P_t, are a fraction, τ, of its real taxable income. (τ is the Greek letter *tau*.) Hence, for simplicity, we do not introduce a graduated-rate tax structure into the model, but use instead a flat-rate tax. Also, we assume at this stage that the tax rate, τ, does not vary over time.

In the model we assume that a family's real taxable income equals its real net product, $y_t - \delta k_{t-1}$, plus real interest income (which can be negative), less the amount of **tax-exempt real income,** e_t. Notice that we treat governmental transfers as nontaxable, which is accurate in most cases. Finally, we assume initially that there is no inflation, so that the real and nominal interest rates on bonds are equal—that is, $r_t = R_t$. Therefore, a household's real taxes are given by

$$\frac{t_t}{P_t} = \tau\left(y_t - \delta k_{t-1} + \frac{r_{t-1}b_{t-1}}{P_t} - e_t\right) \tag{13.1}$$

---

[4]Many other countries use a *value-added tax,* which amounts to a broad-based sales tax. However, rather than applying to final sales, this levy depends on the value added to goods at various stages of production. Recently some members of the U.S. Congress have proposed a "business-transfer tax," which is a form of value-added tax.

If real taxable income is negative, we assume that taxes are negative, rather than zero.[5] Also, we assume that the tax parameters, τ and e_t, are the same for all households. In particular, we neglect any actions that individuals can take to affect either their marginal tax rate, τ, or their quantity of tax-exempt income, e_t. Note that since each household's marginal tax rate is τ, the average marginal tax rate across households is also τ.

A household's average tax rate—that is, the ratio of taxes to income—is

$$\text{average tax rate} = \frac{\tau(y_t - \delta k_{t-1} + r_{t-1}b_{t-1}/P_t - e_t)}{(y_t - \delta k_{t-1} + r_{t-1}b_{t-1}/P_t + v_t/P_t)} \quad (13.2)$$

In the model the average tax rate is below the marginal rate, τ, for two reasons—first, because of the exempt amount, e_t, and second, because of the nontaxable transfers, v_t/P_t. At this point, we still treat the transfer payments as lump sum.

Aggregate real income taxes follow from equation 13.1 as

$$\frac{T_t}{P_t} = \tau(Y_t - \delta K_{t-1} - E_t) \quad (13.3)$$

where E_t is the aggregate amount of tax-exempt income. (Remember that aggregate real interest payments, $r_{t-1}B_{t-1}/P_t$, equal zero.) Therefore, the government's budget constraint in real terms is now

$$G_t + \frac{V_t}{P_t} = \tau(Y_t - \delta K_{t-1} - E_t) + \frac{(M_t - M_{t-1})}{P_t} \quad (13.4)$$

Here we measure aggregate real income taxes on the right side by the expression from equation 13.3.

Suppose that we take as givens the amounts of real government purchases, G_t, aggregate real transfers, V_t/P_t, and the real revenue from money creation, $(M_t - M_{t-1})/P_t$. Then, for a given amount of aggregate net product, $Y_t - \delta K_{t-1}$, the two tax parameters, τ and E_t, must be set so as to satisfy the government's budget constraint. That is, the government has to generate enough income-tax receipts in each period to meet the expenditures that are not covered by printing money. Often, we shall think about changing the marginal tax rate, τ, and then allowing the exempt amount, E_t, to vary in order for equation 13.4 to hold. In that way we can isolate the substitution effect from a change in the tax rate. (The results would be the same if we changed lump-sum transfers, V_t/P_t, instead of E_t, when we shifted the marginal tax rate.) Note that, at this point, we do not allow the government to borrow and lend on the credit market. That is, we wait until the next chapter to allow for budget deficits or surpluses.

---

[5]In the real world taxes can be negative because of the earned-income credit and because individuals or businesses can carry over some losses from one period to the next. For example, the Chrysler Corporation still has past business losses stored up, which it can use to reduce its future taxes.

Households' Budget Constraints

Each household's budget constraint in real terms for period t is

$$y_t - \delta k_{t-1} + \frac{b_{t-1}(1 + r_{t-1})}{P_t} + \frac{m_{t-1}}{P_t} + \frac{v_t}{P_t} - \left(\frac{t_t}{P_t} \right)$$

$$= c_t + i_t - \delta k_{t-1} + \frac{(b_t + m_t)}{P_t} \qquad (13.5)$$

Notice that we subtract depreciation from both sides, so that net product, $y_t - \delta k_{t-1}$, appears on the left, while net investment, $i_t - \delta k_{t-1}$, appears on the right. Notice also that real taxes, t_t/P_t, subtract from the household's disposable funds on the left side.

Now, substitute for real taxes from equation 13.1 into equation 13.5 and rearrange terms to get

$$(1 - \tau)(y_t - \delta k_{t-1}) + \frac{(1 - \tau)r_{t-1}b_{t-1}}{P_t} + \frac{(b_{t-1} + m_{t-1})}{P_t}$$

$$+ \frac{v_t}{P_t} + \tau e_t = c_t + i_t - \delta k_{t-1} + \frac{(b_t + m_t)}{P_t} \qquad (13.6)$$

The first term on the left side equals net product, $y_t - \delta k_{-1}$, less the tax levy on this product, $\tau(y_t - \delta k_{t-1})$. That is, after-tax net product, $(1 - \tau)(y_t - \delta k_{t-1})$, matters for the household. Similarly, the after-tax quantity of real interest income, $(1 - \tau)r_{t-1}b_{t-1}/P_t$, enters on the left side of equation 13.6.

Notice that the previous financial assets, $(b_{t-1} + m_{t-1})/P_t$, and the transfers, v_t/P_t, appear without the tax rate in equation 13.6. That is because the simple income-tax law from equation 13.1 does not tax either the stock of financial assets or the amounts of transfers. But the term, τe_t, does appear as part of the household's sources of funds. This term represents the saving on taxes because the quantity of income, e_t, is exempt from taxation.

Finally, none of the uses of the household's funds on the right side of equation 13.6 involve the tax rate. This result follows because we assume no tax on the expenditures for consumption or net investment. More generally, any sales or excise taxes would enter here.

Tax Rates and Substitution Effects

We want to see how the presence of an income tax alters the various substitution effects on households. For this purpose we have to reconsider our concepts of the real interest rate, the marginal product of labor (or real wage rate), and the return to investment.

The After-Tax Real Interest Rate

People receive real interest at the rate r_t, but they pay the fraction τ of their receipts to the government. Hence, when measured net of tax, people earn interest at the rate $(1 - \tau)r_t$. We refer to this variable as the **after-tax real interest rate.** Notice that this interest rate appears (for period $t - 1$) on the left side of equation 13.6.

In previous chapters we discussed the intertemporal-substitution effects that arise when the real interest rate changes. These effects still apply, but they refer now to the after-tax real interest rate. An increase in this interest rate, $(1 - \tau)r_t$, stimulates saving, which shows up as a reduction in current consumption demand, and as increases in current work effort and the supply of goods.

The After-Tax Marginal Product of Labor

When someone works an additional hour, he or she raises output, y_t, by the marginal product of labor, MPL_t. But people keep only the fraction, $1 - \tau$, of their extra product. Hence, the **after-tax marginal product of labor,** $(1 - \tau)MPL_t$, matters for someone's choices of work and consumption. (With a separate labor market, the after-tax real wage rate, $(1 - \tau)w_t/P_t$, would matter.)

Suppose that there is a given schedule for labor's marginal product, MPL_t, when graphed versus the amount of work, n_t. Then an increase in the tax rate, τ, lowers the schedule when measured net of tax—that is, as $(1 - \tau)MPL_t$. People respond just as they would to a decrease in the schedule for labor's marginal product. Specifically, they reduce work effort, the supply of goods, and consumption demand.

The After-Tax Rate of Return to Investment

If someone raises their stock of capital, k_t, by 1 unit then next period's net product rises by the marginal product of capital less the rate of depreciation, $MPK_t - \delta$. Recall that this term is the real rate of return from an extra unit of investment. But people now keep only the fraction, $1 - \tau$, of this return. Therefore, the **after-tax rate of return to investment** becomes $(1 - \tau)(MPK_t - \delta)$. Producers determine their desired stock of capital, $\hat{k}_t$, by equating this after-tax rate of return to the after-tax real interest rate on bonds, which is $(1 - \tau)r_t$. That is, investors choose the quantity of capital, $\hat{k}_t$, that satisfies the condition

$$(1 - \tau)(MPK_t - \delta) = (1 - \tau)r_t \qquad (13.7)$$

We shall find it convenient not to cancel out the tax terms, $1 - \tau$, which appear on both sides of equation 13.7. Instead, we think of the desired stock of capital as depending separately on the after-tax real interest rate, $(1 - \tau)r_t$, and the tax rate, τ. Then we can write the desired stock of capital, $\hat{k}_t$, as the function

$$\hat{k}_t = \hat{k}[(1 - \tau)r_t, \tau, \quad \delta, \ldots] \qquad (13.8)$$
$$(-) \ (-) \ (-)$$

As before, the term . . . represents characteristics of the production function that affect the schedule for capital's marginal product.

For a given tax rate τ, an increase in the *after-tax* real interest rate on the right side of equation 13.7 raises the required after-tax return from investment. Hence, the desired capital stock falls. For a given after-tax real interest rate, a higher tax rate τ lowers the after-tax return from investment on the left side of equation 13.7. Therefore, the desired capital stock again declines. Finally, as in earlier cases, the desired capital stock rises if the depreciation rate δ falls or if there is an upward shift in the schedule for capital's marginal product, MPK_t.

As before, the desired stock of capital, $\hat{k}_t$, determines a producer's gross investment demand. Namely, the investment demand function is

$$i_t^d = \hat{k}[(1 - \tau)r_t, \tau, \quad \delta, \ldots] - (1 - \delta)k_{t-1}$$
$$(-)\ (-)(-)$$
$$= i_i^d\left[(1 - \tau)r_t, \tau, \quad \delta, k_{t-1}, \ldots\right] \qquad (13.9)$$
$$(-)\ (-)(?)(-)$$

The new features concern the tax rate. First, for a given tax rate, it is the after-tax real interest rate, $(1 - \tau)r_t$, that has a negative effect on gross investment demand. Second, for a given value of the after-tax real interest rate, the tax rate τ has a separate negative effect, which comes from the reduction in the after-tax rate of return to investment, $(1 - \tau)(MPK_t - \delta)$.

A Change in the Tax Rate

Suppose that the tax rate, τ, increases. Aggregate real tax revenues are given from the tax law in equation 13.3 by $T_t/P_t = \tau(Y_t - \delta K_{t-1} - E_t)$. If the exempt amount, E_t, did not change, then real tax revenues would increase unless aggregate net product, $Y_t - \delta K_{t-1}$, fell by a great deal. Let's assume for the moment that this is not the case—that is, real tax receipts would rise if the exempt amount did not change.

Now, suppose that we hold constant the levels of government purchases, G_t, and aggregate real transfers, V_t/P_t, as well as the real revenue from money creation, $(M_t - M_{t-1})/P_t$. Then the government's budget constraint from equation 13.4 says that the amount of real taxes collected cannot change. So if we raise the tax rate, we have to increase the exempt amount, E_t, to keep real tax revenues the same. In effect, we can think of raising the average marginal tax rate, which is what the parameter τ represents in the model, without changing the average tax rate. For example, in the real world, we might increase various exemptions in the income-tax law, but then raise all of the tax rates on taxable income to maintain the level of real revenues. Alternatively, we can think of switching from one type of tax, such as the social security tax on wage earnings, to another, such as the individual income tax. Because the social security tax has a low average marginal tax rate, compared to the revenue that it collects, this type of change tends to raise the average marginal tax rate, while leaving unchanged the aggregate of real tax revenues.

The important point is that, conceptually, we want to keep separate the effects of changes in the average marginal tax rate, τ, from those of changes in government purchases, transfers, or money creation. That is why we want to consider first the case where the exempt amount varies along with the tax rate in order to keep fixed the volume of real tax revenues. Then, when we want to, we can also look at cases where tax revenues do change, along with some combination of shifts in government purchases, transfers, or money creation.

Finally, let's consider whether a change in the tax rate, τ, affects wealth. (Recall that by the term, wealth, we refer to the level of utility that the typical person can attain.) Remember that the aggregate of households' budget constraints over many periods involves the present value of aggregate real transfers less aggregate real taxes. Aside from some monetary terms—which we know cancel in the aggregate—this present value depends only on the level of permanent government purchases, which we called $\bar{G}$. As long as we hold constant the level of permanent purchases, it seems that a change in the tax rate would not change wealth. In fact, this result turns out to be a satisfactory approximation in many cases. However, we shall see later on that it is not exact. But for now, we neglect any effects on wealth from changes in the tax rate.

Clearing of the Commodity Market

Now let's incorporate the various effects from the tax rate into the condition for clearing the commodity market. The condition for period 1 is

$$C^d[r_1(1 - \tau), \tau, \ldots] + I^d[r_1(1 - \tau), \tau, \ldots] + G_1 = Y^s[r_1(1 - \tau), \tau, \ldots]$$
$$\quad (-) \quad (-) \qquad\qquad (-) \quad (-) \qquad\qquad\qquad (+) \quad (-)$$
$$(13.10)$$

To avoid a clutter of terms, we do not write out explicitly some of the variables that influence consumer demand, investment demand, and the supply of goods. These include the initial capital stock, K_0, and the levels of current and permanent government purchases, G_1 and $\bar{G}$.

One new feature is that the after-tax real interest rate, $(1 - \tau)r_1$, appears where the real interest rate, r_1, used to appear. Given the after-tax real interest rate, the tax rate, τ, has some separate effects. First, a higher tax rate reduces the schedule for the after-tax marginal product of labor, $(1 - \tau)\text{MPL}_1$, and thereby reduces the incentive to work. Hence, there are reductions in the aggregates of goods supply, Y_1^s, and consumer demand, C_1^d. Second, a higher tax rate lowers the after-tax rate of return to investment, $(1 - \tau)(\text{MPK}_1 - \delta)$, which means that gross investment demand, I_1^d, decreases. Thus, we see generally that a higher tax rate tends to depress market activity—that is, it reduces the demands for consumption and gross investment, as well as the supply of goods. These results follow because an individual's tax liability rises when he or she engages in more market activity. A higher tax rate motivates people to subsitute away from market activities and toward untaxed areas, such as leisure or the **"underground economy,"** where income is not reported.

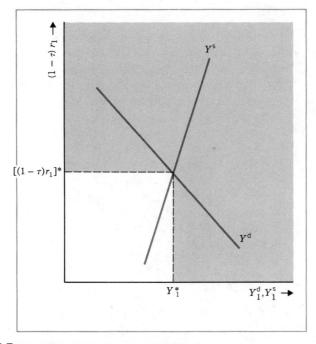

Figure 13.7 Clearing of the Commodity Market
We graph the demand and supply of commodities versus the after-tax real interest rate,
$(1 - \tau)r_1$.

Figure 13.7 shows the clearing of the commodity market. Here we find it convenient to place the after-tax real interest rate, $(1 - \tau)r_1$, on the vertical axis. Then the horizontal axis shows the levels of commodity demand and supply. Note that the graph applies for a given position of the production function, and for given values of the starting capital stock, K_0, current and permanent government purchases, G_1 and $\tilde{G}$, and the tax rate, τ.

Effects of a Higher Tax Rate

Assume now that the tax rate rises permanently from τ to τ' at date 1. Figure 13.8 shows the effects on the commodity market. First, there is a leftward shift in the demand curve, which reflects the decreases in consumption demand and gross investment demand. Second, there is a leftward shift in the supply curve. Since the increase in the tax rate is permanent, we predict little response of desired saving. That is, at the initial value of the after-tax real interest rate, the cutback in goods supply is roughly equal to the fall in consumption demand.[6] Therefore, since investment demand also declines, the overall fall in

---

[6]Recall that we hold constant aggregate real taxes. Therefore, the change in the aggregate of desired saving equals the change in goods supply, Y_1^s, less the change in consumer demand, C_1^d.

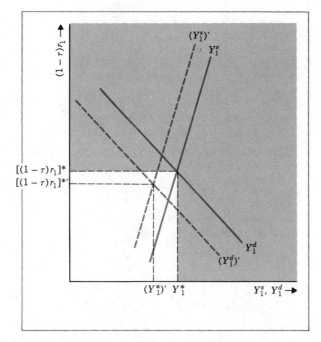

Figure 13.8 **Effects on the Commodity Market of a Higher Income-Tax Rate**
The increase in the income-tax rate from τ to τ' reduces the demand for commodities by more than the supply. Hence, output and the after-tax real interest rate fall.

demand is greater than that in supply. Hence, Figure 13.8 shows that the increase in the tax rate creates an excess supply of commodities at the after-tax real interest rate that initially clears the market.

Figure 13.8 shows that the after-tax real interest rate and the level of output decline. Since the initial capital stock, K_0, is given, the fall in output reflects entirely a decrease in work effort. People work less in this situation because the government extracts a larger fraction of a marginal dollar of income.

Since government purchases do not change, the total of real private spending for consumption and investment must decline. Recall that the disturbance had no initial impact on desired saving. Therefore, with the fall in the after-tax real interest rate, saving must fall in the end. Since saving equals net investment, it follows that net investment decreases. (Gross investment also falls since depreciation is given.)

We can think of the drop in the after-tax real interest rate as signaling a diminished priority for using resources now—in order, specifically, to accumulate and maintain capital—rather than later. Notice that, from the viewpoint of the private sector, the diminished priority for accumulating capital reflects the adverse effect of a higher tax rate on the after-tax rate of return to investment.

The effect on consumption is uncertain. That is because the decrease in the after-tax real interest rate motivates more consumption, while the higher tax rate motivates less consumption. In other words, although total output falls, the higher tax rate may crowd out enough investment to avoid a decline in consumption in the short run.

The Wealth Effect from a Change in the Tax Rate

We carried out the analysis under the assumption that the change in the tax rate left wealth unchanged. This assumption seems reasonable since we varied the amount of tax-exempt income, E_1, in order to hold constant the quantity of real taxes collected, T_1/P_1. But let's consider more carefully whether wealth changes.

As we discussed in Chapter 2, the effect of a disturbance on someone's wealth is positive if it enables him or her to achieve a higher level of utility. Similarly, the effect on wealth is negative if the attainable level of utility declines. Now the increase in the tax rate that we have just considered ends up reducing the utility of the typical household. Therefore, the effect on the typical person's wealth is actually negative, rather than zero.

To see why, note first that someone who produces the quantity of output y_1 gets to keep only the portion, $(1 - \tau)y_1$, while the remainder goes as taxes to the government. Therefore, a person's contribution to the economy's product, y_1, exceeds the contribution to that person's after-tax income, which is $(1 - \tau)y_1$. In deciding how much to work and invest, people consider only the fraction, $1 - \tau$, of the marginal products of their labor and capital. Hence, from a social perspective, people have insufficient incentives to work and invest.[7] In particular, the existence of the tax rate distorts private decisions, so that the aggregates of work, consumption, and investment end up below their desirable levels. Moreover, a higher tax rate means a greater distortion, which leads to a lower level of utility for the typical household.

We could modify our previous analysis to include a negative effect on wealth from an increase in the tax rate. However, the general nature of the results would not change. Therefore, for most purposes, we can use the results that we already obtained while neglecting wealth effects.

---

[7] The fraction τ that goes to taxes reduces the required payments of all other taxpayers (by a very small amount per person). But no individual takes these benefits to others into account when deciding how much to work and invest. Economists call this an "external effect." This effect refers to the benefits that others get from one person's actions, when the person does not take these benefits into account.

Long-Run Effects of a Higher Tax Rate

So far, our analysis does not allow for changes in the capital stock. But since a higher tax rate reduces investment in the short run, we anticipate that the stock of capital will be lower in the long run. To explore this effect, we have to extend the analysis from Chapter 11 of steady-state situations. But we look here only at cases where population and technology do not change in the steady state. Then we know that the levels of the capital stock, etc., also do not change in the steady state.

Recall that the rate of time preference, ρ, tells us the real rate of return that savers insist on in the steady state. If the real rate of return exceeds ρ, then people save and increase their quantities of consumption over time. Alternatively, if the real rate of return is less than ρ, then people dissave, so that consumption declines over time. In the steady state, where consumption is constant and saving is zero, it must be that the real rate of return to saving equals ρ. But this real rate of return is now the after-tax real interest rate, $(1 - \tau)r$. Therefore, in the presence of taxation, it is the after-tax real interest rate that equals the rate of time preference, ρ, in the steady state.

We know also that the after-tax rate of return to investment, $(1 - \tau)$ (MPK $- \delta$), equals the after-tax real interest rate, $(1 - \tau)r$. Therefore, the full condition for the steady state is now

$$(1 - \tau)(\text{MPK} - \delta) = (1 - \tau)r = \rho \qquad (13.11)$$

The condition, $(1 - \tau)(\text{MPK} - \delta) = \rho$, tells us the level of the capital stock in the steady state. Namely, the level of capital corresponds to a marginal product for which the after-tax rate of return to investment, $(1 - \tau)$ (MPK $- \delta$), equals the rate of time preference, ρ. In this situation producers invest just enough to maintain the levels of their capital stocks—that is, aggregate net investment is zero.

So, what happens in the long run when the tax rate, τ, increases? From equation 13.11, the rate of time preference, ρ, pegs the after-tax rate of return to investment, $(1 - \tau)(\text{MPK} - \delta)$. An increase in the tax rate means that the before-tax rate of return to investment, MPK $- \delta$, must rise. But this happens only if the capital stock falls to generate a sufficient increase in the marginal product, MPK. Therefore, in the long run, a higher tax rate means a smaller stock of capital.

Suppose that we compare two steady states: one with the tax rate, τ, and another with the higher tax rate, τ'. We know that the after-tax real interest rate is the same in both steady states, since $(1 - \tau)r$ equals the fixed number ρ. But the one with the higher tax rate has less capital. It also has lower gross and net product, as well as less consumption. However, the comparison for the levels of work effort is uncertain. (Why is that?)

Table 13.3 Summary of Economic Effects from Permanent Changes in Government Purchases and the Tax Rate

Nature of Disturbance	Response of								
	K	Y	$Y - \delta K$	N	C	I	$I - \delta K$	$(1 - \tau)r$	r
1. Permanent rise in government purchases, when financed by lump-sum taxes (short and long run)	0	+	+	+	−	0	0	0	0
2. Permanent increase in tax rate, τ									
a. Short run	0	−	−	−	?	−	−	−	+
b. Long run	−	−	−	?	−	−	0	0	+
3. Permanent rise in government purchases, with permanent increase in tax rate									
a. Short run	0	?	?	?	?	−	−	−	+
b. Long run	−	?	?	?	−	−	0	0	+

Note: We show the effects on the variables in each column from the disturbances shown in each row. The possible responses are positive (+), negative (−), zero (0), or uncertain (?).

Effects of a Permanent Rise in Government Purchases under Income Taxation

In the previous chapter we studied the effects of a permanent increase in government purchases when financed by lump-sum taxes. We found that output increases, partly because the public services are productive, and partly because people work more (in response to a decrease in wealth). Also, consumption decreases, but there are no effects on the real interest rate and investment. The last result suggests that the steady-state stock of capital would not change when government purchases increase permanently.[8] That is, the long- and short-run responses coincide.

In the real world a permanent increase in government purchases generally requires a permanent increase in the average marginal tax rate, which we represent by the parameter τ. That is, the tax rate must rise along with the increase in total real tax revenues. So in assessing the consequences of more government purchases, we want to combine the effects that we found under lump-sum taxes with those that arise when the tax rate increases. (Now we think of a case where the average marginal tax rate τ rises, but the exempt amount E does not change.)

Table 13.3 summarizes the results. Line 1 refers to a permanent increase in government purchases when financed by lump-sum taxes. The responses of the variables are those that we discussed above. Line 2 deals with a permanent increase in the tax rate, τ. Here, we distinguish the short-run results—where

---

[8]Here, we neglect an effect from the increase in work on capital's marginal product. This effect tends to raise investment in the short run and to raise the stock of capital in the long run.

the capital stock does not change—from the long-run ones. The findings are those that we worked out earlier in this chapter.

Finally, line 3 combines the permanent rise in government purchases with a permanent increase in the tax rate. The highlights are as follows. The short- and long-run effects on gross and net product are now ambiguous. That is because the negative effects from the higher tax rate offset the positive effects from more government purchases. Similarly, the effects on work effort are uncertain. However, we find again that the after-tax real interest rate, $(1 - \tau)r$, is pegged in the long run by the rate of time preference, ρ. Therefore, capital's marginal product, MPK, must still increase when the tax rate rises, which leads to the long-run decline in the stock of capital. The counterpart of this result in the short run is the decrease in net investment.

Empirically, it is hard to separate the effects of more government purchases from the effects of a higher tax rate. The reason is that the changes tend to occur simultaneously. We discussed before some empirical estimates for the effect on output of a permanent increase in government purchases. The results suggest a positive effect, although the estimates are imprecise for the case of nondefense purchases. We should interpret these findings as applying to the combined impact of more government purchases and a higher tax rate. Therefore, there is some evidence that this combined effect is positive, although the theory says that the response is ambiguous.

The Relation between the Tax Rate and Tax Revenues

We combined a permanent increase in government purchases with a rise in the tax rate, τ, to generate more real tax revenues for each period, T_t/P_t. But these revenues are given from the tax law as

$$\frac{T_t}{P_t} = \tau(Y_t - \delta K_{t-1} - E_t)$$

Therefore, if we hold the exempt amount, E_t, constant, then real tax receipts increase with the tax rate only if the fall in output, Y_t, reduces real taxable income, $Y_t - \delta K_{t-1} - E_t$, by proportionately less than the increase in the tax rate.

We can view the long-run movements in aggregate output, Y, in terms of the changes in the two productive inputs, K and N. The long-run decline in the capital stock follows from the steady-state condition, which is $(1 - \tau)(\text{MPK} - \delta) = \rho$. When the tax rate rises, capital's marginal product must increase sufficiently in the long run to reestablish this equality. So if we need large reductions in the capital stock to generate this increase in the marginal product—that is, if diminishing marginal productivity sets in slowly—then the capital stock will fall a great deal in response to an increase in the tax rate.

We know that the long-run response of work effort, N, is ambiguous. However, the main force that motivates a reduction in market work is the higher tax rate on income. This higher tax rate induces people to withdraw from the market in order to spend more time on leisure and other nonmarket (nontaxed) activities. So if these alternative uses of time are close substitutes for the things that people can buy on the market, then the negative effect on market work will be strong.

Overall, we require very substantial depressing effects of income taxation on capital and labor for tax revenues to fall when the tax rate rises. However, this outcome does become more likely as the rate of tax, τ, increases. For example, when the tax rate is 10%, a 10% increase means that the new tax rate is 11%. Therefore, the fraction of extra income that people keep, $1 - \tau$, falls from 90 to 89%, or by a percentage of 1.1%. In other words, a 10% increase in the tax rate translates into a decline by only 1.1% in the term, $1 - \tau$, that influences capital and labor. Therefore, we anticipate that the 10% increase in the tax rate would reduce real taxable income by much less than 10%.

Now suppose that we look at higher starting values for the tax rate, but we continue to raise the rate each time by 10%. Then, at a tax rate of 25%, we find that a 10% increase (to a new rate of 27.5%) means that $1 - \tau$ falls from 75 to 72.5%, or by 3.3%. Similarly, at a starting rate of 50%, a 10% increase lowers $1 - \tau$ from 50 to 45%—that is, by 10%. Moreover, at the still higher starting rate of 75%, a 10% increase in the rate reduces $1 - \tau$ by 30%. Overall, the higher is the starting value of the tax rate, the greater is the proportional reduction of the term, $1 - \tau$, from a 10% increase in the tax rate. Table 13.4 summarizes these results.

We have just shown that the term, $1 - \tau$, becomes proportionately more sensitive to a given percentage increase in the tax rate, τ, as the rate of tax increases. But recall that capital and labor—and, therefore, real taxable income—respond to the term, $1 - \tau$. Therefore, we predict that the negative response of real taxable income to the tax rate becomes stronger as the rate of tax increases. At some point—but, surely, for a tax rate below 100%—we shall find that an increase in the tax rate reduces real taxable income by so much that real tax revenues fall.

We show the general form of the relationship between real tax receipts,

Table 13.4 Effects of a 10% Increase in the Tax Rate

Old τ	New τ	Old $(1 - \tau)$	New $(1 - \tau)$	% Change in $(1 - \tau)$
1.0	1.1	99.0	98.9	−0.1
10.0	11.0	90.0	89.0	−1.1
25.0	27.5	75.0	72.5	−3.3
50.0	55.0	50.0	45.0	−10.0
75.0	82.5	25.0	17.5	−30.0
90.0	99.0	10.0	1.0	−90.0

Note: We show the effects of a 10% increase in the tax rate, τ, on the fraction of income that people keep, $1 - \tau$. Notice that the percentage decline of the term, $1 - \tau$, becomes larger as the tax rate rises.

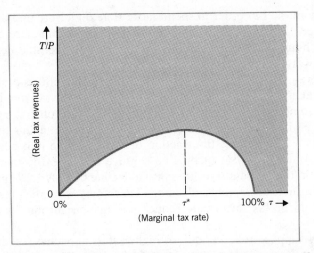

Figure 13.9 **The Relation of Tax Receipts to the Tax Rate (a Laffer Curve)**
Real tax revenues, T/P, initially rise with the tax rate τ. However, revenues reach their peak when the rate is τ^*. If the tax rate rises above τ^*, then revenues fall. Further, revenues approach zero as the tax rate approaches 100%.

T/P, and the tax rate, τ, in Figure 13.9. (Think of this relation as applying in the long run, when capital and labor respond fully to a change in the tax rate.) This relationship is often called a **Laffer curve** (named after the economist, Arthur Laffer). When the tax rate, τ, is zero, the government collects no tax revenues. Then revenues increase as the tax rate rises—hence, the curve has a positive slope. However, as the tax rate rises, the negative response of real taxable income to increases in the tax rate becomes stronger. Since this element reduces revenues, we find that the slope of the curve becomes flatter as the tax rate rises. Eventually, the tax rate becomes high enough so that a further increase in the tax rate reduces real taxable income by the same proportion as the increase in the tax rate. Therefore, real tax revenues do not change, and the curve in Figure 13.9 is flat. We label this tax rate as τ^* in the figure. If the government raises the tax rate above τ^*, then real taxable income falls by proportionately more than the increase in the tax rate. Hence, revenues now decline as the tax rate rises. In fact, as the tax rate approaches 100%, tax receipts approach zero. If the government wishes to maximize its real revenues, it should not choose a tax rate of 100%. Rather, the value τ^* is the tax rate that maximizes receipts.

In 1980–81 some advocates of "**supply-side economics**" used a picture like that in Figure 13.9 to argue for an across-the-board cut in U.S. income-tax rates. These people contended that the average marginal tax rate on income exceeded the value τ^*, so that a general cut in rates would yield a larger volume of real tax revenues. However, there is no evidence that the United States has reached high enough tax rates for this result to apply.

A study for Sweden by Charles Stuart[9] provides some perspective on the U.S. situation. Stuart estimates that the maximum of tax revenues occurs in Sweden when the average marginal tax rate is about 70%. That is, he estimates τ^* to be about 70%. Moreover, the actual value of the average marginal tax rate in Sweden reached 70% in the early 1970s and has since risen to about 80%. (Here, Stuart takes a broad view of taxes to go beyond the income-tax law.) Therefore, Sweden has been operating on the falling portion of the Laffer curve during the 1970s. In fact, Stuart attributes part of Sweden's relatively low average growth rate of per capita gross product during the 1970s (1.7% per year) to this factor.

For the United States in 1983, the average marginal tax rate from the federal income tax and social security was 34% (see Figure 13.6). However, the rate would be higher if we were able to include other taxes. Since we do not have these data, we can draw a rough comparison between the United States and Sweden by considering average tax rates.

For Sweden, the estimated value for τ^* of 70% corresponds to an average tax rate of about 50%. For the United States in 1985, a comparable figure for the tax rate, when calculated as the ratio of total government receipts to GNP, is 32%. So suppose that Sweden and the United States are roughly the same with respect to first the value of τ^*, and second the relation between marginal and average tax rates. Then we conclude that, in 1985, the United States has a long way to go before reaching the average marginal tax rate, $\tau^* = 70\%$, at which tax revenues are maximized. However, we should be cautious about this result for two reasons. First, the estimates for Sweden are rough. Second, we cannot be sure that the United States and Sweden have similar Laffer curves.

Transfer Payments

Suppose now that the government raises the aggregate of real transfers, V/P, and finances these with more tax revenues, T/P. As in the case where government purchases increase, the rise in real taxes typically requires an increase in the average marginal tax rate, τ. Recall that we already discussed the adverse effects on work, production, and investment from an increase in the tax rate. These are summarized in line 2 of Table 13.3. Note especially that an increase in transfers, when financed by an income tax, is no longer neutral in the model.

If transfer payments are lump sum, as we have been assuming, then our analysis is finished. However, lump-sum transfers make little sense. Generally, the point of transfer programs is to provide payments to persons in specified categories—for example, to poor people, to persons who have lost their jobs, to old or sick people, to farmers, to college students, and so on. But none of

[9]Charles E. Stuart, "Swedish Tax Rates, Labor Supply and Tax Revenues," *Journal of Political Economy,* October 1981.

these transfers are lump sum—that is, the amount depends in some way on a persons's status.

Let's think about a welfare program, where the payments depend on a family's current or long-run income. (Similar effects arise for unemployment compensation, food stamps, and a number of other programs.) Typically, individuals face a declining schedule of transfers—possibly subject to some discrete cutoff points—as a function of market income. The important point is that the negative effect of income on benefit payments looks just like a positive marginal tax rate. (Recall our previous example of the earned-income credit in the range where income exceeds $6500 but is less than $11,000.) Since transfers are sometimes cut drastically when a family's income rises, these programs can imply high effective marginal tax rates on the earnings of low-income persons. For example, the Council of Economic Advisers estimated that "typical welfare recipients, namely single mothers with children, face marginal tax rates in excess of 75%."[10] But unfortunately, we do not have estimates for the average marginal tax rate that is implied by the full array of transfer programs.

Suppose again that the government increases taxes to finance more welfare payments. We already noted the adverse effects on work, production, and investment that derive from the increase in the average marginal tax rate, τ. But the expansion of the welfare program means that low-income people stand to lose more benefits if they earn more market income. That is, there is also an increase in the effective marginal tax rate for potential welfare recipients. Hence, the negative influences of this change on work and production add to the effects from the higher tax rate on market income.

In terms of dollar volume, the most important and rapidly growing transfer program in the United States and in most other countries today is the payments to retirees and survivors under social security.[11] We have already discussed the financing of these programs in the United States. From this standpoint, an expansion of social security leads to a higher marginal tax rate on income, τ, which has the usual negative effects on work and production.[12] If people received their social security benefits without restrictions, except for age,[13] then

---

[10] *Economic Report of the President*, 1982, p. 129.

[11] One way to measure the size of this program is by the "replacement ratio." This measure equals the ratio of average benefits of retirees to their average earnings just before retirement. In 1983 this ratio equaled 48%, as compared to only 31% in 1965. (See Colin D. Campbell, "Introduction," in *Controlling the Cost of Social Security*, Lexington Books, Lexington, Massachusetts, 1984, p. xi.)

[12] However, the social security tax depends on labor income, not capital income. Therefore, the effects on investment are different.

[13] Before 1961 recipients had to be over 65. Since 1961, there is an opportunity to receive reduced benefits at age 62. The 1983 law will eventually raise the basic retirement age from 65 to 67.

the distorting influences that arise from welfare programs would not apply. However, the U.S. system involves a test on earned income—specifically, all persons (now below age 70) who earn income above a specified amount experience a partial or total cutoff of social security benefits. This income test works like an income standard for welfare—namely, it imposes a high effective marginal tax rate on the potential recipients. Not surprisingly, researchers find that this income test motivates people to retire earlier than they would otherwise.[14]

Summary

In this chapter we add to the model a simple form of income-tax law. The key parameters of this law are the marginal tax rate and the quantity of tax-exempt income. By the term, marginal tax rate, we refer to the extra tax that the government takes from an additional dollar of income. People take this marginal tax rate into account when deciding how much to work, produce, and invest. By contrast, the government's tax receipts equal the product of the average tax rate (total taxes divided by total income) and the amount of income.

We show that intertemporal-substitution effects now depend on the after-tax real interest rate. Similarly, the decisions to work and invest consider the after-tax marginal products of labor and capital, respectively. Overall—if we hold fixed total real taxes collected—an increase in the marginal tax rate motivates people to substitute away from market activities, which are taxed, and toward leisure (or the underground economy). Therefore, we find that a higher tax rate leads in the short run to less work, output, and investment. In the long run, there are reductions in the stock of capital, as well as in the levels of output and consumption.

When we combine a permanent increase in government purchases with a rise in the marginal tax rate we change some of the results from the previous chapter. Because of the adverse effects of higher taxation, the short-run effects on output and employment become ambiguous. Further, we now conclude that the stock of capital declines in the long run.

As the marginal tax rate rises, the quantity of real taxable income tends to fall. Further, this sensitivity becomes larger the higher is the tax rate. Therefore, we can draw a Laffer curve, which shows a diminishing effect of the tax rate on the quantity of real tax revenues. Eventually, the economy reaches a tax rate for which revenues are at a maximum. At that point further increases in tax rates mean less real tax receipts. For Sweden, there is an

---

[14]See, for example, Michael Boskin, "Social Security and Retirement Decisions," *Economic Inquiry,* January 1977.

estimate that this marginal tax rate is about 70%, which was reached and then surpassed in the early 1970s. But the United States has apparently not yet reached this point.

Finally, we show that transfer payments have allocative effects that resemble those from taxation. Because people tend to lose their welfare payments or social security benefits by earning more income, they effectively face a high marginal tax rate. Thus, an increase in transfers is no longer neutral in the model. Rather, there is a two-dimensional effect, which tends to contract real economic activity. First, tax rates rise to finance the program, and second, the larger transfer payments mean that people stand to lose more benefits by earning income.

Important Terms and Concepts

adjusted gross income

taxable income

flat-rate tax

graduated-rate tax

marginal tax rate

average tax rate

tax-exempt income

after-tax real interest rate

after-tax marginal product of labor

after-tax rate of return to investment

underground economy

Laffer curve

supply-side economics

QUESTIONS AND PROBLEMS

Mainly for Review

13.1 Distinguish between the average tax rate and the marginal tax rate. Must the two be equal for a flat-rate tax?

13.2 Why must we hold tax revenue constant when studying the effect of a change in the tax rate? What wealth effects would operate if we did not?

13.3 Explain briefly why a rise in the tax rate reduces the after-tax real interest rate in the short run but raises the before-tax real interest rate in the long run. How does the latter affect the capital stock?

13.4 Ignoring wealth effects from an increase in the tax rate, does the quantity of work decline in the long run? Explain why.

13.5 Could an increase in the tax rate reduce real tax revenues? How does your answer depend on the response of labor supply to changes in the (after-tax) marginal product of labor?

13.6 Define supply-side economics. How could the economy benefit from lowering the tax rate? Include in your answer a discussion of the wealth effects of taxes.

Problems for Discussion

13.7 **The Flat-Rate Tax**

Some economists advocate shifting from the graduated individual income tax to a flat-rate tax. Under the new system, there would be few deductions from taxable income, and the marginal tax rate would be constant. Because of the elimination of the deductions (sometimes referred to as "loopholes"), the average marginal tax rate would be lower than that under the current law.

a. What would this change do to the aggregate levels of output, employment, and investment?

b. How does the proposed flat-rate tax compare with the present social security tax?

13.8 Subsidies

Suppose that the average marginal tax rate, τ, is zero. We mentioned that an increase in the tax rate, τ, above zero—with total revenues, T/P, held fixed—reduces the utility of the typical household.

a. Explain this result.

b. Does the result mean that a reduction in the tax rate below zero would be desirable? (A negative value of τ means that the government subsidizes increases in production.)

13.9 **Consumption Taxes** (optional)

Instead of an income tax, suppose that taxes are levied on the quantity of consumption during each period. An individual's real tax payments for period t are now given by the formula, $t_t/P_t = \tau(c_t - e_t)$. (A comprehensive sales tax on consumables might operate in this manner.)

a. Write down the budget constraints for the government and the representative household.

b. What is the after-tax real interest rate?

c. How does the tax rate, τ, now enter into the functions for consumption demand, C^d, gross investment demand, I^d, and goods supply, Y^s?

d. What is the short-run effect (while the capital stock is held fixed) of an increase in the tax rate, τ? Consider, in particular, the responses of the real interest rate and the quantities of output, work effort, consumption, and investment. Compare the results with those for an income tax.

13.10 Effects of Inflation on a Graduated Income Tax

In 1985 a married couple in the United States paid income taxes in accordance with the following graduated-rate table:

Range of Taxable Income	Tax Rate on an Extra Dollar of Taxable Income (Marginal Tax Rate) %
$ 3,540– 5,720	11
5,720– 7,910	12
7,910– 12,390	14
12,390– 16,650	16
16,650– 21,020	18
21,020– 25,600	22
25,600– 31,120	25
31,120– 36,630	28
36,630– 47,670	33
47,670– 62,450	38
62,450– 89,090	42
89,090–113,860	45
113,860–169,020	49
169,020–	50

a. Suppose that each person's real income stays constant over time, so that inflation steadily raises everyone's nominal income. If the tax law shown above remains unchanged, what happens over time to the average marginal tax rate? What happens to total real tax collections?

b. Assume now that the dollar bracket limits that appear in the left column of the table are adjusted proportionately (or "indexed") over time for changes in the price level. What then is the effect of inflation on the average marginal tax rate and on total real tax collections? (This indexing rule applies in the United States as of 1985.)

13.11 Taxes, Inflation, and Interest Rates (optional)

Suppose that taxes are levied on nominal interest income, and that the income-tax rate, τ, does not change over time.

a. What is the after-tax real interest rate on bonds?

Consider a permanent increase in the monetary growth rate from μ to μ', which occurs at date 1. Although the acceleration of money is a surprise, people then anticipate that the higher rate of monetary expansion, μ', will continue forever.

b. Given the presence of the income tax, what is the effect of the increase in monetary growth on the inflation rate, π, the nominal interest rate, R, and the aggregate level of real money balances, M/P? (Assume that the income-tax rate, τ, is unaffected by inflation.)

c. Discuss the implications of your answer to part b for the relation between R and π.

13.12 **Effects of Transfer Programs on Work Effort**

Discuss the effects on people's incentives to work of the following governmental programs:

a. The food stamp program, which provides subsidized coupons for purchases of food. The allowable subsidies vary inversely with family income.

b. A negative income tax. This program would provide cash transfers to poor persons. The amount of transfers is reduced as some fraction of increases in family income.

c. Unemployment compensation. People who work for a specified interval and who lose their jobs receive cash payments while unemployed (and "looking for work"). The benefits can last for 6 months or sometimes for longer periods. What difference does it make if businesses with histories of more layoffs have to raise their contributions to the unemployment-insurance fund? (A program that has this feature is said to be "experience rated.")

d. Retirement benefits under social security. What is the consequence of the income test, which reduces benefits to persons (of age less than 70) who earn labor income in excess of a specified amount?

e. The earned-income credit. For families that have no unearned income, the credit is 11% of each dollar earned until income reaches $5000. Then the credit is constant at $550 until income hits $6500. Finally, the credit falls by $12\frac{2}{9}\%$ of each dollar earned, until the credit reaches zero at an income of $11,000.

CHAPTER 14

THE PUBLIC DEBT

In recent years, one of the hottest economic issues concerns the **government's budget deficit** (which we shall define carefully later on). At least from reading the newspapers, we would think that the economy suffers greatly when the government runs a large deficit. The most important task in this chapter will be to evaluate this view. As we shall see, the conclusions depart dramatically from those expressed in the newspapers.

Budget deficits arise when governments finance part of their expenditures by issuing interest-bearing government bonds, rather than levying taxes. The stock of government bonds outstanding is the interest-bearing part of the **public debt.** Hence, a budget deficit means that the public debt increases over time.

In this chapter we study first the historical behavior of the public debt and government deficits. Along the way, we discuss some measurement problems that can seriously distort our view about the size of these deficits. With these facts as a background, we extend the theoretical model to allow for public debt. Now the government can run budget deficits, rather than levy taxes. Then we use the model to assess the effects of deficits on interest rates and other economic variables.

The Behavior of the Public Debt in the United States and the United Kingdom

We can gauge the empirical significance of interest-bearing public debt by looking at the long-term history for the United States and the United Kingdom. Table 14.1 shows the behavior over the past 2 centuries of the central government's nominal interest-bearing public debt, which we denote by B^g. Note that the data for the United States are net of holdings of public debt by parts of the federal government, which include various agencies and trust funds. Also, we think of the monetary authority—that is, the Federal Reserve—as part of the central government. Therefore, we net out the Fed's holdings of

Table 14.1 Values for Public Debt in the United States and the United Kingdom

	United States			United Kingdom		
	B^g ($ Billion)	B^g/P	$B^g/(PY)$	B^g (£ Billion)	B^g/P	$B^g/(PY)$
1700	—	—	—	0.015	0.5	0.22
1710	—	—	—	0.026	0.8	0.33
1720	—	—	—	0.039	1.4	0.57
1730	—	—	—	0.038	1.5	0.56
1740	—	—	—	0.033	1.2	0.44
1750	—	—	—	0.059	2.3	0.79
1760	—	—	—	0.074	2.8	0.91
1770	—	—	—	0.11	3.9	1.22
1780	—	—	—	0.12	4.2	1.01
1790	0.08	0.6	0.31	0.18	5.3	1.04
1800	0.08	0.4	0.18	0.28	5.0	0.78
1810	0.05	0.3	0.08	0.43	7.4	0.93
1820	0.09	0.6	0.11	0.57	13.1	1.32
1830	0.05	0.4	0.04	0.55	13.8	1.13
1840	0.00	0.0	0.00	0.56	15.6	1.01
1850	0.06	0.5	0.03	0.56	17.4	0.94
1860	0.06	0.4	0.01	0.59	14.9	0.69
1865	2.2	8.7	0.24	—	—	—
1870	2.0	9.1	0.25	0.59	17.4	0.51
1880	1.7	9.1	0.13	0.59	17.8	0.43
1890	0.7	4.3	0.05	0.58	18.3	0.37
1900	1.0	6.4	0.05	0.58	17.9	0.29
1910	0.9	4.7	0.03	0.70	20.5	0.29
1919	24.2	69.1	0.31	7.5	95.9	1.30
1920	23.3	58.5	0.27	7.9	83.7	1.21
1930	14.8	46.6	0.16	7.6	120.6	1.55
1940	41.2	141.8	0.41	9.1	126.4	1.18
1945	227.4	600.0	1.07	22.5	234.8	2.27
1950	198.6	370.5	0.69	27.0	224.0	2.03

U.S. government bonds.[1] The table reports also the real quantity of debt, B^g/P, and the ratio of the public debt to nominal GNP, $B^g/(PY)$. We show this last ratio graphically for the United States from 1790 to 1985 in Figure 14.1, and for the United Kingdom from 1700 to 1984 in Figure 14.2

For both countries the two main positive influences on the ratio of public

---

[1]For example, at the end of 1985, the gross amount of interest-bearing debt of the U.S. Treasury was $1950 billion. But $350 billion of this total was held by various United States government agencies and trust funds, and $181 billion by the Federal Reserve. Therefore, the amount in private hands (including about $220 billion with state and local governments) was only $1431 billion.

Table 14.1 (*Continued*)

	United States			United Kingdom		
	B^g ($ Billion)	B^g/P	$B^g/(PY)$	B^g (£ Billion)	B^g/P	$B^g/(PY)$
1960	207.5	302.0	0.41	29.0	161.8	1.12
1970	229.1	250.5	0.23	34.1	125.9	0.66
1980	616.4	345.5	0.23	96.3	96.3	0.42
1984	1212.5	542.1	0.32	143.9	109.5	0.45
1985	1431.3	619.3	0.36	—	—	—

For the United States: B^g is the end-of-year value (midyear value before 1916) of privately held, interest-bearing public debt of the U.S. federal government at nominal par value. The figures are net of holdings by the Federal Reserve and U.S. government agencies and trust funds. (However, they still include holdings by some government-sponsored agencies and by state and local governments.) For the sources, see Robert Barro, "Comment from an Unreconstructed Ricardian, " *Journal of Monetary Economics,* August 1978, Table 1. *P* since 1870 is the GNP deflator (1972 = 1.0, see Figure 1.4 of Chapter 1). Earlier data are wholesale price indices, as reported in U.S. Commerce Department, *Historical Statistics of the U.S., Colonial Times to 1970,* p. 201. *PY* is nominal GNP. (See Figures 1.1 and 1.4 of Chapter 1.) Estimates of real GNP from 1834 to 1871 are unpublished data from Robert Gallman. Earlier figures are calculated from the growth rates of real output that are reported in Paul David, "The Growth of Real Product in the United States before 1840," *Journal of Economic History,* June 1967, Table 1; and Alice Jones, *Wealth of a Nation to Be,* Columbia University Press, New York, 1980, Table 3.15.

For the United Kingdom: B^g since 1917 is the central government's interest-bearing public debt at nominal par value. Before 1917 the figures are the accumulation of the central government's budget deficit, starting with a benchmark stock of public debt in 1700. *P* since 1830 is the GNP deflator (1980 = 1.0). Earlier data are wholesale price indices. *PY* since 1830 is nominal GNP. Earlier data are the product of *P* and an estimate of trend real GNP. The sources for B^g are B. R. Mitchell and P. Deane, *Abstract of British Historical Statistics,* Cambridge University Press, 1962, B. R. Mitchell and H. G. Jones, *Second Abstract of British Historical Statistics,* Cambridge University Press, 1971; and Central Statistical Office, *Annual Abstract of Statistics,* various issues. Recent values are from the Bank of England. Data on *P* and *Y* are from the above and also from C. H. Feinstein, *National Income, Expenditure and Output of the United Kingdom, 1855–1965,* Cambridge University Press, 1972; P. Deane and W. A. Cole, *British Economic Growth, 1688–1959,* 2nd ed., Cambridge University Press, 1969; and *International Financial Statistics,* various issues.

debt to GNP are wartime and major economic contractions. Superimposed on these infrequent positive shocks is a regular pattern where the ratio declines over time.

Let's focus now on the United States. The major peaks in the ratio of public debt to annual GNP occur at the end of the Revolutionary War (the value for 1784 was 0.33), the end of the Civil War (0.25 in 1865), the end of World War I (0.31 in 1919), and the end of World War II (1.07 in 1945). Smaller effects—which amount to pauses in the usual downward trend in the ratio, rather than to actual increases—show up for the Spanish-American and Korean Wars. However, little impact appears for the Vietnam War. (Recall

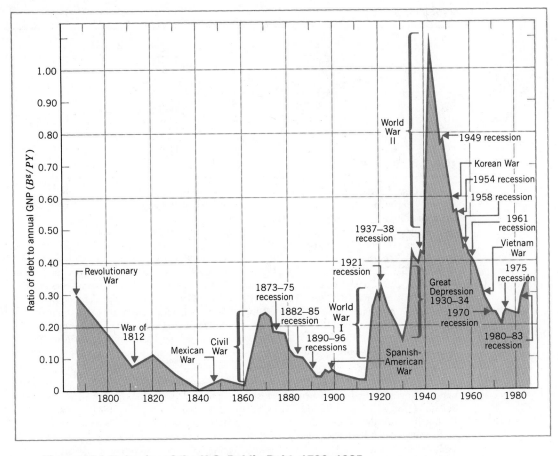

Figure 14.1 **Behavior of the U.S. Public Debt, 1790–1985**
The figure shows the ratio of the public debt to nominal GNP.

that this war exhibited only a small excess of real military spending above trend.)

The positive effect of economic contraction on the ratio of public debt to GNP involves partly a negative effect on GNP and partly a positive effect on public debt. A dramatic response to an economic downturn shows up during the Great Depression, where the ratio of public debt to GNP rose from 0.14 in 1929 to 0.38 in 1933. Qualitatively similar behavior applies to other economic contractions: for example, the ratio rose from 0.23 in 1979 to 0.31 in 1983, from 0.20 in 1973 to 0.23 in 1975, and from 0.039 in 1892 to 0.047 in 1894.

During peacetime, nonrecession years, the ratio of public debt to GNP tends to decline. This pattern applies as much to the (mostly peaceful) post-World War II period from 1945 to 1985—where the ratio fell from 1.07 to 0.36—as to earlier times. For the previous peacetime periods aside from the

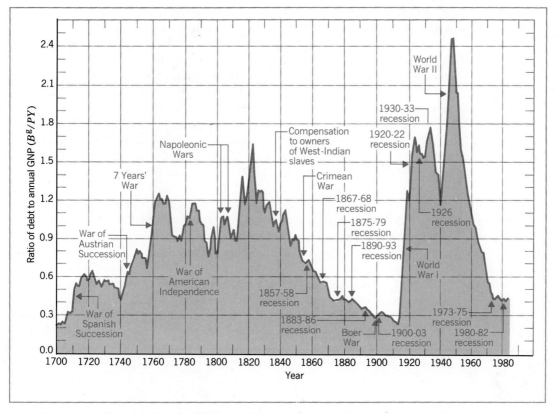

Figure 14.2 Behavior of the British Public Debt, 1700–1984
The figure shows the ratio of the public debt to nominal GNP.

Great Depression, we find that the ratio fell from 0.31 to 0.14 between 1919 and 1929, from 0.24 to 0.02 between 1865 and 1916, from 0.11 to 0.01 between 1820 and 1860, and from 0.33 to 0.08 between 1784 and 1810. Notice also that the ratio for 1985, which is 0.36, is not high by historical standards and is well below the values for the 1950s. However, the ratio has risen substantially from its trough of 0.20 in 1973.

The major element that distinguishes the behavior of the U.S. public debt since the late 1960s is the divergent patterns in nominal and real debt. The rapid inflation of recent years means that a declining ratio of the debt to GNP is consistent with a substantial runup in the nominal debt. For example, the nominal debt for 1985 is $1431 billion, as compared with $228 billion in 1970. (Recall that these figures refer to the privately held part of the interest-bearing public debt.) By contrast, the nominal debt changed very little between 1945 and 1970. But these changes in the behavior of the nominal debt have not translated into dramatically different patterns for the debt when expressed either in real terms or as a ratio to GNP. However, we shall look later at the period since 1981 to see whether the real debt grew "too fast" in these years.

The experience for the United Kingdom is broadly similar to that for the United States. The major peaks in the ratio of public debt to annual GNP are again associated with wartime—1.3 at the end of the Seven-Years' War in 1764, 1.2 after the War of American Independence in 1785, 1.4 after the Napoleonic Wars in 1816, 1.3 at the end of World War I in 1919, and 2.5 after World War II in 1946. It is noteworthy that the high points for the British debt in relation to GNP are more than twice as great as those for the United States. It is also interesting that the public debt amounted to more than 100% of annual GNP as long ago as the 1760s. Large amounts of public debt are not a modern invention.

Economic contractions again have a positive impact on the ratio of the debt to GNP. This response shows up especially for the United Kingdom during the depressed periods from 1920 to 1923 and from 1929 to 1933. The ratio of debt to GNP rose from 1.2 to 1.7 during the first interval, and from 1.5 to 1.8 during the second.

Periods that involve neither war nor economic contraction display a declining pattern in the ratio of public debt to GNP. Again, this behavior applies as much to the post-World War II years as to earlier periods. In particular, the ratio declined from 1.47 in 1946 to 0.45 in 1984. Notice that the ratio for 1984 was not far above the low point over the past 2 centuries, which was 0.23 at the beginning of 1914.

Characteristics of Government Bonds

In our model the government can now borrow from households by selling interest-bearing bonds. We assume that government bonds pay interest and principal in the same way as private bonds, which are already in the model. In particular, we continue to simplify matters by pretending that all bonds have a maturity of one period.[2] In the main analysis we assume also that bondholders regard public and private debts as equivalent. Specifically, we do not treat the government as more credit-worthy than private borrowers. In this case the government's bonds must pay the same nominal interest rate in each period, R_t, as that on privately issued bonds.

Our assumption about public and private bonds contrasts with our treat-

---

[2]The average maturity of marketable, interest-bearing public debt in the United States was around 9 years in 1946. This figure declined fairly steadily to reach a low point of about 2½ years in 1976. During much of this period, the U.S. Treasury was prohibited from issuing long-term bonds at interest rates that would have made them marketable. With the ending of this restriction, the average maturity rose to about 5 years in 1985. (*Source: Economic Report of the President,* 1975, Table C-73; 1986, Table B-82.)

ment of money. Since currency pays no interest, it seems that private enterprises would find it profitable to produce this stuff. In particular, the higher is the nominal interest rate, R_t, the greater is the gain from entering the business of creating currency. But because of legal restrictions or some technical advantages for the government in providing a medium of exchange, we assume that the private sector does not issue currency.

With respect to bonds, we assume no legal restrictions on private issues and no technical advantages for the government in providing these types of securities. Hence, we do not allow the interest rate on government bonds to differ from that on private bonds. This assumption accords reasonably well with the U.S. data if we interpret private bonds as prime corporate obligations. For example, the interest rate on 6-month maturity U.S. treasury bills averaged 6.4% from 1959 to 1985, while that on 4- to 6-month maturity prime commercial paper averaged 7.0%.[3] A similar comparison applies to long-term bonds.

Let's denote by B_t^g the aggregate dollar amount of government bonds outstanding at the end of period t. We still use the symbol b for privately issued bonds. Therefore, an individual's total holdings of bonds for period t are now $b_t + b_t^g$. We still have that the aggregate of privately issued bonds is zero—that is, $B_t = 0$. Hence, the aggregate quantity of bonds held by households now equals the public debt, B_t^g. Usually, we think of cases where the government is a net debtor to the private sector, so that $B_t^g > 0$. However, the government may also become a creditor, where it holds net claims on the private sector.[4] We can represent this case by allowing for $B_t^g < 0$.

The Government's Budget Constraint

The presence of public debt alters the government's budget constraint in two respects. First, the dollar amount of net debt issue for period, t, $B_t^g - B_{t-1}^g$, is a source of funds.[5] In this respect the printing of money and the printing of interest-bearing debt play the same role in the financing of the government's expenditures. Second, the government's nominal interest payments,

---

[3]At least some of the positive differential between the yields on commercial paper and treasury bills reflects two advantages of the government's notes: first, the interest payments are exempt from state and local income taxes, and second, the treasury bills satisfy the requirement that commercial banks hold some amount of government bonds as "backing" for the government's deposits in these banks.

[4]The last time this became a serious possibility for the United States was around 1835. A major concern was the outlet for further governmental revenues once the national debt was fully paid off. (We do not have this problem any more.) See the discussion in Davis Dewey, *Financial History of the United States*, 11th ed., Longmans, Green, New York, 1931, p. 221.

[5]Notice that the simple rollling over or reissue of bonds as they come due is not a net source of funds. What counts is the difference between the stock outstanding at date t, B_t^g, and that outstanding in the previous period, B_{t-1}^g.

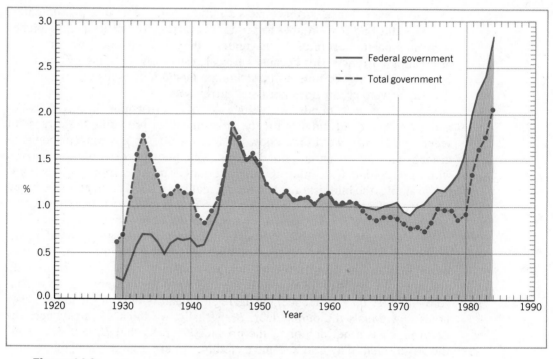

Figure 14.3

The solid line is net federal interest payments as a ratio to GNP. (The figures are interest paid—net of amounts paid by the federal government to the Federal Reserve— less interest received.) The dashed line refers to total government. This line lies below the solid line after the mid 1960s because state and local governments have been net recipients of interest income during this period.

$R_{t-1}B_{t-1}^g$, appear as an expenditure. Recall that this term is zero for the case of money.

The government's budget constraint in dollar terms for period t is now

$$P_t G_t + V_t + R_{t-1}B_{t-1}^g = T_t + (M_t - M_{t-1}) + (B_t^g - B_{t-1}^g) \quad (14.1)$$

The two new terms are the government's interest payments on the left side, $R_{t-1}B_{t-1}^g$, and the net issue of debt on the right side, $(B_t^g - B_{t-1}^g)$. For simplicity, we return to the case where the transfers, V_t, and taxes, T_t, are lump sum.

Figure 14.3 shows how the new item of expenditure—net federal interest payments—has behaved since 1929. When expressed as a ratio to GNP, net federal interest payments were less than 1% until 1945, between 1.3 and 1.8% from 1945 to 1950, and between 0.9 and 1.2% from 1951 to 1978. For much of the latter period, the declining ratio of public debt to GNP (Figure 14.1) was offset by rising interest rates. Since 1978, the ratio of net federal interest payments to GNP has risen sharply, reaching 2.0% in 1981 and 2.7% in 1984. To put this another way, the ratio tripled from 1972 to 1984.

The Government's Deficit

We can think of saving or dissaving for government in the same way as for households. Specifically, the national accounts define the government's nominal saving to be the change in the dollar value of the government's holdings of money and bonds. (Recall that the government holds no capital in our model or in the national accounts.) Since we think of the government as issuing money and bonds—rather than holding them—an increase in money and bonds means that the government is dissaving. Also, economists use the term, surplus, to refer to positive saving by the government, and the term, deficit, to refer to dissaving. (When saving is zero, the government **balances its budget.**)

When we put all this terminology together, we find that the nominal deficit is

nominal deficit (national accounts' version)
$$= \text{government's nominal dissaving} = (M_t + B_t^g) - (M_{t-1} + B_{t-1}^g) \quad (14.2)$$

When we combine the definition from equation 14.2 with the government's budget constraint from equation 14.1, we can express the nominal deficit as

nominal deficit (national accounts' version)
$$= P_t G_t + V_t + R_{t-1} B_{t-1}^g - T_t \quad (14.3)$$

That is, the nominal deficit equals nominal expenditures—for purchases, transfers, and interest payments—less tax revenues. This concept of the budget deficit, amounting to over $200 billion in 1985, is the one that we often see in the newspapers. Finally, to calculate the government's real deficit, we divide through by the price level, P_t, in equation 14.3 to get

real deficit (national accounts' version)
$$= G_t + \frac{V_t}{P_t} + \frac{R_{t-1} B_{t-1}^g}{P_t} - \frac{T_t}{P_t} \quad (14.4)$$

We should note one respect in which our treatment departs from actual practice in the U.S. national accounts. The accounts treat the Federal Reserve as a private corporation, rather than as part of the federal government. By contrast, our analysis consolidates the Federal Reserve with the central government. Thereby, we net out the holdings of government bonds by the Fed when we measure the outstanding public debt, B^g. Similarly, we do not count as government expenditures the part of the Treasury's interest payments that are paid on the bonds held at the Fed. But we also do not count as government receipts the earnings that the Fed transfers back to the Treasury. (This last item roughly equals the Fed's interest receipts on U.S. government bonds.) Finally, we count an increase in the quantity of money, M, as part of the government's deficit. But in the United States, this money is formally a liability of the Federal Reserve, rather than the central government.

As with an individual's saving, the standard definitions of the government's deficit in equations 14.2–14.4 do not take proper account of inflation.[6] Paralleling our treatment for households, we can define the government's real deficit—that is, its real dissaving—to be the change in the real value of its obligations in the forms of money and bonds. (It is these changes that matter later on when we think about future taxes or money creation.) Therefore, the natural definition of the **real deficit** is

$$\text{real deficit} = \frac{(M_t + B_t^g)}{P_t} - \frac{(M_{t-1} + B_{t-1}^g)}{P_{t-1}} \tag{14.5}$$

If we divide through the government's budget constraint from equation 14.1 by the price level, P_t, and use the expression, $P_t/P_{t-1} = 1 + \pi_{t-1}$, then we can show that the real deficit is given by

$$\text{real deficit} = G_t + \frac{V_t}{P_t} + (R_{t-1} - \pi_{t-1})\left(\frac{B_{t-1}^g}{P_t}\right) - \pi_{t-1}\left(\frac{M_{t-1}}{P_t}\right) - \frac{T_t}{P_t} \tag{14.6}$$

Recall that in measuring households' real savings we had to use the real interest rates on assets—that is, $r_{t-1} = R_{t-1} - \pi_{t-1}$ on bonds and $-\pi_{t-1}$ on money. The same holds true for the government's real deficit in equation 14.6.

We can calculate the **nominal deficit** by multiplying through equation 14.6 by the price level, P_t. This result is

$$\text{nominal deficit} = P_t G_t + V_t + (R_{t-1} - \pi_{t-1})B_{t-1}^g - \pi_{t-1}M_{t-1} - T_t \tag{14.7}$$

Notice one tricky aspect of equation 14.7. We calculate the nominal deficit just by multiplying through in equation 14.6 by P_t. That gives us the dollar value of the real deficit. But, although equation 14.7 is a magnitude in dollar terms, it still contains real interest rates, $R_{t-1} - \pi_{t-1}$ on bonds and $-\pi_{t-1}$ on money, rather than nominal interest rates.

Let's compare our concept of the nominal deficit from equation 14.7 with the national accounts' version, which appears in equation 14.3. In both cases the nominal deficit equals total dollar expenditures—for purchases, transfers, and interest payments—less nominal tax revenues. But differences arise in the methods for measuring interest payments. The national accounts' version uses nominal interest rates, while the definition in equation 14.7 adjusts for inflation by using real interest rates.[7]

---

[6]For a discussion of these effects from inflation, see Jeremy J. Siegel, "Inflation-Induced Distortions in Government and Private Saving Statistics," *Review of Economics & Statistics*, April 1979.

[7]Ideally, we would also adjust for changes in the market value of long-term government bonds because of changes in interest rates. Robert Eisner and Paul Pieper, "A New View of the Federal Debt and Budget Deficits," *American Economic Review*, March 1984, make these adjustments as well as those for inflation. They also consider changes in the government's assets, including gold.

Let's construct a simple example to bring out the differences between the two concepts. Suppose that the government's nominal obligations, money and bonds, grow at a steady rate of 10% per year. Assume also that the price level grows at 10% per year, so that the real quantities of money and interest-bearing public debt are constants. Then the national accounts' definition from equation 14.2 says that the nominal deficit is positive and grows at a rate of 10% per year. Hence, when divided by the price level, the national accounts' concept shows a constant positive real deficit. That is, the national accounts report a positive real deficit in every year, but the government's real obligations never change!

We get a more reasonable answer from our concept of the real deficit in equation 14.5. This definition accurately reports a constant real deficit of zero. Also, when we multiply through by the price level, P_t, we find that the nominal deficit is zero in each year.

Typically, a higher growth rate of money generates a higher rate of inflation and a higher nominal interest rate. In this case, the government effectively imposes a higher tax rate on the holdings of real cash, which usually means that the government gets more real revenue from money creation. But we should think of this revenue as reflecting a form of tax, which happens to apply to people's holdings of money. There is no real deficit because the government's real obligations do not change over time.

The differences between the two concepts of the deficit are large when the inflation rate is high. Therefore, it matters a great deal which definition we use for the years since the late 1960s. Table 14.2 compares the national accounts' concept of the deficit with the inflation-adjusted measure for the period 1965–85. The table shows the nominal and real deficits for each year based on the two definitions. (For the years before 1965, where the inflation rate was typically small, the differences are much less significant.)

Notice first that the national accounts' concept shows a deficit for 20 of the 21 years since 1965, while the inflation-adjusted measure indicates one for only 12 of the years. That is because, with substantial inflation, the increases in the government's nominal obligations often do not translate into increases in real obligations.

To go from national accounts' measures of the nominal deficit to the adjusted measure of the real deficit, we make two corrections. First, we eliminate the inflation part of the nominal interest payments (on bonds and money). For example, for 1981, this element reduces the deficit from $86.2 billion to only $17.6 billion. To understand this calculation, observe that the total debt (bonds plus money) at the end of 1980 was $769 billion. Hence, the inflation rate of 8.9% from the end of 1980 until the end of 1981 reduced the real value of the debt outstanding by $0.089 \cdot 769 = \$68$ billion. If the nominal debt had risen by $68 billion, then the real debt would not have changed during 1981. Thus, we subtract $68 billion from the national accounts' version of the deficit to correct for inflation.

After we get the adjusted nominal deficit, which was $17.6 billion in 1981,

Table 14.2 Alternative Measures of the U.S. Government's Deficit, 1965–85

	National Accounts' Basis		Inflation-Adjusted Measure	
	Nominal ($ billion)	Real	Nominal ($ billion)	Real
1965	1.1	1.5	−5.7	−7.7
6	1.9	2.5	−8.3	−10.8
7	7.5	9.5	−1.1	−1.4
8	11.7	14.2	−2.2	−2.6
9	−2.1	−2.4	−17.4	−19.6
1970	12.2	13.4	−2.8	−3.0
1	23.7	24.7	9.0	9.4
2	18.7	18.7	4.9	4.9
3	7.4	7.0	−18.2	−17.1
4	18.5	16.1	−19.9	−13.1
1975	82.4	65.6	53.1	41.8
6	67.0	50.7	44.4	33.2
7	60.0	42.9	26.9	19.0
8	58.4	38.9	10.2	6.7
9	49.1	30.2	−2.9	−1.8
1980	82.0	46.2	13.8	7.8
1	86.2	44.1	17.6	9.0
2	166.2	80.1	127.6	61.5
3	189.8	88.2	149.4	69.4
4	203.1	90.9	158.4	70.9
1985	236.7	102.4	190.9	82.6

Note: For the national accounts' basis, the nominal deficit comes from equation 14.2 as $(M_t + B_t^g) − (M_{t-1} + B_{t-1}^g)$. The real deficit is the nominal one divided by the annual average of the GNP deflator (1972 = 1.0). For the adjusted measure, the real deficit comes from equation 14.5 as $(M_t + B_t^g)/P_t − (M_{t-1} + B_{t-1}^g)/P_{t-1}$. Here, P_t is the seasonally adjusted value of the GNP deflator for the four quarters of year t. The nominal deficit is the real one multiplied by the annual average of the GNP deflator.

Sources (for the table and for Figure 14.4): The data for government bonds, B^g, are described in Table 14.1. M is the aggregate monetary liabilities of the Federal Reserve (called the "monetary base"), which comprises currency outside the U.S. Treasury plus reserves held at the Federal Reserve. The data, which are values for December of each year, come from the *Federal Reserve Bulletin*, various issues. The data for the GNP deflator are from U.S. Commerce Department, *National Income and Product Accounts of the U.S., 1929–76*, and *U.S. Survey of Current Business*, various issues.

we divide by the price level to meaure the real deficit. This adjustment gives us the final figure for the adjusted real deficit, which was $9.0 billion (of 1972 dollars) in 1981. Notice that the first correction to the deficit pertains to the *inflation rate* for the year, while the second involves the *price level*.

Figure 14.4 graphs the adjusted real deficit from 1929 to 1985. The solid line shows the level of the real deficit, while the dotted line expresses it as a ratio to real GNP. There are two important observations from the figure, which correspond to those that we discussed before for the ratio of public debt

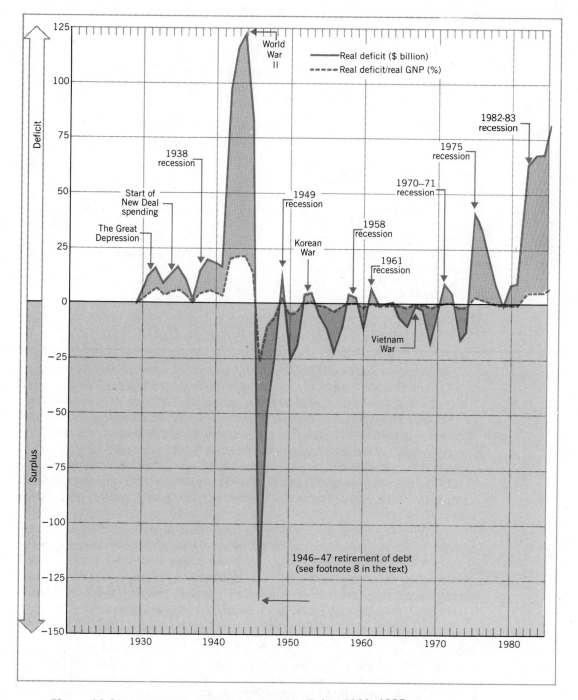

Figure 14.4 **The Behavior of Real Federal Deficits, 1929–1985**
The solid line shows the real deficit, while the dashed line shows the ratio of the real deficit to real GNP.

Table 14.3 **Recession and Real Federal Deficits**

(1) Year of Recession	(2) Percentage Shortfall of Real GNP	(3) Trend Real Federal Receipts (billions of 1972 dollars)	(4) Predicted Real Deficit = 1.8 × col. (2) × col. (3)	(5) Actual Real Deficit
1982	8.6	339	52	62
1975	7.5	264	36	42
1958	4.5	134	11	4
1933	37.6	13.5	9	8

Note: For each year of recession, column 4 shows the predicted real federal deficit. This value is 1.8 times the percentage shortfall in real GNP (col. 2) times the trend value of real federal taxes (col. 3). The trend assumes growth in real taxes at a rate of 3.8% per year (the average over 1948 to 1984) from the benchmark year. Column 5 shows the actual real deficit for each year.

Sources: Column 2 comes from Table 9.1 of Chapter 9. The data on real federal receipts (nominal amounts divided by the GNP deflator) are from *Economic Report of the President*, 1985, and the *National Income and Product Accounts of the U.S., 1929–76*. The values from column 5 are those in Figure 14.4

to GNP. First, there is a positive relation between the real deficit and wars. This relation stands out for World War II, where the real deficits exceeded 20% of real GNP from 1942 to 1944.[8] But there is also some effect during the Korean War for 1952–53 and perhaps during the Vietnam War for 1967–68.

The second important property is the positive relation between the real deficit and economic contraction. This pattern shows up strongly for the Great Depression, where the real deficit exceeded 7% of real GNP in 1932. Also, the real deficit tended to be positive during the post-World War II recessions— for example, in 1949, 1958–59, 1961, 1971, 1975–76, and 1980–83. Note that the ratio of the real deficit to real GNP was 3.4% in 1975 and 4.3% for 1982–83.

Table 14.3 quantifies the linkage between economic contraction and budget deficits. We begin with the estimated shortfall of real GNP in column 2 of the table— for example, the value for 1982 was 8.6%. Note that the trend value of real federal receipts for 1982 was $339 billion (column 3 of the table). If real federal revenues fell below trend by the same fraction as the shortfall in real GNP, then the real deficit on this count for 1982 would have been 8.6% × 339 = $29 billion. In fact, the recession-induced deficit is larger for two rea-

---

[8] For 1946–47, the large negative real deficits reflect first, decreases in the nominal debt, and second, large increases in the reported price level. Much of these increases in the price level arose from the gradual removal of price controls. Probably, the true price level rose more during World War II and much less for 1946–47. (See the discussion in Chapter 12 on p. 325.) Hence, the true real deficits for 1946–47 were not as negative as those shown in the figure.

sons. First, the percentage shortfall of revenues tends to be greater than that of GNP. A major element here is the graduated-rate structure of the federal income tax, which puts people into lower tax-rate brackets when their incomes fall. Second, on the expenditure side, federal transfers tend to rise during recessions. Overall, I estimate[9] that we should multiply the provisional estimate of $29 billion by 1.8 to account for these two factors. Then the estimated effect of the recession on 1982's real budget deficit becomes $52 billion (column 4 of the table). Thus the recession explains most of the total real deficit ($62 billion) for 1982.

Table 14.3 shows similar calculations for some other cases where recession is the major influence on the real deficit. (Significant movements in real federal expenditures would require separate attention.) Notice that we account for $36 billion of the real deficit of $42 billion for 1975. But for 1958, the actual real deficit of $4 billion was well below the projected figure of $11 billion. Finally, for 1933, we predict a real deficit of $9 billion, as compared to the actual value of $8 billion.

Later on we shall return to these types of calculations to consider budget deficits after 1982. But first, we want to see how deficits and the stock of public debt fit into the theoretical model.

Public Debt and Households' Budget Constraints

As in Chapter 13, households care about the anticipated present value of aggregate real taxes. (Recall that we treat the taxes as lump sum at this stage.) Therefore, we want to know how the outstanding stock of public debt and the government's current and prospective deficits affect the present value of real taxes.

To illustrate the main results, let's start with a number of simplifications. First, assume that the price level and aggregate money stock are constants. Then the government obtains no revenue from the creation of money. Second, let's take as given the quantity of government purchases, G_t, in each period. Third, suppose that aggregate transfers, V_t, are zero in each period. Finally, assume that the government starts with no interest-bearing debt—that is, $B_0^g = 0$. Later on we shall demonstrate that the conclusions do not depend on these unrealistic assumptions.

Given our assumptions, the government's budget constraint in real terms for each period is

$$G_t + \frac{RB_{t-1}^g}{P} = T_t + \frac{(B_t^g - B_{t-1}^g)}{P} \qquad (14.8)$$

---

[9]This estimate comes from Robert Barro, "On the Determination of the Public Debt," *Journal of Political Economy,* October 1979, Table 2.

Note that we treat the price level, P, and the nominal interest rate, R, as constants. Also, the real interest rate equals the nominal rate, since there is no inflation.

Recall that the government starts with no interest-bearing debt at date 0. If the government balances its budget from date 1 onward—that is, if $B_t^g - B_{t-1}^g = 0$ in every period—then interest payments would always be nil. Therefore, real purchases, G_t, would equal real taxes, T_t/P, at all times. Now suppose instead that the government runs a deficit of \$1.00 at date 1, so that $B_1^g = 1$. Since we hold fixed the quantity of government purchases, the budget constraint from equation 14.8 says that this period's taxes, T_1, must decline by \$1.00. That is, we are considering a *deficit-financed tax cut*. Note that the cut in taxes by \$1.00 means that the aggregate of current disposable income received by households rises by \$1.00.

Now suppose that the government wants to restore the public debt to zero from date 2 onward—that is, $B_2^g = B_3^g = \ldots = 0$. Then, in period 2, the government must raise taxes enough to pay off the principal and interest on the one dollar of debt that it issued at date 1. Accordingly, the taxes for period 2, T_2, rise by $(1 + R)$ dollars. Since this action pays off the debt, there are no changes in taxes in subsequent periods.

Overall, aggregate taxes fall by \$1.00 during period 1, but rise by $(1 + R)$ dollars for period 2. Thus, the effect on the present value of aggregate real taxes is given by

$$\left(\frac{1}{P}\right) \cdot \left[-1 + \frac{(1 + R)}{(1 + R)}\right] = 0$$

Note that we discount the increase in next period's taxes of $(1 + R)$ dollars by the discount factor, $(1 + R)$. Hence, the net effect on the present value of aggregate real taxes is nil.

Since there is no change in the present value of aggregate real taxes, the government's deficit during period 1 has no aggregate wealth effect for households. Thus, the shift from current taxes to a deficit has no direct impact on the aggregates of consumer demand and work effort. In this sense, people view as equivalent a current aggregate tax of \$1.00 and a current deficit of \$1.00. This finding is the simplest version of the **Ricardian equivalence theorem** on the public debt. (The theorem is named after the famous British economist, David Ricardo, who first enunciated it.[10])

We can interpret the result as follows. Households receive \$1.00 of extra

---

[10]For a discussion, see David Ricardo, "Funding System," in P. Sraffa, ed., *The Works and Correspondence of David Ricardo*, Cambridge University Press, Cambridge, 1951, Vol. 4; James Buchanan, *Public Principles of Public Debt*, Irwin, Homewood, Illinois, 1958, pp. 43–46, 114–22; and Robert Barro, "Public Debt and Taxes," in *Money, Expectations and Business Cycles*, Academic Press, New York, 1981. Gerald O'Driscoll, in "The Ricardian Nonequivalence Theorem," *Journal of Political Economy*, February 1977, points out Ricardo's own doubts about the empirical validity of his famous theorem.

disposable income during period 1 because of the cut in taxes. But they also face $(1 + R)$ dollars of additional taxes during period 2. If people use the extra dollar of disposable income during period 1 to buy an extra $1.00 of bonds, then they will have just enough additional funds—namely, $(1 + R)$ dollars—to pay the extra taxes in period 2. In other words, the tax cut during period 1 provides just enough resources, but no more, for people to pay the higher taxes next period. That is why there is no aggegrate wealth effect and no changes in the aggregates of consumer demand and work effort.

To generate the results, we assumed that the government paid off the entire public debt during period 2. But this assumption is unnecessary for the results. To see this, let's assume instead—and perhaps more realistically—that the government never pays off the principal of $1.00 from the debt that it issued at date 1. That is, after the first period, the government always balances its budget, so that $B_t^g - B_{t-1}^g = 0$ holds from period 2 onward. In this case, the stock of debt stays constant over time, so that $B_1^g = B_2^g = \ldots = 1$. But then the government must finance the interest payments of R dollars in each period. (Remember that these payments would have been zero if the government had not run a deficit during period 1.) Finally, these extra expenses mean that aggregate taxes, T_t, are higher by $R \cdot B^g = R$ dollars for every period after the first.

Overall, aggregate taxes fall by $1.00 during period 1, but rise by R dollars for each subsequent period. Therefore, the change in the present value of aggregate real taxes is now given by the expression

$$\left(\frac{1}{P}\right) \cdot \left\{ -1 + R\left[\frac{1}{(1 + R)} + \frac{1}{(1 + R)^2} + \cdots \right] \right\}$$
$$= \left(\frac{1}{P}\right) \cdot \left\{ -1 + \left[\frac{R}{(1 + R)} \right] \cdot \left[\frac{(1 + R)}{R} \right] \right\} = 0^{11}$$

That is, the net change in the present value of aggregate real taxes is still zero.

We can think of this result as follows. Households receive $1.00 of extra disposable income during period 1 because of the cut in taxes. But they also face the stream of additional future taxes, which equal R dollars in each period. If the households use the extra dollar of disposable income during period 1 to buy an extra dollar of bonds, then in period 2 they receive $1.00 more of principal payments and R dollars more of interest. If they use the interest receipts to pay the higher taxes, households can again buy a bond for $1.00. Continuing in this manner, the households can always use the interest income to meet the extra taxes in each period. In other words, the tax cut during period 1 provides just enough resources, but no more, for the households to pay the stream of higher future taxes. That is why the net change in the present value of aggregate real taxes is again equal to zero. Hence, we still predict no changes in the aggregates of consumer demand and work effort.

---

[11]Use the condition, $(1 + x + x^2 + \cdots) = 1/(1 - x)$, where $x = 1/(1 + R)$.

The basic conclusion is that shifts between taxes and deficits do not generate aggregate wealth effects. Moreover, this result still obtains if we drop many of our simplifying assumptions. For example, if the initial level of public debt is nonzero, then the conclusion follows by considering the extra future interest payments and taxes that result from today's deficit. Also, the results hold if we superimpose an arbitrary pattern of transfers. Suppose, as an example, that the government reacts to higher future interest payments by reducing transfers, rather than by raising taxes. Then we essentially add a new disturbance—namely, equal decreases in future transfers and taxes—to the one that we already considered. But since this new disturbance has a zero aggregate wealth effect, the basic result remains valid.

We can also allow for money creation and inflation. As one possibility, the government may react to higher future interest payments by printing more money, rather than increasing taxes. In this case economists say that the government **monetizes** part of the deficit or monetizes part of the stock of public debt. But then we essentially add another new distubance—namely, an increase in future money creation and a decrease in future taxes—to the one that we treated before. We know that changes in money, which finance a cut in taxes, have no aggregate wealth effect. Therefore, there is again no aggregate wealth effect from deficits. However, monetization of the public debt does have important implications for the behavior of prices. These effects work just like the increases in the quantity of money that we studied before. In particular, the monetization of deficits is inflationary.

Finally, we can allow for nonzero deficits in future periods. But as with a current deficit, these future ones do not generate any aggregate wealth effects. Therefore, we find that the aggregate wealth effect is nil for any path of public debt. It follows that the aggregate of consumer demand does not react either to differences in the initial stock of real government bonds, B_0^g/P, or to variations in current or prospective government deficits.

Fundamentally, there is no aggregate wealth effect from budget deficits because they do not change the government's use of resources. As before, the quantity of government purchases, G_t, determines how much goods the government uses during period t. Therefore, aggregate wealth effects arise when there are changes in the present value of anticipated government purchases—that is, in permanent purchases, $\hat{G}$. But if we hold constant the value of permanent purchases, then there are no aggregate wealth effects from shifts between taxes and deficits.

The Effect of a Deficit-Financed Tax Cut

Recall that, with lump-sum taxes and transfers, the condition for clearing the commodity market in period 1 is

$$C^d(r_1, \ldots) + I^d(r_1, \ldots) + G_1 = Y^s(r_1, \ldots) \qquad (14.9)$$
$$(-) \qquad\qquad (-) \qquad\qquad\qquad (+)$$

Here, we do not write out explicitly in the demand and supply functions the initial stock of capital, K_0, or the levels of actual and permanent government purchases, G_1 and $\tilde{G}$. Also, recall that our previous analysis implies that the initial amount of real government bonds, B_0^g/P_1, does not matter for aggregate consumer demand, C^d, or goods supply, Y^s.

Suppose that the government cuts current taxes, T_1, and substitutes a corresponding increase in its interest-bearing debt, B_1^g. (Economists often refer to this type of action as stimulative **fiscal policy**.) But assume that the government changes neither the current nor the prospective levels of its purchases. Then the replacement of current taxes by a deficit has no aggregate wealth effect. Hence, there are no effects on consumer demand or work effort. It follows that the tax cut has no impact on the condition for clearing the commodity market in equation 14.9. Accordingly, there is no effect on the real interest rate, r_1, or on the quantities of output, Y_1, consumption, C_1, investment, I_1, and so on.

The condition that money be willingly held in period 1 is

$$M_1 = P_1 \cdot L(Y_1, R_1, \ldots) \qquad (14.10)$$
$$(+) \, (-)$$

Suppose that the government does not change either the current money stock, M_1, or the path of prospective money stocks. Then the deficit-financed cut in current taxes has no effect on equation 14.10. Hence, the price level, P_1, and the nominal interest rate, R_1, do not change. Notice also that the inflation rate, π_1, and all future price levels are unaffected by the tax cut.

The government's tax cut means that the stock of public debt, B_1^g/P_1, increases. But why do households willingly hold this higher real amount of government bonds without any changes in the real or nominal interest rate? They do so because the extra real bonds are just sufficient to cover the additional present value of future real taxes. Therefore, the real and nominal interest rates do not have to change to motivate people to hold the bonds.

We have found in our model that a deficit-financed tax cut does not stimulate the economy or affect interest rates. Since these results are controversial and important, we shall want to see later on whether modifications of the model change the conclusions.

Open-Market Operations

With public debt in the model, we can analyze **open-market operations**. An open-market purchase of securities occurs when the government—or a monetary authority like the Federal Reserve—buys government bonds with newly created money. In the opposite case there is an open-market sale of bonds for money. These open-market operations are the main way that the Federal Reserve actually affects the quantity of money in the United States. Therefore,

Table 14.4 Open-Market Purchases of Bonds and Other Government Policies

Government Policy	Change in M_1	Change in B_1^g	Change in T_1
1. Print more money and reduce taxes	+$1	0	−$1
2. Raise taxes and retire public debt	0	−$1	+$1
3. Open-market purchase of bonds	+$1	−$1	0

Note: An open-market purchase of bonds—policy 3—amounts to a combination of policies 1 and 2, which we have already studied.

we want to know whether this realistic way of changing the quantity of money gives us answers that differ from our unrealistic "helicopter drops" of cash.

Consider an open-market purchase during period 1, which results in an increase by $1.00 in the stock of money, M_1, and a decrease by $1.00 in the stock of public debt, B_1^g. Let's assume that no subsequent changes in money occur—that is, there is a one-time increase in the quantity of money at date 1. Also, we hold fixed the quantities of real government purchases and transfers in each period.

Table 14.4 shows that an open-market purchase of bonds amounts to the combination of two governmental policies that we have already examined. Suppose first that the government prints an extra dollar of money, M_1, and correspondingly reduces current taxes, T_1, by $1.00. These changes are labeled as policy 1 in the table. Then suppose that the government raises taxes, T_1, back up by $1.00 and uses the proceeds to pay off $1.00 of the public debt, B_1^g. These changes are called policy 2 in the table. The net effect of combining these two policies is to leave taxes unchanged. But the quantity of government bonds falls by $1.00. Thus, we end up with an open-market purchase of bonds, which is policy 3 in the table.

We know that policy 1 (more money and less taxes) raises the price level in the same proportion as the increase in the quantity of money. But, except for a reduction in the real amount of government bonds, there are no changes in real variables. We know that policy 2 (the fiscal policy where taxes rise and public debt declines) has no effects, except for another reduction in the real quantity of government bonds. We can find the effects from an open-market purchase of bonds by combining these two sets of responses. Namely, the price level and other nominal variables (aside from the quantity of public debt) rise in the same proportion as the increase in the stock of money. But except for the fall in the real amount of government bonds, there are no changes in real variables. Thus, abstracting from the change in the real quantity of government bonds, our previous results about the neutrality of money apply to open-market purchases (or sales) of bonds.

Why Does the Public Debt Matter?

Our results suggest that the public debt and government deficits do not matter much for the economy. But let's think about the parallel with private debt. The aggregate quantity of private debt is always zero, which also seems uninteresting. But the possibilities for borrowing and lending are important because they eliminate the need for individuals to synchronize their incomes and expenditures. The public debt plays a similar role. Since the credit market exists, the government need not match its receipts from taxes and money creation to its expenditures in each period.

Using the government's budget constraint, we can write the real amount of revenue from taxation and money creation for period t as

$$\frac{T_t}{P_t} + \frac{(M_t - M_{t-1})}{P_t} = G_t + \frac{V_t}{P_t} + \frac{R_{t-1}B_{t-1}^g}{P_t} - \frac{(B_t^g - B_{t-1}^g)}{P_t} \quad (14.11)$$

Now imagine given paths for the government's real purchases and transfers. Also, assume for simplicity that the initial stock of interest-bearing debt, B_0^g, is zero. Then if the government never issues any bonds, its real receipts from taxes and money creation for period t must equal the given total of real expenditures for that period, $G_t + V_t/P_t$. In particular, the receipts have to be high whenever expenditures are high, and vice versa. But the possibilities for issuing interest-bearing debt give the government more flexibility. For example, by borrowing a lot when its expenditures are unusually large, the government can lessen the need for unusually high receipts at that time. In general, the government can manage its issues of public debt to alter the quantity of its receipts for a particular period without changing the amount of expenditures for that period. However, remember that the government cannot change the real present value of its receipts from all periods unless it changes the real present value of its spending from all periods.

To bring out the main points, let's assume again that the stock of money is constant over time—that is, there is no revenue from money creation. Then the government's choices of public debt dictate the timing of its real tax receipts, T_t/P_t. But if the taxes are lump sum—as we have been assuming—then this timing is unimportant. That is because people care only about the real present value of taxes, which cannot change unless the real present value of expenditures changes. The important point is that the economy will respond to a different timing of taxes only if the taxes are not lump sum. To see the nature of this response, let's reintroduce the type of income tax that we studied in Chapter 13. Then the aggregate real tax collections for period t are given by

$$\frac{T_t}{P_t} = \tau_t \left(Y_t + \frac{R_{t-1}B_{t-1}^g}{P_t} - E_t \right) \quad (14.12)$$

where τ_t is the marginal tax rate and E_t is the amount of tax-exempt real income for period t. (Note that the interest payments on the public debt—which are taxable—appear in the aggregate of households' real taxable income.)

By managing the public debt over time, the government determines the behavior of real tax revenues, T_t/P_t, which then determines the necessary values of the marginal tax rates, τ_t, from equation 14.12. Suppose, for example, that the government starts with a plan where the marginal tax rate is constant over time. Then reconsider the example where current taxes, T_1, fall by \$1.00, while the public debt rises by \$1.00. Further, assume that the government raises next period's taxes, T_2, by \$(1 + R)$ to pay off the extra debt. Hence, in this example, the taxes collected change only for periods 1 and 2.

Unless the government has gone beyond the point of maximum tax revenues on the Laffer curve, the changes in taxes collected show up as corresponding changes in marginal tax rates. (Here, we assume no changes in the quantities of tax-exempt real income.) Accordingly, to cut today's tax revenues, today's marginal tax rate τ_1 declines, while to raise next period's revenues, the next period's tax rate τ_2 rises. But these changes motivate people to shift their income toward the current period and away from the next period. Specifically, people raise today's work, but plan to reduce work in the next period. Notice that this response operates like some intertemporal-substitution effects that we considered before.[12]

Figure 14.5 shows the effect on the commodity market during period 1. Note that the increase in today's work effort appears as a rightward shift of the supply curve. Since there is no direct stimulus to today's demand,[13] there is an excess supply of goods at the initial value of the after-tax real interest rate, $[(1 - \tau_1)r_1]^*$. Accordingly, Figure 14.5 shows that the after-tax real interest rate declines, while the quantity of output rises. Recall that an increase in work effort underlies the expansion of output. Finally, because of the fall in the after-tax real interest rate, the extra output shows up partly as more consumption and partly as more investment.

The counterpart of this period's lower marginal tax rate is a higher tax rate for period 2. Thus, Figure 14.6 shows that the changes to the market-clearing diagram are opposite to those found before. In comparison with the values that would have arisen with no changes in taxes, there in an increase in the after-tax real interest rate, and declines in output, work effort, consumption, and investment.

To summarize, when we consider income taxes, there are real effects from fiscal policy. Specifically, a deficit-financed cut in today's marginal tax rate leads to increases in today's real economic activity. But the responses reverse later on when the marginal tax rate is higher than otherwise. In our simple example, the higher future tax rate applies only to period 2. But more gen-

---

[12]Since the tax law applies to income, rather than spending, there is no intertemporal-substitution effect on consumer demand.

[13]There may be a direct impact on investment demand, but it depends on the change in the marginal tax rate for the time when the new capital stock is operational. If the changes in marginal tax rates are short-lived, the direct effect on investment demand would be minor. For simplicity, we neglect this effect.

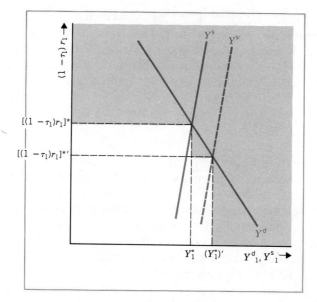

Figure 14.5 The Effect on the Commodity Market of a Deficit-Financed Cut in Today's Marginal Tax Rate

The marginal tax rate falls at date 1. Because of the increase in today's supply of goods, there is an increase in output and a fall in the after-tax real interest rate.

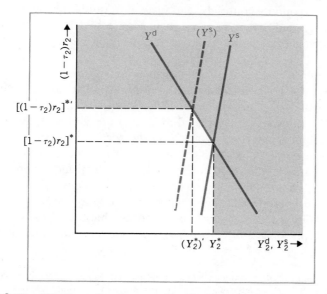

Figure 14.6 The Effect on the Commodity Market of a Temporary Increase in the Marginal Tax Rate

During period 2, when the government pays off public debt, the marginal tax rate is higher. Therefore, output is lower and the after-tax real interest rate is higher.

erally, the higher tax rate could be spread over many periods. Then the tendency for real economic activity to decline would also be spread out into the future. Overall, fiscal policy turns out to be an instrument that can influence the timing of real economic activity. But if we use this policy to get more output today, then we have to accept less output later on.

The Timing of Taxes

The government can manipulate its deficits to change the relative values of marginal tax rates for different periods, and thereby influence the relative levels of output at different times. But it would not be a good idea for the government randomly to make tax rates high in some periods and low in others. These types of fluctuations in tax rates would cause unnecessary distortions, because they would give people the wrong signals in determining how to allocate work and production over time. Fortunately, the U.S. government has not behaved in this erratic manner—rather, the public debt has typically been managed to maintain a pattern of reasonably stable tax rates over time.

One example of this behavior concerns income-tax rates during recessions. Typically, real government expenditures do not decline proportionately as much as aggregate output during a recession. (In fact, items such as unemployment compensation and welfare payments rise automatically.) Therefore, to maintain a balanced budget, the government would have to raise tax rates when the economy contracts. But instead of doing this, the government typically runs a real deficit,[14] as we saw in Figure 14.4.

Another example of the government's debt management shows up during wartime. Here, real government expenditures are much higher than normal. But as mentioned before, real deficits are also especially high at these times. Thereby, the government avoids abnormally high tax rates during wars. In this way the necessary increases in tax rates are spread roughly evenly over time. Tax rates rise somewhat during wartime, but also rise afterward along with the higher interest payments on the accumulated debt.

The general point is that budget deficits would accompany temporary government spending. However, aside from wartime expenditure, it is hard to identify changes in federal spending that people would reasonably perceive as temporary. One example may be the federal government's real interest payments in recent years. As discussed in Chapter 7, real interest rates have risen sharply since 1981. To the extent that real rates exceeded expectations

---

[14]Economists often estimate what the deficit would have been if the economy had been operating at a level of "full capacity" or "full employment." For discussions of the "**full-employment deficit**," see E. Cary Brown, "Fiscal Policy in the Thirties: A Reappraisal:" *American Economic Review,* December 1956; and Council of Economic Advisors, *Economic Report,* 1962, pp. 78–82.

of real rates over the long term, the government's real interest payments were temporarily high. Thus, we predict that these temporary expenditures would be financed by a deficit.

More formally, let r be the real interest rate on the public debt, and let $\bar{r}$ be a measure of long-term real interest rates. Since 1981, a good estimate of $\bar{r}$ comes from the long-term British indexed bonds, which we discussed in Chapter 7. Then our estimate of temporary real interest payments is $(r - \bar{r})B^g/P$. The values of this term for 1981–84 appear in column 2 of Table 14.4. Notice that the values averaged $11 billion for 1982–84.

Column 3 of the table reports the estimated effect of recessions on budget deficits in 1981–84. These calculations parallel those discussed before for Table 14.3. Note that the effect of the recession in 1983 ($51 billion) is comparable to that in 1982 ($52 billion). But the strong recovery meant that the recession-induced real deficit fell to $32 billion in 1984.

The totals of columns 2 and 3 in Table 14.4 give us an overall estimate of the real deficit for each year in column 4. For 1981–83 these values are close to the actual figures, which appear in column 5. In other words, the combined impact of recession and temporarily high real interest payments explains the bulk of real budget deficits through 1983. However, for 1984, the actual real deficit of $71 billion exceeded the estimated value by $26 billion. Equivalently, if we multiply by 1984's price level (2.23), the nominal deficit for 1984 was about $58 billion more than we can explain. Similar values for the excess deficit would apply for 1985 (for which not all data were available at the time of this writing).

The figure of $58 billion corresponds roughly to popular proposals during 1984–85 for deficit reduction via combinations of spending cuts or tax in-

Table 14.5 Real Federal Deficits, 1981–84

(1) Year	(2) Effect of Interest Payments	(3) Effect of Recession	(4) Estimated Real Deficit	(5) Actual Real Deficit	(6) Residual (5) − (4)
1981	−4	22	18	9	−9
1982	10	52	62	62	0
1983	11	51	62	69	7
1984	13	32	45	71	26

Note: Column 2 is $(r_t - \bar{r}_t) \times B^g_{t-1}/P_t$, where r_t is the real interest rate on federal debt and $\bar{r}_t$ is the real interest rate on British long-term index bonds (from Table 7.4). The variable r_t is calculated as $R_t - \pi_t$, where R_t is the ratio of net federal interest payments (Figure 14.3) to the initial stock of debt, B^g_{t-1}, and π_t is the inflation rate, based on the first quarter GNP deflator for each year. Column 3 is 1.8 × estimated percentage shortfall of real GNP × trend real federal receipts (as in column 4 of Table 14.3); column 4 = column 2 + column 3; column 5 is from Figure 14.4; column 6 = column 5 − column 4.

creases.[15] To put the result another way, the Reagan tax-cutting program for 1982–84 can be looked at as a long-term promise of a smaller government. In 1984 this promise was unsatisfied to the extent of $58 billion in excess expenditure, which was the size of the excess budget deficit.

The Standard View of a Deficit-Financed Tax Cut

Our analysis of fiscal policy differs from that of most macroeconomic models. To see why, let's return to the case of lump-sum taxes, which most macromodels assume. For our analysis, the key point is that the typical household regards as equivalent a current aggregate tax of $1.00 or a government deficit of $1.00. In particular, if the behavior of government purchases does not change, then shifts between taxes and deficits entail no aggregate wealth effects. On the other hand, most macroeconomic models assume that a deficit-financed tax cut raises households' wealth, even if there are no changes in government purchases. Let's look first at the results in this case, and then examine briefly the arguments that some economists have made for a positive effect on aggregate wealth.

Suppose again that the government cuts current taxes by $1.00 and runs a deficit. If the tax cut makes people feel wealthier, aggregate consumer demand rises, but work effort and the supply of goods fall. (However, most analyses neglect the wealth effect on work effort.) The excess demand for goods leads to a higher real interest rate and thereby to lower investment. Thus, this analysis predicts that government deficits raise real interest rates and **crowd out** private investment.

What about output and work effort? Because of the increase in wealth, the typical person ends up currently with more leisure to go along with more consumption.[16] But the rise in leisure means less work and hence less output. Recall that the decrease in investment allows the typical person to consume more, even though output is lower.

According to this analysis, the decrease in net investment shows up in the long run as a decrease in the stock of capital. Sometimes, economists refer to this negative effect on the capital stock as a **"burden of the public debt."** That is, each generation "burdens" the next one by bequeathing them a smaller

---

[15]We should also note that state and local governments ran a nominal budget surplus (on a national accounts' basis) of $64 billion in 1984 and $59 billion in 1985. Hence, the excess federal deficit was partly an offset to this surplus by other sectors of government.

[16]Notice that the economy's opportunities for shifting between leisure and consumption, which depend on the schedule for today's marginal product of labor, have not changed. Therefore, current consumption and leisure tend to move in the same direction—namely, upward in this case.

aggregate stock of capital.[17] Note that these effects arise because deficits make people feel wealthier, which leads to a cutback in desired saving.

From an empirical standpoint, a principal prediction from the standard analysis is that larger real government deficits and larger real stocks of public debt lead to higher real interest rates. There is little question that most government officials and news reporters, as well as many economists, believe this prediction to be accurate. Nevertheless, this belief does not have evidence to support it. For example, Charles Plosser[18] carried out a detailed statistical analysis of government deficits and interest rates over the period from 1954 to 1978. His major finding was that the size of the deficit and the quantity of public debt outstanding had no significant effect on the interest rates paid on U.S. treasury bills or long-term U.S. government bonds.[19] Thus, Plosser's evidence directly contradicts the standard theory in which deficit-financed tax cuts make people feel wealthier.

The Effect of a Tax Cut on Wealth

To reach the standard conclusions mentioned above, we had to assume that a tax cut makes people feel wealthier, even if the behavior of government purchases does not change. Here, we consider two of the more interesting justifications for this assumption—one concerning the finiteness of life, and the other imperfections of private loan markets. It is worth exploring these matters in any case, since they come up in other areas, as well as in the context of public debt.

Finite Lives

Suppose again that the government cuts current taxes by $1.00 and runs a deficit. We know that the government has higher interest payments and taxes in the future, and that the present value of the extra future taxes equals $1.00. But assume that some of these taxes will show up after the typical person has already died. Then the present value of the extra future taxes that accrue during the typical person's lifetime falls short of $1.00. Hence, there is a positive effect on wealth when the government replaces current taxes by a deficit.

Why do we get an increase in wealth when people have finite lives? The reason is that the increase in wealth for the aggregate of current taxpayers

---

[17]For some discussion, see James Ferguson, ed., *Public Debt and Future Generations*, University of North Carolina Press, Chapel Hill, 1964. Note especially the paper by Franco Modigliani, "Long-Run Implications of Alternative Fiscal Policies and the Burden of the National Debt."

[18]"The Effects of Government Financing Decisions on Asset Returns," *Journal of Monetary Economics*, May 1982.

[19]Plosser's results refer to nominal interest rates. Therefore, given his findings, a higher deficit would raise real interest rates only if the expected rate of inflation were to decline.

coincides with a decrease for the members of future generations. Individuals will be born with a liability for a portion of taxes to pay interest on the higher stock of public debt. But these people will not share in the benefits from the earlier tax cut. If these future liabilities on descendants were counted fully by present taxpayers, then there would be no aggregate wealth effect. Essentially, government deficits enable members of current generations to die in a state of insolvency by leaving debts for their descendants. Current taxpayers experience an increase in wealth if they view this governmental shifting of incomes across generations as desirable. But in fact, most people already have private opportunities for intergenerational transfers, which they have chosen to exercise to a desired extent. As examples, parents make contributions to children in the form of educational investments, other expenses in the home, and bequests. In the other direction—and especially before the growth of social security—children provide support for their aged parents. To the extent that private transfers of this sort are operative, the shift from taxes to deficits does not offer the typical person a new opportunity to extract funds from his or her descendants. Rather, the response to higher deficits would be a shift in private transfers by an amount sufficient to restore the balance of income across generations that was previously deemed optimal. In this case, the shift from taxes to deficits again has no aggregate wealth effect.[20]

As a concrete example, suppose that a couple plans to leave a bequest with a present value of $5000 for their children. Then the government runs a deficit, which cuts the present value of the couple's taxes by $1000, but raises the present value of their children's taxes by $1000. Our prediction is that the parents use the tax cut to raise the present value of their bequest to $6000. Then the extra $1000 provides the children with the extra funds to pay their higher taxes. Thereby, parents and children end up with the same amounts of consumption and leisure as they enjoyed before the government ran its deficit.

The important idea is that the typical person is connected via family ties to future generations. In fact, we used this idea before to motivate an infinite planning horizon for households. In this setting people effectively plan with an infinite horizon even though they live for only a finite time. But with an infinite horizon it is clear that a deficit-financed tax cut does not change the typical family's wealth. That is, the present value of the extra future taxes balances the cut in current taxes.

Imperfect Loan Markets

The argument that taxes and deficits are equivalent assumes also that private and governmental interest rates are the same. However, the process of lending

---

[20]For a discussion of the interplay between public debt and private intergenerational transfers, see Robert Barro, "Are Government Bonds Net Wealth?," *Journal of Political Economy*, November/December 1974. A different view is that parents use bequests to control their children's behavior, rather than purely out of altruism. For a discussion of this "enforcement theory of giving" see B. Douglas Bernheim, Andrei Shleifer, and Lawrence Summers, "The Strategic Bequest Motive," *Journal of Political Economy*, December 1985.

and borrowing involves transaction costs for loan evaluations, collections, defaults, and so on. It is relatively easy to borrow if a person has a house, car, or factory to put up as collateral. But it is much harder if someone, such as a student, just promises to repay a loan out of future earnings. Therefore, the interest rates for borrowing are especially high for those with poor collateral, who require large costs of supervision to ensure the repayment of loans.

Think of the world as divided into two groups. Group A consists of people who lend or borrow at the same real interest rate, r, as the government. Group B comprises individuals who would like to borrow at this interest rate, but who face higher borrowing rates. Let $\tilde{r}$ be the real discount rate that a person from this group uses in calculating the present value of future incomes and expenses. The main point is that the rate $\tilde{r}$ exceeds the real interest rate, r, for those from group A.

Now suppose that the government cuts taxes and runs a deficit. The cut in taxes applies partly to people from group A and partly to those from group B. As before, the aggregate of future taxes increases. Let's assume that the division of these future taxes between those from group A and those from group B coincides with the division of the current tax cut. (Otherwise, there is a distributional effect, which we would also have to consider.) For the people of type A, the present value of the higher future taxes again equals the amount of the tax cut. Therefore, the wealth effect is nil. But, since the people of type B discount future taxes at the higher rate, $\tilde{r}$, the present value of their extra future taxes is less than their tax cut. Hence, wealth increases for group B, which leads to more consumption demand and less work effort. Further, as type B people raise their current consumption, they tend to reduce the discount rate, $\tilde{r}$, that they apply to future incomes and expenses. Therefore, the investment demand from this group tends also to increase. (Think of a small business that faces a high borrowing rate. When the government cuts taxes, the business uses a portion of its extra funds to finance more investment.)

In the aggregate the deficit-financed tax cut leads to an increase in the current demands for consumption and investment, and to a decrease in the current supply of goods. From our usual analysis, we find that the real interest rate, r, rises. But this rate applies to the people from group A. Therefore, these people end up decreasing their current consumption and investment, and raising their work effort. On the other hand, because of the initial stimulus from the tax cut, those from group B increase current consumption and investment, and reduce work. For these people, the discount rate, $\tilde{r}$, declines. Note especially the narrowing of the spread between the two discount rates, r and $\tilde{r}$.

The overall effects on output, consumption, and investment are uncertain. However, the primary effect is the diversion of current resources away from the consumption and investment of type A people and toward those of type B people. Essentially, the tax cut induces the type A people to hold more than their share of the additional public debt, so as effectively to lend to the type B people at the real interest rate, r. Thus, the members of group B—whose discount rate $\bar{r}$ exceeds r—are better off. But those of type A are also satisfied, because the yield on their bonds is guaranteed by the government. Recall that people of type A require a real interest rate greater than r to lend directly to the people of type B. In other words, the government's issue of public debt somehow avoids the high transaction costs that led in the first place to high borrowing rates for the members of group B.

The analysis assumes implicitly that the government is more efficient than the private market in arranging loans between members of groups A and B. Specifically, we omitted any transaction costs for collecting the additional future taxes from the type B people. But if these individuals are poor credit risks who require close supervision by private lenders, then they are likely to cause similar problems for the government. On the other hand, some economists argue that the ability to levy taxes and to use the police power to enforce collections actually does make the government more efficient in the loan process. Then a deficit-financed tax cut really does raise wealth in the aggregate. Namely, this fiscal policy means that the government carries out more of the loan operations at which, we assume, it is particularly efficient.[21] Of course, if the government is not more efficient, then we no longer get the increase in wealth. The apparent gains disappear when we include the resources that the government uses up to make sure that the people of type B pay their taxes.

Even if private loan markets are imperfect—in the sense of being less efficient than the government—the results do not conform to the standard analysis of a deficit-financed tax cut. For instance, although the real interest rate on the well-secured loans increases, that on less well-secured loans tends to fall. That is, we predict a narrowing of the spread between the two rates, r and $\bar{r}$. Also there need not be crowding-out of private investment. Rather, we find mainly a diversion of all types of spending away from people who have good access to the loan market (the members of group A) and toward those who lack this access (the people of group B).

Social Security and Saving

Benefits paid through social security have expanded enormously in the United States and most other countries. For example, the amounts paid out in 1984 for old age, survivors and disability were 5% of GNP, as compared to 3% in 1970, 2% in 1960, and less than 1% in 1950. Some economists argue that this increase in social security has sharply reduced private saving.[22] Since this effect

---

[21]There is no indication that the U.S. government has superior skills in direct loans, as evidenced by its widespread problems in collecting from students. In fact, the tendency is to subcontract the handling of these loans to private financial institutions.

[22]See Martin Feldstein, "Social Security, Induced Retirement, and Aggregate Capital Accumulation," *Journal of Political Economy*, September/October 1974.

could be quantitatively important, we want to examine it from the standpoint of our model.

The argument for an effect on saving applies when the social security system is not **fully funded.** In a funded setup workers' payments accumulate in a trust fund, which provides later for retirement benefits. The alternative is a **pay-as-you-go system,** in which benefits to old persons are financed by taxes on the currently young. In this case, the people who are at or near retirement age when the program begins or expands receive benefits without paying a comparable present value of taxes. Correspondingly, the people from later generations pay taxes that exceed their expected benefits in present-value terms. (Unfortunately, most readers of this book are in this category.)

The U.S. system operates mainly on a pay-as-you-go basis. Although the plan in 1935 envisioned an important role for the social security trust fund, the system has evolved steadily since 1939 toward primarily a pay-as-you-go operation.[23] In particular, retirees increasingly received benefits that—in present-value terms—exceeded their prior contributions.

Let's consider the effects of social security in a pay-as-you-go system. For this purpose, we neglect the substitution effects from the taxes and transfers, since we already discussed these in the previous chapter. Now we look at possible wealth effects from an increase in retirement benefits, when these are financed by higher taxes on workers.

The usual argument goes as follows. Old persons experience an increase in the present value of their social security transfers net of taxes. Therefore, they respond to the increase in wealth by consuming more. Young persons face higher taxes, but these are offset partly by the expectation of higher retirement benefits. Since the decrease in wealth for the young is smaller in magnitude than the increase for the old, we predict that aggregate consumer demand rises. In other words, more social security reduces the aggregate of desired saving. Therefore, we predict an increase in the real interest rate and a decrease in net investment. In the long run, this decrease in investment shows up as a smaller stock of capital.

The above argument for social security parallels the standard view of a deficit-financed tax cut. In both cases, the increase in aggregate consumer demand arises only if people neglect the adverse effects on descendants. Specifically, an increase in the scale of the social-security program means that the typical person's descendants will be born with a tax liability that exceeds their prospective retirement benefits in present-value terms. If people take full account of these effects on their descendants, the aggregate wealth effect from more social security is nil.

As in the case of a deficit-financed tax cut, more social security enables older persons to extract funds from their descendants. But as before, people

---

[23]For a discussion of the institutional features, see Michael Boskin, ed., *The Crisis in Social Security,* Institute for Contemporary Studies, San Francisco, 1977.

value this change only if they give no transfers to their children and receive nothing from their children. Otherwise, people respond to more social security by shifting private intergenerational transfers, rather than by changing consumption. For example, in the United States the growth of social security has strongly diminished the tendency of children to support their aged parents.

On an empirical level, there has been a great debate about the connection of social security to saving and investment. First, Martin Feldstein (op. cit.) reported a dramatic negative effect of social security on capital accumulation in the United States. But subsequent investigators showed that Feldstein's claims were unsubstantiated.[24] In fact, neither the long-term evidence for the United States nor that from a cross section of countries in recent years support the proposition that social security depresses saving and investment.

Summary

The ability to issue and retire interest-bearing public debt allows the government's expenditures to diverge in the short run from the sum of its tax receipts and its revenue from printing money. As an analogue to households' saving, we define the government's real deficit to be the change in the real value of its outstanding liabilities. This concept involves two adjustments to standard measures of the deficit. First, we remove the inflation part of nominal interest payments, and second, we divide by the price level. Then we find that real deficits are large mainly during wars and recessions, and tend to be negative in "normal" times.

Shifts between taxes and deficits affect the timing of tax collections, but not their overall present value. Hence, if we hold fixed the behavior of government purchases, this type of fiscal policy has no aggregate wealth effect, and consequently no impact on aggregate consumer demand. Equivalently, households save the full amount of their extra disposable income in order to pay for the higher future taxes. For the case of lump-sum taxes, it follows that deficits do not alter the real interest rate, or the quantities of investment and output. This result is called the Ricardian equivalence theorem, which says that taxes and deficits have the same effect on the economy. A related conclusion concerns open-market operations, which are exchanges between money and public debt. These operations change the price level in the same proportion

---

[24]For a summary of the debate, see Louis Esposito, "Effect of Social Security on Saving: Review of Studies Using U.S. Time Series Data," *Social Security Bulletin*, May 1978; and the papers in the May 1979 issue of the *Social Security Bulletin*. For the popular press (*Business Week*, September 22, 1980), the issue was settled by Dean Leimer and Selig Lesnoy in their paper, "Social Security and Private Saving: A Reexamination of the Time Series Evidence Using Alternative Social Security Wealth Variables," Social Security Administration, November 1980. These researchers reported that Feldstein's conclusions stemmed from an error in his computer program!

as the shift in the quantity of money, but, aside from a change in the real public debt, there are no effects on real variables.

When we consider an income tax, there are some real effects from a deficit. These concern the timing of taxes, which generate intertemporal-substitution effects on work and production. Generally, it is optimal for the government to manage the public debt to avoid large random fluctuations in tax rates from period to period. This motivation accounts for the tendency to run large real deficits during wars and recessions, but to run real surpluses in "good times."

The standard view of deficit-financed tax cuts is that they make people feel wealthier. In this case, deficits would raise the real interest rate and crowd out investment. Sometimes, people rationalize the wealth effect from a tax cut by appealing to finite lives or imperfect capital markets. But an examination of these ideas suggests that they are unlikely to support the standard conclusions. Also, some statistical evidence reveals no significant relation between deficits and interest rates.

Finally, we note that social security is analogous to public debt. Thus, if debt-financed tax cuts have little effect on interest rates and capital accumulation, then the same goes for an increase in the scale of the social security program.

Important Terms and Concepts

government deficit (surplus)

public debt

nominal deficit (national accounts' version)

real deficit (national accounts' version)

real deficit

nominal deficit

balanced budget

Ricardian equivalence theorem

monetize the deficit

fiscal policy

open-market operations

full-employment deficit

crowding-out (from government deficits)

burden of the public debt

fully funded system (for social security)

pay-as-you-go system (for social security)

QUESTIONS AND PROBLEMS

Mainly for Review

14.1 What is the real deficit? Why does a rise in the inflation rate reduce the real deficit? Show how the real deficit is altered either by policy changes or by economic events such as recessions.

14.2 Suppose there is a temporary increase in (lump-sum) taxes. Is there any effect on households' wealth? Show how the typical household can use the credit market to offset the reduction in current disposable income.

14.3 Are government budget deficits inflationary? If so, would you expect any effect on the real rate of interest? What about the nominal rate of interest?

14.4 Why are open-market operations neutral?

14.5 Suppose the government announces a reduction in tax rates to take place in some future period. What intertemporal-substitution effect will this have on current work? What effect will it have on consumption?

14.6 Compare the effect of (*a*) government budget deficits and (*b*) social security on the tax liabilities of younger people. Why do the tax liabilities exceed expected future benefits in the case of social security?

Problems for Discussion

14.7 The Aggregate Wealth Effect from a Deficit
Assume that taxes are lump sum. Suppose that the government cuts current taxes and runs a deficit. Then assume that the real public debt remains constant from period 2 onward. Also, the paths of government purchases and real transfers do not change. Discuss the aggregate wealth effect that results from the government's current tax cut. In particular, how does this effect depend on the following considerations:

a. Finite lifetimes?
b. The existence of childless persons?
c. Uncertainty about who will pay the higher future taxes?
d. The possibility that the government will print more money in the future, rather than raising taxes?
e. The imperfection of private loan markets?

14.8 Effects of a Deficit-Financed Tax Cut
Assume that taxes are lump sum. Suppose again that the government cuts current taxes and runs a deficit. Discuss the effects for the current period on first, the real interest rate and the quantities of output and investment, and second, the price level and the nominal interest rate, assuming that

a. The paths of government purchases, real transfers, and money creation do not change.
b. The same as in part a, except that people expect the future growth rate of money to rise.
c. The same as in part a, except that people expect future real transfers to fall.
d. The same as in part a, except that people expect future government purchases to decline.

14.9 The Reagan Tax-Cut Plans

President Reagan's proposal in 1981 for cutting U.S. federal income-tax rates involved roughly a 23% overall reduction in rates. The full cut was to be phased in over a 3-year period ending in 1983. The plan involved also gradual reductions over time in real government expenditures when expressed as a fraction of real GNP.

Consider an alternative plan that yields the same present value of real tax revenues, but which implemented the entire cut in tax rates in 1981. Assume that real government expenditures behave the same way as under Reagan's plan. Compare this plan with Reagan's with respect to the effects on work effort, production, and investment over the period 1981–83.

In 1985–86, the U.S. Congress was considering plans to lower marginal tax rates, effective in 1987. Suppose that these deliberations meant that the typical person's marginal tax rate in 1985–86 was higher than his or her expected rate for 1987. What would be the effect of the deliberations on real economic activity in 1985 and 1986?

14.10 Social Security and Capital Accumulation

Suppose that the government introduces a new social security program, which will pay the real amount s to covered persons when they retire.

a. What long-run effects do you predict on the stock of capital?

b. How does the answer depend on whether the social security program is fully-funded or pay-as-you-go?

14.11 The Government's Stock of Gold

The U.S. Treasury's gold stock is held at the Federal Reserve. Mostly because of changes in the price of gold, the market value of these holdings rose from $12 billion at the end of 1970 to $89 billion at the end of 1985. In terms of 1972 prices, the increase was from $13 billion at the end of 1970 to $39 billion at the end of 1985.

a. How would you modify the measure of the government's deficit to include these changes in the value of gold holdings?

b. Can you apply your reasoning more generally to the government's holdings of other commodities, capital goods, and land?

(Amusingly, the Federal Reserve values its gold holdings at the official price of $42.22 per ounce, rather than at the market price, which was about $340 per ounce at the end of 1985.)

14.12 Temporary Consumption Taxes (optional)

Suppose that taxes are levied on consumption, rather than income. An individual's real tax for period t is then $t_t/P_t = \tau_t c_t - e_t$. Assume that the government runs a deficit during period 1 and cuts the marginal tax rate on consumption, τ_1. For subsequent periods, the marginal tax rates are higher than otherwise.

a. What is the impact of the tax cut on the demand and supply of goods for period 1?

b. What is the effect during period 1 on the real interest rate, output, work effort, consumption, and investment?

PART V

INTERACTIONS BETWEEN THE MONETARY SECTOR AND THE REAL SECTOR

Thus far, our analysis stresses real factors, such as supply shocks, as sources of business fluctuations. The government can affect real variables by changing its purchases of goods and services or its tax rates, but there is little evidence that these fiscal actions have been major sources of business cycles in U.S. history. On the other hand, many economists believe that monetary fluctuations—created mainly by governmental actions—have been a principal cause of these cycles. In this part of the book we examine the theoretical and empirical foundations for these beliefs.

Chapter 15 studies commercial banks and other financial institutions that intermediate between lenders and borrowers. These financial intermediaries create deposits, which can be good alternatives to currency as means of payments. Through the effects on the demand for currency, changes in the nature of financial intermediation have an effect on the price level. We show also that financial intermediation can aid in the allocation of credit, and thereby improve the economy's performance. Accordingly, changes in the amount of financial inter- mediation—including those caused by shifts in governmental regulations—are nonneutral.

However, we still conclude that purely monetary disturbances, such as those generated by open-market operations, are neutral.

In Chapter 16 we survey the various pieces of empirical evidence that concern the relation between nominal and real variables. We find that the theory can explain some of the evidence as reactions to supply shocks or to changes in the nature of financial intermediation. One observation that conflicts with our theory is the apparent sensitivity of real variables to purely nominal disturbances. That is, there is some indication that money is nonneutral and plays a significant role in business fluctuations. Therefore, it is worthwhile to extend the theory to explain why monetary nonneutrality can be important.

Chapter 17 carries out this extension by introducing incomplete information about prices. We retain the setting of cleared markets, and assume that people form rational expectations about prices and other variables. (Because of this last feature, economists often refer to this approach as rational expectations macroeconomics—or sometimes as equilibrium business cycle theory.) In this framework monetary surprises can lead to confusions between nominal and real disturbances, and thereby to changes in real variables. In this way we explain some, but not all, of the observed linkages between money and business cycles. We go on to explore first, the implications for monetary policy, and second, the possible empirical limitations of the approach.

Chapter 18 develops the Keynesian theory of business fluctuations. This approach is another extension of our basic framework—in this approach we replace the assumption of market clearing with the alternative of sticky prices and rationed quantities. As in Chapter 17, where people have incomplete information about prices, the Keynesian theory can explain some nonneutralities of money. However, the two kinds of theories differ in other respects, especially in regard to their implications for government policy. Our discussion brings out the relative theoretical and empirical merits of the theories, although a final verdict is not yet available.

CHAPTER 15
FINANCIAL INTERMEDIATION

Checkable Deposits and *M*1

Up to now our model treats money as currency—that is, as non-interest-bearing pieces of paper issued by the government. When we studied the demand for money in Chapter 4, we focused on the role of money as a medium of exchange. Households held money because they used it for purchases or sales of goods, bonds, or labor services. To reduce their average real cash balances, people had to incur extra transaction costs, which might involve going more often to the bank or the store.

We mentioned in Chapter 4 that currency is not the only medium of exchange in the real world. Typically, the most important alternative is checkable deposits. These deposits are now issued in the United States by various financial institutions, such as commercial banks and savings and loan associations. The holder of a deposit can purchase goods, bonds, or labor services by writing a check on his or her account. The check instructs the financial institution to transfer funds from the account of the check writer to that of another person. The important point is that checkable deposits are often preferable to currency as a medium of exchange.

The most popular definition of money, *M*1, attempts to classify together the assets that serve commonly as media of exchange. Thus, *M*1 is the sum of currency held by the public and checkable deposits (plus some travelers' checks). In the United States and most countries today, checkable deposits account for the bulk of *M*1. For example, in 1985, checkable deposits were 71% of *M*1 in the United States, and 78% of *M*1 in the United Kingdom (see Table 4.1 in Chapter 4).

Some economists have argued that "money" should also include deposits that are not checkable, but can be converted readily into checkable form or into currency. Thus, the broader aggregate *M*2 includes consumer time deposits at various financial institutions, money-market deposit accounts, and some other items. Still broader monetary aggregates, such as *M*3, include additional types of financial assets. Of course, once we go beyond the definition

415

of money as common media of exchange, there is no clear place to draw the line. In the box below we consider some interesting attempts to solve this problem by constructing indices of monetary aggregates.

Indices of Money

Some economists have used an index-number approach to measure the money supply. The general idea is to construct an aggregate that weights different assets according to their "degree of moneyness." One approach (used by William Barnett, Edward Offenbacher and Paul Spindt in "The New Divisia Monetary Aggregates," *Journal of Political Economy*, December 1984) begins with the observation that people hold currency although it bears zero interest. Other assets, such as various kinds of deposits, provide less monetary services and therefore must pay positive interest rates to induce people to hold them. Then the general idea is to weight the quantities of various assets inversely to their interest rates (which are observable) and hence in direct relation to their amounts of monetary services (which are unobservable). Thus, currency counts one-to-one as money, checkable deposits (which bear low but positive interest rates) count somewhat less than one-to-one, time deposits (which bear higher interest rates) count still less, and so on. Using this technique, Barnett *et al.* have constructed a time series of a weighted monetary aggregate, which behaves somewhat differently from $M1$ or other concepts.

One difficulty is that differences in interest rates among assets reflect characteristics other than monetary services. Also it is sometimes hard to measure the implicit interest rate from free services to holders of deposits. To get around these problems, Paul Spindt ("Money Is What Money Does: Monetary Aggregation and the Equation of Exchange," *Journal of Political Economy*, February 1985) took a different approach. He made direct estimates of monetary services by observing how frequently the various kinds of assets were used in exchanges. Thus, currency and checkable deposits—which have high velocities—received a high weight for monetary services. In contrast, time deposits—which have low velocity—received a low weight as money. Using this procedure, Spindt calculated a time series for another weighted monetary aggregate, which showed somewhat different behavior from the one described above. It is likely that economists will make increasing use of these weighted monetary aggregates in future research.

For our purposes, it is unimportant to settle on a precise definition of money. But we do want to extend our model to assess the economic consequences from the existence of various types of deposits and various kinds of financial institutions.

Let's begin by noting that deposits in the United States differ in the following ways:

- Whether they can be withdrawn on demand at face value. This privilege applies to **demand deposits** and usually to **savings deposits,** which often have passbooks and legally allow for 30-day notice of withdrawal. In contrast, **time deposits** have a stated maturity date, with some penalties typically attached to premature withdrawals.
- Whether people can write checks that instruct the financial intermediary to make payments to a third party. In the United States, all demand deposits are checkable.
- Whether they pay interest and at what rate.
- Whether they are insured by the federal government. Since 1980 this insurance applies to deposits up to $100,000 at most commercial banks, savings and loan associations, and mutual savings banks.

Households decide how much to hold of the various deposits by considering the above characteristics as well as the interest rate paid. The main point is that these deposits are often more attractive to households than either currency or bonds. By bonds, we mean interest-bearing obligations of governments, businesses, or households. By holding a bond, a household lends funds directly to governments or businesses or other households. In contrast, deposits are liabilities of financial institutions. Thus, by holding a deposit, a household lends funds to a financial institution. As we shall see, the financial institution then acts as an intermediary by lending its funds to governments, businesses, or households.

One thing we want to understand in this chapter is why households use the services of financial intermediaries, rather than making loans directly. Then we can also see how the existence of financial intermediaries and the amount of financial intermediation affect the performance of the economy.

Financial Intermediaries and the Credit Market

Thus far in our model, the people who hold bonds make direct loans to others. For example, a lender may hold a mortgage on someone's house, or a loan collateralized by someone's car, or a loan to a business for investment purposes. But this type of direct lending is often inefficient. First, it requires people to evaluate the credit-worthiness of borrowers, which is costly when strangers are involved (or even when we loan funds to a friend or relative!). Second, unless individuals hold portions of many different types of loans, they may have substantial risks of losing a large part of their assets when a single loan goes bad. But it is hard for an individual to diversify by holding lots of different loans. Finally, the form of claim that someone holds—say, a home mortgage—must match the form of the loan in terms of its maturity. In the case of a 20-

Table 15.1 Balance Sheet of First National Bank of Rochester December 31, 1984 (amounts in millions of dollars)

Assets		Liabilities	
Cash (includes deposits held at Fed and other financial institutions)	8.0	Demand deposits	16.0
Loans (net of loss reserve)	60.5	Time deposits	73.2
Securities	18.7	Borrowing from Federal	
Federal Funds	7.1	Funds Market	0
Other assets	3.2	Borrowing from Fed	0
		Other liabilities	2.3
		Shareholders' equity	6.0
Total	97.5	Total	97.5

year loan to a homeowner, the lender can cash in this claim only by selling it to someone else or by convincing the borrower to pay it off.

Financial intermediaries, such as commercial banks,[1] can solve the problems that we just mentioned. First, these institutions are in a good position to evaluate and collect on loans, and to assemble a variety of loans by type and maturity. In particular, the credit market works better when loans are evaluated and administered by financial specialists, rather than households. Second, as we already noted, financial institutions can attract funds by offering deposits, which are desirable forms of assets for households. In normal times, where financial institutions hold a sound, well-diversified portfolio of assets, the deposits are safe and easy to understand. These features make deposits attractive for most households.

The Balance Sheet of a Financial Intermediary

A financial institution's deposits appear on the liabilities side of its balance sheet, while various loans appear on the assets side. Table 15.1 shows a typical balance sheet. To be concrete (and to advertise the fine city of Rochester, N.Y.), the figures apply in 1984 to an actual, small commercial bank—The First National Bank of Rochester—which had total assets of about $100 million.

Let's look first at the main items on the asset side of the balance sheet. Here we have

Cash of $8.0 million. This item includes currency (often called **vault cash**), deposits held on the books of the Federal Reserve, and deposits held at

---

[1]Others are savings and loan associations, money-market funds, mutual savings banks, pension funds, investment companies, insurance companies, and the government's mortgage associations.

other financial institutions. The total of currency and deposits held at the Fed is called **reserves.**

Loans of $60.5 million. The principal items are commercial loans, mortgages, and installment loans. Most large banks would also have substantial foreign loans.[2]

Securities of $18.7 million. This category includes government bonds and short-term "money-market instruments" (such as commercial paper and certificates of deposit issued by other financial institutions).

Federal Funds of $7.1 million. These are short-term (often overnight) loans to other financial intermediaries through the **Federal Funds market.** The interest rate charged on these loans is called the **Federal Funds rate.** Typically, the smaller institutions—like the First National Bank of Rochester—lend funds in this market, while the large commercial banks are the main borrowers.

Now, let's look at the liability side of the ledger. The principal items are

Demand deposits of $16.0 million.

Time deposits of $73.2 million.

Borrowings from the Federal Funds market of $0. (First National is a lender of federal funds.)

Borrowings from the Federal Reserve (*also called the Fed*), *which are nil in this case.* The Federal Reserve lends to financial institutions—principally commercial banks that are members of the Federal Reserve System—at the "discount window." The interest rate charged on these loans is called the Fed's **discount rate.**

Shareholders' equity of $6.0 million. This "book value" is the sum of paid-in capital plus accumulated profits (as measured by accountants).

Reserves—Required and Excess

Financial intermediaries hold "earning assets"—by which we mean loans and securities—to obtain a flow of interest income. They hold physical capital and deposits at other financial institutions to carry out their business efficiently. What about cash? Since banks and some other depository institutions stand ready to convert their deposits into currency on demand, they would hold some currency to meet the possible withdrawals of depositors. But in the United States in recent years, the main determinant of cash holdings by these institutions is the **reserve requirement** imposed by the Federal Reserve. (We shall discuss the Federal Reserve System later on.) The Fed specifies the

---

[2]In the United States there are legal restrictions on the types of earning assets that financial intermediaries can hold. For example, commercial banks cannot hold corporate stock.

quantity of reserves that must be held against various categories of deposits. Legally, the reserves can be held either as currency (vault cash) or as non-interest-bearing deposits on the books of the Federal Reserve.[3] Before 1980, the Fed's requirements applied only to commercial banks that were members of the Federal Reserve System. However, the Monetary Control Act of 1980 extended the reserve requirements to all depository institutions (not including money-market funds), but at lower average percentages than before. The requirements in 1985 were 12% of checkable deposits[4] and 3% of business time deposits of maturity less than $1\frac{1}{2}$ years. But the Fed retains some discretionary authority to vary these requirements.

Figure 15.1 shows how the ratio of required reserves to checkable deposits changed from 1918 to 1985. (For years before the mid 1970s, checkable deposits coincided with demand deposits at commercial banks.) The main source of changes in this ratio is shifts in legal requirements. But some requirements attach also to time and savings deposits, which do not enter into the total of checkable deposits. Also, the requirements depend on the total volume of deposits of the financial institution (or, before 1972, on whether a bank was located in a city or in the "country"). Therefore, some changes in the ratio of required reserves to checkable deposits reflect shifts in the composition of deposits (between checkable and time or savings, and among the categories of financial institutions). We shall discuss later some details and implications of shifts in the required-reserve ratio.

Instead of keeping non-interest-bearing cash, financial institutions prefer to hold assets that bear interest. Since these institutions can shift rapidly in and out of short-term securities or the Federal Funds market, even a moderate interest rate induces them to hold very little reserves above the required amount. Economists use the term, **excess reserves,** for the difference between total and required reserves. Figure 15.2 shows that excess reserves were less than 1% of total reserves throughout the 1970s, when interest rates were high. However, at the lower interest rates that prevailed earlier during the post-World War II period, excess reserves were as much as 5% of the total. Notice also the large holdings of excess reserves from 1933 to 1941. Here, the ratio of excess reserves to the total averaged 37%. This behavior reflects the financial crises of the Great Depression, as well as the extremely low interest rates on safe assets. We shall discuss this period in detail later on.

We should note that excess reserves provide funds that a financial institution can dip into during emergencies. By contrast, required reserves do not serve this purpose. For a given amount of deposits, a depository institution is not permitted to let its reserves fall below the required amount.

---

[3]Before December 1959 (and since 1917), vault cash did not count at all toward satisfying the reserve requirements. But since November 1960 all vault cash counts.

[4]The requirement was only 3% of an institution's checkable deposits up to a total of $31.7 million. For further discussion of the Monetary Control Act, see Robert Auerbach, *Money, Banking and Financial Markets,* 2nd ed., Macmillan, New York, 1985, Chapters 6–8.

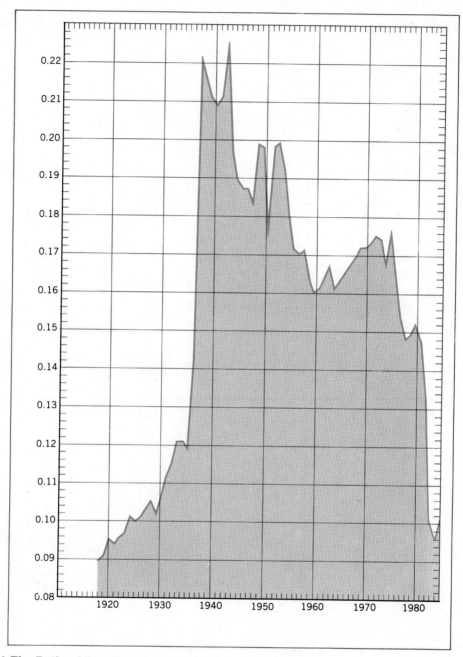

Figure 15.1 The Ratio of Required Reserves to Checkable Deposits

Sources (for Figure 15.1 and subsequent figures): Board of Governors of the Federal Reserve System, *Banking and Monetary Statistics, 1941–1970; Annual Statistical Digest, 1970–79;* and *Federal Reserve Bulletin,* various issues.

Figure 15.2 The Behavior of Excess Reserves

Deposits and Earnings Assets

Suppose that a depository institution attracts an additional $100 of deposits. For concreteness, let's think about a checkable deposit for which the required-reserve ratio is 12%. Then the institution holds $12 out of the extra $100 as required reserves. The rest of the $100 may be divided as the institution chooses between loans and securities (which bear interest) or excess reserves (which do not bear interest). The change in the institution's net earnings equals the interest on the additional earning assets, less the added costs of evaluating and collecting on loans or dealing in securities, less any extra costs of servicing the deposits (if no separate fees are charged), less the interest paid on the new deposits. For the institution to profit from this enterprise, it must be that the interest rate on deposits, call it R^d, is less than that on loans and securities, which we still call R.[5] In particular, the spread, $R - R^d$, must cover at least the following: first, the cost of the funds that the intermediary holds in non-interest-bearing form, second, the transaction costs associated with handling the additional deposits and earnings assets, and third, some return on the capital invested in the business of being an intermediary—that is, some amount of "normal profit." Let's call the total of these items the **costs of intermediation.** Then suppose that we neglect for the moment any governmental regulations that limit interest rates on deposits. In this case, competition among intermediaries would drive the interest rate on deposits high enough so that the net earnings from an extra dollar of deposits covered only the normal profit. That is, the spread, $R - R^d$, would just balance the costs of intermediation.[6]

As an illustration, suppose that the interest rate on earning assets, R, is 10%, and that the reserve requirement is 12% of deposits. Also, suppose that financial institutions hold no excess reserves. Further, assume that transaction costs are 1% of earning assets and 0.5% of deposits. Finally, suppose that normal profit is 1% of deposits (although this profit would actually relate to the amount of invested capital, rather than directly to the volume of deposits). Then an extra $100 of deposits means

- $88 of added earning assets, which yield $8.80 per year in interest (10% of $88),
- $12 of added reserves, which yield zero interest,
- $0.88 of added transaction costs on earning assets (1% of $88),
- $0.50 of added transaction costs on deposits (0.5% of $100), and
- $1.00 more of normal profit.

Before paying interest on the deposits, the net return (after an allowance for normal profit) is $6.42 ($8.80 − $0.88 − $0.50 − $1.00). Hence, an interest rate on deposits, R^d, of 6.4% would drive the net earnings on an extra dollar of deposits down to the normal profit.

Overall, competition among intermediaries tells us the following things about the interest rate paid on deposits, R^d. This rate rises with

- An increase in the interest rate on loans and securities, R (but by less than one-to-one).

---

[5] In practice, interest rates differ on different types of loans and securities. The rates depend on the risks of default and on how costly the assets are to evaluate and collect.

[6] For further discussion, see Ben Klein, "Competitive Interest Payments on Bank Deposits and the Long-Run Demand for Money," *American Economic Review,* December 1974.

- A decrease in the required-reserve ratio, which was 12% in the example
- A decline in the transaction costs associated with handling earning assets and deposits.

Deposit Interest Rates and Financial Intermediation

The amount of deposits that people want to hold—and hence the amount of funds that financial intermediaries have to loan out—depends on the interest rate on deposits, R^d. Deposits become more attractive relative to currency if R^d increases. (Note that the nominal interest rate on currency is fixed at zero.) On the other hand, deposits become less attractive relative to bonds if the spread, $R - R^d$, rises.

Suppose, for example, that the required-reserve ratio declines as it did from 1980 to 1984 (see Figure 15.1). For a given value of R, our analysis of competition among financial intermediaries predicts that the deposit interest rate, R^d, would rise. Therefore, households would hold more deposits at the expense of currency and bonds. The increase in deposits means that financial intermediaries would expand their holdings of assets. Thus overall, we find that a lower reserve requirement leads first, to more of $M1$ held as deposits rather than currency, and second, to more financial intermediation.

As another example, assume that the interest rate R increases, perhaps because of an increase in expected inflation. We noted before that the deposit rate, R^d, would rise but by less than the increase in R. Therefore, the higher spread, $R - R^d$, induces households to hold less deposits and more bonds. On the other hand, the rise in R^d motivates people to hold less currency and more deposits. Overall, we find that the demand for currency declines, but the net effect on the demand for deposits is uncertain. (The empirical evidence shows that checkable deposits—but not necessarily other kinds of deposits—fall when interest rates rise.) Therefore—at least when deposit interest rates are free to adjust (see below)—the overall effect of higher interest rates on the amount of financial intermediation is uncertain.

Regulation of Interest Rates on Deposits

Since the 1930s, the federal government has regulated the interest rates that banks and other financial intermediaries can pay on deposits. With the Banking Acts of 1933 and 1935, the government prohibited interest payments on demand deposits. This restriction stayed in force until the middle and late 1970s, when interest-bearing checking accounts began to develop. These mainly took the form of negotiable-order-of-withdrawal (or NOW) accounts. Of course, a negotiable-order-of-withdrawal is just another name for a check. These types of accounts, which bear interest, began in New England in the mid 1970s, but became available nationwide with the Monetary Control Act of 1980.

The Federal Reserve has limited interest rates on time deposits through its **Regulation Q.** Figure 15.3 shows how the legal limit for the rate on short

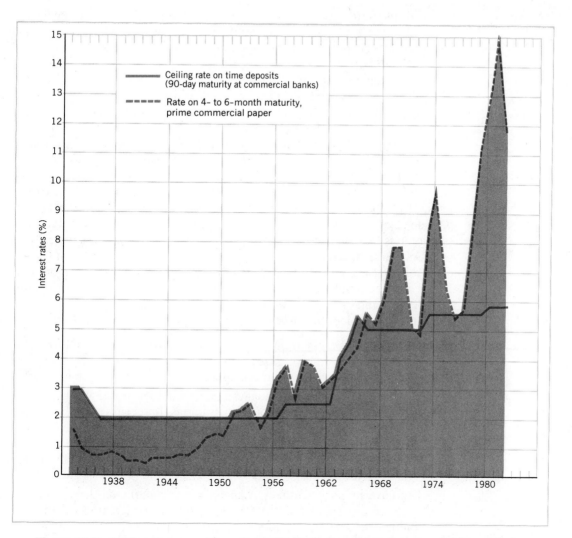

Figure 15.3 **Ceiling Rates on Time Deposits as Compared to Commercial Paper Rates, 1933—82**

maturity time deposits of commercial banks compared with an open-market interest rate, which we measure as the rate on 4- to 6-month prime commercial paper. The figure suggests that the ceiling rates on time deposits were high enough not to be binding at least until the 1950s. But the rate on commercial paper rose above this ceiling in the middle and late 1950s, in the late 1960s, and in much of the 1970s. In particular, for 1979–82, the gap exceeded 5 percentage points. So in these periods—and especially in 1979–82—the government's restrictions constrained the interest rates that banks and some other financial institutions could offer to their depositors. However, effective October 1983, the government removed the restrictions on the interest rates that institutions could pay on most time deposits. (The final restrictions lapsed at the end of 1985.)

What happens when the legal limit on deposits is below the interest rate that would otherwise be paid? One point is that the limits apply only to explicit interest. Institutions often compete for profitable deposits by providing services at below cost. The services that people receive by holding deposits amount to implicit interest, which substitutes for the explicit interest that the government prohibits. But, despite the possibilities for evading restrictions on interest rates, we should not conclude that legal restrictions are irrelevant. Basically, the implicit methods of paying interest tend to be less efficient than the explicit ones. That is because there are limits to the services that banks can conveniently provide as close substitutes for explicit interest. (However, an offsetting consideration is that explicit interest is taxable, whereas free services typically are not.) As market interest rates rose since the 1950s, the ceiling rates on deposits made it increasingly difficult for the regulated institutions to compete for funds. In this case the regulation of interest payments meant that the deposit interest rate, R^d, offered by these intermediaries was lower than otherwise. Our previous analysis of deposit interest rates predicts some of the outcomes:

- People moved away from deposits and toward direct holding of assets such as bonds and mortgages. This process, which is the reverse of intermediation, is called **disintermediation.**
- New types of unregulated financial intermediaries arose, which attracted funds away from banks and other institutions. In recent years, the primary example was money-market funds, whose assets grew from near zero in 1977 to over $200 billion by the end of 1982 (and with little net change from 1982 to 1985). The money-market funds hold various securities and offer deposit-like instruments to their customers.
- The government eventually changed its regulations on deposit interest rates, so that banks and other depository intermediaries could again compete effectively for funds. However, according to the regulations established through 1985, there are two remaining distinctions between money-market funds and other depository institutions. First, there are no reserve requirements on the money-market funds. But second, unlike the deposits at banks and some other intermediaries, the shares in money-market funds are not insured by the federal government.

Borrowing from the Federal Reserve

From the start of the Federal Reserve System in 1914 until 1980, banks that were members of the Federal Reserve System could borrow short-term funds at the discount rate from a Federal Reserve bank. With the Monetary Control

Act of 1980, all depository institutions with checkable deposits can borrow from the Fed.

Borrowing from the Federal Reserve can be advantageous if the Fed's discount rate is below the rates at which banks can otherwise borrow. However, such borrowing may not always be desirable even if the discount rate is relatively low. That is because first, the Fed examines banks more carefully when they borrow frequently at the discount window, and second, the Fed can refuse to lend to banks that ask "too often." In any case the lower the discount rate, relative to market interest rates, the greater the incentive for banks to borrow from the Fed.

Figure 15.4 shows the ratio of borrowings from the Fed to checkable deposits from 1918 to 1985. Notice that these borrowings were important during World War I and through the 1920s. Borrowings peaked at 13% of checkable deposits in 1920,[7] and still amounted to 4% of these deposits in 1929, 3% in 1932, and 2% in 1933. However, borrowings fell to near zero for 1935–43. During the post-World War II period, some borrowing occurred, but the ratio to checkable deposits never exceeded 1%. For these years, the peaks in the ratio occurred in 1974 and 1984. For 1974, the average amount borrowed of $2.0 billion constituted about 1% of checkable deposits. Most of these loans were to the Franklin National Bank of Long Island, which was a large bank that engaged in questionable speculations and subsequently failed. For 1984, the average borrowing of $3.7 billion was again about 1% of checkable deposits. Most of these loans went to the Continental Illinois National Bank (which has a beautiful marble building in Chicago).

Figure 15.5 shows how the annual average discount rate at the New York Fed compares to the interest rate on 4- to 6-month maturity prime commercial paper.[8] (The discount rates at the Federal Reserve banks in different cities stay very close to each other.) Although the two interest rates shown in Figure 15.5 tended to move together, the discount rate was typically lower than the commercial paper rate since World War II. Therefore, in these years the loans from the Fed usually involved a subsidy to the borrower. In some years— 1966–67, 1969–70, 1973–74, 1981, and 1984—the discount rate was more than a full percentage point below the commercial paper rate. Looking at the earlier years, we see that the discount rate exceeded the commercial paper rate from 1932 to 1946, but was lower than the commercial paper rate during the 1920s and especially for 1918–20.

---

[7]The borrowings of member banks actually exceeded their total reserves for 1919–21. For example, the average amount borrowed during 1920 was $2.5 billion, while the average amount of reserves was $1.8 billion. Hence, the banks' "unborrowed reserves" (total reserves less borrowings) were negative at this time.

[8]The comparison is similar if we look at the federal funds rate. But these data are available only since 1954.

Figure 15.4 Borrowings from the Federal Reserve as a Ratio to Checkable Deposits

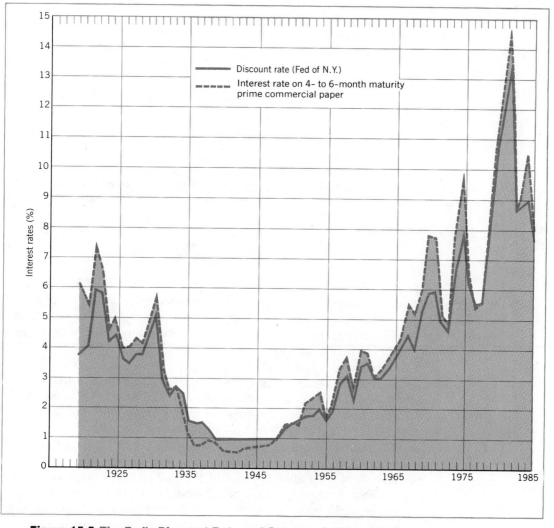

Figure 15.5 The Fed's Discount Rate and Commercial Paper Rates

The Federal Reserve System

Since 1914 the Federal Reserve System has functioned as the central bank in the United States. There are 12 regional Federal Reserve banks, each of which was set up as a separate, quasi-private corporation. In the early days of the system, the 12 presidents of the regional banks served on the Governors' Conference, which had substantial influence over the Fed's policies. However, following the Great Depression and the Banking Act of 1935, the Governors' Conference was abolished and the Fed's power was centralized in Washington,

**Table 15.2 Balance Sheet of All Federal Reserve Banks
(December 31, 1984) (amounts in billions of dollars)**

Assets		Liabilities and Capital Account	
Gold account	11.1	Federal Reserve notes (currency)	168.3
Loans to depository institutions	3.6	Deposits of depository institutions	21.8
U.S. government and agency		U.S. Treasury deposits	5.3
securities	169.7	Other deposits and liabilities	3.0
Other assets[a]	17.3	Paid-in capital and surplus	3.3
Total	201.7	Total	201.7

[a]Consists of special drawing rights at the International Monetary Fund ($4.6 billion), accounts due from the Federal Deposit Insurance Corporation (FDIC) ($3.9 billion), assets denominated in foreign currency ($3.6 billion), coin ($0.4 billion), accrued interest ($2.5 billion), physical capital ($0.8 billion), and some other items.

Source: U.S. Board of Governors of the Federal Reserve System, *Annual Report,* 1984, pp. 218–19.

D.C. Since 1935 the main authority has resided with the **Board of Governors of the Federal Reserve System.** The seven members of this board are appointed by the President (and confirmed by the Senate) for staggered 14-year terms. The board is often dominated by its chairman—currently Paul Volcker—who is appointed by the President for a 4-year term.

The Fed carries out its open-market operations—purchases or sales of government securities in the open-market—through the **Federal Open Market Committee** (or **FOMC**). This important committee consists of the seven members of the Board of Governors plus five presidents of the regional banks (including the president of the New York bank and rotating membership among the other 11 banks). We shall discuss the FOMC when we deal later with open-market operations.

We have already mentioned some of the Fed's activities, which include the setting of reserve requirements, the regulation of interest rates on deposits, and the lending to financial institutions at the discount window.[9] Now we want to focus on the Fed's instruments for controlling the quantity of money. We begin by looking at the balance sheet of the Federal Reserve System.

Table 15.2 shows the balance sheet at the end of 1984. The main items on the asset side are the following:

- Gold account of $11.1 billion (carried at the official price of $42.22 per ounce). The Fed holds this gold on behalf of the U.S. Treasury. In past years, when the United States was on the gold standard, variations in the quantity of gold resulted mainly from dealings with foreign central

[9]For discussions of the Federal Reserve System and its policy instruments, see Robert Auerbach, *Money, Banking and Financial Markets,* Macmillan, 2nd ed., New York, 1985, Chapters 14–16; and Milton Friedman, *A Program for Monetary Stability,* Fordham University Press, New York, 1960, Chapter 2.

banks. Now there are changes if the Treasury auctions off gold or if there are adjustments in the official price of gold. (These changes in price occurred in 1933 and a few times in the 1970s.)

- Loans to Depository Institutions of $3.6 billion. These are borrowings of depository intermediaries at the discount rate, which we mentioned before.
- U.S. Government and Agency Securities of $169.7 billion. As the balance sheet makes clear, the bulk of the Fed's assets are held in this form.

The sum of loans to depository institutions, U.S. government and agency securities, and some miscellaneous assets is called **Federal Reserve credit.** This amount represents the total of the Fed's claims on the government and the private sector. Note that the great bulk of Federal Reserve credit takes the form of U.S. government securities. That is, unlike the central banks of many countries, the Fed engages in little direct lending to the private sector.

On the liability side of the Fed's ledger, we have the following main items:

- Federal Reserve Notes (currency) of $168.3 billion. At present these notes are the only form of currency outstanding. But at earlier dates, currency was issued by the U.S. Treasury and—even earlier—as notes from private banks.
- Deposits of Depository Institutions of $21.8 billion. These are the non-interest-bearing reserves of depository intermediaries, which we mentioned before.
- U.S. Treasury deposits of $5.3 billion. Essentially, these deposits are the federal government's checking account, which is held at the Federal Reserve.

The total of federal reserve notes and deposits of depository institutions ($190.1 billion) is called the **monetary base** or **high-powered money** (or sometimes $M0$). This sum represents the total of the Fed's monetary liabilities (aside from those held by the U.S. Treasury or as foreign deposits). Note that, in 1984, about 89% of the monetary base took the form of currency, while only 11% consisted of deposits of depository institutions.

Figure 15.6 shows how the monetary base evolved from 1918 to 1985. For recent years, the definition of the base is the one given above. But at earlier times it included also private holdings of monetary gold (until 1933), as well as paper currency issued by the U.S. Treasury.

Control of the Monetary Base
Open-Market Operations

When the Federal Reserve began operations in 1914, open-market operations were not viewed as an element of monetary policy. The plan was instead to focus on loans through the discount window, which we discuss below. However,

Figure 15.6 The Monetary Base

Source: Milton Friedman and Anna J. Schwartz, *A Monetary History of the United States, 1867–1960,* Princeton University Press, Princeton, New Jersey, Table B-3; and the sources listed in Figure 15.1.

especially since the 1930s, open-market operations have become the principal instrument for controlling the monetary base.

Since 1935, decisions on open-market operations have been made by the Federal Open Market Committee (FOMC), which we mentioned earlier. The directives of this committee are carried out by the trading desk of the New York Federal Reserve Bank. Although the directives to the trading desk are explicit in terms of quantities of government bonds to buy or sell, the FOMC's reports on its policy stance are often vague. Typically, these reports mention the "condition of the market" or targets for the interest rate on Federal Funds. But it is unclear how to relate these targets to the volume of open-market operations, which is what the FOMC actually determines.

For awhile in the early 1980s, the targets of Federal Reserve policy were expressed more in terms of monetary aggregates, such as M1 or M2, and less in terms of interest rates. As we shall see later, we can relate the behavior of monetary aggregates to changes in the monetary base and hence to open-market operations. Therefore, it would be meaningful to guide open-market operations by a target for a specified monetary aggregate. But there is not much evidence that the Fedral Reserve has actually paid much attention to its announced targets (which it began to release in 1978 at the insistence of Congress).

Finally, it is interesting to note that the FOMC delays for 30–60 days the publication of its statements on open-market policy. (These appear eventually in the *Federal Reserve Bulletin*.) The Fed believes that this secrecy helps it to maintain "orderly" securities markets. Anybody who can explain this reasoning deserves at least an A in the course![10]

Let's consider now how open-market operations affect the monetary base. In the case of an open-market purchase, the Fed writes a check to buy, say $1 million of U.S. government securities. Suppose that the seller of the bonds is a commercial bank, which we call People's Bank. (We would end up with the same results if the seller were a household or, more likely, a large corporation.) Then the Fed credits this bank with $1 million more of reserves in the form of book-entry deposits at the Fed. At this point, the balance sheets of the Fed and People's Bank change as shown in Table 15.3. Notice that the Fed has $1 million more in assets in the form of government bonds. This amount balances the extra $1 million of liabilities, which show up as more deposits of depository institutions (in this case of People's Bank). Correspondingly, People's Bank has $1 million more in assets in the form of deposits held at the Fed, but $1 million less of government bonds, which are a part of the bank's portfolio of loans and securities.

The balance sheets shown in Table 15.3 are not the end of the story,

---

[10]The FOMC's secrecy was challenged under the Freedom-of-Information Act. The Supreme Court finally decided in favor of the FOMC. For a discussion, including the FOMC's defense of secrecy, see Marvin Goodfriend, "Monetary Mystique: Secrecy and Central Banking," *Journal of Monetary Economics,* January 1986.

Table 15.3 **Effects on the Balance Sheets of the Fed and Depository Institutions from an Open-Market Purchase of Government Bonds**

Assets	Liabilities
Federal Reserve	
U.S. Government securities: + $1 million	Deposits of depository institutions: + $1 million
People's Bank	
Loans and securities: − $1 million Deposits at Fed: + $1 million	

because People's Bank probably does not want to hold $1 million more of non-interest-bearing reserves at the Fed. But let's hold off on this matter for now in order to focus on the behavior of the monetary base. The open-market purchase of securities shown in Table 15.3 raises the monetary base by $1 million, which shows up initially as an extra $1 million in reserves held by depository institutions at the Fed. Note also that an open-market sale of securities would just reverse the process. If the Fed sells $1 million of U.S. government bonds, then the monetary base declines by $1 million.

In the United States, open-market operations involve government bonds, rather than private bonds, mortgages, shares in General Motors, and so on. That is because the Fed does not hold these types of private obligations. With respect to controlling the monetary base, it would make no difference if the Fed dealt instead in private securities. In fact, it would make little difference all together (except perhaps on political grounds) if the Fed switched from holdings of the public debt to holdings of private bonds. If this switch were made, then the private sector would end up holding more of the public debt, but would owe correspondingly more to the Fed. The Fed would have more claims on the private sector, but less on the U.S. Treasury. Overall, there would be no changes in the net positions of the private sector, the Federal Reserve, or the U.S. Treasury.

Loans to Depository Institutions

The Fed can also control the monetary base by varying the quantity of loans to depository institutions. Here, the Fed can change either the discount rate or other aspects of its lending policies to induce depository institutions to borrow more or less at the discount window. Suppose, for example, that People's Bank decides to borrow an additional $1 million from the Fed. Then the Fed records a loan of $1 million to People's Bank, and also credits this bank with an extra $1 million of deposits. If People's Bank just holds these deposits at the Fed (perhaps because if would otherwise have fallen short of its reserve requirement), then the balance sheet of the Fed and People's Bank change as shown in Table 15.4.

Table 15.4 **Effects on the Balance Sheets of the Fed and Depository Institutions from Fed Lending at the Discount Window**

Assets	Liabilities
Federal Reserve	
Loans to depository institutions: +$1 million	Deposits of depository institutions: +$1 million
People's Bank	
Deposits at Fed: +$1 million	Borrowing from Fed: +$1 million

Notice that the borrowings show up as $1 million more in loans to depository institutions on the asset side of the Fed's books. Simultaneously, on the liability side, there is an increase by $1 million in the deposits of depository institutions. There are corresponding changes on the books of People's Bank. The main point is that, as before, the monetary base rises by $1 million.

It is important to recognize that an increase in borrowings by depository institutions at the discount window is essentially the same as an open-market purchase of securities by the Fed. In both cases the monetary base increases. The only difference is that in one case (the open-market purchase) the Fed ends up holding more U.S. government bonds, while in the other (lending at the discount window) the Fed ends up with more loans to depository institutions.[11] Correspondingly, People's Bank ends up holding less government bonds in the first case, and more debt to the Fed in the second. Overall, the difference amounts to a shift from the Fed's holding U.S. government bonds to the Fed's holding obligations on a private bank. But as mentioned before, these types of changes have no major consequences. The only significant difference concerns the subsidy that the Fed provides to depository institutions, because the discount rate is typically set below the competitive interest rate.

Economists often say that a shift in the discount rate is significant not for its direct impact on borrowings, but rather as an announcement of the Fed's intentions. Over the longer term, the Fed moves the discount rate to match changes in market interest rates (see Figure 15.5). Hence, most of the movements in the discount rate are reactions to changes in the economy, rather than vice versa. But the timing and sometimes the amount of a shift in the discount rate are at the Fed's discretion. It is possible that some of these changes are a useful signal about the future behavior of the monetary base or of other policy instruments, such as the regulation of interest rates on deposits. However, no one has yet shown that changes in the discount rate can actually help to predict the future quantity of the monetary base or other economic

---

[11]Moreover, the depository institutions typically provide U.S. government securities as collateral for their borrowings at the Fed.

variables. So the suggestion that shifts in the discount rate have an "announcement effect" amounts to an interesting idea, which has not been proven.

Many economists think that the Fed should stop subsidizing borrowers—that is, it should set the discount rate at a penalty level above market interest rates. Of course, if the discount rate were actually a penalty rate, it would have to be above the rate at which an individual institution could otherwise borrow. For example, for a risky bank like Franklin National in 1974 or Continental Illinois in 1984, the penalty rate would be well above the interest rate on commercial paper. But then, no institution would ever borrow from the Fed. So the suggestion for a penalty discount rate amounts to a proposal for closing the discount window.

From the standpoint of controlling the monetary base, the existence of the discount window adds nothing to open-market operations. Thus, the argument for the Fed's lending to depository institutions comes down to the desirability of subsidizing selected financial institutions—presumably, mainly institutions that are in trouble. So far, no one has come up with good arguments to justify this policy.

The Monetary Base and Monetary Aggregates

Thus far, our discussion shows how the Fed can control the monetary base. But we already mentioned that the Fed might adjust the base to achieve a target value for a monetary aggregate, such as M1 or M2. Recall that these aggregates add various categories of deposits to the amount of currency held by the public. Therefore, to study the relation between the monetary base and monetary aggregates, we have to understand the behavior of deposits.

Let's return to the case shown in Table 15.3, where the open-market purchase of government bonds raised the monetary base by $1 million. (For the analysis in this section, we would get the same results if the change in the base reflected more lending at the discount window, as shown in Table 15.4.) Instead of thinking of a single bank, we consider now the effects on financial intermediaries as a whole. Thus, Table 15.5 shows that in step 1 these intermediaries have $1 million more of deposits at the Fed and $1 million less of loans and securities.

Suppose that the extra $1 million of deposits at the Fed are excess reserves, which the financial intermediaries do not wish to hold. (We assume that they also do not wish to pay off borrowings from the Fed.) Rather, these institutions place these funds into earning assets. To be concrete, we assume that they make an additional $1 million of loans to households. However, the results would be the same if the intermediaries bought more securities. In any event, the recipients of the loans have an extra $1 million, which we suppose that they hold initially as deposits at a financial intermediary. Thus the balance sheet of these intermediaries changes as shown in step 2 of Table 15.5. On the asset side there is an additional $1 million of loans and securities, which

Table 15.5 Effect of Open-Market Purchases of Bonds on the Financial System

	Financial Intermediaries (FI'S)		Households		The Fed	
	Assets	Liabilities	Assets	Liabilities	Assets	Liabilities
Step 1	Loans and securities: −$1 million Deposits at Fed: +$1 million				U.S. Govt. Bonds: +$1 million	Deposits of FI's: +$1 million
Step 2	Loans and securities: +$1 million	Customer deposits: +$1 million	Deposits at FI's: +$1 million	Loans from FI's: +$1 million		
Step 3	Loans and securities: +$880,000	Customer deposits: +$880,000	Deposits at FI's: +$880,000	Loans from FI's: +$880,000		

offsets the initial decline by this amount. On the liability side there is an added $1 million of customer deposits.

The recipients of the loan probably do not want to hold an extra $1 million of deposits. But as they spend these funds they are transferred to the accounts of others. Ultimately, people are either induced[12] to hold an extra $1 million of deposits at financial intermediaries, or else people are motivated to redeem all or part of this $1 million for currency (which the intermediaries stand ready to provide to depositors). For the moment, suppose that we forget about this important possibility of moving into currency. Then we eventually reach the situation shown as step 2 in Table 15.5.

The extra $1 million in customer deposits raises the required reserves of the financial intermediaries. For illustrative purposes, we use a reserve ratio of 12%, which applies currently to most checkable deposits. (But it is important to note that whether these deposits are checkable does not affect the essence of the subsequent analysis.) Thus, required reserves rise by $120,000. But then the financial institutions still have $880,000 ($1 million less the $120,000) of excess reserves. Therefore, they are again motivated to place these funds into earning assets, which we assume take the form of loans. When people are motivated to hold these additional funds as deposits we arrive at step 3 in Table 15.5. Here, the intermediaries' loans and securities and deposits each rise by another $880,000.

If we continue to work through this process, we find that the deposits held

---

[12]As we show in the following section, the inducement derives in the present case from a higher price level.

Figure 15.7 The Ratio of the Public's Currency to Checkable Deposits

at financial institutions rise by a large multiple of the expansion in the monetary base. Specifically, the deposits increase eventually by the amount, $1 million $\cdot$ (1/0.12) = $8.33 million. At this point, the intermediaries' required reserves are up by 0.12 $\cdot$ $8.33 million = $1 million—that is, the additional base money is all held as required reserves.

An important amendment to this **multiple expansion of deposits** concerns the household's demand for currency. Figure 15.7 shows the ratio of currency to checkable deposits since 1918. For 1985, the ratio was 0.39. Using the value 0.4 for this ratio, and assuming no changes in the relative attractiveness of currency and deposits, we predict that people will hold an additional 40 cents of currency along with each extra dollar of deposits.

In Table 15.6 we modify the analysis to take account of currency. Now, with an extra $1 million of funds in step 2a, the public is eventually motivated to hold (approximately) $700,000 more in deposits and $300,000 more in currency (assuming that the ratio of currency to deposits remains at 0.4). As the public redeems deposits to obtain this extra currency, the financial intermediaries must get this currency by running down their deposits at the Fed. (Equivalently, the intermediaries could reduce their vault cash.) Thus, in step 2a, the liabilities of financial institutions show $700,000 more in customer

Table 15.6 Effect of Open-Market Purchases of Bonds on the Financial System Including the Responses of Currency

	Financial Intermediaries (FI's)		Households		The Fed	
	Assets	Liabilities	Assets	Liabilities	Assets	Liabilities
Step 1a	Loans and securities: −$1 million Deposits at Fed: +$1 million				U.S. Govt. bonds: +$1 million	Deposits of FI's: +$1 million
Step 2a	Loans and securities: +$1 million Deposits at Fed: −$300,000	Customer deposits: +$700,000	Deposits at FI's: +$700,00 Currency: +$300,000	Loans from FI's: +$1 million		Deposits of FI's: −$300,000 Currency: +$300,000
Step 3a	Loans and securities +$616,000 Deposits at Fed: −$176,000	Customer deposits: +$440,000	Deposits at FI's: +$440,000 Currency: +$176,000	Loans from FI's: +$616,000		Deposits of FI's: −$176,000 Currency: +$176,000

deposits, while their assets show $300,000 less in deposits at the Fed. Notice that required reserves are now up by $84,000 (0.12 · $700,000 of deposits), rather than the $120,000 in the previous step 2. But actual reserves are higher by only $700,000, rather than the previous $1 million. Thus, excess reserves are higher by $616,000 ($700,000 less $84,000), instead of the previous $800,000 ($1 million less $120,000). The "leakage" of funds into currency means that the financial intermediaries end up with less excess reserves than otherwise.

For the Fed, the additional currency outstanding of $300,000 corresponds to an equivalent reduction in the book-entry deposits of financial institutions. As shown in step 2a of Table 15.6, there is no change in the monetary base, which consists of currency plus the deposits of the financial institutions at the Fed. Thus, the monetary base remains higher by $1 million.

The rest of the analysis proceeds as before, except that some funds leak out to currency at each stage. We can find the ultimate position from the following set of equations, where the symbol Δ represents the change in the associated variable:

$$\Delta(\text{monetary base}) \quad = \Delta(\text{required reserves}) + \Delta(\text{currency}) = \$1 \text{ million}$$
$$\Delta(\text{required reserves}) = 0.12 \cdot \Delta(\text{deposits})$$
$$\Delta(\text{currency}) \quad\quad = 0.4 \cdot \Delta(\text{deposits})$$

Substituting the second and third conditions into the first leads to

$$0.12 \cdot \Delta(\text{deposits}) + 0.4 \cdot \Delta(\text{deposits}) = \$1 \text{ million}$$

Solving for the change in deposits, we get the results

$$\Delta(\text{deposits}) \quad\quad = \$1 \text{ million}/0.52 = \$1,920,000$$
$$\Delta(\text{currency}) \quad\quad = 0.4 \cdot \Delta(\text{deposits}) = \$770,000$$
$$\Delta(\text{required reserves}) = 0.12 \cdot \Delta(\text{deposits}) = \$230,000$$

Thus, the incorporation of currency has a dramatic effect on the results—instead of rising by $8.33 million, the deposits held at financial intermediaries end up increasing by only $1.92 million. Generally, the ultimate expansion of deposits is larger the smaller is the ratio of reserves to deposits (fixed at 0.12 above) and the smaller is the ratio of currency to deposits (0.4 above).

Given the changes in deposits and currency, we can calculate how an open-market operation affects various monetary aggregates. If we limit attention to checkable deposits (with a required-reserve ratio of 0.12), then the change in M1 is the sum of the changes in deposits and currency, or $2,690,000 above. Since an increase by $1,000,000 in high-powered money leads to an expansion by $2,690,000 in M1, we can say that the **money multiplier** (the ratio of M1 to the base) is 2.69. Generally, the money multiplier is higher the lower the ratios of reserves and currency to deposits.

Figure 15.8 The Ratio of *M*1 to the Monetary Base (the Money Multiplier)

Figure 15.8 shows the behavior of the money multiplier from 1918 to 1985. This multiplier has been relatively stable since World War II, with a range of 2.4 to 2.9. However, this stability reflects some long-term changes that happened to cancel. First, as shown in Figures 15.1 and 15.2, the ratios of required and excess reserves to checkable deposits declined from a total of 0.22 in 1950 to 0.10 in 1985. This change tended to raise the money multiplier. But second, as shown in Figure 15.7, the ratio of currency to checkable deposits rose from 0.26 in 1960 to 0.39 in 1985.[13] This factor tended to lower the money multiplier.

The other striking feature of Figure 15.8 is the dramatic drop in the money multiplier from 3.9 in 1930 to 1.9 in 1940. This change reflected increases in the ratios of reserves and currency to checkable deposits. We shall discuss the details of these changes later on.

Effects of Federal Reserve Actions

The Neutrality of Open-Market Operations

In the previous chapter we found that open-market operations were neutral. In particular, a one-time shift in the monetary base led only to proportional responses in the price level and other nominal variables (except for the quantity of public debt).

This result does not change when we introduce financial intermediation. But we have to include as nominal variables the dollar quantities of the various deposits and reserves. Then we find that these nominal magnitudes rise along with the other nominal variables in proportion to the change in the monetary base. An open-market operation leaves unchanged the real quantities of deposits and reserves, the ratio of deposits to currency, the ratio of reserves to deposits, and so on.

Among the variables that do not change when there is a one-time open-market operation are the nominal interest rate on earning assets, R, and the (explicit or implicit) nominal interest rate, R^d, paid on customer deposits by financial intermediaries. Since these interest rates are unchanged, households would not alter their desired holdings of currency and deposits in real terms. Thus, the results are consistent with the unchanged real quantities of currency and deposits, which we mentioned above.

The financial intermediaries also end up in the same real position as before the open-market operation. Specifically, there are no changes in the intermediaries' real quantities of deposits, reserves, and loans and securities. If these institutions held reserves initially only because of requirements—say, 12% of deposits—then the final holdings of reserves again equal the required amount.

---

[13]The following forces probably underlie this change. First, various financial innovations reduced the real demand for checkable deposits by more than they reduced the real demand for currency. Second, increases in tax rates and criminal activity motivated people to use more currency to conceal their transactions from governments. Third, there may be relatively more U.S. currency held abroad than there used to be.

The Amount of Financial Intermediation

Financial intermediation is important because it facilitates the matching of borrowers and lenders,[14] as well as the carrying out of transactions. The reflection of this process is the real quantity of deposits and the real quantity of loans and securities held by financial intermediaries. We can think of these real quantities as a measure of the amount of financial intermediation in an economy.

Generally, the amount of financial intermediation that occurs depends on the benefits and costs. As mentioned before, the benefits relate to the efficient evaluation of loans, the diversification of assets by risk and maturity, and the convenience of deposits. The costs include the expenses of servicing deposits and loans, the return to capital in the intermediary business, reserve requirements, and the costs of evading restrictions for paying interest on deposits. If these costs of intermediation rise, then we predict that there would be less intermediation.

As an example, suppose that the Fed increases reserve requirements. Since financial intermediaries must hold more non-interest-bearing reserves for each dollar of deposits, these institutions end up paying a lower interest rate, R^d, on deposits. Consequently, households are motivated to switch out of deposits and into either currency or direct holding of earning assets. Ultimately, we find that the real quantity of deposits and the real amount of loans and securities held by financial intermediaries decrease. That is, there is less financial intermediation in the economy. Note that we would reach the same conclusion if, instead of assuming an increase in reserve requirements, we postulated a higher cost for financial intermediaries to service deposits or police loans. Again, we would end up with less financial intermediation.

When there is less financial intemediation it becomes harder for resources to flow toward investors whose projects have the greatest marginal products or toward consumers who have the greatest desires to consume now rather than later. On both counts, the economy operates less efficiently. Typically, this loss in efficiency shows up as smaller aggregates of the capital stock and output. But the principal conclusion is that less financial intermediation means a poorer match of resources to their ultimate uses.

To some extent, the costs of intermediation reflect the underlying expenses of policing borrowers and servicing deposits. We can think of these elements as part of the technology or production function that generates intermediating services. Then the amount of intermediation that results tends to be optimal, given this technology. But as already noted, reserve requirements, government regulations of interest rates on deposits, and so on, artificially raise the cost of intermediation. More restrictive policies—such as higher reserve require-

---

[14]Although we focus on financial institutions in this chapter, there are other forms of intermediaries that assist in the efficient channeling of credit. A prime example is the publicly held corporation.

ments—tend to discourage intermediation, which leads to a less efficient allocation of resources. Often, the reduction in intermediation shows up as smaller levels of the capital stock and output. But in any case, these types of government policies are surely nonneutral.[15]

Financial Intermediation and the Price Level

The degree of financial intermediation also interacts with the determination of the price level. To see how this works, let's use our analysis of price level determination from previous chapters. We now identify money with the monetary base—that is, as the sum of currency in circulation plus the reserves held by financial institutions at the Fed. Suppose that the Fed controls the dollar quantity of base money, M, through open-market operations, as discussed above. Then the process of financial intermediation influences the price level because it affects the real demand for base money, M^d/P. For a given dollar quantity of base money, anything that raises the real demand for base money leads to a fall in the price level. Note that this effect works just like the various increases in the real demand for money that we considered in previous chapters.

As an example, suppose again that the Fed raises the required-reserve ratio on deposits. For a given quantity of deposits there is an increase in the demand for reserves by depository institutions. Hence, on this count, there is an increase in the real demand for the monetary base.

There are some additional effects because, as noted before, the higher reserve ratio tends to reduce the interest rate paid on deposits, which makes them less attractive to households. To the extent that households shift out of deposits and into currency, there is a further increase in the real demand for the monetary base. (That is because the demand for base money varies one-to-one with the demand for currency, but varies only fractionally with the amount of deposits.) But to the extent that people move away from deposits and into direct holdings of earnings assets, the real demand for base money tends to decline. (That is because the reduction in deposits reduces the real demand for reserves by financial institutions.) Thus, the shifting of households' assets among deposits, currency, and earning assets has an ambiguous overall effect on the real demand for the monetary base.[16]

Because of the direct positive effect on the demand for reserves, we can be pretty sure that the overall effect of an increase in the required-reserve ratio is to raise the real demand for base money. Therefore, for a given nominal

---

[15]For the argument that the financial industry should be fully deregulated, see Fischer Black, "Banking and Interest Rates in a World without Money," *Journal of Bank Research,* Autumn 1970; and Eugene Fama, "Financial Intermediation and Price Level Control," *Journal of Monetary Economics,* July 1983.

[16]For further discussion of these types of effects, see James Tobin, "A General Equilibrium Approach to Monetary Theory," and "Deposit Interest Ceilings as a Monetary Control," in James Tobin, *Essays in Economics,* Vol. 1, *Macroeconomics,* Markham, Chicago, 1971.

quantity of base money, the rise in the real demand for base money means that the price level falls.

Historically, the main examples of large short-term variations in the real demand for base money involve banking panics and an experiment with changes in reserve requirements in 1936–37. Therefore, we now consider some details of these episodes.

Banking Panics

Banks and other financial intermediaries promise to convert their demand deposits into currency immediately at face value. Typically, these institutions also extend this instantaneous conversion privilege to savings deposits, for which some notice of withdrawal (usually 30 days) can legally be required. However, intermediaries do not hold nearly enough cash or liquid securities to allow for the simultaneous conversion of all deposits into currency at face value.[17] Even if the underlying loans and securities are sound, financial institutions can get into trouble if too many customers want their cash at the same time. If people become concerned about a bank's ability to convert its deposits into currency at face value, then each individual has an incentive to get into line first to cash in. This incentive is especially great when the deposits are not insured by the government, as was the case in the United States until 1934. When many people attempt to cash in their deposits simultaneously, there is a "run on the bank." Sometimes a bank responds by temporarily "suspending" the privilege of converting demand deposits into currency. When this happens simultaneously at many banks or other financial institutions, we say that a **banking panic** occurs.

The hallmark of a banking panic is a sudden increase in the demand for currency, rather than deposits. As a response, banks and other intermediaries tend to increase their demands for excess reserves and other liquid assets in order to meet their customers' possible demands for cash. Overall, the banking panic leads to increases in the real demand for base money—partly in the form of the public's currency and partly as reserves of financial institutions. Hence, from our previous analysis, a banking panic has two types of effects. First, it makes financial intermediation more difficult, which has adverse consequences for the efficient allocation of resources. Specifically, real output and investment are likely to decline. Then second, unless there is substantial increase in the nominal quantity of base money, the sharp increase in the real demand for base money puts strong downward pressure on the price level.

Banking panics occurred fairly often in the United States before the Federal Reserve began operations in 1914. There were 12 episodes between 1800 and 1914 that are generally called banking panics. For the period after the

---

[17]By "liquid," we mean that little cost attaches to the quick sale of an asset. Thus, government bonds are liquid, but real estate is relatively illiquid. Loans that are costly to evaluate—such as those to local businesses and consumers—may also be illiquid.

Civil War, where better data are available, the most severe crises were those in 1873, 1893, and 1907. Typically, the panics exhibited increases in the ratios of the public's currency and banks' excess reserves to deposits. They also tended to show decreases in prices and in real economic activity. However, it is hard to sort out the independent influence of the banking panics on output and other real variables. That is because, under the monetary system that was in place before the establishment of the Federal Reserve, bad economic conditions tended automatically to generate financial crises.[18] Economists think that these crises also made real economic conditions worse, but it is not easy to prove this through statistical analysis.

A major reason for the creation of the Federal Reserve was the desire to avoid banking panics. The initial idea was that the Fed would serve as the **lender of last resort** through the operation of its discount window. Especially when a financial crisis threatened, the Fed would lend liberally to member institutions at the discount rate, which would be set below market interest rates. Thereby, the Fed would provide the extra reserves that banks desired. In fact, this process of direct lending by the Fed was important during World War I and in the 1920s, but has since become less significant.

During the 1920s, the Fed was successful in averting banking panics. In particular, it is likely that the sharp economic contraction of 1921 would have resulted in a banking panic under the pre-World War I monetary regime. However, the worst banking panics in U.S. history occurred from 1930 to 1933 during the Great Depression. Further, Milton Friedman and Anna Schwartz[19] argue convincingly that this financial crisis would have been much less severe if the Fed had not existed. That is because, under the earlier environment, the banks would not have relied on corrective measures from the Fed, which turned out not to materialize.

Between 1930 and 1933 there was an unprecedented number of bank suspensions—roughly 9000 out of about 25,000 banks that existed at the end of 1929. Then in March 1933, President Roosevelt proclaimed a "banking holiday," which temporarily closed all of the banks. About one-third of those that had existed in 1929 never reopened.

Because of the banking panics from 1930 to 1933, there were sharp increases in the public's holdings of currency, relative to deposits. Figure 15.7 shows that the ratio of currency to checkable deposits rose from 0.17 in 1930 to 0.34 in 1933. Similarly, the banking panics increased the ratio of excess reserves to checkable deposits from near zero in 1930 to 0.04 in 1933 and 0.12

---

[18]Phillip Cagan, in *Determinants and Effects of Changes in the Stock of Money, 1875–1960*, Columbia University Press, New York, 1965, pp. 265 ff., argues that the banking panics have major elements that are independent of changes in business conditions. But Gary Gorton, in "Banking Panics and Business Cycles," Federal Reserve Bank of Philadelphia, February 1986, finds a close relationship between business failures and banking panics.

[19]For an excellent discussion of this period, see Milton Friedman and Anna J. Schwartz, *A Monetary History of the United States, 1867–1960*, Princeton University Press, Princeton, New Jersey, 1963, Chapter 7.

in 1935 (see Figure 15.2). As mentioned before, these types of increases in the real demand for base money depress the price level if the nominal quantity of base money does not change.[20] In fact, base money increased from an average of $6.6 billion in 1930 to $7.9 billion in 1933 (see Figure 15.6). Yet the price level, as measured by the GNP deflator, fell at an annual rate of 7.9% over this period.

The reaction to the banking panics of the Great Depression was a substantial amount of banking legislation. As mentioned before, the various regulations on deposit interest rates began at this time. Also, the Fed obtained the power to change reserve requirements. However, the principal innovation was the federal insurance of deposits at banks and some other financial intermediaries. This insurance came into effect in 1934.[21] When the government guarantees the redemption of deposits, people lose most of their incentive to withdraw their funds when they are unsure about an institution's financial position. Therefore, it becomes harder for a bank run to start, or for one bank's problems to spread to others. In fact, there have been no banking panics since 1933. Accordingly, we no longer have this major source of instability in the real demand for base money and, hence, in the price level. We can be pretty confident that this dramatic change from the earlier experience derives from the implementation of federal deposit insurance.

Changes in Reserve Requirements in 1936–37

There were no changes in legal reserve requirements from 1917 until 1936. Then, nervous about the large quantity of banks' excess reserves (49% of total reserves and 12% of checkable deposits in 1935), the Fed decided to "mop them up" by sharply raising reserve requirements.[22] The required-reserve ratio for member commercial banks in major cities other than New York and Chicago (the "central-reserve cities")[23] went from 10% of net demand deposits in 1935 to 15% in August 1936, 17.5% in March 1937, and 20% in May 1937.

---

[20]The costs of financial intermediation also rise. Ben Bernanke stresses this feature of banking panics during the Great Depression in "Non-Monetary Effects of the Financial Collapse in the Propagation of the Great Depression," *American Economic Review,* June 1983.

[21]The Federal Deposit Insurance Corporation—or FDIC—insures the deposits of most banks. The funds for this purpose come from a levy on the deposits of the insured banks. Formally, there is a ceiling for the size of insured deposits, which is presently $100,000. But in practice, the government seems to guarantee even the larger deposits. This practice was made explicit for the depositors of the Continental Illinois National Bank in 1984.

[22]The Fed received the authority to make these sorts of changes in reserve requirements only with the Banking Acts of 1933 and 1935. Not surprisingly, it took little time for the Fed to exercise its new power.

[23]This designation gives rise to a major trivia question: What city, other than New York and Chicago, was designated as a central-reserve city in 1914? (The answer is St. Louis, which lost the title in 1922.) In 1962 New York and Chicago were also reclassified as reserve cities. Since 1972, reserve requirements depend on an institution's total volume of deposits, rather than its location.

(Comparable changes applied to banks in New York City and Chicago, as well as to "country banks.") Overall, the ratio of required reserves to checkable deposits rose from an average of 12% in 1935 to 22% in 1937 (see Figure 15.1).

Apparently, the Fed believed that banks would hold required reserves instead of excess reserves, with no major change occurring in total reserves. But the massive holdings of excess reserves after 1933 (see Figure 15.2) reflected the banks' precautions in order to avoid the kinds of banking panics that occurred from 1930 to 1933. (The interest rate on safe assets was also extremely low at this time—for example, the yield on commercial paper was only 0.75% in 1935.) Although the ratio of excess reserves to checkable deposits fell from 12% in 1935 to 5% in 1937, the banks then rebuilt this ratio to 10% in 1938 and 16% in 1939. Accordingly, while the monetary base grew at an annual rate of 13% from 1937 to 1939 (see Figure 15.6), the GNP deflator declined over this period at an annual rate of about 1.5%. We can attribute this behavior of prices to the growing demand for reserves by banks, which followed from the steep rise in required reserves during 1936–37.

Many economists also attribute the recession of 1936–38 to the Fed's steep increase in reserve requirements. Starting from the trough of the Great Depression in 1933, real GNP grew rapidly at the average rate of 9.6% per year until 1936. But the average growth rate was near zero between 1936 and 1938 (before rising strongly at the average rate of 7.3% per year from 1938 to 1940). At this point, our theory predicts a real effect from the increase in reserve requirements only because of the adverse effect on financial intermediation—that is, on the matching of lenders and borrowers. In particular, we do not predict real effects because of the depressing influence of higher reserve requirements on prices and other nominal variables. However, we shall reexamine the important issue of linkages between nominal and real variables in Chapters 16–18.

Probably because of the economy's poor performance in 1936–38, the Fed has never again engineered a sharp short-run increase in reserve requirements. Although the legal requirements shifted many times—mostly downward—between 1938 and 1980, Figure 15.1 does not show any short-run movements in the required-reserve ratio that rival those of 1936–37. However, one notable development is the decline in the ratio from 15% in 1979 to less than 10% in 1984. This change reflected the spread of checkable deposits outside of commercial banks and the reduced reserve requirements under the banking legislation of 1980.

Summary

Financial institutions use the funds generated from deposits to make loans to households, businesses, and the government. The intermediation between deposit holders and businesses is useful because it allows financial specialists to evaluate and collect loans. In addition, the process creates various types of deposits, which are convenient as stores of value and as media of exchange. The conventional definition of money, $M1$, adds those deposits that are checkable to the public's holding of currency. Thus, $M1$ attempts to measure the assets that serve as common media of exchange.

The amount of financial intermediation depends on the costs of intermediating, which include expenses for servicing deposits and loans, returns to capital in the intermediary business, requirements to hold non-interest-bearing reserves, and costs of avoiding restrictions on the payments of interest on deposits. An increase in these costs—such as a rise in reserve requirements on deposits—leads to less financial intermediation. Consequently, there are adverse real effects, which include a greater difficulty of matching borrowers and lenders. These effects tend to show up as reductions in the quantities of investment and output.

The Federal Reserve controls the size of the monetary base (the sum of the public's currency and the reserves of financial institutions) mainly through open-market operations. In the United States these operations typically involve exchanges between base money and U.S. government bonds. However, the Fed's loans to financial institutions affect the monetary base in a similar manner.

An increase in the monetary base leads to a multiplicative expansion of deposits and of monetary aggregates, such as $M1$. The money multiplier, which is the ratio of $M1$ to the base, is greater the smaller are the ratios of reserves and currency to deposits. The money multiplier has been reasonably stable since World War II, but fell sharply in the 1930s.

Open-market operations are still neutral in the model. That is, they affect the price level and other nominal variables, but do not change any real variables (aside from the private sector's holdings of real government bonds). Among the real variables that do not change are the ratios of deposits to currency and of deposits to reserves.

Given the quantity of base money, the price level depends inversely on the real demand for the monetary base. Historically for the United States, the major short-term movements in this demand stemmed from banking panics. These panics featured sharp increases in the public's demand for currency and in banks' demands for excess reserves. However, the implementation of deposit insurance in 1934 apparently eliminated banking panics.

Important Terms and Concepts

financial intermediaries	vault cash
demand deposits	reserves (of depository institutions)
savings deposits	Federal Funds market
time deposits	Federal Funds rate

discount rate (of Fed)

reserve requirement

excess reserves

costs of intermediation

Regulation Q

disintermediation

Board of Governors of the Federal Reserve System

Federal Open Market Committee (FOMC)

Federal Reserve credit

monetary base

high-powered money

multiple expansion of deposits

money multiplier

banking panic

lender of last resort

QUESTIONS AND PROBLEMS

Mainly for Review

15.1 What considerations limit the amount of excess reserves held by financial institutions? Explain how the volume of reserves can be less than the volume of deposits.

15.2 What factors account for the spread between the interest rate on earning assets and the interest rate on checkable deposits? Is an increase in the spread associated with a lower volume of deposits?

15.3 Show that for an increase in the monetary base to be matched by an equivalent increase in reserves and currency held by the public, there must be a multiplicative expansion of deposits. How much would deposits expand if the reverse requirement were 100%?

15.4 Why does the expectation of a bank failure give individuals an incentive to cash in their deposits? Show that this expectation can be a "self-fulfilling prophecy." How does the provision of deposit insurance reduce the likelihood of this event?

15.5 Explain why a shift by households away from currency and toward demand deposits would raise the price level.

Problems for Discussion

15.6 **The Fed's Discount Rate and Borrowing at the Fed**
How does the volume of borrowing at the Fed depend on the discount rate and the interest rate on earning assets? Do the data shown in Figures 15.4 and 15.5 support the answer?

Suppose that the Fed lowers the discount rate, so that borrowings increase. Are the effects on the economy the same as those from an open-market purchase of bonds?

15.7 **Reserve Requirements**

Suppose that the Fed increases the required-reserve ratio on checkable deposits.

a. How does this change affect the real demand for base money?

b. How does it affect the price level?

c. How does it affect the nominal quantity of $M1$?

d. What real effects occur from the increase in reserve requirements?

Let's pretend now that the government imposes reserve requirements on something that has nothing to do with "money." For example, the requirement could be on refrigerators—anyone who owns a refrigerator must hold $10 of non-interest-bearing reserves at the Fed.

How does this new policy affect the real demand for base money and the price level? What other effects arise (for example, on the number of refrigerators)? In what ways do the answers differ from those above, where the requirements apply to checkable deposits?

15.8 **Vault Cash and Reserve Requirements**

From 1917 until December 1959, vault cash did not count toward satisfying the Fed's reserve requirements. Part of it counted until November 1960, after which all of vault cash counted toward the requirements. Just before the change in 1959–60, vault cash at banks that were members of the Federal Reserve System was $2.2 billion, which amounted to about 2% of all checkable deposits.

If the monetary base did not change for 1960–61, how would the new treatment of vault cash affect the price level? (In fact, base money declined from an average of $50.4 billion in 1959 to $50.0 billion in 1960 and $49.1 billion in 1961.)

15.9 **Interest on Reserves Held at the Fed**

At present, reserves held at the Federal Reserve bear no interest. Suppose that reserves were paid interest at a rate that was some fraction of the interest rate on commercial paper. If the quantity of base money stayed the same, how would this change affect the following:

a. The interest rate paid on checkable deposits?

b. The dollar amount of checkable deposits?

c. The price level?

d. The amount of intermediation in the economy?

e. The profits of the Federal Reserve (which go to the U.S. Treasury)?

15.10 **Gold and the Monetary Base**

Suppose that the U.S. Treasury receives $1 billion of gold from abroad. Then the Treasury deposits the gold at the Fed, so that the Fed's gold account and the Treasury's deposits at the Fed each rise by $1 billion.

a. What happens to the monetary base if the Treasury holds the extra $1 billion in deposits?

b. What happens if the Treasury spends the extra $1 billion and thereby restores its deposits to their initial level?

c. How can the Fed offset the effect of the gold inflow on the monetary base? (If it takes this action, the Fed is said to "sterilize" the inflow of gold.)

d. Suppose that the government raises the official price of gold from $42.22 per ounce to the market price of around $340 (at the end of 1985). Then the capital gain on the Fed's gold holdings (valued at $11.1 billion at the end of 1985, using the official price of $42.22) is credited to the Treasury's deposits at the Fed. What might this action do to the monetary base (which was $221 billion at the end of 1985)? What could the Fed do to keep the monetary base from changing?

15.11 Membership in the Federal Reserve System

Until 1980 only commercial banks that were members of the Federal Reserve System were subject to the Fed's reserve requirements. (There were also some services, such as check-clearing and access to the discount window, which were provided free to members.) Membership was optional for banks with state charters, but required for those with federal charters. (In 1980 only 30% of all commercial banks had national charters. But these accounted for 55% of the deposits at commercial banks.)

The fraction of state banks that were members of the Federal Reserve System declined from 21% in 1948 to 10% in 1980. Why do you think this happened?

15.12 Runs on Financial Institutions

In the text we discussed runs on banks. How does the analysis differ if the run applies to other financial intermediaries, which do not offer checkable deposits? (For example, this description would apply until recently to savings and loan associations.)

15.13 Deposit Insurance (optional)

We discussed the role of federal deposit insurance, which has apparently prevented banking panics since 1933. A number of unsolved questions arise here, which you might want to think about.

a. Could private companies satisfactorily provide insurance on deposits? In particular, would the private sector end up providing the "right" amount of insurance? Would private companies also charge for this insurance in accordance with the riskiness of an institution's earnings? More generally, why is deposit insurance an area where the government should be involved?

b. Is there a reason for the government to be in the insurance business for deposits, but not for other things, such as corporate obligations? (In fact, the federal government has gotten into the business of insuring the debt of doubtful borrowers—such as New York City and the Chrysler Corporation—as well as pension obligations and accounts at stockbrokers. But, so far, the government has not bailed out the Washington State Public Power Supply System.)

CHAPTER 16

THE INTERPLAY BETWEEN NOMINAL AND REAL VARIABLES—WHAT IS THE EVIDENCE?

Thus far, our analysis has not stressed monetary variables as a source of fluctuations in real economic activity. Yet many economists think that movements in money and prices—that is, nominal disturbances—have a great deal to do with the short-term behavior of real variables, such as aggregate output and employment. In this chapter we concern ourselves mostly with the empirical evidence on this important issue. But before we look at the evidence, let's summarize what our theory says so far about the interaction between nominal and real variables.

The theory predicts that changes in the monetary base are neutral. In particular, a one-time shift in the quantity of base money leads to proportional changes in the nominal variables, but to no changes in the real variables. So we get responses in the price level, the nominal wage rate, and the dollar values of output, investment, and so on. But there are no changes in the quantities of output and employment, the real interest rate, and so on.

We can also consider complicated monetary disturbances, where the changes do not occur entirely at the present time. Then the anticipations of future monetary changes lead to complicated responses of the price level, as well as to shifts in the nominal interest rate. But the model still predicts no changes in the real variables. At least, the only exception in our theory concerns the transaction costs for moving between money and either goods or interest-bearing assets. Since changes in the nominal interest rate affect the real demand for money, we can get some real effects through this channel. But these influences are probably insufficient to account for sizable fluctuations in aggregate real economic activity.

The results differ if monetary fluctuations reflect shifts in the cost of intermediation, rather than changes in the quantity of base money. For example, there might be a banking panic, which causes people to lose confidence in deposits.[1] Alternatively, there might be changes in reserve requirements. In these cases, as with contractions of the monetary base, there tend to be reductions in the price level and other nominal variables. But because of the higher cost of intermediation, there are also some adverse effects on real variables. Specifically, since it becomes harder to match borrowers and lenders, the levels of investment and output tend to decline. Therefore, these types of disturbances move nominal and real variables in the same direction.

There are also real disturbances, such as the oil crises of 1973–74 and 1979–80, which we can represent as shifts to production functions.[2] An adverse shock reduces output, which lowers the quantity of real money demanded. For a given amount of base money, the price level rises. Since the price level now moves in the opposite direction of output, we find that the pattern of response differs markedly from the one associated with changes in the cost of intermediation.

Overall, our theory does allow for some relationships between nominal and real variables, although the sign of the interaction depends on the nature of the underlying disturbance. However, let's stress the key theoretical proposition, which concerns monetary neutrality. Purely monetary disturbances—in the sense of changes in the monetary base—have no real effects. To put this another way, although these monetary disturbances can create substantial variations in prices and other nominal variables, we still predict no response in the aggregates of output, employment, and so on.[3]

Most economists regard the proposition of monetary neutrality as incorrect, at least in some short-run contexts. In fact, many researchers attribute a large portion of aggregate business fluctuations to monetary disturbances, which our theory says have no important real effects. The common view is that monetary expansion tends to stimulate real economic activity, whereas monetary contraction tends to cause recessions.

---

[1] Banking panics are typically not independent of prior changes in business conditions. However, the potential for panics does depend on some features of the financial structure. In particular, as discussed in Chapter 15, the implementation of federal deposit insurance in 1934 has apparently prevented panics since that time.

[2] For most purposes, we can also include here changes in government purchases and shifts in taxes and transfers. For example, an increase in marginal tax rates is analogous to an adverse shift of the production function.

[3] The variations in prices lead to changes in the distribution of real assets. Specifically, nominal debtors gain from surprise inflation, while nominal creditors lose. But the theory does not allow for effects of these types of distributional shifts on the aggregates of output and employment. One possibility would be to extend the theory, so that these distributional changes do have aggregate consequences.

The Phillips Curve

Economists often express their ideas about the relation between real and nominal variables in terms of the **Phillips curve** (named after the British economist A. W. Phillips). This curve is intended to summarize the relation between a measure of real economic activity—such as the unemployment rate or the level or growth rate of output—and a nominal variable—such as the rate of change of prices or nominal wages or the stock of money. The basic notion behind the Phillips curve is that more inflation (and more monetary growth underlying this inflation) brings about an economic boom, which shows up as less unemployment and a higher growth rate of real gross national product (GNP). Initially, this idea was presented (by Phillips) as an empirical, inverse relation between the unemployment rate and the rate of growth of nominal wages. But subsequently, researchers have often replaced the rate of wage change by the growth rate of either prices or money. Figure 16.1 shows a simple version of the Phillips curve. In this figure a lower inflation rate, π, is associated with a higher unemployment rate, u.

Economists sometimes argue that more inflation or more monetary growth results in less unemployment and higher growth of output only in the "short run." Eventually, the economy adjusts to any established rate of inflation, so that the real variables no longer depend on the behavior of the nominal variables. Suppose that we think of the expected rate of inflation, π^e, as the rate

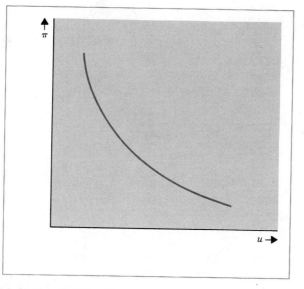

Figure 16.1 **A Simple Phillips Curve**
The Phillips curve associates a lower value of the inflation rate, π, with a higher unemployment rate, u.

of inflation to which the economy has adjusted itself. Then, as shown in Figure 16.2, it is only the surprise part of inflation, $\pi - \pi^e$, that would relate systematically (and presumably negatively) to the unemployment rate. This type of relation is called an **expectational Phillips curve** because the inflation rate enters relative to the amount of expected inflation. One important property of this curve is that a given unemployment rate can coexist with any amount of inflation. For example, an unemployment rate of 6% is consistent with an inflation rate of 0, 10, 20%, etc. Equal changes in actual and expected inflation, which leave unchanged the amount of unexpected inflation, $\pi - \pi^e$, have no significance for the unemployment rate. Equivalently, we can say that the simple Phillips curve in Figure 16.1 applies for a fixed value of the expected inflation rate, π^e. When π^e changes, the curve in this figure shifts—specifically, a higher value of π^e means that a higher inflation rate is associated with any given value of the unemployment rate.

We can view much of the macrotheorizing since the 1930s as attempts to explain versions of the Phillips curve and, as a related matter, the absence of monetary neutrality. This perspective applies as much to the Keynesian theory as to the more recent monetary theories of business fluctuations. But before we explore these theories, we should understand the nature of the facts that they are trying to explain. In particular, we want to know to what extent the

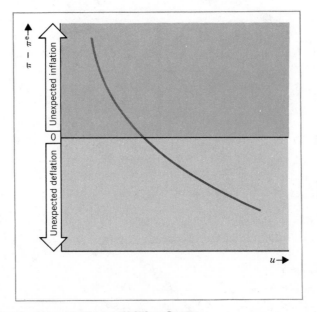

Figure 16.2 An Expectational Phillips Curve
The expectational Phillips curve associates a lower value of unexpected inflation, $\pi - \pi^e$, with a higher unemployment rate, u. Thus, a given unemployment rate (say 6%) can coexist with any rate of inflation.

Phillips curve—either the simple one or the expectational variety—and monetary nonneutrality are "facts." So in this chapter we bring out the major pieces of empirical evidence that concern the interplay between nominal and real variables. Throughout this discussion, we look especially for findings that demonstrate the existence of the Phillips curve and the nonneutrality of money.

The Relationship between Unemployment and the Rates of Change of Wages, Prices, and Money—Long-Term Evidence for the United Kingdom and the United States

The term, Phillips curve, derives from studies of the relationship between unemployment and the growth rate of nominal wages, which were carried out by A. W. Phillips and Richard Lipsey.[4] Lipsey's statistical analysis documents a significant inverse relationship between the unemployment rate and the growth rate of nominal wages in the United Kingdom for the period, 1862–1913. The nature of his findings shows up in Figure 16.3, which plots the British data over the period, 1862–1984, excluding the years that are associated with World Wars I and II. The growth rate of the nominal wage, Δw, appears on the vertical axis, while the unemployment rate, u, is on the horizontal. We use dots for the observations from 1862–1913. For these years, we can discern a negative slope, which is also confirmed by a formal statistical analysis.

We see also from Figure 16.3 that the inverse relation between unemployment and the growth rate of nominal wages does not hold up when we look at the behavior after World War I. For the interwar period, 1923–39, the observations appear as asterisks in the figure. Notice that these years exhibit exceptionally high unemployment rates. The average value of 14.3% contrasts with that of 4.7% for 1862–1913. But there is no significant correlation between the unemployment rate and the rate of change of wages over the period, 1923–39.

A different pattern of association between wage-rate changes and unemployment arises when we look at the post-World War II period (plotted by +'s in Figure 16.3). For the years 1947–84, the relation between the unemployment rate and the rate of change of wages turns out to be significantly positive. In other words, the Phillips curve slopes in the "wrong" direction since World War II! However, the most notable change from the pre-World War I period is the higher average growth of nominal wages—7.7% per year in 1947–84, versus 0.8% for 1862–1913 (and −0.1% for 1923–39). In comparison with the period before World War I, the recent years involve mainly

---

[4]A. W. Phillips, "The Relation between Unemployment and the Rate of Change of Money Wage Rates in the United Kingdom, 1861–1959," *Economica,* November 1958; and Richard Lipsey, "The Relation between Unemployment and the Rate of Change of Money Wage Rates in the United Kingdom, 1862–1957: A Further Analysis," *Economica,* February 1960.

Figure 16.3 **The Relation between the Unemployment Rate and the Rate of Change of Wages in the United Kingdom, 1862–1984**

For the years, 1862–1913 (shown by dots), there is a negative relation between the two variables. But for the interwar period, 1923–39 (shown by asterisks), there is no significant relation. For the recent years, 1947–84 (shown by +'s), the relation is positive.

an increase in the average rate of wage change, with no major difference in the unemployment rate. (The average unemployment rate for 1947–84 is 3.6%, but the rate has risen recently to 13% in 1983–84.)

The results for the United Kingdom look basically similar if we replace the growth rate of nominal wages by the growth rate of either prices or the $M1$ definition of money. The only indication of an inverse relation between unemployment and the growth rate of the nominal variables—wages, prices, or $M1$—appears in the years before World War I. Also, for the nominal variables, the slope of the Phillips curve has the wrong sign in the recent period.

The pattern of results for the United States resembles that for the United Kingdom.[5] In Figure 16.4 we show the U.S. data for the period, 1890–1985,

[5]Irving Fisher carried out an early statistical study of this type of relationship for the United States. But he used price changes, rather than wage changes. The results appear in Irving Fisher, "A Statistical Relation between Unemployment and Price Changes," *International Labor Review*, June 1926. This paper is reprinted (under the cute title, "I Discovered the Phillips Curve") in the *Journal of Political Economy*, April 1973.

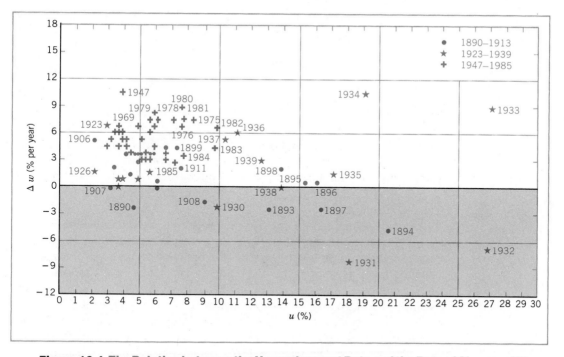

Figure 16.4 **The Relation between the Unemployment Rate and the Rate of Change of Wages in the United States, 1890–1985**

For the period, 1890–1913 (shown by dots), the relation between the two variables is negative. There is no significant relation over the other two periods. *Sources of data for Figures 16.3 and 16.4.* United Kingdom: The unemployment rate is from B. R. Mitchell and P. Deane, *Abstract of British Historical Statistics,* Cambridge University Press, Cambridge, 1962; B. R. Mitchell, *European Historical Statistics, 1750–1970,* Macmillan, New York, 1975; and *Monthly Digest of Statistics,* various issues. The wage rate index is from B. R. Mitchell, *European Historical Statistics, 1750–1970;* Department of Employment and Productivity, *British Labour Statistics, Historical Abstract 1886–1968,* London, 1971; and *Monthly Digest of Statistics,* various issues. United States: The unemployment rate is from Figure 1.3 of Chapter 1. The wage-rate index is from Albert Rees, "Patterns of Wages, Prices and Productivity," in Charles Myers, ed., *Wages, Prices, Profits and Productivity,* Columbia University Press, New York, 1959; and *Economic Report of the President,* various issues. The recent data include an adjustment for overtime pay.

excluding the years that are associated with World Wars I and II. The growth rate of nominal wages, Δw, appears on the vertical axis, while the unemployment rate, u, is on the horizontal.

A significant negative association between the unemployment rate and the growth rate of wages appears again in the pre-World War I period, 1890–1913 (the observations are indicated by dots in Figure 16.4). As with the United

Kingdom, there is no significant correlation between the two variables over the interwar period, 1923–39 (shown by asterisks in the figure). Notice that, unlike the United Kingdom, the unemployment rates in the United States are low for 1923–29. But for the 1930s, the unemployment rates are similar in the two countries.

For the post-World War II period in the United States, 1947–85 (shown by +'s in Figure 16.4), we also find no significant correlation between the unemployment rate and the growth rate of nominal wages. Recall that, for the United Kingdom, we found a positive association between the two variables during these years. Some weak indication of a positive relationship—that is, of a wrongly sloped Phillips curve—shows up for the United States from 1947–85 if we replace the growth rate of wages by that of either prices or a monetary aggregate, such as $M1$.

What conclusions can we draw from the long-period relationships between the unemployment rate and the growth rates of the nominal variables? First, there is no stable relation between the unemployment rate—or, it turns out, real economic activity more generally—and the growth rates of nominal wages, prices, or money.[6] Thus, the sharply higher growth rates of the nominal variables since World War II, as compared with those before World War I, correspond to little change in the average rate of unemployment (or in average growth rates of real GNP). Hence, we can firmly reject the notion of a Phillips curve, such as that shown in Figure 16.1, which is stable over the long term. At least in the long run, it is untrue that more inflation leads to a lower unemployment rate, or that to have low inflation a country must accept a high unemployment rate.

What about the negative relation between unemployment and the growth rates of the nominal variables before World War I? One important consideration is that the United Kingdom and the United States (after 1879) were on the gold standard during these years. Under this type of monetary regime, the monetary policy in each country had to conform to maintaining a fixed nominal price of gold. (In this period, the U.S. price of gold was $20.67 per ounce.) In particular, it would be infeasible to have high growth rates of money and prices over long periods without having to abandon the gold standard. (We discuss these matters more in Chapter 19.) The main point is that under the gold standard we observe long-term average rates of change of nominal wages and prices that are close to zero. For example, in the case of the United Kingdom, the average rate of change of nominal wages from 1862–1913 was 0.8% per year, while that for prices was −0.4% per year. For the United States from 1890 to 1913, the average growth rate of nominal wages was 1.8% per year, while that for prices was 0.9% per year.

---

[6]Formal statistical support for this proposition appears in Robert Lucas, "Two Illustrations of the Quantity Theory of Money," *American Economic Review*, December 1980; and John Geweke, "The Superneutrality of Money in the United States: An Interpretation of the Evidence," *Econometrica*, January 1986.

Under the gold standard, high rates of inflation represented rates that were high relative to the long-term average rate of inflation, which was close to zero. If we think of zero as the expected rate of inflation (at least over long periods), then the results suggest an inverse relation between unexpected inflation, $\pi - \pi^e \approx \pi$, and the unemployment rate. That is, we have an expectational Phillips curve of the form shown in Figure 16.2. Note that this form of the Phillips curve can also accommodate the breakdown of the relationship over the longer term. Once countries moved off the gold standard—as happened in part around World War I and more so in the 1930s and around World War II—we find that the inflation rates no longer average close to zero. Rather, inflation rates tend to be high and unstable. But the general rise in actual and expected rates of inflation—which shows up especially after World War II—does not mean that unexpected inflation, $\pi - \pi^e$, is systematically high or low. Therefore, we no longer see an inverse association between the rate of inflation and the unemployment rate.

What about the positive relation between unemployment and the growth rates of the nominal variables, which shows up for the United Kingdom and weakly for the United States in the post-World War II period? There are two elements that explain at least part of this behavior. First, as noted before, disturbances to production functions ("supply shocks") tend to generate this pattern. Second, any tendency of governments to raise monetary growth during recessions reinforces this outcome. That is, lower output triggers more money, which raises the price level. This pattern of active monetary policy applies to the United States and the United Kingdom since World War II, but not during the earlier years under the gold standard.

Overall, the main phenomenon that our theory does not yet explain is the tendency for higher than expected growth rates of the nominal variables to accompany low rates of unemployment. So far, the data indicate the presence of this type of expectational Phillips curve for the period before World War I.

Cross-Country Relations between Nominal and Real Variables

Suppose that we look at average growth rates of real GNP for various countries[7] and compare these with the average growth rates of prices, money, and so on. If we look at averages over one or more decades, then the main variations across countries reflect differences in the long-term average growth rates of real GNP, prices, money, etc. Hence, the relations among these variables should tell us something about how differences in the growth rates of the nominal variables associate in the long run with differences in the real growth

---

[7]Because of differences in concepts and lack of data, it is hard to compare unemployment rates across countries.

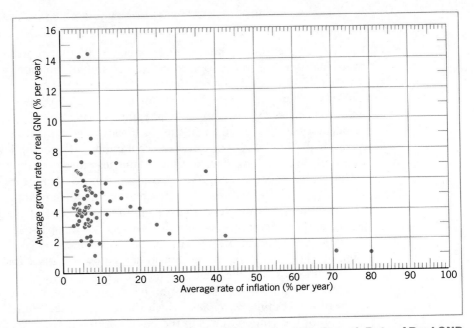

Figure 16.5 **The Cross-Country Relation between Inflation and the Growth Rate of Real GNP**
Looking at 78 countries, there is no significant relation between the average rate of inflation and the average growth rate of real GNP.

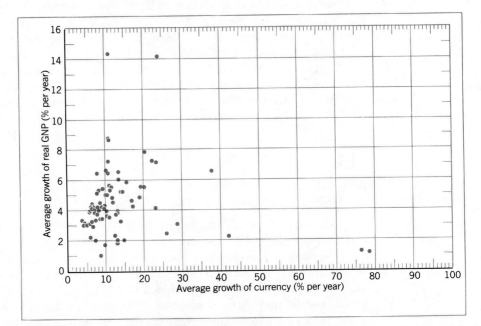

Figure 16.6 **The Cross-Country Relation between Monetary Growth (Currency) and the Growth Rate of Real GNP**
For the 78 countries, there is no significant relation between the average growth rate of currency and the average growth rate of real GNP.

rates. That is, the cross-country evidence should resemble the longer-term findings on Phillips curves that we discussed before for the United States and the United Kingdom.

Figure 16.5 uses data from 78 countries to relate the average growth rate of real GNP (over intervals of 1 to 3 decades since World War II) with the average rate of inflation. (Recall that we looked at these data before in Chapter 7.) There is no apparent relation between the two variables in Figure 16.5, as we can verify from a formal statistical analysis.

Figures 16.6 and 16.7 plot the average growth rate of real GNP against the average growth rate of either currency or $M1$. Again, the average growth rate of real GNP bears no relation to the growth rate of the nominal variables. Thus, as with the long-period evidence for the United States or the United Kingdom, the cross-country data indicate no connection between the growth rates of the nominal variables and the behavior of real variables, such as the growth rate of real GNP.

Roger Kormendi and Phil Meguire ("Macroeconomic Determinants of

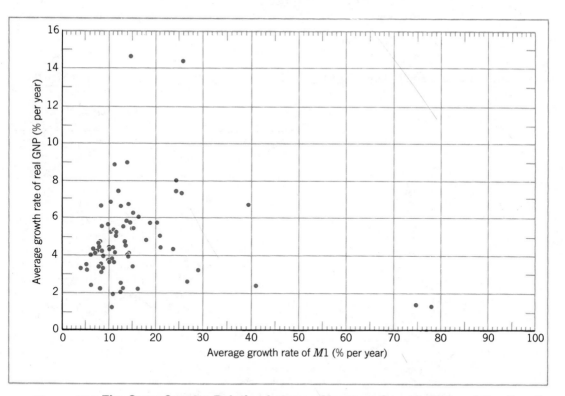

Figure 16.7 **The Cross-Country Relation between Monetary Growth ($M1$) and the Growth Rate of Real GNP**

For the 78 countries, there is no significant relation between the average growth rate of $M1$ and the average growth rate of real GNP.

Growth: Cross-Country Evidence," *Journal of Monetary Economics,* September 1985, p. 147) carried out a detailed statistical analysis of the growth experience of 46 countries in the post-World War II period. One of their findings is that *increases* in inflation rates are associated with lower average growth rates of real output. This result suggests that a higher rate of inflation leads to a lower *level* of output. Thus there is some indication of a form of Phillips curve with the "wrong" sign. One possibility is that the transaction costs associated with higher inflation reduce the incentive for people to engage in market activity.

The Relation between Real and Nominal Variables during the Major Recessions before World War II

Some of the evidence already discussed suggests that the main short-term interplay between nominal and real variables arises when the nominal variables behave in an unusual or surprising manner. Hence, we should focus on shocks or surprises in money and prices to find interesting short-run interactions with the real variables. Table 16.1 brings out this type of relationship for the five

Table 16.1 **Real and Nominal Variables during Five Major Recessions before World War II**

	1894	1908	1921	1933	1938
Final Year of Recession	1894	1908	1921	1933	1938
Benchmark Year for Comparison	1892	1906	1920	1929	1937
Y	104.3	183.7	199.9	222.1	296.7
Y^0	114.0	199.1	220.8	356.0	319.6
$Y^0 - Y$	9.7	15.4	20.9	133.9	22.9
% shortfall	8.5	7.7	9.5	37.6	7.2
M	1.57	3.09	6.33	7.92	14.4
M^0	1.65	2.89	7.15	7.03	14.9
$M^0 - M$	0.08	−0.20	0.82	−0.89	0.5
% shortfall	4.8	−6.9	11.5	−12.7	3.4
P	0.150	0.183	0.340	0.251	0.286
P^0	0.153	0.185	0.404	0.332	0.301
$P^0 - P$	0.003	0.002	0.064	0.081	0.015
% shortfall	2.0	1.1	15.8	24.4	5.0
% change in $M1/M$	−5.4	−12.0	0.3	−32.9	−8.6

Note: Y is real GNP, M is the monetary base, P is the GNP deflator, and $M1$ is the $M1$ definition of the money stock. (For the two earliest cases, we estimate $M1$ from the available data on $M2$.) The normal or expected values, Y^0, M^0, and P^0, equal the values from the benchmark year, adjusted by the normal growth rates. For real GNP, we use the long-term average growth rate of 3.0% per year. For the monetary base and the price level, we use the average growth rates over the five years prior to the benchmark year. An exception is 1921, where we generate the normal values, M^0, and P^0, by using the average growth rates of these variables from 1909 to 1914. We then apply these rates to the values for 1920.

Sources: See Figures 1.1 and 1.4, Table 7.2, and Figure 15.6.

principal U.S. recessions between 1890 and 1940. Three of these—1892–94, 1906–08, and 1929–33—contain banking panics. Another one, 1937–38, involves the Fed's steep increase in reserve requirements. The fifth episode, 1920–21, occurs along with a dramatic fall in money and prices after World War I.

The first section of Table 16.1 shows the estimated shortfall of real GNP for each recession. Aside from the Great Depression of 1929–33, where the shortfall was a remarkable 38%, the values are similar to the most severe of the post-World War II recessions, which are 1980–82 and 1974–75. (See Table 9.1 of Chapter 9.)

The second section of the table shows the monetary base, M,[8] along with an estimate of the "normal" or expected amount, which we call M^0. For example, M = \$1.57 billion in 1894. To calculate M^0, consider what the quantity of base money would have been in 1894 if it had grown at a normal or expected rate from the benchmark year, 1892. By a normal rate, we mean the rate that someone would have predicted in 1892 for monetary growth over the next 2 years (pretending that people were thinking about such matters!). Operationally, we estimate this rate as the average value, 3.4% per year, that applied over the 5 years prior to 1892. Then we estimate the normal amount of base money, M^0, for 1894 as \$1.65 billion. The actual stock, M, was 4.8% below this normal value. Although the precise figure depends on the procedure for estimating the normal growth rate of money, we can satisfactorily use a value of 5% to gauge the rough size of the shortfall in base money for 1892–94.

We apply a similar procedure for three of the other recessions. Thereby, we find that base money actually exceeded the normal amount for two cases— by 6.9% in 1906–08 and 12.7% in 1929–33. But for the 1937–38 recession, the shortfall of base money was 3.4%.

We have some difficulties in generating the normal growth rate of money for 1920–21. The 5 years prior to 1920 featured the rapid growth of money during World War I. But people would have had no reason to expect these high rates of expansion to continue after 1920. So to get a rough estimate, we use the growth rate of the monetary base that applied before World War I from 1909–14, which was 2.7% per year. Then we find that the shortfall in the monetary base for 1920–21 was 11.5%. In any event, there is no doubt that the sharp drop in base money during 1921 represented a substantial decline relative to anyone's predictions.

Overall, the five major recessions between 1890 and 1940 do not suggest a close association between contractions of output and shortfalls in the monetary base. In fact, for two of the cases—1929–33 and 1906–08—the movements in base money were expansionary. Only in the case of the post-World War I contraction, 1920–21, do the figures suggest a dominant role for the

---

[8] Gold and silver coins and certificates accounted for roughly half of the monetary base through World War I, and still retained a substantial role until 1933. The reserves held at the Fed appear in the monetary base after the start of the Federal Reserve System in 1914.

shortfall in base money. It is also interesting that, for this episode, the fall in the monetary base reflected mostly a sharp decline in borrowing from the Fed. This decline stemmed at least in part from a dramatic increase in the Fed's discount rate—that is, from a reduction in the subsidy to borrowing by banks.

Conceivably, our focus on the episodes of major economic contraction would mislead us about the overall role of shortfalls in base money. But the notion that this role is minor is confirmed by a more thorough analysis of Mark Rush.[9] His study uses all the data from 1885 to 1913 and also employs more sophisticated techniques for measuring the normal growth rate of the monetary base. In addition, he allows for lagged effects of changes in the monetary base on real variables. But his basic finding is that unusual movements in the monetary base played at most a minor role in influencing output and employment over this period.

The third section of Table 16.1 makes calculations for the price level, which parallel those that we made for the monetary base. We find shortfalls in prices relative to the normal or expected level, P^0, by no more than 2% for two cases—1892–94 and 1906–08—by 5% for 1937–38, 16% for 1920–21, and 24% for 1929–33.

Given our earlier results, we know that much of these shortfalls in prices cannot be explained by contractions in base money. That is, increases in the real demand for base money must be important during these recessions. But we expect precisely this behavior during banking panics—which occurred in 1893, 1907, and 1930–33—or in response to the sharp increase in reserve requirements in 1936–37.

We can get some idea about the size of the change in the real demand for base money by examining the relation between base money, M, and a broader monetary aggregate, such as $M1$ (the public's currency and checkable deposits). The ratio of $M1$ to M tells us something about the amount of financial intermediation in the economy. Our previous analysis implies that this ratio declines when the real demand for base money expands, as in a banking panic.[10] Looking at the fourth section of Table 16.1, we see that the ratio, $M1/M$, declined substantially for four of the five cases. The declines by 5% for 1892–94, 12% for 1906–08, and 33% for 1929–33 reflected the impacts of the banking panics. The reduction by 9% for 1937–38 stemmed from the increase in reserve requirements. But for 1920–21, the ratio was virtually unchanged.

In any event, the results suggest a positive relation between changes in financial intermediation—as proxied by the ratio of $M1$ to the monetary base—and real economic activity. Further, this indication from the five recessions that we considered is reinforced by the more detailed analysis of Mark Rush,

---

[9]See Mark Rush, "Unexpected Monetary Disturbances during the Gold Standard Era," *Journal of Monetary Economics,* May 1985.

[10]Before 1914, data on $M1$ are unavailable because we cannot separate banks' time deposits from their demand deposits. But we can estimate $M1$ by looking at a broader monetary aggregate, which includes the banks' time deposits. This aggregate used to be called $M2$, although this term now encompasses some additional assets.

which we mentioned earlier. Over the period, 1885–1913, and again for the 1930s,[11] he finds an important linkage between shifts in the ratio of $M1$ to the monetary base and subsequent changes in output and employment.

An important point is that neither Rush's analysis nor ours tells us for sure whether banking panics cause recessions or, in reverse, that hard economic times make banking panics more likely. But we do know a couple of things about this direction of causation. First, the implementation of deposit insurance in 1934 apparently eliminated the potential for banking panics and thereby lessened the typical size of business fluctuations. This observation suggests that the potential for banking panics explains part of the magnitude of economic contractions, even if not the timing of these contractions. Second, the increase in reserve requirements in 1936–37 isolates the effect of a financial change on economic activity, rather than the reverse effect.

Overall, the evidence from before World War II indicates important real effects from shifts in financial intermediation, which reflect especially banking panics and changes in reserve requirements. Further, the movements in the ratio of $M1$ to the monetary base serve as a rough proxy for these effects. But there is not much connection between shifts to the monetary base—even when they are surprisingly large—and changes in real economic activity. The one suggestion of this linkage comes from the sharp, but brief, contraction of 1920–21. But even here, the dramatic reduction in the monetary base reflects a major decrease in the Fed's subsidy for borrowing at the discount window. Thus, even this episode does not decisively demonstrate important real effects from a pure reduction in the monetary base (when generated, for example, through open-market sales of bonds).

The Relation between Real and Nominal Variables since World War II

For the post-World War II period, there are many detailed studies that attempt to isolate the effects on real variables from unusual movements in the nominal variables. Let's consider first some research that deals with shocks to the price level, and then some work that focuses on monetary disturbances.

Effects from Changes in Prices

An econometric study by Ray Fair[12] analyzes the relation between surprise movements in the price level and the amount of real economic activity in the post-World War II United States. He focuses on the unemployment rate, u_t, as the measure of real economic performance. The statistical procedure seeks

---

[11]The results for the 1930s are in Mark Rush, "Unexpected Money and Unemployment," unpublished, University of Florida, September 1985.

[12]Ray Fair, "An Analysis of the Accuracy of Four Macroeconometric Models," *Journal of Political Economy,* August 1979.

to estimate the effect on unemployment from surprises in prices, $P_t - P_t^e$, where P_t is the actual price level and P_t^e is the price that the typical person expected for period t. In other words, the study provides estimates of expectational Phillips curves. Operationally, Fair interprets the expected price, P_t^e, as the best forecast for the actual price, P_t, that people could have made with the data available through the previous period, $t - 1$. In practice, the periods are treated as quarters of years. Fair uses statistical techniques to obtain a best fit between the actual price level, P_t, and the lagged values of a group of explanatory variables. Then he uses the fitted value from this relationship as a proxy for the expected price, P_t^e—that is, for the best prediction of prices that could have been made from the assumed list of explanatory variables, when observed up to date $t - 1$.

Fair finds no significant relationship between the unemployment rate and the price surprise over the period, 1954–73. Moreover, when he adds data from 1974 to 1977, the estimated effect of price shocks on unemployment becomes positive. That is, the expectational Phillips curve has the wrong sign.

Recall that our analysis in previous chapters implies that the relation between a real variable, such as the unemployment rate or the level of output, and surprise movements in the price level depends on the nature of the underlying disturbance. Specifically, shifts to production functions can generate a negative relation between movements in output and movements in prices. Hence, this element can account for the positive relation between price shocks and unemployment that Fair reports when he adds the data for 1974–77. Recall that these years include the effects from the first oil crisis of 1973–74, which we can interpret as a major supply shock. For this reason, the expectational Phillips curve, which is the relation between unemployment and price surprises, tends to confound two types of effects. First, there would be the positive relation caused by supply shocks. Second, if monetary disturbances raise prices and lower unemployment, then the expectational Phillips curve would tend to have a negative slope. Thus, even if money is nonneutral, the slope of the Phillips curve could have the wrong (positive) sign. Instead of estimating expectational Phillips curves as Fair did, it would be useful to isolate the real effects of monetary disturbances. Then we get a clearer test for the neutrality of monetary shocks.

Monetary Shocks and Real Economic Activity in the Post-World War II United States

I have analyzed the real effects of monetary shocks in a number of papers.[13] The starting point is the division of monetary growth into anticipated and unanticipated components. Conceptually, I identified the anticipated part with

---

[13]This work is summarized in Robert Barro, "Unanticipated Money Growth and Economic Activity in the U.S.," in *Money, Expectations and Business Cycles*, Academic Press, New York, 1981.

the prediction that could have been made by exploiting the historical relation between money and a specified set of explanatory variables. Using the $M1$ definition of money over the period since World War II, I found that monetary growth for year t depends positively on three variables: last year's monetary growth, last year's unemployment rate, and this year's level of federal expenditure relative to a measure of normal spending. The positive relation to past unemployment may reflect the Fed's desire to expand money during a recession, which is a form of "countercyclical" or "activist" monetary policy. The positive effect of federal spending may involve the incentive for inflationary finance. Some further research indicates a negative reaction of monetary growth to previous increases in nominal interest rates, which can also be added to the analysis.

I used the estimated relation of monetary growth to the explanatory variables to construct a series labeled **anticipated money growth.** Then I took the difference between actual and anticipated monetary change as the empirical counterpart of **unanticipated money.** Essentially, this procedure does for money what Fair did for prices in the study that we discussed above.

I estimated equations for real GNP and the unemployment rate over the post-World War II period to ascertain the real effects of anticipated and unanticipated changes in money. Basically, I found that unanticipated money had expansionary real effects that lasted over a 1 to 2 year period. On the other hand, the anticipated parts of monetary change did not have important real effects. Quantitatively, I estimated that a 1% rise in money above expectations raises next year's output by about 1% and lowers next year's unemployment rate by about six-tenths of a percentage point. Thus, unlike the price shocks that Fair studied, positive monetary surprises seem to have important expansionary effects on real economic activity.[14]

The results just mentioned pertain to the monetary aggregate, $M1$. But we can think of disturbances to $M1$ as composed partly of shocks to the monetary base, M, and partly to the ratio of $M1$ to the base. Remember that the ratio of $M1$ to the monetary base tends to proxy for the state of financial intermediation. We found that this ratio—but not the movements in the monetary base—were associated with business fluctuations prior to World War I. If we look just at the monetary base since World War II, then the association with real variables is much weaker than that for $M1$. However, Mark Rush[15] reports that shocks to the base do have a significant positive association with

---

[14]Empirical analysis of anticipated versus unanticipated money has become popular in recent years. Some of the contributions are C. L. F. Attfield, D. Demery, and N. W. Duck, "A Quarterly Model of Unanticipated Monetary Growth, Output and the Price level in the U.K.," *Journal of Monetary Economics,* November 1981; Roger Kormendi and Philip Meguire, "Cross-Regime Evidence of Macroeconomic Rationality," *Journal of Political Economy,* October 1984; and Frederic Mishkin, "Does Anticipated Monetary Policy Matter? An Econometric Investigation," *Journal of Political Economy,* February 1982.

[15]"Unexpected Money and Unemployment," op. cit.

U.S. real economic activity in the annual data since World War II (as well as for the 1920s).

If shocks to the monetary base matter for business fluctuations, then this observation would conflict with our theory. Remember that the theory predicts that changes in the monetary base would be neutral, at least if we neglect transaction costs and distributional effects. In the next chapter we explore some extensions of the theory that can accommodate nonneutral effects from changes in the monetary base. In evaluating this extension, we should keep in mind the empirical evidence. There is some suggestion of nonneutralities to be explained, but the evidence is not very strong.

Summary

Much of the macrotheorizing since the 1930s can be viewed as attempts to rationalize a strong interplay between nominal and real variables, which shows up in various versions of the Phillips curve. We can view the Keynesian theory and more recent monetary theories of business fluctuations in this context. But before considering these theories, we should think about how much evidence there is to explain.

Neither the long-period evidence nor that from across countries suggests important effects on real variables from differences in the average growth rates of money, prices, or wages. That is, in the long run there is no systematic relation between real variables and nominal variables.

Before World War II, the evidence suggests important real effects from banking panics and changes in reserve requirements, which show up as fluctuations in the ratio of $M1$ to the monetary base. Also, these episodes typically involve some surprise decreases in prices (and nominal wages). But there is not much evidence for real effects from changes in the monetary base.

After World War II, there is an indication that monetary shocks—but not price surprises—have positive effects on real economic activity. The strongest evidence for real effects of money show up when we use a broad aggregate like $M1$. But there is also some evidence of real effects from shocks to the monetary base.

Basically, it is the nonneutral effect of the monetary base—to the extent that it exists—that conflicts with our theory. Although this result deserves some weight in our thinking, it is probable that the weight has usually been too large. The interplay between nominal and real variables is neither as large nor as pervasive as most people believe.

Important Terms and Concepts

Phillips curve	anticipated money growth
expectational Phillips curve	unanticipated money growth

QUESTIONS AND PROBLEMS

Mainly for Review

16.1 What is the theoretical link between the price level and real variables? The inflation rate and real variables? Why do you think it might be important to distinguish between expected and unexpected inflation?

16.2 Consider the statement, "Makers of economic policy face a cruel choice between unemployment and inflation." Explain why this statement is not supported by either (a) theoretical results or (b) empirical findings on the Phillips curve.

16.3 How does the expectational Phillips curve explain the negative association between inflation and unemployment rates in the United States prior to World War I? Could the absence of this negative association in subsequent years be "explained" by shifts in the Phillips curve?

16.4 To what extent was the Great Depression (1929–33) accompanied by a change in the nominal quantity of money? In the real quantity of money?

16.5 Explain why it is important to distinguish between shifts in the nominal quantity of money and shifts in money demand. What association would we expect between the price level and real output in periods where both types of shifts occur?

CHAPTER 17

MONEY AND BUSINESS FLUCTUATIONS IN THE MARKET-CLEARING MODEL

In recent years, some macroeconomists have developed a new line of theory to explain the role of money in business fluctuations. The new approach has been called at least the following: *the equilibrium approach to business cycles*, *rational expectations macroeconomics*, and the *new classical macroeconomics*. Here we refer to it, somewhat more descriptively, as the *market-clearing model with incomplete information about prices*.[1]

It is important to stress that the theory developed in this chapter applies mainly to the interaction between monetary and real phenomena. Thus, the evidence surveyed in Chapter 16 indicates the potential scope for the theory. That evidence suggests something interesting to explain, but does not imply that monetary shocks are the most important source of business fluctuations. In particular, the theory in this chapter is not crucial for understanding the real effects of supply shocks or of government purchases and tax rates.

As with the models that we have discussed so far, the approach in this chapter relies on the conditions for general market clearing as its central analytical device. The approach also retains the assumption that people behave rationally, even including the manner in which they form expectations of inflation and other variables. However, we introduce an important source of

---

[1]For surveys of the research, see Robert Barro, "The Equilibrium Approach to Business Cycles," in Robert Barro, *Money, Expectations and Business Cycles,* Academic Press, New York, 1981; and Ben McCallum, "The Current State of the Policy-Ineffectiveness Debate," *American Economic Review,* proceedings, May 1979. See also the papers collected in Robert Lucas, *Studies in Business-Cycle Theory,* MIT Press, Cambridge, Massachusetts, 1981. Two early papers that stimulated much of the subsequent work are Milton Friedman, "The Role of Monetary Policy," *American Economic Review,* March 1968; and Edmund Phelps, ed., *Microeconomic Foundations of Employment and Inflation Theory,* Norton, New York, 1970.

"friction" by allowing for incomplete information about prices. An important way in which people receive information—and thereby make their allocative decisions—is by observing prices of various goods. But it would be prohibitively expensive for individuals to observe all prices instantly. Therefore, people typically make do with partial knowledge about the prices of different goods, about wage rates in alternative jobs, and so on. In this situation people's decisions often depart from those that they would make with full information.

Variations in money and the general price level make it difficult for people to interpret the limited set of prices that they observe. Hence, when there is an increase in the general price level, people may mistakenly think that the price of their output or their nominal wage rate has increased *relative* to other prices and wages. Consequently, they tend to produce more goods and work more than they would under full information. Because of these responses, we shall find that surprise increases in money and the general price level can lead to expansions in the aggregate level of real economic activity.

In this chapter we work out the details of a representative model from this new line of macroeconomic theory. To bring out the role of incomplete information, we have to move away from the simplified model with an economy-wide market for commodities. Now we make things more realistic by including a variety of local markets on which people buy and sell commodities.

The Structure of a Model with Local Markets

Consider again the model where households produce goods and sell them on a commodity market. Instead of assuming that all goods are the same, let's now imagine products that differ by physical characteristic, location, and so on. Accordingly, we now index commodities by the symbol z, which takes on the possible values, $1, 2, \ldots, q$, where q is a large number. To be concrete and to simplify matters, we usually think of z as a location—that is, as a "local market." But more generally, we could identify this index with various characteristics of goods, occupations, methods of production, and so on. So the value $z = 1$ might signify the automobile industry, $z = 2$ the computer industry, etc.

Since changes in job location or in type of product entail substantial costs, people do not move too often from one place or line of work to another. To capture this idea in a workable model, we assume that each household produces and sells goods in only one location during each period. But there is mobility in the sense that people may change locations at some cost from one period to the next.

We now distinguish prices by type or location of product and by date, so that $P_t(z)$ is the price of goods of type z during period t. Thus, $P_t(1)$ might be the dollar price of a market basket of goods in Detroit, while $P_t(2)$ is the price of the same market basket in Pittsburgh. Correspondingly, the ratio, $P_t(1)/P_t(2)$, is the price of goods of type or location 1, relative to that of type or location 2. It is important to distinguish this concept of a *relative price* from the general price level, which we have stressed in previous chapters. By the general price level P_t we mean an average of the individual prices at date t.

To keep things manageable, we neglect any long-lasting differences among locations or other characteristics of goods. That is, we ignore a variety of things that make goods permanently more or less expensive in different places. (For example, a market basket of goods always costs more in Alaska than in New York.) So, in our model, if the "local price," $P_t(z)$, exceeds the average price, P_t, then market z looks relatively favorable for sellers during period t. But this situation attracts producers from elsewhere. Then the expansion of goods supplied to market z tends to drive down the local price toward the general level of prices. Similarly, if the local price is lower than the average price, then producers move to other territory. Again, this process tends to bring the local price in line with the general price level. Overall there is a process of entry to and exit from local markets that keeps each local price reasonably close to the average price. Hence, if someone makes long-range forecasts, then the expected price in any local market equals that for the average of the markets.

Supply of Goods in a Local Market

At the beginning of period t, a producer in market z has the stock of capital, $k_{t-1}(z)$. Correspondingly, the amount of goods that he or she produces at location z during period t is given from the production function as

$$y_t(z) = f[k_{t-1}(z), n_t(z)] \qquad (17.1)$$

where $n_t(z)$ is the producer's work effort. Note that we again think of each household as working on its own production process, although we could extend things to include hired workers. Also, we think of last period's capital, $k_{t-1}(z)$, as stuck in market z, rather than movable across locations.

The dollar revenue from sales equals output, $y_t(z)$, multiplied by the local price, $P_t(z)$. But people buy goods from many locations. As an approximation, the typical household pays the average price, P_t, for its purchases of consumables and capital goods. In this case, people calculate the real value of the revenue from local sales—that is, the value in terms of the goods that they buy—by dividing the dollar amount by the general price level, P_t. Hence the real revenue from production is

$$\left[\frac{P_t(z)}{P_t}\right] \cdot y_t(z) = \left[\frac{P_t(z)}{P_t}\right] \cdot f[k_{t-1}(z), n_t(z)] \qquad (17.2)$$

The term, $P_t(z)/P_t$, is the price of goods sold in market z relative to the average price of goods. Notice that for a given amount of physical product, $y_t(z)$, an increase in the relative price, $P_t(z)/P_t$, means a greater real value of sales.

When deciding how much to work during period t, producers (and workers) looked before at the physical marginal product of labor, $\mathrm{MPL}_t(z)$. (Here, the index z means that the marginal product applies to additional work and output in market z.) Now, to compute the effect on real sales revenue, producers multiply the change in physical product by the relative price, $P_t(z)/P_t$. Hence, the real value of labor's marginal product is $[P(z)/P_t] \cdot \mathrm{MPL}_t(z)$.[2] An increase in the relative price looks to the producer just like a proportional upward shift in the schedule for labor's physical marginal product. Therefore, producers respond to changes in the relative price, $P_t(z)/P_t$, just as they did before to changes in the schedule for labor's marginal product.

Consider the response to an increase in the relative price, $P_t(z)/P_t$. Suppose that this increase applies only for period t, so that people do not anticipate a higher relative price for subsequent periods. Then the change amounts to a temporary upward shift in the schedule for labor's marginal product. Therefore, producers increase work effort, $n_t(z)$, and the supply of goods, $y_t^s(z)$. Recall that these responses involve two types of substitution effects. First, there is a shift away from leisure and toward consumption, and second, there is a shift away from today's leisure and toward tomorrow's leisure. The second channel, which is an intertemporal-substitution effect, suggests that the current responses of work and production will be large.[3] As an example, we can think of the strong response of labor supply to the unusually high wages that firms offer during overtime periods.

Let's consider now the determination of investment demand. We can use the approach developed in Chapter 9, but amended for a model with local markets. Suppose first that producers in market z buy capital goods from other markets at the *general* price level, P_t. If capital, $k_t(z)$, rises by one unit, then next period's output, $y_{t+1}(z)$, increases by the marginal product of capital, $\mathrm{MPK}_t(z)$. Since this output will sell at the *local* price, $P_{t+1}(z)$, revenues next period will rise by the amount, $P_{t+1}(z) \cdot \mathrm{MPK}_t(z)$. As before, we can pretend that producers sell their used capital at the *general* price, P_{t+1}. This price applies as long as producers in market z are still buying capital from other markets (at price P_{t+1}) during the next period.

If we neglect depreciation for simplicity, then the nominal rate of return

---

[2]With separate labor markets, we would say that a worker looks at the local dollar wage rate, $w_t(z)$, divided by the average price of commodities, P_t. The real wage rate, $w_t(z)/P_t$, is the value of the local wage in terms of the goods that it can buy on the average commodity market. Firms would hire labor until the local marginal product, $\mathrm{MPL}_t(z)$, equaled the local cost of labor, $w_t(z)$, expressed relative to the price of the firm's product, $P_t(z)$. That is, firms would operate where $\mathrm{MPL}_t(z) = w_t(z)/P_t(z)$. Substituting for $\mathrm{MPL}_t(z)$, we find that $[P_t(z)/P_t]\mathrm{MPL}_t(z) = w_t(z)/P_t$. Thus, by responding to $w_t(z)/P_t$, labor suppliers end up reacting to the term, $[P_t(z)/P_t]\mathrm{MPL}_t(z)$, that we used in the text. Since the answer is the same, we again simplify by not introducing firms or separate labor markets.

[3]The higher relative price, $P_t(z)/P_t$, also increases wealth for sellers in market z. However, for buyers, the effect on wealth is negative. In any case, since the changes in relative prices are temporary, the wealth effects will be small. In order to focus on the main points, we neglect these wealth effects.

to investment is $[P_{t+1}(z) \cdot \text{MPK}_t(z) + P_{t+1}]/P_t - 1$. Letting π_t be the inflation rate (for the general price level), this expression becomes $(1+\pi_t)[(P_{t+1}(z)/P_{t+1})\text{MPK}_t(z) + 1] - 1$. As in Chapter 9, producers would invest enough to equate this rate of return to the nominal interest rate, R_t. (We still treat R_t as determined on an economy-wide market for credit.) Writing out this equation and simplifying leads to the condition for investment demand,

$$\left[\frac{P_{t+1}(z)}{P_{t+1}}\right] \text{MPK}_t(z) = r_t \qquad (17.3)$$

where r_t is the economy-wide real interest rate (as defined by $1+r_t = (1+R_t)/(1+\pi_t)$). The condition in equation 17.3 is the same as in Chapter 9, except that capital's marginal product, $\text{MPK}_t(z)$, is multiplied by the prospective relative price, $P_{t+1}(z)/P_{t+1}$. Thus, investment demand for period t rises with either an upward shift in the schedule for capital's marginal product or an increase in $P_{t+1}(z)/P_{t+1}$. Also, as before, investment demand falls with an increase in r_t.

To carry out investment projects, producers typically have to buy some goods and labor services locally at the price $P_t(z)$. (Think of a gold rush, where the prospectors have to pay high local prices for labor and shovels.) In this case the main change to our formal analysis is that the purchase price of capital would be $P_t(z)$ rather than P_t. The result of this modification is that, other things equal, investment demand falls with an increase in the current relative price, $P_t(z)/P_t$. However, if the prospective relative price, $P_{t+1}(z)/P_{t+1}$, increases at the same time, demand for local goods can rise despite the increase in $P_t(z)/P_t$.

Consumer Demand

So far, we have examined the behavior of producers. Now we consider the incentives of consumers, who may come from elsewhere to purchase goods from these producers. For buyers, a high relative price, $P_t(z)/P_t$, deters consumption demand, $c_t^d(z)$. (Note that the index z refers to goods bought in market z, although the buyers may use the goods in other locations.)

Clearing of the Local Market

If we put the pieces of the analysis together, then the condition for clearing the local market is

$$Y_t^s(z)[\underset{(+)}{P_t(z)/P_t}, \underset{(+)}{r_t}, \ldots] = C_t^d(z)[\underset{(-)}{P_t(z)/P_t}, \underset{(-)}{r_t}, \ldots]$$
$$+ I_t^d(z)[\underset{(-)}{P_t(z)/P_t}, \underset{(+)}{P_{t+1}(z)/P_{t+1}}, \underset{(-)}{r_t}, \ldots] \qquad (17.4)$$

Here, we use capital letters to denote the quantity of goods supplied or demanded in market z. Notice that a higher current relative price, $P_t(z)/P_t$, raises the supply of goods, but lowers consumption and investment demand. Also, a higher prospective relative price, $P_{t+1}(z)/P_{t+1}$, increases investment demand.

We also include in the supply and demand functions the real interest rate, r_t. As before, an increase in r_t raises the supply of goods, $Y_t^s(z)$, but lowers the demands, $C_t^d(z)$ and $I_t^d(z)$.

Figure 17.1 depicts the clearing of a local commodity market. We put the current relative price, $P_t(z)/P_t$, on the vertical axis. The supply and demand curves in the figure assume given values for the prospective relative price, $P_{t+1}(z)/P_{t+1}$, and the real interest rate, r_t. (We also hold fixed the initial stock of capital in the local market, $K_{t-1}(z)$, and the forms of production functions.) Notice that the intersection of the curves determines the market-clearing values of the relative price, $[P_t(z)/P_t]^*$, and local output, $Y_t^*(z)$. Also, for the average market—which, by definition, has not experienced unusual changes in its supply and demand curves—the market-clearing relative price must equal one. That is, in the average market, the local price, $P_t^*(z)$, equals the average price, P_t^*.

Disturbances to Local Markets

We can imagine a variety of changes in tastes and technology that affect the clearing of a local market for goods. For example, there may be shifts in the numbers of producers, or in production functions, or in the numbers of demanders, and so on. Let's think of an increase in local consumption demand, $C_t^d(z)$, which might reflect an increase in the number of shoppers in market z. Alternatively, we can think of an increase in demand that reflects the popularity of some new or improved product, such as video games or personal computers.

Figure 17.2 shows the effect on a local commodity market from the increase in consumer demand. The solid lines reproduce the supply and demand curves from Figure 17.1. The new demand curve is the dashed line, labeled $Y^d(z)'$, which lies to the right of the original curve. Note that we hold constant the real interest rate, r_t, and the prospective relative price, $P_{t+1}(z)/P_{t+1}$. Since the disturbance applies only to the local market, it is reasonable to hold fixed the real interest rate. That is, this economy-wide variable responds to movements in the aggregates of supply and demand, rather than to changes in a single location or for a single type of product. However, we consider in a moment the behavior of the prospective relative price.

Figure 17.2 shows that the current relative price and local output increase. Notice that the rise in the relative price motivates producers to work more and supply more goods. Thus, we can think of the high relative price as the signal that generates the unusually large volume of work and production. However, the higher relative price means that investment falls. Since total output is higher, it follows that consumption, $C_t(z)$, must be up on net. Finally, if the

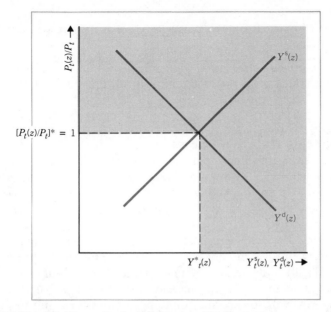

Figure 17.1 The Clearing of a Local Commodity Market
We show the dependence of commodity supply and demand on the relative price, $P_t(z)/P_t$. Here we hold fixed the effects of other variables, including the real interest rate, r_t, and the prospective relative price, $P_{t+1}(z)/P_{t+1}$. Note that, for the average market, the market-clearing relative price is one.

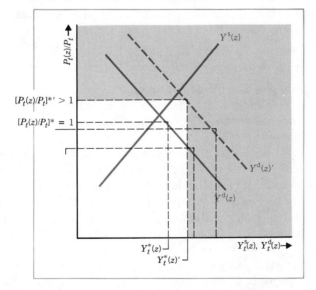

Figure 17.2 The Responses to an Increase in Local Demand
The change in consumer demand shows up as a positive shift to the local demand curve. Hence, the relative price and local output increase. Notice that the suppliers respond to the higher relative price by producing more goods (and by working harder). Also, if the market-clearing relative price is initially one (which holds for the average market), then the new value exceeds one.

479

market-clearing relative price were initially equal to one—as is true for the average market—then the new relative price must exceed one.

Prospective Relative Prices

The increase in consumer demand tends also to raise the prospective relative price, $P_{t+1}(z)/P_{t+1}$. The reason is that the disturbance—which in our case is an upward shift in demand—tends to persist. Further, we assume that the entry of new suppliers is insufficient to return the relative price to unity within a single period.

An increase in the prospective relative price raises investment demand, $I_t^d(z)$. Therefore, we modify the analysis from Figure 17.2 to include a larger rightward shift of demand. The main point of this modification is that investment may now increase. This increase is likely if it is crucial for investors to move aggressively to capitalize on opportunities for high prospective relative prices.

Note that, so far, we have considered only the response of a local market to a local disturbance. Hence, we have not yet explained movements in aggregate output and investment. But in later sections we show how a monetary disturbance may look, in each market, like a shift to local demand. Then producers in each market change output and investment, just as they do in response to a shift in local demand. When all producers act this way, we end up with movements in the aggregate variables.

Changes in the Stock of Money

Consider a once-and-for-all increase in the quantity of base money, M_t. As in some cases that we explored before, this change might involve an open-market purchase of bonds by the Fed.

Previously, we found that an increase in the quantity of money raises the general price level proportionately, but leaves unchanged real variables like aggregate output and employment. This conclusion still obtains when there are a variety of locations in which people produce and trade goods. As in previous analyses, we can think of people as attempting to spend their excess real cash balances on the goods in various markets. Then the price in each market, $P_t(z)$, ends up rising by the same proportion as the increase in money. It follows that the general or average price level, P_t, also moves one-to-one with the quantity of money. Therefore, the relative price, $P_t(z)/P_t$, does not change. There is also no change in the level of output, $Y_t(z)$, in each market. At this point, we still lack any connection between money and the real variables, which include the quantities of output and the relative prices of the different goods.

Imperfect Information about Money and the General Price Level

Now we make a crucial change in the setup to remove some information that individuals have about money and prices. The basic idea is that people know the prices of things that they recently bought or sold. So they know the wage rate for their labor services (at least on the present job), the price of groceries at the local market, the price of a car that they looked at last week, the rent on their apartment, and so on. Similarly, producers know a good deal about the costs of labor and other inputs, as well as the price of their own product (at least in a local market). However, people have much poorer knowledge about the prices of objects that they shopped for last year or perhaps have never examined.

We can model these general ideas by assuming that sellers and buyers know the local price of goods, $P_t(z)$, but are less sure about the general or average price, P_t. So the local goods correspond to the items that people have dealt with recently, and on which they know the current price. On the other hand, the general price applies to other goods, which are potential alternatives to local product, but for which people have a blurrier notion of the price.

As before, sellers and buyers in market z respond to their perception of the relative price, $P_t(z)/P_t$. But although they know the local price, $P_t(z)$, they no longer are sure about the general price level, P_t. Therefore, we have to analyze how people compute expectations of this average price under incomplete information. Here, we use the idea of rational expectations, which we mentioned before in Chapter 7. This approach says that if people do not observe something directly—such as the current price level—then they form the best possible estimate of this variable, given the information that they possess. In other words people make efficient use of their limited data, so as not to commit avoidable errors.[4]

Consider the expectations that people have about prices for period t. For simplicity, let's imagine that all markets look the same beforehand. That is, before period t, people cannot predict whether the price in market z, $P_t(z)$, will be higher or lower than the average price, P_t. Then we can just think about the expectations that people have before period t for the general price level, P_t. To keep things manageable, let's pretend that everyone has the same information beforehand and therefore calculates the same expectation, which we denote by P_t^e.

Generally, the expectation of prices depends on past information and on knowledge about the workings of the economy. We can think of this expec-

---

[4]The basic idea of rational expectations comes from John Muth, "Rational Expectations and the Theory of Price Movements," *Econometrica,* July 1961. For a discussion of applications to macroeconomics see Robert Lucas, "Understanding Business Cycles," *Carnegie-Rochester Conference Series on Public Policy,* 1976.

tation as incorporating information about the quantity of money and about variables that influence the aggregate real demand for .money. Often people will get useful information about these variables from lagged values of money and prices, from interest rates, and possibly from the government's announcements about monetary and fiscal policy. Therefore, the expectation, P_t^e, typically depends on all of these variables.

Clearing of a Local Commodity Market When Information Is Incomplete

Given the expected general price level, P_t^e, people compute the **perceived relative price** for market z as $P_t(z)/P_t^e$. We assume that sellers and buyers react to this price ratio just as they did to the actual ratio, $P_t(z)/P_t$, in the model with complete information. That is, an increase in the perceived relative price, $P_t(z)/P_t^e$, raises the supply of local goods, $Y_t^s(z)$, but lowers the demands, $C_t^d(z)$ and $I_t^d(z)$.

Figure 17.3 shows the supply and demand in a local market when people do not observe the general price level. We plot the perceived relative price, $P_t(z)/P_t^e$, on the vertical axis. For the moment, we hold fixed the prospective relative price, $P_{t+1}(z)/P_{t+1}$, and the real interest rate, r_t. Notice that the local market clears when the price ratio, $P_t(z)/P_t^e$, equals one. This result applies

Figure 17.3 **Response of a Local Market to the Perceived Relative Price**
A higher perceived relative price, $P_t(z)/P_t^e$, raises supply and lowers demand. The typical market clears when $P_t(z)/P_t^e = 1$.

to the average market, which, by definition, has not experienced unusual recent changes in local supply and demand. In other words, for the typical market, supply equals demand when the local price, $P_t(z)$, equals the expected price elsewhere, P_t^e.

Prospective Relative Prices

Thus far, we have neglected the prospective relative price, $P_{t+1}(z)/P_{t+1}$. Before, when people had full information about the general price level, there was a tendency for high relative prices to persist. These effects still arise when sellers and buyers do not observe the current general price level. In particular, an increase in the perceived relative price, $P_t(z)/P_t^e$, tends to raise expectations of the relative price in market z for the next period. Then this expectation raises today's investment demand, $I_t^d(z)$.

We add this effect to the supply and demand curves in Figure 17.4. As $P_t(z)/P_t^e$ increases, the higher prospective relative price raises $I_t^d(z)$. Therefore, the demand curve is more nearly vertical than before. Note that the demand curve now combines two types of effects. First, the effect from a change in $P_t(z)p_t^e$, and second, the effect from the accompanying change in expectations of $P_{t+1}(z)/P_{t+1}$. For now, the main thing to note from Figure 17.4 is that the typical local market still clears at the point where $P_t(z)/P_t^e = 1$.

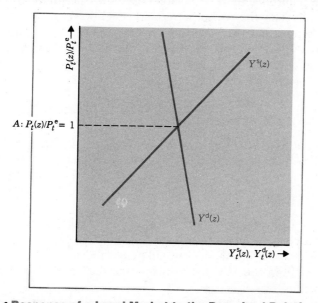

Figure 17.4 Response of a Local Market to the Perceived Relative Price, Including the Response of the Prospective Relative Price

As the price ratio, $P_t(z)/P_t^e$, rises the higher prospective relative price stimulates investment demand. Hence, as compared with Figure 17.3, the demand curve is more nearly vertical.

Changes in Money When There Is Incomplete Information

Now let's reconsider the effects of a once-and-for-all increase in the stock of money, M_t. Here, we deal with a surprise increase in money—that is, one that people could not anticipate when they formed their expectation of prices, P_t^e. Although this expectation was rational, it could not incorporate the effects from unanticipated changes in money.

Suppose, as before, that the local price, $P_t(z)$, rises in the typical market. (As usual, we can think of people attempting to spend their excess cash balances, which tends to bid up prices.) Then, since the expectation P_t^e is given, there must be an increase in $P_t(z)/P_t^e$. In other words the typical person now thinks that he or she is located in a market where the relative price is high. Of course, this belief must be incorrect, since the average across markets of the local prices, $P_t(z)$, always equals the general price level, P_t. But the surprise increase in money and prices—together with the lack of direct information about either the average price, P_t, or the quantity of money, M_t—means that the typical person underestimates the rise in the general price level. Thus, this person overestimates the relative price that he or she faces, and reacts by raising goods supply and lowering consumption demand. However, the net impact on investment demand is ambiguous. The direct effect from an increase in $P_t(z)/P_t^e$ is negative. But the higher expectation of $P_{t+1}(z)/P_{t+1}$ offsets this effect.

The point labeled A in Figure 17.5 shows the price ratio, $P_t(z)/P_t^e = 1$, that would clear the typical local market. However, the surprise increase in money means that the price in a typical market, $P_t(z)$, must exceed the expectation, P_t^e, as shown at point B in the figure. Then the supply of goods would exceed the demand in the typical market. So something else has to happen for this market to clear.

Effects on the Real Interest Rate

Recall that the real interest rate, r_t, still equals the nominal rate R_t—which everyone observes on the economy-wide credit market—less the general rate of inflation, π_t. The expected real interest rate, r_t^e—which matters for supply and demand decisions—equals the nominal rate, R_t, less the expected inflation rate, π_t^e.

So far, we have not allowed for any effects of the monetary disturbance on the expected real interest rate. But, for a given value of r_t^e, Figure 17.5 shows that the supply of goods would exceed the demand in the typical market. We know from previous analyses that the real interest rate must decline in this situation.

Here we pretend that everyone has the same expectation, r_t^e. In fact, these can differ because of differences in expected inflation rates, π_t^e. However, the basic results would not change if we added this complication.

Let's consider the results from the perspective of the typical commodity market. First, we reproduce the supply and demand curves from Figure 17.5 as the solid lines in Figure 17.6. Then, as r_t^e declines, the demand curve shifts

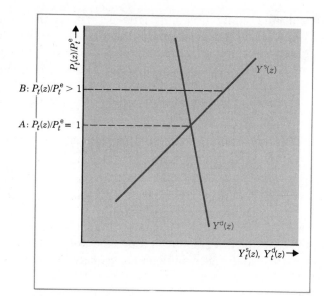

Figure 17.5 The Effect of a Surprise Increase in Money on the Typical Commodity Market
For given values of prospective relative prices and the real interest rate, the typical market would clear at point A, where $P_t(z)/P_t^e = 1$. But the surprise increase in money and prices means that the ratio, $P_t(z)/P_t^e$, exceeds one, as shown at point B. Here, the supply of goods, $Y_t^s(z)$, exceeds the demand, $Y_t^d(z)$.

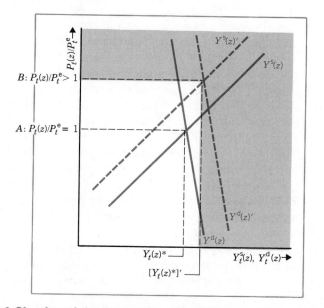

Figure 17.6 Clearing of the Typical Commodity Market after a Surprise Increase in Money
The solid lines for supply and demand come from Figure 17.5. The decline in the expected real interest rate shifts the demand curve rightward and the supply curve leftward. Hence, the typical commodity market clears where $P_t(z)/P_t^e$ exceeds one.

rightward, while the supply curve shifts leftward. That is, the fall in r_t^e motivates people to consume and invest more, but to work and produce less. We show the new curves as dashed lines in the figure. Notice that these curves intersect along the line labeled B, where $P_t(z)/P_t^e$ exceeds one. Thus, although people still perceive a high relative price in the typical commodity market, the reduction in the expected real interest rate allows the market to clear.

Monetary Effects on Output, Work, and Investment

Figure 17.6 shows an increase in local output, $Y_t(z)$, although the sign of this change is generally ambiguous. Let's consider the various forces that affect output in the typical market. (By typical, we mean that no unusual shifts in local supply or demand apply to this market.)

First, the high price ratio, $P_t(z)/P_t^e$, stimulates supply but deters consumption and investment demand. Second, the anticipation of a high future relative price, $P_{t+1}(z)/P_{t+1}$, encourages investment. Finally, the decrease in the expected real interest rate, r_t^e, boosts investment and consumption demand but discourages supply.

The presumption that output increases in the typical market depends on a strong positive effect from the prospective relative price, $P_{t+1}(z)/P_{t+1}$, on local investment demand. Given this property, the monetary disturbance tends to raise local investment, output, and work effort. Further, since this result applies to the typical market, it shows up also in the aggregates of investment, output, and work.

Let's review the main process by which a surprise increase in money and prices can lead to higher work, output, and investment. First, the general rise in prices looks to local suppliers like an increase in their relative price. Therefore, they work more and increase production, just as they would in the case of a true expansion of local demand. In other words the suppliers confuse the change in the general price level with the type of local disturbance that warrants an expansion of their real activity. (Recall that we considered this type of local disturbance before in Figure 17.2.)

Second, the increase in $P_t(z)/P_t^e$ makes people think that the local market will remain favorable to sellers for awhile. Thus, people raise their expectations of the future relative price, $P_{t+1}(z)/P_{t+1}$. Then just as in the case of a true increase in local demand, this belief stimulates investment. Further, the investment shows up currently as purchases of goods and services at the local price, which people perceive to be relatively high. Investors make these purchases to position themselves for the expected high returns later on.

Finally, since the disturbance causes an excess supply of goods in the typical commodity market, the expected real interest rate, r_t^e, must decline. This response clears the typical commodity market by raising the demand for goods and lowering the supply. Moreover, our previous analysis (from Chapter 9) suggests that investment demand would be especially responsive to the reduction in the real interest rate. Therefore, the model predicts a strong positive response of investment to a surprise increase in money.

Overall, the expansion of work, output, and investment occurs because the typical person confuses a high general price level for a high relative price in his or her location. Of course, individuals strive to avoid these kinds of mistakes. But given the available information, they cannot distinguish all changes in general prices from those in relative prices. Also, people have to weigh their mistaken reactions to changes in general prices against the potential errors from not responding to true shifts in relative prices. In most instances the local price, $P_t(z)$, accurately signals the reward for local production and investment. An overly cautious producer who fails to react to these signals—in order to avoid the mistaken responses to changes in the general price level—will also fail to exploit a variety of true opportunities for profit.

To summarize, the theory shows how surprise injections of money can be nonneutral. Moreover, unanticipated changes in money can generate the responses in quantities that typify aggregate business fluctuations. For example, the theory explains how a surprise contraction in the monetary base can cause a recession, in which output, employment, and especially investment decline. Recall that, at least for the post-World War II period, there is some evidence that movements in the monetary base have these sorts of effects.

Persisting Effects of Money on Real Variables

During recessions, variables like output, employment, and investment tend to be depressed for periods of a year or more. Therefore, we want to know whether the theory can account for persisting effects of monetary disturbances on real variables. One possibility is that misperceptions about the general price level persist for a long time, such as a year or more. Then any real effects from these misperceptions would also persist. But this argument is implausible. Earlier, we argued that people have incomplete information about prices in other markets and about monetary developments, which means that they can be ignorant for awhile about shifts in the general price level. But people presumably receive enough information about prices so that they would not make the same mistake in estimating the general price level for very long. Thus, it seems unlikely that the persistence in these errors would be as long as the persistence of booms and recessions.

The theory does not require that confusions about prices persist to explain why the responses of quantities persist. For example, we showed that the confusions from a monetary disturbance can lead to more investment. Then, perhaps a few months later, investors recognize that they confused an increase in the general price level for an increase in their relative price. But once people start investment projects, it does not always pay to terminate them, even when the past mistakes become clear. Hence, investment demand may remain high even after the confusion about prices disappears. Further, the higher level of investment shows up later as more productive capacity, which tends to raise output and employment even after people learn the truth about past money and prices. Through this type of mechanism, we find that a monetary disturbance can have a long-lasting influence on output and employment.

The Neutrality of Perceived Changes in Money

The analysis in the previous sections applies to surprise changes in money and the general price level. It is important to recognize that the confusion between general and relative prices cannot arise if people understand fully the movements in money and prices. To see this, suppose that everyone accurately anticipates a once-and-for-all increase in the quantity of money between dates $t - 1$ and t. Then the higher value of the money stock, M_t, shows up one-to-one as a higher rational expectation of prices, P_t^e. Hence, the increase of the price level in a typical market, $P_t(z)$, no longer represents a shift relative to expectations. Rather, actual and expected prices end up increasing in the same proportion. In this case there are no effects on commodity supply and demand in the typical market, which means no effects on the quantities of output and work, or on the real interest rate. Fully understood movements in money and prices are neutral, just as in our earlier models.

Changes in the long-run averages of monetary growth and inflation would be accompanied by corresponding changes in expectations of monetary growth and inflation. The theory predicts no effect from these long-term changes on real variables, such as the growth rate of output or the rate of unemployment.[5] Therefore, the theory is consistent with the long-term evidence for the United States and the United Kingdom, and with the data across countries for the post-World War II period. Remember that this evidence indicates that the average rate of monetary growth or inflation bears no relation to the unemployment rate or the growth rate of output.

Implications for Monetary Policy

If changes in money have real effects, then it is natural to think about a systematic policy of varying money to stabilize the economy. Specifically, economists often advise the Federal Reserve to accelerate money—for example, through open-market purchases of bonds—to bring the economy out of a recession. However, the theory developed in this chapter does not suggest that monetary policy could smooth out business fluctuations.

We can think of monetary policy as a regular procedure for adjusting the quantity of money, M_t, in relation to the state of the economy. For example, the monetary authority may expand money more rapidly than usual in response to a recession, but then hold down the growth rate of money in response to a boom. As noted before, there is some evidence that the Federal Reserve has pursued this sort of countercyclical monetary policy since World War II.

What does the theory predict for the real effects of this type of monetary policy? Given that the policy is in place, our best guess is that people take it into account when they formulate expectations of prices. In particular, if everyone knows that the Fed tends to inflate the economy in response to a recession,

---

[5]As in most of our analysis, we neglect the effects of expected inflation on transaction costs. Otherwise, there are some real effects, which economists typically regard as small.

then people raise their forecasts of money and prices accordingly. Hence, the expectation of prices, P_t^e, incorporates the typical response of the Fed to the observed state of the economy. But this means that the Fed changes money and prices relative to people's perceptions only when it departs from its usual practice. It follows that only the erratic part of the Fed's behavior has real effects. The systematic part of monetary policy—which is the predictable acceleration of money in response to a recession and the contraction in response to a boom—does not create any confusions between general and relative prices. Therefore, these monetary changes are neutral in the model. Sometimes, people call this finding the **irrelevance result for systematic monetary policy.**[6]

Of course, a great portion of actual fluctuations in money are unpredictable. Therefore, the irrelevance result does not apply to these types of monetary movements. But we also cannot think of this erratic behavior as representing useful policy. Rather, sometimes the changes are expansionary and sometimes contractionary, but not in a way that systematically improves the workings of the economy.

Stagflation

Economists use the term, **stagflation,** to describe a situation where inflation is either high or rising during a recession. For example, during the recession of 1974–75, the civilian unemployment rate reached a peak of 9.0% in May 1975, but the annual rate of change of the GNP deflator increased from about 4% in 1972 to 9% in 1975. Similarly, during 1979–80, the unemployment rate peaked at 7.8% in July 1980, but the inflation rate rose from about 7% in 1978 to 9% in 1980.

The theory in this chapter has no problem accounting for stagflation. First, there is no relation in the theory between the perceived parts of monetary growth or inflation and the real variables. So the increase in the average growth rates of money and prices from the late 1960s to the early 1980s, which were presumably perceived by everyone, give us no reason to predict low unemployment rates. Second, the oil crises of 1973–74 and 1979–80 constituted supply shocks, which tend to raise the general price level for a given behavior of the money stock. Thus, we predict in these cases that a burst of inflation would accompany the shortfalls in output.

Current Information on Prices

Thus far, expectations of prices, P_t^e, depend only on information available before period, t. Now we develop some interesting new results by allowing people to adjust their beliefs based on current information.

Recall that, during period t, people find that goods sell locally at the price

---

[6]For discussions of this result, see Thomas J. Sargent and Neil Wallace, "Rational Expectations, the Optimal Monetary Instrument, and the Optimal Money Supply Rule," *Journal of Political Economy,* April 1975, and Ben McCallum, "The Current State of the Policy-Ineffectiveness Debate," *American Economic Review,* proceedings, May 1979.

$P_t(z)$. If this price differs from P_t^e, then there are two possibilities. First, some local condition—such as a shift to demand in market z—may make the relative price of goods in this market either high or low. Second, the forecast of general prices may be inaccurate. That is, the general price level, P_t, may turn out to be either higher or lower than P_t^e. But by assumption, people cannot check things out directly by immediately sampling lots of prices in other markets or by observing a useful published index of current prices. Because the process of obtaining information is costly, sellers and buyers make do with incomplete knowledge about the prices of alternative goods. But the observation of the local price, $P_t(z)$, does convey some information about the current general price level, P_t. It is this information that we want to consider now.

Suppose first that people can predict the general price level, P_t, with a high degree of accuracy. This would be true if the monetary authority pursued a policy that usually provided for overall price stability. To carry out such a policy, the authority would have to avoid large random changes in the quantity of money, M_t. In this kind of stable environment, people would not make significant adjustments to their expectations, P_t^e, when they observed the local price, $P_t(z)$. Rather, they would be confident that movements of $P_t(z)$ signaled changes in relative prices, $P_t(z)/P_t$, rather than movements in P_t. Of course, this also means that people get fooled substantially on the rare occasions when monetary surprises do generate large movements in the overall price level.

In contrast, consider an economy where money is volatile and the general price level, P_t, often departs substantially from the forecast, P_t^e. In this setting people would be much less confident that a movement in $P_t(z)$ reflected a change in the relative price, $P_t(z)/P_t$. At least to some extent they would think that a high value of $P_t(z)$ signals a higher than expected value of P_t. It follows that perceptions of the relative price, $P_t(z)/P_t$, become less responsive to observed changes in $P_t(z)$. That is because people partially adjust P_t^e in the same direction as the movement in $P_t(z)$.

Recall that the response of perceived relative prices is the mechanism whereby surprise movements in money have real effects. Since people are now less willing to believe that relative prices have changed, we find that monetary shocks have smaller real effects than before. The general result is that *the greater the historical volatility of money, the smaller the real effect of a monetary shock*. This follows because more historical volatility of money makes people more inclined to associate observed increases in local prices with unexpectedly high general price levels. Therefore, it is harder for monetary shocks to fool people into thinking that relative prices have changed.

These propositions receive empirical support from some studies of various countries during the post-World War II period.[7] First, it turns out that monetary

---

[7]See Roger Kormendi and Philip Meguire, "Cross-Regime Evidence of Macroeconomic Rationality," *Journal of Political Economy*, October 1984; and C. L. F. Attfield and N. W. Duck, "The Influence of Unanticipated Money Growth on Real Output: Some Cross-Country Estimates," *Journal of Money, Credit and Banking*, November 1983.

disturbances (measured by surprise movements in $M1$) have a positive relation to real GNP for the majority of the countries. But most importantly for the theory, the strength of this relation diminishes as a country's rate of monetary growth becomes less predictable. Countries such as the United States that display relative stability of money turn out to be the ones where monetary shocks (for $M1$) have a strong positive relation to real GNP. In places like Argentina and Brazil where monetary growth fluctuates unpredictably, there is essentially no connection between monetary disturbances and real GNP.

Let's return now to the theory to derive another result. We already noted that greater fluctuations in money mean that perceived relative prices become less responsive to changes in local prices. On the one hand, this means that people make fewer mistakes when the changes in prices reflect surprises in money and the general price level. But it implies also that people make more mistakes when there actually are shifts in relative prices. Overall, more uncertainty about money and the overall price level means that observed prices become less useful as signals of changes in relative prices. Thus, in a general sense, the price system becomes less effective as a mechanism for channeling resources. For example, the economy becomes less responsive to shifts in the composition of tastes and technology, which require resources to shift from one place to another.[8] Note especially that—in contrast to variations in the average growth rate of money—changes in the predictability of money are nonneutral in this model. From this standpoint the best monetary policy is the one that is the most predictable.

Some Problems with the Theory

So far, we have shown how the market-clearing model with incomplete information about prices generates some results that compare favorably with empirical evidence. But before we accept the theory and its intriguing implications for monetary policy, we should investigate more of its properties. Here, we consider some serious criticisms of the theory.

The Behavior of Prices and Real Interest Rates

According to the theory, the real effects of monetary disturbances operate through the channels of price surprises and movements in the real interest rate. But the empirical evidence does not verify these channels of effect. For example, as discussed in Chapter 16, the post-World War II data do not indicate much of a connection between price surprises and fluctuations in real economic

---

[8]For discussions of the adverse consequences of monetary uncertainty, see F. A. Hayek, "The Use of Knowledge in Society," *American Economic Review,* September 1945; and Henry Simons, "Rules versus Authorities in Monetary Policy," in Henry Simons, *Economic Policy for a Free Society,* University of Chicago Press, Chicago, 1948.

activity.[9] Also, some studies for the post-World War II period do not find much connection between monetary disturbances and real interest rates.[10]

Overall, the theory gets mixed reviews for its predictions about monetary disturbances. On the one hand, the analysis neatly accommodates the positive responses of production, employment, and investment to monetary shocks. But on the other hand, the available evidence does not support the model's story about the channels of transmission from monetary changes to the real variables.

Incomplete Information about Prices and Money

A central element in the theory is that people do not observe immediately the general price level or the quantity of money. For instance, if people always know the general level of prices—perhaps because they look regularly at a useful index, such as the CPI or the deflator for the GNP—then they cannot confuse shifts in the general price level for changes in relative prices. Alternatively, suppose that people observe quickly the quantity of money, but not the general price level. Then—at least if they understand the economics taught in this book!—they can figure out the implications of the monetary movements for the general price level. Therefore, they would not confuse at least the monetary-induced parts of changes in general prices with shifts in relative prices. But then the model predicts that the monetary changes would be neutral.

In fact, it is not difficult for people to observe quickly an index of prices (with a 1-month lag for the CPI) or measures of monetary aggregates (with a 1-week lag for $M1$). Lately, the press reports quickly and with great publicity (and often with conflicting interpretations!) the size of each week's monetary aggregate, $M1$. Also, if people read the *Wall Street Journal,* they can observe the value of each week's monetary base. Of course, most people do not bother to collect and interpret these types of data. But presumably, that is because the information is of minor value to them.[11]

Let's think about the usefulness of the available indices of prices. One reason that they may not be very helpful is that each individual cares about a market basket of goods that differs substantially from the one used in the index. Also, the indices sometimes have conceptual problems, which limit

---

[9]However, as noted in Chapter 16, it is possible that supply shocks obscure the relation. Since these shocks lead to an inverse relation between prices and output, the available studies may not isolate the positive relation that results from monetary shocks.

[10]Some results are in Robert Barro, "Intertemporal Substitution and the Business Cycle," *Carnegie-Rochester Conference Series on Public Policy,* Spring 1981. See also Robert Litterman and Laurence Weiss, "Money, Real Interest Rates, and Output: A Reinterpretation of Postwar U.S. Data," *Econometrica,* January 1985.

[11]Traders of stocks and bonds pay close attention to monetary developments. So it is likely that all the useful information from observing the quantity of money is already reflected in stock prices and interest rates. Then as long as people look at stock prices and interest rates, they have no reason to look separately at the monetary statistics.

their value. (The CPI's treatment of mortgage interest costs was an example, until the recent change in procedures.) Then to keep well informed about prices, people would have to take detailed samples from a variety of markets. But this process is costly. Hence, this viewpoint suggests that people would sometimes make significant errors in their interpretations of observed prices.

A similar argument is that the data on monetary aggregates provide little useful information. Possibly because of seasonal adjustments and the arbitrariness in defining money, the reported measures bear little relation to the concept of money that matters in the theory. However, this argument leads to a puzzle. Namely, it is the reported figures—on $M1$ and perhaps on the monetary base—that seem to have a positive relation to real economic activity in the post-World War II period. But if the data are meaningless, it is hard to explain this relation. Alternatively, if the reported measures are important, then why would people not bother to observe them?

To put the various points together, it seems reasonable that ignorance about the general price level and the quantity of money can account for small and short-lived confusions about relative prices. That is because people would find it too costly to monitor continuously and interpret the behavior of general prices and the quantity of money. But it is unlikely that large or long-lasting confusions would arise. The costs of being misinformed about relative prices— and therefore making incorrect decisions about production, work, and investment—seem excessive relative to the costs of gathering the necessary information. Hence, this view suggests that monetary-induced confusions of general for relative prices can account only for small fluctuations in the aggregate economy. We cannot use this line of theory to explain massive contractions of output and employment.

In terms of the U.S. history, the theory has promise for explaining a role for money in the relatively mild recessions of the post-World War II period. Recall that, if we identify money with the monetary base, then there is some evidence that this role was significant. But it is unlikely that the approach can account for a major portion of the more severe contractions from before the war. In particular, the confusion between general and relative prices probably played only a minor part in the Great Depression of 1929–33. On the other hand, we also suggested before that this episode—and some others from before World War I that featured banking panics—involved a cutback in financial intermediation, rather than a contraction of the monetary base. So we probably do not need to rely on incomplete information about money and prices to understand these experiences.

Summary

There is a new line of macroeconomic theory, which attempts to explain the role of money in business fluctuations. This approach retains the framework of market clearing and rational behavior, but introduces incomplete information about prices to explain some real effects from monetary disturbances.

In this model surprise increases in money and the general price level make individuals in local markets think that the relative price of their output has risen. Thereby, monetary injections can induce people to expand the quantities of production, work, and investment. In this respect the theory accords with some evidence, which suggests that surprise variations in the quantity of base money may be nonneutral.

Perceived changes in money and the general price level do not lead to confusions about relative prices. Therefore, the perceived parts of monetary changes are still neutral. This result conforms with the absence of a strong long-term relation of real variables to either monetary growth or inflation.

The systematic part of monetary policy causes no confusions about relative prices. Therefore, the theory predicts that this part of policy has no significance for real variables. However, an increase in monetary uncertainty is nonneutral, because it alters the information that people receive by observing local prices. Since people recognize that monetary shocks are often large, the real variables become less sensitive to monetary disturbances. But because the observed prices become less useful as allocative signals, there is also a worsening in the allocation of resources. Specifically, the economy becomes less responsive to variations in the composition of tastes and technology. Thus, the model's main lesson is that monetary policy should be predictable, rather than erratic.

Although the theory accords with some empirical evidence, it also has problems. For example, the data do not support either the role of price shocks during recessions or the prediction that monetary disturbances depress the real interest rate. Also, since the costs of obtaining information about money and prices are not very large, the theory cannot explain major business contractions such as the Great Depression. But the theory may help to understand some aspects of mild recessions, such as those experienced since World War II.

Important Terms and Concepts

perceived relative price

stagflation

irrelevance result for systematic monetary policy

QUESTIONS AND PROBLEMS

Mainly for Review

17.1 Explain why it is reasonable to assume that individuals have imperfect information about the general price level. What are the costs of collecting information about prices?

17.2 Explain what a relative price is. Is the real wage an example of a relative price? Show how a proportional increase in $P_t(z)$ and P_t^e leaves buyers and sellers unaffected.

17.3 What are the factors that might cause the relative price in a market to remain high for many periods of time? What are the factors that cause changes in the relative price to be offset in later periods? (Include in your answer the effect of changes in the numbers of buyers and sellers and changes in the capital stock.)

17.4 Can there be unexpected changes in the quantity of money when expectations are rational? If so, does a policymaker have the option of counteracting business cycles through "surprise" increases in money?

17.5 When expectations are rational, any errors made in estimating the price level will not persist. How then can we explain persistent deviations of aggregate output from trend?

Problems for Discussion

17.6 Investment Demand in a Local Market
   a. Suppose that producers in market z buy capital at the price, P_t. What is the condition that determines investment demand if old capital sells next period at the price P_{t+1}?
   b. What is the condition for investment demand if producers in market z buy capital locally at the price $P_t(z)$? How does the result depend on whether old capital sells the next period at price $P_{t+1}(z)$ or P_{t+1}?

17.7 Changes in the Predictability of Money
Suppose that the fluctuations of money become less predictable from year to year. What happens to the following:
   a. The responsiveness of the perceived value of the relative price, $P_t(z)/P_t$, to the observed local price, $P_t(z)$?
   b. The effect of a given size monetary disturbance on output?
   c. The allocation of resources?

17.8 Money and the Dispersion of Relative Prices (optional)
The local price, $P_t(z)$, differs across locations because each market experiences local shocks to supply and demand. (Think here of changes in the composition of tastes and technology.) Thus, the model generates a dispersion of relative prices across markets at each point in time. Now suppose, as in problem 17.7, that the fluctuations in money become less predictable from year to year. Then what happens to the dispersion of relative prices across markets at a point in time?

   (There is evidence that this effect is important during extreme inflations, such as the German hyperinflation, but not for the U.S. experience. See Zvi Hercowitz, "Money and the Dispersion of Relative Prices," *Journal of Monetary Economics,* July 1982. For a survey of the related literature on price dispersion, see Alex Cukierman, "Relative Price Variability and Inflation: A

Survey and Further Results," *Carnegie-Rochester Conference Series on Public Policy,* Autumn 1983.)

17.9 Monetary Effects on Consumption (optional)

In the text we noted some shortcomings of the market-clearing model with incomplete information on prices. Here, we explore another problem, which concerns the behavior of consumption.

We argued that a positive monetary shock could increase output, employment, and investment. Suppose, in fact, that work effort increases, so that leisure declines.

a. What must be the effect on consumption? (*Hint:* Does the monetary shock alter the terms on which people can substitute today's leisure for today's consumption?)

b. Would the results change if the monetary disturbance raised perceived wealth?

c. How do the theoretical results about consumption conform with the data on U.S. recessions?

17.10 Monetary Effects on Real Wage Rates (optional)

Another problem with the theory concerns the behavior of real wage rates. We explore this problem here.

Suppose that we allow each locality to have a labor market, on which the wage rate is $w_t(z)$. How would a surprise increase in money affect the real wage, $w_t(z)/P_t(z)$, in the typical market? (See footnote 2 above for a suggestion on how to proceed.) How does the result compare with empirical evidence on real wage rates during recessions and booms?

17.11 Revisions of the Monetary Data

a. Suppose that people observe the monetary base as it is reported from week to week. Then what does the theory predict about the effects of changes in base money on real variables?

b. The Federal Reserve often revises its data on money—especially $M1$—several months after the initial reports. (Mostly, these revisions arise because the Fed has to estimate the monthly figures on checkable deposits for nonmember banks and some other financial institutions.) What does the theory say about the economic effects of these revisions in the monetary figures? (Empirically, the revisions bear no relation to real economic activity—see Robert Barro and Zvi Hercowitz, "Money Stock Revisions and Unanticipated Money Growth," *Journal of Monetary Economics,* April 1980.)

17.12 The Effects of Anticipated Policy

a. What is the irrelevance result for systematic monetary policy?

b. Does the result mean that the unpredictable parts of money do not matter?

c. Does the result mean that the systematic parts of all government policies are irrelevant? Consider, as examples, the following:

i. The unemployment-insurance program.

ii. A policy of raising government purchases during a recession.

iii. A policy of cutting income-tax rates during a recession.

17.13 **The Fed's Information and Monetary Policy**

Suppose that the Fed has a regular policy of accelerating money during a recession.

a. Why does the theory say that this policy does not matter?

b. If the Fed observes the recession before others do, does the policy still not matter?

c. Suppose that the Fed knows no more about recessions than anyone else does. But the Fed also knows that real activity expands when monetary growth is surprisingly high. Thus, when the economy is in a recession, the Fed attempts to expand money by more than the amount people expect. What problems arise here? (*Hint:* Suppose that people understand that the Fed is pursuing this type of policy. What then is the rational expectation of monetary growth and inflation?)

CHAPTER 18

THE KEYNESIAN THEORY OF BUSINESS FLUCTUATIONS

The Keynesian theory was developed to understand the tendency of private enterprise economies to experience fluctuations in aggregate business activity. More specifically, Keynes's analysis[1] sought to explain and suggest policy remedies for the prolonged depressions that occurred in the United States during the 1930s and in the United Kingdom during the 1920s and 1930s.

The Keynesian theory focuses on the process by which private markets match up suppliers and demanders. Notably, the theory assumes that prices on some markets do not adjust perfectly to ensure continual balance between the quantities supplied and demanded. Hence, unlike our previous models, some markets do not always clear. (The imbalance between supply and demand is often referred to as "disequilibrium," but we shall avoid that ambiguous term.) Because of the absence of general market clearing, output and employment typically end up below the efficient amounts. That is, although everyone could be made better off by an expansion of economic activity, the private market sometimes fails to generate this higher level of activity.

Keynesian models assume, at least implicitly, that there are constraints on the flexibility of some prices. For example, the models assume that the nominal wage rate or the dollar price of commodities responds only sluggishly to changes in market conditions. In extreme cases the wage rate or price level is rigid—or at least fully determined from the past. Then current market forces have no influence on these prices. But economists' willingness to accept this type of assumption as reasonable has diminished with the advent of high and variable inflation in the United States and other industrialized countries. Thus we shall also consider the possibilities for introducing some flexibility of prices into the Keynesian model.

---

[1] John Maynard Keynes, *The General Theory of Employment, Interest and Money*, Harcourt Brace, New York, 1935.

499

A Simple Keynesian Model

Keynes's analysis and some subsequent treatments[2] focused on "sticky" nominal wage rates and the resultant lack of balance between labor supply and demand. Prices for commodities were sometimes assumed to be perfectly flexible (leading to the so-called **complete Keynesian model**), but were more often treated also as sticky. In our framework, we can generate the basic Keynesian results without explicitly considering a separate labor market. Here, we treat as sticky the dollar price, P_t, for goods and services that people exchange on the commodity market. (We return now to the case of an economy-wide market for goods.) We should stress that the neglect of the labor market is purely a simplification. The same sorts of conclusions emerge if we choose instead to examine this market and postulate a sticky nominal wage rate.

Some early analyses assumed that prices were rigid. This assumption turns out to be unnecessary because the Keynesian framework can accommodate nonzero inflation rates. The crucial feature is not completely fixed prices, but rather the failure of prices to clear all markets instantly. However, it is convenient to begin with a model in which the price level is fixed. Then after we develop this model we can introduce a nonzero inflation rate.

Let's begin by writing down our standard conditions for general market clearing. For the commodity market, the condition for period t is

$$Y^s(R_t, \ G_t, \ldots) = C^d(R_t, \ G_t, \ldots) + I^d(R_t, \ldots) + G_t \quad (18.1)$$
$$(+) \ (+) \qquad\qquad (-) \ (-) \qquad\qquad (-)$$

Notice first that we enter the nominal interest rate, R_t, because the price level is fixed. Hence, the real interest rate, r_t, equals the nominal rate. Second, we include the level of government purchases, G_t. Recall that a higher quantity of purchases, G_t, means a larger amount of goods supplied (because public services are productive), but a smaller amount of consumer goods demanded. We assume lump-sum taxes, although an income tax could also be considered. Finally, equation 18.1 takes as given the stock of capital, K_{t-1}, the characteristics of the production function, and the level of permanent government purchases, $\bar{G}$.

Next we have the condition that money be willingly held

$$M_t = P_t \cdot L(Y_t, \ R_t, \ldots) \quad (18.2)$$
$$(+) \ (-)$$

[2]See Don Patinkin, *Money, Interest and Prices*, Harper & Row, New York, 1956, Chapter 13; and Robert Barro and Herschel Grossman, "A General Disequilibrium Model of Income and Employment," *American Economic Review*, March 1971, and *Money, Employment and Inflation*, Cambridge University Press, Cambridge, England, 1976, Chapter 2.

where M_t is the nominal quantity of money for period t. As usual, the aggregate real demand for money depends positively on output, Y_t, and negatively on the nominal interest rate, R_t.

Equations 18.1 and 18.2 determine the general-market-clearing values of the interest rate and the price level, which we denote by R_t^* and P_t^*. Correspondingly, we denote the general-market-clearing level of output by Y_t^*.

The departure for Keynesian analysis is that the fixed price level, P_t, differs from the general-market-clearing value, P_t^*. Specifically, the standard Keynesian results emerge when the price level is excessive—that is, $P_t > P_t^*$ —which amounts to assuming downward rigidity of prices. Then it will generally be impossible for the economy to attain full market clearing, as specified in equations 18.1 and 18.2. Consequently, we have to search for some concept other than supply equals demand to determine the interest rate and the level of output.

Think of starting from a position of general market clearing and then arbitrarily raising the price level above its market-clearing value. In this case, equation 18.2 can no longer hold at the general-market-clearing values of output, Y_t^*, and the interest rate, R_t^*. The excessive price level means that the quantity of money, M_t, would fall short of the aggregate quantity demanded. Then we can think of individuals as attempting to replenish their cash balances, partly by selling bonds and partly by reducing consumer demand and leisure. The first channel suggests upward pressure on the interest rate, which raises the supply of goods, Y_t^s, and lowers the demand, $C_t^d + I_t^d$. Hence, excess supply of commodities results. The second channel—whereby consumer demand and leisure decline—reinforces this outcome. Thus, the excessive price level leads to an excess supply of goods.

The Rationing of Sales

How does the commodity market operate under conditions of excess supply? That is, what happens when—at the going price, P_t—the total of offers to sell goods exceeds the overall willingness to buy? Normally, we expect a decline in the price level, but that mechanism is ruled out by assumption. Therefore, we have to study the commodity market when excess supply prevails, but the price level cannot fall.

Some type of quantity-rationing rule must allocate sales when there is an imbalance between the quantities supplied and demanded. The usual mechanism assumes two properties. First, no supplier or demander can be forced to sell or buy more than he or she desires, which follows in a setting of voluntary exchange. Second, trade proceeds as long as some seller and some buyer are both made better off—that is, the market ensures the execution of all mutually advantageous exchanges, given that the fixed price, P_t, applies to all trades. The first condition means that the total quantity of goods sold, Y_t, cannot exceed the smaller of aggregate supply and demand—otherwise, some involuntary sales or purchases would occur. The second condition guarantees that the amount sold is at least as great as the minimum of aggregate supply and demand—if not, some mutually advantageous trade at price P_t would be missed. Thus, the combination of the two properties ensures that output is determined by the **short side** of the market—that is, by the condition

$$Y_t = \text{MIN} \ (Y_t^s, \ Y_t^d) \tag{18.3}$$

where MIN denotes the minimum of the variables that appear in the parentheses. Note that we deal here with the rationing of sales on the commodity market. In a more general Keynesian framework, we would include also the rationing of jobs—that is, sales of labor services—on a separate labor market. Then the people who seek jobs but cannot find them are considered to be **involuntarily unemployed.**

Under conditions of excess supply—that is, $Y_t^s > Y_t^d$—output is determined by aggregate demand, Y_t^d, which defines the short side of the commodity market. Therefore, the typical demander experiences no difficulty in finding goods to purchase from the eager suppliers. However, the representative supplier faces an insufficiency of buyers for the products that he or she offers for sale at the price, P_t.[3] Thus, we now have to reconsider households' decisions in the presence of this constraint. These modifications play an essential role in Keynesian analysis.

In the standard model of a competitive market, individual sellers and buyers are able to transact any amount desired at the going price. But this condition cannot hold for all suppliers when an excess supply of goods prevails. Here, we want to specify the constraint that confronts an individual supplier of goods. We assume that the total quantity of real sales available, Y_t, is somehow apportioned via a nonprice mechanism among the sellers, who offer the larger quantity, Y_t^s. In other words, there is a rationing process, which assigns each individual producer the quantity of real sales, y_t. Notice that we consider a ration on sales rather than on purchases, which would arise if goods were in excess demand.

We assume that each producer regards his or her real sales limit, y_t, as a given, in the same way that people take as givens the price level, P_t, and the interest rate, R_t. We do not allow an individual to take any actions that would influence the size of his or her ration. That is, we exclude such possibilities as greater search for buyers, black-market activities that could involve price cutting, overstatement of the true sales offers in order to secure a larger individual ration, political influence to change official rations (in this case, of sales) and so on. Basically, the allowance for these features would amount to relaxing the constraint of the fixed price, P_t.

---

[3]In a disaggregated setup, excess supply could appear in some markets and excess demand in others. The standard Keynesian model applies when the great majority of markets experience excess supply.

The Choice of Work Effort

The production function implies

$$y_t = f(k_{t-1}, n_t, \quad G_t) \qquad (18.4)$$
$$(+) \ (+) \ (+)$$

Here, we assume that the ration is an effective constraint on sales—that is, $y_t < y_t^s$ applies for the typical producer.[4] Therefore, the level of output, y_t, is now a given to the producer, rather than a choice variable.

Given the quantity of capital, k_{t-1}, and the level of government purchases, G_t, the quantity of work, n_t, is the minimum amount necessary to produce the assigned level of output, y_t. Therefore, the production function from equation 18.4 determines n_t for given values of y_t, k_{t-1}, and G_t. We can write the quantity of work as the function

$$n_t = n(y_t, \quad k_{t-1}, \quad G_t) \qquad (18.5)$$
$$(+) \ (-) \ (-)$$

For given values of the other inputs, n_t varies directly with y_t, as shown by the graph of the production function in Figure 18.1. For any value of y_t on the vertical axis, we can read off n_t on the horizontal. Note that more output means more labor input. With the labor market included, more work also means less involuntary unemployment.

Increases in either of the other inputs, k_{t-1} and G_t, mean that less work is needed to produce a given amount of output. Therefore, n_t declines in equation 18.5. (In Figure 18.1 we can verify these results by shifting the production function upward.)

In the model without sales constraints, people set the level of work to equate the marginal product of labor to the value placed on an extra unit of leisure time. But an effective restraint on sales means that work effort is smaller than otherwise. Because of diminishing marginal productivity, labor's marginal product now exceeds the value placed on an extra unit of leisure. People would like to work and produce more, if only the goods could be sold at the going price. But the constraint on sales prevents the expansion of work and production. We can also say that the constraint on sales means that the economy operates inefficiently. Everyone could be made better off if work and production were higher—as they would be if all markets cleared. But in the Keynesian model, where the commodity market (and the labor market) do not clear, these efficient adjustments are assumed not to occur.

---

[4]Note that we do not allow producers to store up excess output as inventories. This option becomes especially important if people perceive the state of excess supply to be temporary. For extensions of the Keynesian model to include inventories, see Ajit Chaudhury, "Output, Employment and Inventories under General Excess Supply," *Journal of Monetary Economics,* October 1979; and Alan Blinder, "Inventories in the Keynesian Macro Model," *Kyklos,* No. 4, 1980.

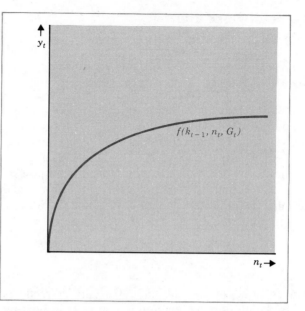

Figure 18.1 The Determination of Labor Input
The graph of the production function shows the effect on output of more labor input for given quantities of capital and government purchases. For a given level of output on the vertical axis, the graph determines the quantity of work on the horizontal. Notice that more output means more labor input.

The Keynesian Consumption Function

The restraint on sales means that people receive less real income than otherwise. In fact, in our model where the households are also the producers, each household's current real receipts from the commodity market equal the real sales ration, y_t. If prospective real sales equal the current value, then variations in y_t have a one-to-one effect on permanent income. Then the effect on consumption demand would also be roughly one-to-one. More generally—when the constraint on sales is temporary—there is a weaker effect on permanent income. Consequently, consumption demand becomes less responsive to variations in y_t.

The main point is that an increase in current output, y_t, has a positive effect on consumer demand. Hence, the consumption function, now denoted by $\hat{c}^d$, takes the form

$$c_t^d = \hat{c}^d(y_t, \ R_t, \ . \ . \ .) \tag{18.6}$$
$$(+) \ (-)$$

Notice that the interest rate, R_t, still has a negative intertemporal-substitution effect on current consumer demand.

The expression in equation 18.6 is often called the **Keynesian consumption**

function. The distinctive feature of this function is the presence of the quantity of real sales, y_t. In our previous analysis, people chose consumption by considering the real interest rate, the possibilities for substituting between consumption and leisure, the position of the production function, and the nature of their preferences. But now there is a separate effect from the given level of real sales in the commodity market. Anything that raises the quantity of someone's real sales, y_t, spills over to increase consumption demand.

Another argument that people use to derive the Keynesian consumption function concerns the credit market. Up to now we have assumed that this market allows people to borrow or lend any amount they desire at the going interest rate R_t. An alternative view is that households cannot borrow readily unless they have good collateral, such as a house, car, or business, to secure the loan. In particular, because of the costs of collection and customer evaluation, people cannot usually borrow based solely on a promise to repay out of future labor income. Economists describe as **liquidity constrained** a person who would like to borrow at the going interest rate to raise current consumption, but cannot obtain a loan (at a "reasonable" interest rate). People in this situation would alter their consumption demand, c_t^d, virtually one-to-one in response to changes in their current income, y_t. Therefore, this viewpoint can also explain why the variable, y_t, appears on the right side of equation 18.6 for some consumers. We shall try to evaluate the importance of liquidity constraints later on.

Determination of Output in the Keynesian Model

Putting together the results thus far, we can write the level of aggregate demand in the form

$$Y_t^d = \hat{C}^d(Y_t, \; R_t, \; \ldots) + I^d(R_t, \; \ldots) + G_t$$
$$\quad\;\; (+) \, (-) \qquad\qquad (-)$$

where $\hat{C}^d$ is an aggregate version of the Keynesian consumption function, and I^d is the investment demand function, which we have studied previously. Recall that the price level exceeds the general-market-clearing value—that is, $P_t > P_t^*$—which means that goods are in excess supply. Consequently, output is demand determined, as follows

$$Y_t = Y_t^d = \hat{C}^d(Y_t, \; R_t, \; \ldots) + I^d(R_t, \; \ldots) + G_t \qquad (18.7)$$
$$\qquad\quad (+) \, (-) \qquad\qquad (-)$$

Equation 18.7 is the key relation in the Keynesian model. It says that output, Y_t, equals aggregate demand, Y_t^d. But the tricky aspect is that the consumption part of aggregate demand is itself a function of output. Thus, equation 18.7 says that the level of output, Y_t, determines a level of demand, Y_t^d, which is, in turn, equal to output.

An important element in the determination of output is the responsiveness

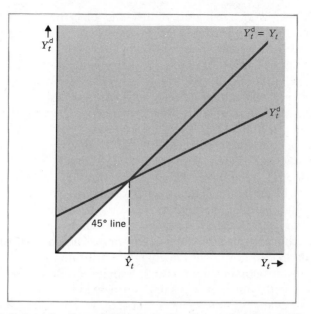

Figure 18.2 Determination of Ouput via the Keynesian Cross Diagram
The line denoted Y_t^d shows the response of aggregate demand to changes in output, Y_t. But output equals demand only along the 45° line. Therefore, we determine the level of output at the intersection of the curves as the value $\hat{Y}_t$.

of aggregate consumer demand to variations in output—that is, the aggregate "marginal propensity to consume" out of changes in current real income, Y_t. Typically this marginal propensity is between zero and one, with the value approximating one when people view a change in output as permanent. We denote the marginal propensity to consume by ν (the Greek letter *nu*).

For now, let's consider an extreme version of the Keynesian model, where the interest rate, as well as the price level, is fixed. Later on, we shall allow the interest rate to be flexible. Figure 18.2, which is called the **Keynesian cross diagram,** shows how equation 18.7 determines the level of output for a given interest rate, R_t. First, the line labeled Y_t^d indicates the dependence of aggregate demand on the level of output. Note that I_t^d and G_t in equation 18.7 do not depend on Y_t. Therefore, the Y_t^d line reflects only the positive effect of Y_t on C_t^d. Hence the slope is the marginal propensity to consume ν. Notice that the figure assumes a marginal propensity that is positive, but less than one. (We show Y_t^d as a straight line only for convenience.)

Next, the 45° line in Figure 18.2 indicates positions where output, Y_t, equals the level of demand, Y_t^d. Therefore, equation 18.7 holds when the aggregate demand curve intersects the 45° line. We denote the level of output at this intersection by $\hat{Y}_t$. The Keynesian model with a given interest rate predicts that the economy's output will be this quantity $\hat{Y}_t$.

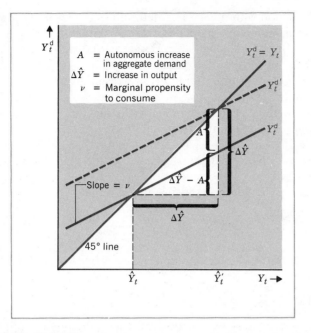

Figure 18.3 The Multiplier

Aggregate demand increases by the amount A. The figure shows that the response of output, $\Delta\hat{Y}$, exceeds the initial expansion of demand. The geometry implies that $(\Delta\hat{Y} - A)/\Delta\hat{Y} = v$ so that $\Delta\hat{Y} = A/(1 - v)$. The term, $1/(1 - v)$, is the multiplier.

The Multiplier

To illustrate the determination of output in the Keynesian model, let's consider an increase in aggregate demand, Y_t^d. This increase could apply either to consumption demand or investment demand. However, the Keynesian model usually focuses on shifts to investment demand that reflect changing beliefs about the marginal product of capital.[5]

The increase in aggregate demand leads to an increase in output, Y_t. (Recall that, with excess supply of goods, output is demand determined.) The increase in output means more real income and hence a further increase in aggregate demand. This leads to another rise in output, which generates more demand, and so on. However, each successive increase in output turns out to be smaller than the one before, and the process implies that output rises ultimately by a finite multiple of the initial expansion of demand. To calculate the exact change, we can use the Keynesian cross diagram.

In Figure 18.3, the aggregate demand curve is initially the one labeled Y_t^d.

---

[5]Keynes attributed a large part of these disturbances to *animal spirits*. Here, he referred to spontaneous shifts in optimism or pessimism, which lead businesses to alter their expectations for the profitability of investment. See Keynes, op. cit., Chapter 12.

The intersection with the 45° line determines the level of output, $\hat{Y}_t$. Then an **autonomous increase in demand** of size A shifts the aggregate demand curve upward to the one labeled $Y_t^{d'}$. (By autonomous, we mean that the change comes from out of the blue, rather than being explained within the model.) Accordingly, the level of output, $\hat{Y}_t'$, corresponds to the new intesection with the 45° line.

The geometry of the Keynesian cross diagram in Figure 18.3 reveals the relation between the initial and final levels of output, $\hat{Y}_t$ and $\hat{Y}_t'$. Let $\Delta\hat{Y}$ be the change in output, $\hat{Y}_t' - \hat{Y}_t$. Then observe the smaller right-angle triangle with base $\Delta\hat{Y}$. Note that the slope of the line marked with an arrow is the marginal propensity to consume, v. Since the vertical side of the triangle is of length $\Delta\hat{Y} - A$, the slope satisfies the relation

$$v = \frac{(\Delta\hat{Y} - A)}{\Delta\hat{Y}}$$

It follows that the change in output is given by

$$\Delta\hat{Y} = \frac{A}{(1 - v)} \tag{18.8}$$

Thus, output changes by a multiple of the autonomous shift in demand, A. The **multiplier** is the term, $1/(1 - v)$, which is positive and greater than one. Note that the higher is the marginal propensity to consume, v, the larger is the multiplier. Also, for the analysis to make sense, the marginal propensity to consume must be less than one, as we have assumed.

We can better understand the source of the multiplier by deriving equation 18.8 in an alternative manner. The autonomous increase in demand leads initially to an increase in output by the amount A. Then the rise in real income by the amount A leads to an increase in aggregate demand by the quantity, $v \cdot A$. Hence, there is an additional increase in output of size $v \cdot A$, which then causes demand to rise further by the amount $v \cdot vA$. In other words, there is a continuing sequence where each round's increase in output is the amount v multiplied by the previous round's increase. It follows that the full increase in output comes from summing up all the rounds—namely,[6]

$$\Delta\hat{Y} = A + vA + v^2A + \cdots = A(1 + v + v^2 + \cdots) = \frac{A}{(1 - v)} \tag{18.9}$$

Notice that the result coincides with the one in equation 18.8.

We should stress two points about the derivation of the change in output, $\Delta\hat{Y}$. First, we assume that excess supply of goods prevails throughout, so that producers never hesitate to meet extra demand with more output. (The producers also do not raise their prices, since these prices were already too high.)

---

[6]The formula for a geometric series implies that $1 + v + v^2 + \cdots = 1/(1 - v)$ if $-1 < v < 1$.

Second, although part of the discussion mentions a sequence of rounds, we do not actually allow any time to elapse while people make adjustments. That is, we do not introduce any lags for the adjustment of either demand or production. Therefore, an autonomous increase in demand leads immediately to the full multiplicative response of output, as shown in equation 18.9. More generally, we could include some dynamics, whereby output adjusts gradually toward the value dictated by the Keynesian cross diagram in Figure 18.3.

Before going on, let's work out a third way to look at the multiplier. We can rewrite the condition for determining output from equation 18.7 as

$$Y_t - \hat{C}^d(Y_t, R_t, \ldots) = I^d(R_t, \ldots) + G_t \qquad (18.10)$$
$$(+)\,(-) \qquad\qquad (-)$$

The left side is the sum of households' desired saving plus taxes. Hence equation 18.10 says that the level of output is determined so that desired saving plus taxes equals investment demand plus government purchases.

Suppose that an autonomous increase in demand means that the right side of equation 18.10 rises by the amount A. (Equivalently, part of this change could show up as an increase in consumer demand and hence, as a decrease in the left side of the equation.) If taxes do not change, output must rise enough to generate a matching expansion of desired saving on the left side of the equation. Since the marginal propensity to consume is v, the marginal propensity to save is $1 - v$. Hence the change in saving is the amount, $(1 - v)\Delta\hat{Y}$. Since this extra saving, $(1 - v)\Delta\hat{Y}$, must balance the autonomous increase in demand, A, it follows at once that

$$\Delta\hat{Y} = \frac{A}{(1 - v)} \qquad (18.11)$$

The answer for the change in output coincides with those in equations 18.8 and 18.9.

The multiplier is a distinctive feature of the Keynesian model, and would not arise under conditions of general market clearing. To see this, let's assume again an autonomous increase in aggregate demand, Y_t^d, with no shift in aggregate supply, Y_t^s. In a market-clearing setting, as in Chapter 5, we know that the real interest rate, r_t, rises to clear the commodity market. Since the higher real interest rate reduces the quantity of goods demanded, we know that output, Y_t, must end up rising by less than the autonomous increase in demand. (Remember that consumer demand does not depend directly on output in the market-clearing model.) Thus, the market-clearing model features a *dampener* rather than a multiplier. The general point is that a well-functioning economy—with cleared markets—operates to buffer disturbances rather than to magnify them. The presence of a multiplier in the Keynesian model reflects the assumption that private markets fail to clear and therefore operate inefficiently.

The Determination of Employment

For a given level of output, Y_t, the amount of work, N_t, is the minimum amount necessary to produce this quantity of goods. That is, using an aggregate version of equation 18.5, we have

$$N_t = N(Y_t, \ K_{t-1}, \ G_t) \tag{18.12}$$
$$(+) \ (-) \ (-)$$

Notice that for given values of the capital stock and government purchases, any disturbance that leads to a change in output leads to a change of the same sign for employment. For example, our previous discussion showed that an autonomous increase in aggregate demand led to a multiplicative expansion of output. Now we find that an increase in employment accompanies this rise in output.

Recall that the analysis applies in the range where goods are in excess supply. Here, the marginal product of labor exceeds the value attached to leisure time. Therefore, people eagerly work more whenever it becomes feasible to sell more goods. With a separate labor market where the nominal wage was sticky, we would find that suppliers of labor—who face rationing of jobs—readily accept more work whenever the employers raise their demands. Then the amount of involuntary unemployment corresponds to the gap between the aggregate supply of labor, N_t^s, and the quantity of work. Thus, increases in employment show up as decreases in involuntary unemployment.

The Keynesian Investment Function

Because of the multiplier, small disturbances to the aggregate demand for goods can be magnified into sizable fluctuations in aggregate output. For example, a small cutback in investment demand could generate a recession where real GNP and consumption fell significantly below trend. On the other hand, at least since World War II, U.S. recessions have featured large shortfalls in investment with relatively small contractions in consumer expenditures on nondurables and services. In particular, recessions do not typically involve small reductions of investment that are accompanied by major declines in consumption. To explain these aspects of the data, we have to modify the Keynesian model in two respects. First, we have to allow for reactions of investment demand to economic conditions. Then second, we have to moderate the response of consumption to current income, which we can do by incorporating the idea of permanent income.

Recall that, with excess supply of goods, producers reduce their inputs of labor services. Thereby the marginal product of labor exceeds the value of leisure time. Similar reasoning suggests that producers would cut back on their inputs of capital services. That is, when sales are rationed, producers reduce their desired stocks of capital. Thereby the marginal product of capital (less the depreciation rate) exceeds the real interest rate. The main point is that a reduction in the available real sales leads to a smaller desired stock of capital and hence to less investment demand.

We can write the **Keynesian investment function** as

$$i_t^d = \hat{i}^d(y_t, \; R_t, \; \ldots) \qquad (18.13)$$
$$(+) \; (-)$$

Notice that by including the level of output, y_t, the Keynesian investment function looks similar to the Keynesian consumption function, which we introduced in equation 18.6. Actually, what matters for desired capital and therefore for investment demand is the prospective quantity of real sales and output, y_{t+1}. Therefore, a cutback in current output, y_t, reduces investment demand, i_t^d, to the extent that prospective output, y_{t+1}, also declines.

The Investment Accelerator

The Keynesian investment function is related to the **investment accelerator,** which was discussed frequently in earlier literature on business cycles. The main difference is that the accelerator relates investment demand to the change in output, whereas the investment demand function in equation 18.13 involves the level of output. In fact, it is the prospective amount of output, y_{t+1}, that matters here. Recall that the level of the capital stock, k_{t-1}, appears with a negative sign among the omitted terms of the investment demand function in equation (18.13). If we allow for changes over time in the quantity of capital, then we could generate a dynamic relation for investment, which can resemble the accelerator. For an analysis of a model with an accelerator and a multiplier, see Paul Samuelson, "A Synthesis of the Principle of Acceleration and the Multiplier," *Journal of Political Economy*, December 1939.

Our formal analysis of the determination of output and employment does not change when we introduce the Keynesian investment function. The only difference is that we have to redefine the parameter v to be the **marginal propensity to spend**—that is, the total effect of a change in current output, y_t, on the demand for goods, y_t^d. This total effect is the sum of the marginal propensity to consume and the **marginal propensity to invest.** The latter term is the impact of a change in output, y_t, on investment demand in equation 18.13. For the analysis to go through, the marginal propensity to spend, v, must be less than one.

Recall that the multiplier in equation 18.8 is the expression $1/(1 - v)$. The term, $1 - v$, is no longer the marginal propensity to save. Rather, it is one minus the marginal propensity to spend or, equivalently, the difference between the marginal propensity to save and the marginal propensity to invest. Note that if the marginal propensity to spend, v, is less than 1, then the term, $1 - v$, is positive.

The new results concern the composition of output during business fluctuations. The Keynesian investment function implies that an autonomous contraction of demand can lead to a major decline of investment. At least this response follows if the contraction lasts long enough for prospective output, y_{t+1}, to decline.

On the other hand, the recession may not persist so long that it has a major effect on permanent income. In this case the cutback in current output, y_t, has only a minor impact on consumer demand, c_t^d. Therefore, most of the shortfall in output could show up as less investment, rather than less consumption. In other words, the Keynesian model can now be consistent with this important feature of recessions in the real world.

We mentioned before that liquidity constraints, where some people cannot borrow readily at the going interest rate, could be a basis for the Keynesian consumption function. But if such constraints were important, we would expect recessions to exhibit major shortfalls in consumer expenditures on non-durables and services. In fact, the data show relatively little fluctuation in these categories of spending. The components that do decline substantially during recessions are—aside from business investment—the purchases of consumer durables, including residential housing, automobiles, and appliances. These goods are relatively easy to buy on credit because durables serve as good collateral for loans. Therefore, the data suggest that liquidity constraints do not play a major role in U.S. business fluctuations.

The Supply Side in the Keynesian Model

The Keynesian model—whether the simple version that we have been studying or more sophisticated versions—views aggregate demand as the central determinant of output and employment. Specifically, the analysis pays little attention to aggregate supply. In formal terms the neglect of the supply side arises because the postulated excessive price level, $P_t > P_t^*$, means that excess supply of goods and services prevails. Thereby, the model assumes that productive capacity and the willingness to work do not represent effective constraints on output—only the willingness to spend limits the extent of economic activity in this model. This perspective explains why Keynesian analyses typically pay little attention to some matters that are important in a market-clearing framework. Among these are shifts to the production function, variations in the stock of capital, effects of the tax system on the willingness to work, and so on.[7] The neglect of these elements became especially embarrassing with the supply shocks of the 1970s. In fact, the failure to handle supply shocks was one of the major elements that led many economists to look for alternatives to the Keynesian model.

---

[7]The Keynesian model considers these factors to the extent that they influence investment or consumption demand. Also, the supply of labor services matters when computing the amount of involuntary unemployment.

IS/LM Analysis and the Role of the Interest Rate

Our previous analysis, which includes the multiplier, shows how to determine the level of output for a given interest rate. As long as there is excess supply of goods, the condition for determining output is

$$Y_t = Y_t^d = \hat{C}^d(Y_t, R_t, \ldots) + \hat{I}^d(Y_t, R_t, \ldots) + G_t \qquad (18.14)$$
$$ (+) \, (-) \qquad\qquad (+) \, (-)$$

Now we want to go further by considering the determination of the interest rate, R_t, in the Keynesian model. To carry out this analysis, we have to reintroduce the condition that all money be willingly held. This condition is

$$M_t = P_t \cdot L(Y_t, R_t, \ldots) \qquad (18.15)$$
$$ (+) \, (-)$$

Given the price level, P_t, equations 18.14 and 18.15 determine simultaneously the interest rate and the level of output. Notice first that equation 18.14 determines Y_t for a given value of R_t. But a change in R_t would affect aggregate demand, Y_t^d, and thereby the level of output. What we want to do now is figure out the value of Y_t that corresponds to each value of R_t. That is, we want to trace out the combinations of R_t and Y_t that are consistent with the equality between output and aggregate demand, as specified in equation 18.14.

An increase in the interest rate lowers aggregate demand on the right side of equation 18.14. As with any decline in aggregate demand, the level of output falls. Therefore, if we map out the combinations of R_t and Y_t that satisfy equation 18.14, we determine a downward-sloping relationship. Following standard notation, we label as **IS** the curve in Figure 18.4 that shows this relation.[8] Along the **IS curve,** the interest rate and the level of output are consistent with the equality between output and aggregate demand.

Consider now the condition that money be willingly held, as specified in equation 18.15. Given the quantity of money, M_t, and the price level, P_t, this condition defines another array of combinations for the interest rate and output. What we want to do here is trace out the combinations of R_t and Y_t that are consistent with the condition that all money be willingly held. Note that a higher value of Y_t raises the demand for money on the right side of equation 18.15. Therefore, R_t must rise to lower the demand for money back to the given level, M_t. Hence, when we map out the combinations of R_t and Y_t that satisfy equation 18.15, we determine an upward-sloping relationship. Again following the conventional notation, the curve designated **LM** in Figure

---

[8]The terminology, IS, refers to an equation of investment demand to desired saving. Recall from equation 18.10 that the condition, $Y_t = Y_t^d$, is equivalent to an equality between desired saving (plus taxes) and investment demand (plus government purchases). The apparatus in Figure 18.4 comes from John Hicks, "Mr. Keynes and the 'Classics,' " *Econometrica*, April 1937.

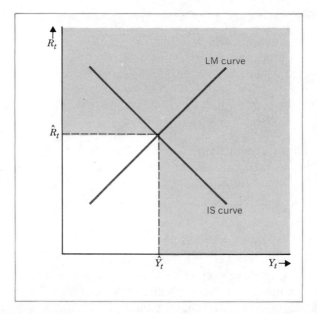

Figure 18.4 Use of IS/LM Curves to Determine Output and the Interest Rate
The IS curve shows the combinations of Y_t and R_t that satisfy the condition, $Y_t = Y_t^d$. The LM curve shows the combinations that induce people to hold all the existing money, M_t. Thus, the levels of output and the interest rate correspond to the intersection of the two curves.

18.4 shows this relation. Along the **LM curve,** the interest rate and the level of output are consistent with the condition that all money be willingly held.

The intersection of the IS and LM curves in Figure 18.4 picks out the combination of output and the interest rate—labeled as $\hat{Y}_t$ and $\hat{R}_t$—that satisfies two conditions: First, output equals aggregate demand, and second, all money is willingly held. As long as the price level is fixed, the Keynesian model predicts that the level of output will be the amount $\hat{Y}_t$ and the interest rate will be the value $\hat{R}_t$. Hence, we can use the IS/LM apparatus to analyze simultaneously the determination of output and the interest rate in the Keynesian model. In fact, because of the popularity of the Keynesian model, the IS/LM diagram has been the favorite analytical tool of most macroeconomists in the last two decades.

Variations in Output and the Interest Rate

To bring out the role of the interest rate, let's consider again a case where aggregate demand rises autonomously by the amount A. If the interest rate did not change, then output would rise multiplicatively. However, the expansion of output increases the demand for money above the given quantity, M_t.

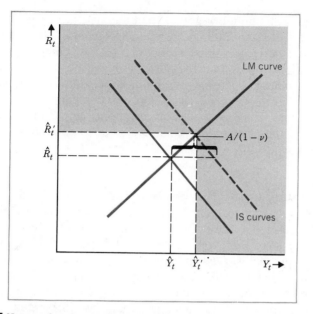

Figure 18.5 **Keynesian Analysis of the Effect of an Increase in Aggregate Demand on Output and the Interest Rate**

The increase in aggregate demand shifts the IS curve rightward. The size of the shift is the autonomous rise in demand, A, times the multiplier, $1/(1 - v)$. We find that output and the interest rate increase. But the rise in output falls short of the full multiplier amount, $A/(1 - v)$.

Consequently, people attempt to move out of bonds and into money. But then the interest rate must increase to restore balance on the credit market. This increase in the interest rate reduces the demand for money, but it also decreases aggregate demand. Hence, the overall effect on output turns out to be less than the full multiplicative amount, which we derived before. In fact, it is now possible that the increase in output, $\Delta \hat{Y}$, is less than the autonomous expansion of demand, A. The increase in the interest rate may make the multiplier be less than one in the Keynesian model (as it is for sure in the market-clearing model).

Figure 18.5 uses the IS/LM apparatus to show the results. We reproduce the solid lines from Figure 18.4. The boost to aggregate demand appears as a rightward shift in the IS curve—that is, output increases for a given value of the interest rate. The size of this shift is the change in aggregate demand, A, times the multiplier, $1/(1 - v)$. In this example, the LM curve does not shift. Therefore, the figure shows that output and the interest rate rise. But the increase in output is less than the full multiplier amount, which equals the rightward shift of the IS curve. Finally, underlying the expansion of output is an increase in employment (and a decrease in unemployment).

For a given amount of government purchases, it is clear that total private spending for consumption and investment increases. But because of the rise in the interest rate, it is possible that one of these components would decline. For example, suppose that the autonomous disturbance is an increase in investment demand. Then the rise in output stimulates consumer demand, but the increase in the interest rate depresses this demand. Thus, consumption may fall along with the expansion of output, employment, and investment. Similarly, if the autonomous change applies to consumer demand, then investment may decline.

Fiscal Policy in the Keynesian Model

The government can influence aggregate demand directly by changing the level of its purchases, G_t. Suppose that the government raises its purchases by 1 unit, and finances this extra spending with lump-sum taxes. Assume also that permanent purchases, $\bar{G}$, do not change. Then, as in our analysis from Chapter 12, consumer demand falls by a fraction of the increase in purchases.[9] It follows that aggregate demand expands, but by less than 1 unit. In terms of the IS/LM diagram, the disturbance can again be represented by Figure 18.5.[10] Now the rightward shift of the IS curve equals some fraction of the increase in government purchases, times the multiplier, $1/(1 - v)$. Notice that output and the interest rate again increase. But the increase in output is again less than the full multiplier amount, which equals the rightward shift of the IS curve.

The effects of more government purchases on private spending are uncertain. On the one hand, the expansion of output stimulates private demands, but on the other hand, the higher interest rate reduces these demands. In addition, there is the direct negative effect of government purchases on consumer spending. Recall that empirically for the United States, a temporary burst of wartime expenditure tends to crowd out investment, but has little effect on consumer expenditures for nondurables and services.

Another type of fiscal policy that economists consider is a reduction in taxes, which the government finances by issuing more bonds. Often, people argue that this policy is expansionary in the Keynesian model. But to get this answer, we have to assume that deficit-financed tax cuts make people feel wealthier. Then the tax cut stimulates consumer demand, which shifts the IS curve rightward, as shown in Figure 18.5. Given this shift, there would again be increases in output and the interest rate.

Because of the higher future taxes, it can still be true (as it was in Chapter

---

[9]Remember that public services substitute for α units of private consumer spending, where α is a positive fraction. If permanent purchases increase, then there is effectively a decrease in permanent income. Hence, consumer demand falls further on this count.

[10]This diagram applies if the change in government purchases has no direct effect on the demand for money. Otherwise, there is also a shift of the LM curve.

14) that a deficit-financed tax cut has no aggregate wealth effect on consumer demand. Then the IS curve does not shift, which means that output and the interest rate do not change. In other words, the Ricardian theorem—which states that taxes and deficits are equivalent—can remain valid within the Keynesian model.

If people treat a tax cut as a signal of more wealth, then the Keynesian model predicts an expansion of output. Since production and employment are constrained initially by lack of demand, the typical person ends up better off in the situation. Thus, people actually do end up being wealthier. But this result has nothing to do with tax cuts, as such. In the Keynesian model *anything* that makes people feel wealthier generates the increases in output and employment that actually make them wealthier. (Think about what would happen in this model if we assumed that people felt poorer when they saw a tax cut.) This type of result can occur only because the Keynesian model assumes that outcomes are inefficient in the first place.

Changes in the Price Level

Recall that the starting point for the Keynesian model was the excessive price level, $P_t > P_t^*$. This constraint on prices meant that the quantity of money, M_t, fell short of the amount demanded at the general market-clearing values of the interest rate, R_t^*, and output, Y_t^*. Then people's efforts to exchange bonds for money led to a higher interest rate, $\hat{R}_t > R_t^*$, which meant lower levels of aggregate demand, Y_t^d, and hence output, $\hat{Y}_t < Y_t^*$.

If the price level declines toward the general market-clearing value, P_t^*, then the basic constraint on the economy relaxes. Therefore, we should anticipate that the interest rate, $\hat{R}_t$, would fall toward the general market-clearing value, R_t^*, while the level of output, $\hat{Y}_t$, would rise toward the general market-value, Y_t^*. To see how this works, we can use the IS/LM diagrams.

Recall from equation 18.15 that the LM curve shows the combinations of R_t and Y_t that equate the amount of money demanded to the given quantity of money, M_t. A decline in the price level lowers the nominal demand for money, $M_t^d = P_t \cdot L(R_t, Y_t, \ldots)$. Therefore, to restore equality with the given supply of money, we need changes in R_t or Y_t that raise the real demand for money, $L(R_t, Y_t, \ldots)$. It follows that the LM curve shifts rightward, as shown in Figure 18.6.

Notice that the new LM curve intersects the unchanged IS curve at a lower interest rate—$(\hat{R}_t)' < \hat{R}_t$—and a higher level of output—$(\hat{Y}_t)' > \hat{Y}_t$. We can understand these changes by recalling that a lower price level reduces the nominal demand for money, $M_t^d = P_t \cdot L(R_t, Y_t, \ldots)$, at the initial values of the interest rate, $\hat{R}_t$, and output, $\hat{Y}_t$. People's attempts to exchange their excess cash for bonds tends to depress the interest rate. Then a lower interest rate means greater aggregate demand for goods and hence higher output.

Consider a sequence of reductions in the price level from its initial value toward the general market-clearing value, P_t^*. Each reduction in the price level

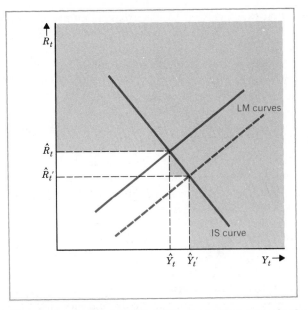

Figure 18.6 **Keynesian Analysis of the Effect of a Decrease in the Price Level on Output and the Interest Rate**
A decrease in the price level shifts the LM curve rightward. Therefore, the interest rate falls and the level of output rises.

shifts the LM curve rightward as shown in Figure 18.6. Correspondingly, the interest rate falls and the level of output rises. When the price level falls all the way to the value P_t^*, the interest rate will have fallen to its general market-clearing value, R_t^*, and output will have risen to its general market-clearing value, Y_t^*.

Once the price level reaches P_t^*, further reductions in the price level would not generate more increases in output. That is because the commodity market shifts at this point to excess demand, $Y_t^d > Y_t^s$, rather than excess supply. Then the suppliers no longer produce the quantity demanded, but rather produce the lesser amount Y_t^s. Recall that the IS curve assumes that producers accommodate demand fully—that is, $Y_t = Y_t^d$. Therefore, we cannot use this curve to study the determination of output when there is excess demand for goods.[11]

---

[11]Under excess demand it is purchases of goods and services, rather than sales, that have to be rationed. For a theoretical discussion, see Robert Barro and Herschel Grossman, "Suppressed Inflation and the Supply Multiplier," *Review of Economic Studies,* January 1974. For empirical applications to the centrally planned economies of eastern Europe, see David Howard, "The Disequilibrium Model in a Controlled Economy: An Empirical Test of the Barro-Grossman Model," *American Economic Review,* December 1976; and Richard Portes and David Winter, "Disequilibrium Estimates for Consumption Goods Markets in Centrally Planned Economies," *Review of Economic Studies,* January 1980.

Changes in the Quantity of Money

Assume again that the price level is fixed above the general market-clearing value—that is, $P_t > P_t^*$. Then consider an increase in the quantity of money, M_t, which could arise as an open-market purchase of bonds. Since P_t is fixed, equation 18.15 implies that the real amount of money demanded, $L(R_t, Y_t, \ldots)$, must go up for the additional money to be willingly held. Therefore, the increase in M_t works just like a reduction in P_t, which we studied before. We can again use Figure 18.6 to analyze the effects. The rightward shift of the LM curve leads to a lower interest rate and a higher level of output.

We can interpret these results by noting that the quantity of money, M_t, rises above the amount demanded at the initial values of the interest rate, $\hat{R}_t$, and output, $\hat{Y}_t$. As before, people's efforts to exchange their excess cash for bonds leads to a lower interest rate and hence to higher output.

The important finding is that an increase in the quantity of money is a substitute for a reduction in the price level toward the general market-clearing value. One way to correct for the excessive price level, $P_t > P_t^*$, is for prices to fall. But an alternative is to raise the stock of money, which we know has a proportional effect on the general market-clearing level of prices, P_t^*. Monetary expansion closes the gap between P_t and P_t^* by raising P_t^*, rather than lowering P_t.

Shifts in the Demand for Money

Notice from equation 18.15 that a reduction in the real demand for money, $L(R, Y, \ldots)$, works exactly like a decrease in the price level. Both changes lead to an excess of money, M_t, over the amount demanded, M_t^d. If the demand for money falls—for example, because of a financial innovation—then the LM curve shifts rightward as shown in Figure 18.6. Therefore, we again have a decrease in the interest rate and an expansion of output.

These results obtain because the decline in the demand for money raises the general market-clearing value of the price level, P_t^*. Therefore, the gap diminishes between P_t^* and the fixed price level, P_t. From this perspective, a decrease in the real demand for money works in the same way as an increase in M_t. Both changes reduce the spread between P_t and P_t^* by raising the value of P_t^*.

IS/LM Analysis and General Market Clearing

The IS/LM framework is designed to bring out the interaction between monetary phenomena (the LM curve) and real phenomena (the IS curve). In the Keynesian model the main source of this interaction is the stickiness of the general price level. That is why the IS/LM apparatus was helpful when we studied various disturbances in the context of a fixed price level.

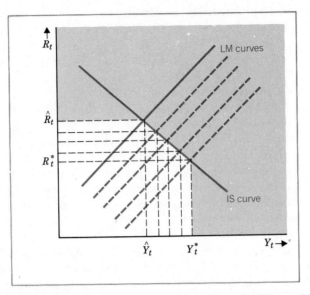

Figure 18.7 Effects of Declines in the Price Level to the General Market-Clearing Value, P_t^*

Each decrease in the price level shifts the LM curve rightward. Therefore, the interest rate falls and the level of output rises. When the price level reaches its general market-clearing value, P_t^*, the interest rate and output attain their general market-clearing values, R_t^* and Y_t^*.

Suppose now that we return to a setting of general market clearing, where the price level is flexible. Then Figure 18.7 shows how we could use the IS/LM diagram to find the general market-clearing values of the interest rate, R_t^*, and output, Y_t^*. However, the apparatus would now be cumbersome. That is because disturbances to the economy generally imply shifts of the IS and LM curves, as well as changes in the market-clearing price level, P_t^*.

When we allow the price level to be flexible we eliminate the main source of interaction between monetary and real phenomena in the model.[12] Thereby we also lose the main point of the IS/LM diagram—namely to study the interplay between monetary and real factors. If we want to analyze the economy under conditions of general market clearing, then we can return to the

---

[12]The interaction can arise also if transaction costs or the level of real cash balances influence the amounts of commodities supplied and demanded. Recall that the neglect of transaction costs is only an approximation, but probably a good one in most circumstances. We discussed in Chapters 4 and 7 why we could ignore the amount of real money balances when we analyzed the clearing of the commodity market. Another source of interaction between monetary and real phenomena involves incomplete information about prices, as studied in Chapter 17. But, since the IS/LM model assumes an economy-wide market for commodities, it is not helpful in this context.

framework that we developed in Chapter 5. Although we could get the same answers from the IS/LM model, our earlier framework is more straightforward.

Keynesian Predictions about Business Fluctuations

As we developed the market-clearing model in previous chapters, one of our major concerns was the identification of types of disturbances that have been important in real-world business fluctuations. The possibilities include supply shocks, shifts to investment demand (which could reflect supply shocks), autonomous changes in consumption demand or labor supply, monetary disturbances, and variations in the government's expenditures or tax rates. It is important to realize that the Keynesian model does not enlarge the set of possibilities. Rather, the model narrows the list by limiting attention to disturbances that impinge on aggregate demand. As mentioned before, the neglect of the supply side is a basic weakness of the Keynesian model.

Decreases in aggregate demand may reflect autonomous declines in investment and consumption demand, or reductions in government purchases. In the Keynesian model, these changes tend to produce a recession, whereby output, employment, investment, and consumption all decline. Although the model does not explain the initial disturbance, it does show why the aggregate variables tend to move together during recessions and booms.

The presence of the multiplier suggests that small disturbances can be magnified into significant fluctuations in aggregate activity. By including the Keynesian investment function and the permanent income theory of consumption, the model can explain why the shortfall of output during a recession shows up mostly as less investment.

The Keynesian model predicts an expansionary effect from an increase in the quantity of money (relative to the given price level). This effect operates via a reduction in the interest rate. However, this prediction tends to explain too much, since the empirical evidence indicates no long-term connection between monetary growth and real variables. To reconcile the model with this observation, we have to introduce some flexibility of prices (see below). But there is another problem, since the data do not suggest even a short-run relation between monetary fluctuations and changes in real interest rates. Recall that this last finding also caused difficulties for the market-clearing model in the previous chapter.

Notice that shifts to aggregate demand, which affect the IS curve, change the real interest rate in the same direction. But movements in the quantity of money (or shifts to velocity), which affect the LM curve, cause inverse movements in the real interest rate. Therefore, the Keynesian model does not predict a definite cyclical pattern for the real interest rate. (Remember that the data also reveal no definite pattern.) In the Keynesian model the behavior of the real interest rate depends on whether the dominant disturbance involves aggregate demand or the supply and demand for money.

Inflation in the Keynesian Model

Thus far, we assumed that the price level was fixed. This assumption is generally unsatisfactory, especially for present-day economies, where inflation rates are typically positive and often highly variable over time. Since the Keynesian model does not rely on market-clearing conditions to determine the price level, we need some other mechanism to replace the assumption that prices are rigid. The usual device is an ad hoc adjustment relationship, whereby the price level adjusts gradually toward the general market-clearing value, P_t^*. Recall that the condition, $P_t > P_t^*$, corresponds to an excess supply of commodities. Therefore, an adjustment of the price level toward the market-clearing value, P_t^*, means that prices decline when goods are in excess supply, and vice versa for excess demand. This type of price-adjustment relation is sometimes called the **law of supply and demand.**

Formally, the price-adjustment rule says that the inflation rate π_t is given by

$$\pi_t = \lambda(Y_t^d - Y_t^s) \tag{18.16}$$

where λ (the Greek letter *lambda*) is positive. Note that the higher the parameter λ the more rapidly prices adjust to an imbalance between supply and demand. Sometimes, economists regard the reaction of prices to excess demand as different from that to excess supply. Prices are thought to rise quickly in the face of excess demand, but to fall sluggishly when there is excess supply. This asymmetry would support the Keynesian focus on cases where the price level exceeds its market-clearing value. But the reason for this asymmetry in the law of supply and demand has not been explained.

As it stands, the price-adjustment formula in equation 18.16 has some problems. First, inflation is nonzero only if the commodity market does not clear—that is, if $Y_t^d \neq Y_t^s$. But the theory should allow inflation and cleared markets to coexist. Second, as a related matter, inflation is negative in the Keynesian case where goods are in excess supply. Thus, we cannot use equation 18.16 to incorporate positive inflation into the Keynesian analysis.

Recall that equation 18.16 implies that the price level, P_t, moves toward the general market-clearing price, P_t^*. But monetary growth or some other factors can lead to continuing changes in P_t^*. Then our intuition suggests that P_t would respond to two things: first, the gap between P_t and P_t^*, which relates to the amount of excess demand for goods; and second, the change over time in P_t^*. Let's call this last element π_t^*—that is, π_t^* is the expected rate of change of P_t^*. Using this concept, we might modify equation 18.16 to the form

$$\pi_t = \lambda(Y_t^d - Y_t^s) + \pi_t^* \tag{18.17}$$

Equation 18.17 says that actual inflation, π_t, exceeds the anticipated rate of change of the market-clearing price, π_t^*, when there is excess demand, and vice versa for excess supply. Thus, the actual price level, P_t, tends to approach the target, P_t^*, even when the target moves over time.

Note that equation 18.17 is consistent with nonzero inflation when the commodity market clears. For example, a high rate of anticipated monetary growth would imply a high value for π_t^*, and hence for π_t. Moreover, if π_t^* is positive, then π_t can be positive even when goods are in excess supply. Hence, positive inflation can appear in the Keynesian model.

We now have the following general description of a recession. First, there is some adverse shock to aggregate demand, perhaps stemming from an autonomous decline in firms' desires to invest. Then output, employment, and investment (and probably consumption) fall below their general market-clearing values. Correspondingly, there is an increase in unemployment.

The shortfalls in quantities persist because prices (and wages) do not adjust downward immediately to reestablish general market clearing. That is, although prices are no longer rigid, they are still sticky. But equation 18.17 says that the inflation rate, π_t, falls below the rate of change of the market-clearing price, π_t^*. Therefore, the price level, P_t, tends to fall relative to the target price, P_t^*. Then there are gradual increases in real cash balances,[13] which lead to decreases in interest rates, and thereby to expansions of aggregate demand. Through this process, the economy returns eventually to a position of general market clearing (which economists often call a position of "full employment").

The role for active policy in the Keynesian model appears as a substitute for the economy's automatic, but sluggish, reaction through price adjustment. Either expansions in the growth rate of money (monetary policy) or increases in government purchases (fiscal policy) can spur aggregate demand. Thereby, the model says that the recovery from a recession can be quickened.

Sticky Prices in the Keynesian Model

All of the novel features in the Keynesian analysis derive from the assumption that prices (or wages) are sticky. The key postulate is that prices do not fall quickly (relative to the movements in the market-clearing price) when there is excess supply of goods. Among other things, this assumption delivers the following results:

- Output is determined by aggregate demand—supply-side elements play no important role.
- There may be a multiplier connecting autonomous shifts in aggregate demand to the responses of output.
- Whenever people feel wealthier and raise consumer demand, the expansions of output and employment actually make them wealthier.
- There are real effects from changes in the quantity of money.
- There is a desirable role for active monetary and fiscal policies.

---

[13]We assume here that the growth rate of the market-clearing price, π_t^*, reflects an equal growth rate for the quantity of money. Therefore, the growth rate of money exceeds that of prices.

Given all the results that follow from sticky prices, we should look further into the meaning of this assumption. Presumably, the stickiness of prices does not to a significant degree reflect the costs of changing prices, as such. (In fact, the costs of changing production and employment—which Keynesian models usually ignore—are clearly much more important.) Instead, economists intend to use sluggish price adjustment as a proxy for other problems that make it difficult for the private sector to operate efficiently. For example, there are costs of obtaining various kinds of information, costs of moving from one job to another, costs of changing methods of production, and so on. These types of coordination problems mean that the economy does not always react appropriately to changes in the composition of tastes and technology, or to shifts in the levels of aggregate demand and supply.

There is no question that the elements just mentioned are important for explaining variations in the aggregates of output and employment and for understanding unemployment. But it is unclear that we can represent these matters by the Keynesian device of imposing an excessive price level on the trades that the private sector can carry out. For example, incomplete information does not imply that aggregate demand is more important than aggregate supply. Also, the gaps in people's knowledge do not necessarily imply a desirable role for activist monetary and fiscal policies.

When we allow for incomplete information and various adjustment costs, we find that the allocation of resources is a hard problem for the private sector to solve. Thus, there are often mistakes, which sometimes show up as unemployment and underproduction. But the challenge to Keynesian analysis is to explain why these problems are eased if the government occasionally throws in a lot of money or steps up its purchases of goods. In the type of model that we explored in this chapter, these policy actions look good because the assumption of an excessive price level forces the private economy to commit easily correctable mistakes. Namely, output and employment fall short of the levels at which labor's marginal product equals the value of workers' time. Similarly, the marginal product of capital (less the rate of depreciation) exceeds the real interest rate. But these types of problems are transparent and easy for the private sector to solve without governmental assistance. What has not been shown is that activist governmental policies can assist when the economy has to deal with incomplete information or other serious problems.

Long-Term Contracts

It has long been recognized that the weak link in Keynesian analysis is the absence of a theory of sticky prices. Probably the most interesting attempt to explain this behavior involves the role of **long-term contracts.** This approach recognizes that buyers and sellers often form long-term relationships, rather than dealing exclusively on auction markets, such as wholesale markets for agricultural commodities, organized securities markets, and so on. For example, the associations between employers and workers or between firms and their suppliers often extend over many years. Frequently, these types of continuing interchanges involve formal—though more often implicit—contractural obligations between the parties. Some presetting of prices—or, more likely, of wages—may be one feature of these contracts.[14]

Prior agreement on prices or wages may allow one party, which might be a group of workers, to shift some risk from themselves to the other party, say a large corporation. For example, an automobile company may shield its workers from some—but surely not all—of the fluctuations in the demand for automobiles. This setup is desirable if the company is in a better position than the workers to assume risks—perhaps because the company has better access to insurance and other financial markets.

The presetting of some prices may also prevent one person from demanding "unreasonable" terms, ex post. For example, a firm might lower the wage rate after its employee had incurred significant costs in moving to a job. Similarly, a builder might raise the price for a construction project at a time when delays become prohibitively expensive. In these cases the market—for builders, workers, and employers—may be competitive beforehand, but more likely a monopoly later on. People can avoid some of the problems with these monopolies by entering initially into contractual arrangements about prices and other considerations.

Some economists have used the contracting approach to rationalize the stickiness of prices or wages in Keynesian models.[15] For example, suppose that two parties agree on a price, P, over the life of a contract.[16] In some cases the chosen price will be the best estimate of the average market-clearing price during the contract, P^*, given the information available at the outset. But unanticipated events—such as monetary disturbances—create departures of

---

[14]Some major papers in this area are Donald Gordon, "A Neo-Classical Theory of Keynesian Unemployment," *Economic Inquiry,* December 1974; Costas Azariadis, "Implicit Contracts and Underemployment Equilibria," *Journal of Political Economy,* December 1975; Martin N. Baily, "Wages and Employment under Uncertain Demand," *Review of Economic Studies,* January 1974; and Herschel Grossman, "Risk Shifting, Layoffs and Seniority," *Journal of Monetary Economics,* November 1978.

[15]See, for example, Jo Anna Gray, "Wage Indexation: A Macroeconomic Approach," *Journal of Monetary Economics,* April 1976; Stan Fischer, "Long-Term Contracts, Rational Expectations and the Optimal Money Supply Rule," *Journal of Political Economy,* February 1977; and John Taylor, "Aggregate Dynamics and Staggered Contracts," *Journal of Political Economy,* February 1980.

[16]Actually, the contracting theory motivates the presetting of a relative price or a real wage rate, rather than dollar prices or wages. Yet most contracts in the United States are not explicitly "indexed"—that is, do not contain automatic adjustments of nominal prices or wages for changes in the general cost of living. Apparently people find it convenient to frame their contracts in terms of the standard unit of account—namely, the dollar—even when inflation is moderately high and variable. But inflation does tend to produce contracts with shorter durations.

the price from its market-clearing value. When the contract expires, the parties will agree to a new price, which equals the anticipated market-clearing price over the next period.

At any point in time, there is an array of existing contracts, which specify prices that likely depart somewhat from market-clearing values. In particular, if there has been a recent monetary contraction, then the typical price will be above its market-clearing value (and vice versa for monetary expansion). As more people renegotiate contracts, the average price adjusts gradually toward the average market-clearing value. In other words, we can use this model to rationalize the law of supply and demand for price adjustment, which is again (from equation 18.17)

$$\pi_t = \lambda(Y_t^d - Y_t^s) + \pi_t^*$$

The gradual response of the average price to excess demand corresponds to the process of recontracting. Then the anticipated rate of change of the market-clearing price, π_t^*, reflects the known factors that negotiators take into account when setting prices or wages at the start of contracts. Note that an excessive price—that is, excess supply of goods and services—is no more likely than too low a price. The law of supply and demand would be a symmetric relation, which does not support the Keynesian stress on cases where the average price level is too high.

Although the contracting viewpoint may rationalize the law of supply and demand, there are difficulties in using this approach to explain Keynesian unemployment and underproduction. The Keynesian results emerge when prices or wages are above market-clearing values *and* when the quantities of output and employment equal the smaller of supply and demand. Recall that this short-side rule for determining quantities accords with voluntary exchange on an impersonal market. But the rule is not generally sensible in a long-term contract, which is now the theoretical basis for sluggish price adjustment.

In an enduring relationship, where long-term contracts arise, people do not have to change prices or wages every instant in order to get the "right" behavior of quantities. For example, workers can agree in advance that they will work harder when there is more work to do—that is, when the demand for a firm's product is high—and vice versa when there is little work. Unlike in an auction market, these efficient adjustments in work and production can occur even if wages do not change from day to day. (For large short-term increases in work, contracts sometimes prescribe overtime premia or other types of bonuses.) The important point is that stickiness of wages does not necessarily imply mistakes in determining the levels of employment and production.

Similarly, suppose that inflation is sometimes higher than expected and sometimes lower. People know that inflation—if not accompanied by some real changes—does not alter the efficient levels of work and production. Therefore, it is reasonable to agree on a contract that insulates the choices of quantities from the rate of inflation. Over many periods—where the effects of unanticipated inflation on real wage rates tend to average out—both parties to a labor contract would benefit from this type of provision. (However, when inflation gets very high and unpredictable, people prefer either to index wages to the price level or to renegotiate contracts more frequently.)

Consider as an example the salaries of college professors. These payments are typically set in nominal terms at the beginning of each academic year. Hence the real value of these salaries depends on the inflation rate during the year. But—as far as I can tell by observing my colleagues—the quantity of effort does not respond to differences in the inflation rate.

One important lesson from the contracting viewpoint is that stickiness of prices or wages need not lead to underproduction and unemployment. Within a long-term agreement, it is unnecessary for prices and wages to move all the time to attain the general-market-clearing values of output and employment. Thus, stickiness in prices and wages no longer tends to generate Keynesian results. Rather than supporting the Keynesian model, the perspective of long-term contracting demonstrates that output and employment can be determined efficiently—as if prices and wages always adjusted to clear markets—even if prices and wages are sticky.[17]

Some Empirical Evidence on the Contracting Approach

Despite the theoretical counterarguments, many economists believe that some version of the contracting story will eventually deliver Keynesian style results. Therefore, it is interesting to look at some recent empirical evidence, provided by Shaghil Ahmed in a direct test of long-term contracts as a basis for the Keynesian model.[18] His data set covered 19 industries in Canada over the period from 1961 to 1974. He used these data because an earlier study by David Card[19] calculated the amount of indexation—that is, automatic adjustment of wages for general inflation—in each industry's labor contracts. (Indexation ranged across the industries from zero to roughly 100%.) According to theories in which contracts are the basis for the Keynesian model, industries with little indexation should show substantial response of real wages, and hence of employment and output, to nominal disturbances. On the other hand, those with lots of indexation would be affected little by nominal disturbances.

---

[17]For an elaboration of this argument, see Robert Barro, "Long-Term Contracts, Sticky Prices and Monetary Policy," *Journal of Monetary Economics,* July 1977; and Robert Hall and David Lilien, "Efficient Wage Bargains under Uncertain Supply and Demand," *American Economic Review,* December, 1979.

[18]See "Wage Indexation and the Phillips Curve Slope: A Cross-Industry Analysis," unpublished, Brown University, 1985.

[19]"Determinants of the Form of Long-Term Contracts," Princeton University working paper No. 135, June 1980.

Ahmed found that nominal shocks—based on unanticipated changes in money or some other nominal variables—had positive effects on hours worked in most of the 19 industries. These results are consistent with some other findings that we discussed in Chapter 16 for the United States and other countries. However, the important point for present purposes is that the extent of an industry's response to nominal disturbances bore no relation to the amount of indexation in that industry. Those with lots of indexation were as likely as those with little indexation to respond to nominal disturbances. This finding is damaging to theories that use long-term contracts as the basis for the Keynesian model. Therefore, these empirical results are consistent with the theoretical reasoning that questioned this use for the contracting approach.

Summary

In the Keynesian model the price level (or the nominal wage rate) exceeds the market-clearing value. Then the excess supply of goods and services means that output is determined by aggregate demand. Correspondingly, there is underproduction and unemployment.

In the simplest Keynesian model, where the interest rate is given, an increase in aggregate demand leads to a multiplicative expansion of output. The increase in demand could reflect an autonomous shift to investment or consumption demand, or could come from an increase in government purchases. Along with the expansion of output, there tend to be increases in employment, investment, and consumption. If we include the Keynesian investment function and the permanent-income view of consumption, then we find that investment would be more volatile than consumption.

The IS/LM analysis shows how to determine the interest rate along with the level of output. In this model, an increase in aggregate demand may no longer have a multiplicative effect on output. That is because the increase in the interest rate crowds out the demands for consumption and investment.

In the Keynesian model a decrease in the price level leads to more real cash balances and thereby to a lower interest rate. The fall in the interest rate stimulates consumption and investment demand, which results in an expansion of output and employment. Similarly, an increase in the quantity of money or a cutback in the demand for money leads to a lower interest rate, and thereby to higher levels of output and employment.

We can incorporate inflation into the Keynesian model by using the law of supply and demand. This relation says that inflation responds positively to excess demand for goods, and negatively to excess supply. Also, when the commodity market clears, the inflation rate equals the anticipated rate of change of the market-clearing price. This mechanism allows the price level to fall, relative to the market-clearing value, during a recession. Then the increases in real cash balances lead to decreases in the interest rate, which stimulate aggregate demand. Thus, the economy adjusts toward the market-clearing levels of output and employment. However, in the Keynesian model, active monetary and fiscal policies can usefully substitute for this slow process of automatic adjustment.

Some novel features of the Keynesian analysis are the following:

- Output is determined by aggregate demand—supply-side elements play no important role.
- There may be a multiplier connecting autonomous shifts in aggregate demand to the responses of output.
- Whenever people feel wealthier and raise consumer demand, the expansions of output and employment actually make them wealthier.
- There are real effects from changes in the quantity of money.
- There is a desirable role for active monetary and fiscal policies.

These features all follow from the assumption that prices are sticky downward. Fundamentally, economists use sticky prices to proxy for the private sector's coordination problems in reacting to fluctuations in aggregate supply and demand and in the composition of tastes and technology. But when we model these problems in terms of incomplete information, costs of moving, and so on, the Keynesian features noted above do not tend to emerge.

An interesting rationale for sticky prices concerns long-term contracts. Each (explicit or implicit) contract specifies a wage or price over an interval of time. Then the gradual process of recontracting means that the average wage or price adjusts gradually toward the average market-clearing value. Although this perspective may account for sticky prices, it is less successful in explaining the Keynesian predictions about quantities. That is because sensible agreements would allow for efficient adjustment of work and production even if wages or prices do not change from day to day. Thus, the existence of long-term contracts does not explain the type of unemployment and underproduction that arises in Keynesian models.

Important Terms and Concepts

complete Keynesian model
short-side rule (for determining quantities)
involuntary unemployment
Keynesian consumption function
liquidity constraint
Keynesian cross diagram
autonomous change in demand
Keynesian investment function

investment accelerator
marginal propensity to spend
marginal propensity to invest
IS curve
LM curve
law of supply and demand (for adjusting the price level)
long-term contracts

QUESTIONS AND PROBLEMS

Mainly for Review

18.1 (*a*) Contrast the form of consumption demand in the Keynesian model with that in Chapter 5. Why doesn't a change in current income affect consumption demand in the market-clearing model? (*b*) Make the same comparisons for investment demand.

18.2 What is involuntary unemployment? Are the temporary layoffs of workers on long-term contracts an example of involuntary unemployment?

18.3 How does output adjust to ensure the aggregate-consistency condition for the commodity market (equation 18.7)? Would this result apply if goods were not in excess supply?

18.4 Explain how an increase in the quantity of money reduces the real interest rate in the Keynesian model. Why doesn't this effect arise in the market-clearing model?

18.5 What is the output multiplier for an increase in government purchases? Discuss how the size of the muliplier is affected by (*a*) whether government purchases are tax financed or deficit financed; (*b*) any increases in the interest rate; (*c*) whether government purchases are temporary or permanent.

18.6 If the price level is fixed at a level that is "too high," show that the interest rate and output must adjust to ensure the condition that all money be willingly held. Can the interest rate be too high as a result? How does a downward adjustment of the price level bring down the interest rate and eliminate excess supply of commodities?

Problems for Discussion

18.7 The Paradox of Thrift

Suppose that people become "thriftier" and thereby decide to save more and consume less.

a. For a given interest rate, what happens to the quantities of output and employment? What happens to the amount of saving? (*Hint:* What happens to the quantity of investment?) If the amount of saving falls when people become thriftier, there is said to be a *paradox of thrift*.

b. Redo the analysis when the interest rate is allowed to adjust. What happens now to the amount of saving? Is there a paradox of thrift?

c. Can there by a paradox of thrift in the market-clearing model, where the price level is also allowed to adjust? What accounts for the differences in results?

18.8 The Multiplier

Consider an autonomous increase in investment demand.

a. Why is there a multiplicative effect on output if we hold fixed the interest rate?

b. Is there still a multiplier when the interest rate adjusts? In particular, how does this answer depend on the magnitudes of the following:
   i. The sensitivity of aggregate demand to the interest rate?
   ii. The sensitivity of money demand to output?
   iii. The sensitivity of money demand to the interest rate?

18.9 Perceived Wealth in the Keynesian Model

Suppose that the President makes a speech and announces that we are all wealthier than we previously thought. If we all believe the President, then what does the Keynesian model predict for the changes in output, employment, and "wealth?" Explain these results and contrast them with the predictions from the market-clearing model.

18.10 A Change in Inflationary Expectations

Consider an (unexplained) increase in inflationary expectations, π^e.

a. How does this change affect the IS curve? In answering, assume now that we place the expected real interest rate, $r^e = R - \pi^e$, rather than the nominal interest rate, on the vertical axis.

b. How does the increase in expected inflation affect the LM curve? Assume again that we place the expected real interest rate on the vertical axis.

c. What happens to the level of output, the real interest rate, and the nominal interest rate? Explain these results and contrast them with those in the market-clearing model. (*Hint:* How does the change in inflationary expectations compare to an autonomous shift in the demand for money?)

18.11 Extreme Cases in the IS/LM Analysis

Consider the following extreme cases (which have sometimes been suggested, but have not been supported empirically).

a. Suppose that money demand is insensitive to the interest rate. What does the LM curve look like? In this case what is the effect on output and the interest rate from a disturbance that shifts the IS curve?

b. Suppose that money demand is extremely sensitive to the interest rate (which is sometimes called a *liquidity trap*). How does the LM curve look in this case? What is the effect now from shifts in the IS curve?

c. Suppose that the interest rate has a negligible effect on aggregate demand. How does the IS curve look in this situation? What are the effects from shifts in the LM curve?

d. Finally, suppose that aggregate demand is extremely sensitive to the interest rate. Draw the IS curve and describe the effects from shifts in the LM curve.

18.12 Stagflation in the Keynesian Model

Suppose that we define stagflation as an increase in inflation during a recession.

a. Assume that a recession stems from an autonomous decline in aggregate demand. Can we get stagflation from this disturbance in the Keynesian model?

b. Is there some other way to generate stagflation in the Keynesian model?

PART VI

THE INTERNATIONAL ECONOMY

CHAPTER 19

THE INTERNATIONAL ECONOMY

Thus far, we have dealt with the macroeconomic performance of a single economy. In particular, we have neglected the interactions among countries on international markets. In this chapter we extend the model to allow for trade in goods and credit across national borders.

We shall find that our previous analysis of a single economy now applies to the macroeconomics of the world economy, whereas our earlier treatment of individuals carries over to the behavior of a small economy that operates on world markets. We can use this perspective to think about international borrowing and lending, changes in the prices of commodities such as oil, and the factors that determine a country's balance of international payments. Since the U.S. economy is so large, we can view it as an intermediate case between the small economy and the entire world.

Aside from the parallels to our previous discussion, there are some entirely new issues that concern the determination of exchange rates between different currencies. As part of this analysis, we have to assess the linkages across countries of prices, interest rates, and monetary policies.

Because of space considerations, this chapter provides only an overview of some basic points in the international aspects of macroeconomics. More detailed treatments appear in textbooks that are designed for courses in international economics (see, for example, Wilfred Ethier, *Modern International Economics,* Norton, New York, 1983, parts 3 and 4).

The United States in the World Economy

Consider a world economy, within which the United States is one of many countries. For now, we assume that the goods produced in each country are physically identical. We also abstract from transport costs or barriers to trade across national borders.

For the moment, we assume that all countries quote prices of goods in units of U.S. dollars. Then, given the conditions mentioned above, it follows that goods in all countries must sell at the same dollar price P_t. Otherwise, people would want to buy all goods at the lowest price and to sell all goods at the highest price. This is the simplest version of the **law of one price.** At this point, we also abstract from inflation, so that the dollar price level is the constant P.

We suppose that the central bank of each country holds a quantity of **international currency.** This currency could be pieces of paper denominated in U.S. dollars or other national units, or could be a commodity such as gold. The precise form of the international currency is unimportant for our purposes, except that we assume that the interest rate on this currency is zero.

Let $\bar{H}_t$ denote the world quantity in units of U.S. dollars of international currency for period t. (An overbar means that the variable pertains to the entire world.) The domestic central bank demands the real quantity, H_t/P, of this currency to facilitate transactions between domestic residents and foreigners. Basically, this demand for money by the central bank is analogous to the demand for real cash balances by individuals.[1] In particular, a greater amount of real transactions with foreigners increases the real demand for international currency, whereas a higher nominal interest rate, R_t, reduces this demand.

We assume that a single credit market exists in the world. The aggregate dollar quantity of bonds on this credit market, $\bar{B}_t$, is zero, just as it was for a single country when we neglected foreigners. If we abstract from differences in credit-worthiness among borrowers, the real interest rate, r_t, must be the same for all lenders and borrowers in every country. When measured in U.S. dollars—that is, as future dollars paid per current dollar per year—the nominal interest rate is R_t. Since we abstract at this point from inflation, the real interest rate, r_t, equals the nominal rate.

Now consider the situation from the standpoint of the residents of a single country, which might be the United States. We refer to this country as the domestic or home country, while we refer to other countries as the rest of the world. Let Y_t represent the total of goods and services produced domestically, which is the real gross domestic product. Correspondingly, the dollar income from this source is the amount, PY_t.

For the residents of a single country, the total of funds lent need no longer

---

[1]Many researchers have studied the demand for **international reserves** by central banks. These reserves include the currency that our model considers, but consist largely of "liquid," interest-bearing assets, such as U.S. treasury bills. In practice, there is considerable ambiguity about which assets to include as part of a country's international reserves, and which to exclude. For a survey of the demand for international reserves see Stanley Black, "International Money and International Monetary Arrangements," in Ronald Jones and Peter Kenen, eds, *Handbook of International Economics,* Vol. 2, North-Holland, Amsterdam, 1985. Two interesting studies of the demand for international reserves are Nasser Saidi, "The Square-Root Law, Uncertainty and International Reserves under Alternative Regimes: Canadian Experience, 1950–1976," *Journal of Monetary Economics,* May 1981; and Sebastian Edwards, "On the Interest-Rate Elasticity of the Demand for International Reserves: Some Evidence from Developing Countries," *Journal of International Money and Finance,* August 1985.

equal the total borrowed. Rather, the total amount lent on net by domestic residents (including the government) corresponds to the total borrowed on net from this country by foreigners. Let B_t represent the net holding of bonds by domestic residents at the end of period t.[2] Then, if $B_t > 0$, the home country is a net creditor to the rest of the world, whereas if $B_t < 0$, the country is a net debtor. Correspondingly, the amount $R_t B_t$ is the net interest income for period $t + 1$ to domestic residents from abroad.[3]

We suppose for convenience that the net interest income from abroad, $R_t B_t$, is the only source of net income from the rest of the world. In particular, we neglect any net labor income from abroad, which is the labor income of domestic residents working in foreign countries, less that of foreigners working in the home country. This category of income is unimportant for most countries. However, it is a significant negative item for Germany, which imports many foreign workers as *gastarbeiter,* and a significant positive item for countries like Pakistan and Turkey, which export workers to other places. If we include this net labor income, then we would add it to the net interest income to measure the overall **net factor income from abroad.** The term, factor income, means that the income flows either to the factor, labor, or to the factor, "capital," which includes here the net claims on assets abroad, B. Then the total dollar income accruing out of productive activity to domestic residents during period t is the amount, $PY_t + R_{t-1}B_{t-1}$. This total, which is the gross national product, equals gross domestic product plus the net factor income from abroad. In our simplified setup the last item includes only the net receipts of interest income from abroad.

Suppose that we neglect any transfer payments that flow from one country to another. (These include gifts, governmental foreign aid, pension payments, and the like.) Then the gross national product is the total income of domestic residents. This income can be spent in the following ways:

- Personal consumption expenditures, PC_t, whether on goods and services produced domestically or abroad.
- Private domestic gross investment, PI_t, which is the expenditure on capital goods located at home.
- Government purchases of goods and services, PG_t.
- **Net foreign investment,** which is the name given to the net acquisition of interest-bearing claims from abroad, $B_t - B_{t-1}$, plus any accumulation of international currency, $H_t - H_{t-1}$.

---

[2]Note that we have changed the notation from before, so that B_t is now the total holding of bonds (including government bonds) by the domestic private sector less any net debt outstanding of the home government. The last term includes the public debt less any assets held by the government. In other words, we have consolidated the asset position of the government with that of the private sector.

[3]More generally, the variable B_t includes not only interest-bearing securities but also any other net claims of domestic residents on the rest of the world. Specifically, it includes ownership of capital abroad, which arises from **"direct investment"** in foreign countries. Hence, the term, $R_t B_t$, encompasses the income from this ownership of capital.

Putting the results together, we have the budget constraint for the home country during period t

$$PY_t + R_{t-1}B_{t-1} = P(C_t + I_t + G_t) + (B_t - B_{t-1}) + (H_t - H_{t-1}) \quad (19.1)$$

When we consider a single economy in isolation (a closed economy), we find that the gross domestic product, PY_t, equals the total expenditure by domestic residents for goods and services, $P(C_t + I_t + G_t)$. When we open the economy to the rest of the world—that is, when we allow for an open economy—we introduce some new items, which creates a divergence between the gross domestic product and the domestic expenditures on goods and services. On the left side of equation 19.1 we include the net factor income from abroad, $R_{t-1}B_{t-1}$. On the right side we include net foreign investment, which equals the net acquisition of interest-bearing claims, $B_t - B_{t-1}$, plus the accumulation of international currency, $H_t - H_{t-1}$.

The term, $B_t - B_{t-1}$, is called the **balance on capital account** for the home country. If $B_t - B_{t-1}$ is positive, then there is an **outflow of capital.** (If it is negative, there is an **inflow of capital.**) That is, by acquiring interest-bearing claims on foreigners, the home country provides funds for the purchase of capital goods abroad.

Consider the difference between the value of goods and services produced by domestic residents (including the net factor income from abroad), $PY_t + R_{t-1}B_{t-1}$, and the expenditure by these residents on goods and services, $P(C_t + I_t + G_t)$. This difference corresponds to the additional assets that domestic residents acquire currently from the rest of the world, and is called the **current-account balance.** Notice from equation 19.1 that

$$\text{Current-account balance} = PY_t + R_{t-1}B_{t-1} - P(C_t + I_t + G_t)$$
$$= \text{net foreign investment}$$
$$= B_t - B_{t-1} + H_t - H_{t-1} \quad (19.2)$$

This expression is the basic identity for the balance of international payments. The equation says that the current-account balance equals net foreign investment, which is the sum of the net capital flow, $B_t - B_{t-1}$, plus the change in international currency, $H_t - H_{t-1}$. If the current-account balance is positive (or negative), then a country is said to have a **surplus** (or **deficit**) **on current account.** Notice that, as an accounting identity, a surplus on current account must have an offsetting financial transaction in the form of an increase in interest-bearing claims, B, or international currency, H.

Now let us take an alternative view of a country's position with respect to the rest of the world. First, the gross national product, $PY_t + R_{t-1}B_{t-1}$, is the total value of the goods and services produced this period by domestic residents. Therefore, the difference between GNP and domestic expenditures equals the value of goods and services produced by domestic residents less the value of goods and services used currently by these residents. If the difference is positive, then the home country must be selling goods and services on net to the rest of the world. Otherwise, the home country must be buying goods and services on net. We define exports to be the goods and services produced by domestic residents that are sold to foreigners and define imports to be the goods and services produced by foreigners that are bought by domestic residents. Hence, we have shown that the difference between the gross national product, $PY_t + R_{t-1}B_{t-1}$, and domestic expenditure, $P(C_t + I_t + G_t)$, equals the value of exports less the value of imports. That is, using equation 19.2,

$$\text{Current-account balance} = PY_t + R_{t-1}B_{t-1} - P(C_t + I_t + G_t)$$

$$= \text{value of exports less value of imports}^4 \quad (19.3)$$

By rearranging equation 19.3 we obtain the customary definition of the gross national product

$$\text{GNP} = PY_t + R_{t-1}B_{t-1} = P(C_t + I_t + G_t)$$
$$+ \text{value of exports less value of imports} \quad (19.4)$$

Economists refer to exports less imports as "net exports." Thus, GNP equals consumption plus domestic investment plus government purchases plus net exports.

We can get another perspective on international borrowing and lending by thinking about the home country's saving and investment. From equation 19.2, the current-account balance is $PY_t + R_{t-1}B_{t-1} - P(C_t + I_t + G_t)$. But the expression, $PY_t + R_{t-1}B_{t-1} - P(C_t + G_t)$, is the total of private saving and the government surplus.[5] Hence, this term equals national saving, which we denote by S. It follows that the current-account balance is the difference between national saving and domestic investment—that is,

$$\text{Current-account balance} = PY_t + R_{t-1}B_{t-1} - P(C_t + I_t + G_t) = S - I$$
$$(19.5)$$

Thus a country runs a surplus on current account—and thereby lends funds abroad—when its saving exceeds its investment.

Figure 19.1 shows the ratio of the U.S. current-account balance to GNP from 1869 to 1985. One thing to note is that the current account was in deficit during the period from 1869 to 1896, except for 1894 and the years from 1876 to 1881. (The current account was also in deficit for most of the years from

---

[4]If the net transfers from foreigners to the home country are nonzero, then these add to exports less imports in the calculation of the current-account balance.

[5]Assuming that the net factor income from abroad, $R_{t-1}B_{t-1}$, accrues to the private sector, private saving is $PY_t + R_{t-1}B_{t-1} + R_{t-1}B^g_{t-1} + V_t - PC_t - T_t$, where B^g_{t-1} is government debt, V_t is transfers, and T_t is taxes. The government's surplus is $T_t - PG_t - V_t - R_{t-1}B^g_{t-1}$. Therefore, the sum of private saving and the government's surplus is $PY_t + R_{t-1}B_{t-1} - P(C_t + G_t)$. This last result does not change if some of the net income from abroad, $R_{t-1}B_{t-1}$, accrues to the government. However, if a part of the government's purchases, G_t, represent public investment, then the government's (and national) saving would be correspondingly higher. Our treatment regards all government purchases as a form of consumption expenditure.

Figure 19.1 The U.S. Current-Account Balance, 1869–1985
The Figure shows the ratio to GNP of the current-account balance. The data are from
Historical Statistics of the U.S., pp. 866–68; *Economic Report of the President*, 1986,
Table B-99; and *U.S. Survey of Current Business*, February 1986, p. 9.

1830 to 1868.) The deficit averaged 1.6% of GNP from 1869 to 1875, and
1.4% of GNP from 1886 to 1891.

The current account was in surplus for most years after 1896, averaging
0.8% of GNP from 1897 to 1914, 1.2% for the 1920s, and 0.5% for the 1930s.
Because of World War I, the surplus on current account averaged 4.6% of
GNP from 1915 to 1919. This surplus represented the substantial lending from
the United States to its foreign allies. During World War II the account was
in surplus in 1940–41 (averaging 1.3% of GNP) before the U.S. entered the
war, but was in deficit from 1942 to 1945 (averaging −0.7% of GNP). However, the large foreign lending for 1946–47 implied substantial current-account
surpluses, which averaged 3.1% of GNP.

From 1948 to 1976 the current account was typically in surplus, but by an
amount that averaged only 0.3% of GNP. Subsequently, there were deficits

of 0.7% of GNP in 1977–78, followed by near balance in 1979–81, and a deficit of 0.3% of GNP in 1982. Then the current account shifted sharply toward deficit, reaching -1.3% of GNP in 1983, and -2.8% of GNP for 1984 and 1985. We have to go back to the 1880s and 1870s to find U.S. current-account deficits that were comparable in relation to GNP.

Inflation in the International Accounts

As in a closed economy, inflation makes conventional accounting practices less useful as measures of economic changes. For example, in equation 19.2, we would want to measure the flow of interest earnings on the net holding of assets, B_{t-1}, by using the real interest rate, r_{t-1}, rather than the nominal rate, R_{t-1}. Then, when divided by the price level, net foreign investment on the right side of equation 19.2 would measure the change in the real value of a nation's assets. Unfortunately, the available data do not make these adjustments for inflation.[6]

The Role of the International Credit Market

For an individual in a closed economy, the credit market allows for divergences between income and spending. For example, if a disturbance temporarily lowers someone's income, then he or she can borrow—or spend out of accumulated assets—to avoid a temporary decline in consumption or investment. Similarly, an individual can save most of a windfall of income to spread it over extra consumption in many periods.

On the other hand, when a closed economy experiences an economy-wide disturbance—such as a temporary decline in everyone's production opportunities—it is impossible for everyone to borrow more. In this case, the real interest rate adjusts so that the aggregate of desired borrowing equals the aggregate of desired lending. Hence, in a closed economy, the credit market cannot cushion spending against an economy-wide disturbance, even if it is temporary.

Basically, a single country functions in a world credit market much like an individual functions in the credit market of a closed economy. Assume that the home country initially has a zero balance on current account. Then suppose that a temporary supply shock, such as a harvest failure or a natural disaster, makes everyone in the home country desire to decrease saving at the initial real interest rate. If the home country's economy is small, the world credit market can accommodate this decrease in saving without significant changes in the world's real interest rate. By using equation 19.5, we see that the

---

[6]They also do not adjust for other changes in the real values of assets. For gold, long-term bonds, and direct investments, these capital gains and losses can be important. Generally, there turn out to be numerous "errors and omissions" in the international accounts.

reduction in saving, for a given value of investment, implies a deficit on current account.

Now suppose that the supply shock applies to the entire world, instead of just to the home country. Then the universal desire to save less and borrow from abroad cannot be satisfied. In these circumstances the real interest rate would rise on the international credit market to ensure that the world aggregate of desired borrowing equaled the world aggregate of desired lending. Thus $S = I$ would still apply for the typical country, and the typical country would not (and could not) run a deficit on current account.

Figure 19.2 illustrates the case of a temporary supply shock that applies only to the home country. The vertical axis plots the real interest rate, r_t, which prevails on the international credit market. Because we think of a small economy that has little effect on world markets, we hold this real interest rate fixed in the present context. Then the downward-sloping solid curve in the figure shows the domestic residents' aggregate demand for goods, $Y_t^d = C_t^d + I_t^d + G_t$. As in our previous analysis of a closed economy, a lower real interest rate stimulates this demand.

The upward-sloping solid curve in the figure shows the domestic residents' aggregate supply of goods, $Y_t^s + R_{t-1}B_{t-1}/P$. Note that this concept corresponds to real GNP, which is the total of goods produced by domestic residents,

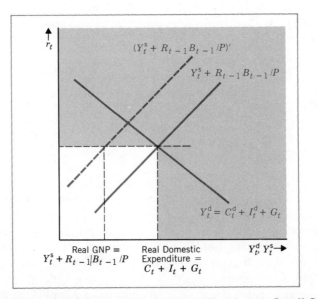

Figure 19.2 The Effect of a Temporary Supply Shock on a Small Open Economy
The supply shock lowers the domestic residents' aggregate supply of goods, but has a negligible effect on demand. Thus, at the going world real interest rate, there is a fall in real GNP relative to real domestic expenditure. Consequently, the home country runs a current-account deficit, which corresponds to an inflow of capital from abroad.

including the real net factor income from abroad. As in previous analyses, a higher real interest rate raises the quantity of goods supplied.

We draw the solid lines in the figure so that, at the given world real interest rate, the domestic residents' aggregate quantity of goods demanded, Y_t^d, is initially equal to the aggregate quantity supplied, $Y_t^s + R_{t-1}B_{t-1}/P$. Hence, real domestic expenditure on goods and services initially equals real GNP. It follows from equation 19.2 that the current account is in balance. Hence, if the home country's holding of international currency is constant ($H_t = H_{t-1}$), then the capital account is initially in balance ($B_t = B_{t-1}$).

Now suppose that a temporary supply shock reduces the home country's supply of goods but has a negligible effect on demand. Then the new supply curve is the one shown by the dashed line in Figure 19.2. At the going world real interest rate, r_t, the quantity of goods demanded by domestic residents now exceeds the quantity supplied. In the world economy this imbalance can be accommodated by the home country's borrowing from abroad. Namely, the real domestic expenditure, $C_t + I_t + G_t$, equals the quantity of goods demanded, Y_t^d; the real GNP equals the quantity of goods supplied, $Y_t^s + R_{t-1}B_{t-1}/P$; and the difference between the two is the real deficit on current account (see equation 19.2). Furthermore, if there is no change in the home country's holding of international currency, then equation 19.2 says that the current-account deficit corresponds to a capital inflow from abroad—that is, to a negative value for the change in earning assets, $B_t - B_{t-1}$. Hence, the temporary supply shock induces the home country to borrow from abroad to avoid a cutback in current spending.

Notice that a worldwide supply shock would be different. In this case, the construction shown in Figure 19.2 applies to each country and, thereby, to the world aggregates of goods demanded and supplied. Consequently, the world real interest rate has to rise to clear the international credit market—that is, to equate the quantities of goods demanded and supplied in the world. Then, for the typical country, we end up at the point where the new supply curve intersects the demand curve in Figure 19.2. At this point, there is a balance on current account—that is, as must always be the case, the typical country does not borrow from abroad. Notice that this treatment of a worldwide disturbance—including the determination of the world real interest rate— corresponds to the type of analysis that we carried out previously for a closed economy.

We can identify several situations in which a country ends up borrowing heavily on the world credit market. First, consider the example of Poland for 1978–81, where harvest failures and labor-force problems meant that output fell well below the anticipated average level of future output. In particular, an estimate of real product for Poland shows a decline of about 20% from 1978 to 1981.[7] Thus, the situation resembles that shown in Figure 19.2, where

---

[7]The data on Poland are from the Economist Intelligence Unit, Ltd. (U.K.), *Quarterly Economic Review of Poland,* Annual Supplement 1982, and no. 1, 1983.

external borrowing avoids a sharp decline in current real spending. In fact, the gross foreign debt of Poland reached $25 billion in 1981, which was about one-half of annual GNP.

For a second situation where a country borrows heavily, we can consider Mexico. In this case, there was a major discovery of a natural resource, namely oil, which promised large amounts of income in future periods. For example, by 1974, Mexico's oil prospects were great, but a significant volume of production had not yet appeared. In this situation, the increase in permanent income motivates external borrowing to finance higher consumption (and marvelous government projects) before most of the oil revenue materializes. (In Figure 19.2 we would show this by shifting the demand curve rightward, while keeping the supply curve fixed.) Thus Mexico's gross external debt rose from $3.5 billion or 9% of GDP in 1971 to $61 billion or 26% of GDP in 1981.[8] Of course, this type of foreign borrowing can run into trouble when, as in 1982–86, the relative price of oil falls unexpectedly, so that Mexico's permanent income turns out to be lower than predicted.

As another example, consider a developing country that has a relatively small amount of capital per worker and thus a high marginal product of capital. This type of country borrows abroad to finance large amounts of investment and, thereby, high growth rates of output. Furthermore, the potential to borrow abroad means that a developing country's level of consumption need not be depressed drastically during the period of high investment.

A recent example of this behavior is Brazil, which sustained an average growth rate of per capita real gross domestic product of about 5% per year from 1971 to 1980. Over this period, Brazil's gross external debt grew from $6 billion, or 11% of GDP, to $55 billion, or 22% of GDP. For an earlier example of a developing country that borrowed heavily abroad, we can look at the United States in 1890 when the net foreign debt reached $2.9 billion,[9] which amounted to 21% of GNP. (Recall from Figure 19.1 that the United States was an international borrower for most years prior to 1890.) Thus the situation of the United States in the late nineteenth century was roughly comparable to that for Brazil in recent years.

Recall that borrowing from abroad reflects a shortfall of national saving, *S*, from domestic investment, *I*. For Poland and Mexico the borrowing reflected a drop in saving, which resulted from either a drop in current income (Poland) or an increase in permanent income (Mexico). For Brazil—or other rapidly growing countries—the borrowing reflects especially the high value of investment demand.

---

[8]The data on gross domestic product for Mexico and Brazil (mentioned below) are from *International Financial Statistics,* 1982 Yearbook and April 1983. The data on external debt for Mexico and Brazil are from Organization of American States, *Statistical Bulletin of the OAS,* vol. 4, no. 1–2, January–June 1982, Table SA-5, p. 30; and Morgan Guaranty Trust, *World Financial Markets,* February 1983, Table 2, p. 5.

[9]U.S. Commerce Department, *Historical Statistics of the U.S., Colonial Times to 1970,* series U40, p. 869.

By contrast, the countries that lend internationally are those with high desired saving—where current income is high relative to permanent income— or with relatively low investment demand. Included in the category of international lenders are the mature industrialized countries, such as the United States through 1984 and Switzerland. For example, the net international investment position of the United States (U.S. assets held abroad including international reserves less foreign assets held in the United States) was estimated to be $147 billion at the end of 1982, but then fell to $28 billion at the end of 1984 and became negative in 1985.[10] The reduction in this net asset position reflected the U.S. current-account deficits from 1983 to 1985. The most likely explanation for these deficits is the strong investment boom since 1983, which led to an excess of investment demand over desired national saving. In this sense the shift of status from international creditor to international debtor is not necessarily a bad mark for the United States.

Another example of an important international creditor is Saudi Arabia, whose flow of oil income through 1981 was high relative to the long-term prospective flow. The estimate for the net international investment position of Saudi Arabia (including international reserves) was about $150 billion in 1982, but declined to about $115 billion in 1985 because of the drop in oil revenues.[11]

One important point is that—just as in the case of a credit market in a closed economy—the existence of an international credit market tends to be advantageous for both borrowers and lenders. Obviously, this market enables borrowing countries to spend more than their current income, which is warranted in the cases mentioned above. But the potential to lend abroad also allows countries that have a relatively large amount of desired saving to achieve higher rates of return than would be available domestically. Therefore, although there have been some recent troubles about foreign loans, we should not conclude that the existence of the international credit market is a bad idea overall.

Notice that throughout this analysis we assumed a "perfect" world credit market, where the real interest rate was the same for each country. But economists sometimes argue that there are "country risks" associated with loans. As the residents of a country increase their borrowing—with the government of the country often doing the borrowing or guaranteeing the loans—there may be an increasing risk of default. Then the real interest rate paid by that country rises as the amount borrowed increases.[12] (Similar results apply to an

---

[10]*Economic Report of the President,* 1986, Table B-103. The estimates are very rough because of incomplete coverage and because the assets are carried at book value rather than market value. For example, gold—which is included in the net international investment position—is valued at the official price, which is about 10% of the market price.

[11]The data are from the Economist Intelligence Unit, Ltd. (U.K.), *Quarterly Economic Review of Saudi Arabia,* Annual Supplement 1985, p. 29.

[12]For a discussion of these issues see Jonathan Eaton, Mark Gersovitz, and Joseph E. Stiglitz, "The Pure Theory of Country Risk," *European Economic Review,* June 1986.

individual when borrowing funds on the credit market in a closed economy.) Because of these considerations, a single country, or a single person, has difficulty in using the credit market to smooth out spending when there are major fluctuations in income. In this case, the results turn out to be something like an average of those that we found before for a closed economy with those discussed in this chapter for a single world credit market. Specifically, a temporary disturbance to a country's income shows up partly as a change in that country's real interest rate and level of real expenditure, and partly in the amount of borrowing from abroad. International borrowing then buffers only a portion of the variations in a country's income.

The Terms of Trade

Up to now we assumed that the home country and the rest of the world produced goods that were physically identical. Also, by neglecting transport costs, we assumed that all goods were **tradable** across countries. Let us continue to assume for now that all goods are tradable, but suppose that different countries specialize in the production of different goods. For example, Chile produces a substantial fraction of the world's copper, whereas Brazil produces a large share of the world's coffee. Under these circumstances countries are affected significantly when the prices of their principal products change relative to the prices of other goods.

To keep things simple, pretend that the home country produces a single good (or market basket of goods) that sells at the dollar price P, while the rest of the world produces another good (or market basket of goods) that sells at the price $\bar{P}$. Then we want to study changes in the ratio, $P/\bar{P}$. If the ratio increases, we say that the home country's **terms of trade** improve. That is, for each unit of goods that a home country produces and sells abroad (exports), it can now purchase more units of foreign goods (imports).

Consider a change in the terms of trade, $P/\bar{P}$, that reflects a disturbance in the rest of the world. For example, Chile may face a change in the relative price of copper, or Brazil may experience a shift in the relative price of coffee. But, since the disturbance originates from the rest of the world, we assume here that Chile's capacity to produce copper or Brazil's to produce coffee does not change.

The shift in the terms of trade, $P/\bar{P}$, looks to the residents of the home country like a change in the local relative price, $P(z)/P$, looked to the producers in a local market in the model that we considered in Chapter 17. Specifically, an improvement in the terms of trade raises the real values of marginal products in the home country. If the change is temporary, then wealth effects are small enough to neglect. The substitution effects imply increases in work effort, production, and the physical volume of exports, with only a small increase in current consumption. The greater real value of exports— reflecting partly the higher relative price and partly the higher physical volume—shows up as a surplus on current account. Thus there is an outflow of capital, which domestic residents accumulate as greater claims on foreigners. Note that the residents of the domestic country willingly accumulate these extra assets at going interest rates—that is, they raise their desired saving— because the improvement in the terms of trade is temporary. People plan to use the additional assets to finance higher consumption (in the form of imports) in future periods, when they expect the terms of trade to return to its normal value.

If the improvement in the terms of trade is permanent, then there is a strong wealth effect, which motivates an increase in consumption. In fact, there would now be little change in the home country's desired saving. In this situation, we find little change in the assets accumulated from abroad—that is, imports of goods rise (in terms of dollar value) along with exports. Correspondingly, there is no longer a surplus on current account. Thus a surplus on current account accompanies a temporary improvement in the terms of trade but not a permanent improvement.

Another element is investment. The improvement in the terms of trade raises the real value of the marginal product of domestic capital. Hence—at least if people expect the improved terms of trade to persist for awhile— investment demand rises.[13] If this increase in demand exceeds the rise in desired saving, then the home country ends up borrowing from abroad. Thus overall, an improvement in the terms of trade leads to a surplus on current account only if the rise in desired saving exceeds the increase in investment demand. The spur to saving is greater the more temporary is the disturbance, whereas the reverse tends to hold for investment (refer to footnote 13). Therefore, we still conclude that a temporary improvement in the terms of trade leads to a surplus on current account. However, because of the spur to investment, a permanent improvement in the terms of trade may lead to a deficit on current account.[14]

As an empirical example of effects from changes in the terms of trade, consider the current-account balance for the Organization of Petroleum-Exporting Countries (OPEC). Table 19.1 shows that OPEC's current account was nearly balanced in 1972. Then the sharp increases in oil prices during 1973–74 led to a current-account surplus of $60 billion in 1974. From 1974 to 1978, the relative price of oil fell somewhat. But more importantly, the OPEC countries adjusted their expenditures to their higher permanent incomes, which corresponded to the growing perception that the relative price of oil would remain high. Thus by 1978 the current account of OPEC was again nearly

---

[13]If changes in the capital stock entail adjustment costs, then investment demand would respond little to a temporary change in the terms of trade.

[14]For further analysis of effects from changes in the terms of trade, see Jeffrey Sachs, "The Current Account and Macroeconomic Adjustment in the 1970s," *Brookings Papers on Economic Activity,* no. 1, 1981; and Jeremy Greenwood, "Expectations, the Exchange Rate and the Current Account," *Journal of Monetary Economics,* November 1983.

Table 19.1 **Current-Account Balance of Oil-Exporting Countries (OPEC)**

Year	Current-Account Balance ($ billion)
1972	1
1974	60
1976	37
1978	−3
1980	103
1982	−18
1984	−18

Source: OCED, *OECD Economic Outlook,* December 1985, July 1983, July 1979.

balanced—but at much higher dollar levels of exports and imports. Then the surprise increases in oil prices in 1979–80 led again to a large surplus on current account, which reached $103 billion in 1980. In this case the upward adjustment of expenditures and the fall in oil's relative price moved the current account to a deficit position by 1982.

Nontraded Goods

Thus far we have assumed that all goods are tradable across countries. But some items, such as services and real estate, are difficult to transport across national borders. Economists account for this phenomenon by including **nontraded goods** in the model.[15] Recall that the terms of trade refers to the price of tradables produced in the home country relative to the price of tradables produced in the rest of the world. Given the terms of trade, it is possible for the price of the home country's nontradables to change relative to the price of its tradables. In particular, since the nontradables do not enter into international commerce (by definition), the home country's relative price of nontradables and tradables tends to be more sensitive than the terms of trade to disturbances that originate at home. (In the extreme case of a closed economy, none of its goods enter into international trade and only the domestic disturbances matter.)

Let us see how the presence of nontraded goods affects the analysis of a change in the terms of trade. The main consideration is that an improvement in the terms of trade raises the price of the home country's tradables relative to its nontradables. This change motivates the home country to shift production and employment away from nontradables and toward tradables. Hence, the

---

[15]There are problems in implementing this idea, since considerations such as transport costs mean that tradability is a relative matter. Although some goods enter more easily than others into international trade, with enough incentive, almost anything—including the services of workers—becomes a tradable good.

existence of the nontradable sector reinforces the positive effect of the terms of trade on the production of tradables. However, the expansion in the tradables sector may go along with a contraction of production and employment in the nontradables sector.

International Flows of Money

Recall that the change in a country's holdings of international currency, $H_t - H_{t-1}$, is one component of the current-account balance in equation 19.2. Any element that increases a country's demand for international currency, such as a rise in that country's aggregate real income, shows up as a positive value for $H_t - H_{t-1}$. Generally, a country can finance this increase in currency either by running a current-account surplus—that is, exporting more than it imports— or by borrowing from abroad.

Suppose that the total world supply of international currency is the fixed number, $\bar{H}$. Then the world's aggregate demand for international currency must accommodate itself to the given amount that is available. But this situation is analogous to the one that we worked out previously for a closed economy, where the nominal quantity of money, M, was a given number. In that situation we found that the domestic price level, P, adjusted so that the real quantity of cash, M/P, equaled the real amount demanded. The same idea applies to the world economy. Namely, the world price level, $\bar{P}$, adjusts so that the real value of international currency, $\bar{H}/\bar{P}$, equals the real quantity demanded. It follows that the world price level depends positively on the world's "money supply," $\bar{H}$, and negatively on the world's real demand for money. This dependence parallels our previous findings for a closed economy.

Different Monies and Exchange Rates

In the real world, each country issues currency in its own unit, whether dollars, pounds, yen, or whatever. To allow for this fact, let M^i be the quantity of domestic money—that is, the monetary base—for country i. We measure this money in domestic currency units, such as Japanese yen. A typical setup is that the central bank of country i holds the international currency, H, and then issues the domestic monetary base, M^i. Thus we would have the simplified balance sheet of a central bank as shown in Table 19.2. Note that the central

Table 19.2 Simplified Balance Sheet of a Central Bank

Assets	Liabilities
International Currency (H^i)	Monetary base, M^i (currency and
Foreign interest-bearing assets	deposits of domestic financial
Domestic interest-bearing assets	institutions)
(domestic credit)	

bank's assets consist of international currency, H, foreign interest-bearing assets, and domestic interest-bearing assets, which include bonds issued by the home government. As mentioned in Chapter 15, the holdings of domestic earning assets are called the central bank's domestic credit. Then on the liabilities side are currency and deposits of domestic financial institutions held at the central bank. The sum of these two items constitutes the home country's monetary base, M^i. (For simplicity, we neglect foreign deposits held at the central bank.)

The domestic price level in country i, P^i, now expresses the number of local currency units, say yen, that exchange for a unit of goods. To simplify matters, think again of a case where all goods are physically identical. Hence, the same physical object sells for P^i units of one currency (yen) in country i, and for P^j units of another currency (say, Swiss francs) in country j. Note also that the ratio, M^i/P^i, is the real value of cash held in the form of country i's currency. We assume that this cash is held only by the residents of country i, which is realistic in most instances.

We now must introduce a new market, called an exchange market, on which people trade the currency of one country for that of another. For example, people might trade Japanese yen for U.S. dollars or for Swiss francs. The exchange market establishes exchange rates among the various currencies. For convenience, we express all exchange rates in terms of the number of units of domestic currency that trade for $1.00 (U.S.). For example, on July 15, 1986, 159 Japanese yen exchanged for $1.00, which means that each yen was worth about 0.6 cents. Similarly, 1.74 Swiss francs exchanged for $1.00, so that a Swiss franc was worth about 57 cents.

Notice that the exchange rates for Japanese yen and Swiss francs in terms of U.S. dollars tell us the exchange rate between yen and francs. Namely, 159 Japanese yen could buy $1.00, which could then be converted into 1.74 Swiss francs. Hence, $159/1.74 = 91$ Japanese yen could buy one Swiss franc. Thus the exchange rate between yen and francs was 91 yen per franc. (In practice, people can make these exchanges directly, rather than going through U.S. dollars.)

Let ϵ^i (the Greek letter *epsilon*) be the exchange rate for country i. In other words, ϵ^i units of country i's currency (say, yen) exchange for $1.00 (U.S.). Alternatively, we see that the dollar value of 1 unit of country i's currency (1 yen) is $1/\epsilon^i$. Notice that a *higher* value of the exchange rate, ϵ^i, means that country i's currency is *less* valuable in terms of dollars, because it takes more of country i's currency to buy $1.00.

For any two countries, i and j, we observe the exchange rates, ϵ^i and ϵ^j. These rates prescribe the number of units of each currency that trade for $1.00. Hence, ϵ^i units of currency i (say, 159 Japanese yen) can buy ϵ^j units of currency j (say, 1.74 Swiss francs). Therefore, the exchange rate between currencies i and j—that is, the number of units of currency i needed to buy one unit of currency j—equals ϵ^i/ϵ^j ($159/1.74 = 91$ yen per franc). Alternatively, for one unit of currency, i, we can get ϵ^j/ϵ^i units of currency j.

Purchasing-Power Parity

We are now ready to derive the central theoretical proposition of international finance. This result connects the exchange rate between two currencies to the price levels that prevail in the two countries.

Suppose again that we can think of all goods as tradable and physically identical. Then a resident of country i can choose between first, using local currency to buy goods domestically at the price P^i, or second, exchanging money into the currency of country j to buy goods at the price P^j. For each unit of currency i, a person gets $1/P^i$ units of goods domestically. In the exchange market, he or she gets ϵ^j/ϵ^i units of currency j for each unit of currency i. Then, buying at the price P^j, the person gets $(\epsilon^j/\epsilon^i) \cdot (1/P^j)$ units of goods. But for things to make sense, the two options must result in the same amount of goods. Otherwise, everyone would want to buy goods in the cheap country and sell goods in the expensive country. This idea is a version of the law of one price, which we mentioned before. Thus we must have that $1/P^i = (\epsilon^j/\epsilon^i) \cdot (1/P^j)$ or, when we arrange terms,

$$\frac{\epsilon^j}{\epsilon^i} = \frac{P^j}{P^i} \tag{19.6}$$

Equation 19.6 says that the ratio of the exchange rates for any two currencies, ϵ^j/ϵ^i, equals the ratio of the prices of goods in the two countries, P^j/P^i. This condition is called **purchasing-power parity (PPP).** It ensures that the purchasing power in terms of goods for each currency is the same regardless of where someone uses the currency to buy goods.

Define the rate of change of country i's exchange rate to be $\Delta\epsilon^i$—that is, $\epsilon^i_{t+1} = (1 + \Delta\epsilon^i)\epsilon^i_t$. Note that a positive value for $\Delta\epsilon^i$ means that country i's currency becomes less valuable over time in terms of dollars. Alternatively, we can say that country i's currency depreciates in value relative to the dollar. Conversely, if $\Delta\epsilon^i$ is negative, then country i's currency appreciates over time relative to the dollar.

The PPP condition in equation 19.6 implies that the rates of change of any two exchange rates, $\Delta\epsilon^j$ and $\Delta\epsilon^i$, are related to the inflation rates in the two countries. Specifically, equation 19.6 implies

$$\Delta\epsilon^j - \Delta\epsilon^i \simeq \pi^j - \pi^i \tag{19.7}$$

where π^j and π^i are the respective inflation rates. Equation 19.7 says that the higher a country's inflation rate, π^j, the higher the rate of depreciation of that country's currency, $\Delta\epsilon^j$. Equation 19.7 is called the **relative form of PPP,** whereas equation 19.6 is called the **absolute form of PPP** (in the sense of involving levels of prices and exchange rates rather than changes). For most purposes, we shall use the relative PPP condition, which is weaker than the absolute condition.

Equations 19.6 and 19.7 apply when the prices, P^i and P^j, refer to the same tradable goods. But, since economists are usually interested in the general levels of prices in different countries, let us think of P^i and P^j as referring to the prices of market baskets of goods produced or consumed in countries i and j, respectively. (In practice, we might measure these prices by the deflators for the GDP or by consumer or wholesale price indices.) When we think of prices in this way the PPP conditions do not hold exactly. That is because, first, different countries specialize in the production of different tradable goods, whose relative prices can change, and second, countries produce and consume nontradables. Since nontradables cannot move from one country to another, it does not necessarily follow that the purchasing power of a currency in terms of nontradables is independent of where one buys them. That is, equation 19.6 need not hold if P^i and P^j include prices of nontradables.

Suppose, as an example, that country j's terms of trade improve. That is, the price of tradables produced in country j rise relative to the prices of tradables produced elsewhere. Then, if P^i and P^j refer to market baskets of produced goods, it follows that P^j/P^i must rise for a given ratio of the exchange rates, ϵ^j/ϵ^i. The general point is that various real disturbances can shift the PPP condition in equation 19.6. Aside from changes in the terms of trade, some other real factors that can affect this condition are changes in trade restrictions or transport costs, some aspects of tax policies, and a variety of disturbances that shift the relative prices of traded and nontraded goods.

Interest-Rate Parity

Suppose that there is a market-determined nominal interest rate in each country. The nominal rate in country i, R^i, will be expressed in units of its own currency—for example, as yen paid per period per yen lent out today. Let us think about this interest rate from the standpoint of U.S. dollars. At date t we can exchange \$1.00 for ϵ_t^i units of country i's currency. Then by lending at the interest rate R^i, we receive $\epsilon_t^i(1 + R^i)$ units of country i's currency at date $t + 1$. If we convert back to dollars, using period $t + 1$'s exchange rate ϵ_{t+1}^i, then we obtain the dollar amount

$$\frac{\epsilon_t^i(1 + R^i)}{\epsilon_{t+1}^i} = \frac{(1 + R^i)}{(1 + \Delta\epsilon^i)}$$

where $\Delta\epsilon^i$ is again the rate of change of country i's exchange rate. If the exchange rate rises at a faster rate over time, then the dollar value of next period's holdings falls for a given value of the nominal interest rate R^i.

If there are no restrictions on the flows of assets across national borders, then people can hold assets in any country. If people choose country i, then the dollar value of next period's holdings is $(1 + R^i)/(1 + \Delta\epsilon^i)$. But if this amount is not the same for all countries, then everyone would want to lend where the amount is largest and borrow where it is smallest. Thus, as another implication of the law of one price, applied here to the returns on assets, we find that the amounts must be the same for all countries,

$$\frac{(1 + R^j)}{(1 + \Delta\epsilon^j)} = \frac{(1 + R^i)}{(1 + \Delta\epsilon^i)}$$

We can use this result to derive a condition that is called **interest-rate parity,** namely,[16]

$$R^j - R^i \simeq \Delta\epsilon^j - \Delta\epsilon^i \qquad (19.8)$$

Thus the higher the rate of change of a country's exchange rate, $\Delta\epsilon^j$—that is, the faster the depreciation in value relative to the U.S. dollar—the higher must be that country's nominal interest rate, R^j.

In practice, the changes in the exchange rates would not be known in advance. Then we would replace the variables, $\Delta\epsilon^j$ and $\Delta\epsilon^i$, by their expected values. With this modification, equation 19.8 says that a higher expected rate of change of the exchange rate, $(\Delta\epsilon^j)^e$, implies a correspondingly higher nominal interest rate, R^j. However, there are a number of real-world considerations that prevent interest-rate parity from holding exactly. These include varying tax treatments of interest income across countries, as well as uncertainties about the various returns and exchange-rate movements.

Finally, if purchasing-power parity holds in relative form, then equation 19.7 says that the difference in the growth rates of the exchange rates, $\Delta\epsilon^j - \Delta\epsilon^i$, equals the difference in the inflation rates, $\pi^j - \pi^i$. Then the interest-rate parity condition from equation 19.8 implies that (expected) real interest rates are the same in all countries.

Recall that the PPP conditions in equations 19.6 and 19.7 need not hold when the price levels, P^i and P^j, refer to market baskets of goods produced or consumed in the two countries. In particular, if relative PPP from equation 19.7 does not hold, then (expected) real interest rates differ across countries. There is some evidence of systematic differences in expected real interest rates across countries.[17] However, for the industrialized countries, these differences tend to be small.

Fixed Exchange Rates

Until the early 1970s and except during major wars, most countries typically maintained **fixed exchange rates** among their currencies. For example, during the post-World War II period, many countries established narrow bands within which they pegged the exchange rate, ϵ^i, between their currency and the U.S. dollar. In these cases, the central bank of country i stood ready to buy and to sell its currency at the rate of ϵ^i units per U.S. dollar. For example, the German central bank (*Bundesbank*) provided dollars for marks when people wanted to reduce their holdings of marks, and vice versa when people wished to

---

[16]Multiply through by the term, $(1 + \Delta\epsilon^i)(1 + \Delta\epsilon^j)$. Then we get the interest-rate parity condition in equation 19.8 if we neglect the terms, $R^i \cdot \Delta\epsilon^j$ and $R^j \cdot \Delta\epsilon^i$. As the length of the period declines, the approximation becomes more accurate.

[17]See Robert Cumby and Maurice Obstfeld, "International Interest Rate and Price Level Linkages under Flexible Exchange Rates: A Review of Recent Evidence," in John Bilson and Richard Marston, eds., *Exchange Rate Theory and Practice*, University of Chicago Press, Chicago, 1984.

increase their holdings of marks. To manage these exchanges, each central bank maintained a stock of liquid assets in the form of U.S. dollars or in other forms that could be readily converted into dollars. Then the United States stood ready to exchange dollars for gold (on the request of foreign official institutions) at a fixed price, which happened to be $35 per ounce.[18] Thus, by maintaining a fixed exchange rate with the U.S. dollar, each country indirectly pegged its currency to gold.

Let P be the dollar price of goods in the United States and note that the U.S. exchange rate with itself is unity. Then, if the absolute purchasing-power-parity condition from equation 19.6 holds, country i's price level is

$$P^i = \epsilon^i \cdot P \tag{19.9}$$

If the exchange rate ϵ^i is fixed, it follows that the price level in country i, P^i, is determined by the U.S. price level P. For a given U.S. price level, and assuming that absolute purchasing-power parity holds, the choice of an exchange rate with the U.S. dollar, ϵ^i, translates into a choice of domestic price level P^i.

We can generalize the result by introducing possibilities for deviations from purchasing-power parity. These include a variety of real disturbances, which we mentioned previously. But we would retain the basic result, namely, a country cannot choose independently its exchange rate ϵ^i and its general price level P^i. Given the variety of real factors mentioned above, a fixed exchange rate means that a country's price level is determined by the U.S. price level.

If the U.S. price level, P, changes, then equation 19.9 says that country i's price level, P^i, changes in the same proportion. In other words, any country that maintains a fixed exchange rate with the U.S. dollar experiences roughly the same inflation rate, π^i, as the U.S. rate, π. (This result requires relative PPP from equation 19.7, but not absolute PPP.)

The interest-rate parity condition from equation 19.8 implies that country's i's nominal interest rate, R^i, equals the U.S. rate, R. Thus, under fixed exchange rates, there is a single nominal interest rate in the world. (Again, differences in taxes and in riskiness of returns mean that this result does not hold exactly.)

The Quantity of Money under Fixed Exchange Rates

Before, when considering a closed economy, we stressed the relation between a country's quantity of base money, M^i, and its price level, P^i. Yet we have determined a country's price level in equation 19.9 without saying anything

---

[18]The arrangement is called the **Bretton-Woods System,** in honor of the meeting in 1944 at Bretton Woods, New Hampshire, where the regime was set up. For a discussion of this system, see James Ingram, *International Economics*, Wiley, New York, 1983, Chapter 9.

about that country's quantity of money. Let us now investigate the relation between money and prices in an open economy under fixed exchange rates.

It is still the case that the residents of country i demand a quantity of real cash, M^i/P^i, which depends on variables like output, Y^i, and the world nominal interest rate, R. (Recall our assumption that the residents of country i use and hold their own currency, rather than that of other countries.) The condition that all money in country i be willingly held is

$$M^i = P^i \cdot L(Y^i, R, \ldots) \qquad (19.10)$$
$$(+) \ (-)$$

If absolute purchasing-power parity holds, then we can substitute in equation 19.10 for the domestic price level as $P^i = \epsilon^i \cdot P$ from equation 19.9. Then we get the condition for the domestic quantity of money

$$M^i = \epsilon^i \cdot P \cdot L(Y^i, R, \ldots) \qquad (19.11)$$

Given the exchange rate ϵ^i, the U.S. price level P, and the determinants of the real demand for money in country i, $L(\bullet)$, equation 19.11 determines the nominal quantity of money, M^i, that must be in country i. Hence, this quantity of money cannot be regarded as a free element of choice by the monetary authority in country i. If the monetary authority wants to peg the exchange rate, ϵ^i, there is a specific quantity of money, M^i, that is consistent with this exchange rate.

To understand these findings, let us assume first that the domestic price level, P^i, accords with absolute purchasing-power parity, as specified in equation 19.9, and that the quantity of money M^i is the amount prescribed by equation 19.11. Then the quantity of money equals the amount demanded, as expressed in equation 19.10. Now suppose that the monetary authority increases the quantity of base money M^i, for example, by an open-market purchase of government securities. In Table 19.3 we illustrate this case in step 1 by assuming that the monetary base and the central bank's holdings of domestic assets each rise by $1 million.

Our previous analysis of a closed economy suggests that the domestic price level P^i would rise. But then, the price level in country i would exceed the value dictated by purchasing-power parity in equation 19.9. Hence, for a given exchange rate, goods bought in country i would become more expensive than goods bought elsewhere. Therefore, people would move away from buying goods in country i and toward buying goods in other countries. This response tends to keep the domestic price level P^i in line with prices in the rest of the world. But at this price level, the domestic residents would be unwilling to hold a larger quantity of domestic money, M^i. We can think of people as returning their excess domestic currency to the central bank to obtain U.S. dollars or

Table 19.3 **Effects of Open-Market Operations on the Central Bank's Balance Sheet**

	Assets	Liabilities
Step 1	Domestic interest-bearing assets: +$1 million	Monetary base, M^i: +$1 million

	Assets	Liabilities
Step 2	International currency: −$1 million	Monetary base, M^i: −$1 million

Note: In step 1 the open-market purchase raises the monetary base by $1 million. But in step 2, the loss of international currency means that the monetary base declines by $1 million.

other currencies. (Since the central bank pegs the exchange rate, it stands willing to make these exchanges at a fixed conversion ratio.) Thus, in step 2 of Table 19.3, we show that the monetary base and the central bank's holdings of international currency each decline by $1 million. Alternatively, the central bank could sell off other liquid assets to get the international currency that people are demanding. The main point is that the open-market purchase leads eventually to the loss of international currency or other liquid assets by the central bank.

To complete the story, we must assess the central bank's reaction to its loss of international currency or other assets. As one possibility, the bank allows the domestic quantity of money M^i to decline. Then as people return money to the central bank, the domestic quantity of money falls toward the level that is again consistent with purchasing-power parity in equation 19.11. In fact, this automatic response of domestic money to the loss of international currency is a central element of the gold standard or other systems of fixed exchange rates.

On the other hand, whenever the automatic mechanism tends to reduce the quantity of domestic money, M^i, the central bank can offset this tendency— for example, by further open-market purchases of securities. When the central bank acts this way, economists say that it **sterilizes** the flow of international currency. Thus, by sterilization, we mean that the central bank attempts to insulate the domestic quantity of base money, M^i, from changes in its holding of international currency. Eventually, this type of policy can lead to a sufficient drain on liquid assets so that the central bank becomes unwilling or unable to maintain the exchange rate. That is, the central bank may no longer provide dollars at the fixed rate of ϵ^i units of domestic currency per dollar. Instead, there may be a **devaluation,** which means that the exchange rate rises above ϵ^i units of domestic currency per dollar. Thus the tendency of central banks to sterilize the flows of international currency threatens the viability of fixed exchange rates.[19] We shall discuss these matters further in a later section.

We should mention another possible reaction of government policy to the loss of international currency. Recall that this drain results in the present example from excessive monetary creation at home, which tends to make domestic goods more expensive than foreign goods. To counter this tendency, the government might impose trade restrictions, which artificially raise the cost of foreign goods for domestic residents. Alternatively, the government might subsidize exports to make these goods cheaper for foreigners. The main idea is that the government can interfere with free trade across national borders to prevent purchasing-power parity from holding. Thus there are two types of potential ill effects that result from excessive monetary expansion under fixed exchange rates. One is the loss of international currency, which leads eventually to devaluation. But to avoid either this outcome or domestic monetary contraction, governments may pursue a course of interference with international trade. In fact, the frequency of these interferences during the post-World War II period was a major argument used by opponents of fixed exchange rates.[20]

World Prices under Fixed Exchange Rates

A system of fixed exchange rates, centered on the U.S. dollar, determines each country's price level, P^i, as a ratio to the U.S. price P. To complete the picture, we have to determine the U.S. price level. Basically, the analysis is similar to our earlier determination of the world price level. Namely, we have to equate the world's demand for international currency to the supply.

Suppose that we add up the total real demand for U.S. money, whether by U.S. residents or by foreigners in the form of international currency. Then, given the dollar quantity of U.S. money, M, we can determine the U.S. price level, P, in the usual manner. Specifically, a greater amount of money, M, means a higher U.S. price level, P, and a correspondingly higher price level, P^i, in each other country.

Under the international regime that prevailed after World War II, there were a number of factors that constrained the Federal Reserve's choice of the quantity of U.S. money, M. First, if the Federal Reserve pursued a monetary policy that was inconsistent with stabilization of the U.S. price level P, then U.S. currency would become less attractive as an international medium of

---

[19]Our discussion in this and the following sections follows a viewpoint that is often called the **monetary approach to the balance of payments.** This approach was developed by Robert Mundell (see, for example, his books, *International Economics,* Macmillan, New York, 1968, part II, and *Monetary Theory*, Goodyear, Pacific Palisades, California, 1971, Part II). The early origins of this view are in the eighteenth-century writings of David Hume—see his "Of the Balance of Trade" in Eugene Rotwein, ed., *David Hume Writings on Economics*, University of Wisconsin Press, Madison, 1970.

[20]See Milton Friedman, "Free Exchange Rates," in his *Dollars and Deficits*, Prentice-Hall, Englewood Cliffs, N.J., 1968, Chapter 9.

exchange. Consequently, other countries might no longer find it desirable to peg their exchange rates to the U.S. dollar, or to hold dollars as a form of international currency. Second, the U.S. had a commitment to exchange U.S. dollars for gold at the rate of $35 per ounce. Therefore, if the U.S. price level rose substantially, as it did during the late 1960s, it would become attractive for foreign central banks to trade their dollars for gold. As the United States lost more and more gold, it would become unable to maintain the dollar price of gold. Eventually, the system would break down, as it did at the beginning of the 1970s.

Devaluation

Let's return now to the situation of a typical country in a regime of exchange rates tied to the U.S. dollar. As we suggested before, a country that typically pegs its exchange rate, ϵ^i, occasionally faces pressures to shift this rate. In particular, any force that tends to increase the domestic price level P^i, relative to the U.S. price P, leads to losses of international currency by the central bank. These pressures could arise, for example, from rapid expansion of the domestic monetary base, M^i, or from a decrease in the demand for country i's real cash balances, M^i/P^i. (The decline in real money demanded might reflect a domestic supply shock, which reduces output in country i.) In response to its loss of international currency, the central bank has an incentive to raise the exchange rate, ϵ^i, which implies a devaluation of the domestic currency in terms of the U.S. dollar. Conversely, any pressure toward reduction in the domestic price level P^i, relative to the U.S. price P, implies gains in international currency, which motivate a reduction in the exchange rate ϵ^i. Since the domestic currency then becomes more valuable in terms of the dollar, there is an appreciation of the currency, which economists call a **revaluation.**

Typically, devaluations and revaluations do not involve long periods during which the central bank gradually loses or gains international currency. That is because the expectation of a shift in the exchange rate leads to **speculation,** which tends to hasten the central bank's actions. For example, if people anticipate a devaluation, then they have incentives to return their domestic money to the central bank to get international currency, which might be U.S. dollars. People react this way because they expect the domestic money to become less valuable relative to other moneys. But since this decline in the demand for domestic money leads to further losses of international currency by the central bank, the devaluation tends to occur sooner.

Consider now the effects of a devaluation—that is, an increase in the exchange rate ϵ^i. As noted before, this change may be a symptom of pressure for inflation in the devaluing country, such as excessive expansion of the domestic money stock, M^i. But let us consider here the effects of an autonomous devaluation—that is, a devaluation that comes out of the blue, rather than as a response to changes in domestic money supply or demand.

If the domestic price level P^i (yen per good) did not change, then an

increase in the exchange rate ϵ^i (yen per dollar) means that goods in country
i would become cheaper in terms of dollars. Therefore, for a given U.S. price
level P, there would be an increase in the demand for goods sold in country
i. Hence, as shown by the purchasing-power parity condition in equation 19.9,
a devaluation leads to a higher domestic price level, $P^i = \epsilon^i \cdot P$.

Suppose that we treat the devaluation and the rise in domestic prices as
one-time events. Then the higher domestic price means a greater demand for
domestic money in nominal terms, M^i (see equation 19.11). The rise in the
quantity of money, M^i, can come about in two ways. First, the central bank
may create more money through open-market operations or other means. Then
second, if the central bank does not act, individuals would bring their international currency to the central bank to get more domestic currency. As the
bank exchanges domestic for international currency, the quantity of domestic
money, M^i, tends to rise. Thus, a one-time devaluation can lead to an expansion
of the central bank's international currency, which accompanies the increase
in the quantity of domestic money, M^i.

Notice that there is a two-way direction of association between devaluations and the behavior of domestic prices and money. First, expansionary
monetary policy creates pressure for devaluation. In this sense we would say
that domestic inflation causes devaluation. Second, a devaluation tends to
raise domestic prices and money. In this sense devaluation is itself inflationary.

Our analysis treats the changes in the exchange rate ϵ^i and the domestic
price level P^i as one-time happenings. But, in practice, countries that devalue
once tend to devalue again. This outcome makes sense if we think of devaluations as primarily symptoms of pressures for domestic inflation—in particular, as signals that the domestic central bank is pursuing an expansionary
monetary policy. Countries that act this way today are likely to continue this
behavior later on. Hence, a devaluation can create expectations of future
increases in the exchange rate ϵ^i. Then the interest-rate parity condition from
equation 19.8 implies that the domestic nominal interest rate, R^i, must rise
above that in the United States. But this change reduces the demand for
country i's money, M^i. As a consequence, a devaluation of country i's currency
may not generate the increase in international currency that we discussed
previously.

Flexible Exchange Rates

The international system of fixed exchange rates, centered on the U.S. dollar,
broke down in the early 1970s. One reason for the breakdown was the excessive
creation of U.S. dollars after the mid-1960s, which led to increases in the U.S.
price level. Thereby, it became difficult for the United States to maintain
convertibility of the dollar into gold at the rate of $35 per ounce. Finally,
President Nixon acted in 1971 to raise the dollar price of gold. This action
signaled the end of the fixed-rate system linked through the U.S. dollar to
gold, which had operated since World War II.

Since the early 1970s, countries have allowed their exchange rates to vary or float more or less freely to clear the markets for foreign exchange. Thus, despite occasional interventions by various central banks (sometimes referred to as "dirty floating"), we can say that the last decade and a half featured **flexible exchange rates,** rather than fixed rates.

If we think of the goods produced in various countries as physically identical, then the condition for absolute purchasing-power parity, $P^i = \epsilon^i P$ from equation 19.9, would still hold under flexible exchange rates. That is, the purchasing power of any currency in terms of goods is still the same regardless of where someone uses the currency to buy goods. Also, deviations from purchasing-power parity can still arise from various real effects, such as shifts in the terms of trade, changes in trade restrictions, and so on.

A new result under flexible exchange rates is that country i's price level, P^i, is no longer tied to the U.S. price P. Instead, the monetary authority of country i can independently determine its money supply, M^i, through open-market operations or other means. Given the quantity of money, the domestic price level, P^i, is determined, as in our earlier analysis of a closed economy, to ensure that the money is willingly held. Then the exchange rate adjusts to satisfy the condition for purchasing-power parity, $P^i = \epsilon^i \cdot P$ from equation 19.9. In relative form the PPP condition now says that the rate of change of country i's exchange rate with the U.S. dollar, $\Delta\epsilon^i$, equals the difference between country i's inflation rate and the U.S. rate, $\pi^i - \pi$ (see equation 19.7).

The last proposition turns out to work especially well if we examine countries with high average rates of inflation. Not surprisingly, these countries turn out also to be the ones that have maintained flexible exchange rates with the U.S. dollar over most years, even before the 1970s. Table 19.4 reports the relative inflation rates and growth rates of the exchange rate for some high-inflation countries, mainly over the period, 1955–80. (The table covers the high-inflation countries for which data are available). Notice that the difference between each country's average inflation rate and the U.S. rate, $\pi^i - \pi$, matches up closely with the average percentage change per year in the exchange rate, $\Delta\epsilon^i$. Thus the relative form of PPP works well here.

The interest-parity condition in equation 19.8 implies that the difference between a country's nominal interest rate and the U.S. rate, $R^i - R$, equals the (expected) rate of change of the exchange rate, $\Delta\epsilon^i$. Therefore, if relative PPP holds, so that $\Delta\epsilon^i = \pi^i - \pi$, the (expected) real interest rate in country i, $R^i - \pi^i$, still equals the U.S. rate, $R - \pi$. In other words, the nominal interest rate is $R^i = r + \pi^i$, where r is the world real interest rate.

An important point about flexible exchange rates is that they allow each country to pursue an independent monetary policy. Suppose that the demand for domestic real money balances is given again by $M^i/P^i = L(Y^i, R^i, \ldots)$. Then the PPP condition, $P^i = \epsilon^i \cdot P$, means that the exchange rate must satisfy

$$\epsilon^i = \frac{M^i}{P \cdot L(Y^i, R^i, \ldots)} \qquad (19.12)$$

Suppose that we neglect variations in the U.S. price level P or in the world real interest rate, r. Then variations in the exchange rate with the U.S. dollar, $\Delta\epsilon^i$, reflect growth in the domestic money supply, M^i, relative to growth in the real demand for domestic money, $L(\bullet)$. (This result requires only the relative form of PPP.)

It is important to recognize that flexible exchange rates do not isolate a country economically from the rest of the world. Basically, the nature of the exchange rate system does not have a great deal to do with the role of international trade in commodities (which allows for specialization in production across countries) or of international borrowing and lending. At least, this conclusion holds if we neglect the possible interplay between the exchange rate regime and the extent of restrictions on international commerce. Recall that countries might resort to various restrictions to defend a fixed exchange rate without having to undergo domestic monetary contraction. Aside from this possibility, our previous analysis of international trade in goods and earning assets applies as well under flexible exchange rates as with fixed rates.

Table 19.4 A Comparison of Inflation Rates with Changes in Exchange Rates for Some High-Inflation Countries

	% per Year over 1955–80	
	$\pi^i - \pi$	$\Delta\epsilon^i$
Argentina	40.8	39.3
Brazil	26.6	26.4
Chile	47.0	44.1
Colombia	9.7	11.7
Iceland	14.2	13.5
Indonesia*	16.4	10.8
Israel	13.2	13.4
Peru**	13.1	11.8
South Korea	11.4	10.0
Uruguay	33.3	31.3
Zaire	12.1	16.1

*1967–80.
**1960–80.

Note: We show each country's average inflation rate, π^i, less the average U.S. rate, π. These values match up closely with the average percentage change per year in the exchange rate with the U.S. dollar, $\Delta\epsilon^i$.

Sources: The data on price levels (deflators for the gross domestic product) and exchange rates are from IMF, *International Financial Statistics*.

Purchasing-Power Parity under Flexible and Fixed Exchange Rates

Many economists have noted that purchasing-power parity holds less well under flexible exchange rates since the early 1970s than under the fixed rates that prevailed earlier for most countries. Table 19.5 provides evidence on this idea from the experience of the major industrialized countries: Canada, France, Germany, Italy, Japan, Switzerland, the United Kingdom, and the United States.[21]

Panel 1 of the table shows the exchange rates with the U.S. dollar for selected years from 1950 to 1985. For convenience, we normalize each rate to be 1.0 in 1970, and then express the rate for each year relative to that for 1970. For example, for France the exchange rate in 1970 was 5.5 francs per dollar. Hence, the value 0.63 shown for 1950 means that the exchange rate was $0.63 \times 5.5 = 3.5$ francs per dollar.

Note that there were few significant changes in exchange rates between 1950 and 1970, because these countries operated mainly under fixed rates. However, Canada did have a flexible rate over part of this period. Also, there were devaluations by France and the United Kingdom, and revaluations by Germany. On the other hand, during the flexible-rate period since the early 1970s, the exchange rates have fluctuated substantially.

Panel 2 of the table shows the ratio of each country's general price level, P^i, to the U.S. price level, P. We measure the price levels by deflators for the gross domestic product (or, in some cases, for the gross national product). Also, we normalize the numbers in each case so that the ratio is 1.0 for 1970. Then the number for any other year shows how the price level moved in country i relative to that in the United States. For example, the value 1.08 for Canada in 1975 means that Canada's price level rose 8% more than the U.S. price level from 1970 to 1975.

Panel 3 computes the ratio of the exchange rate, ϵ^i, to the relative price, P^i/P. Under relative purchasing-power parity, this ratio would be a constant (equal to 1.0) for each country. Therefore, deviations in relative PPP show up as movements in the ratio above or below 1.0.

Economists often call the ratio of ϵ^i to P^i/P the **real exchange rate.** That is because the expression, $\epsilon^i P/P^i$, indicates the quantity of goods produced in country i that exchange for 1 unit of goods produced in the U.S. (A person can sell 1 unit of U.S. goods for P dollars, which can then be exchanged for $\epsilon^i P$ units of country i's currency. Then this much currency buys $(1/P^i) \cdot \epsilon^i P$ units of country i's goods.) If the real exchange rate rises, it means that goods produced in country i have become relatively cheaper than those produced in

---

[21]For a discussion of a wide array of developing countries, see Sebastian Edwards and Francis Ng, "Trends in Real Exchange Rate Behavior in Selected Developing Countries," World Bank, CPD discussion paper no. 1985–16, April 1985.

Table 19.5 **Real Exchange Rates in Industrialized Countries**

Panel 1: Exchange Rates, ϵ^i, Domestic Currency per U.S. Dollar (1970 = 1.0)

	Canada	France	Germany	Italy	Japan	Switzerland	United Kingdom
1950	1.05	0.63	1.15	1.00	1.01	1.00	0.86
55	0.95	0.63	1.15	1.00	1.01	1.00	0.86
60	0.93	0.89	1.14	1.00	1.01	1.00	0.86
65	1.04	0.89	1.09	1.00	1.01	1.00	0.86
70	1.00	1.00	1.00	1.00	1.00	1.00	1.00
75	0.98	0.78	0.67	1.04	0.83	0.60	1.07
80	1.12	0.76	0.50	1.37	0.63	0.40	1.02
1985	1.32	1.63	0.81	3.04	0.67	0.57	1.83

Panel 2: Relative Price Levels, P^i/P (1970 = 1.0), Based on Deflators for GDP or GNP

	Canada	France	Germany	Italy	Japan	Switzerland	United Kingdom
1950	0.97	0.57	0.87	0.78	0.60	0.92	0.76
55	1.01	0.71	0.91	0.87	0.72	0.89	0.87
60	1.00	0.87	0.93	0.85	0.78	0.87	0.89
65	1.00	0.99	1.02	1.05	0.94	1.04	0.99
70	1.00	1.00	1.00	1.00	1.00	1.00	1.00
75	1.08	1.09	0.97	1.27	1.16	1.08	1.33
80	1.16	1.23	0.83	1.99	1.01	0.84	1.87
1985	1.22	1.47	0.73	2.91	0.85	0.82	1.97

Panel 3: Real Exchange Rates, $\epsilon^i (P/P^i)$ (1970 = 1.0)

	Canada	France	Germany	Italy	Japan	Switzerland	United Kingdom
1950	1.08	1.11	1.32	1.28	1.68	1.09	1.13
55	0.94	0.89	1.26	1.15	1.40	1.12	0.99
60	0.93	1.02	1.23	1.18	1.29	1.15	0.97
65	1.04	0.90	1.07	0.95	1.07	0.96	0.87
70	1.00	1.00	1.00	1.00	1.00	1.00	1.00
75	0.91	0.72	0.69	0.82	0.72	0.56	0.80
80	0.97	0.62	0.60	0.69	0.62	0.48	0.55
1985	1.08	1.11	1.11	1.04	0.79	0.70	0.93

Source: Data are from International Monetary Fund, *International Financial Statistics*; *O.E.C.D.*, *National Accounts, Main Aggregates*, Vol. 1, 1952–81, and *Main Economic Indicators*; and (for Japan for 1950) Irving Kravis, Alan Heston, and Robert Summers, *World Product and Income, International Comparisons of Real Gross Product*, Johns Hopkins University Press, Baltimore, 1982, Table 8-4.

the United States. Or, to put it the other way, U.S. goods have become relatively more expensive.

As an example, for Japan in 1950 the value 1.68 in panel 3 means that in 1950 the dollar bought 68% more goods in Japan relative to the United States in comparison to the relative purchasing power in 1970. Thus Japanese goods became substantially more expensive relative to U.S. goods from 1950 to 1970. Since the exchange rate was essentially fixed at this time (see panel 1), the fall in the real exchange rate reflected a higher average inflation rate in Japan from 1950 to 1970 (5.2% per year) than in the United States (2.7% per year).

The value 0.62 for Japan in 1980 means that in 1980 the dollar bought only 62% as much in Japan as in the United States, relative to the situation in 1970. But matters reversed from 1980 to 1985. In 1985 the purchasing power of the dollar in Japan relative to that in the United States returned to 79% of the 1970 level. Notice that over the period from 1970 to 1985, the movements in the real exchange rate for Japan reflected primarily the variations in the exchange rate (see panel 1). Namely, the Japanese currency appreciated sharply from 1970 to 1980, but then depreciated somewhat from 1980 to 1985. Over the period 1970–85, the average annual inflation rates for Japan and the United States were not too different (5.3% and 6.4%, respectively).

The pattern of real exchange rates for Germany was roughly parallel to that for Japan, except that German goods did not start out relatively as cheap in the 1950s. Thus, the real exchange rate in 1950 for Germany was 1.32, as compared with 1.68 for Japan. Notice that, as in the Japanese case, the German currency appreciated sharply relative to the dollar from 1970 to 1980 (see panel 1). But, even more than Japan, the situation reversed from 1980 to 1985.

Interestingly, the behavior of real exchange rates in Italy was very close to that for Germany. This result obtains even though the average Italian inflation rate for 1970–85 (13.5% per year) was roughly 3 times the German rate (4.3% per year). (In terms of relative price levels, P^i/P, panel 2 shows that the value for Germany fell from 1.0 in 1970 to 0.7 in 1985, while that for Italy rose from 1.0 to 2.9.) Note that the Italian exchange rate rose (the currency depreciated in dollar value) from 1970 to 1980 (panel 1 of the table) at the same time that the real exchange rate declined (panel 3). Then from 1980 to 1985 the exchange rate and the real exchange rate both depreciated sharply.

The lesson from the comparison between Germany and Italy is that very different patterns for nominal variables—namely domestic price levels, exchange rates, and, it turns out, underlying rates of monetary growth—seem to have little to do with the determination of real exchange rates. That is because the exchange rates, which were flexible since the early 1970s, behaved sufficiently differently in Germany and Italy so as to offset the divergent trends in domestic price levels. Thus, although the real exchange rates moved substantially since the early 1970s, the suggestion is that some real disturbances, rather than the nominal policies that differed substantially across the countries, were at work. However, economists have not been so successful in isolating the important real disturbances.

Looking at Table 19.5 for France, Switzerland, and the United Kingdom, we again observe the pattern where the real exchange rate fell from 1970 to 1980, but then rose at least part of the way back from 1980 to 1985. For Switzerland, these movements reflected mainly changes in the exchange rate, including the sharp appreciation of the Swiss franc from 1970 to 1980. But for the United Kingdom and France, the shifts in the real exchange rates from 1970 to 1980 reflected the excesses of the inflation rates in these countries (13.1% and 9.0%, respectively) over those in the United States (6.9%). On the other hand, from 1980 to 1985, the British and French currencies depreciated relative to the U.S. dollar. When we add these experiences to those of Germany, Italy, and Japan, we again find that similar patterns in real exchange rates arose since the early 1970s despite widely divergent patterns in the nominal variables.

Finally, for Canada, the shifts in the real exchange rate were relatively small. Since the average Canadian inflation rate from 1950 to 1985 (4.9% per year) exceeded that in the United States (4.3%), we do find a net depreciation of the Canadian dollar over this period.

Let us try to summarize some of the major facts about real exchange rates in the post-World War II period.[22] Some of these follow readily from observing the data in Table 19.5 whereas others come from more detailed statistical analysis of these and other data.

1. Real exchange rates were not constant, and did move around more in the flexible-rate period since the early 1970s than in the earlier period where most exchange rates were fixed. Therefore, if we think of purchasing-power parity in terms of prices of market baskets of goods in different countries (measured say by GDP deflators), departures from relative PPP have been important, especially since the early 1970s. However, there were some substantial movements in real exchange rates in the earlier period when exchange rates were fixed (for example, for Japan, Germany, and Italy from 1950 to 1970). Thus, fixed exchange rates do not guarantee stability in real exchange rates.

2. The real exchange rates for Canada remained relatively stable even under flexible exchange rates. Thus flexible rates do not lead necessarily to fluctuations in real exchange rates.

3. It turns out that we cannot use the past experience of movements in real exchange rates to predict future changes. For example, the fact that all the real exchange rates with the U.S. dollar declined from 1970 to

---

[22]For a related discussion, see Michael Mussa, "Empirical Regularities in the Behavior of Exchange Rates and Theories of the Foreign Exchange Market," *Carnegie-Rochester Conference Series on Public Policy*, Vol. 11, 1979, pp. 10–27.

1975 (panel 3 of the table) would not have allowed us to predict the changes after 1975. Similarly, the rise in the real exchange rates from 1980 to 1985 gives us no basis to forecast changes after 1985. People who state confidently that the U.S. dollar is overvalued or undervalued at any particular date should not be taken seriously.

4. There is no clear connection between the behavior of real exchange rates and a country's experience with inflation (or monetary growth). As an example, recall our comparison of Germany and Italy. Probably, we can think of the movements in real exchange rates as reflecting primarily real changes—such as shifts in the terms of trade, in the relative prices of traded and nontraded goods, in trade restrictions and tax policies, and so on. But the details of the links between these real variables and the real exchange rates have not been worked out empirically.

5. The large fluctuations in real exchange rates under flexible exchange rates probably have more to do with explaining why we have flexible rates, rather than vice versa. That is, since the early 1970s, there have been larger than usual variations in the terms of trade and other real factors, which have implied larger than usual fluctuations in real exchange rates. If exchange rates had been fixed, then we would have observed dramatic fluctuations (up or down) in each country's price level relative to that in the United States. Policymakers may have resisted these tendencies by carrying out offsetting monetary policies which, with fixed exchange rates, may have led to restrictions on trade in goods and assets. This finding explains the usefulness of flexible exchange rates at a time when real exchange rates are unstable. But the important point is that we cannot conclude that the existence of flexible rates was the underlying source of fluctuations in real exchange rates.

Summary

We began by introducing international trade in goods and credit. These possibilities allow for the efficient specialization of production across countries, and for an individual country's spending to diverge temporarily from its income.

The current-account balance equals national saving less domestic investment. A temporary supply shock in one country reduces desired saving and thereby leads to a deficit on current account. Similarly, temporary movements in the terms of trade have a strong interaction with a country's current-account balance. Generally, countries borrow abroad either when a shortfall of current income from permanent income reduces desired saving, or when favorable investment opportunities raise investment demand.

Purchasing-power parity (PPP) connects a country's exchange rate with, say, the U.S. dollar to the ratio of that country's price level to the U.S. price level. However, a variety of real factors, including changes in the terms of trade, shifts in the relative prices of traded and nontraded goods, and variations in trade restrictions and tax policies, can lead to deviations from PPP. Interest-rate parity implies that differences in nominal interest rates across countries correspond to differences in (expected) rates of change of exchange rates. However, differences in taxes and in riskiness of returns can lead to violations of interest-rate parity.

When the exchange rate is fixed to the U.S. dollar, a country's price level is determined mainly by the U.S. price level. Then, to satisfy the PPP condition, there is a specific quantity of money that is consistent with a country's chosen exchange rate. The flows of international currency tend to generate this quantity of money automatically. However, countries sometimes sterilize the flows of international currency to maintain a higher quantity of domestic money. These actions tend to lead either to devaluation of the currency or to trade restrictions. Overall, we find a two-way association, where domestic inflation tends to cause devaluation, but where an autonomous devaluation is itself inflationary.

Flexible exchange rates leave intact the main results about international trade in goods and credit. In particular, the conditions for PPP and interest-rate parity apply in the same manner as before. However, under flexible exchange rates, a country can pursue an independent monetary policy, which allows for an independent choice of inflation rate.

Important Terms and Concepts

law of one price

international currency

international reserves

net factor income from abroad

direct investment abroad

net foreign investment

balance on capital account

outflow (inflow) of capital

current-account balance

surplus (deficit) on current account

tradable goods

terms of trade

nontraded goods

purchasing-power parity (PPP)

absolute form of PPP

relative form of PPP

interest-rate parity

fixed exchange rate

Bretton-Woods System

sterilization

devaluation

monetary approach to the balance of payments

revaluation

speculation (on exchange rate)

flexible exchange rate

real exchange rate

QUESTIONS AND PROBLEMS

Mainly for Review

19.1 Equation 19.2 states that the current-account balance is identically equal to net foreign investment. If GNP or domestic expenditure changes, why is there a change in foreign investment (or borrowing) rather than a change in the interest rate? What is the accompanying change in net exports?

19.2 Explain why an improvement in the terms of trade need not be associated with an increase in net exports.

19.3 Explain the conditions for absolute and relative purchasing-power parity in equations 19.6 and 19.7. How do these relate to the behavior of real exchange rates?

19.4 Under fixed exchange rates, does the monetary authority have discretion over the money supply? Show how an attempt to exercise an independent monetary policy may result in devaluation or revaluation. Why might the attempt lead to trade restrictions?

19.5 Under flexible exchange rates, a country that has a persistently high rate of inflation will experience a steady increase in its exchange rate. Why might the monetary authority like this system?

Problems for Discussion

19.6 Wealth Effects from Changes in the Real Interest Rate
Consider the wealth effects from a change in the world real interest rate.
a. What is the effect for a single country?
b. What is the aggregate effect for the world?
c. How do these results compare with our earlier findings for a closed economy?

19.7 Shifts in the Demand for Money
Consider an increase in the real demand for money in country i.
a. Under a fixed exchange rate, what happens to country i's price level, P^i, and quantity of money, M^i? What happens to the country's quantity of international currency, H^i?
b. Under a flexible exchange rate—with a fixed quantity of money, M^i—what happens to the country's price level, P^i, and exchange rate, ϵ^i?

19.8 Supply Shocks for a Single Country
Consider a supply shock that adversely affects the home country's production of tradable goods. Assume that the shock is temporary and that no significant change occurs in the terms of trade.
a. If the country can borrow abroad at the world real interest rate, what happens to the home country's consumption and current-account balance?
b. How do the results differ if the home country cannot borrow from abroad?
c. Return to part a, but assume now that the domestic industries were owned

primarily by foreigners. (In other words, domestic residents had diversified their ownership of assets internationally, so as not to be too susceptible to local supply shocks.) How does this change affect the answers?

19.9 A Change in the Terms of Trade

In the text we considered a change in the terms of trade that reflected a disturbance from the rest of the world. Suppose instead that a supply shock at home leads to an increase in the relative price of the home country's tradable goods. For example, a harvest failure in Brazil would raise the relative price of coffee. What are the effects from this type of disturbance for the home country's

a. wealth and consumption of various goods, and

b. current-account balance?

(*Hint*: Did you assume that the disturbance was temporary or permanent?)

19.10 Monetary Growth Under Flexible Exchange Rates

Equation 19.12 relates a country's exchange rate with the U.S. dollar, ϵ^i, to domestic money supply and demand. Suppose that a country raises its growth rate of money, μ^i, once and for all. Describe the effect of this change on the path of ϵ^i. (Assume here that the U.S. price level, P, the world real interest rate, r, and the path of domestic output, Y^i, do not change.)

19.11 Flexible Exchange Rates and Inflation Rates

a. Show, by using the conditions for purchasing-power parity, that the percentage change in the exchange rate, $\Delta\epsilon^i$, equals the difference between country i's inflation rate, π^i, and the U.S. inflation rate, π.

b. Using the IMF's *International Financial Statistics* (yearbook issue), calculate the values of $\Delta\epsilon^i$ and $\pi^i - \pi$ for some countries in the post-World War II period. (Pick some other than those appearing in Table 19.4.) What conclusions emerge?

19.12 Nixon's Departure from Gold in 1971

Under the Bretton-Woods System, which prevailed from the end of World War II until 1971, the United States pegged the price of gold at $35 per ounce.

a. Why did trouble about the gold price arise in 1971?

b. Was President Nixon right in eliminating the U.S. commitment to buy and sell gold (from and to foreign official institutions) at a fixed price? What other alternatives were there—in particular,

    i. What was the classical prescription of the gold standard?

    ii. The French suggested a doubling in the price of gold—would that have helped?

19.13 Tariffs (optional)

Suppose that a small country levies a tariff on imports of a tradable good from abroad. Thus, if the good sells at price $\overline{P}$ abroad and if the rate of tariff is 10%, then domestic residents pay $1.1\,\overline{P}$ for each unit of the good. Assuming that the tariff is permanent, what are its effects on the home country's

a. consumption of the various tradable and nontradable goods,

b. production of tradables and nontradables, and

c. balance on current account?

(*Hint*: What did you assume happened to the revenue collected from the tariff?) Redo the analysis for the case where the tariff is temporary.

19.14 Nontraded Goods and Real Exchange Rates (optional)

Suppose that each country produces some goods and services (such as haircuts and rents on buildings) that are not traded internationally. Assume that the price of nontraded goods in country i rises relative to the price of traded goods. But no change occurs in the relative price of nontraded and traded goods in the United States. What happens to country i's real exchange rate, $(\epsilon^i/P^i) \cdot P$? In answering, note the following: First, the general price levels, P^i and P, include the prices of traded and nontraded goods. Second, the law of one price says that the purchasing power of any currency should be the same for traded goods, regardless of where they are produced, but the same may not hold for nontraded goods.

Can you use the result to suggest an explanation for the movement in Japan's real exchange rate from 1.68 in 1950 to 1.0 in 1970 (see Table 19.5, panel 3)?

BIBLIOGRAPHY

Abraham, Katharine G. and Lawrence F. Katz, "Cyclical Unemployment: Sectoral Shifts or Aggregate Disturbances," *Journal of Political Economy,* **94,** June 1986, 507–522.

Adams, Larry T., "Changing Employment Patterns of Organized Workers," *Monthly Labor Review,* **108,** February 1985, 25–31.

Ahmed, Shaghil, "Wage Indexation and the Phillips Curve Slope: a Cross-Industry Analysis," unpublished, Brown University, Providence, RI, 1985.

Alchian, Armen A. and Harold Demsetz, "Production, Information Costs, and Economic Organization," *American Economic Review,* **62,** December 1972, 777–795.

Ando, Albert and Franco Modigliani, "The 'Life-Cycle' Hypothesis of Saving: Aggregate Implications and Tests," *American Economic Review,* **53,** March 1963, 55–84.

Archibald, G. C. and Richard G. Lipsey, "Monetary and Value Theory: A Critique of Lange and Patinkin," *Review of Economic Studies,* **26,** October 1958, 1–22.

Aschauer, David A., "Fiscal Policy and Aggregate Demand," *American Economic Review,* March 1985, 117–127.

Attfield, C. L. F., D. Demery and N. W. Duck, "A Quarterly Model of Unanticipated Monetary Growth, Output and the Price Level in the U.K.," *Journal of Monetary Economics,* **8,** November 1981, 331–350.

———— and N. W. Duck, "The Influence of Unanticipated Money Growth on Real Output: Some Cross-Country Estimates," *Journal of Money, Credit and Banking,* **15,** November 1983, 442–454.

Auerbach, Robert D., *Money, Banking and Financial Markets,* 2nd ed., Macmillan, New York, 1985.

Azariadas, Costas, "Implicit Contracts and Underemployment Equilibria," *Journal of Political Economy,* **83,** December 1975, 1183–1202.

Bailey, Martin J., *National Income and the Price Level,* 2nd ed., McGraw-Hill, New York, 1971.

Baily, Martin N., "Wages and Employment under Uncertain Demand," *Review of Economic Studies,* **33,** January 1974, 37–50.

Bank of England, *Quarterly Bulletin,* various issues.

Barnett, William, A., Edward K. Offenbacher and Paul A. Spindt, "The New Divisia Monetary Aggregates," *Journal of Political Economy,* **92,** December 1984, 1049–1085.

Barro, Robert J., "Inflationary Finance and the Welfare Cost of Inflation," *Journal of Political Economy,* **80,** September/October 1972, 978–1001.

——, "Are Government Bonds Net Wealth?" *Journal of Political Economy*, **82,** November/December 1974, 1095–1118.

——, "Long-Term Contracts, Sticky Prices and Monetary Policy," *Journal of Monetary Economics,* **3,** July 1977, 305–316.

——, "Comment from an Unreconstructed Ricardian," *Journal of Monetary Economics,* **4,** August 1978, 569–581.

——, "Unanticipated Money, Output and the Price Level in the United States," *Journal of Political Economy,* **86,** August 1978, 548–580.

——, "On the Determination of the Public Debt," *Journal of Political Economy,* **87,** October 1979, 940–971.

——, "Intertemporal Substitution and the Business Cycle," *Carnegie-Rochester Conference Series on Public Policy,* **14,** Spring 1981, 237–268.

——, *Money, Expectations and Business Cycles,* Academic Press, New York, 1981.

——, "Output Effects of Government Purchases," *Journal of Political Economy,* **89,** December 1981, 1086–1121.

——, "Measuring the Fed's Revenue from Money Creation," *Economics Letters,* **10,** 1982, 327–332.

——, "Government Spending, Interest Rates, Prices and Budget Deficits in the United Kingdom, 1730–1918," Rochester Center for Economic Research, working paper number 1, March 1985.

——, "U.S. Deficits since World War I," *Scandinavian Journal of Economics,* **88,** number 1, 1986, 195–222.

—— and Chaipat Sahasakul, "Average Marginal Tax Rates from Social Security and the Individual Income Tax," *Journal of Business,* **59,** October 1986.

—— and Herschel I. Grossman, "A General Disequilibrium Model of Income and Employment," *American Economic Review,* **61,** March 1971, 82–93.

——, "Suppressed Inflation and the Supply Multiplier," *Review of Economic Studies,* **41,** January 1974, 87–104.

——, *Money, Employment and Inflation,* Cambridge University Press, Cambridge, 1976.

—— and Zvi Hercowitz, "Money Stock Revisions and Unanticipated Money Growth," *Journal of Monetary Economics,* **6,** April 1980, 257–268.

Baumol, William J., "The Transactions Demand for Cash: an Inventory Theoretic Approach," *Quarterly Journal of Economics,* **66,** November 1952, 545–556.

Becker, Gary S., "The Demand for Children," in *A Treatise on the Family,* Harvard University Press, Cambridge, MA, 1981.

—— and Robert J. Barro, "A Reformulation of the Economic Theory of Fertility," Rochester Center for Economic Research, working paper number 25, October 1985.

Benjamin, Daniel K. and Levis A. Kochin, "War, Prices and Interest Rates: Gibson's Paradox Revisited," in Michael D. Bordo and Anna J. Schwartz, eds., *A Retrospective on the Classical Gold Standard, 1821–1931.* University of Chicago Press, Chicago, 1984.

Bernanke, Ben S., "Non-Monetary Effects of the Financial Collapse in the Propagation of the Great Depression," *American Economic Review,* **73,** June 1983, 257–276.

Bernheim, B. Douglas, Andrei Shleifer, and Lawrence H. Summers, "The Strategic Bequest Motive," *Journal of Political Economy,* **93,** December 1985, 1045–1076.

Bienefeld, M. A., *Working Hours in British Industry,* Weidenfeld and Nicolson, London, 1972.

Bird, Roger C. and Ronald G. Bodkin, "The National Service Life Insurance Dividend of 1950 and Consumption: A Further Test of the 'Strict' Permanent Income Hypothesis," *Journal of Political Economy,* **73,** October 1965, 499–515.

Black, Fischer, "Banking and Interest Rates in a World without Money," *Journal of Bank Research,* Autumn 1970, 9–20.

Black, Stanley W., "International Money and International Monetary Arrangements," in Ronald W. Jones and Peter B. Kenen, eds., *Handbook of International Economics,* volume 2, North-Holland, Amsterdam, 1985.

Blinder, Alan S., "Inventories in the Keynesian Macro Model," *Kyklos,* **33,** number 4, 1980, 585–614.

Board of Governors of the Federal Reserve System, *Annual Report,* 1984.

———, *Annual Statistical Digest 1970–1979,* Washington, DC, 1981.

———, *Banking and Monetary Statistics, 1941–1970,* Washington, DC, 1976.

———, *Federal Reserve Bulletin,* various issues.

Bordo, Michael D. and Lars Jonung, "The Long-Run Behavior of the Income Velocity of Money in Five Advanced Countries, 1870–1975: an Institutional Approach," *Economic Inquiry,* **19,** January 1981, 96–116.

Boskin, Michael J., "Social Security and Retirement Decisions," *Economic Inquiry,* **15,** January 1977, 1–25.

———, ed., *The Crisis in Social Security,* Institute for Contemporary Studies, San Francisco, 1977.

Bresciani-Turroni, Costantino, *The Economics of Inflation,* Allen & Unwin, London, 1937.

Brown, Charles, Curtis Gilroy, and Andrew Koehn, "The Effect of the Minimum Wage on Employment and Unemployment: a Survey," *Journal of Economic Literature,* **20,** June 1982, 487–528.

Brown, E. Cary, "Fiscal Policy in the Thirties: a Reappraisal," *American Economic Review,* **46,** December 1956, 857–879.

Brunner, Karl, "The Role of Money and Monetary Policy," Federal Reserve Bank of St. Louis, *Review,* July 1968, 9–24.

Buchanan, James M., *Public Principles of Public Debt,* Irwin, Homewood, IL, 1958.

Buckmaster and Moore, *Index-Linked Gilt Book,* London, May 1985.

Cagan, Phillip D., "The Monetary Dynamics of Hyperinflation," in Milton Friedman, ed., *Studies in the Quantity Theory of Money,* University of Chicago Press, Chicago, 1956.

———, "The Demand for Currency Relative to the Total Money Supply," *Journal of Political Economy,* **66,** August 1958, 303–328.

———, *Determinants and Effects of Changes in the Stock of Money, 1875–1960,* Columbia University Press, New York, 1965.

Campbell, Colin D., "Introduction," In *Controlling the Cost of Social Security,* Lexington, MA, 1984.

Card, David, "Determinants of the Form of Long-Term Contracts," Princeton University working paper number 135, June 1980.

Carlson, John A. "A Study of Price Forecasts," *Annals of Economic and Social Measurement,* **6,** winter 1977, 27–56.

Caskey, John, "Modeling the Formation of Price Expectations: a Bayesian Approach," *American Economic Review,* **75,** September 1985, 768–776.

Central Statistical Office, *Annual Abstract of Statistics,* London, various issues.

———, *Monthly Digest of Statistics,* London, various issues.

Chaudhury, Ajit K., "Output, Employment and Inventories under General Excess Supply," *Journal of Monetary Economics,* **5,** October 1979, 505–514.

Clark, Kim B. and Lawrence H. Summers, "Labor Market Dynamics and Unemployment: a Reconsideration," *Brookings Papers on Economic Activity,* number 1, 1979, 13–60.

———, "Unemployment Insurance and Labor Market Transitions," in Martin N. Baily, ed., *Workers, Jobs and Inflation,* Brookings Institution, Washington, DC, 1982.

Coase, Ronald H., "The Nature of the Firm," *Economica,* **4,** November 1937, 386–405.

Cukierman, Alex, "Relative Price Variability and Inflation, a Survey and Further Results," *Carnegie–Rochester Conference Series on Public Policy,* **19,** autumn 1983, 103–158.

Cumby, Robert and Maurice Obstfeld, "International Interest Rate and Price Level Linkages under Flexible Exchange Rates: a Review of Recent Evidence," in John F. O. Bilson and Richard C. Marston, eds., *Exchange Rate Theory and Practice,* University of Chicago Press, Chicago, 1984.

Darby, Michael R., "Three-and-a-Half Million U.S. Employees Have Been Mislaid: or an Explanation of Unemployment, 1934–1941," *Journal of Political Economy,* **84,** February 1976, 1–16.

———, John C. Haltiwanger, Jr. and Mark W. Plant, "Unemployment Rate Dynamics and Persistent Unemployment under Rational Expectations," *American Economic Review,* **75,** September 1985, 614–637.

David, Paul A., "The Growth of Real Product in the United States before 1840," *Journal of Economic History,* **27,** June 1967, 151–197.

Deane, P. and W. A. Cole, *British Economic Growth 1688–1959,* 2nd ed., Cambridge University Press, Cambridge, 1969.

Department of Employment and Productivity, *British Labour Statistics, Historical Abstract 1886–1968,* London, 1971.

Dewey, Davis R., *Financial History of the United States,* 11th ed., Longmans, Green, New York, 1931.

Dotsey, Michael, "The Use of Electronic Funds Transfers to Capture the Effect of Cash Management Practices on the Demand for Demand Deposits," *Journal of Finance,* **40,** December 1985, 1493–1503.

Easterlin, Richard A., *Population, Labor Force, and Long Swings in Economic Growth,* Columbia University Press, New York, 1968.

Eaton, Jonathan, Mark Gersovitz, and Joseph E. Stiglitz, "The Pure Theory of Country Risk," *European Economic Review,* **30,** June 1986, 481–513.

Economic Report of the President, United States Government Printing Office, Washington, DC, various issues.

Economist Intelligence Unit, Ltd. (U.K.), *Quarterly Economic Review of Poland,* Annual Supplement 1982; number 1, 1983.

———, *Quarterly Economic Review of Saudi Arabia,* Annual Supplement 1985.

Edwards, Sebastian, "On the Interest Rate Elasticity of the Demand for International Reserves: Some Evidence from Developing Countries," *Journal of International Money and Finance,* **4,** August 1985, 287–295.

——— and Francis Ng, "Trends in Real Exchange Rate Behavior in Selected Developing Countries," World Bank, CPD discussion paper number 1985–16, April 1985.

Eisner, Robert and Robert H. Strotz, "Determinants of Business Investment," in Commission on Money and Credit, *Impacts of Monetary Policy,* Prentice–Hall, Englewood Cliffs, NJ, 1963.

——— and Paul Pieper, "A New View of the Federal Debt and Budget Deficits," *American Economic Review,* **74,** March 1984, 11–29.

Esposito, Louis, "Effect of Social Security on Saving: Review of Studies Using U.S. Time Series Data," *Social Security Bulletin,* **41,** May 1978, 9–17.

Ethier, Wilfred J., *Modern International Economics,* Norton, New York, 1983.

Fair, Ray C., "An Analysis of the Accuracy of Four Macroeconometric Models," *Journal of Political Economy,* **87,** August 1979, 701–718.

Fama, Eugene F., "Short-Term Interest Rates as Predictors of Inflation," *American Economic Review,* **65,** June 1975, 269–282.

———, "Financial Intermediation and Price Level Control," *Journal of Monetary Economics,* **12,** July 1983, 7–28.

Feinstein, C. H., *National Income, Expenditures and Output of the United Kingdom 1855–1965,* Cambridge University Press, Cambridge, 1972.

Feldstein, Martin S., "Social Security, Induced Retirement, and Aggregate Capital Accumulation," *Journal of Political Economy,* **82,** September/October 1974, 905–928.

Ferguson, James M., ed., *Public Debt and Future Generations,* University of North Carolina Press, Chapel Hill, 1964.

Fischer, Stanley, "Long-Term Contracts, Rational Expectations and the Optimal Money Supply Rule," *Journal of Political Economy,* **85,** February 1977, 191–206.

———, "Seigniorage and The Case for a National Money," *Journal of Political Economy,* **90,** April 1982, 295–313.

Fisher, Irving, "A Statistical Relation between Unemployment and Price Changes," *International Labor Review,* **13,** June 1926, 785–792, reprinted as "I Discovered the Phillips Curve," *Journal of Political Economy,* **81,** March/April 1973, 496–502.

———, *The Theory of Interest,* Macmillan, New York, 1930.

———, *The Purchasing Power of Money,* 2nd ed. (1922), Augustus Kelley, New York, 1963.

Flavin, Marjorie A., "The Adjustment of Consumption to Changing Expectations about Future Income," *Journal of Political Economy,* **89,** October 1981, 974–1009.

Fleisher, Belton M. and Thomas J. Kniesner, *Labor Economics: Theory, Evidence and Policy,* 3rd ed., Prentice–Hall, Englewood Cliffs, NJ, 1984.

Flood, Robert P. and Peter M. Garber, "An Economic Theory of Monetary Reform," *Journal of Political Economy,* **88,** February 1980, 24–58.

Foley, Duncan K. and Miguel Sidrauski, *Monetary and Fiscal Policy in a Growing Economy,* Macmillan, New York, 1971.

Friedman, Milton, "The Quantity of Money—A Restatement," in *Studies in the Quantity Theory of Money,* University of Chicago Press, Chicago, 1956.

———, *A Theory of the Consumption Function,* Princeton University Press, Princeton, NJ, 1957.

———, *A Program for Monetary Stability,* Fordham University Press, New York, 1960.

———, "Free Exchange Rates," in *Dollars and Deficits,* Prentice–Hall, Englewood Cliffs, NJ, 1968.

———, "Inflation: Causes and Consequences," in *Dollars and Deficits,* Prentice–Hall, Englewood Cliffs, NJ, 1968.

———, "The Role of Monetary Policy," *American Economic Review,* **58,** March 1968, 1–17.

———, *The Optimum Quantity of Money and other Essays,* Aldine, Chicago, 1969.

——— and Anna J. Schwartz, *A Monetary History of the United States, 1867–1960,* Princeton University Press, Princeton, NJ, 1963.

———, *Monetary Statistics of the United States,* Columbia University Press, New York, 1970.

Garber, Peter M., "Transition from Inflation to Price Stability," *Carnegie–Rochester Conference Series on Public Policy,* **16,** Spring 1982, 11–42.

Geweke, John, "The Superneutrality of Money in the United States: an Interpretation of the Evidence," *Econometrica,* **54,** January 1986, 1–22.

Goldfeld, Steven M. "The Demand for Money Revisited," *Brookings Papers on Economic Activity,* number 3, 1973, 577–638.

——— "The Case of the Missing Money," *Brookings Papers on Economic Activity,* number 3, 1976, 683–730.

Goodfriend, Marvin, "Monetary Mystique: Secrecy and Central Banking," *Journal of Monetary Economics,* **17,** January 1986, 63–92.

Gordon, Donald F., "A Neo-Classical Theory of Keynesian Unemployment," *Economic Inquiry,* **12,** December 1974, 431–459.

Gordon, Roger H., "Social Security and Labor Supply Incentives," National Bureau of Economic Research, working paper number 986, September 1982.

Gorton, Gary, "Banking Panics and Business Cycles," unpublished, Federal Reserve Bank of Philadelphia, February 1986.

Gray, Jo Anna, "Wage Indexation: a Macroeconomic Approach," *Journal of Monetary Economics,* **2,** April 1976, 221–236.

Greenwood, Jeremy, "Expectations, the Exchange Rate and the Current Account," *Journal of Monetary Economics,* **12,** November 1983, 543–570.

Grossman, Herschel I., "Risk Shifting, Layoffs and Seniority," *Journal of Monetary Economics,* **4,** November 1979, 661–686.

Haberler, Gottfried, *Prosperity and Depression,* 2nd ed., League of Nations, Geneva, 1939.

Hall, Robert E., "Investment, Interest Rates, and the Effects of Stabilization Policies," *Brookings Papers on Economic Activity,* number 1, 1977, 61–103.

———, "A Theory of the Natural Unemployment Rate and the Duration of Unemployment," *Journal of Monetary Economics,* **5,** April 1979, 153–170.

———, "Employment Fluctuations and Wage Rigidity," *Brookings Papers on Economic Activity,* number 1, 1980, 91–123.

———, "Labor Supply and Aggregate fluctuations," *Carnegie-Rochester Conference Series on Public Policy,* **12,** spring 1980, 7–33.

——— "The Importance of Lifetime Jobs in the U.S. Economy," *American Economic Review,* **72,** September 1982, 716–724.

——— and David M. Lilien, "Efficient Wage Bargains under Uncertain Supply and Demand," *American Economic Review,* **69,** December 1979, 868–879.

——— and Frederic S. Mishkin, "The Sensitivity of Consumption to Transitory Income: Estimates from Panel Data on Households," *Econometrica,* **50,** March 1982, 461–482.

Hamermesh, Daniel, *Jobless Pay and the Economy,* Johns Hopkins University Press, Baltimore, 1977.

Hamilton, James D., "Oil and the Macroeconomy since World War II," *Journal of Political Economy,* **91,** April 1983, 228–248.

———, "Uncovering Financial Market Expectations of Inflation," *Journal of Political Economy,* **93,** December 1985, 1224–1241.

Hayashi, Fumio, "Why is Japan's Saving Rate so Apparently High?" presented at the National Bureau of Economic Research Conference on Macroeconomics, Cambridge, MA, March 1986.

Hayek, Friedrich A., "The Use of Knowledge in Society," *American Economic Review,* **35,** September 1945, 519–530.

Hercowitz, Zvi, "Money and the Dispersion of Relative Prices," *Journal of Political Economy,* **89,** April 1981, 328–356.

———, "Money and Price Dispersion in the United States," *Journal of Monetary Economics,* **10,** July 1982, 25–38.

Hicks, John, "Mr. Keynes and the 'Classics'," *Econometrica,* **5,** April 1937, 147–159.

———, *Value and Capital,* 2nd ed., Oxford University Press, Oxford, 1946.

Howard, David H., "The Disequilibrium Model in a Controlled Economy: an Empirical Test of the Barro-Grossman Model," *American Economic Review,* **66,** December 1976, 871–879.

Ingram, James C., *International Economics,* Wiley, New York, 1983.

International Monetary Fund, *International Financial Statistics,* various issues.

Jevons, W. Stanley, *Money and the Mechanism of Exchange,* D. Appleton, New York, 1896.

Jones, Alice H., *Wealth of a Nation to Be,* Columbia University Press, New York, 1980.

Jones, Robert A., "The Origin and Development of Media of Exchange," *Journal of Political Economy,* **84,** August 1976, 757–776.

Judd, John P. and John L. Scadding, "The Search for a Stable Money Demand Function," *Journal of Economic Literature,* **20,** September 1982, 993–1023.

Kendrick, John W., *Productivity Trends in the United States,* Princeton University Press, Princeton, New Jersey, 1961.

Keynes, John Maynard, *The General Theory of Employment, Interest and Money,* Harcourt Brace, New York, 1935.

King, Robert G. and Charles I. Plosser, "Money, Credit and Prices in a Real Business Cycle," *American Economic Review,* **74,** June 1984, 363–380.

Klein, Ben, "Competitive Interest Payments on Bank Deposits and the Long-Run Demand for Money," *American Economic Review,* **64,** December 1974, 931–949.

Kohler, Heinz, *Intermediate Microeconomics,* Scott, Foresman, Glenview, IL, 1982.

Kormendi, Roger C., "Government Debt, Government Spending, and Private Sector Behavior," *American Economic Review,* **73,** December 1983, 994–1010.

—— and Phillip G. Meguire, "Cross-Regime Evidence of Macroeconomic Rationality," *Journal of Political Economy,* **92,** October 1984, 875–908.

——, "Macroeconomic Determinants of Growth: Cross-Country Evidence," *Journal of Monetary Economics,* **16,** September 1985, 141–164.

Kravis, Irving B., Alan Heston, and Robert Summers, *World Product and Income, International Comparisons of Real Gross Product,* Johns Hopkins University Press, Baltimore, 1982.

Kreinin, Mordechai E., "Windfall Income and Consumption—Additional Evidence," *American Economic Review,* **51,** June 1961, 388–390.

Kuznets, Simon, "Discussion of the New Department of Commerce Income Series," *Review of Economics and Statistics,* **30,** August 1948, 151–179.

Lahaye, Laura, "Inflation and Currency Reform," *Journal of Political Economy,* **93,** June 1985, 537–560.

Laidler, David E., *The Demand for Money: Theories and Evidence,* 3rd ed., Harper & Row, New York, 1985.

Landsberger, Michael, "Restitution Receipts, Household Savings and Consumption Behavior in Israel," unpublished, Research Department, Bank of Israel, 1970.

Law, John, *Money and Trade Considered (1705),* Augustus Kelley, New York, 1966.

Leimer, Dean and Selig Lesnoy, "Social Security and Private Saving: a Reexamination of the Time Series Evidence Using Alternative Social Security Wealth Variables," unpublished, Social Security Administration, November 1980.

Lilien, David M., "Sectoral Shifts and Cyclical Unemployment," *Journal of Political Economy,* **90,** August 1982, 777–793.

Lipsey, Richard E., "The Relation between Unemployment and the Rate of Change of Money Wage Rates in the United Kingdom, 1862–1957: a Further Analysis," *Economica,* **27,** February 1960, 1–31.

Litterman, Robert B. and Laurence Weiss, "Money, Real Interest Rates, and Output: a Reinterpretation of Postwar U.S. Data," *Econometrica,* **53,** January 1985, 129–156.

Long, John B., Jr. and Charles I. Plosser, "Real Business Cycles," *Journal of Political Economy,"* **91,** February 1983, 39–69.

Loungani, Prakash, "Oil Price Shocks and the Dispersion Hypothesis," *Review of Economics and Statistics*, **68**, August 1986, 536–539.

Lucas, Robert E., Jr., "Adjustment Costs and the Theory of Supply," *Journal of Political Economy*, **75**, August 1967, 321–334.

———, "Understanding Business Cycles," *Carnegie–Rochester Conference Series on Public Policy*, **5**, 1976, 7–29.

———, "Two Illustrations of the Quantity Theory of Money," *American Economic Review*, **70**, December 1980, 1005–1014.

———, *Studies in Business-Cycle Theory*, M.I.T. Press, Cambridge, MA, 1981.

Macaulay, Frederick R., *The Movement of Interest Rates, Bond Yields and Stock Prices in the United States since 1856*, National Bureau of Economic Research, New York, 1938.

MaCurdy, Thomas E., "An Empirical Model of Labor Supply in a Life–Cycle Setting," *Journal of Political Economy*, **89**, December 1981, 1059–1085.

Mansfield, Edwin, *Microeconomics*, 5th ed., Norton, New York, 1985.

Marston, Stephen T., "Employment Stability and High Unemployment," *Brookings Papers on Economic Activity*; number 1, 1976, 169–203.

McCallum, Ben T., "The Current State of the Policy-Ineffectiveness Debate," *American Economic Review*, **69**, proceedings, May 1979, 240–245.

McCulloch, J. Huston, "The Ban on Indexed Bonds, 1933–77," *American Economic Review*, **70**, December 1980, 1018–1021.

Mishan, Edward J., "A Fallacy in the Interpretation of the Cash Balance Effect," *Econometrica*, **25**, May 1958, 106–118.

Mishkin, Frederic S., "Does Anticipated Monetary Policy Matter?" *Journal of Political Economy*, **90**, February 1982, 22–51.

Mitchell, B. R., *European Historical Statistics, 1750–1970*, Macmillan, New York, 1975.

——— and P. Deane, *Abstract of British Historical Statistics*, Cambridge University Press, Cambridge, 1962.

——— and H. G. Jones, *Second Abstract of British Historical Statistics*, Cambridge University Press, Cambridge, 1971.

Modigliani, Franco, "Long-Run Implications of Alternative Fiscal Policies and the Burden of the National Debt," in James M. Ferguson, ed., *Public Debt and Future Generations*, University of North Carolina Press, Chapel Hill, 1964.

——— and Richard Brumberg, "Utility Analysis and the Consumption Function: an Interpretation of Cross-Section Data," in Kenneth Kurihara, ed., *Post-Keynesian Economics*, Rutgers University Press, New Brunswick, NJ, 1954.

Morgan Guaranty Trust, *World Financial Markets*, New York, February 1983.

Mundell, Robert A., *International Economics*, Macmillan, New York, 1968.

———, *Monetary Theory*, Goodyear, Pacific Palisades, California, 1971.

Musgrave, John C., "Fixed Capital Stock in the United States: Revised Estimates," *Survey of Current Business*, February 1981.

———, "Fixed Reproducible Tangible Wealth in the United States," *Survey of Current Business*, August 1984.

Musgrave, Richard, *Theory of Public Finance*, McGraw-Hill, New York, 1959.

Mussa, Michael, "Empirical Regularities in the Behavior of Exchange Rates and Theories of the Foreign Exchange Market," *Carnegie–Rochester Conference Series on Public Policy,* **11,** 1979, 9–58.

Muth, John F., "Rational Expectations and the Theory of Price Movements," *Econometrica,* **29,** July 1961, 315–335.

Nelson, Charles R. and G. William Schwert, "Short-Term Interest Rates as Predictors of Inflation: on Testing the Hypothesis that the Real Rate of Interest is Constant," *American Economic Review,* **67,** June 1977, 478–486.

Ochs, Jack and Mark Rush, "The Persistence of Interest Rate Effects on the Demand for Currency," *Journal of Money, Credit and Banking,* **15,** November 1983, 499–505.

O'Driscoll, Gerald, P., Jr., "The Ricardian Nonequivalence Theorem," *Journal of Political Economy,* **85,** February 1977, 207–210.

Organization for Economic Cooperation and Development, *Main Economic Indicators,* Paris, various issues.

———, *National Accounts, Main Aggregates,* volume 1, 1952–1981, Paris, 1983.

———, *National Accounts of OECD Countries,* Paris, various issues.

———, *OECD Economic Outlook,* Paris, various issues.

Organization of American States, *Statistical Bulletin of the OAS,* various issues.

Patinkin, Don, "Price Flexibility and Full Employment," *American Economic Review,* **38,** September 1948, 543–564.

———, *Money, Interest and Prices,* Harper & Row, New York, 1956.

Phelps, Edmund S., "The New Microeconomics in Employment and Inflation Theory," in *Microeconomic Foundations of Employment and Inflation Theory,* Norton, New York, 1970.

Phillips, A. W., "The Relation between Unemployment and the Rate of Change of Money Wage Rates in the United Kingdom, 1861–1959," *Economica,* **25,** November 1958, 283–299.

Pigou, Arthur C., "Economic Progress in a Stable Environment," *Economica,* **14,** August 1947, 180–188.

Plosser, Charles I., "The Effects of Government Financing Decisions on Asset Returns," *Journal of Monetary Economics,* **9,** May 1982, 325–352.

Portes, Richard and David Winter, "Disequilibrium Estimates for Consumption Goods Markets in Centrally Planned Economies," *Review of Economic Studies,* **47,** January 1980, 137–159.

Ramaswami, Chitra, "Equilibrium Unemployment and the Efficient Job-Finding Rate," *Journal of Labor Economics,* **1,** April 1983, 171–196.

Ramsey, Frank P., "A Mathematical Theory of Saving," *Economic Journal,* **38,** December 1928, 543–549.

Rees, Albert E., "Patterns of Wages, Prices and Productivity," in Charles Myers, ed., *Wages, Prices, Profits and Productivity,* Columbia University Press, New York, 1959.

Ricardo, David, "Funding System," in P. Sraffa, ed., *The Works and Correspondence of David Ricardo,* Cambridge University Press, Cambridge, 1957.

Romer, Christina, "The Prewar Business Cycle Reconsidered: New Estimates of Gross National Product, 1872–1918," unpublished, Princeton University, May 1985.

———, "Spurious Volatility in Historical Unemployment Data," *Journal of Political Economy,* **94,** February 1986, 1–37.

Rotwein, Eugene, ed., *David Hume—Writings on Economics,* University of Wisconsin Press, Madison, 1970.

Rush, Mark, "Unexpected Monetary Disturbances during the Gold Standard Era," *Journal of Monetary Economics,* **15,** May 1985, 309–322.

———, "Unexpected Money and Unemployment: 1920 to 1983," *Journal of Money, Credit and Banking,* **18,** August 1986, 259–274.

Sachs, Jeffrey D., "The Current Account and Macroeconomic Adjustment in the 1970s," *Brookings Papers on Economic Activity,* number 1, 1981, 201–268.

Saidi, Nasser, "The Square-Root Law, Uncertainty and International Reserves under Alternative Regimes: Canadian Experience, 1950–1976," *Journal of Monetary Economics,* **7,** May 1981, 271–290.

Samuelson, Paul A., "A Synthesis of the Principle of Acceleration and the Multiplier," *Journal of Political Economy,* **47,** December 1939, 786–797.

Sargent, Thomas J. and Neil Wallace, "Rational Expectations, the Optimal Monetary Instrument, and the Optimal Money Supply Rule," *Journal of Political Economy,* **83,** April 1975, 241–254.

Siegel, Jeremy J., "Inflation-Induced Distortions in Government and Private Saving Statistics," *Review of Economics and Statistics,* **61,** April 1979, 83–90.

Simons, Henry C., "Rules versus Authorities in Monetary Policy," in *Economic Policy for a Free Society,* University of Chicago Press, Chicago, 1948.

Solon, Gary, "Work Incentive Effects of Taxing Unemployment Benefits," *Econometrica,* **53,** March 1985, 295–306.

Spindt, Paul A., "Money Is What Money Does: Monetary Aggregation and the Equation of Exchange," *Journal of Political Economy,* **93,** February 1985, 175–204.

Stuart, Charles E., "Swedish Tax Rates, Labor Supply and Tax Revenues," *Journal of Political Economy,* **89,** October 1981, 1020–1038.

Taylor, John B., "Aggregate Dynamics and Staggered Contracts," *Journal of Political Economy,* **88,** February 1980, 1–23.

Thornton, Henry, *An Enquiry into the Nature and Effects of the Paper Credit of Great Britain (1802),* Augustus Kelly, Fairfield, NJ, 1978.

Timberlake, Richard H., Jr., *The Origins of Central Banking in the United States,* Harvard University Press, Cambridge, MA, 1978.

Tobin, James, "The Interest-Elasticity of Transactions Demand for Cash," *Review of Economics and Statistics,* **38,** August 1956, 241–247.

———, "A General Equilibrium Approach to Monetary Theory," in *Essays in Economics,* volume 1, *Macroeconomics,* Markham, Chicago, 1971.

———, "Deposit Interest Ceilings as a Monetary Control," in *Essays in Economics,* volume 1, *Macroeconomics,* Markham, Chicago, 1971.

Topel, Robert and Finis Welch, "Unemployment Insurance: Survey and Extensions," *Economica,* **47,** August 1980, 351–379.

United Nations, *Statistical Yearbook,* various issues.

U.S. Bureau of Labor Statistics, *Employment and Earnings,* various issues.

U.S. Department of Commerce, *Historical Statistics of the U.S., Colonial Times to 1970,* Washington, DC, 1975.

———, *National Income and Product Accounts of the U.S.,* 1929–1976, Washington, DC, 1981.

———, *Statistical Abstract of the United States,* various issues.

———, *Survey of Current Business,* various issues.

Walre de Bordes, J. van, *The Austrian Crown,* King, London, 1927.

Warburg, Paul M., *The Federal Reserve System, its Origin and Growth,* volumes 1 and 2, Macmillan, New York, 1930.

Winston, Gordon C., "An International Comparison of Income and Hours of Work," *Review of Economics and Statistics,* **48,** February 1966, 28–39.

GLOSSARY

absolute form of PPP   The version of **purchasing-power-parity** that involves levels of exchange rates and prices.

adjusted gross income   Gross income less adjustments for tax purposes, such as business and moving expenses and deferred compensation through pension plans.

after-tax marginal product of labor   The **marginal product of labor** less the tax levied on the resulting increase in product.

after-tax rate of return to investment   The **real rate of return from investment** less the tax levied on the resulting increase in net product.

after-tax real interest rate   The **real interest rate** less the tax paid on the interest earnings.

aggregate-consistency conditions   Conditions on quantities that must hold when we add up the actions of all participants in a market—for example, the total of goods sold equals the total bought and the total of funds lent equals the total borrowed; in the basic model we use **market-clearing conditions** to ensure that the aggregate-consistency conditions are satisfied.

anticipated money growth   The public's forecast of the **rate of monetary growth,** based on the historical relationship between the quantity of money and economic variables.

autonomous change in demand   An unexplained shift in the aggregate demand for commodities.

average tax rate   The ratio of taxes to a measure of income. See **marginal tax rate.**

balance on capital account   The net acquisition of interest-bearing assets from abroad.

balance of international payments   The summary statement of a country's international trade in commodities, bonds, and **international currency.**

balanced budget   A situation in which there is no change in the real amount of money and bonds issued by government; zero real saving by government.

banking panic   Simultaneous runs on many banks and financial institutions, where depositors attempt to convert their deposits to cash.

barter   Direct exchange of one good for another, without the use of money. See **medium of exchange.**

Board of Governors of the Federal Reserve System   The seven-member group, appointed by the U.S. President, that makes most decisions of the Federal Reserve System.

bond   A contract that gives the holder (lender) a claim to a specified stream of payments from the issuer (borrower).

boom   A period in which aggregate economic activity or real GNP is high and rising.

Bretton-Woods System   A system of international payments established after World War II in which each country pegged the exchange rate between its currency and the U.S. dollar; the United States exchanged dollars for gold at a fixed price ($35 per ounce), thus pegging the value of each country's currency to gold.

budget constraint   The equation relating the sources of funds in a period, such as income from the commodity market and initial assets, to the uses of funds in that period, such as consumption and end-of-period assets.

budget line   A graph of the combinations of consumptions over two periods that satisfy the two-period **budget constraint.**

burden of the public debt   The possible negative effect of the **public debt** on saving and investment, and hence on the stock of capital available later.

closed economy   An economy that is isolated from the rest of the world.

complete Keynesian model   A version of the Keynesian theory that assumes sticky nominal **wage rates** but a perfectly flexible **general price level.**

constant returns to scale   The property of some production functions that a proportionate increase in all inputs results in an equi-proportionate increase in output.

consumer durables   Consumable commodities purchased by households that last for a long time, such as homes, automobiles, and appliances.

consumer nondurables and services   Consumable commodities purchased by households that last for a short time.

consumer price index (CPI)   A weighted average of prices of consumer goods relative to a base year.

costs of intermediation   The total cost of operating a financial intermediary, including a return (normal profit) on the capital invested.

crowding out (from government deficits)   The decline in private investment that may result from a tax cut that is financed by a **government budget deficit.**

crowding out (from government purchases)   The decrease in consumption and investment that accompanies an increase in government purchases.

current-account balance   The value of goods produced by domestic residents (including the **net factor income from abroad**) plus net transfers from abroad, less the expenditure by domestic residents on goods; if the current-account balance is positive (negative), then there is a **surplus (deficit) on current account.**

currency   Noninterest-bearing paper money issued by the government.

deflation   A sustained decrease in the **general price level** over time. See **inflation.**

demand deposits   Deposits held at a financial institution that can be withdrawn at face value without restrictions.

demand for money   The amount of money that someone desires to hold, expressed as a function of the volume of spending, the interest rate, **transaction costs,** and other variables.

depreciation   The wearing out of **capital goods** over time; often expressed as a fraction of the stock of capital.

desired stock of capital   The stock of capital that is chosen by a producer, depending on factors such as the **marginal product of capital,** the **real interest rate,** and the **depreciation rate.**

devaluation   An action by the central bank of a country that raises the number of units of its **currency** that exchange for other currencies; a rise in the **exchange rate.**

diminishing marginal productivity   A characteristic of the **production function** by which successive increments of an input yield progressively smaller increments in output.

direct investment abroad   Purchase of capital goods that are located in foreign countries.

discount factor   The relative value of a dollar in different periods of time; for example, between one period and the next the nominal discount factor is one plus the **nominal interest rate.**

discount rate of Fed   The interest rate charged on loans from the Federal Reserve to financial institutions.

discouraged workers   Workers who leave the **labor force** following a period of **unemployment.**

disintermediation   The decline in the use of the services of **financial intermediaries** that results when the public moves away from holding deposits toward direct holding of bonds and mortgages.

disposable personal income   **Personal income** less taxes.

distributional effects   Shifts in the distribution of resources across households, with no change in the aggregate of resources; changes such that some sectors in the economy gain at the expense of others.

double coincidence of wants   The situation required for **barter** to take place, in which the type and quantity of goods offered by one trader match those desired by the other trader.

duration of jobs   The average length of time that a job is expected to last; the duration of jobs is inversely related to the **job-separation rate.**

duration of unemployment   The length of time that a period of **unemployment** is expected to last; the duration of unemployment is inversely related to the **job-finding rate.**

economies of scale in the demand for money   The property of the **demand for money** that the desired average cash holding increases less than proportionately with a rise in income.

employment   The number of persons working at jobs in the market sector.

excess demand   A situation in a market where, at the prevailing market price, the quantity demanded exceeds the quantity supplied.

excess reserves   The difference between the total **reserves** held by financial institutions and the amount required to be held under the **reserve requirement** of the Federal Reserve.

excess supply   A situation in a market where, at the prevailing market price, the quantity supplied exceeds the quantity demanded.

exchange rate   The number of units of the **currency** of a country that trade for 1 unit of another currency, such as the U.S. dollar.

expectation of inflation   The public's forecast of the **inflation rate.**

expectational Phillips curve   The relation between **unexpected inflation** and the **unemployment rate;** according to this curve, an unexpected increase in the **inflation rate** has a negative effect on the unemployment rate.

expected real interest rate   The **real interest rate** that is expected to be earned (or paid) after adjusting the **nominal interest rate** by the **expectation of inflation.**

experience rating (for unemployment insurance)   The feature of the U.S. program of **unemployment insurance** that taxes employers more heavily if they have a history of a higher **job-separation rate.**

exports   Goods that are produced by the residents of a country but are sold to foreigners.

Federal Funds Market   The market for very short-term borrowing and lending between financial institutions, primarily commercial banks.

Federal Funds Rate   The interest rate on loans made in the **Federal Funds Market.**

Federal Open-Market Committee (FOMC)   A committee of the Federal Reserve that has responsibility for **open-market operations.**

Federal Reserve credit   The sum of the Fed's holdings of loans to depository institutions, U.S. government securities, and miscellaneous assets. The total of the Fed's claims on the government and the private sector.

financial intermediaries   Institutions that obtain funds from deposits made by individuals and make loans to households and businesses. Examples are banks, savings and loan associations, and money-market funds.

firm   An economic organization that employs and supervises various factors of production, and then sells its products to consumers or other firms.

fiscal policy The choice of levels of government spending, taxation, and borrowing in order to influence the level of aggregate economic activity.

fixed exchange rate The system of international payments prevalent until the early 1970s, in which a country pegs the rate at which its **currency** exchanges against another currency, such as the U.S. dollar; by buying or selling its currency the central bank would limit variations in the **exchange rate** to a narrow range.

flat-rate tax A kind of income tax in which the amount of tax is a constant fraction of **taxable income.** See **graduated-rate tax.**

flexible exchange rate The system of international payments, prevalent since the early 1970s, in which countries allow the **exchange rates** for their currencies to fluctuate so as to clear the exchange market.

full-employment deficit The **government deficit** after adjusting for the automatic response of government spending and taxes to **recession** or **boom;** an estimate of what the deficit would be if the economy were operating at a full-employment level.

fully funded system (for social security) A system in which each individual's payments accumulate in a trust fund and retirement benefits are paid out of the accumulated funds. See **social security; pay-as-you-go system.**

general market clearing Simultaneous clearing of all markets. See **market-clearing approach; Walras' Law of Markets.**

general price level The dollar price per unit of a (physically uniform) aggregate of commodities.

gold standard A system of international payments under which countries agree to buy or sell gold for a fixed amount of their **currencies;** the high point of this system was from 1879 to 1914.

government budget deficit (or surplus) In **real terms,** the increase (or decrease) in the real value of the government's obligations to the private sector in the forms of money and bonds.

government purchases of goods and services Expenditures by government on commodities and services produced by the private sector.

governmental budget constraint The equation showing the balance between total expenditures and total revenues of the government.

government's revenue from printing money The real income that government obtains by increasing the quantity of **high-powered money.** See **inflation tax.**

graduated-rate tax A kind of income tax in which the **marginal tax rate** rises with **taxable income.** See **flat-rate tax.**

Great Depression The decline in the aggregate economic activity in the United States that occurred from 1929 to 1933.

gross domestic product (GDP) The market value of an economy's domestically produced goods and services over a specified period of time.

gross investment   The purchases of capital goods.

gross national product (GNP)   The total market value of the goods and serices produced by the residents of a country over a specified period of time; GNP equals **gross domestic product** plus the **net factor income from abroad.**

high-powered money   The total amount of Federal Reserve Notes (**currency**) and noninterest-bearing deposits (**reserves**) held at the Fed by depository institutions; the **monetary base.**

human capital   Skills and training that are embodied in workers and add to productivity.

hyperinflation   A period with an extraordinarily high **inflation rate,** such as that in Germany after World War I.

implicit GNP price deflator   The **price index** that relates the **gross national product,** measured in **nominal** terms, to **real GNP.**

imports   Goods that are produced in foreign countries and purchased by the domestic residents of a country.

income effect   Another term for a **wealth effect.**

increasing (or decreasing) returns to scale   A characteristic of the production function such that a proportionate increase in all inputs results in a more than (or less than) proportionate increase in output.

indexation   A system of contracts in which payments are revised upward or downward according to increases or decreases in the **general price level,** so as to keep the real value of payments independent of **inflation; inflation correction.**

indifference curve   A graph showing the combinations of two items, such as consumption and work effort, that yield the same level of **utility.**

inferior goods   Goods for which the **wealth effect** is negative.

infinite horizon   The household's planning horizon when plans extend into the indefinite future; used in models that stress the role of intergenerational transfers.

inflation   A sustained increase in the **general price level** over time.

inflation correction   Another term for **indexation.**

inflation rate   The percentage change in a **price index** between two periods of time.

inflation tax   The revenue that the government gets by printing money at a faster rate (and thereby causing more **inflation**). See **government's revenue from printing money.**

interest rate   The ratio of the interest payment to the amount borrowed; the return to lending or the cost of borrowing.

interest-rate parity   The equalization of **interest rates** across countries, taking account of an adjustment for prospective changes in **exchange rates.**

intermediate goods   Commodities that are purchased for resale or for use in the production and sale of other commodities.

international currency International **media of exchange,** such as gold or U.S. currency, held by central banks.

international reserves The total quantity of liquid assets, including **international currency,** that central banks use for international transactions.

intertemporal-substitution effect The effect on current consumption (leisure) when the cost of future consumption (leisure) changes relative to that of current consumption (leisure).

inventories Stores of commodities held by businesses either for sale or for use in production.

investment accelerator The positive effect of changes in output on investment demand. See **Keynesian investment function.**

investment demand The quantity of **investment** that is desired by firms and households, expressed as a function of the **real interest rate,** the **depreciation rate,** and the existing stock of capital.

involuntary unemployment The inability of workers to obtain **employment** at the prevailing market wage; a feature of Keynesian theory.

irrelevance result for systematic monetary policy The theoretical finding that a policy of changing the quantity of money in response to the state of economy is predictable and therefore powerless to affect the economy.

IS curve A graph used in Keynesian theory showing the combinations of aggregate output and the **interest rate** that satisfy the condition that aggregate output equals the aggregate demand for commodities.

IS/LM model The analytical tool used in Keynesian theory to study the simultaneous determination of aggregate output and the **interest rate.**

job-finding rate The rate at which workers move from being **unemployed** or **outside of the labor force** to being **employed.**

job-separation rate The rate at which workers move from being **employed** to being **unemployed** or **outside of the labor force.**

Keynesian consumption function The relationship between consumption demand on the one hand and income and the **interest rate** on the other; a central element of Keynesian theory.

Keynesian cross diagram The graph depicting the determination of the level of aggregate output for a given **interest rate.**

Keynesian investment function The relationship between investment demand on the one hand and output and the **interest rate** on the other hand; an important element of Keynesian theory.

Keynesian model The theory developed by John Maynard Keynes that sought to explain aggregate business fluctuations.

labor force The total number of **employed** workers plus the number of **unemployed.**

Laffer curve A graph showing that tax revenues initially rise as the **marginal tax rate** rises but eventually reach a maximum and decline with further increases in the marginal tax rate.

law of one price The condition that identical goods in different countries must sell at the same dollar price.

law of supply and demand (for adjusting the price level) The assumption that the price level declines when goods are in **excess supply** and rises when goods are in **excess demand.**

legal tender A characteristic of money, whereby its use as a **medium of exchange** is reinforced by government statute.

lender of last resort The role of the central bank as a provider of loans to financial institutions during crises.

life-cycle model The theory of the choices of consumption and leisure that are made when the **planning horizon** is equal to the individual's expected remaining lifetime; it predicts that the individual will build up savings during working years and exhaust them during retirement years. See **infinite horizon.**

liquidity constraint The negative effect on consumer demand from the inability to borrow at the "going" **interest rate.**

LM curve A graph used in Keynesian theory showing the combinations of aggregate output and the **interest rate** that satisfy the condition that the **demand for money** equals the given quantity of money.

long-term contracts Agreements between buyers and sellers or between firms and workers that specify the terms of exchange over a number of periods.

lump-sum taxes Taxes paid to the government so that the amount paid does not depend on any characteristic of the individual, such as income or wealth.

lump-sum transfer A **transfer payment** from government to an individual in which the amount paid does not depend on any characteristic of the recipient, such as income or wealth.

M1 The definition of money as the sum of **currency** plus checkable deposits plus travelers' checks; a measure of the volume of assets that serve regularly as **media of exchange.**

marginal product of capital (MPK) The increment of output obtained per unit increment in the input of **physical capital,** while holding fixed any other inputs.

marginal product of labor (MPL) The increment of output obtained per unit increment in labor input while holding fixed any other inputs; the slope of the graph of the **production function** relating output to labor input.

marginal propensity to consume The effect of a change in income on consumption demand.

marginal propensity to invest The effect of a change in output on investment demand.

marginal propensity to save The effect of a change in income on desired saving.

marginal propensity to spend The effect of a change in income (or output) on the total demand for goods, whether for consumption or investment.

marginal tax rate The fraction of an additional dollar of income that must be paid as tax. This rate varies according to the level of **adjusted gross income.** See **average tax rate.**

market-clearing approach The viewpoint that prices, such as the **interest rate** and the **general price level,** are determined to clear all markets, such as those for credit and commodities; that is, supply equals demand in each market.

medium of exchange The commodity or other item that people use as a means of paying for purchases; money.

microeconomic foundations The theoretical analysis of individual behavior that underlies the macroeconomic model of the economy.

minimum wage The amount below which the **wage rate** paid by a firm cannot legally fall.

monetarism A school of thought, based on the **quantity theory of money,** that changes in the nominal quantity of money primarily account for movements in the price level in the long run and for fluctuations in **real GNP** in the short run.

monetary approach to the balance of payments Analyses of the **balance of international payments** and **exchange rates** that stress the quantity of money and the **demand for money** in each country.

monetary base See **high-powered money.**

monetary reform A fundamental change in the monetary system or in the formulation of monetary policy.

monetize the deficit Raise revenue to meet interest payments on government debt by increasing the quantity of money.

money multiplier The ratio of **M1** to the **monetary base.**

multiple expansion of deposits The effect of an increase in the **monetary base** on the volume of deposits held at financial institutions.

multiplier The change in aggregate output per dollar **autonomous** increase in aggregate demand; assumed in simple **Keynesian models** to be positive and greater than one.

national income The income earned from aggregate production; **GNP** adjusted for **depreciation** and sales and excise taxes.

national-income accounts The summary statement of **GNP** and the components of GNP during a year.

natural unemployment rate The average **unemployment rate** that prevails in the economy, depending on the average rates of **job separation** and **job finding.**

net exports The difference between the value of **exports** and the value of **imports.**

net factor income from abroad   Income earned by the residents of a country from labor supplied to foreign countries or from net claims on foreign assets.

net foreign investment   The change in a country's net holdings of interest-bearing assets from abroad plus the change in its **international currency.**

net investment   The change in the capital stock; **gross investment** minus the amount of **depreciation.**

net national product (NNP)   Gross national product minus the **depreciation** of capital.

neutrality of money   The theoretical finding that once-and-for-all changes in the **nominal** quantity of money affect nominal variables such as the **general price level** but leave real variables such as **real GNP** unaffected.

nominal   Measured in current dollar magnitudes; valued at current dollar prices; unadjusted for changes in the **general price level.**

nominal deficit   The current dollar value of the **real deficit** of the government. See **nominal deficit (national accounts' version).**

nominal deficit (national accounts' version)   The change in the nominal value of government-issued money and bonds. See **nominal deficit.**

nominal interest rate   The amount paid as **interest** per dollar borrowed for one period; the rate at which the nominal value of assets that are held as **bonds** grows over time.

nominal saving   The current dollar value of **real saving,** calculated by multiplying real saving by a **price index.**

nontraded goods   Goods, such as services and real estate, that do not enter readily into international commerce.

open economy   An economy that conducts trade with the rest of the world.

open-market operations   The purchase or sale of government securities by the Federal Reserve in exchange for newly created **high-powered money.**

outflow (inflow) of capital   The positive (negative) **balance on capital account** for a country.

outside of the labor force   The classification of a person who is neither employed nor currently looking for a job.

pay-as-you-go system (for social security)   A system in which benefits to old persons are financed by taxes on the current young generation.

perceived relative price   The ratio of the observed price in a local market to the perceived **general price level.**

perfect competition   The assumption that individuals participating in a market each view themselves as sufficiently small that they can buy or sell any amount without affecting the established price.

perfect foresight   An assumption that **expectations of inflation** or of other variables are accurate, so that there are no forecast errors.

permanent government purchases   The hypothetical level of government purchases that, if maintained permanently, would have the same total present value as the actual pattern of government purchases; the per-period equivalent of the **present value** of government purchases.

permanent income   The hypothetical amount of real income that, when received constantly throughout the individual's **planning horizon,** has the same total present value as the actual pattern of the individual's income; the per-period equivalent of the total present value of income. A temporary change in income entails a less than equivalent change in permanent income.

personal consumption expenditure   Purchases of goods and services by households for use in consumption.

personal income   Income received directly by persons; **national income** adjusted for undistributed corporate profits, social security contributions, transfer payments, and some other items.

Phillips curve   The relationship between **nominal** variables such as the **inflation rate** and real variables such as the **unemployment rate** or growth rate of aggregate output.

physical capital   Capital inputs into production, such as machinery and buildings.

planning horizon   The number of future periods that enter the household's **budget constraint;** the length of time for which the household plans consumption and leisure choices.

present value   The value of future dollar amounts, after dividing by the **discount factor.**

price index   A weighted average of individual prices in a particular year, relative to prices in some given base year; a measure of how much the average price has changed since the base year.

principal of bond   The amount borrowed, to be repaid at maturity.

private fixed capital   The sum of **producers' durable equipment and structures** and residential structures; a measure of the capital stock that excludes business **inventories** and **consumer durables** other than homes.

producer price index (PPI)   A weighted average of prices of raw materials and semifinished goods, relative to base-year prices.

producers' durable equipment and structures   The measure of **physical capital** that includes machinery and buildings used in production.

production function   The relationship between the quantity of output obtained and the quantities of inputs into production, such as labor and capital.

profit   The difference between revenues and costs for a firm.

public debt   The volume of interest-bearing government obligations to the public.

public goods   Goods that are enjoyed jointly by many people, such as the space program and national defense.

purchasing-power parity (P.P.P.)   The condition that the ratio of the **exchange rates** for the **currencies** of any two countries must equal the ratio of the prices of goods in each country.

quantity theory of money   The theory that changes in the **nominal** quantity of money account for the majority of long-run movements in the **general price level.**

rate of monetary growth   The percentage increase in the nominal quantity of money between two periods.

rate of time preference   The parameter that determines the relative weights applied to **utility** in different periods. The higher the rate of time preference, the higher the discount applied to future utility.

rational expectations   The viewpoint that individuals make forecasts or estimates of unknown variables, such as the **general price level,** in the best possible manner, utilizing all information currently available.

real-balance effect   The effect of a change in wealth resulting from a change in the **general price level;** the **wealth effect** of a rise in the real value of money balances.

real deficit   The change in the real value of the government's obligations to the public in the form of money and bonds. See **real deficit (national accounts' version).**

real deficit (national accounts' version)   The change in the nominal value of the government's obligations to the public in the form of money and bonds, divided by the current price level. See **real deficit.**

real exchange rate   The **exchange rate** between two **currencies** divided by the ratio of the price levels in the two countries.

real gross national product   The **gross national product** divided by a **price index** to adjust for changes in the average level of market prices; **GNP** in constant dollars.

real interest rate   The rate at which the real value of dollar assets that are held as bonds grows over time; the **interest rate** on an asset after adjusting for **inflation.**

real rate of return from investment   The net real proceeds from investment over one period expressed relative to the real cost of the investment.

real saving   The change in the real value of assets of a household or of the economy as a whole.

real terms   Measured in units of commodities; valued at base-year prices; dollar magnitudes that are adjusted for **inflation** by deflating by a **price index.**

real wage rate   The value in **real terms** of the dollar amount paid for an hour of labor services.

recession   A period of decline in the level of aggregate economic activity or **real GNP.**

Regulation Q   The legal limit imposed by the Federal Reserve on the **interest rate** payable on time deposits and savings deposits held at banks.

relative form of PPP   The version of **purchasing-power parity** that involves changes in **exchange rates** and prices.

relative price   The price of a commodity or service relative to the price of other goods or services; the ratio of the dollar price of a commodity to the **general price level.**

replacement ratio (for unemployment insurance)   The ratio of unemployment benefits to the prior wage earnings of a worker.

reservation wage   The **wage rate** that is just high enough to induce someone to accept a job.

reserve requirement   The requirement imposed by the Federal Reserve that depository institutions must hold a certain quantity of **reserves.** For each category of deposits, the requirement is specified as a fraction of the amount of deposits.

reserves (of depository institutions)   The total amount of **currency** and non-interest-bearing deposits at the Fed held by banks and other depository institutions.

revaluation   An increase in the value of a country's **currency** in terms of another currency, such as the U.S. dollar.

Ricardian Equivalence Theorem   The theoretical finding that, given the amounts of government purchases, an increase in current taxes has the same effect on the economy as an equal increase in the **government budget deficit.**

saving   The change in an individual's assets during a period of time.

savings deposits   Deposits held at banks that usually allow funds to be withdrawn without penalty with a 30-day notice of withdrawal.

short-side rule (for determining quantities)   The condition that the quantity of output or sales in a situation of **excess demand** or **excess supply** is determined by the lesser of the quantity demanded and the quantity supplied.

social security   **Transfer payments** made by government to households through social insurance programs such as old age and survivors insurance and disability insurance.

speculation (on exchange rates)   Sale (or purchase) of a **currency** in exchange for another currency whenever a **devaluation** (or **revaluation**) is expected.

stagflation   A situation where a **recession** is accompanied by high and rising **inflation.**

steady state   A situation where the rate of growth of the economy is zero and output, consumption, gross investment, and work effort are all constant.

steady-state growth   A situation in a growing economy where output, the stock of **physical capital,** consumption, and work effort all grow at the same rate as population, so that the amounts of output, etc., per person are constant.

steady state per capita growth   A situation in a growing economy where the amounts of output, capital stock, and consumption per person all grow at some constant rate.

sterilization   An action by the central bank of a country that prevents increases (decreases) in the amount of **international currency** from increasing (decreasing) the quantity of money in the country.

substitution effects   The response of households to changes in the relative cost of obtaining any two goods such as consumption and leisure.

superior goods (or normal goods)   Goods for which the **wealth effect** is positive.

superneutrality of money   The theoretical finding that a change in the pattern over time of monetary growth does not affect real variables such as aggregate output and the **real interest rate.** See **neutrality of money.**

supply shock   Changes that alter the **production function,** that is, raise or lower the output obtainable from given inputs or alter the **marginal products** of the inputs. Examples are harvest failures and **technological changes.**

supply-side economics   The study of the causes and effects of changes in the supply and productivity of factors of production. This approach emphasizes the negative effect of income taxes on the incentive to work.

surplus (deficit) on current account   A positive (negative) **current-account balance.**

taxable income   **Adjusted gross income** minus the value of tax exemptions.

tax exempt income   Income from production, interest earnings, or government transfers that is not liable for income taxes.

technological change   Improved knowledge about methods of production that shifts the **production function** upward.

temporary layoffs   **Job separations** where the worker is usually rehired within a few months.

terms of trade   The price of a country's **tradable goods** expressed relative to the price of a market basket of the world's tradable goods; often approximated by the ratio of a country's **export** prices to its **import** prices.

time deposits   Deposits at banks and other depository institutions that have a stated maturity date and carry penalties for early withdrawal.

tradable goods   Goods that are actually exchanged or could potentially be exchanged with foreign countries.

transaction costs   Costs incurred in the process of making sales or purchases, such as brokerage fees or the cost of the time involved.

transfer payments   Transfers of funds from government to individuals, such as welfare payments, which do not constitute payments for goods and services.

unanticipated money growth   The difference between the actual amount of monetary growth and **anticipated money growth.**

underground economy   The collection of economic activities from which the income earned is not reported and therefore not taxed.

unemployment   The situation of a worker who has no job and is looking for work.

unemployment insurance   The government program of providing temporary benefits to workers who have lost their jobs and are eligible by virtue of their work history.

unemployment rate   The ratio of the number of **unemployed** workers to the total number of **employed** and unemployed workers; the fraction of the **labor force** that is unemployed.

unexpected inflation   The difference between the actual **rate of inflation** and the **expectation of inflation;** the forecast error made in predicting inflation.

utility   The level of happiness of a household, measured in units called utils. Utility increases with increases in either consumption or leisure. See **utility function.**

utility function   The relationship between the amount of **utility** obtained and the amounts of consumption and labor chosen by the household.

utilization rate   The percentage of time that capital is used in production. For example, an increase in the number of shifts per day in a factory increases the utilization rate of machinery.

vacancies   The difference between the number of job openings at firms and the level of **employment.**

value added   The increase in value of product at a particular stage of production.

vault cash   **Currency** that is held by a depository institution.

velocity of money   The ratio of the dollar volume of transactions per period to the average money holding; the number of times per period that the average dollar turns over in making transactions.

wage rate   The dollar amount that is paid to a worker in exchange for an hour of labor services.

Walras' Law of Markets   The finding that if all but one of the conditions for **general market clearing** hold, then the final one must hold as well; this result follows because, in the aggregate, households' **budget constraints** must be satisfied.

wealth effects   The response of consumption and leisure (or labor) to changes in the household's opportunities for increasing **utility.** An increase (decrease) in wealth occurs when the household can raise (must reduce) consumption while leisure remains unchanged.

AUTHOR INDEX

SUBJECT INDEX